Pro JavaFX 8

A Definitive Guide to Building Desktop, Mobile, and Embedded Java Clients

Johan Vos
Weiqi Gao
Stephen Chin
Dean Iverson
James Weaver

Apress®

Pro JavaFX 8: A Definitive Guide to Building Desktop, Mobile, and Embedded Java Clients

ISBN-13 (pbk): 978-1-4302-6574-0

ISBN-13 (electronic): 978-1-4302-6575-7

Publisher: Heinz Weinheimer
Lead Editor: Steve Anglin
Technical Reviewer: Mark Heckler
Editorial Board: Steve Anglin, Mark Beckner, Ewan Buckingham, Gary Cornell, Louise Corrigan, James T. DeWolf, Jonathan Gennick, Jonathan Hassell, Robert Hutchinson, Michelle Lowman, James Markham, Matthew Moodie, Jeff Olson, Jeffrey Pepper, Douglas Pundick, Ben Renow-Clarke, Dominic Shakeshaft, Gwenan Spearing, Matt Wade, Steve Weiss
Coordinating Editor: Anamika Panchoo
Copy Editor: Teresa Horton
Compositor: SPi Global
Indexer: SPi Global
Artist: SPi Global
Cover Designer: Anna Ishchenko

Distributed to the book trade worldwide by Springer Science+Business Media New York, 233 Spring Street, 6th Floor, New York, NY 10013. Phone 1-800-SPRINGER, fax (201) 348-4505, e-mail `orders-ny@springer-sbm.com`, or visit `www.springeronline.com`. Apress Media, LLC is a California LLC and the sole member (owner) is Springer Science + Business Media Finance Inc (SSBM Finance Inc). SSBM Finance Inc is a Delaware corporation.

For information on translations, please e-mail `rights@apress.com`, or visit `www.apress.com`.

Apress and friends of ED books may be purchased in bulk for academic, corporate, or promotional use. eBook versions and licenses are also available for most titles. For more information, reference our Special Bulk Sales–eBook Licensing web page at `www.apress.com/bulk-sales`.

Any source code or other supplementary materials referenced by the author in this text is available to readers at `www.apress.com`. For detailed information about how to locate your book's source code, go to `www.apress.com/source-code`.

Contents at a Glance

Contents

About the Authors

Johan Vos is a Java Champion who started to work with Java in 1995. As part of the Blackdown team, he helped port Java to Linux. With LodgON, the company he cofounded, he has been mainly working on Java-based solutions for social networking software. His main focus is on end-to-end Java, combining the strengths of back-end systems and embedded devices. His favorite technologies are currently Java EE/Glassfish at the back end and JavaFX at the front end. He contributes to a number of open source projects, including DataFX and the Android port of JavaFX. Johan's blog can be followed at `http://blogs.lodgon.com/johan`, he tweets at `http://twitter.com/johanvos`, and can be reached at `johan@lodgon.com`.

Weiqi Gao is a principal software engineer with Object Computing, Inc. in St. Louis, Missouri. He has decades of software development experience and has been using Java technology since 1998. He is interested in programming languages, object-oriented systems, distributed computing, and graphical user interfaces. He is a member of the steering committee of the St. Louis Java Users Group. Weiqi holds a PhD in mathematics.

Stephen Chin is a Java Ambassador at Oracle specializing in embedded and user interface technology and the JavaOne Content Chair. He has been featured at Java conferences around the world including Devoxx, JFokus, OSCON, JFall, GeeCON, JustJava, and JavaOne, where he three times received a Rock Star Award. Stephen is an avid motorcyclist who has done several Pan-European evangelism tours, interviewing hackers in their natural habitat and posting the videos on `http://nighthacking.com/`. When he is not traveling, he enjoys teaching kids how to do embedded and robot programming together with his 11-year-old daughter.

Dean Iverson has been writing software professionally for more than 15 years. He is employed by the Virginia Tech Transportation Institute, where he is a senior researcher and rich client application developer. He also has a small software consultancy called Pleasing Software Solutions, which he cofounded with his wife.

James Weaver is a developer, author, teacher, and international speaker focused on client-side Java and the Internet of Things. He tweets at `@JavaFXpert`.

About the Technical Reviewer

Mark Heckler is a Java Software Architect/Engineer with development experience in numerous environments. He has worked for and with key players in the manufacturing, emerging markets, retail, medical, telecom, and financial industries to develop and deliver critical capabilities on time and on budget. Currently, he works primarily with enterprise customers using Java throughout the stack. He also participates in open source development at every opportunity, being a JFXtras project committer, developer of DialogFX and MonologFX, codeveloper of Autonomous4j, and more. When Mark isn't working with Java, he enjoys sharing his experiences at conferences and via the Java Jungle web site (`https://blogs.oracle.com/javajungle`), his personal web site (`http://www.thehecklers.org`), and Twitter (`@MkHeck`). Mark lives with his very understanding wife, three kids, and dog in St. Louis, Missouri.

Acknowledgments

Writing a book is often done in spare time. I want to thank my wife Kathleen and our children Merlijn and Linde, for allowing me to spend evening and weekend time in front of my computer. I want to thank authors Jim Weaver, Weiqi Gao, Stephen Chin, and Dean Iverson; technical reviewer Mark Heckler; and the Apress team for their trust in me. A special thanks to my LodgON colleagues Joeri Sykora and Erwin Morrhey for helping me with the examples. The JavaFX team at Oracle did a great job releasing JavaFX 8. The combination of their efforts and those of the Java community makes JavaFX an excellent platform for an increasing number of clients.

—Johan Vos

I would like to thank my wife, Youhong Gong, for her support, understanding, and encouragement during the writing process. My thanks also go to the author and technical review team: Johan Vos, Jim Weaver, Stephen Chin, Dean Iverson, and Mark Heckler for making this book a fun project. I share with my coauthors the appreciation for the JavaFX team at Oracle and the editorial team at Apress.

—Weiqi Gao

To my wife Justine, and daughters Cassandra and Priscilla, who supported me in writing this book on top of all my other responsibilities. Also, a huge thanks to the entire author team, including our newest members, Johan Vos and Mark Heckler, who both went above and beyond in their contributions to this title. Finally, a great debt of gratitude to the JavaFX team and JVM language designers who have produced technology that will profoundly change the way we design and code user interfaces going forward.

—Stephen Chin

I would like to thank my family, Sondra, Alex, and Matt, for their support and understanding during yet another writing project. You guys make this possible. I would also like to thank the writing and review team of Jim Weaver, Stephen Chin, Weiqi Gao, Johan Vos, and Mark Heckler for their dedication and their patience. The editorial team at Apress was, as usual, first rate and utterly professional. And, of course, none of this would be possible without the hard work of an extremely talented team of engineers on the JavaFX team at Oracle.

—Dean Iverson

To my wife Julie, daughters Lori and Kelli, son Marty, and grandchildren Kaleb and Jillian. Thanks Merrill and Barbara Bishir, Ken and Marilyn Prater, and Walter Weaver for being such wonderful examples. My contributions to this book are dedicated to the memory of Merrill Bishir and Ken Prater. *"I have told you these things, so that in me you may have peace. In this world you will have trouble. But take heart! I have overcome the world." (John 16:33)*

—Jim Weaver

Foreword

I remember it distinctly, like it was yesterday: standing center stage at Moscone Center when we launched JavaFX at JavaOne 2007. We promised to build a world-class client platform for Java. With the world watching with skeptical eyes and in a crowded client arena, we set out to build the dream. In hindsight, it was a rather ambitious goal.

Fast forward seven years, with the release of Java SE 8, we have taken a huge leap forward in fulfilling that promise. As the vision unfolded, our product plans have shifted to match the evolving RIA market and what developers and the Java community told us they were looking for. As someone who was there at the inception of JavaFX and has watched it mature over the last seven years to this current release, my feelings are akin to a parent watching a toddler blossom.

James Weaver and Stephen Chin have been traveling through the evolution of JavaFX with me. They have both presented on JavaFX at numerous international conferences and have been developing with and blogging about JavaFX since 2007. James is a 30-year software veteran and has authored several books on Java, as well as articles for Java Magazine and Oracle Technology Network. He has also developed numerous JavaFX applications for a wide variety of customers.

Stephen is passionate about open source technologies and is the founder of WidgetFX and JFXtras. He also has a deep passion for improving development technologies and processes, as well as agile development methodologies.

Johan Vos is co-founder of LodgON, holds a PhD in applied physics, and has been a very prolific member of the JavaFX community. His interest lies in the enterprise communication aspects of JavaFX, combining the world of large servers with end-user devices. Johan's analogy to physics: The grand unified theory combines quantum mechanics (small) with relativity theory (large); similarly in software, Java combines JavaFX with Java EE.

Dean Iverson is a longtime client developer with a great eye for creating elegant user interfaces. He develops GroovyFX libraries and is a contributor to the JFXtras project. He has been developing and blogging about JavaFX since 2007. Weiqi Gao holds a PhD in mathematics. His expertise is in the language aspects of JavaFX, as reflected in the chapters on Properties and Bindings and Collections and Concurrency.

Today, the core JavaFX team at Oracle still has several of the developers who were part of the early versions of JavaFX and we also have new engineers who have joined us. As we move ahead and open source JavaFX, we are looking forward to having more developers and experts from the extended Java community join us in making JavaFX the number one choice for client development.

I am proud and honored to be part of this key software technology. Given their length of experience and depth of expertise in all aspects of JavaFX and across the Java platform, I cannot think of a better group of authors to bring you JavaFX 8. I hope you will enjoy this book and find JavaFX as satisfying as I have found it over the years. I hope it piques your interest sufficiently to join the JavaFX community in making JavaFX the platform of choice for clients.

—Nandini Ramani

Vice President, Java Client Development

Oracle Corporation

Introduction

As a developer, author, speaker, and advocate for JavaFX since its inception in 2007, I am very excited about JavaFX 8. It was released in March 2014 as an integral part of Java SE 8, and is the successor to Java Swing. As you'll read in the pages of this book, JavaFX runs on desktops (Mac, Windows, Linux), as well as embedded devices such as the Raspberry Pi. As the Internet of things (IoT) is increasingly realized, JavaFX is well positioned to enable the user interface of IoT. Also, because of community projects led by folks such as Johan Vos and Niklas Therning, developers are deploying JavaFX apps on Android and iOS devices.

The JavaFX community has many talented, passionate, and cordial developers, and I count it a privilege to call them my colleagues. One such colleague, Johan Vos, is a coauthor of our Pro JavaFX 2 book, and is the lead author of this Pro JavaFX 8 book. It has been my pleasure to continue working with Johan on this book under his leadership. Please join me in welcoming and congratulating him in this role, perhaps by tweeting him at `@JohanVos` or posting a review of this book on Amazon. It is my hope that you'll find this book both enjoyable and instrumental in helping you learn JavaFX!

—James L. Weaver

Java Technology Ambassador

Oracle Corporation

CHAPTER 1

Getting a Jump Start in JavaFX

Don't ask what the world needs. Ask what makes you come alive, and go do it. Because what the world needs is people who have come alive.

—Howard Thurman

At the annual JavaOne conference in May 2007, Sun Microsystems announced a new product family named JavaFX. Its stated purpose includes enabling the development and deployment of content-rich applications on consumer devices such as cell phones, televisions, in-dash car systems, and browsers. Josh Marinacci, a software engineer at Sun, made the following statement, very appropriately, in a Java Posse interview: "JavaFX is sort of a code word for reinventing client Java and fixing the sins of the past." He was referring to the fact that Java Swing and Java 2D have lots of capability, but are also very complex. By using FXML, JavaFX allows us to simply and elegantly express user interfaces (UIs) with a declarative programming style. It also leverages the full power of Java, because you can instantiate and use the millions of Java classes that exist today. Add features such as binding the UI to properties in a model and change listeners that reduce the need for setter methods, and you have a combination that will help restore Java to the client-side Internet applications.

In this chapter, we give you a jump start in developing JavaFX applications. After bringing you up to date on the brief history of JavaFX, we show you how to get the required tools. We also explore some great JavaFX resources and walk you through the process of compiling and running JavaFX applications. In the process you'll learn a lot about the JavaFX application programming interface (API) as we walk through application code together.

A Brief History of JavaFX

JavaFX started life as the brainchild of Chris Oliver when he worked for a company named SeeBeyond. They had a need for richer user interfaces, so Chris created a language that he dubbed F3 (Form Follows Function) for that purpose. In the article "Mind-Bendingly Cool Innovation" (cited in the Resources section at the end of this chapter), Chris is quoted as follows: "When it comes to integrating people into business processes, you need graphical user interfaces for them to interact with, so there was a use case for graphics in the enterprise application space, and there was an interest at SeeBeyond in having richer user interfaces."

SeeBeyond was acquired by Sun, who subsequently changed the name of F3 to JavaFX, and announced it at JavaOne 2007. Chris Oliver joined Sun during the acquisition and continued to lead the development of JavaFX.

The first version of JavaFX Script was an interpreted language, and was considered a prototype of the compiled JavaFX Script language that was to come later. Interpreted JavaFX Script was very robust, and there were two JavaFX books published in the latter part of 2007 based on that version. One was written in Japanese, and the other was written in English and published by Apress (*JavaFX Script: Dynamic Java Scripting for Rich Internet/Client-Side Applications,* Apress, 2007).

While developers were experimenting with JavaFX and providing feedback for improvement, the JavaFX Script compiler team at Sun was busy creating a compiled version of the language. This included a new set of runtime API libraries. The JavaFX Script compiler project reached a tipping point in early December 2007, which was commemorated in a blog post entitled "Congratulations to the JavaFX Script Compiler Team—The Elephant Is Through the Door." That phrase came from the JavaFX Script compiler project leader Tom Ball in a blog post, which contained the following excerpt.

> *An elephant analogy came to me when I was recently grilled about exactly when the JavaFX Script compiler team will deliver our first milestone release. "I can't give you an accurate date," I said. "It's like pushing an elephant through a door; until a critical mass makes it past the threshold you just don't know when you'll be finished. Once you pass that threshold, though, the rest happens quickly and in a manner that can be more accurately predicted."*

A screenshot of the silly, compiled JavaFX application written by one of the authors, Jim Weaver, for that post is shown in Figure 1-1, demonstrating that the project had in fact reached the critical mass to which Tom Ball referred.

Figure 1-1. *Screenshot for the "Elephant Is Through the Door" program*

Much progress continued to be made on JavaFX in 2008:

- The NetBeans JavaFX plug-in became available for the compiled version in March 2008.
- Many of the JavaFX runtime libraries (mostly focusing on the UI aspects of JavaFX) were rewritten by a team that included some very talented developers from the Java Swing team.
- In July 2008, the JavaFX Preview Software Development Kit (SDK) was released, and at JavaOne 2008, Sun announced that the JavaFX 1.0 SDK would be released in fall 2008.
- On December 4, 2008, the JavaFX 1.0 SDK was released. This event increased the adoption rate of JavaFX by developers and IT managers because it represented a stable codebase.
- In April 2009, Oracle and Sun announced that Oracle would be acquiring Sun. The JavaFX 1.2 SDK was released at JavaOne 2009.
- In January 2010, Oracle completed its acquisition of Sun. The JavaFX 1.3 SDK was released in April 2010, with JavaFX 1.3.1 being the last of the 1.3 releases.

At JavaOne 2010, JavaFX 2.0 was announced. The JavaFX 2.0 roadmap was published by Oracle and included items such as the following.

- Deprecate the JavaFX Script language in favor of using Java and the JavaFX 2.0 API. This brings JavaFX into the mainstream by making it available to any language (e.g., Java, Groovy, and JRuby) that runs on the Java Virtual Machine (JVM). As a consequence, existing developers do not need to learn a new language, but they can use existing skills and start developing JavaFX applications.
- Make the compelling features of JavaFX Script, including binding to expressions, available in the JavaFX 2.0 API.
- Offer an increasingly rich set of UI components, building on the components already available in JavaFX 1.3.
- Provide a Web component for embedding HTML and JavaScript content into JavaFX applications.
- Enable JavaFX interoperability with Swing.
- Rewrite the media stack from the ground up.

JavaFX 2.0 was released at JavaOne 2011, and has enjoyed a greatly increased adoption rate due to the innovative features articulated previously.

JavaFX 8 marks another important milestone. JavaFX is now an integral part of the Java Platform, Standard Edition.

- This is a clear indication that JavaFX is considered mature enough, and that it is the future of Java on the client.
- This greatly benefits developers, as they don't have to download two SDKs and tool suites.
- The new technologies in Java 8, in particular the Lambda expressions, Stream API, and default interface methods, are very usable in JavaFX.
- Many new features have been added, including native 3D support, a printing API, and some new controls including a datepicker.

Now that you've had the obligatory history lesson in JavaFX, let's get one step closer to writing code by showing you where some examples, tools, and other resources are.

Prepare Your JavaFX Journey

Required Tools

Because JavaFX is now part of Java, you don't have to download a separate JavaFX SDK. The whole JavaFX API and implementation is part of the Java 8 SE SDK that can be downloaded from `http://www.oracle.com/technetwork/java/javase/downloads/index.html`.

This SDK contains everything you need to develop, run, and package JavaFX applications. You can compile JavaFX applications using command-line tools contained in the Java 8 SE SDK.

Most developers, however, prefer an integrated development environment (IDE) for increased productivity. By definition, an IDE that supports Java 8 also supports JavaFX 8. Hence, you can use your favorite IDE and develop JavaFX applications. In this book, we mainly use the NetBeans IDE, as it allows for a tighter integration with SceneBuilder (see the next paragraph). The NetBeans IDE can be downloaded from `https://netbeans.org/downloads`.

SceneBuilder is a stand-alone tool that allows you to design JavaFX interfaces rather than coding them. We discuss SceneBuilder in Chapter 3. Although SceneBuilder produces FXML—and we discuss FXML in Chapter 3 as well—that can be used in any IDE, NetBeans provides a tight integration with SceneBuilder. The SceneBuilder tool can be downloaded at `http://www.oracle.com/technetwork/java/javase/downloads/sb2download-2177776.html`.

JavaFX, the Community

JavaFX is not a closed-source project, developed in a secret bunker. To the contrary, JavaFX is being developed in an open spirit, with an open source code base, open mailing lists, and an open and active community sharing knowledge.

The source code is developed in the OpenJFX project, which is a subproject of the OpenJDK project in which Java SE is being developed. If you want to examine the source code or the architecture, or if you want to read the technical discussions on the mailing list, have a look at `http://openjdk.java.net/projects/openjfx`.

The developer community is very active, both in OpenJFX as well as in application-specific areas. The starting point for developers is the JavaFX Community at `http://javafxcommunity.com`. This is a community site created by Oracle, but with input from many JavaFX developers. The content of the JavaFX Community changes often, and in Figure 1-2 we show a snapshot on how this community site looked at the time of writing.

***Figure 1-2.** A snapshot of the JavaFX community web site*

In addition, blogs maintained by JavaFX engineers and developers are great resources for up-to-the-minute technical information on JavaFX. For example, Oracle JavaFX Engineers Richard Bair, Jasper Potts, and Jonathan Giles keep the developer community apprised of the latest JavaFX innovations at `http://fxexperience.com`. The Resources section at the end of this chapter contains the URLs of the blogs that the authors of this book use to engage the JavaFX developer community.

Two important characteristics of the JavaFX Community are its own creativity and the desire to share. There are a number of open-source efforts bringing added value to the JavaFX Platform. Because of good cooperation between the JavaFX Platform engineers and the external JavaFX developers, these open-source projects fit very well with the official JavaFX Platform.

Some of the most interesting efforts are listed here:

- RoboVM allows you to create iOS applications using Java and JavaFX. As a consequence, your JavaFX application can be used to create an app for the iPhone or the iPad.
- The JavaFX-Android project maintains a JavaFX SDK for Android development. As a consequence, your JavaFX application can be used to create an app for Android devices.

The iOS and the Android port of JavaFX are discussed in more detail in Chapter 12.

- `JFXtras.org` is a project working on adding high-quality controls and add-ons to the JavaFX Platform.
- ControlsFX is another project adding high-quality controls and tools to the JavaFX Platform.

It is worth mentioning that the JavaFX team is closely watching the efforts in both `JFXtras.org` and ControlsFX, and ideas that are started in one of those projects might make it into one of the next releases of JavaFX.

- DataFX is an open-source project aiming to facilitate the retrieval of external data in JavaFX applications, and to provide JavaFX developers with enterprise functionality like injection and flow management.
- OpenDolphin is another project helping developers in separating and synchronizing client and server development, by implementing the highest degree of Model-View-Controller separation.

Take a few minutes to explore these sites. Next we point out some more valuable resources that are helpful.

Use the Official Specifications

While developing JavaFX applications, it is very useful to have access to the API JavaDoc documentation, which is available at `http://download.java.net/jdk8/jfxdocs/index.html` and shown in Figure 1-3.

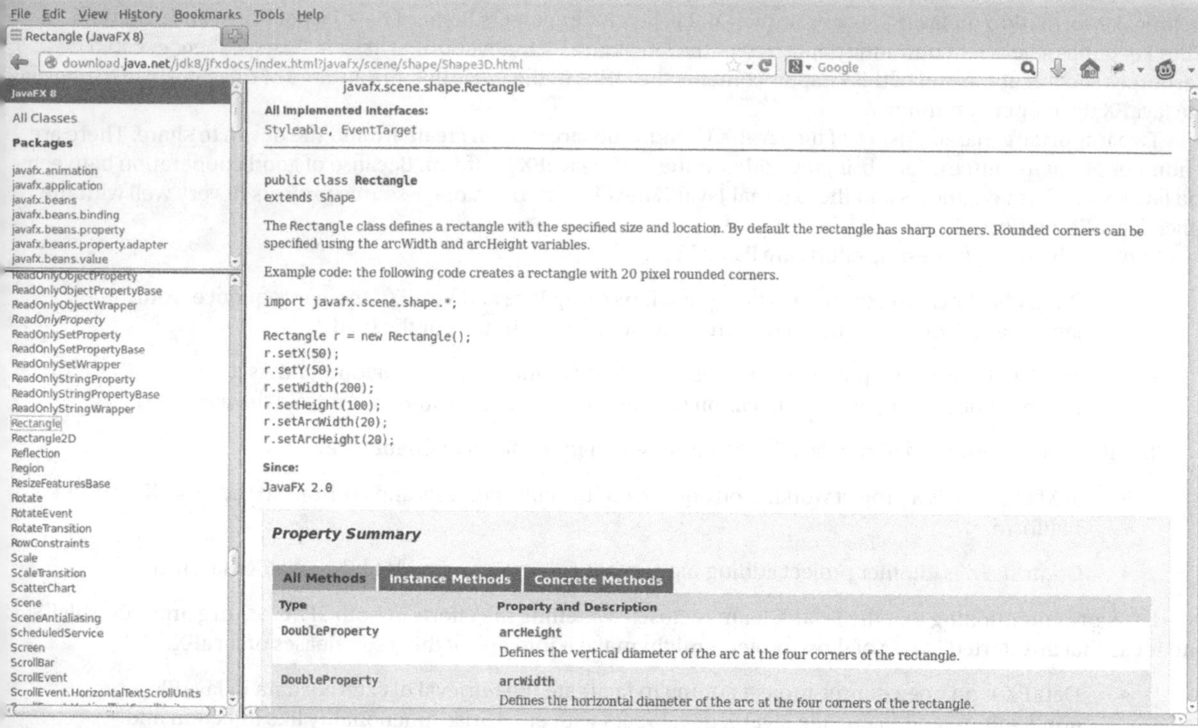

Figure 1-3. JavaFX SDK API Javadoc

The API documentation in Figure 1-3, for example, shows how to use the `Rectangle` class, located in the `javafx.scene.shape` package. Scrolling down this web page shows the properties, constructors, methods, and other helpful information about the `Rectangle` class. By the way, this API documentation is available in the Java 8 SE SDK that you downloaded, but we wanted you to know how to find it online as well.

Apart from the JavaDoc, it is very useful to have the Cascading Style Sheets (CSS) style reference at hand as well. This document explains all the style classes that can be applied to a particular JavaFX element. You can find this document at `http://download.java.net/jdk8/jfxdocs/javafx/scene/doc-files/cssref.html`.

ScenicView

You already downloaded SceneBuilder, which is the tool that allows you to create UIs by designing them, rather than writing code. We expect that there will be more tools developed by companies and individuals that help you create JavaFX applications. One of the first tools that was made available for free and that is very helpful when debugging JavaFX applications is ScenicView, originally created by Amy Fowler at Oracle, and later maintained by Jonathan Giles. You can download ScenicView at `http://fxexperience.com/scenic-view/`.

ScenicView is particularly helpful because it provides a convenient UI that allows developers to inspect properties of nodes (i.e., dimensions, translations, CSS) at runtime.

Packaging and Distribution

The techniques used for delivering software to the end user are always changing. In the past, the preferred way for delivering Java applications was via the Java Network Launch Protocol (JNLP). Doing so, both applets and stand-alone applications can be installed on a client. However, there are a number of issues with this technique. The idea only works if the end user has a JVM installed that is capable of executing the application. This is not always true. Even in the desktop world, where a system can be delivered preinstalled with a JVM, there are issues with versioning and security. Indeed, some applications are hard-coded against a specific version of the JVM. Although vulnerabilities in the JVM are in most cases fixed very fast, this still requires the end user to always install the latest version of the JVM, which can be pretty frustrating.

On top of that, browser manufacturers are increasingly reluctant to support alternative embedded platforms. In summary, relying on a browser and on a local, preinstalled JVM does not provide the best end-user experience.

The client software industry is shifting more and more toward the so-called AppStores. In this concept, applications can be downloaded and installed that are self-containing. They do not rely on preinstalled execution environments. The principles originated in the mobile space, where Apple with the AppStore and Android with the Play store are leading the market. Especially in these markets, single-click installs have a huge advantage over local downloads, unpacking, manual configuration, and more nightmares.

In Java terminology, a self-contained application means that the application is bundled together with a JVM that is capable of running the application. In the past, this idea was often rejected because it made the application bundle too big. However, with increasing memory and storage capacities, and with decreasing costs of sending bytes over the Internet, this disadvantage is becoming less relevant.

There are a number of technologies being developed currently that help you bundle your application with the correct JVM version and package it.

The JavaFXPackager, which is developed inside the OpenJFX project area, contains an API for creating self-contained bundles. This tool is used by NetBeans, and it can be used to generate self-contained bundles with just a few clicks.

Users of maven can use a maven plug-in created by Daniel Zwolenski. This plug-in, which is documented at `http://zenjava.com/javafx/maven/` allows the creation of JavaFX self-contained bundles using familiar maven commands.

Now that you have the tools installed, we show you how to create a simple JavaFX program, and then we walk through it in detail. The first program that we've chosen for you is called "Hello Earthrise," which demonstrates more features than the typical beginning "Hello World" program.

Developing Your First JavaFX Program: Hello Earthrise

On Christmas Eve in 1968 the crew of Apollo 8 entered lunar orbit for the first time in history. They were the first humans to witness an "Earthrise," taking the magnificent picture shown in Figure 1-4. This image is dynamically loaded from this book's web site when the program starts, so you'll need to be connected to the Internet to view it.

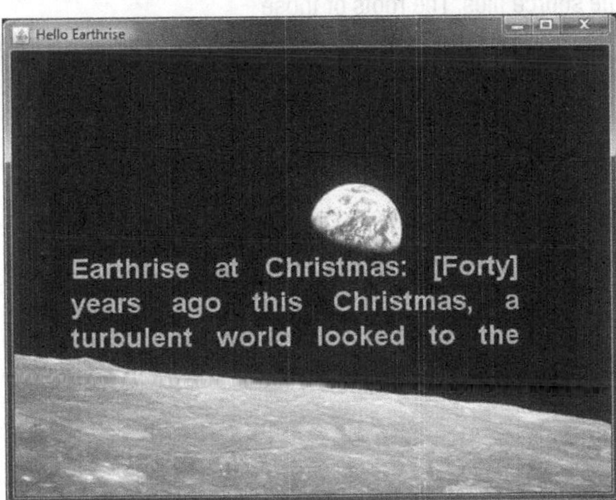

Figure 1-4. *The Hello Earthrise program*

In addition to demonstrating how to dynamically load images over the Internet, this example shows you how to use animation in JavaFX. Now it's time for you to compile and run the program. We show you two ways to do this: from the command line and using NetBeans.

Compiling and Running from the Command Line

We usually use an IDE to build and run JavaFX programs, but to take all of the mystery out of the process we use the command-line tools first.

■ **Note** For this exercise, as with most others in the book, you need the source code. If you prefer not to type the source code into a text editor, you can obtain the source code for all of the examples in this book from the code download site. See the Resources section at the end of this chapter for the location of this site.

Assuming that you've downloaded and extracted the source code for this book into a directory, follow the directions in this exercise, performing all of the steps as instructed. We dissect the source code after the exercise.

COMPILING AND RUNNING THE HELLO EARTHRISE PROGRAM FROM THE COMMAND LINE

You'll use the javac and java command-line tools to compile and run the program in this exercise. From the command-line prompt on your machine:

1. Navigate to the `Chapter01/Hello` directory.
2. Execute the following command to compile the `HelloEarthRiseMain.java` file.

```
javac -d . HelloEarthRiseMain.java
```

3. Because the `-d` option was used in this command, the class files generated are placed in directories matching the package statements in the source files. The roots of those directories are specified by the argument given for the `-d` option, in this case the current directory.
4. To run the program, execute the following command. Note that we use the fully qualified name of the class that will be executed, which entails specifying the nodes of the path name and the name of the class, all separated by periods.

```
java projavafx.helloearthrise.ui.HelloEarthRiseMain
```

The program should appear as shown in Figure 1-4 earlier, with the text scrolling slowly upward, reminiscent of the *Star Wars* opening crawls.

Congratulations on completing your first exercise as you explore JavaFX!

Understanding the Hello Earthrise Program

Now that you've run the application, let's walk through the program listing together. The code for the Hello Earthrise application is shown in Listing 1-1.

Listing 1-1. The `HelloEarthRiseMain.java` Program

```
package projavafx.helloearthrise.ui;

import javafx.animation.Interpolator;
import javafx.animation.Timeline;
import javafx.animation.TranslateTransition;
import javafx.application.Application;
import javafx.geometry.VPos;
import javafx.scene.Group;
import javafx.scene.Scene;
import javafx.scene.image.Image;
import javafx.scene.image.ImageView;
import javafx.scene.paint.Color;
import javafx.scene.shape.Rectangle;
import javafx.scene.text.Font;
import javafx.scene.text.FontWeight;
import javafx.scene.text.Text;
import javafx.scene.text.TextAlignment;
import javafx.stage.Stage;
import javafx.util.Duration;

/**
 * Main class for the "Hello World" style example
 */
public class HelloEarthRiseMain extends Application {

    /**
     * @param args the command line arguments
     */
    public static void main(String[] args) {
        Application.launch(args);
    }

    @Override
    public void start(Stage stage) {

        String message
                = "Earthrise at Christmas: "
                + "[Forty] years ago this Christmas, a turbulent world "
                + "looked to the heavens for a unique view of our home "
                + "planet. This photo of Earthrise over the lunar horizon "
                + "was taken by the Apollo 8 crew in December 1968, showing "
                + "Earth for the first time as it appears from deep space. "
                + "Astronauts Frank Borman, Jim Lovell and William Anders "
                + "had become the first humans to leave Earth orbit, "
                + "entering lunar orbit on Christmas Eve. In a historic live "
```

```
            + "broadcast that night, the crew took turns reading from "
            + "the Book of Genesis, closing with a holiday wish from "
            + "Commander Borman: \"We close with good night, good luck,"
            + "a Merry Christmas, and God bless all of you -- all of "
            + "you on the good Earth.\"";

        // Reference to the Text
        Text textRef = new Text(message);
        textRef.setLayoutY(100);
        textRef.setTextOrigin(VPos.TOP);
        textRef.setTextAlignment(TextAlignment.JUSTIFY);
        textRef.setWrappingWidth(400);
        textRef.setFill(Color.rgb(187, 195, 107));
        textRef.setFont(Font.font("SansSerif", FontWeight.BOLD, 24));

        // Provides the animated scrolling behavior for the text
        TranslateTransition transTransition = new TranslateTransition(new Duration(75000), textRef);
        transTransition.setToY(-820);
        transTransition.setInterpolator(Interpolator.LINEAR);
        transTransition.setCycleCount(Timeline.INDEFINITE);

        // Create an ImageView containing the Image
        Image image = new Image ("http://projavafx.com/images/earthrise.jpg");
        ImageView imageView = new ImageView(image);

        // Create a Group containing the text
        Group textGroup = new Group(textRef);
        textGroup.setLayoutX(50);
        textGroup.setLayoutY(180);
        textGroup.setClip(new Rectangle(430, 85));

        // Combine ImageView and Group
        Group root = new Group(imageView, textGroup);
        Scene scene = new Scene(root, 516, 387);

        stage.setScene(scene);
        stage.setTitle("Hello Earthrise");
        stage.show();

        // Start the text animation
        transTransition.play();
    }
```

Now that you've seen the code, let's take a look at its constructs and concepts in some more detail.

What Happened to the Builders?

If you were using JavaFX 2 before, you are probably familiar with the so-called builder pattern. Builders provide a declarative style of programming. Rather than calling `set()` methods on a class instance to specify its fields, the builder pattern uses an instance of a Builder class to define how the target class should be composed.

Builders were very popular in JavaFX. However, it turned out that there were major technical hurdles with keeping them in the platform. As a consequence, it has been decided to phase builders out. In Java 8, `Builder` classes are still usable, but they are deprecated. In Java 9, `Builder` classes might be removed entirely.

More information on the reason why `Builder` classes are not preferred anymore can be found in a mailing list entry by JavaFX Chief Architect Richard Bair at `http://mail.openjdk.java.net/pipermail/openjfx-dev/2013-March/006725.html`. The bottom of this entry contains a very important statement: "I believe that FXML or Lambda's or alternative languages all provide other avenues for achieving the same goals as builders but without the additional cost in byte codes or classes."

This is what we will show throughout this book. Near the end of this chapter, we show a first example of a Lambda expression in our code. In Chapter 3, we show how SceneBuilder and FXML allow you to use a declarative way of defining a UI.

In the current example, we programmatically define the different components of the UI, and we glue them together. In Chapter 3, we show the same example using a declarative FXML-based approach.

The JavaFX Application

Let's have a look at the class declaration in our first example:

```
public class HelloEarthRiseMain extends Application
```

This declaration states that our application extends the `javafx.application.Application` class. This class has one abstract method that we should implement:

```
public void start(Stage stage) {}
```

This method will be called by the environment that executes our JavaFX application.

Depending on the environment, JavaFX applications will be launched in a different way. As a developer, you don't have to worry about how your application is launched, and where the connection to a physical screen is made. You have to implement the "start" method and use the provided `Stage` parameter to create your UI, as discussed in the next paragraph.

In our command-line example, we launched the applications by executing the main method of the application class. The implementation of the main method is very simple:

```
public static void main(String[] args) {
    Application.launch(args);
}
```

The only instruction in this main method is a call to the static launch method of the application, which will launch the application.

■ **Tip** A JavaFX application always has to extend the `javafx.application.Application` class.

A Stage and a Scene

A `Stage` contains the UI of a JavaFX app, whether it is deployed on the desktop, on an embedded system, or on other devices. On the desktop, for example, a `Stage` has its own top-level window, which typically includes a border and title bar.

The initial stage is created by the JavaFX runtime, and passed to you via the start() method, as described in the previous paragraph. The Stage class has a set of properties and methods. Some of these properties and methods, as shown in the following code snippet from the listing, are as follows.

- A scene that contains the graphical nodes in the UI
- A title that appears in the title bar of the window (when deployed on the desktop)
- The visibility of the Stage

```
stage.setScene(scene);
stage.setTitle("Hello Earthrise");
stage.show();
```

A Scene is the top container in the JavaFX scene graph. A Scene holds the graphical elements that are displayed on the Stage. Every element in a Scene is a graphical node, which is any class that extends javafx.scene.Node. The scene graph is a hierarchical representation of the Scene. Elements in the scene graph may contain child elements, and all of them are instances of the Node class.

The Scene class contains a number of properties, such as its width and height. A Scene also has a property named root that holds the graphical elements that are displayed in the Scene, in this case a Group instance that contains an ImageView instance (which displays an image) and a Group instance. Nested within the latter Group is a Text instance (which is a graphical element, usually called a graphical node, or simply node).

Notice that the root property of the Scene contains an instance of the Group class. The root property may contain an instance of any subclass of javafx.scene.Node, and typically contains one capable of holding its own set of Node instances. Take a look at the JavaFX API documentation that we showed you how to access in the "Use the Official Specifications" section earlier and check out the Node class to see the properties and methods available to any graphical node. Also, take a look at the ImageView class in the javafx.scene.image package and the Group class in the javafx.scene package. In both cases, they inherit from the Node class.

■ **Tip** We can't emphasize enough the importance of having the JavaFX API documentation handy while reading this book. As classes, variables, and functions are mentioned, it's a good idea to look at the documentation to get more information. In addition, this habit helps you become more familiar with what is available to you in the API.

Displaying Images

As shown in the following code, displaying an image entails using an ImageView instance in conjunction with an Image instance.

```
Image image = new Image ("http://projavafx.com/images/earthrise.jpg");
ImageView imageView = new ImageView(image);
```

The Image instance identifies the image resource and loads it from the URL assigned to its URL variable. Both of these classes are located in the javafx.scene.image package.

Displaying Text

In the example, we created a Text Node as follows:

```
Text textRef = new Text(message);
```

If you consult the JavaFX API documentation, you will notice that a Text instance, contained in package javafx.scene.text, extends a Shape that extends a Node. As a consequence, a Text instance is a Node as well, and all the properties on Node apply on Text as well. Moreover, Text instances can be used in the scene graph the same way other nodes are used.

As you can detect from the example, a Text instance contains a number of properties that can be modified. Most of the properties are self-explanatory, but again, it is always useful to consult the JavaFX API documentation when manipulating objects.

Because all graphical elements in JavaFX directly or indirectly extend the Node class, and because the Node class already contains many useful properties, the amount of properties on a specific graphical element such as Text can be rather high.

In our example, we set a limited number of properties that we briefly explain next.

The method

```
textRef.setLayoutY(100)
```

applies a vertical translation of 100 pixels to the Text content.

The fill method is used to specify the color of the text.

While you're looking at the javafx.scene.text package in the API documentation, take a look at the font function of the Font class, which is used to define the font family, weight, and size of the Text.

The textOrigin property specifies how the text is aligned with its area.

Referring again to the JavaFX API documentation, notice that the VPos enum (in the javafx.geometry package) has fields that serve as constants, for example, BASELINE, BOTTOM, and TOP. These control the origin of the text with respect to vertical locations on the displayed Text:

- The TOP origin, as we're using it in the previous code snippet, places the top of the text (including ascenders) at the layoutY position, relative to the coordinate space in which the Text is located.
- The BOTTOM origin would place the bottom of the text, including descenders (located in a lowercase g, for example) at the layoutY position.
- The BASELINE origin would place the baseline of the text (excluding descenders) at the layoutY position. This is the default value for the textOrigin property of a Text instance.

The wrappingWidth property enables you to specify at what number of pixels the text will wrap.

The textAlignment property enables you to control how the text will be justified. In our example, TextAlignment.JUSTIFY aligns the text on both the left and right sides, expanding the space between words to achieve that.

The text that we're displaying is sufficiently long to wrap and be drawn on the Earth, so we need to define a rectangular region outside of which that text cannot be seen.

■ **Tip** We recommend you modify some of the values, recompile the example, and run it again. This will help you understanding how the different properties work. Alternatively, by using ScenicView you can inspect and modify the different properties at runtime.

Working with Graphical Nodes as a Group

One powerful graphical feature of JavaFX is the ability to create scene graphs, which consist of a tree of graphical nodes. You can then assign values to properties of a Group located in the hierarchy, and the nodes contained in the Group will be affected. In our current example from Listing 1-1, we're using a Group to contain a Text node and to clip a specific rectangular region within the Group so that the text doesn't appear on the moon or the Earth as it animates upward. Here's the relevant code snippet:

```
Group textGroup = new Group(textRef);
textGroup.setLayoutX(50);
textGroup.setLayoutY(180);
textGroup.setClip(new Rectangle(430, 85));
```

Notice that the Group is located 50 pixels to the right and 180 pixels down from where it would have been located by default. This is due to the values assigned to the layoutX and layoutY variables of the Group instance. Because this Group is contained directly by the Scene, its upper-left corner's location is 50 pixels to the right and 180 pixels down from the upper-left corner of the Scene. Take a look at Figure 1-5 to see this example illustrated as you read the rest of the explanation.

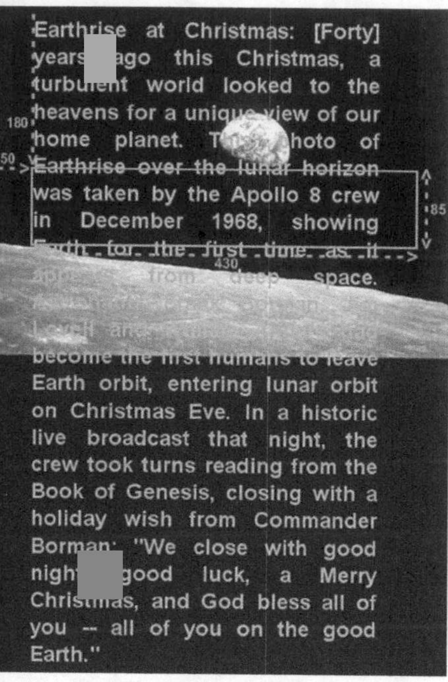

Figure 1-5. *The Scene, Group, Text, and clip illustrated*

A Group instance contains instances of Node subclasses by assigning a collection of them to itself via the children() method. In the previous code snippet, the Group contains a Text instance that has a value assigned to its layoutY property. Because this Text is contained by a Group, it assumes the two-dimensional space (also called the coordinate space) of the Group, with the origin of the Text node (0,0) coincident with the top-left corner of the Group. Assigning a value of 100 to the layoutY property causes the Text to be located 100 pixels down from the top of the Group, which is just below the bottom of the clip region, thus causing it to be out of view until the animation begins. Because a value isn't assigned to the layoutX variable, its value is 0 (the default).

The layoutX and layoutY properties of the Group just described are examples of our earlier statement that nodes contained in a Group will be affected by values assigned to properties of the Group. Another example is setting the opacity property of a Group instance to 0.5, which causes all of the nodes contained in that Group to become translucent. If the JavaFX API documentation is handy, look at the properties available in the javafx.scene.Group class. Then look at the properties available in the javafx.scene.Node class properties, which is where you'll find the layoutX, layoutY, and opacity variables that are inherited by the Group class.

Clipping Graphical Areas

To define a clipping area, we assign a Node subclass to the clip property that defines the clipping shape, in this case a Rectangle that is 430 pixels wide and 85 pixels high. In addition to keeping the Text from covering the moon, when the Text scrolls up as a result of animation, the clipping area keeps the Text from covering the earth.

Animating the Text to Make It Scroll Up

When the HelloEarthriseMain program is invoked, the Text begins scrolling up slowly. To achieve this animation, we're using the TranslateTransition class located in the javafx.animation package, as shown in the following snippet from Listing 1-1.

```
TranslateTransition transTransition = new TranslateTransition(new Duration(75000), textRef);
transTransition.setToY(-820);
transTransition.setInterpolator(Interpolator.LINEAR);
transTransition.setCycleCount(Timeline.INDEFINITE);
...code omitted...
// Start the text animation
transTransition.play();
```

The javafx.animation package contains convenience classes for animating nodes. This TranslateTransition instance translates the Text node referenced by the textRef variable from its original Y position of 100 pixels to a Y position of -820 pixels, over a duration of 75 seconds. The Interpolator.LINEAR constant is assigned to the interpolator property, which causes the animation to proceed in a linear fashion. A look at the API docs for the Interpolator class in the javafx.animation package reveals that there are other forms of interpolation available, one of which is EASE_OUT, which slows down the animation toward the end of the specified duration.

■ **Note** Interpolation in this context is the process of calculating the value at any point in time, given a beginning value, an ending value, and a duration.

The last line in the previous snippet begins executing the play method of the TranslateTransition instance created earlier in the program. This makes the Text begin scrolling upward. Because of the value assigned to the cycleCount variable, this transition will repeat indefinitely.

Now that you've compiled and run this example using the command-line tools and we've walked through the code together, it is time to begin using the NetBeans IDE to make the development and deployment process faster and easier.

Building and Running the Program with NetBeans

Assuming that you've downloaded and extracted the source code for this book into a directory, follow the directions in this exercise to build and run the Hello Earthrise program in NetBeans. If you haven't yet downloaded the Java SDK and NetBeans, please do so from the site listed in the Resources section at the end of this chapter.

BUILDING AND RUNNING HELLO EARTHRISE WITH NETBEANS

To build and run the Hello Earthrise program, perform the following steps.

1. Start up NetBeans.
2. Choose File ➤ New Project from the menu bar. The first window of the New Project Wizard will appear. Select the JavaFX category, and you will see wizard shown in Figure 1-6:

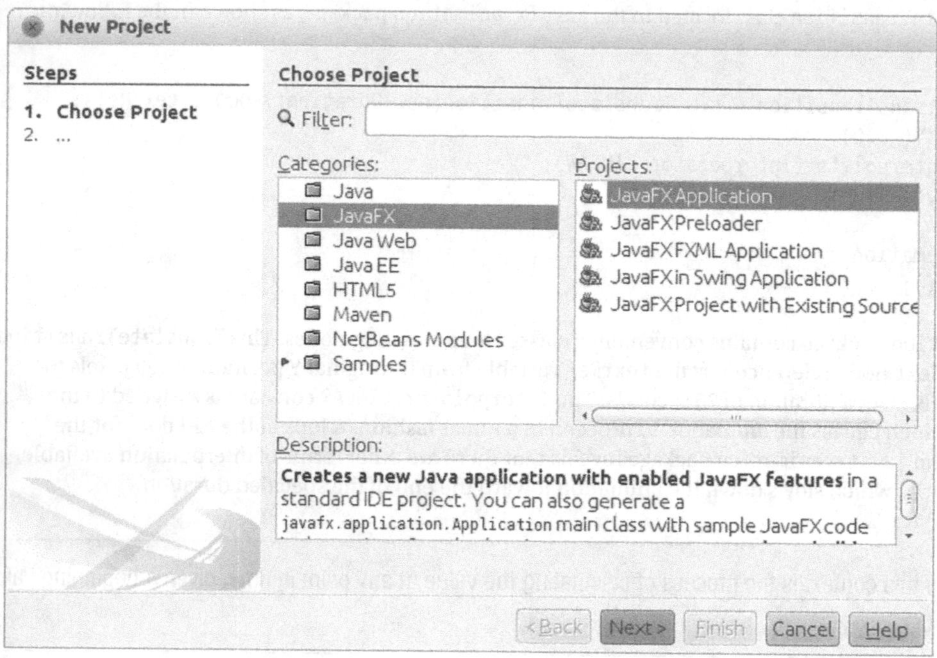

Figure 1-6. *New Project Wizard*

3. Choose JavaFX Application in the Projects pane, and click Next. The next page in the New Project Wizard, shown in Figure 1-7, should appear:

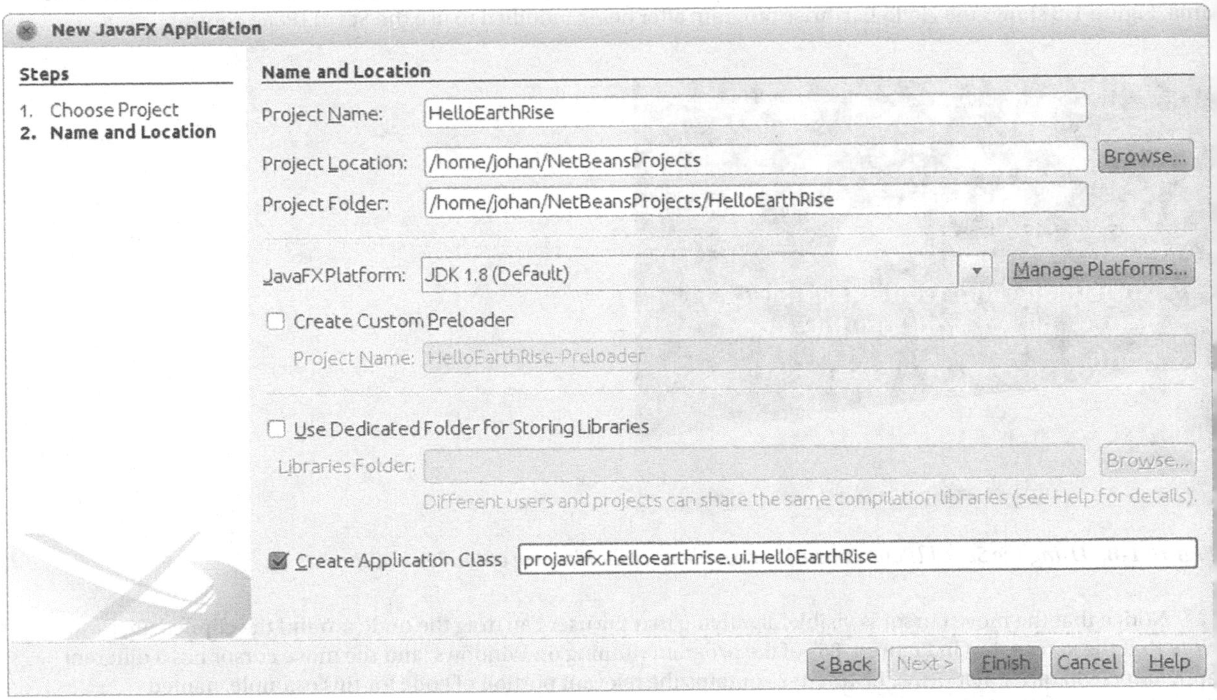

Figure 1-7. *The next page of the New Prjoect Wizard*

4. On this screen, type the project name (we used HelloEarthRise) and click Browse.
5. Select a Project Location, either by typing it directly into the text box or by clicking Browse to navigate to the desired directory (we used `/home/johan/NetBeansProjects`).
6. Select the Create Application Class check box, and change the supplied package/class name to `projavafx.helloearthrise.ui.HelloEarthRiseMain`.
7. Click Finish. The HelloEarthRise project with a default main class created by NetBeans should now be created. If you'd like to run this default program, right-click the HelloEarthRise project in the Projects pane and select Run Project from the shortcut menu.
8. Enter the code from Listing 1-1 into the HelloEarthRiseMain.java code window. You can type it in, or cut and paste it from the `HelloEarthRiseMain.java` file located in the `Chapter01/HelloEarthRise/src/projavafx/helloearthrise/ui` directory of this book's source code download.
9. Right-click the HelloEarthRise project in the Projects pane and select Run Project from the shortcut menu.

The HelloEarthRise program should begin executing, as you saw in Figure 1-4 earlier in the chapter.

At this point, you've built and run the "Hello Earthrise" program application, both from the command line and using NetBeans. Before leaving this example, we show you another way to achieve the scrolling `Text` node. There is a class in the `javafx.scene.control` package named `ScrollPane` whose purpose is to provide a scrollable view of a node that is typically larger than the view. In addition, the user can drag the node being viewed within the scrollable area. Figure 1-8 shows the Hello Earthrise program after being modified to use the `ScrollPane` control.

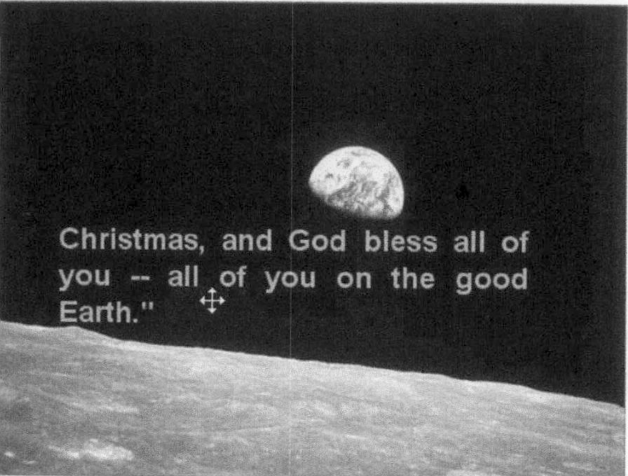

***Figure 1-8.** Using the `ScrollPane` control to provide a scrollable view of the `Text` node*

Notice that the move cursor is visible, signifying that the user can drag the node around the clipped area. Note that the screenshot in Figure 1-8 is of the program running on Windows, and the move cursor has a different appearance on other platforms. Listing 1-2 contains the relevant portion of code for this example, named `HelloScrollPaneMain.java`.

Listing 1-2. The `HelloScrollPaneMain.java` Program

```
...code omitted...
    // Create a ScrollPane containing the text
        ScrollPane scrollPane = new ScrollPane();
        scrollPane.setLayoutX(50);
        scrollPane.setLayoutY(180);
        scrollPane.setPrefWidth(400);
        scrollPane.setPrefHeight(85);
        scrollPane.setHbarPolicy(ScrollPane.ScrollBarPolicy.NEVER);
        scrollPane.setVbarPolicy(ScrollPane.ScrollBarPolicy.NEVER);
        scrollPane.setPannable(true);
        scrollPane.setContent(textRef);
        scrollPane.setStyle("-fx-background-color: transparent;");

        // Combine ImageView and ScrollPane
        Group root = new Group(iv, scrollPane);
        Scene scene = new Scene(root, 516, 387);
```

Now that you've learned some of the basics of JavaFX application development, let's examine another sample application to help you learn more JavaFX concepts and constructs.

Developing Your Second JavaFX Program: "More Cowbell!"

If you're familiar with the *Saturday Night Live* television show, you may have seen the "More Cowbell" sketch, in which Christopher Walken's character keeps asking for "more cowbell" during a Blue Oyster Cult recording session. The following JavaFX example program covers some of the simple but powerful concepts of JavaFX in the context of an imaginary application that lets you select a music genre and control the volume. Of course, "Cowbell Metal," shortened to "Cowbell," is one of the available genres. Figure 1-9 shows a screenshot of this application, which has a sort of retro iPhone application look.

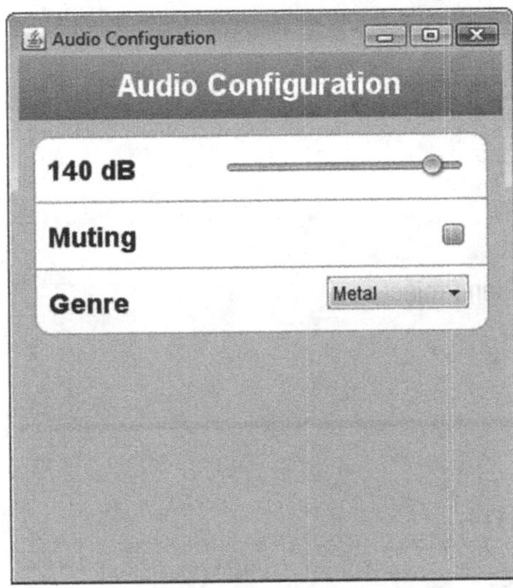

Figure 1-9. *The Audio Configuration "More Cowbell" program*

Building and Running the Audio Configuration Program

Earlier in the chapter, we showed you how to create a new JavaFX project in NetBeans. For this example (and the rest of the examples in the book), we take advantage of the fact that the code download bundle for the book contains both NetBeans and Eclipse project files for each example. Follow the instructions in this exercise to build and run the Audio Configuration application.

BUILDING AND RUNNING THE AUDIO CONFIGURATION PROGRAM USING NETBEANS

To build and execute this program using NetBeans, perform the following steps.

1. From the File menu, select the Open Project menu item. In the Open Project dialog box, navigate to the Chapter01 directory where you extracted the book's code download bundle, as shown in Figure 1-10.

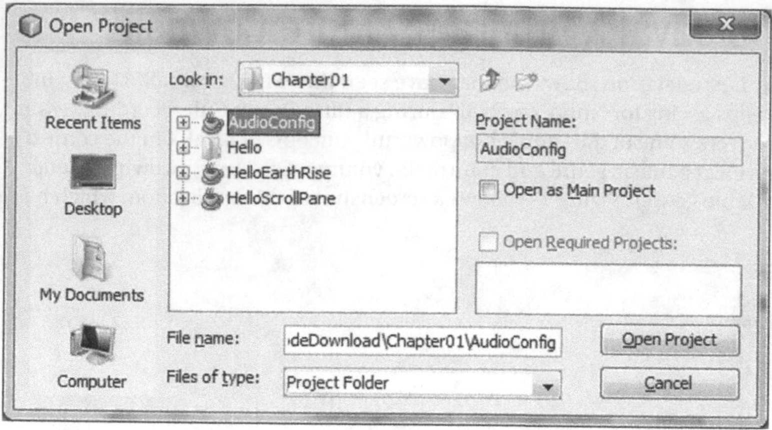

Figure 1-10. *The Chapter 01 directory in the Open Project dialog box*

2. Select the AudioConfig project in the pane on the left, and click Open Project.
3. Run the project as discussed previously.

The application should appear as shown in Figure 1-9.

The Behavior of the Audio Configuration Program

When you run the application, notice that adjusting the volume slider changes the associated decibel (dB) level displayed. Also, selecting the Muting check box disables the slider, and selecting various genres changes the volume slider. This behavior is enabled by concepts that are shown in the code that follows, such as the following:

- Binding to a class that contains a model
- Using change listeners
- Creating observable lists

Understanding the Audio Configuration Program

The Audio Configuration program contains two source code files, shown in Listing 1-3 and Listing 1-4:

- The `AudioConfigMain.java` file in Listing 1-3 contains the main class, and expresses the UI in a manner that you are familiar with from the Hello Earthrise example in Listing 1-1.
- The `AudioConfigModel.java` file in Listing 1-4 contains a model for this program, which holds the state of the application, to which the UI is bound.

Listing 1-3. The `AudioConfigMain.java` Program

```
package projavafx.audioconfig.ui;

import javafx.application.Application;
import javafx.geometry.VPos;
import javafx.scene.Group;
import javafx.scene.Scene;
```

```
import javafx.scene.control.CheckBox;
import javafx.scene.control.ChoiceBox;
import javafx.scene.control.Slider;
import javafx.scene.paint.Color;
import javafx.scene.paint.CycleMethod;
import javafx.scene.paint.LinearGradient;
import javafx.scene.paint.Stop;
import javafx.scene.shape.Line;
import javafx.scene.shape.Rectangle;
import javafx.scene.text.Font;
import javafx.scene.text.FontWeight;
import javafx.scene.text.Text;
import javafx.stage.Stage;
import projavafx.audioconfig.model.AudioConfigModel;

public class AudioConfigMain extends Application {

    // A reference to the model
    AudioConfigModel acModel = new AudioConfigModel();

    Text textDb;
    Slider slider;
    CheckBox mutingCheckBox;
    ChoiceBox genreChoiceBox;
    Color color = Color.color(0.66, 0.67, 0.69);

    public static void main(String[] args) {
        Application.launch(args);
    }

    @Override
    public void start(Stage stage) {
        Text title = new Text(65,12, "Audio Configuration");
        title.setTextOrigin(VPos.TOP);
        title.setFill(Color.WHITE);
        title.setFont(Font.font("SansSerif", FontWeight.BOLD, 20));

        Text textDb = new Text();
        textDb.setLayoutX(18);
        textDb.setLayoutY(69);
        textDb.setTextOrigin(VPos.TOP);
        textDb.setFill(Color.web("#131021"));
        textDb.setFont(Font.font("SansSerif", FontWeight.BOLD, 18));

        Text mutingText = new Text(18, 113, "Muting");
        mutingText.setTextOrigin(VPos.TOP);
        mutingText.setFont(Font.font("SanSerif", FontWeight.BOLD, 18));
        mutingText.setFill(Color.web("#131021"));

        Text genreText = new Text(18,154,"Genre");
        genreText.setTextOrigin(VPos.TOP);
```

```
        genreText.setFill(Color.web("#131021"));
        genreText.setFont(Font.font("SanSerif", FontWeight.BOLD, 18));

        slider = new Slider();
        slider.setLayoutX(135);
        slider.setLayoutY(69);
        slider.setPrefWidth(162);
        slider.setMin(acModel.minDecibels);
        slider.setMax(acModel.maxDecibels);

        mutingCheckBox = new CheckBox();
        mutingCheckBox.setLayoutX(280);
        mutingCheckBox.setLayoutY(113);

        genreChoiceBox = new ChoiceBox();
        genreChoiceBox.setLayoutX(204);
        genreChoiceBox.setLayoutY(154);
        genreChoiceBox.setPrefWidth(93);
        genreChoiceBox.setItems(acModel.genres);
        Stop[] stops = new Stop[]{new Stop(0, Color.web("0xAEBBCC")), new Stop(1,
Color.web("0x6D84A3"))};

        LinearGradient linearGradient = new LinearGradient(0, 0, 0, 1, true,
CycleMethod.NO_CYCLE, stops);
        Rectangle rectangle = new Rectangle(0, 0, 320, 45);
        rectangle.setFill(linearGradient);

        Rectangle rectangle2 = new Rectangle(0, 43, 320, 300);
        rectangle2.setFill(Color.rgb(199, 206, 213));

        Rectangle rectangle3 = new Rectangle(8, 54, 300, 130);
        rectangle3.setArcHeight(20);
        rectangle3.setArcWidth(20);
        rectangle3.setFill(Color.WHITE);
        rectangle3.setStroke(color);

        Line line1 = new Line(9, 97, 309, 97);
        line1.setStroke(color);

        Line line2 = new Line(9, 141, 309, 141);
        line2.setFill(color);

        Group group = new Group(rectangle, title, rectangle2, rectangle3,
                textDb,
                slider,
                line1,
                mutingText,
                mutingCheckBox, line2, genreText,
                genreChoiceBox);
        Scene scene = new Scene(group, 320, 343);
```

```
        textDb.textProperty().bind(acModel.selectedDBs.asString().concat(" dB"));
        slider.valueProperty().bindBidirectional(acModel.selectedDBs);
        slider.disableProperty().bind(acModel.muting);
        mutingCheckBox.selectedProperty().bindBidirectional(acModel.muting);
        acModel.genreSelectionModel = genreChoiceBox.getSelectionModel();
        acModel.addListenerToGenreSelectionModel();
        acModel.genreSelectionModel.selectFirst();

        stage.setScene(scene);
        stage.setTitle("Audio Configuration");
        stage.show();
    }
}
```

Take a look at the AudioConfigMain.java source code in Listing 1-3, after which we examine it together, focusing on concepts not covered in the previous example.

Now that you've seen the main class in this application, let's walk through the new concepts.

The Magic of Binding

One of the most powerful aspects of JavaFX is binding, which enables the application's UI to easily stay in sync with the state, or model, of the application. The model for a JavaFX application is typically held in one or more classes, in this case the AudioConfigModel class. Look at the following snippet, taken from Listing 1-3, in which we create an instance of this model class.

```
AudioConfigModel acModel = new AudioConfigModel();
```

There are several graphical node instances in the scene of this UI (recall that a scene consists of a sequence of nodes). Skipping past several of them, we come to the graphical nodes shown in the following snippet that have a property bound to the selectedDBs property in the model.

```
textDb = new Text();
... code omitted
slider = new Slider();
...code omitted...
textDb.textProperty().bind(acModel.selectedDBs.asString().concat(" dB"));
slider.valueProperty().bindBidirectional(acModel.selectedDBs);
```

As shown in this code, the text property of the Text object is bound to an expression. The bind function contains an expression (that includes the selectedDBs property), which is evaluated and becomes the value of the text property. Look at Figure 1-9 (or check the running application) to see the content value of the Text node displayed to the left of the slider.

Notice also in the code that the value property of the Slider node is bound to the selectedDBs property in the model as well, but that it uses the bindBidirectional() method. This causes the bind to be bidirectional, so in this case when the slider is moved, the selectedDBs property in the model changes. Conversely, when the selectedDBs property changes (as a result of changing the genre), the slider moves.

Go ahead and move the slider to demonstrate the effects of the bind expressions in the snippet. The number of decibels displayed at the left of the slider should change as the slider is adjusted.

There are other bound properties in Listing 1-3 that we point out when we walk through the model class. Before leaving the UI, we point out some color-related concepts in this example.

Colors and Gradients

The following snippet from Listing 1-3 contains an example of defining a color gradient pattern, as well as defining colors.

```
Stop[] stops = new Stop[]{new Stop(0, Color.web("0xAEBBCC")), new Stop(1, Color.web("0x6D84A3"))};
LinearGradient linearGradient = new LinearGradient(0, 0, 0, 1, true, CycleMethod.NO_CYCLE, stops);
Rectangle rectangle = new Rectangle(0, 0, 320, 45);
rectangle.setFill(linearGradient);
```

If the JavaFX API docs are handy, first take a look at the `javafx.scene.shape.Rectangle` class and notice that it inherits a property named `fill` that is of type `javafx.scene.paint.Paint`. Looking at the JavaFX API docs for the `Paint` class, you'll see that the `Color`, `ImagePattern`, `LinearGradient`, and `RadialGradient` classes are subclasses of `Paint`. This means that the fill of any shape can be assigned a color, pattern, or gradient.

To create a `LinearGradient`, as shown in the code, you need to define at least two stops, which define the location and color at that location. In this example, the offset value of the first stop is 0.0, and the offset value of the second stop is 1.0. These are the values at both extremes of the unit square, the result being that the gradient will span the entire node (in this case a `Rectangle`). The direction of the `LinearGradient` is controlled by its `startX`, `startY`, `endX`, and `endY` values, which we pass via the constructor. In this case, the direction is only vertical because the `startY` value is 0.0 and the `endY` value is 1.0, whereas the `startX` and `endX` values are both 0.0.

Note that in the Hello Earthrise example in Listing 1-1, the constant named `Color.WHITE` was used to represent the color white. In the previous snippet, the web function of the `Color` class is used to define a color from a hexadecimal value.

The Model Class for the Audio Configuration Example

Take a look at the source code for the `AudioConfigModel` class in Listing 1-4.

Listing 1-4. The Source Code for `AudioConfigModel.java`

```
package projavafx.audioconfig.model;

import javafx.beans.Observable;
import javafx.beans.property.BooleanProperty;
import javafx.beans.property.IntegerProperty;
import javafx.beans.property.SimpleBooleanProperty;
import javafx.beans.property.SimpleIntegerProperty;
import javafx.collections.FXCollections;
import javafx.collections.ObservableList;
import javafx.scene.control.SingleSelectionModel;

/**
 * The model class that the AudioConfigMain class uses
 */
public class AudioConfigModel {
  /**
   * The minimum audio volume in decibels
   */
  public double minDecibels = 0.0;
```

```
    /**
     * The maximum audio volume in decibels
     */
    public double maxDecibels = 160.0;

    /**
     * The selected audio volume in decibels
     */
    public IntegerProperty selectedDBs = new SimpleIntegerProperty(0);

    /**
     * Indicates whether audio is muted
     */
    public BooleanProperty muting = new SimpleBooleanProperty(false);

    /**
     * List of some musical genres
     */
    public ObservableList genres = FXCollections.observableArrayList(
      "Chamber",
      "Country",
      "Cowbell",
      "Metal",
      "Polka",
      "Rock"
    );

    /**
     * A reference to the selection model used by the Slider
     */
    public SingleSelectionModel genreSelectionModel;

    /**
     * Adds a change listener to the selection model of the ChoiceBox, and contains
     * code that executes when the selection in the ChoiceBox changes.
     */
  public void addListenerToGenreSelectionModel() {
      genreSelectionModel.selectedIndexProperty().addListener((Observable o) -> {
          int selectedIndex = genreSelectionModel.selectedIndexProperty().getValue();
          switch(selectedIndex) {
              case 0: selectedDBs.setValue(80);
              break;
              case 1: selectedDBs.setValue(100);
              break;
              case 2: selectedDBs.setValue(150);
              break;
              case 3: selectedDBs.setValue(140);
              break;
```

```
            case 4: selectedDBs.setValue(120);
            break;
            case 5: selectedDBs.setValue(130);
        }
    });

  }
}
```

Using InvalidationListeners and Lambda Expressions

In the earlier section "The Magic of Binding," we showed how you can use property binding for dynamically changing parameters. There is another, more low-level but also more flexible way of achieving this, using `ChangeListeners` and `InvalidationListeners`. These concepts are discussed in more detail in Chapter 4.

In our example, we add an `InvalidationListener` to the `selectedIndexProperty` of the `genreSelectionModel`. When the value of the `selectedIndexProperty` changes, and when we didn't retrieve it yet, the `invalidated(Observable)` method on the added `InvalidationListener` will be called. In the implementation of this method, we retrieve the value of the `selectedIndexProperty`, and based on its value, the value of the `selectedDBs` property is changed. This is achieved with the following code:

```
public void addListenerToGenreSelectionModel() {
    genreSelectionModel.selectedIndexProperty().addListener((Observable o) -> {
        int selectedIndex = genreSelectionModel.selectedIndexProperty().getValue();
        switch(selectedIndex) {
            case 0: selectedDBs.setValue(80);
            break;
            case 1: selectedDBs.setValue(100);
            break;
            case 2: selectedDBs.setValue(150);
            break;
            case 3: selectedDBs.setValue(140);
            break;
            case 4: selectedDBs.setValue(120);
            break;
            case 5: selectedDBs.setValue(130);
        }
    });

  }
```

Note that we are using a Lambda expression here rather than creating a new instance of the `InvalidationListener` and implementing its single abstract method invalidated.

■ **Tip** One of the major enhancements in JavaFX 8 is the fact that it is using Java 8. As a consequence, abstract classes with a single abstract method can easily be replaced by Lambda expressions, which clearly enhances readability of the code.

What causes selectedIndexProperty of the genreSelectionModel to change? To see the answer to this, we have to revisit some code in Listing 1-3. In the following code snippet, the setItems method of ChoiceBox is used to populate the ChoiceBox with items that each contain a genre.

```
genreChoiceBox = new ChoiceBox();
genreChoiceBox.setLayoutX(204);
genreChoiceBox.setLayoutY(154);
genreChoiceBox.setPrefWidth(93);
genreChoiceBox.setItems(acModel.genres);
```

This snippet from the model code in Listing 1-4 contains the collection to which the ComboBox items are bound:

```
/**
 * List of some musical genres
 */
public ObservableList genres = FXCollections.observableArrayList(
  "Chamber",
  "Country",
  "Cowbell",
  "Metal",
  "Polka",
  "Rock"
);
```

When the user chooses a different item in the ChoiceBox, the invalidationListener is invoked. Looking again at the code in the invalidationListener, you'll see that the value of the selectedDBs property changes, which as you may recall, is bidirectionally bound to the slider. This is why the slider moves when you select a genre in the combo box. Go ahead and test this by running the Audio Config program.

■ **Note** Associating the items property of the ChoiceBox with an ObservableList causes the items in the ChoiceBox to be automatically updated when the elements in the underlying collection are modified.

Surveying JavaFX Features

We close this chapter by surveying many of the features of JavaFX, some of which are a review for you. We do this by describing several of the more commonly used packages and classes in the Java SDK API.

The javafx.stage package contains the following:

- The Stage class, which is the top level of the UI containment hierarchy for any JavaFX application, regardless of where it is deployed (e.g., the desktop, a browser, or a cell phone).
- The Screen class, which represents the displays on the machine in which a JavaFX program is running. This enables you to get information about the screens, such as size and resolution.

The javafx.scene package contains some classes that you'll use often:

- The Scene class is the second level of the UI containment hierarchy for JavaFX applications. It includes all of the UI elements contained in the application. These elements are called graphical nodes, or simply nodes.
- The Node class is the base class of all of the graphical nodes in JavaFX. UI elements such as text, images, media, shapes, and controls (e.g., text boxes and buttons) are all subclasses of Node. Take a moment to look at the variables and functions in the Node class to appreciate the capabilities provided to all of its subclasses, including bounds calculation and mouse and keyboard event handling.
- The Group class is a subclass of the Node class. Its purpose includes grouping nodes together into a single coordinate space and allowing transforms (e.g., rotate) to be applied to the whole group. Also, attributes of the group that are changed (e.g., opacity) apply to all of the nodes contained within the group.

Several packages begin with javafx.scene that contain subclasses of Node of various types. Examples include the following:

- The javafx.scene.image package contains the Image and ImageView classes, which enable images to be displayed in the Scene. The ImageView class is a subclass of Node.
- The javafx.scene.shape package contains several classes for drawing shapes such as Circle, Rectangle, Line, Polygon, and Arc. The base class of the shapes, named Shape, contains an attribute named fill that enables you to specify a color, pattern, or gradient with which to fill the shape.
- The javafx.scene.text package contains the Text class for drawing text in the scene. The Font class enables you to specify the font name and size of the text.
- The javafx.scene.media package has classes that enable you to play media. The MediaView class is a subclass of Node that displays the media.
- The javafx.scene.chart package has classes that help you easily create area, bar, bubble, line, pie, and scatter charts. The corresponding UI classes in this package are AreaChart, BarChart, BubbleChart, LineChart, PieChart, and ScatterChart.

Here are some other packages in the JavaFX 8 API.

- The javafx.scene.control package contains several UI controls, each one having the ability to be skinned and styled via CSS.
- The javafx.scene.transform package enables you to transform nodes (scale, rotate, translate, shear, and affine).
- The javafx.scene.input package contains classes such as MouseEvent and KeyEvent that provide information about these events from within an event handler function such as the Node class's onMouseClicked event.
- The javafx.scene.layout package contains several layout containers, including HBox, VBox, BorderPane, FlowPane, StackPane, and TilePane.
- The javafx.scene.effect package contains easy-to-use effects such as Reflection, Glow, Shadow, BoxBlur, and Lighting.

- The `javafx.scene.web` package contains classes for easily embedding a web browser in your JavaFX applications.
- The `javafx.animation` package contains time-based interpolations typically used for animation and convenience classes for common transitions.
- The `javafx.beans`, `javafx.beans.binding`, `javafx.beans.property`, and `javafx.beans.value` packages contain classes that implement properties and binding.
- The `javafx.fxml` package contains classes that implement a very powerful facility known as FXML, a markup language for expressing JavaFX UIs in XML.
- The `javafx.util` package contains utility classes such as the `Duration` class used in the HelloEarthRise example earlier in this chapter.
- The `javafx.print` package contains utilities for printing (parts of) the layout of a JavaFX application.
- The `javafx.embed.swing` package contains the required functionality for embedded JavaFX applications in a Swing application.
- The `javafx.embed.swt` package contains the required functionality for embedding JavaFX applications in an SWT application.

Take a look at the JavaFX API docs again in light of this information to get a deeper sense of how you can use its capabilities.

Summary

Congratulations! You learned a lot about JavaFX in this chapter, including:

- JavaFX is rich-client Java, and is needed by the software development industry.
- Some of the high points of the history of JavaFX.
- Where to find JavaFX resources, including the Java SDK, NetBeans, SceneBuilder, ScenicView, and the API documentation.
- How to compile and run a JavaFX program from the command line.
- How to build and run a JavaFX program using NetBeans.
- How to use several of the classes in the JavaFX API.
- How to create a class in JavaFX and use it as a model that contains the state of a JavaFX application.
- How to use property binding to keep the UI easily in sync with the model.

We also looked at many of the available API packages and classes, and you learned how you can leverage their capabilities. Now that you have a jump start in JavaFX, you can begin examining the details of JavaFX in Chapter 2.

Resources

For some background information on JavaFX, you can consult the following resources.

- This book's code examples: The Source Code/Download section at the Apress web site (`www.apress.com`).
- Java Posse #163: Newscast for February 8, 2008: This is a podcast of a Java Posse interview with Josh Marinacci and Richard Bair on the subject of JavaFX. The URL is `http://javaposse.com/java_posse_163_newscast_for_feb_8th_2008`.
- "Congratulations to the JavaFX Script Compiler Team—The Elephant Is Through the Door": A blog post by one of this book's authors, Jim Weaver, that congratulated the JavaFX compiler team for reaching a tipping point in the project. The URL is `http://learnjavafx.typepad.com/weblog/2007/12/congratulations.html`.
- Oracles's `JavaFX.com` site: The home page for JavaFX where you can download the JavaFX SDK and other resource for JavaFX. The URL is `http://www.javafx.com`.
- The JavaFX Community site, with content from a wide source of contributors that are active in the JavaFX world. The URL is `https:// javafxcommunity.com`.
- FX Experience: A blog maintained by Oracle JavaFX Engineers Richard Bair, Jasper Potts, and Jonathan Giles. The URL is `http://fxexperience.com`.
- Jim Weaver's JavaFX Blog: A blog, started in October 2007, the stated purpose of which is to help the reader become a "JavaFXpert." The URL is `http://javafxpert.com`.
- Weiqi Gao's Observation: A blog in which Weiqi Gao shares his experience in software development. The URL is `http://weiqigao.blogspot.com/`.
- Dean Iverson's Pleasing Software Blog: A blog in which Dean Iverson shares his innovations in JavaFX and GroovyFX. The URL is `http://pleasingsoftware.blogspot.com`.
- Steve on Java: A blog in which Stephen Chin keeps the world updated on his tireless exploits in the areas of JavaFX, Java, and Agile development. The URL is `http://steveonjava.com`.
- Johan's blog: A blog in which Johan Vos discusses JavaFX and Java Enterprise. The URL is `http://blogs.lodgon.com/johan`.
- JavaFX Eclipse Plugin: Eclipse tooling for JavaFX 2.0, being developed by Tom Shindl. The URL for the announcement is `http://tomsondev.bestsolution.at/2011/06/24/introducing-efxclipse/`.
- ScenicView: An application for inspecting the scenegraph of your JavaFX applications. The URL is `http://scenic-view.org`.
- RoboVM, allowing you to port JavaFX Applications to iOS. The URL is `http://robovm.org`.
- JavaFX-Android port, allowing you to run JavaFX applications on Android. The URL is `https://bitbucket.org/javafxports/android/wiki/Home`.
- JavaFXPorts, a web site dedicated to the mobile ports of JavaFX. The URL is `http://javafxports.org`.
- ControlsFX, high-quality custom JavaFX controls. The URL is `http://controlsfx.org`.
- JFXtras.org, high-quality custom JavaFX controls. The URL is `http://jfxtras.org`.

CHAPTER 2

Creating a User Interface in JavaFX

Life is the art of drawing without an eraser.

—John W. Gardner

Chapter 1 gave you a jump start using JavaFX by covering the basics in developing and executing JavaFX programs. Now we cover many of the details about creating a UI in JavaFX that were glossed over in Chapter 1. First on the agenda is to get you acquainted with the *theater* metaphor used by JavaFX to express UIs and to cover the significance of what we call a *node-centric UI*.

Programmatic Versus Declarative Creation of the User Interface

The JavaFX platform provides two complementary ways for creating a UI. In this chapter, we discuss how you can use the Java API to create and populate a UI. This is a convenient way for Java developers who are used to writing code to leverage APIs.

Designers often use graphical tools that allow them to declare rather than program a UI. The JavaFX platform defines FXML, which is an XML-based markup language that can be used to declaratively describe a UI. Furthermore, a graphical tool called SceneBuilder is made available by Oracle, and this tool is capable of working with FXML files. The use of SceneBuilder is demonstrated in Chapter 3.

Note that parts of a UI can be created using the API, where other parts can be created using SceneBuilder. The FXML APIs provide the bridge and the integration glue between the two approaches.

Introduction to Node-Centric UIs

Creating a UI in JavaFX is like creating a theater play, in that it typically consists of these very simple steps:

1. *Create a stage on which your program will perform.* The realization of your stage will depend on the platform on which it is deployed (e.g., a desktop, a tablet, or an embedded system).

2. *Create a scene in which the actors and props (nodes) will visually interact with each other and the audience (the users of your program).* Like any good set designer in the theater business, good JavaFX developers endeavor to make their scenes visually appealing. To this end, it is often a good idea to collaborate with a graphic designer on your "theater play."

3. *Create nodes in the scene.* These nodes are subclasses of the `javafx.scene.Node` class, which include UI controls, shapes, Text (a type of shape), images, media players, embedded browsers, and custom UI components that you create. Nodes can also be containers for other nodes, often providing cross-platform layout capabilities. A scene has a scene graph that contains a directed graph of nodes. Individual nodes and groups of nodes can be manipulated in many ways (e.g., moving, scaling, and setting opacity) by changing the values of a very rich set of `Node` properties.
4. *Create variables and classes that represent the model for the nodes in the scene.* As discussed in Chapter 1, one of the very powerful aspects of JavaFX is binding, which enables the application's UI to stay in sync easily with the state, or model, of the application.

■ **Note** Most of the examples in this chapter are small programs intended to demonstrate UI concepts. For this reason, the model in many of these examples consists of variables appearing in the main program, rather than being contained by separate Java classes (e.g., the `AudioConfigModel` class in Chapter 1).

---

5. *Create event handlers, such as* `onMousePressed`, *that allow the user to interact with your program.* Often these event handlers manipulate instance variables in the model. Many of these handlers require a single abstract method to be implemented, and as a consequence provide a perfect opportunity to use lambda expressions.
6. *Create timelines and transitions that animate your scene.* For example, you might want the thumbnail images of a list of books to move smoothly across the scene or a page in the UI to fade into view. You might simply want a ping pong ball to move across the scene, bouncing off walls and paddles, which is demonstrated later in this chapter in the section, "The Zen of Node Collision Detection."

Let's get started with a closer look at Step 1, in which we examine the capabilities of the stage.

Setting the Stage

The appearance and functionality of your stage will depend on the platform on which it is deployed. For example, if deployed in an embedded device with a touch screen, your stage might be the whole touch screen. The stage for a JavaFX program deployed via Java Web Start will be a window.

Understanding the Stage Class

The `Stage` class is the top-level container for any JavaFX program that has a graphical UI. It has several properties and methods that allow it, for example, to be positioned, sized, given a title, made invisible, or given some degree of opacity. The two best ways that we know of to learn the capabilities of a class are to study the JavaFX API documentation and to examine (and write) programs that use it. In this section, we ask you to do both, beginning with looking at the API docs.

The JavaFX API docs may be found in the `docs/api` directory subordinate to where you installed the JavaFX SDK. Also, they are available online at the URL given in the Resources section at the end of this chapter. Open the `index.html` file in your browser, navigate to the `javafx.stage` package, and select the `Stage` class. That page should contain tables of Properties, Constructors, and Methods, including select ones shown in the excerpt in Figure 2-1.

Property Summary

All Methods | **Instance Methods** | **Concrete Methods**

Type	Property and Description
`ObjectProperty<java.lang.String>`	`fullScreenExitHint`
`ObjectProperty<KeyCombination>`	`fullScreenExitKey` Get the property for the Full Screen exit key combination.
`ReadOnlyBooleanProperty`	`fullScreen` Specifies whether this `Stage` should be a full-screen, undecorated window.
`ReadOnlyBooleanProperty`	`iconified` Defines whether the `Stage` is iconified or not.
`DoubleProperty`	`maxHeight` Defines the maximum height of this `Stage`.
`ReadOnlyBooleanProperty`	`maximized` Defines whether the `Stage` is maximized or not.
`DoubleProperty`	`maxWidth` Defines the maximum width of this `Stage`.
`DoubleProperty`	`minHeight` Defines the minimum height of this `Stage`.
`DoubleProperty`	`minWidth` Defines the minimum width of this `Stage`.
`BooleanProperty`	`resizable` Defines whether the `Stage` is resizable or not by the user.
`StringProperty`	`title` Defines the title of the `Stage`.

Properties inherited from class javafx.stage.Window

`eventDispatcher, focused, height, onCloseRequest, onHidden, onHiding, onShowing, onShown, opacity, scene, showing, width, x, y`

Constructor Summary

Constructors

Constructor and Description
`Stage()` Creates a new instance of decorated `Stage`.
`Stage(StageStyle style)` Creates a new instance of `Stage`.

Method Summary

All Methods | **Instance Methods** | **Concrete Methods**

Modifier and Type	Method and Description
`void`	`close()` Closes this `Stage`.

Figure 2-1. *A portion of the `Stage` class documentation in the JavaFX API*

Go ahead and explore the documentation for each of the properties and methods in the `Stage` class, remembering to click the links to reveal more detailed information. When you're finished, come back and we'll show you a program that demonstrates many of the properties and methods available in the `Stage` class.

Using the `Stage` Class: The StageCoach Example

A screenshot of the unassuming, purposely ill-fitting StageCoach example program is shown in Figure 2-2.

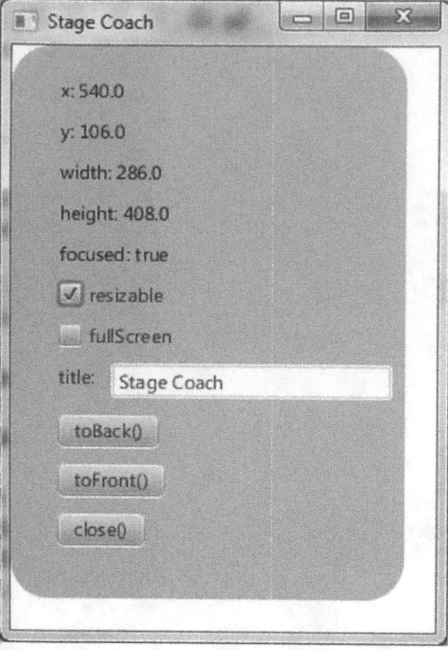

Figure 2-2. *A screenshot of the StageCoach example*

The StageCoach program was created to coach you through the finer points of using the `Stage` class and related classes such as `StageStyle` and `Screen`. Also, we use this program to show you how to get arguments passed into the program. Before walking through the behavior of the program, go ahead and open the project and execute it by following the instructions for building and executing the Audio-Config project in Chapter 1. The project file is located in the Chapter02 directory subordinate to where you extracted the book's code download bundle.

EXAMINING THE BEHAVIOR OF THE STAGECOACH PROGRAM

When the program starts, its appearance should be similar to the screenshot in Figure 2-2. To fully examine its behavior, perform the following steps. Note that for instructional purposes, the property and method names on the UI correspond to the properties and methods in the `Stage` instance.

1. Notice that the StageCoach program's window is initially displayed near the top of the screen, with its horizontal position in the center of the screen. Drag the program's window and observe that the x and y values near the top of the UI are dynamically updated to reflect its position on the screen.

2. Resize the program's window and observe that the width and height values change to reflect the width and height of the `Stage`. Note that this size includes the decorations (title bar and borders) of the window.

3. Click the program (or cause it to be in focus some other way) and notice that the focused value is true. Cause the window to lose focus, perhaps by clicking somewhere else on the screen, and notice that the focused value becomes false.

4. Clear the resizable check box and then notice that the resizable value becomes false. Then try to resize the window and note that it is not permitted. Select the resizable check box again to make the window resizable.

5. Select the fullScreen check box. Notice that the program occupies the full screen and that the window decorations are not visible. Clear the fullScreen check box to restore the program to its former size.

6. Edit the text in the text field beside the title label, noticing that the text in the window's title bar is changed to reflect the new value.

7. Drag the window to partially cover another window, and click toBack(). Notice that this places the program behind the other window, therefore causing the z-order to change.

8. With a portion of the program's window behind another window, but with the toFront() button visible, click that button. Notice that the program's window is placed in front of the other window.

9. Click close(), noticing that the program exits.

10. Invoke the program again, passing in the string `"undecorated"`. If invoking from NetBeans, use the Project Properties dialog box to pass this argument as shown in Figure 2-3. The `"undecorated"` string is passed as a parameter without a value.

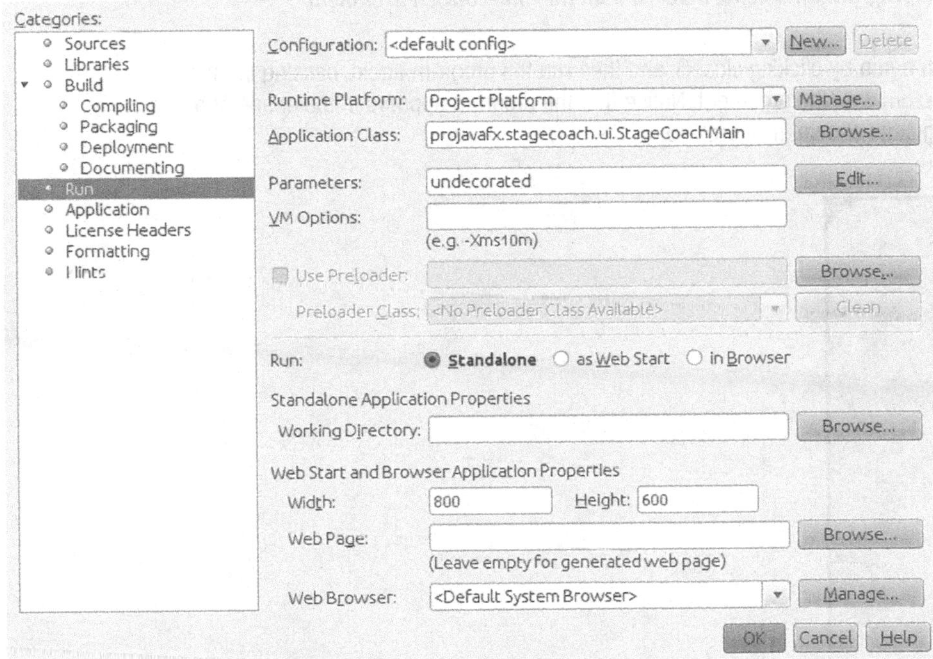

Figure 2-3. *Using NetBeans' Project Properties dialog box to pass an argument into the program*

11. Notice that this time the program appears without any window decorations, but the white background of the program includes the background of the window. The black outline in the screenshot shown in Figure 2-4 is part of the desktop background.

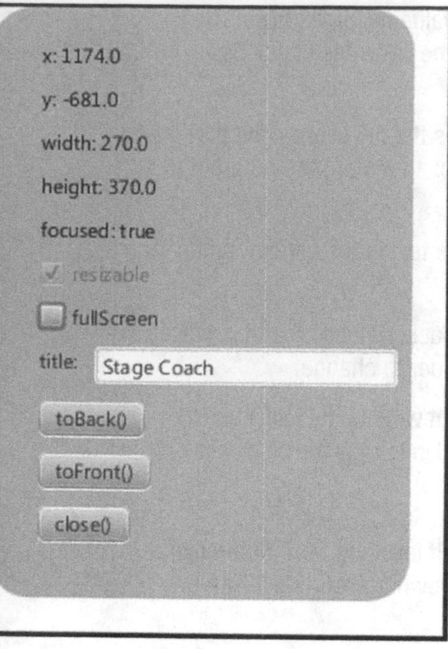

Figure 2-4. The StageCoach program after being invoked with the undecorated argument

12. Exit the program again by clicking close(), and then run the program again, passing in the string `"transparent"` as the argument. Notice that the program appears in the shape of a rounded rectangle, as shown in Figure 2-5.

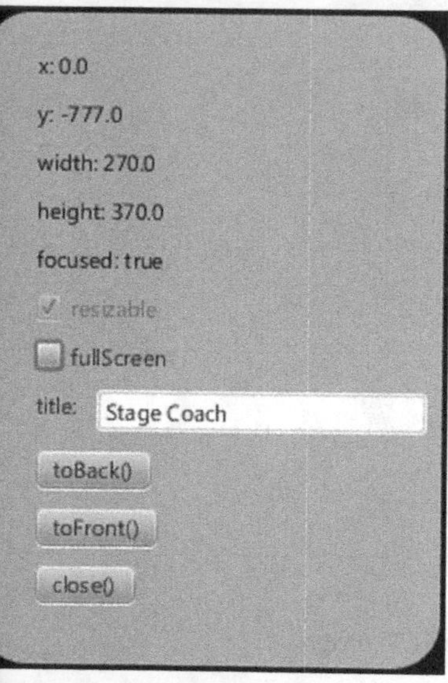

Figure 2-5. The StageCoach program after being invoked with the transparent argument

■ **Note** You might have noticed that the screenshots in Figures 2-4 and 2-5 have y values that are negative. This is because the application was positioned on the secondary monitor, logically above the primary monitor, when the screenshots were taken.

13. Click the application's UI, drag it around the screen, and click close() when finished. Congratulations on sticking with this 13-step exercise! Performing this exercise has prepared you to relate to the code behind it, which we now walk through together.

Understanding the StageCoach Program

Take a look at the code for the StageCoach program in Listing 2-1 before we point out new and relevant concepts.

Listing 2-1. StageCoachMain.java

```
package projavafx.stagecoach.ui;
import java.util.List;
import javafx.application.Application;
import javafx.beans.property.SimpleStringProperty;
import javafx.beans.property.StringProperty;
import javafx.geometry.Rectangle2D;
import javafx.geometry.VPos;
import javafx.scene.Group;
import javafx.scene.Scene;
import javafx.scene.control.Button;
import javafx.scene.control.CheckBox;
import javafx.scene.control.Label;
import javafx.scene.control.TextField;
import javafx.scene.input.MouseEvent;
import javafx.scene.layout.HBox;
import javafx.scene.layout.VBox;
import javafx.scene.paint.Color;
import javafx.scene.shape.Rectangle;
import javafx.scene.text.Text;
import javafx.stage.Screen;
import javafx.stage.Stage;
import javafx.stage.StageStyle;
import javafx.stage.WindowEvent;

public class StageCoachMain extends Application {

    StringProperty title = new SimpleStringProperty();

    Text textStageX;
    Text textStageY;
    Text textStageW;
    Text textStageH;
    Text textStageF;
```

```
    CheckBox checkBoxResizable;
    CheckBox checkBoxFullScreen;

    double dragAnchorX;
    double dragAnchorY;

    public static void main(String[] args) {
        Application.launch(args);
    }

    @Override
    public void start(Stage stage) {
        StageStyle stageStyle = StageStyle.DECORATED;
        List<String> unnamedParams = getParameters().getUnnamed();
        if (unnamedParams.size() > 0) {
            String stageStyleParam = unnamedParams.get(0);
            if (stageStyleParam.equalsIgnoreCase("transparent")) {
                stageStyle = StageStyle.TRANSPARENT;
            } else if (stageStyleParam.equalsIgnoreCase("undecorated")) {
                stageStyle = StageStyle.UNDECORATED;
            } else if (stageStyleParam.equalsIgnoreCase("utility")) {
                stageStyle = StageStyle.UTILITY;
            }
        }
        final Stage stageRef = stage;
        Group rootGroup;
        TextField titleTextField;
        Button toBackButton = new Button("toBack()");
        toBackButton.setOnAction(e -> stageRef.toBack());
        Button toFrontButton = new Button("toFront()");
        toFrontButton.setOnAction(e -> stageRef.toFront());
        Button closeButton = new Button("close()");
        closeButton.setOnAction(e -> stageRef.close());
        Rectangle blue = new Rectangle(250, 350, Color.SKYBLUE);
        blue.setArcHeight(50);
        blue.setArcWidth(50);
        textStageX = new Text();
        textStageX.setTextOrigin(VPos.TOP);
        textStageY = new Text();
        textStageY.setTextOrigin(VPos.TOP);
        textStageH = new Text();
        textStageH.setTextOrigin(VPos.TOP);
        textStageW = new Text();
        textStageW.setTextOrigin(VPos.TOP);
        textStageF = new Text();
        textStageF.setTextOrigin(VPos.TOP);
        checkBoxResizable = new CheckBox("resizable");
        checkBoxResizable.setDisable(stageStyle == StageStyle.TRANSPARENT
                || stageStyle == StageStyle.UNDECORATED);
        checkBoxFullScreen = new CheckBox("fullScreen");
        titleTextField = new TextField("Stage Coach");
```

```
Label titleLabel = new Label("title");
HBox titleBox = new HBox(titleLabel, titleTextField);
VBox contentBox = new VBox(
        textStageX, textStageY, textStageW, textStageH, textStageF,
        checkBoxResizable, checkBoxFullScreen,
        titleBox, toBackButton, toFrontButton, closeButton);
contentBox.setLayoutX(30);
contentBox.setLayoutY(20);
contentBox.setSpacing(10);
rootGroup = new Group(blue, contentBox);

Scene scene = new Scene(rootGroup, 270, 370);
scene.setFill(Color.TRANSPARENT);

//when mouse button is pressed, save the initial position of screen
rootGroup.setOnMousePressed((MouseEvent me) -> {
    dragAnchorX = me.getScreenX() - stageRef.getX();
    dragAnchorY = me.getScreenY() - stageRef.getY();
});

//when screen is dragged, translate it accordingly
rootGroup.setOnMouseDragged((MouseEvent me) -> {
    stageRef.setX(me.getScreenX() - dragAnchorX);
    stageRef.setY(me.getScreenY() - dragAnchorY);
});

textStageX.textProperty().bind(new SimpleStringProperty("x: ")
        .concat(stageRef.xProperty().asString()));
textStageY.textProperty().bind(new SimpleStringProperty("y: ")
        .concat(stageRef.yProperty().asString()));
textStageW.textProperty().bind(new SimpleStringProperty("width: ")
        .concat(stageRef.widthProperty().asString()));
textStageH.textProperty().bind(new SimpleStringProperty("height: ")
        .concat(stageRef.heightProperty().asString()));
textStageF.textProperty().bind(new SimpleStringProperty("focused: ")
        .concat(stageRef.focusedProperty().asString()));
stage.setResizable(true);
checkBoxResizable.selectedProperty()
        .bindBidirectional(stage.resizableProperty());
checkBoxFullScreen.selectedProperty().addListener((ov, oldValue, newValue) -> {
    stageRef.setFullScreen(checkBoxFullScreen.selectedProperty().getValue());
});
title.bind(titleTextField.textProperty());

stage.setScene(scene);
stage.titleProperty().bind(title);
stage.initStyle(stageStyle);
stage.setOnCloseRequest((WindowEvent we) -> {
    System.out.println("Stage is closing");
});
```

```
        stage.show();
        Rectangle2D primScreenBounds = Screen.getPrimary().getVisualBounds();
        stage.setX((primScreenBounds.getWidth() - stage.getWidth()) / 2);
        stage.setY((primScreenBounds.getHeight() - stage.getHeight()) / 4);
    }
}
```

Obtaining Program Arguments

The first new concept introduced by this program is the ability to read the arguments passed into a JavaFX program. The javafx.application package includes a class named Application that has application life cycle-related methods such as launch(), init(), start(), and stop(). Another method in the Application class is getParameters(), which gives the application access to the arguments passed on the command line, as well as unnamed parameters and <name,value> pairs specified in a JNLP file. Here's the relevant code snippet from Listing 2-1 for your convenience:

```
StageStyle stageStyle = StageStyle.DECORATED;
List<String> unnamedParams = getParameters().getUnnamed();
if (unnamedParams.size() > 0) {
  String stageStyleParam = unnamedParams.get(0);
  if (stageStyleParam.equalsIgnoreCase("transparent")) {
    stageStyle = StageStyle.TRANSPARENT;
  }
  else if (stageStyleParam.equalsIgnoreCase("undecorated")) {
    stageStyle = StageStyle.UNDECORATED;
  }
  else if (stageStyleParam.equalsIgnoreCase("utility")) {
    stageStyle = StageStyle.UTILITY;
  }
}
...code omitted...
stage.initStyle(stageStyle);
```

Setting the Style of the Stage

We're using the getParameters() method described previously to get an argument that tells us whether the stage style of the Stage instance should be its default (StageStyle.DECORATED), StageStyle.UNDECORATED, or StageStyle.TRANSPARENT. You saw the effects of each in the preceding exercise, specifically in Figures 2-2, 2-4, and 2-5.

Controlling Whether a Stage Is Resizable

As shown in the following excerpt from Listing 2-1, to make this application's window initially resizable we're calling the setResizable() method of the Stage instance. To keep the resizable property of the Stage and the state of the resizable check box synchronized, the check box is bidirectionally bound to the resizable property of the Stage instance.

```
stage.setResizable(true);
checkBoxResizable.selectedProperty()
        .bindBidirectional(stage.resizableProperty());
```

■ **Tip** A property that is bound cannot be explicitly set. In the code preceding the snippet, the resizable property is set with the `setResizable()` method *before* the property is bound in the next line.

Making a Stage Full Screen

Making the `Stage` show in full-screen mode is done by setting the `fullScreen` property of the `Stage` instance to true. As shown in the following snippet from Listing 2-1, to keep the `fullScreen` property of the `Stage` and the state of the fullScreen check box synchronized, the `fullScreen` property of the `Stage` instance is updated whenever the selected property of the `checkBox` changes.

```
checkBoxFullScreen.selectedProperty().addListener((ov, oldValue, newValue) -> {
    stageRef.setFullScreen(checkBoxFullScreen.selectedProperty().getValue());
});
```

Working with the Bounds of the Stage

The bounds of the `Stage` are represented by its `x`, `y`, `width`, and `height` properties, the values of which can be changed at will. This is demonstrated in the following snippet from Listing 2-1 where the `Stage` is placed near the top and centered horizontally on the primary screen after the `Stage` has been initialized.

```
Rectangle2D primScreenBounds = Screen.getPrimary().getVisualBounds();
stage.setX((primScreenBounds.getWidth() - stage.getWidth()) / 2);
stage.setY((primScreenBounds.getHeight() - stage.getHeight()) / 4);
```

We're using the `Screen` class of the `javafx.stage` package to get the dimensions of the primary screen so that the desired position may be calculated.

■ **Note** We intentionally made the `Stage` in Figure 2-2 larger than the `Scene` contained within to make the following point. The width and height of a `Stage` include its decorations (title bar and border), which vary on different platforms. It is therefore usually better to control the width and height of the `Scene` (we show you how in a bit) and let the `Stage` conform to that size.

Drawing Rounded Rectangles

As pointed out in Chapter 1, you can put rounded corners on a `Rectangle` by specifying the `arcWidth` and `arcHeight` for the corners. The following snippet from Listing 2-1 draws the sky-blue rounded rectangle that becomes the background for the transparent window example in Figure 2-5.

```
Rectangle blue = new Rectangle(250, 350, Color.SKYBLUE);
blue.setArcHeight(50);
blue.setArcWidth(50);
```

In this snippet, we use the three-argument constructor of `Rectangle`, in which the first two parameters specify the width and the height of the `Rectangle`. The third parameter defines the fill color of the `Rectangle`.

As you can detect from this code snippet, rounded rectangles are easily created using the arcWidth(double v) and arcHeight(double v) methods, where the parameter v defines the diameter of the arc.

Dragging the Stage on the Desktop When a Title Bar Isn't Available

The Stage may be dragged on the desktop using its title bar, but in the case where its StageStyle is UNDECORATED or TRANSPARENT, the title bar isn't available. To allow dragging in this circumstance, we added the code shown in the following code snippet from Listing 2-1.

```
//when mouse button is pressed, save the initial position of screen
rootGroup.setOnMousePressed((MouseEvent me) -> {
    dragAnchorX = me.getScreenX() - stageRef.getX();
    dragAnchorY = me.getScreenY() - stageRef.getY();
});

//when screen is dragged, translate it accordingly
rootGroup.setOnMouseDragged((MouseEvent me) -> {
    stageRef.setX(me.getScreenX() - dragAnchorX);
    stageRef.setY(me.getScreenY() - dragAnchorY);
});
```

Event handlers are covered a little later in the chapter, but as a preview, the lambda expression that is supplied to the onMouseDragged() method is called when the mouse is dragged. As a result, the values of the x and y properties are altered by the number of pixels that the mouse was dragged, which moves the Stage as the mouse is dragged.

Using UI Layout Containers

When developing applications that will be deployed in a cross-platform environment or are internationalized, it is good to use *layout containers*. One advantage of using layout containers is that when the node sizes change, their visual relationships with each other are predictable. Another advantage is that you don't have to calculate the location of each node that you place in the UI.

The following snippet from Listing 2-1 shows how the VBox layout class, located in the javafx.scene.layout package, is used to arrange the Text, CheckBox, HBox, and Button nodes in a column. This snippet also shows that layout containers may be nested, as demonstrated by the HBox with the name titleBox that arranges the Label and TextField nodes horizontally. Note that several lines of code are omitted from this snippet to show the layout nesting clearly:

```
HBox titleBox = new HBox(titleLabel, titleTextField);
VBox contentBox = new VBox(
        textStageX, textStageY, textStageW, textStageH, textStageF,
        checkBoxResizable, checkBoxFullScreen,
        titleBox, toBackButton, toFrontButton, closeButton);
```

The VBox layout class is similar to the Group class discussed in the Hello Earthrise example in Chapter 1, in that it contains a collection of nodes within it. Unlike the Group class, the VBox class arranges its contained nodes vertically, spacing them apart from each other by the number of pixels specified in the spacing property.

Ascertaining Whether the Stage Is in Focus

To know whether your JavaFX application is the one that currently is in focus (e.g., keys pressed are delivered to the application), simply consult the focused property of the Stage instance. The following snippet from Listing 2-1 demonstrates this.

```
textStageF.textProperty().bind(new SimpleStringProperty("focused: ")
        .concat(stageRef.focusedProperty().asString()));
```

Controlling the Z-Order of the Stage

In the event that you want your JavaFX application to appear on top of other windows or behind other windows onscreen, you can use the toFront() and toBack() methods, respectively. The following snippet from Listing 2-1 shows how this is accomplished.

```
Button toBackButton = new Button("toBack()");
toBackButton.setOnAction(e -> stageRef.toBack());
Button toFrontButton = new Button("toFront()");
toFrontButton.setOnAction(e -> stageRef.toFront());
```

Once again, note how using lambda expressions enhances the readability of the code. It is clear from the first line of the snippet that a Button named toBackButton is created with a text "toBack()" being displayed on the button. The second line defines that when an action is performed on the button (i.e., the button is clicked), the stage is sent to the back.

Without using a lambda expression, the second line would be replaced by a call to an anonymous inner class as follows:

```
toBackButton.setOnAction(new EventHandler<javafx.event.ActionEvent>() {
  @Override public void handle(javafx.event.ActionEvent e) {
    stageRef.toBack();
  }
})
```

This approach not only requires more code, it doesn't allow the Java runtime to optimize calls and it is much less readable.

Closing the Stage and Detecting When It Is Closed

As shown in the following code snippet from Listing 2-1, you can programmatically close the Stage with its close() method. This is important when the stageStyle is undecorated or transparent, because the close button supplied by the windowing system is not present.

```
Button closeButton = new Button("close()");
closeButton.setOnAction(e -> stageRef.close());
```

By the way, you can detect when there is an external request to close the Stage by using the onCloseRequest event handler as shown in the following code snippet from Listing 2-1.

```
stage.setOnCloseRequest((WindowEvent we) -> {
        System.out.println("Stage is closing");
});
```

To see this in action, run the application without any arguments so that it has the appearance of Figure 2-2 shown previously, and then click the close button on the decoration of the window.

■ **Tip** The onCloseRequest event handler is only called when there is an external request to close the window. This is why the "Stage is closing" message doesn't appear in this example when you click the button labeled "close()".

Making a Scene

Continuing on with our theater metaphor for creating JavaFX applications, we now discuss putting a Scene on the Stage. The Scene, as you recall, is the place in which the actors and props (nodes) visually interact with each other and the audience (the users of your program).

Using the Scene Class: The OnTheScene Example

As with the Stage class, we're going to use a contrived example application to demonstrate and teach the details of the available capabilities in the Scene class. See Figure 2-6 for a screenshot of the OnTheScene program.

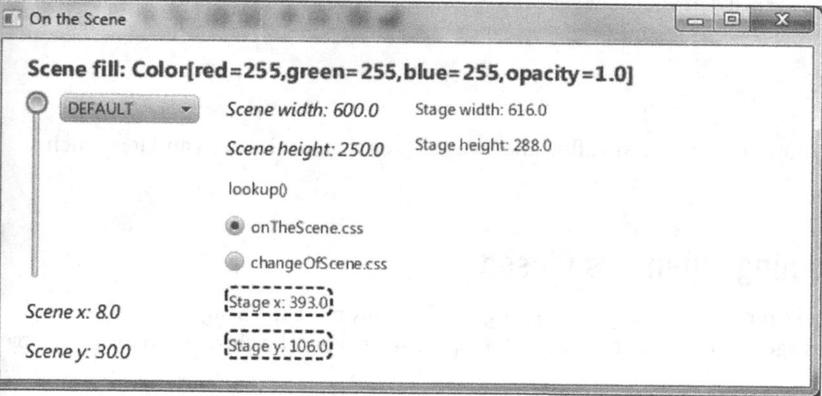

Figure 2-6. *The OnTheScene program when first invoked*

Go ahead and run the OnTheScene program, putting it through its paces as instructed in the following exercise. We follow up with a walkthrough of the code so that you can associate the behavior with the code behind it.

EXAMINING THE BEHAVIOR OF THE ONTHESCENE PROGRAM

When the OnTheScene program starts, its appearance should be similar to the screenshot in Figure 2-6. To fully examine its behavior, perform the following steps. Note that the property and method names on the UI correspond to the property and methods in the `Scene`, `Stage`, and `Cursor` classes, as well as Cascading Style Sheets (CSS) file names.

1. Drag the application around, noticing that although the `Stage` `x` and `y` values are relative to the screen, the `Scene`'s `x` and `y` values are relative to the upper-left corner of the exterior of the `Stage` (including decorations). Similarly, the width and height of the `Scene` are the dimensions of the interior of the `Stage` (which doesn't include decorations). As noted earlier, it is best to set the `Scene` width and height explicitly (or let them be set implicitly by assuming the size of the contained nodes), rather than setting the width and height of a decorated `Stage`.
2. Resize the program's window and observe that the width and height values change to reflect the width and height of the `Scene`. Also notice that the position of much of the content in the scene changes as you change the height of the window.
3. Click the lookup() hyperlink and notice that the string "Scene height: XXX.X" prints in the console, where XXX.X is the `Scene`'s height.
4. Hover the mouse over the choice box drop-down list and notice that it becomes slightly larger. Click the choice box and choose a cursor style in the list, noticing that the cursor changes to that style. Be careful about choosing NONE, as the cursor might disappear, and you'll need to use the keyboard (or psychic powers while moving the mouse) to make it visible.
5. Drag the slider on the left, noticing that the fill color of the `Scene` changes and that the string at the top of the `Scene` reflects the red-green-blue (RGB) and opacity values of the current fill color.
6. Notice the appearance and content of the text on the `Scene`. Then click changeOfScene.css, noticing that the color and font and content characteristics for some of the text on the `Scene` changes as shown in the screenshot in Figure 2-7.

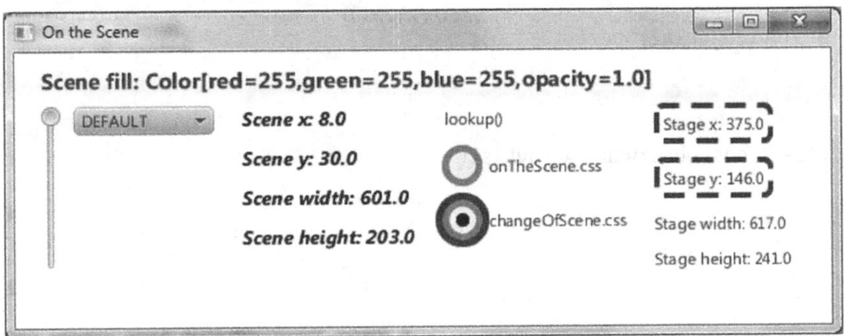

***Figure 2-7.** The OnTheScene program with the changeOfScene CSS style sheet applied*

7. Click OnTheScene.css, noticing that the color and font characteristics return to their previous state.

Now that you've explored this example program that demonstrates features of the Scene, let's walk through the code

Understanding the OnTheScene Program

Take a look at the code for the OnTheScene program in Listing 2-2, before we point out new and relevant concepts.

Listing 2-2. OnTheSceneMain.java

```
import javafx.application.Application;
import javafx.beans.property.DoubleProperty;
import javafx.beans.property.SimpleDoubleProperty;
import javafx.beans.property.SimpleStringProperty;
import javafx.collections.FXCollections;
import javafx.collections.ObservableList;
import javafx.geometry.HPos;
import javafx.geometry.Insets;
import javafx.geometry.Orientation;
import javafx.geometry.VPos;
import javafx.scene.Cursor;
import javafx.scene.Scene;
import javafx.scene.control.ChoiceBox;
import javafx.scene.control.Hyperlink;
import javafx.scene.control.Label;
import javafx.scene.control.RadioButton;
import javafx.scene.control.Slider;
import javafx.scene.control.ToggleGroup;
import javafx.scene.layout.FlowPane;
import javafx.scene.layout.HBox;
import javafx.scene.paint.Color;
import javafx.scene.text.Font;
import javafx.scene.text.FontWeight;
import javafx.scene.text.Text;
import javafx.stage.Stage;

public class OnTheSceneMain extends Application {

  DoubleProperty fillVals = new SimpleDoubleProperty(255.0);

  Scene sceneRef;

  ObservableList cursors = FXCollections.observableArrayList(
          Cursor.DEFAULT,
          Cursor.CROSSHAIR,
          Cursor.WAIT,
          Cursor.TEXT,
          Cursor.HAND,
          Cursor.MOVE,
          Cursor.N_RESIZE,
          Cursor.NE_RESIZE,
          Cursor.E_RESIZE,
          Cursor.SE_RESIZE,
          Cursor.S_RESIZE,
          Cursor.SW_RESIZE,
```

```
            Cursor.W_RESIZE,
            Cursor.NW_RESIZE,
            Cursor.NONE
    );

    public static void main(String[] args) {
        Application.launch(args);
    }

    @Override
    public void start(Stage stage) {
        Slider sliderRef;
        ChoiceBox choiceBoxRef;
        Text textSceneX;
        Text textSceneY;
        Text textSceneW;
        Text textSceneH;
        Label labelStageX;
        Label labelStageY;
        Label labelStageW;
        Label labelStageH;

        final ToggleGroup toggleGrp = new ToggleGroup();
        sliderRef = new Slider(0, 255, 255);
        sliderRef.setOrientation(Orientation.VERTICAL);
        choiceBoxRef = new ChoiceBox(cursors);
        HBox hbox = new HBox(sliderRef, choiceBoxRef);
        hbox.setSpacing(10);
        textSceneX = new Text();
        textSceneX.getStyleClass().add("emphasized-text");
        textSceneY = new Text();
        textSceneY.getStyleClass().add("emphasized-text");
        textSceneW = new Text();
        textSceneW.getStyleClass().add("emphasized-text");
        textSceneH = new Text();
        textSceneH.getStyleClass().add("emphasized-text");
        textSceneH.setId("sceneHeightText");
        Hyperlink hyperlink = new Hyperlink("lookup");
        hyperlink.setOnAction((javafx.event.ActionEvent e) -> {
            System.out.println("sceneRef:" + sceneRef);
            Text textRef = (Text) sceneRef.lookup("#sceneHeightText");
            System.out.println(textRef.getText());
        });
        RadioButton radio1 = new RadioButton("onTheScene.css");
        radio1.setSelected(true);
        radio1.setToggleGroup(toggleGrp);
        RadioButton radio2 = new RadioButton("changeOfScene.css");
        radio2.setToggleGroup(toggleGrp);
        labelStageX = new Label();
        labelStageX.setId("stageX");
        labelStageY = new Label();
        labelStageY.setId("stageY");
```

```
        labelStageW = new Label();
        labelStageH = new Label();

        FlowPane sceneRoot = new FlowPane(Orientation.VERTICAL, 20, 10, hbox,
                textSceneX, textSceneY, textSceneW, textSceneH, hyperlink,
                radio1, radio2,
                labelStageX, labelStageY,
                labelStageW,
                labelStageH);
        sceneRoot.setPadding(new Insets(0, 20, 40, 0));
        sceneRoot.setColumnHalignment(HPos.LEFT);
        sceneRoot.setLayoutX(20);
        sceneRoot.setLayoutY(40);

        sceneRef = new Scene(sceneRoot, 600, 250);

        sceneRef.getStylesheets().add("onTheScene.css");
        stage.setScene(sceneRef);

        choiceBoxRef.getSelectionModel().selectFirst();

        // Setup various property binding
        textSceneX.textProperty().bind(new SimpleStringProperty("Scene x: ")
                .concat(sceneRef.xProperty().asString()));
        textSceneY.textProperty().bind(new SimpleStringProperty("Scene y: ")
                .concat(sceneRef.yProperty().asString()));
        textSceneW.textProperty().bind(new SimpleStringProperty("Scene width: ")
                .concat(sceneRef.widthProperty().asString()));
        textSceneH.textProperty().bind(new SimpleStringProperty("Scene height: ")
                .concat(sceneRef.heightProperty().asString()));
        labelStageX.textProperty().bind(new SimpleStringProperty("Stage x: ")
                .concat(sceneRef.getWindow().xProperty().asString()));
        labelStageY.textProperty().bind(new SimpleStringProperty("Stage y: ")
                .concat(sceneRef.getWindow().yProperty().asString()));
        labelStageW.textProperty().bind(new SimpleStringProperty("Stage width: ")
                .concat(sceneRef.getWindow().widthProperty().asString()));
        labelStageH.textProperty().bind(new SimpleStringProperty("Stage height: ")
                .concat(sceneRef.getWindow().heightProperty().asString()));
        sceneRef.cursorProperty().bind(choiceBoxRef.getSelectionModel()
                .selectedItemProperty());
        fillVals.bind(sliderRef.valueProperty());

        // When fillVals changes, use that value as the RGB to fill the scene
        fillVals.addListener((ov, oldValue, newValue) -> {
            Double fillValue = fillVals.getValue() / 256.0;
            sceneRef.setFill(new Color(fillValue, fillValue, fillValue, 1.0));
        });
```

```
        // When the selected radio button changes, set the appropriate style sheet
        toggleGrp.selectedToggleProperty().addListener((ov, oldValue, newValue) -> {
            String radioButtonText = ((RadioButton) toggleGrp.getSelectedToggle())
                    .getText();
            sceneRef.getStylesheets().clear();
            sceneRef.getStylesheets().addAll(radioButtonText);
        });

        stage.setTitle("On the Scene");
        stage.show();

        // Define an unmanaged node that will display Text
        Text addedTextRef = new Text(0, -30, "");
        addedTextRef.setTextOrigin(VPos.TOP);
        addedTextRef.setFill(Color.BLUE);
        addedTextRef.setFont(Font.font("Sans Serif", FontWeight.BOLD, 16));
        addedTextRef.setManaged(false);

        // Bind the text of the added Text node to the fill property of the Scene
        addedTextRef.textProperty().bind(new SimpleStringProperty("Scene fill: ").
                concat(sceneRef.fillProperty()));

        // Add to the Text node to the FlowPane
        ((FlowPane) sceneRef.getRoot()).getChildren().add(addedTextRef);
    }
}
```

Setting the Cursor for the Scene

The cursor can be set for a given node, for the entire scene, or for both. To do the latter, set the cursor property of the Scene instance to one of the constant values in the Cursor class, as shown in the following snippet from Listing 2-2.

```
sceneRef.cursorProperty().bind(choiceBoxRef.getSelectionModel()
      .selectedItemProperty());
```

These cursor values can be seen by looking at the javafx.scene.Cursor class in the JavaFX API docs; we've created a collection of these constants in Listing 2-2.

Painting the Scene's Background

The Scene class has a fill property of type javafx.scene.paint.Paint. Looking at the JavaFX API will reveal that the known subclasses of Paint are Color, ImagePattern, LinearGradient, and RadialGradient. Therefore, a Scene's background can be filled with solid colors, patterns, and gradients. If you don't set the fill property of the Scene, the default color (white) will be used.

■ **Tip** One of the Color constants is Color.TRANSPARENT, so you may make the Scene's background completely transparent if desired. In fact, the reason that the Scene behind the rounded-cornered rectangle in the StageCoach screenshot in Figure 2-5 isn't white is that its fill property is set to Color.TRANSPARENT (see Listing 2-1 again).

To set the fill property in the OnTheScene example, instead of using one of the constants in the Color class (e.g., Color.BLUE), we're using an RGB formula to create the color. Take a look at the javafx.scene.paint.Color class in the JavaFX API docs and scroll down past the constants such as ALICEBLUE and WHITESMOKE to see the constructors and methods. We're using a constructor of the Color class, setting the fill property to it, as shown in the following snippet from Listing 2-2.

```
sceneRef.setFill(new Color(fillValue, fillValue, fillValue, 1.0));
```

As you move the Slider, to which the fillVals property is bound, each of the arguments to the Color() constructor is set to a value from 0 to 255, as indicated in the following code snippet from Listing 2-2.

```
fillVals.bind(sliderRef.valueProperty());
```

Populating the Scene with Nodes

As covered in Chapter 1, you can populate a Scene with nodes by instantiating them and adding them to container nodes (e.g., Group and VBox) that can contain other nodes. These capabilities enable you to construct complex *scene graphs* containing nodes. In the example here, the root property of the Scene contains a Flow layout container, which causes its contents to flow either vertically or horizontally, wrapping as necessary. The Flow container in our example contains an HBox (which contains a Slider and a ChoiceBox) and several other nodes (instances of Text, Hyperlink, and RadioButton classes).

Finding a Scene Node by ID

Each node in a Scene can be assigned an ID in the id property of the node. For example, in the following snippet from Listing 2-2, the id property of a Text node is assigned the String "sceneHeightText". When the action event handler in the Hyperlink control is called, the lookup() method of the Scene instance is used to obtain a reference to the node with the id of "sceneHeightText". The event handler then prints the content of the Text node to the console.

■ **Note** The Hyperlink control is essentially a button that has the appearance of hyperlink text. It has an action event handler in which you could place code that opens a browser page or any other desired functionality.

```
textSceneH = new Text();
textSceneH.getStyleClass().add("emphasized-text");
textSceneH.setId("sceneHeightText");
Hyperlink hyperlink = new Hyperlink("lookup");
hyperlink.setOnAction((javafx.event.ActionEvent e) -> {
    System.out.println("sceneRef:" + sceneRef);
    Text textRef = (Text) sceneRef.lookup("#sceneHeightText");
    System.out.println(textRef.getText());
});
```

A close examination of the action event handler reveals that the lookup() method returns a Node, but the actual type of object returned in this snippet is a Text object. Because we need to access a property of the Text class (text) that isn't in the Node class, it is necessary to coerce the compiler into trusting that at runtime the object will be an instance of the Text class.

Accessing the Stage from the Scene

To obtain a reference to the Stage instance from the Scene, we use a property in the Scene class named window. The accessor method for this property appears in the following snippet from Listing 2-2 to get the x and y co-ordinates of the Stage on the screen.

```
labelStageX.textProperty().bind(new SimpleStringProperty("Stage x: ")
      .concat(sceneRef.getWindow().xProperty().asString()));
labelStageY.textProperty().bind(new SimpleStringProperty("Stage y: ")
      .concat(sceneRef.getWindow().yProperty().asString()));
```

Inserting a Node into the Scene's Content Sequence

Sometimes it is useful to add a node dynamically to the children of a UI container class. The code snippet from Listing 2-2 that follows demonstrates how this may be accomplished by dynamically adding a Text node to the children of the FlowPane instance:

```
// Define an unmanaged node that will display Text
Text addedTextRef = new Text(0, -30, "");
addedTextRef.setTextOrigin(VPos.TOP);
addedTextRef.setFill(Color.BLUE);
addedTextRef.setFont(Font.font("Sans Serif", FontWeight.BOLD, 16));
addedTextRef.setManaged(false);

// Bind the text of the added Text node to the fill property of the Scene
addedTextRef.textProperty().bind(new SimpleStringProperty("Scene fill: ").
      concat(sceneRef.fillProperty()));

// Add the Text node to the FlowPane
((FlowPane) sceneRef.getRoot()).getChildren().add(addedTextRef);
```

This particular Text node is the one at the top of the Scene shown in Figures 2-6 and 2-7, in which the value of the Scene's fill property is displayed. Note that in this example the managed property of the addedTextRef instance is set to false, so its position isn't governed by the FlowPane. By default, nodes are "managed," which means that their parent (the container to which this node is added) is responsible for the layout of the node. By setting the managed property to false, the developer is assumed to be responsible for laying out the node.

CSS Styling the Nodes in a Scene

A very powerful aspect of JavaFX is the ability to use CSS to style the nodes in a Scene dynamically. You used this capability in Step 6 of the previous exercise when you clicked changeOfScene.css to change the appearance of the UI from what you saw in Figure 2-6 to what was shown in Figure 2-7. Also, in Step 7 of the exercise, the appearance of the UI changed back to what was shown in Figure 2-6 when you selected the onTheScene.css radio button. The relevant code snippet from Listing 2-2 is shown here:

```
sceneRef.getStylesheets().add("onTheScene.css");
...code omitted...
// When the selected radio button changes, set the appropriate stylesheet
toggleGrp.selectedToggleProperty().addListener((ov, oldValue, newValue) -> {
String radioButtonText = ((RadioButton) toggleGrp.getSelectedToggle())
       .getText();
```

```
sceneRef.getStylesheets().clear();
sceneRef.getStylesheets().addAll("/"+radioButtonText);
});
```

In this snippet, the stylesheets property of the Scene is initialized to the location of the onTheScene.css file, which in this case is the root directory. Also shown in the snippet is the assignment of the CSS files to the Scene as the appropriate buttons are clicked. The text of the RadioButton instances is equal to the names of the style sheets, hence we can easily set the corresponding style sheet to the scene. Take a look at Listing 2-3 to see the style sheet that corresponds to the screenshot in Figure 2-6. Some of the CSS *selectors* in this style sheet represent the nodes whose id property is either "stageX" or "stageY". There is also a selector in this style sheet that represents nodes whose styleClass property is "emphasized-text". In addition, there is a selector in this style sheet that maps to the ChoiceBox UI control by substituting the camel-case name of the control to a lowercase hyphenated name (choice-box). The *properties* in this style sheet begin with "-fx", and correspond to the type of node with which they are associated. The *values* in this style sheet (e.g., black, italic, and 14pt) are expressed as standard CSS values.

Listing 2-3. onTheScene.css

```
#stageX, #stageY {
  -fx-padding: 1;
  -fx-border-color: black;
  -fx-border-style: dashed;
  -fx-border-width: 2;
  -fx-border-radius: 5;
}

.emphasized-text {
  -fx-font-size: 14pt;
  -fx-font-weight: normal;
  -fx-font-style: italic;
}

.choice-box:hover {
    -fx-scale-x: 1.1;
    -fx-scale-y: 1.1;
}

.radio-button .radio  {
   -fx-background-color: -fx-shadow-highlight-color, -fx-outer-border,
                         -fx-inner-border, -fx-body-color;
   -fx-background-insets: 0 0 -1 0,  0,  1,  2;
   -fx-background-radius: 1.0em;
   -fx-padding: 0.333333em;
}

.radio-button:focused .radio {
    -fx-background-color: -fx-focus-color, -fx-outer-border,
                          -fx-inner-border, -fx-body-color;
    -fx-background-radius: 1.0em;
    -fx-background-insets: -1.4, 0, 1, 2;
}
```

Listing 2-4 is the style sheet that corresponds to the screenshot in Figure 2-7. For more information on CSS style heets, see the Resources section at the end of this chapter.

Listing 2-4. changeOfScene.css

```
#stageX, #stageY {
  -fx-padding: 3;
  -fx-border-color: blue;
  -fx-stroke-dash-array: 12 2 4 2;
  -fx-border-width: 4;
  -fx-border-radius: 5;
}

.emphasized-text {
  -fx-font-size: 14pt;
  -fx-font-weight: bold;
  -fx-font-style: normal;
}

.radio-button *.radio  {
    -fx-padding: 10;
    -fx-background-color: red, yellow;
    -fx-background-insets: 0, 5;
    -fx-background-radius: 30, 20;
}

.radio-button:focused *.radio {
    -fx-background-color: blue, red, yellow;
    -fx-background-insets: -5, 0, 5;
    -fx-background-radius: 40, 30, 20;
}
```

Now that you've had some experience with using the Stage and Scene classes, several of the Node subclasses, and CSS styling, we show you how to handle events that can occur when your JavaFX program is running.

Handling Input Events

So far we've shown you a couple of examples of event handling. For example, we used the onAction event handler to execute code when a button is clicked. We also used the onCloseRequest event handler of the Stage class to execute code when the Stage has been requested externally to close. In this section, we explore more of the event handlers available in JavaFX.

Surveying Mouse, Keyboard, Touch, and Gesture Events and Handlers

Most of the events that occur in JavaFX programs are related to the user manipulating input devices such as a mouse, a keyboard, or a multitouch screen. To see the available event handlers and their associated event objects, we take yet another look at the JavaFX API documentation. First, navigate to the javafx.scene.Node class and look for the properties that begin with the letters "on". These properties represent the event handlers common to all nodes in JavaFX. Here is a list of these event handlers in the JavaFX 8 API:

- Key event handlers: onKeyPressed, onKeyReleased, onKeyTyped
- Mouse event handlers: onMouseClicked, onMouseDragEntered, onMouseDragExited, onMouseDragged, onMouseDragOver, onMouseDragReleased, onMouseEntered, onMouseExited, onMouseMoved, onMousePressed, onMouseReleased

- Drag-and-drop handlers

  :onDragDetected, onDragDone, onDragDropped, onDragEntered, onDragExited, onDragOver
- Touch handlers: onTouchMoved, onTouchPressed, onTouchReleased, onTouchStationary
- Gesture handlers: onRotate, onRotationFinished, onRotationStarted, onScroll, onScrollStarted, onScrollFinished, onSwipeLeft, onSwipeRight, onSwipeUp, onSwipeDown, onZoom, onZoomStarted, onZoomFinished

Each of these is a property that defines a method to be called when particular input events occur. In the case of the key event handlers, as shown in the JavaFX API docs, the method's parameter is a javafx.scene.input.KeyEvent instance. The method's parameter for the mouse event handlers is a javafx.scene.input.MouseEvent. Touch handlers consume a javafx.scene.input.TouchEvent instance, and when a gesture event occurs, the method's parameter for the handle event is an instance of javax.scene.input.GestureInput.

Understanding the KeyEvent Class

Take a look at the JavaFX API docs for the KeyEvent class, and you'll see that it contains several methods, a commonly used one being getCode(). The getCode() method returns a KeyCode instance representing the key that caused the event when pressed. Looking at the javafx.scene.input.KeyCode class in the JavaFX API docs reveals that a multitude of constants exist that represent keys on an international set of keyboards. Another way to find out what key was pressed is to call the getCharacter() method, which returns a string that represents the unicode character associated with the key pressed.

The KeyEvent class also enables you to see whether the Alt, Ctrl, Meta, and/or Shift keys were down at the time of the event by calling the isAltDown(), isControlDown(), isMetaDown(), or isShiftDown() methods, respectively.

Understanding the MouseEvent Class

Take a look at the MouseEvent class in the JavaFX API docs, and you see that significantly more methods are available than in KeyEvent. Like KeyEvent, MouseEvent has the isAltDown(), isControlDown(), isMetaDown(), and isShiftDown() methods, as well as the source field, which is a reference to the object in which the event originated. In addition, it has several methods that pinpoint various coordinate spaces where the mouse event occurred, all expressed in pixels:

- getX() and getY() return the horizontal and vertical position of the mouse event, relative to the origin of the node in which the mouse event occurred.
- getSceneX() and getSceneY() return the horizontal and vertical position of the mouse event, relative to the Scene.
- getScreenX() and getScreenY() return the horizontal and vertical position of the mouse event, relative to the screen.

Here are a few other commonly useful methods:

- isDragDetect() returns true if a drag event is detected.
- getButton(), isPrimaryButtonDown(), isSecondaryButtonDown(), isMiddleButtonDown(), and getClickCount() contain information about what button was clicked, and how many times it was clicked.

A little later in this chapter you get some experience with creating key and mouse event handlers in the ZenPong example program. To continue preparing you for the ZenPong example, we now give you a look at how you can animate the nodes that you put in your scene.

Understanding the TouchEvent Class

With more and more devices being equipped with a touch screen, built-in support for touch events makes JavaFX a state-of-the art platform for creating applications that leverage multitouch capabilities, by which we mean that the platform is able to track more than one touchpoint in a single set of events.

The `TouchEvent` class provides the `getTouchPoint()` method, which returns a specific touch point. The methods on this `TouchPoint` are similar to the methods on a `MouseEvent`, for example, you can retrieve the relative and absolute positions by calling `getX()` and `getY()`, or `getSceneX()` and `getSceneY()`, or `getScreenX()` and `getScreenY()`.

The `TouchEvent` class also allows the developer to get information about the other touch points that belong to the same set. By calling `getEventSetId()`, you get the unique identifier of the set of `TouchEvent` instances, and the list of all touch points in the set can be obtained by calling `getTouchPoints()`, which returns a list of `TouchPoint` instances.

Understanding the GestureEvent Class

Besides handling multitouch events, JavaFX also supports the creation and dispatching of gesture events. Gestures are increasingly used on smartphones, tablets, touch screens, and other input devices. They provide an intuitive way of performing an action, for example, by having the user swipe his or her finger. The `GestureEvent` class currently has four subclasses, each representing a specific gesture: `RotateEvent`, `ScrollEvent`, `SwipeEvent`, and `ZoomEvent`. All of these events have methods comparable to the `MouseEvent` for retrieving the position of the action—the `getX()` and `getY()`, `getSceneX()` and `getSceneY()`, and the `getScreenX()` and `getScreenY()` methods.

The specific subclasses all allow for retrieving a more detailed type of the event. A `SwipeEvent`, for example can be a swipe to the right or the left, to the top or the bottom. This information is obtained by calling the `getEventType()` method on the `GestureEvent`.

Animating Nodes in the Scene

One of the strengths of JavaFX is the ease with which you can create graphically rich UIs. Part of that richness is the ability to animate nodes that live in the `Scene`. At its core, animating a node involves changing the value of its properties over a period of time. Examples of animating a node include the following.

- Gradually increasing the size of a node when the mouse enters its bounds, and gradually decreasing the size when the mouse exits its bounds. Note that this requires scaling the node, which is referred to as a transform.
- Gradually increasing or decreasing the opacity of a node to provide a fade-in or fade-out effect, respectively.
- Gradually altering values of properties in a node that change its location, causing it to move from one location to another. This is useful, for example, when creating a game such as Pong. A related capability is detecting when a node has collided with another node.

Animating a node involves the use of the `Timeline` class, located in the `javafx.animation` package. Depending on the requirements of an animation and personal preference, use one of two general techniques:

- Create an instance of the `Timeline` class directly and supply key frames that specify values and actions at specific points in time.
- Use the `javafx.animation.Transition` subclasses to define and associate specific transitions with a node. Examples of transitions include causing a node to move along a defined path over a period of time, and rotating a node over a period of time. Each of these transition classes extends the `Timeline` class.

We now cover these techniques, showing examples of each, beginning with the first one listed.

Using a Timeline for Animation

Take a look at the `javafx.animation` package in the JavaFX API docs, and you see three of the classes that are used when directly creating a timeline: `Timeline`, `KeyFrame`, and `Interpolator`. Peruse the docs for these classes, and then come back so we can show you some examples of using them.

■ **Tip** Remember to consult the JavaFX API docs for any new packages, classes, properties, and methods that you encounter.

The Metronome1 Example

We use a simple metronome example to demonstrate how to create a timeline.

As the screenshot in Figure 2-8 shows, the Metronome1 program has a pendulum as well as four buttons that start, pause, resume, and stop the animation. The pendulum in this example is a `Line` node, and we're going to animate that node by *interpolating* its `startX` property over the period of one second. Go ahead and take this example for a spin by doing the following exercise.

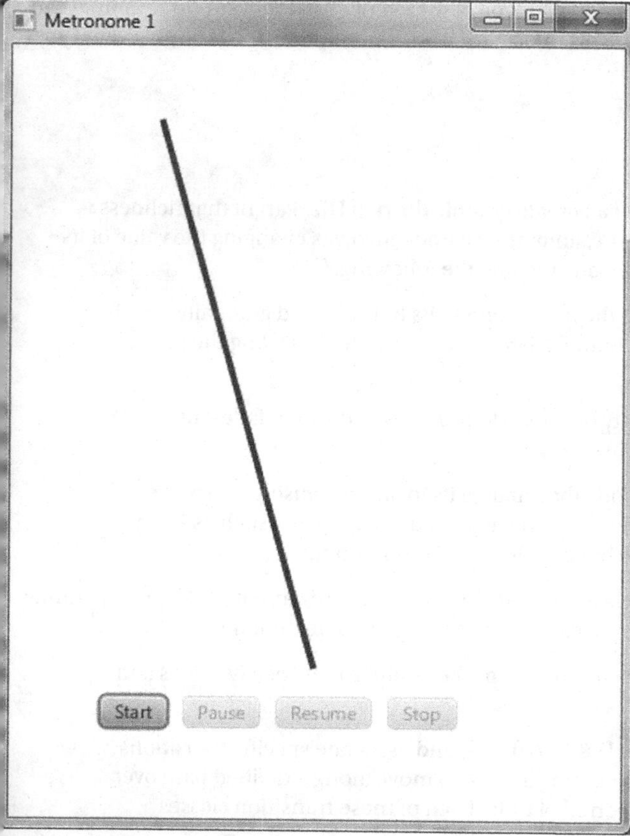

***Figure 2-8.** The Metronome1 program*

EXAMINING THE BEHAVIOR OF THE METRONOME1 PROGRAM

When the Metronome1 program starts, its appearance should be similar to the screenshot in Figure 2-8. To fully examine its behavior, perform the following steps.

1. Observe that of the four buttons on the scene, only the Start button is enabled.
2. Click Start. Notice that the top of the line moves back and forth, taking one second to travel each direction. Also, observe that the Start and Resume buttons are disabled and that the Pause and Stop buttons are enabled.
3. Click Pause, noticing that the animation pauses. Also, observe that the Start and Pause buttons are disabled and that the Resume and Stop buttons are enabled.
4. Click Resume, noticing that the animation resumes from where it was paused.
5. Click Stop, noticing that the animation stops and that the button states are the same as they were when the program was first started (see Step 1).
6. Click Start again, noticing that the line jumps back to its starting point before beginning the animation (rather than simply resuming as it did in Step 4).
7. Click Stop.

Now that you've experienced the behavior of the Metronome1 program, let's walk through the code behind it.

Understanding the Metronome1 Program

Take a look at the code for the Metronome1 program in Listing 2-5, before we discuss relevant concepts.

Listing 2-5. `Metronome1Main.java`

```
package projavafx.metronome1.ui;

import javafx.animation.Animation;
import javafx.animation.Interpolator;
import javafx.animation.KeyFrame;
import javafx.animation.KeyValue;
import javafx.animation.Timeline;
import javafx.application.Application;
import javafx.beans.property.DoubleProperty;
import javafx.beans.property.SimpleDoubleProperty;
import javafx.scene.Group;
import javafx.scene.Scene;
import javafx.scene.control.Button;
import javafx.scene.layout.HBox;
import javafx.scene.paint.Color;
import javafx.scene.shape.Line;
```

```
import javafx.stage.Stage;
import javafx.util.Duration;

public class Metronome1Main extends Application {

    DoubleProperty startXVal = new SimpleDoubleProperty(100.0);

    Button startButton;
    Button pauseButton;
    Button resumeButton;
    Button stopButton;
    Line line;
    Timeline anim;

    public static void main(String[] args) {
        Application.launch(args);
    }

    @Override
    public void start(Stage stage) {
        anim = new Timeline(
                new KeyFrame(new Duration(0.0), new KeyValue(startXVal, 100.)),
                new KeyFrame(new Duration(1000.0), new KeyValue(startXVal, 300., Interpolator.LINEAR))
        );
        anim.setAutoReverse(true);
        anim.setCycleCount(Animation.INDEFINITE);
        line = new Line(0, 50, 200, 400);
        line.setStrokeWidth(4);
        line.setStroke(Color.BLUE);
        startButton = new Button("start");
        startButton.setOnAction(e -> anim.playFromStart());
        pauseButton = new Button("pause");
        pauseButton.setOnAction(e -> anim.pause());
        resumeButton = new Button("resume");
        resumeButton.setOnAction(e -> anim.play());
        stopButton = new Button("stop");
        stopButton.setOnAction(e -> anim.stop());
        HBox commands = new HBox(10,
                startButton,
                pauseButton,
                resumeButton,
                stopButton);
        commands.setLayoutX(60);
        commands.setLayoutY(420);
        Group group = new Group(line, commands);
        Scene scene = new Scene(group, 400, 500);
```

```
        line.startXProperty().bind(startXVal);
        startButton.disableProperty().bind(anim.statusProperty()
                .isNotEqualTo(Animation.Status.STOPPED));
        pauseButton.disableProperty().bind(anim.statusProperty()
                .isNotEqualTo(Animation.Status.RUNNING));
        resumeButton.disableProperty().bind(anim.statusProperty()
                .isNotEqualTo(Animation.Status.PAUSED));
        stopButton.disableProperty().bind(anim.statusProperty()
                .isEqualTo(Animation.Status.STOPPED));

        stage.setScene(scene);
        stage.setTitle("Metronome 1");
        stage.show();
    }
}
```

Understanding the Timeline Class

The main purpose of the Timeline class is to provide the ability to change the values of properties in a gradual fashion over given periods of time. Take a look at the following snippet from Listing 2-5 to see the timeline being created, along with some of its commonly used properties.

```
DoubleProperty startXVal = new SimpleDoubleProperty(100.0);

  ...code omitted...

Timeline anim = new Timeline(
                new KeyFrame(new Duration(0.0), new KeyValue(startXVal, 100.)),
                new KeyFrame(new Duration(1000.0), new KeyValue(startXVal, 300., Interpolator.LINEAR))
        );
        anim.setAutoReverse(true);
        anim.setCycleCount(Animation.INDEFINITE);

  ...code omitted...

line = new Line(0, 50, 200, 400);
        line.setStrokeWidth(4);
        line.setStroke(Color.BLUE);

  ...code omitted...

    line.startXProperty().bind(startXVal);
```

■ **Note** In JavaFX 2, it was recommended to use the builder pattern for creating Nodes. As a consequence, creating a Line would be done as follows:

```
line = LineBuilder.create()
.startY(50)
.endX(200)
.endY(400)
.strokeWidth(4)
.stroke(Color.BLUE)
.build();
```

The advantage of this approach is that it is clear what the parameter "50" in the second line means: The line has a start-coordinate of 50 in the vertical position. The same readability can be achieved by calling setter methods, for example

```
line.setStartY(50);
```

In practice, however, many parameters are passed via the constructor of the Node. In the case of a Line instance, the second parameter is the startY parameter. This approach leads to fewer lines of code, but the developer should be careful about the order and the meaning of the parameters in the constructor. Once again, we strongly recommend having the JavaDoc available while writing JavaFX applications.

Inserting Key Frames into the Timeline

Our timeline contains a collection of two KeyFrame instances. Using the KeyValue constructor, one of these instances assigns 100 to the startXVal property at the beginning of the timeline, and the other assigns 300 to the startXVal property when the timeline has been running for one second. Because the startX property of the Line is bound to the value of the startXVal property, the net result is that the top of the line moves 200 pixels horizontally over the course of one second.

In the second KeyFrame of the timeline, the KeyValue constructor is passed a third argument that specifies that the interpolation from 100 to 300 will occur in a linear fashion over the one-second duration. Other Interpolation constants include EASE_IN, EASE_OUT, and EASE_BOTH. These cause the interpolation in a KeyFrame to be slower in the beginning, ending, or both, respectively.

The following are the other Timeline properties, inherited from the Animation class, used in this example:

- autoReverse, which we're initializing to true. This causes the timeline to automatically reverse when it reaches the last KeyFrame. When reversed, the interpolation goes from 300 to 100 over the course of one second.
- cycleCount, which we're initializing to Animation.INDEFINITE. This causes the timeline to repeat indefinitely until stopped by the stop() method of the Timeline class.

Speaking of the methods of the Timeline class, now is a good time to show you how to control the timeline and monitor its state.

Controlling and Monitoring the Timeline

As you observed when using the Metronome1 program, clicking the buttons causes the animation to start, pause, resume, and stop. This in turn has an effect on the states of the animation (running, paused, or stopped). Those states are reflected in the buttons in the form of being enabled or disabled. The following snippet from Listing 2-5 shows how to start, pause, resume, and stop the timeline, as well as how to tell whether the timeline is running or paused.

```
startButton = new Button("start");
startButton.setOnAction(e -> anim.playFromStart());
pauseButton = new Button("pause");
pauseButton.setOnAction(e -> anim.pause());
resumeButton = new Button("resume");
resumeButton.setOnAction(e -> anim.play());
stopButton = new Button("stop");
stopButton.setOnAction(e -> anim.stop());

...code omitted...

startButton.disableProperty().bind(anim.statusProperty()
        .isNotEqualTo(Animation.Status.STOPPED));
pauseButton.disableProperty().bind(anim.statusProperty()
        .isNotEqualTo(Animation.Status.RUNNING));
resumeButton.disableProperty().bind(anim.statusProperty()
        .isNotEqualTo(Animation.Status.PAUSED));
stopButton.disableProperty().bind(anim.statusProperty()
        .isEqualTo(Animation.Status.STOPPED));
```

As shown here in the action event handler of the Start button, the `playFromStart()` method of the `Timeline` instance is called, which begins playing the timeline from the beginning. In addition, the `disable` property of that `Button` is bound to an expression that evaluates whether the status property of the timeline is not equal to `Animation.Status.STOPPED`. This causes the button to be disabled when the timeline is not stopped (in which case it must be either running or paused).

When the user clicks the Pause button, the action event handler calls the timeline's `pause()` method, which pauses the animation. The `disable` property of that `Button` is bound to an expression that evaluates whether the timeline is not running.

The Resume button is only disabled when the timeline is not paused. To resume the timeline from where it was paused, the action event handler calls the `play()` method of the timeline.

Finally, the Stop button is disabled when the timeline is stopped. To stop the timeline, the action event handler calls the `stop()` method of the timeline.

Now that you know how to animate nodes by creating a `Timeline` class and creating `KeyFrame` instances, it's time to learn how to use the transition classes to animate nodes.

Using the Transition Classes for Animation

Using a `TimeLine` allows for very flexible animations. There are a number of common animations facilitating the translation from one state to another that are out-of-the box supported by JavaFX. The `javafx.animation` package contains several classes whose purpose is to provide convenient ways to do these commonly used animation tasks. Both `TimeLine` and `Transition` (the abstract root class for all concrete transitions) extend the `Animation` class.

Table 2-1 contains a list of transition classes in that package.

Table 2-1. Transition Classes in the javafx.animation Package for Animating Nodes

Transition Class Name	Description
TranslateTransition	Translates (moves) a node from one location to another over a given period of time. This was employed in the Hello Earthrise example program in Chapter 1.
PathTransition	Moves a node along a specified path.
RotateTransition	Rotates a node over a given period of time.
ScaleTransition	Scales (increases or decreases the size of) a node over a given period of time.
FadeTransition	Fades (increases or decreases the opacity of) a node over a given period of time.
FillTransition	Changes the fill of a shape over a given period of time.
StrokeTransition	Changes the stroke color of a shape over a given period of time.
PauseTransition	Executes an action at the end of its duration; designed mainly to be used in a SequentialTransition as a means to wait for a period of time.
SequentialTransition	Allows you to define a series of transitions that execute sequentially.
ParallelTransition	Allows you to define a series of transitions that execute in parallel.

Let's take a look at a variation on the metronome theme in which we create a metronome using TranslateTransition for the animation.

The MetronomeTransition Example

When using the transition classes, we take a different approach toward animation than when using the Timeline class directly:

- TIn the timeline-based Metronome1 program, we bound a property of a node (specifically, startX) to a property in the model (startXVal), and then used the timeline to interpolate the value of the property in the model.
- When using a transition class, however, we assign values to the properties of the Transition subclass, one of which is a node. The net result is that the node itself is affected, rather than just a bound attribute of the node being affected.

The distinction between these two approaches becomes clear as we walk through the MetronomeTransition example. Figure 2-9 shows a screenshot of this program when it is first invoked.

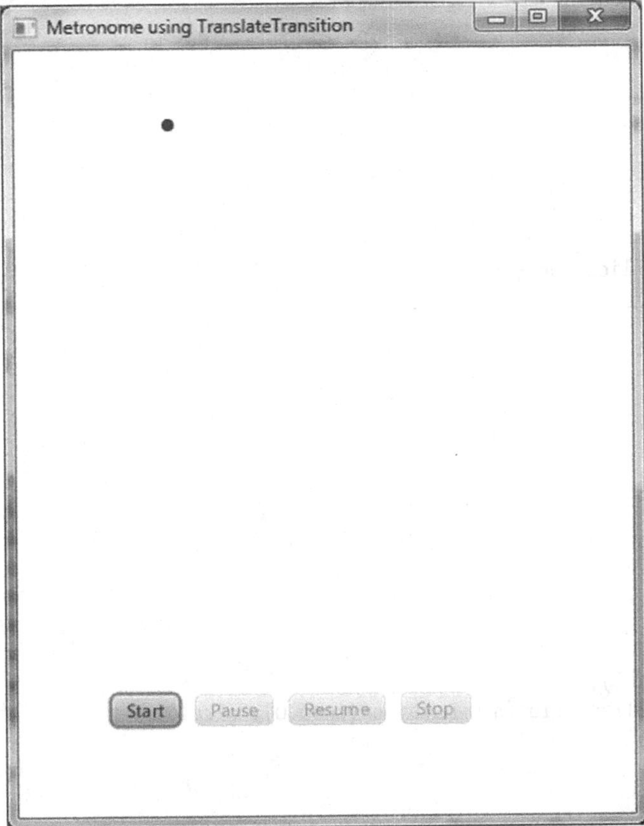

Figure 2-9. *The MetronomeTransition program*

The first noticeable difference between this example and the previous (Metronome1) example is that instead of one end of a line moving back and forth, we're going to make a `Circle` node move back and forth.

The Behavior of the MetronomeTransition Program

Go ahead and run the program, and perform the same steps that you did in the previous exercise with Metronome1. Everything should function the same, except for the visual difference pointed out previously.

Understanding the MetronomeTransition Program

Take a look at the code for the MetronomeTransition program in Listing 2-6, before we point out relevant concepts.

Listing 2-6. `MetronomeTransitionMain.fx`

```
package projavafx.metronometransition.ui;

import javafx.animation.Animation;
import javafx.animation.Interpolator;
import javafx.animation.TranslateTransition;
import javafx.application.Application;
```

```
import javafx.scene.Group;
import javafx.scene.Scene;
import javafx.scene.control.Button;
import javafx.scene.layout.HBox;
import javafx.scene.paint.Color;
import javafx.scene.shape.Circle;
import javafx.stage.Stage;
import javafx.util.Duration;

public class MetronomeTransitionMain extends Application {

    Button startButton;
    Button pauseButton;
    Button resumeButton;
    Button stopButton;
    Circle circle;

    public static void main(String[] args) {
        Application.launch(args);
    }

    @Override
    public void start(Stage stage) {
        circle = new Circle(100, 50, 4, Color.BLUE);
        TranslateTransition anim = new TranslateTransition(new Duration(1000.0), circle);
        anim.setFromX(0);
        anim.setToX(200);
        anim.setAutoReverse(true);
        anim.setCycleCount(Animation.INDEFINITE);
        anim.setInterpolator(Interpolator.LINEAR);
        startButton = new Button("start");
        startButton.setOnAction(e -> anim.playFromStart());
        pauseButton = new Button("pause");
        pauseButton.setOnAction(e -> anim.pause());
        resumeButton = new Button("resume");
        resumeButton.setOnAction(e -> anim.play());
        stopButton = new Button("stop");
        stopButton.setOnAction(e -> anim.stop());
        HBox commands = new HBox(10, startButton,
                pauseButton,
                resumeButton,
                stopButton);
        commands.setLayoutX(60);
        commands.setLayoutY(420);
        Group group = new Group(circle, commands);
        Scene scene = new Scene(group, 400, 500);
        startButton.disableProperty().bind(anim.statusProperty()
                .isNotEqualTo(Animation.Status.STOPPED));
        pauseButton.disableProperty().bind(anim.statusProperty()
                .isNotEqualTo(Animation.Status.RUNNING));
```

```
        resumeButton.disableProperty().bind(anim.statusProperty()
                .isNotEqualTo(Animation.Status.PAUSED));
        stopButton.disableProperty().bind(anim.statusProperty()
                .isEqualTo(Animation.Status.STOPPED));

        stage.setScene(scene);
        stage.setTitle("Metronome using TranslateTransition");
        stage.show();
    }
}
```

Using the TranslateTransition Class

As shown in the following snippet from Listing 2-6, to create a `TranslateTransition` we're supplying values that are reminiscent of the values that we used when creating a timeline in the previous example. For example, we're setting `autoReverse` to true and `cycleCount` to `Animation.INDEFINITE`. Also, just as when creating a `KeyFrame` for a timeline, we're supplying a duration and an interpolation type here as well.

In addition, we're supplying some values to properties that are specific to a `TranslateTransition`, namely `fromX` and `toX`. These values are interpolated over the requested duration and assigned to the `layoutX` property of the node controlled by the transition (in this case, the circle). If we also wanted to cause vertical movement, assigning values to `fromY` and `toY` would cause interpolated values between them to be assigned to the `layoutY` property.

An alternative to supplying `toX` and `toY` values is to provide values to the `byX` and `byY` properties, which enables you to specify the distance to travel in each direction rather than start and end points. Also, if you don't supply a value for `fromX`, the interpolation will begin with the current value of the node's `layoutX` property. The same holds true for `fromY` (if not supplied, the interpolation will begin with the value of `layoutY`).

```
circle = new Circle(100, 50, 4, Color.BLUE);
TranslateTransition anim = new TranslateTransition(new Duration(1000.0), circle);
anim.setFromX(0);
anim.setToX(200);
anim.setAutoReverse(true);
anim.setCycleCount(Animation.INDEFINITE);
anim.setInterpolator(Interpolator.LINEAR);
```

Controlling and Monitoring the Transition

The `TranslateTransition` class, as do all of the classes in Table 2-1 earlier, extends the `javafx.animation.Transition` class, which in turn extends the `Animation` class. Because the `Timeline` class extends the `Animation` class, as you can see by comparing Listings 2-5 and 2-6, all of the code for the buttons in this example is identical to that in the previous example. Indeed, the functionality required to start, pause, resume, and stop an animation is defined on the `Animation` class itself, and inherited by both the `Translation` classes as well as the `Timeline` class.

The MetronomePathTransition Example

As shown in Table 2-1 earlier, `PathTransition` is a transition class that enables you to move a node along a defined geometric path. Figure 2-10 shows a screenshot of a version of the metronome example, named MetronomePathTransition, that demonstrates how to use the `PathTransition` class.

Figure 2-10. The MetronomePathTransition program

The Behavior of the MetronomePathTransition Program

Go ahead and run the program, performing once again the same steps that you did for the Metronome1 exercise. Everything should function the same as it did in the MetronomeTransition example, except that the node is an ellipse instead of a circle, and the node moves along the path of an arc.

Understanding the MetronomePathTransition Program

Listing 2-7 contains code snippets from the MetronomePathTransition program that highlight the differences from the preceding (MetronomeTransition) program. Take a look at the code, and then we review relevant concepts.

Listing 2-7. Portions of `MetronomePathTransitionMain.java`

```
package projavafx.metronomepathtransition.ui;

...imports omitted...

public class MetronomePathTransitionMain extends Application {

    Button startButton;
    Button pauseButton;
```

```
    Button resumeButton;
    Button stopButton;
    Ellipse ellipse;

    Path path;

    public static void main(String[] args) {
        Application.launch(args);
    }

    @Override
    public void start(Stage stage) {
        ellipse = new Ellipse(100, 50, 4, 8);
        ellipse.setFill(Color.BLUE);
        path = new Path(
                new MoveTo(100, 50),
                new ArcTo(350, 350, 0, 300, 50, false, true)
        );
        PathTransition anim = new PathTransition(new Duration(1000.0), path, ellipse);
        anim.setOrientation(OrientationType.ORTHOGONAL_TO_TANGENT);
        anim.setInterpolator(Interpolator.LINEAR);
        anim.setAutoReverse(true);
        anim.setCycleCount(Timeline.INDEFINITE);
        startButton = new Button("start");
        startButton.setOnAction(e -> anim.playFromStart());
        pauseButton = new Button("pause");
        pauseButton.setOnAction(e -> anim.pause());
        resumeButton = new Button("resume");
        resumeButton.setOnAction(e -> anim.play());
        stopButton = new Button("stop");
        stopButton.setOnAction(e -> anim.stop());
        HBox commands = new HBox(10, startButton,
                pauseButton,
                resumeButton,
                stopButton);
        commands.setLayoutX(60);
        commands.setLayoutY(420);
        Group group = new Group(ellipse, commands);
        Scene scene = new Scene(group, 400, 500);

        startButton.disableProperty().bind(anim.statusProperty()
                .isNotEqualTo(Animation.Status.STOPPED));
        pauseButton.disableProperty().bind(anim.statusProperty()
                .isNotEqualTo(Animation.Status.RUNNING));
        resumeButton.disableProperty().bind(anim.statusProperty()
                .isNotEqualTo(Animation.Status.PAUSED));
        stopButton.disableProperty().bind(anim.statusProperty()
                .isEqualTo(Animation.Status.STOPPED));

        stage.setScene(scene);
        stage.setTitle("Metronome using PathTransition");
        stage.show();
    }
}
```

Using the PathTransition Class

As shown in Listing 2-7, defining a PathTransition includes supplying an instance of type Path to the path property that represents the geometric path that the node is to travel. Here we're creating a Path instance that defines an arc beginning at 100 pixels on the x axis and 50 pixels on the y axis, ending at 300 pixels on the x axis and 50 pixels on the y axis, with 350 pixel horizontal and vertical radii. This is accomplished by creating a Path that contains the MoveTo and ArcTo path elements. Take a look at the javafx.scene.shape package in the JavaFX API docs for more information on the PathElement class and its subclasses, which are used for creating a path.

■ **Tip** The properties in the ArcTo class are fairly intuitive except for sweepFlag. If sweepFlag is true, the line joining the center of the arc to the arc itself sweeps through increasing angles. Otherwise, it sweeps through decreasing angles.

Another property of the PathTransition class is orientation, which controls whether the node's orientation remains unchanged or stays perpendicular to the path's tangent as it moves along the path. Listing 2-7 uses the OrientationType.ORTHOGONAL_TO_TANGENT constant to accomplish the latter, as the former is the default.

Drawing an Ellipse

As shown in Listing 2-7, drawing an Ellipse is similar to drawing a Circle, the difference being that an additional radius is required (radiusX and radiusY instead of just radius).

Now that you've learned how to animate nodes by creating a timeline and by creating transitions, we create a very simple Pong-style game that requires animating a ping pong ball. In the process, you learn how to detect when the ball has hit a paddle or wall in the game.

The Zen of Node Collision Detection

When animating a node, you sometimes need to know when the node has collided with another node. To demonstrate this capability, our colleague Chris Wright developed a simple version of the Pong-style game that we call ZenPong. Originally we asked him to build the game with only one paddle, which brought the famous Zen koan (philosophical riddle), "What is the sound of one hand clapping," to mind. Chris had so much fun developing the game that he snuck a second paddle in, but we're still calling this example ZenPong. Figure 2-11 shows this very simple form of the game when first invoked.

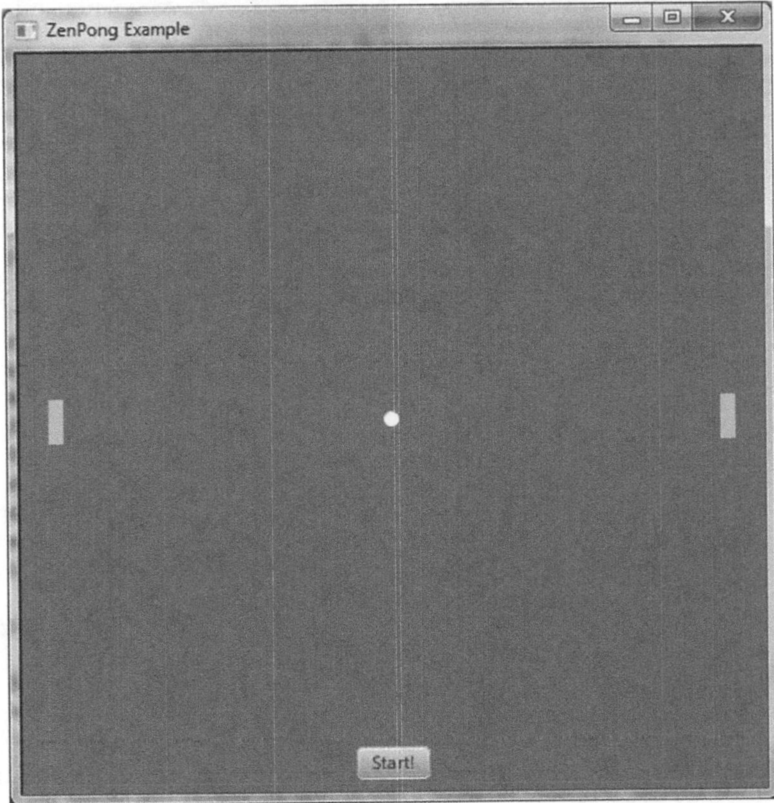

Figure 2-11. *The initial state of the ZenPong game*

Try out the game by following the instructions in the upcoming exercise, remembering that you control both paddles (unless you can get a colleague to share your keyboard and play).

EXAMINING THE BEHAVIOR OF THE ZENPONG GAME

When the program starts, its appearance should be similar to the screenshot in Figure 2-11. To fully examine its behavior, perform the following steps.

1. Before clicking Start, drag each of the paddles vertically to other positions. One game cheat is to drag the left paddle up and the right paddle down, which will put them in good positions to respond to the ball after being served.
2. Practice using the A key to move the left paddle up, the Z key to move the left paddle down, the L key to move the right paddle up, and the comma (,) key to move the right paddle down.
3. Click Start to begin playing the game. Notice that the Start button disappears and the ball begins moving at a 45° angle, bouncing off paddles and the top and bottom walls. The screen should look similar to Figure 2-12.

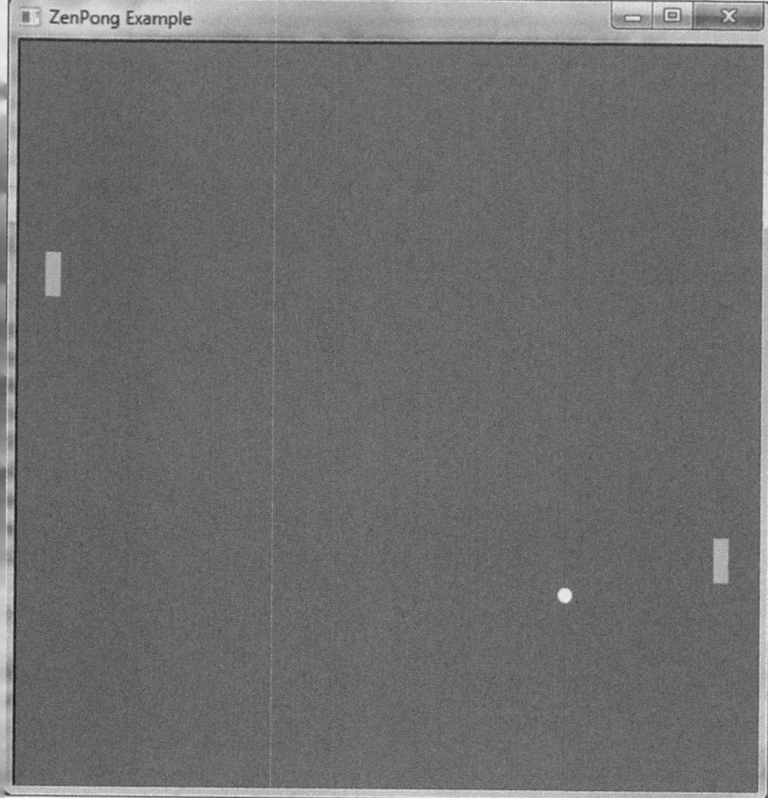

Figure 2-12. The ZenPong game in action

4. If the ball hits the left or right wall, one of your hands has lost the game. Notice that the game resets, looking again like the screenshot in Figure 2-11.

Now that you've experienced the behavior of the ZenPong program, let's review the code behind it.

Understanding the ZenPong Program

Examine the code for the ZenPong program in Listing 2-8, before we highlight some concepts demonstrated within.

Listing 2-8. ZenPongMain.java

```
package projavafx.zenpong.ui;
...imports omitted...
public class ZenPongMain extends Application {

  /**
   * The center points of the moving ball
   */
  DoubleProperty centerX = new SimpleDoubleProperty();
  DoubleProperty centerY = new SimpleDoubleProperty();
```

```
/**
 * The Y coordinate of the left paddle
 */
DoubleProperty leftPaddleY = new SimpleDoubleProperty();

/**
 * The Y coordinate of the right paddle
 */
DoubleProperty rightPaddleY = new SimpleDoubleProperty();

/**
 * The drag anchor for left and right paddles
 */
double leftPaddleDragAnchorY;
double rightPaddleDragAnchorY;

/**
 * The initial translateY property for the left and right paddles
 */
double initLeftPaddleTranslateY;
double initRightPaddleTranslateY;

/**
 * The moving ball
 */
Circle ball;

/**
 * The Group containing all of the walls, paddles, and ball. This also
 * allows us to requestFocus for KeyEvents on the Group
 */
Group pongComponents;

/**
 * The left and right paddles
 */
Rectangle leftPaddle;
Rectangle rightPaddle;

/**
 * The walls
 */
Rectangle topWall;
Rectangle rightWall;
Rectangle leftWall;
Rectangle bottomWall;

Button startButton;
```

```
    /**
     * Controls whether the startButton is visible
     */
    BooleanProperty startVisible = new SimpleBooleanProperty(true);

    /**
     * The animation of the ball
     */
    Timeline pongAnimation;

    /**
     * Controls whether the ball is moving right
     */
    boolean movingRight = true;

    /**
     * Controls whether the ball is moving down
     */
    boolean movingDown = true;

    /**
     * Sets the initial starting positions of the ball and paddles
     */
    void initialize() {
        centerX.setValue(250);
        centerY.setValue(250);
        leftPaddleY.setValue(235);
        rightPaddleY.setValue(235);
        startVisible.set(true);
        pongComponents.requestFocus();
    }

    /**
     * Checks whether or not the ball has collided with either the paddles,
     * topWall, or bottomWall. If the ball hits the wall behind the paddles, the
     * game is over.
     */
    void checkForCollision() {
        if (ball.intersects(rightWall.getBoundsInLocal())
                || ball.intersects(leftWall.getBoundsInLocal())) {
            pongAnimation.stop();
            initialize();
        } else if (ball.intersects(bottomWall.getBoundsInLocal())
                || ball.intersects(topWall.getBoundsInLocal())) {
            movingDown = !movingDown;
        } else if (ball.intersects(leftPaddle.getBoundsInParent()) && !movingRight) {
            movingRight = !movingRight;
        } else if (ball.intersects(rightPaddle.getBoundsInParent()) && movingRight) {
            movingRight = !movingRight;
        }
    }
```

```
            pongAnimation.playFromStart();
            pongComponents.requestFocus();
        });
        pongComponents = new Group(ball,
                topWall,
                leftWall,
                rightWall,
                bottomWall,
                leftPaddle,
                rightPaddle,
                startButton);
        pongComponents.setFocusTraversable(true);
        pongComponents.setOnKeyPressed(k -> {
            if (k.getCode() == KeyCode.SPACE
                    && pongAnimation.statusProperty()
                    .equals(Animation.Status.STOPPED)) {
                rightPaddleY.setValue(rightPaddleY.getValue() - 6);
            } else if (k.getCode() == KeyCode.L
                    && !rightPaddle.getBoundsInParent().intersects(topWall.getBoundsInLocal())) {
                rightPaddleY.setValue(rightPaddleY.getValue() - 6);
            } else if (k.getCode() == KeyCode.COMMA
                    && !rightPaddle.getBoundsInParent().intersects(bottomWall.getBoundsInLocal())) {
                rightPaddleY.setValue(rightPaddleY.getValue() + 6);
            } else if (k.getCode() == KeyCode.A
                    && !leftPaddle.getBoundsInParent().intersects(topWall.getBoundsInLocal())) {
                leftPaddleY.setValue(leftPaddleY.getValue() - 6);
            } else if (k.getCode() == KeyCode.Z
                    && !leftPaddle.getBoundsInParent().intersects(bottomWall.getBoundsInLocal())) {
                leftPaddleY.setValue(leftPaddleY.getValue() + 6);
            }
        });
        Scene scene = new Scene(pongComponents, 500, 500);
        scene.setFill(Color.GRAY);

        ball.centerXProperty().bind(centerX);
        ball.centerYProperty().bind(centerY);
        leftPaddle.translateYProperty().bind(leftPaddleY);
        rightPaddle.translateYProperty().bind(rightPaddleY);
        startButton.visibleProperty().bind(startVisible);

        stage.setScene(scene);
        initialize();
        stage.setTitle("ZenPong Example");
        stage.show();
    }
```

```
    /**
     * @param args the command line arguments
     */
    public static void main(String[] args) {
        Application.launch(args);
    }

    @Override
    public void start(Stage stage) {
        pongAnimation = new Timeline(
                new KeyFrame(new Duration(10.0), t -> {
                    checkForCollision();
                    int horzPixels = movingRight ? 1 : -1;
                    int vertPixels = movingDown ? 1 : -1;
                    centerX.setValue(centerX.getValue() + horzPixels);
                    centerY.setValue(centerY.getValue() + vertPixels);
                })
        );
        pongAnimation.setCycleCount(Timeline.INDEFINITE);
        ball = new Circle(0, 0, 5, Color.WHITE);
        topWall = new Rectangle(0, 0, 500, 1);
        leftWall = new Rectangle(0, 0, 1, 500);
        rightWall = new Rectangle(500, 0, 1, 500);
        bottomWall = new Rectangle(0, 500, 500, 1);
        leftPaddle = new Rectangle(20, 0, 10, 30);
        leftPaddle.setFill(Color.LIGHTBLUE);
        leftPaddle.setCursor(Cursor.HAND);
        leftPaddle.setOnMousePressed(me -> {
            initLeftPaddleTranslateY = leftPaddle.getTranslateY();
            leftPaddleDragAnchorY = me.getSceneY();
        });
        leftPaddle.setOnMouseDragged(me -> {
            double dragY = me.getSceneY() - leftPaddleDragAnchorY;
            leftPaddleY.setValue(initLeftPaddleTranslateY + dragY);
        });
        rightPaddle = new Rectangle(470, 0, 10, 30);
        rightPaddle.setFill(Color.LIGHTBLUE);
        rightPaddle.setCursor(Cursor.CLOSED_HAND);
        rightPaddle.setOnMousePressed(me -> {
            initRightPaddleTranslateY = rightPaddle.getTranslateY();
            rightPaddleDragAnchorY = me.getSceneY();
        });
        rightPaddle.setOnMouseDragged(me -> {
            double dragY = me.getSceneY() - rightPaddleDragAnchorY;
            rightPaddleY.setValue(initRightPaddleTranslateY + dragY);
        });
        startButton = new Button("Start!");
        startButton.setLayoutX(225);
        startButton.setLayoutY(470);
        startButton.setOnAction(e -> {
            startVisible.set(false);
```

Using the KeyFrame Action Event Handler

We're using a different technique in the timeline than demonstrated in the Metronome1 program earlier in the chapter (see Figure 2-8 and Listing 2-5). Instead of interpolating two values over a period of time, we're using the action event handler of the KeyFrame instance in our timeline. Take a look at the following snippet from Listing 2-8 to see this technique in use.

```
pongAnimation = new Timeline(
                new KeyFrame(new Duration(10.0), t -> {
                    checkForCollision();
                    int horzPixels = movingRight ? 1 : -1;
                    int vertPixels = movingDown ? 1 : -1;
                    centerX.setValue(centerX.getValue() + horzPixels);
                    centerY.setValue(centerY.getValue() + vertPixels);
                })
);
pongAnimation.setCycleCount(Timeline.INDEFINITE);
```

As shown in the snippet, we use only one KeyFrame, and it has a very short time (10 milliseconds). When a KeyFrame has an action event handler, the code in that handler—which in this case is once again a lambda expression—is executed when the time for that KeyFrame is reached. Because the cycleCount of this timeline is indefinite, the action event handler will be executed every 10 milliseconds. The code in this event handler does two things:

- Calls a method named checkForCollision(), which is defined in this program, the purpose of which is to see whether the ball has collided with either paddle or any of the walls
- Updates the properties in the model to which the position of the ball is bound, taking into account the direction in which the ball is already moving

Using the Node `intersects()` Method to Detect Collisions

Take a look inside the checkForCollision() method in the following snippet from Listing 2-8 to see how we check for collisions by detecting when two nodes intersect (share any of the same pixels).

```
void checkForCollision() {
  if (ball.intersects(rightWall.getBoundsInLocal()) ||
      ball.intersects(leftWall.getBoundsInLocal())) {
    pongAnimation.stop();
    initialize();
  }
  else if (ball.intersects(bottomWall.getBoundsInLocal()) ||
           ball.intersects(topWall.getBoundsInLocal())) {
    movingDown = !movingDown;
  }
  else if (ball.intersects(leftPaddle.getBoundsInParent()) && !movingRight) {
    movingRight = !movingRight;
  }
  else if (ball.intersects(rightPaddle.getBoundsInParent()) && movingRight) {
    movingRight = !movingRight;
  }
}
```

The intersects() method of the Node class shown here takes an argument of type Bounds, located in the javafx.geometry package. It represents the rectangular bounds of a node, for example, the leftPaddle node shown in the preceding code snippet. Notice that to get the position of the left paddle in the Group that contains it, we're using the boundsInParent property that the leftPaddle (a Rectangle) inherited from the Node class.

The net results of the intersect method invocations in the preceding snippet are as follows.

- If the ball intersects with the bounds of the rightWall or leftWall, the pongAnimation Timeline is stopped and the game is initialized for the next play. Note that the rightWall and left Wall nodes are one-pixel-wide rectangles on the left and right sides of the Scene. Take a peek at Listing 2-8 to see where these are defined.
- If the ball intersects with the bounds of the bottomWall or topWall, the vertical direction of the ball will be changed by negating the program's Boolean movingDown variable.
- If the ball intersects with the bounds of the leftPaddle or rightPaddle, the horizontal direction of the ball will be changed by negating the program's Boolean movingRight variable.

■ **Tip** For more information on boundsInParent and its related properties, layoutBounds and boundsInLocal, see the "Bounding Rectangles" discussion at the beginning of the javafx.scene.Node class in the JavaFX API docs. For example, it is a common practice to find out the width or height of a node by using the expression myNode.getLayoutBounds().getWidth() or myNode.getLayoutBounds().getHeight().

Dragging a Node

As you experienced previously, the paddles of the ZenPong application may be dragged with the mouse. The following snippet from Listing 2-8 shows how this capability is implemented in ZenPong for dragging the right paddle.

```
DoubleProperty rightPaddleY = new SimpleDoubleProperty();
...code omitted...
double rightPaddleDragStartY;
double rightPaddleDragAnchorY;
...code omitted...
void initialize() {
...code omitted...
   rightPaddleY.setValue(235);

}
...code omitted...
rightPaddle = new Rectangle(470, 0, 10, 30);
rightPaddle.setFill(Color.LIGHTBLUE);
rightPaddle.setCursor(Cursor.CLOSED_HAND);
rightPaddle.setOnMousePressed(me -> {
    initRightPaddleTranslateY = rightPaddle.getTranslateY();
    rightPaddleDragAnchorY = me.getSceneY();
});
```

called the Hierarchy, and the Controller that provides event handler code for the various controls in the UI. On the right side is the Inspector area that has subareas that allow you to manipulate Properties, Layout, and Code hookup of the currently selected control.

Understanding the FXML File

Listing 3-1 shows the FXML file that is saved by JavaFX SceneBuilder from the UI we have created.

Listing 3-1. StageCoach.fxml

```
<?xml version="1.0" encoding="UTF-8"?>

<?import javafx.scene.control.Button?>
<?import javafx.scene.control.CheckBox?>
<?import javafx.scene.control.Label?>
<?import javafx.scene.control.TextField?>
<?import javafx.scene.Group?>
<?import javafx.scene.layout.HBox?>
<?import javafx.scene.layout.VBox?>
<?import javafx.scene.shape.Rectangle?>
<?import javafx.scene.text.Text?>
<Group fx:id="rootGroup"
       onMouseDragged="#mouseDraggedHandler"
       onMousePressed="#mousePressedHandler"
       xmlns="http://javafx.com/javafx/8"
       xmlns:fx="http://javafx.com/fxml/1"
       fx:controller="projavafx.stagecoach.ui.StageCoachController">
    <children>
        <Rectangle fx:id="blue"
                   arcHeight="50.0"
                   arcWidth="50.0"
                   fill="SKYBLUE"
                   height="350.0"
                   strokeType="INSIDE"
                   width="250.0"/>
        <VBox fx:id="contentBox"
              layoutX="30.0"
              layoutY="20.0"
              spacing="10.0">
            <children>
                <Text fx:id="textStageX"
                      strokeType="OUTSIDE"
                      strokeWidth="0.0"
                      text="x:"
                      textOrigin="TOP"/>
                <Text fx:id="textStageY"
                      layoutX="10.0"
                      layoutY="23.0"
                      strokeType="OUTSIDE"
                      strokeWidth="0.0"
                      text="y:"
                      textOrigin="TOP"/>
```

```
                <Text fx:id="textStageH"
                      layoutX="10.0"
                      layoutY="50.0"
                      strokeType="OUTSIDE"
                      strokeWidth="0.0"
                      text="height:"
                      textOrigin="TOP"/>
                <Text fx:id="textStageW"
                      layoutX="10.0"
                      layoutY="77.0"
                      strokeType="OUTSIDE"
                      strokeWidth="0.0"
                      text="width:"
                      textOrigin="TOP"/>
                <Text fx:id="textStageF"
                      layoutX="10.0"
                      layoutY="104.0"
                      strokeType="OUTSIDE"
                      strokeWidth="0.0"
                      text="focused:"
                      textOrigin="TOP"/>
                <CheckBox fx:id="checkBoxResizable"
                          mnemonicParsing="false"
                          text="resizable"/>
                <CheckBox fx:id="checkBoxFullScreen"
                          mnemonicParsing="false"
                          text="fullScreen"/>
                <HBox fx:id="titleBox">
                    <children>
                        <Label fx:id="titleLabel"
                               text="title"/>
                        <TextField fx:id="titleTextField"
                                   text="Stage Coach"/>
                    </children>
                </HBox>
                <Button fx:id="toBackButton"
                        mnemonicParsing="false"
                        onAction="#toBackEventHandler"
                        text="toBack()"/>
                <Button fx:id="toFrontButton"
                        mnemonicParsing="false"
                        onAction="#toFrontEventHandler"
                        text="toFront()"/>
                <Button fx:id="closeButton"
                        mnemonicParsing="false"
                        onAction="#closeEventHandler"
                        text="close()"/>
            </children>
        </VBox>
    </children>
</Group>
```

■ **Note** The FXML file created by JavaFX SceneBuilder has longer lines. We reformatted the FXML file to fit the page of the book.

Most of this FXML file can be understood intuitively: It represents a Group holding two children, a Rectangle and a VBox. The VBox in turn holds five Text nodes, two CheckBoxes, an HBox, and three Buttons. The HBox holds a Label and a TextField. Various properties of these nodes are set to some sensible values; for example, the text on the three Buttons is set to "toBack()", "toFront()" and "close()".

Some of the constructs in this FXML file need a little bit more explanation. The XML processing instructions at the top of the file

```
<?import javafx.scene.control.Button?>
<?import javafx.scene.control.CheckBox?>
<?import javafx.scene.control.Label?>
<?import javafx.scene.control.TextField?>
<?import javafx.scene.Group?>
<?import javafx.scene.layout.HBox?>
<?import javafx.scene.layout.VBox?>
<?import javafx.scene.shape.Rectangle?>
<?import javafx.scene.text.Text?>
```

inform the consumer of this file, either JavaFX SceneBuilder at design time or FXMLLoader at runtime, to import the mentioned Java classes. These have the same effect as import directives in Java source files.

Two namespace declarations are provided for the top-level element Group. JavaFX SceneBuilder puts these namespaces in every FXML file it creates:

```
xmlns="http://javafx.com/javafx/8"
xmlns:fx="http://javafx.com/fxml/1"
```

■ **Caution** The FXML file is not validated against any XML schemas. The namespaces specified here are used by the FXMLLoader, JavaFX SceneBuilder, and Java IDEs such as NetBeans, Eclipse, and IntelliJ IDEA to provide assistance when editing FXML files. The actual prefix, empty string for the first namespace and "fx" for the second namespace, should not be altered.

This FXML file contains two kinds of attributes with the fx prefix, fx:controller and fx:id. The fx:controller attribute appears on the top-level element Group. It informs the JavaFX runtime that the UI designed in the current FXML file is meant to work together with a Java class called its *controller*:

```
fx:controller="projavafx.stagecoach.ui.StageCoachController"
```

The preceding attribute declares that StageCoach.fxml will work together with the Java class projavafx.stagecoach.ui.StageCoachController. The fx:id attribute can appear in every element that represents a JavaFX Node. The value of fx:id is the name of a field in the controller that represents the Node after the FXML file has been loaded. The StageCoach.fxml file declares the following fx:ids (only lines with fx:id attribute are shown):

```
<Group fx:id="rootGroup"
      <Rectangle fx:id="blue"
      <VBox fx:id="contentBox"
              <Text fx:id="textStageX"
              <Text fx:id="textStageY"
              <Text fx:id="textStageH"
              <Text fx:id="textStageW"
              <Text fx:id="textStageF"
              <CheckBox fx:id="checkBoxResizable"
              <CheckBox fx:id="checkBoxFullScreen"
              <HBox fx:id="titleBox">
                      <Label fx:id="titleLabel"
                      <TextField fx:id="titleTextField"
              <Button fx:id="toBackButton"
              <Button fx:id="toFrontButton"
              <Button fx:id="closeButton"
```

Thus after the FXMLLoader is done loading the FXML file, the top-level Group node in the FXML file can be accessed and manipulated in Java code as the rootGroup field of the StageCoachController class. In this FXML file, we assigned an fx:id to all the nodes that we create. This is done for illustration purposes only. If there is no reason to manipulate a node programmatically, such as is the case for a static label, both the fx:id attribute and the corresponding field in the controller can be omitted.

Providing programmatic access to the nodes in an FXML file is one role that the controller plays. Another role the controller plays is to provide the methods that handle user input and interaction events originating from the nodes in an FXML file. These event handlers are specified by attributes whose name begins with "on", such as onMouseDragged, onMousePressed, and onAction. They correspond to the setOnMouseDragged(), setOnMousePressed(), and setOnAction() methods in the Node classes or its subclasses. To set the event handlers to a method in the controller, use the method name preceded with a "#" character as the value of the onMouseDragged, onMousePressed, and onAction attributes. The StageCoach.fxml file declares the following event handlers (only lines with event handlers are shown):

```
<Group fx:id="rootGroup"
      onMouseDragged="#mouseDraggedHandler"
      onMousePressed="#mousePressedHandler"
              <Button fx:id="toBackButton"
                      onAction="#toBackEventHandler"
              <Button fx:id="toFrontButton"
                      onAction="#toFrontEventHandler"
              <Button fx:id="closeButton"
                      onAction="#closeEventHandler"
```

The event handler methods in the controller class should in general conform to the signature of the single method in the EventHandler<T> interface

```
void handle(T event)
```

where T is the appropriate event object, MouseEvent for the onMouseDragged and onMousePressed event handlers, and ActionEvent for the onAction event handlers. A method that does not take any arguments can also be set as event handler methods. You can use such a method if you do not plan to use the event object.

Now that we understand the FXML file, we move on to the controller class next.

Understanding the Controller

Listing 3-2 shows the controller class that works with the FXML file we created in the last subsection.

Listing 3-2. StageCoachController.java

```
package projavafx.stagecoach.ui;

import javafx.beans.property.SimpleStringProperty;
import javafx.beans.property.StringProperty;
import javafx.event.ActionEvent;
import javafx.fxml.FXML;
import javafx.scene.control.Button;
import javafx.scene.control.CheckBox;
import javafx.scene.control.Label;
import javafx.scene.control.TextField;
import javafx.scene.input.MouseEvent;
import javafx.scene.layout.HBox;
import javafx.scene.layout.VBox;
import javafx.scene.shape.Rectangle;
import javafx.scene.text.Text;
import javafx.stage.Stage;
import javafx.stage.StageStyle;

public class StageCoachController {
    @FXML
    private Rectangle blue;

    @FXML
    private VBox contentBox;

    @FXML
    private Text textStageX;

    @FXML
    private Text textStageY;

    @FXML
    private Text textStageH;

    @FXML
    private Text textStageW;

    @FXML
    private Text textStageF;
```

```
    @FXML
    private CheckBox checkBoxResizable;

    @FXML
    private CheckBox checkBoxFullScreen;

    @FXML
    private HBox titleBox;

    @FXML
    private Label titleLabel;

    @FXML
    private TextField titleTextField;

    @FXML
    private Button toBackButton;

    @FXML
    private Button toFrontButton;

    @FXML
    private Button closeButton;

    private Stage stage;
    private StringProperty title = new SimpleStringProperty();
    private double dragAnchorX;
    private double dragAnchorY;

    public void setStage(Stage stage) {
        this.stage = stage;
    }

    public void setupBinding(StageStyle stageStyle) {
        checkBoxResizable.setDisable(stageStyle == StageStyle.TRANSPARENT
            || stageStyle == StageStyle.UNDECORATED);
        textStageX.textProperty().bind(new SimpleStringProperty("x: ")
            .concat(stage.xProperty().asString()));
        textStageY.textProperty().bind(new SimpleStringProperty("y: ")
            .concat(stage.yProperty().asString()));
        textStageW.textProperty().bind(new SimpleStringProperty("width: ")
            .concat(stage.widthProperty().asString()));
        textStageH.textProperty().bind(new SimpleStringProperty("height: ")
            .concat(stage.heightProperty().asString()));
        textStageF.textProperty().bind(new SimpleStringProperty("focused: ")
            .concat(stage.focusedProperty().asString()));
        stage.setResizable(true);
        checkBoxResizable.selectedProperty()
            .bindBidirectional(stage.resizableProperty());
        checkBoxFullScreen.selectedProperty().addListener((ov, oldValue, newValue) ->
            stage.setFullScreen(checkBoxFullScreen.selectedProperty().getValue()));
```

```
        title.bind(titleTextField.textProperty());
        stage.titleProperty().bind(title);
        stage.initStyle(stageStyle);
    }

    @FXML
    public void toBackEventHandler(ActionEvent e) {
        stage.toBack();
    }

    @FXML
    public void toFrontEventHandler(ActionEvent e) {
        stage.toFront();
    }

    @FXML
    public void closeEventHandler(ActionEvent e) {
        stage.close();
    }


    @FXML
    public void mousePressedHandler(MouseEvent me) {
        dragAnchorX = me.getScreenX() - stage.getX();
        dragAnchorY = me.getScreenY() - stage.getY();
    }

    @FXML
    public void mouseDraggedHandler(MouseEvent me) {
        stage.setX(me.getScreenX() - dragAnchorX);
        stage.setY(me.getScreenY() - dragAnchorY);
    }
}
```

This class is extracted from the StageCoachMain class of Chapter 2, and this is the class that we specified as the controller class for the FXML file StageCoach.fxml. Indeed, it includes fields whose types and names match the fx:ids in the FXML file. It also includes methods whose names and signatures match those specified as the event handlers for the various nodes in the FXML file.

The only thing that needs some explanation is the @FXML annotation. It belongs to the javafx.fxml package. This is a marker annotation with a runtime retention that can be applied to fields and methods. When applied to a field, the @FXML annotation tells JavaFX SceneBuilder the field's name can be used as the fx:id of the appropriately typed elements in an FXML file. When applied to a method, the @FXML annotation tells JavaFX SceneBuilder the method's name can be used as the value of the appropriately typed event handler attributes. Fields and methods annotated with @FXML are made accessible to the FXML loading facility regardless of the modifiers. Therefore it is safe to change all the @FXML annotated fields from public to private without adversely affecting the FXML loading process.

The StageCoachController class includes matching fields for all the fx:ids declared in the FXML file. It also includes the five event handler methods to which the event handler attributes in the FXML file point. All of these fields and methods are annotated with @FXML.

The StageCoachController also includes some fields and methods that are not annotated with the @FXML annotation. These fields and methods are present in the class for other purposes. For example, the stage field, the setStage(), and the setupBindings() methods are used directly in Java code.

Understanding the FXMLLoader

Now that we understand both the FXML file and the controller class that works with the FXML file, we turn our attention to the loading of the FXML file at runtime. The `FXMLLoader` class in the `javafx.fxml` package does the bulk of the work of loading FXML files. In our example, the FXML file loading is done in the `StageCoachMain` class. Listing 3-3 shows the `StageCoachMain` class.

Listing 3-3. StageCoachMain.java

```
package projavafx.stagecoach.ui;

import javafx.application.Application;
import javafx.fxml.FXMLLoader;
import javafx.geometry.Rectangle2D;
import javafx.scene.Group;
import javafx.scene.Scene;
import javafx.scene.paint.Color;
import javafx.stage.Screen;
import javafx.stage.Stage;
import javafx.stage.StageStyle;

import java.io.IOException;
import java.util.List;

public class StageCoachMain extends Application {
    @Override
    public void start(Stage stage) throws IOException {
        final StageStyle stageStyle = configStageStyle();

        FXMLLoader fxmlLoader = new FXMLLoader(StageCoachMain.class
            .getResource("/projavafx/stagecoach/ui/StageCoach.fxml"));
        Group rootGroup = fxmlLoader.load();

        final StageCoachController controller = fxmlLoader.getController();
        controller.setStage(stage);
        controller.setupBinding(stageStyle);

        Scene scene = new Scene(rootGroup, 250, 350);
        scene.setFill(Color.TRANSPARENT);

        stage.setScene(scene);
        stage.setOnCloseRequest(we -> System.out.println("Stage is closing"));
        stage.show();
        Rectangle2D primScreenBounds = Screen.getPrimary().getVisualBounds();
        stage.setX((primScreenBounds.getWidth() - stage.getWidth()) / 2);
        stage.setY((primScreenBounds.getHeight() - stage.getHeight()) / 4);
    }

    public static void main(String[] args) {
        launch(args);
    }
```

```
    private StageStyle configStageStyle() {
        StageStyle stageStyle = StageStyle.DECORATED;
        List<String> unnamedParams = getParameters().getUnnamed();
        if (unnamedParams.size() > 0) {
            String stageStyleParam = unnamedParams.get(0);
            if (stageStyleParam.equalsIgnoreCase("transparent")) {
                stageStyle = StageStyle.TRANSPARENT;
            } else if (stageStyleParam.equalsIgnoreCase("undecorated")) {
                stageStyle = StageStyle.UNDECORATED;
            } else if (stageStyleParam.equalsIgnoreCase("utility")) {
                stageStyle = StageStyle.UTILITY;
            }
        }
        return stageStyle;
    }
}
```

Before looking at the FXMLLoader code, let me point out that for this example, we choose to put the StageCoach.fxml file together with the StageCoachMain.java and the StageCoachController.java files. And they all reside in the projavafx/stagecoach/ui directory. That relation is preserved when we compile the source files. Therefore when we run this program, the FXML file appears as a resource /projavafx/stagecoach/ui/StageCoach.fxml in the classpath. Figure 3-2 illustrates the file layout of our example.

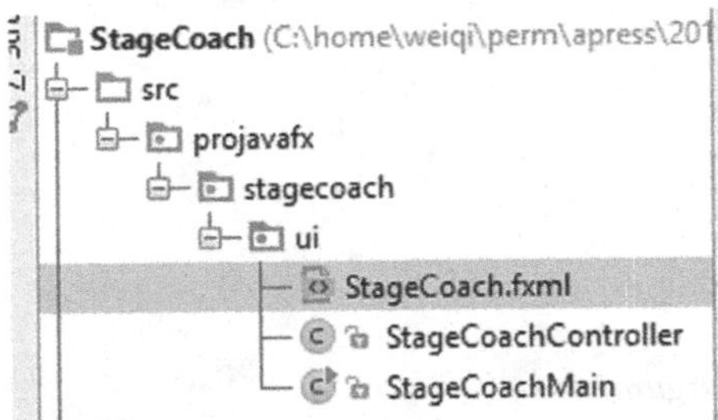

***Figure 3-2.** The file layout of the StageCoach example*

The loading of the FXML file is performed by the following snippet of code:

```
FXMLLoader fxmlLoader = new FXMLLoader(StageCoachMain.class
    .getResource("/projavafx/stagecoach/ui/StageCoach.fxml"));
Group rootGroup = fxmlLoader.load();

final StageCoachController controller = fxmlLoader.getController();
```

Here we use the one-parameter constructor of the FXMLLoader class to construct an fxmlLoader object and pass in a URL object returned by the getResource() call on the Class object of StageCoachMain. This URL object is a jar URL or a file URL, depending on whether you run this program from a jar. We then call the load() method on the fxmlLoader object. This method reads the FXML file, parses it, instantiates all the nodes it specified, and hooks them up according to the containment relationships it specified. Because a controller is specified in the FXML file, the method also instantiates a StageCoachController instance and assigns the nodes to the fields of the controller instance according to the fx:ids. This step is usually called *injecting* the FXML nodes into the controller. The event handlers are also hooked up. The `load()` method returns the top-level object in the FXML file, which in our example is a `Group`. This returned `Group` object is assigned to the `rootGroup` variable and is used in subsequent code the same way as the programmatically created `rootGroup` in Chapter 2 is used. We then call the `getController()` method to get the controller with its node fields already injected by the `FXMLLoader`. This controller is assigned to the `controller` variable and is used in subsequent code as if we have just created it and assigned its node fields programmatically.

Now that we've finished switching the Stage Coach program from programmatic to declarative UI creation, we can run it. It behaves just like in Chapter 2. Figure 3-3 shows the program running with the `transparent` command-line argument.

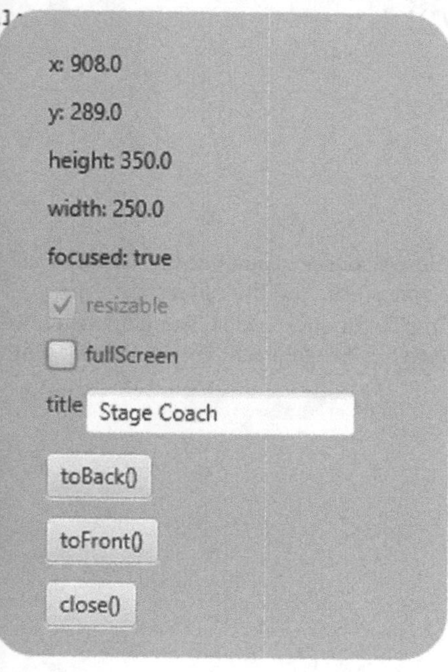

Figure 3-3. The Stage Coach program run with transparent command-line argument

In this section we touched on all aspects of the FXML design-time and runtime facilities. However, we described only parts of each facility, barely enough to get our example program going. In the rest of this chapter, we study each of the facilities in detail.

Understanding the FXML Loading Facility

The FXML file loading facility is made up of two classes, an interface, an exception, and an annotation in the `javafx.fxml` package. The `FXMLLoader` is the class that does the bulk of the work, such as reading and parsing the FXML file, recognizing processing instructions in the FXML file, and responding with the necessary actions, recognizing each element and attribute of the FXML file and delegating the object creation tasks to a set of builders, creating the controller object if necessary and injecting the nodes and other objects into the controller. The `JavaFXBuilderFactory` is responsible for creating builders in response for `FXMLLoader`'s requests for builders for a particular class. The `Initializable` interface can be implemented by controller classes to receive information from the `FXMLLoader` as in previous versions of JavaFX; however, this functionality has been superseded by the injection approach, so we do not discuss it. A `LoadException` is thrown if the FXML file contains errors that make it impossible for the `FXMLLoader` to construct all the objects specified in the FXML file. The `@FXML` annotation can be used in controller classes to mark certain fields as injection targets and certain methods as event handler candidates.

Understanding the FXMLLoader Class

The FXMLLoader class has the following public constructors:

- FXMLLoader()
- FXMLLoader(URL location)
- FXMLLoader(URL location, ResourceBundle resources)
- FXMLLoader(URL location, ResourceBundle resources, BuilderFactory builderFactory)
- FXMLLoader(URL location, ResourceBundle resources, BuilderFactory BuilderFactory builderFactory, Callback<Class<?>, Object> controllerFactory)
- FXMLLoader(Charset charset)
- FXMLLoader(URL location, ResourceBundle resources, BuilderFactory BuilderFactory builderFactory, Callback<Class<?> controllerFactory, Object>, Charset charset)
- FXMLLoader(URL location, ResourceBundle resources, BuilderFactory BuilderFactory builderFactory, Callback<Class<?>, Object> controllerFactory, Charset charset, LinkedList<FXMLLoader> loaders)

Constructors with fewer parameters delegate to constructors with more parameters, with the missing parameters filled in with default values. The location parameter is the URL of the FXML file to be loaded. It defaults to null. The resources parameter is the resource bundle to be used with the FXML file. This is necessary if internationalized strings are used in the FXML file. It defaults to null. The builderFactory parameter is the builder factory that FXMLLoader uses to get the builders of the various objects that it creates. It defaults to an instance of the JavaFXBuilderFactory. This builder factory has knowledge about all the standard JavaFX types that are likely to appear in FXML files, so a customized builder factory is rarely used. The controllerFactory is a javafx.util.CallBack that is capable of returning an instance of the controller when provided with the class of the controller. It defaults to null, in which case the FXMLLoader will instantiate the controller through reflection by calling the no-parameters constructor of the controller class. Therefore you need to supply a controllerFactory only if the controller cannot be constructed that way. The charset is used when the FXML is parsed. It defaults to UTF-8. The loaders parameter is a list of FXMLLoaders. It defaults to an empty list.

The FXMLLoader class has the following getter and setter methods that alter the states of the FXMLLoader:

- URL getLocation()
- void setLocation(URL location)
- ResourceBundle getResources()
- void setResources(ResourceBundle resources)
- ObservableMap<String, Object> getNamespace()
- <T> T getRoot()
- void setRoot(Object root)
- <T> T getController()
- void setController(Object controller)
- BuilderFactory getBuilderFactory()
- void setBuilderFactory(BuilderFactory builderFactory)

- `Callback<Class<?>, Object> getControllerFactory()`
- `void setControllerFactory(Callback<Class<?>, Object> controllerFactory)`
- `Charset getCharset()`
- `void setCharset(Charset charset)`
- `ClassLoader getClassLoader()`
- `void setClassLoader(ClassLoader classLoader)`

As you can see from this list, the `location`, `resources`, `builderFactory`, `controllerFactory`, and the `charset` can also be set after the `FXMLLoader` is constructed. In addition, we can get and set the `root`, `controller`, `classLoader`, and get the `namespace` of the `FXMLLoader`. The `root` is relevant only if the FXML file uses `fx:root` as its root element, in which case `setRoot()` must be called before the FXML file is loaded. We go into more detail about the usage of `fx:root` in the next section. The `controller` needs to be set before the FXML file is loaded only if the `fx:controller` attribute is not present in the top-level element in the FXML file. The `classLoader` and `namespace` are mostly used internally by the `FXMLLoader` and usually are not called by user code.

The actual loading of the FXML file happens when one of the `load()` methods is called. The `FXMLLoader` class has the following load methods:

- `<T> T load() throws IOException`
- `<T> T load(InputStream input) throws IOException`
- `static <T> T load(URL location) throws IOException`
- `static <T> T load(URL location, ResourceBundle resources) throws IOException`
- `static <T> T load(URL location, ResourceBundle resources, BuilderFactory builderFactory) throws IOException`
- `static <T> T load(URL location, ResourceBundle resources, BuilderFactory builderFactory, Callback<Class<?>, Object> controllerFactory) throws IOException`
- `static <T> T load(URL location, ResourceBundle resources, BuilderFactory builderFactory, Callback<Class<?>, Object> controllerFactory, Charset charset) throws IOException`

The `load()` method with no argument can be called on an `FXMLLoader` instance that has all the necessary fields already initialized. The `load()` method that takes an `InputStream` argument will load the FXML from the specified input. All the static `load()` methods are convenience methods that will instantiate an `FXMLLoader` with the supplied parameters and then call one of its nonstatic `load()` methods.

In our next example, we deliberately did not specify `fx:controller` in the FXML file. We also added a one-parameter constructor to the controller class. The FXML file, the controller class, and the main class are shown in Listings 3-4, 3-5, and 3-6.

Listing 3-4. FXMLLoaderExample.fxml

```
<?xml version="1.0" encoding="UTF-8"?>

<?import javafx.geometry.Insets?>
<?import javafx.scene.control.Button?>
<?import javafx.scene.control.TextField?>
<?import javafx.scene.layout.HBox?>
<?import javafx.scene.layout.VBox?>
<?import javafx.scene.web.WebView?>
```

```
<VBox maxHeight="-Infinity"
      maxWidth="-Infinity"
      minHeight="-Infinity"
      minWidth="-Infinity"
      prefHeight="400.0"
      prefWidth="600.0"
      spacing="10.0"
      xmlns="http://javafx.com/javafx/8"
      xmlns:fx="http://javafx.com/fxml/1">
    <children>
        <HBox spacing="10.0">
            <children>
                <TextField fx:id="address"
                           onAction="#actionHandler"
                           HBox.hgrow="ALWAYS">
                    <padding>
                        <Insets bottom="4.0" left="4.0" right="4.0" top="4.0"/>
                    </padding>
                </TextField>
                <Button fx:id="loadButton"
                        mnemonicParsing="false"
                        onAction="#actionHandler"
                        text="Load"/>
            </children>
        </HBox>
        <WebView fx:id="webView"
                 prefHeight="200.0"
                 prefWidth="200.0"
                 VBox.vgrow="ALWAYS"/>
    </children>
    <padding>
        <Insets bottom="10.0" left="10.0" right="10.0" top="10.0"/>
    </padding>
</VBox>
```

Listing 3-5. FXMLLoaderExampleController.java

```
import javafx.event.ActionEvent;
import javafx.fxml.FXML;
import javafx.scene.control.Button;
import javafx.scene.control.TextField;
import javafx.scene.web.WebView;

public class FXMLLoaderExampleController {
    @FXML
    private TextField address;

    @FXML
    private WebView webView;
```

```
    @FXML
    private Button loadButton;

    private String name;

    public FXMLLoaderExampleController(String name) {
        this.name = name;
    }

    @FXML
    public void actionHandler() {
        webView.getEngine().load(address.getText());
    }
}
```

Listing 3-6. FXMLLoaderExampleMain.java

```
import javafx.application.Application;
import javafx.fxml.FXMLLoader;
import javafx.scene.Scene;
import javafx.scene.layout.VBox;
import javafx.stage.Stage;

public class FXMLLoaderExampleMain extends Application {
    @Override
    public void start(Stage primaryStage) throws Exception {
        FXMLLoader fxmlLoader = new FXMLLoader();
        fxmlLoader.setLocation(
            FXMLLoaderExampleMain.class.getResource("/FXMLLoaderExample.fxml"));
        fxmlLoader.setController(
            new FXMLLoaderExampleController("FXMLLoaderExampleController"));
        final VBox vBox = fxmlLoader.load();
        Scene scene = new Scene(vBox, 600, 400);
        primaryStage.setTitle("FXMLLoader Example");
        primaryStage.setScene(scene);
        primaryStage.show();
    }

    public static void main(String[] args) {
        launch(args);
    }
}
```

Because we did not specify the `fx:controller` attribute in the top-level element of the FXML file, we need to set the controller on `fxmlLoader` before loading the FXML file:

```
FXMLLoader fxmlLoader = new FXMLLoader();
fxmlLoader.setLocation(
    FXMLLoaderExampleMain.class.getResource("/FXMLLoaderExample.fxml"));
fxmlLoader.setController(
    new FXMLLoaderExampleController("FXMLLoaderExampleController"));
final VBox vBox = fxmlLoader.load();
```

If the controller is not set, a `LoaderException` will be thrown, with a message "No controller specified." This is because we did specify the controller method `actionHandler` as the action event handler for both the text field and the button. The `FXMLLoader` needs the controller to fulfill these specifications in the FXML file. Had the event handlers not been specified, the FXML file would have been loaded successfully because there is no need for a controller.

This program is a very primitive web browser with an address bar `TextField`, a load `Button`, and a `WebView`. Figure 3-4 shows the FXMLLoaderExample program at work.

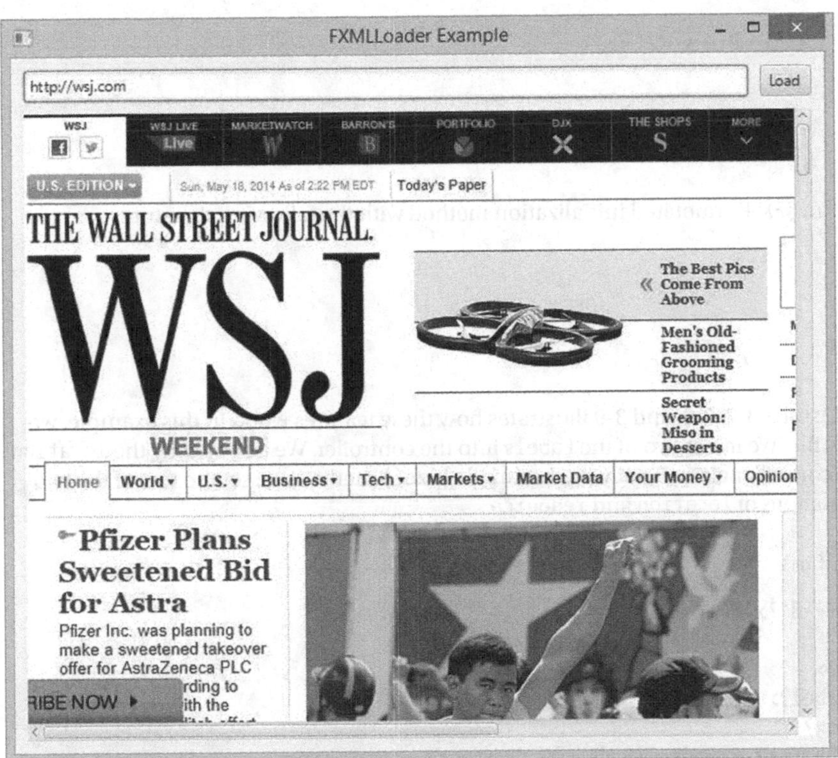

Figure 3-4. The FXMLLoaderExample program

Our next example, ControllerFactoryExample, is nearly identical to the FXMLLoaderExample with only two differences, so we do not show the complete code here. You can find it in the code download bundle. Unlike in `FXMLLoaderExample`, we do specify `fx:controller` in the FXML file. This forces us to remove the `setController()` call in the main class, because otherwise we get a `LoadException` with a message "Controller value already specified." However, because our controller does not have a default constructor, `FXMLLoader` will throw a `LoadException` caused by its inability to instantiate the controller. This exception can be remedied by a simple controller factory that we set on the `fxmlLoader`:

```
fxmlLoader.setControllerFactory(
    clazz -> new ControllerFactoryExampleController("ExampleController"));
```

Here we used a simple lambda expression to implement the functional interface `Callback<Class<?>, Object>`, which has a single

```
Object call(Class<?>)
```

method. In our implementation we simply return an instance of `ControllerFactoryExampleController`.

Understanding the @FXML Annotation

We have seen two uses of the @FXML annotation. It can be applied to fields in the controller of an FXML file whose name and type match the fx:id attribute and element name of an FXML element to be injected with the node. It can be applied to void methods that take either no parameter or one parameter of type javafx.event.Event or its subtype, making them eligible for use as event handlers for elements in FXML files.

The FXMLLoader will inject its location and resources into the controller if it has the fields to receive them:

```
@FXML
private URL location;

@FXML
private ResourceBundle resources;
```

The FXMLLoader will also invoke an @FXML annotated initialization method with the following signature:

```
@FXML
public void initialize() {
    // ...
}
```

The FXMLInjectionExample in Listings 3-7, 3-8, and 3-9 illustrates how these features work. In this example, we put four Labels in a VBox in the FXML file. We inject two of the Labels into the controller. We also specify the location and resources injection fields in the controller class. Finally, in the initialize() method, we set the text of the two injected Labels to the string representations of location and resource.

Listing 3-7. FXMLInjectionExample.fxml

```
<?xml version="1.0" encoding="UTF-8"?>

<?import javafx.geometry.Insets?>
<?import javafx.scene.control.Label?>
<?import javafx.scene.layout.VBox?>
<?import javafx.scene.text.Font?>
<VBox alignment="CENTER_LEFT"
      maxHeight="-Infinity"
      maxWidth="-Infinity"
      minHeight="-Infinity"
      minWidth="-Infinity"
      prefHeight="150.0"
      prefWidth="700.0"
      spacing="10.0"
      xmlns="http://javafx.com/javafx/8"
      xmlns:fx="http://javafx.com/fxml/1"
      fx:controller="FXMLInjectionExampleController">
    <children>
        <Label text="Location:">
            <font>
                <Font name="System Bold" size="14.0"/>
            </font>
        </Label>
```

```
        <Label fx:id="locationLabel" text="[location]"/>
        <Label text="Resources:">
            <font>
                <Font name="System Bold" size="14.0"/>
            </font>
        </Label>
        <Label fx:id="resourcesLabel" text="[resources]"/>
    </children>
    <opaqueInsets>
        <Insets/>
    </opaqueInsets>
    <padding>
        <Insets bottom="10.0" left="10.0" right="10.0" top="10.0"/>
    </padding>
</VBox>
```

Listing 3-8. FXMLInjectionExampleController.java

```
import javafx.fxml.FXML;
import javafx.scene.control.Label;

import java.net.URL;
import java.util.ResourceBundle;

public class FXMLInjectionExampleController {
    @FXML
    private Label resourcesLabel;

    @FXML
    private Label locationLabel;

    @FXML
    private URL location;

    @FXML
    private ResourceBundle resources;

    @FXML
    public void initialize() {
        locationLabel.setText(location.toString());
        resourcesLabel.setText(resources.getBaseBundleName());
    }
}
```

Listing 3-9. FXMLInjectionExampleMain.java

```
import javafx.application.Application;
import javafx.fxml.FXMLLoader;
import javafx.scene.Scene;
import javafx.scene.layout.VBox;
import javafx.stage.Stage;
```

```
import java.util.ResourceBundle;

public class FXMLInjectionExampleMain extends Application {
    @Override
    public void start(Stage primaryStage) throws Exception {
        FXMLLoader fxmlLoader = new FXMLLoader();
        fxmlLoader.setLocation(
            FXMLInjectionExampleMain.class.getResource("/FXMLInjectionExample.fxml"));
        fxmlLoader.setResources(ResourceBundle.getBundle("FXMLInjectionExample"));
        VBox vBox = fxmlLoader.load();
        Scene scene = new Scene(vBox);
        primaryStage.setTitle("FXML Injection Example");
        primaryStage.setScene(scene);
        primaryStage.show();
    }

    public static void main(String[] args) {
        launch(args);
    }
}
```

Notice that we also created an empty `FXMLInjectionExample.properties` file to use as the resource bundle to illustrate the injection of the resources field into the controller. We explain how to use resource bundles with FXML files in the next section. When the FXMLInjectionExample is run on my machine, the FXML Injection Example window in Figure 3-5 is displayed on the screen.

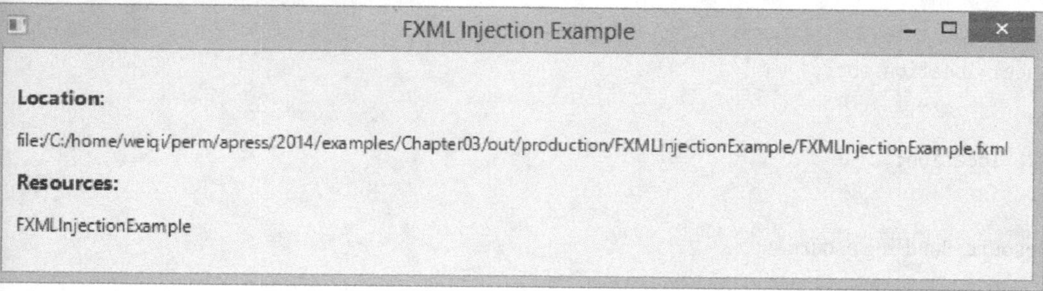

***Figure 3-5.** The FXMLInjection program*

The `@FXML` annotation can also be used for included FXML file controller injection, and for marking controller properties of `javafx.event.EventHandler` type for use as event handlers in FXML files. We cover them in detail when we discuss the relevant features of the FXML file in the next section.

Exploring the Capabilities of FXML Files

In this section, we go over the features of the FXML file format. Because a major goal of the `FXMLLoader` is to deserialize an FXML file into Java objects, it should be no surprise that it provides facilities that help to make writing FXML files easier.

The Deserialization Power of the FXML Format

Because the features that we cover in this section have more to do with deserializing generic Java objects, we will move away from the GUI world and work with plain Java classes. We use the JavaBean defined in Listing 3-10 in our discussion. It is a made-up class meant to illustrate the different FXML features.

Listing 3-10. FXMLBasicFeaturesBean.java

```
package projavafx.fxmlbasicfeatures;

import javafx.scene.paint.Color;

import java.util.ArrayList;
import java.util.HashMap;
import java.util.List;
import java.util.Map;

public class FXMLBasicFeaturesBean {
    private String name;
    private String address;
    private boolean flag;
    private int count;
    private Color foreground;
    private Color background;
    private Double price;
    private Double discount;
    private List<Integer> sizes;
    private Map<String, Double> profits;
    private Long inventory;
    private List<String> products = new ArrayList<String>();
    private Map<String, String> abbreviations = new HashMap<>();

    public String getName() {
        return name;
    }

    public void setName(String name) {
        this.name = name;
    }

    public String getAddress() {
        return address;
    }

    public void setAddress(String address) {
        this.address = address;
    }

    public boolean isFlag() {
        return flag;
    }
```

```
    public void setFlag(boolean flag) {
        this.flag = flag;
    }

    public int getCount() {
        return count;
    }

    public void setCount(int count) {
        this.count = count;
    }

    public Color getForeground() {
        return foreground;
    }

    public void setForeground(Color foreground) {
        this.foreground = foreground;
    }

    public Color getBackground() {
        return background;
    }

    public void setBackground(Color background) {
        this.background = background;
    }

    public Double getPrice() {
        return price;
    }

    public void setPrice(Double price) {
        this.price = price;
    }

    public Double getDiscount() {
        return discount;
    }

    public void setDiscount(Double discount) {
        this.discount = discount;
    }

    public List<Integer> getSizes() {
        return sizes;
    }

    public void setSizes(List<Integer> sizes) {
        this.sizes = sizes;
    }
```

```
    public Map<String, Double> getProfits() {
        return profits;
    }

    public void setProfits(Map<String, Double> profits) {
        this.profits = profits;
    }

    public Long getInventory() {
        return inventory;
    }

    public void setInventory(Long inventory) {
        this.inventory = inventory;
    }

    public List<String> getProducts() {
        return products;
    }

    public Map<String, String> getAbbreviations() {
        return abbreviations;
    }

    @Override
    public String toString() {
        return "FXMLBasicFeaturesBean{" +
            "name='" + name + '\'' +
            ",\n\taddress='" + address + '\'' +
            ",\n\tflag=" + flag +
            ",\n\tcount=" + count +
            ",\n\tforeground=" + foreground +
            ",\n\tbackground=" + background +
            ",\n\tprice=" + price +
            ",\n\tdiscount=" + discount +
            ",\n\tsizes=" + sizes +
            ",\n\tprofits=" + profits +
            ",\n\tinventory=" + inventory +
            ",\n\tproducts=" + products +
            ",\n\tabbreviations=" + abbreviations +
            '}';
    }
}
```

The FXML file in Listing 3-11 is loaded and printed out to the console in the program in Listing 3-12.

Listing 3-11. FXMLBasicFeatures.fxml

```
<?import javafx.scene.paint.Color?>
<?import projavafx.fxmlbasicfeatures.FXMLBasicFeaturesBean?>
<?import projavafx.fxmlbasicfeatures.Utilities?>
<?import java.lang.Double?>
```

```
<?import java.lang.Integer?>
<?import java.lang.Long?>
<?import java.util.HashMap?>
<?import java.lang.String?>
<FXMLBasicFeaturesBean name="John Smith"
                       flag="true"
                       count="12345"
                       xmlns:fx="http://javafx.com/fxml/1">
    <address>12345 Main St.</address>
    <foreground>#ff8800</foreground>
    <background>
        <Color red="0.0" green="1.0" blue="0.5"/>
    </background>
    <price>
        <Double fx:value="3.1415926"/>
    </price>
    <discount>
        <Utilities fx:constant="TEN_PCT"/>
    </discount>
    <sizes>
        <Utilities fx:factory="createList">
            <Integer fx:value="1"/>
            <Integer fx:value="2"/>
            <Integer fx:value="3"/>
        </Utilities>
    </sizes>
    <profits>
        <HashMap q1="1000" q2="1100" q3="1200" a4="1300"/>
    </profits>
    <fx:define>
        <Long fx:id="inv" fx:value="9765625"/>
    </fx:define>
    <inventory>
        <fx:reference source="inv"/>
    </inventory>
    <products>
        <String fx:value="widget"/>
        <String fx:value="gadget"/>
        <String fx:value="models"/>
    </products>
    <abbreviations CA="California" NY="New York" FL="Florida" MO="Missouri"/>

</FXMLBasicFeaturesBean>
```

Listing 3-12. FXMLBasicFeaturesMain.java

```
package projavafx.fxmlbasicfeatures;

import javafx.fxml.FXMLLoader;

import java.io.IOException;
```

```
public class FXMLBasicFeaturesMain {
    public static void main(String[] args) throws IOException {
        FXMLBasicFeaturesBean bean = FXMLLoader.load(
            FXMLBasicFeaturesMain.class.getResource(
                "/projavafx/fxmlbasicfeatures/FXMLBasicFeatures.fxml")
        );
        System.out.println("bean = " + bean);
    }
}
```

We made use of a small utility class that contains a few constants and a factory method that creates a `List<Integer>`, as shown in Listing 3-13.

Listing 3-13. `Utilities.java`

```
package projavafx.fxmlbasicfeatures;

import java.util.ArrayList;
import java.util.List;

public class Utilities {
    public static final Double TEN_PCT = 0.1d;
    public static final Double TWENTY_PCT = 0.2d;
    public static final Double THIRTY_PCT = 0.3d;

    public static List<Integer> createList() {
        return  new ArrayList<>();
    }
}
```

The `FXMLBasicFeaturesBean` object is being created in the FXML file; this is indicated by the fact that the top-level element of the FXML file is `FXMLBasicFeaturesBean`. The `name` and `address` fields illustrate that a field can be set either as an attribute or as a subelement:

```
<FXMLBasicFeaturesBean name="John Smith"
                       flag="true"
                       count="12345"
                       xmlns:fx="http://javafx.com/fxml/1">
    <address>12345 Main St.</address>
```

The `foreground` and `background` fields illustrate two ways of setting a `javafx.scene.paint.Color` subelement, either through a hex string, or using a `Color` element (remember `Color` is an immutable object without a default constructor):

```
<foreground>#ff8800</foreground>
<background>
    <Color red="0.0" green="1.0" blue="0.5"/>
</background>
```

The price field illustrates a way to construct a Double object. The fx:value attribute invokes the valueOf(String) method on Double. This works on any Java class that has a factory method valueOf(String):

```
<price>
    <Double fx:value="3.1415926"/>
</price>
```

The discount field illustrates how to use a constant defined in a Java class. The fx:constant attribute accesses constant (public static final) fields of the type of its element. The following sets the discount field to Utilities.TEN_PCT, which is 0.1:

```
<discount>
    <Utilities fx:constant="TEN_PCT"/>
</discount>
```

The sizes field illustrates the use of factory methods to create objects. The fx:factory attribute invokes the specified factory method on the type of its element. In our case, it calls Utilities.createList() to create a list of Integers, which is then populated with three Integers. Notice that sizes is a read-write property. You will see an example of how a read-only list property is populated later.

```
<sizes>
    <Utilities fx:factory="createList">
        <Integer fx:value="1"/>
        <Integer fx:value="2"/>
        <Integer fx:value="3"/>
    </Utilities>
</sizes>
```

The profits field illustrates how to populate a read-write map. Here we set the profits field to a HashMap that we create with key/value pairs:

```
<profits>
    <HashMap q1="1000" q2="1100" q3="1200" a4="1300"/>
</profits>
```

The inventory field illustrates how to define an object in one place and reference it in another place. The fx:define element creates a stand-alone object that has an fx:id attribute. The fx:reference element creates a reference to an object defined elsewhere, and its source attribute points to the fx:id of a previously defined object:

```
<fx:define>
    <Long fx:id="inv" fx:value="9765625"/>
</fx:define>
<inventory>
    <fx:reference source="inv"/>
</inventory>
```

The products field illustrates how to populate a read-only list. The following fragment of FXML is equivalent to invoking bean.getProducts().addAll("widget", "gadget", "models"):

```
<products>
    <String fx:value="widget"/>
    <String fx:value="gadget"/>
    <String fx:value="models"/>
</products>
```

The abbreviations field illustrates how to populate a read-only map:

```
<abbreviations CA="California" NY="New York" FL="Florida" MO="Missouri"/>
```

When the FXMLBasicFeaturesMain program is run, the following output is printed to the console, as expected:

```
bean = FXMLBasicFeaturesBean{name='John Smith',
        address='12345 Main St.',
        flag=true,
        count=12345,
        foreground=0xff8800ff,
        background=0x00ff80ff,
        price=3.1415926,
        discount=0.1,
        sizes=[1, 2, 3],
        profits={q1=1000, q2=1100, q3=1200, a4=1300},
        inventory=9765625,
        products=[widget, gadget, models],
        abbreviations={MO=Missouri, FL=Florida, NY=New York, CA=California}}
```

Understanding Default and Static Properties

Many JavaFX classes have a default property. *Default properties* are specified with a @DefaultProperty annotation on the class. The @DefaultProperty annotation belongs to the javafx.beans package. The default property of the javafx.scene.Group class, for example, is its children property. In FXML files, when a default property is specified via a subelement, the beginning and ending tag of the default property itself can be omitted. As an example, the following snippet, which you saw in Listing 3-1,

```
<HBox fx:id="titleBox">
    <children>
        <Label fx:id="titleLabel"
               text="title"/>
        <TextField fx:id="titleTextField"
                   text="Stage Coach"/>
    </children>
</HBox>
```

can be simplified to

```
<HBox fx:id="titleBox">
    <Label fx:id="titleLabel"
           text="title"/>
    <TextField fx:id="titleTextField"
               text="Stage Coach"/>
</HBox>
```

A *static property* is a property that is set on an object not by calling a setter method on the object itself, but by calling a static method of a different class, passing both the object and the value of the property as parameters. Many of JavaFX's container Nodes have such static methods. These methods are called on a Node prior to adding it to the container to affect certain results. Static properties are represented in FXML files as attributes on the inner object (the object that is passed in as the first parameter to the static method) with a name that includes both the class name and the static method name separated by a dot. You can spot an example of a static property in Listing 3-4:

```
<WebView fx:id="webView"
         prefHeight="200.0"
         prefWidth="200.0"
         VBox.vgrow="ALWAYS"/>
```

Here we are adding a `WebView` to a `VBox`, and the `VBox.vgrow` attribute indicates that the `FXMLLoader` needs to call

```
VBox.vgrow(webView, Priority.ALWAYS)
```

prior to adding `webView` to the `VBox`. Static properties can also appear as subelements in addition to appearing as attributes.

Understanding Attribute Resolutions and Bindings

As you have seen in earlier parts of this chapter, object properties can be represented both as attributes and as subelements. Sometimes it is as effective to model a property as a subelement or an attribute. However, the `FXMLLoader` will perform additional processing for attributes, making it more attractive to use attributes. When processing attributes, the `FXMLLoader` will perform three kinds of attribute value resolutions and expression binding.

When an attribute's value starts with an "@" character, `FXMLLoader` will treat the value as a location relative to the current file. This is called *location resolution*. When an attribute's value starts with a "%" character, `FXMLLoader` will treat the value as a key in a resource bundle and substitute the locale-specific value for the key. This is called *resource resolution*. When an attribute's value starts with a "$" character, `FXMLLoader` will treat the value as a variable name, and substitute the value of the referenced variable as the value of the attribute. This is called *variable resolution*.

When an attribute's value starts with "${" and ends with "}", and if the attribute represents a JavaFX property, `FXMLLoader` will treat the value as a binding expression, and binds the JavaFX property to the enclosed expression. This is called *expression binding*. You will learn about JavaFX properties and bindings in Chapter 4. For now simply understand that when a property is bound to an expression, every time the expression changes value, the change is reflected in the property. Supported expressions include string literals, boolean literals, numeric literals, the unary -(minus) and !(negation) operators, the arithmetic operators (+, -, *, /, %), the logical operators (&&, ||), and the relational operators (>, >=, <, <=, ==, !=).

The ResolutionAndBindingExample, shown in Listings 3-14 to 3-19, illustrates the use of location resolution, resource resolution, and variable resolution as well as expression binding.

Listing 3-14. `ResolutionAndBindingExample.fxml`

```
<?xml version="1.0" encoding="UTF-8"?>

<?import javafx.geometry.Insets?>
<?import javafx.scene.control.Label?>
<?import javafx.scene.control.TextField?>
<?import javafx.scene.layout.HBox?>
<?import javafx.scene.layout.VBox?>
<?import javafx.scene.text.Font?>
<?import java.util.Date?>
<VBox id="vbox" alignment="CENTER_LEFT" maxHeight="-Infinity" maxWidth="-Infinity" minHeight="-Infinity"
    minWidth="-Infinity" prefHeight="200.0" prefWidth="700.0" spacing="10.0"
    stylesheets="@ResolutionAndBindingExample.css" xmlns="http://javafx.com/javafx/8"
    xmlns:fx="http://javafx.com/fxml/1" fx:controller="ResolutionAndBindingController">
```

```
        <children>
            <Label text="%location">
                <font>
                    <Font name="System Bold" size="14.0"/>
                </font>
            </Label>
            <Label fx:id="locationLabel" text="[location]"/>
            <Label text="%resources">
                <font>
                    <Font name="System Bold" size="14.0"/>
                </font>
            </Label>
            <Label fx:id="resourcesLabel" text="[resources]"/>
            <Label text="%currentDate">
                <font>
                    <Font name="System Bold" size="14.0"/>
                </font>
            </Label>
            <HBox alignment="BASELINE_LEFT" spacing="10.0">
                <children>
                    <fx:define>
                        <Date fx:id="capturedDate"/>
                    </fx:define>
                    <Label fx:id="currentDateLabel" text="$capturedDate"/>
                    <TextField fx:id="textField"/>
                    <Label text="${textField.text}"/>
                </children>
            </HBox>
        </children>
        <opaqueInsets>
            <Insets/>
        </opaqueInsets>
        <padding>
            <Insets bottom="10.0" left="10.0" right="10.0" top="10.0"/>
        </padding>
    </VBox>
```

Listing 3-15. ResolutionAndBindingController.java

```
import javafx.fxml.FXML;
import javafx.scene.control.Label;

import java.net.URL;
import java.util.ResourceBundle;

public class ResolutionAndBindingController {
    @FXML
    private Label resourcesLabel;

    @FXML
    private Label locationLabel;
```

```
    @FXML
    private Label currentDateLabel;

    @FXML
    private URL location;

    @FXML
    private ResourceBundle resources;

    @FXML
    public void initialize() {
        locationLabel.setText(location.toString());
        resourcesLabel.setText(resources.getBaseBundleName() +
            " (" + resources.getLocale().getCountry() +
            ", " + resources.getLocale().getLanguage() + ")");
    }
}
```

Listing 3-16. ResolutionAndBindingExample.java

```
import javafx.application.Application;
import javafx.fxml.FXMLLoader;
import javafx.scene.Scene;
import javafx.scene.layout.VBox;
import javafx.stage.Stage;

import java.util.ResourceBundle;

public class ResolutionAndBindingExample extends Application {
    @Override
    public void start(Stage primaryStage) throws Exception {
        FXMLLoader fxmlLoader = new FXMLLoader();
        fxmlLoader.setLocation(
            ResolutionAndBindingExample.class.getResource(
                "/ResolutionAndBindingExample.fxml"));
        fxmlLoader.setResources(
            ResourceBundle.getBundle(
                "ResolutionAndBindingExample"));
        VBox vBox = fxmlLoader.load();
        Scene scene = new Scene(vBox);
        primaryStage.setTitle("Resolution and Binding Example");
        primaryStage.setScene(scene);
        primaryStage.show();
    }

    public static void main(String[] args) {
        launch(args);
    }
```

Listing 3-17. `ResourceAndBindingExample.properties`

```
location=Location:
resources=Resources:
currentDate=CurrentDate:
```

Listing 3-18. `ResolutionAndBindingExample_fr_FR.properties`

```
location=Emplacement:
resources=Resources:
currentDate=Date du jour:
```

Listing 3-19. `ResolutionAndBindingExample.css`

```
#vbox {
    -fx-background-color: azure ;
}
```

Location resolution is used in the FXML file to specify the location of the CSS file. The `stylesheet` attribute is set to the location "`@ResolutionAndBindingExample.css`":

```
<VBox id="vbox" alignment="CENTER_LEFT" maxHeight="-Infinity" maxWidth="-Infinity" minHeight="-Infinity"
      minWidth="-Infinity" prefHeight="200.0" prefWidth="700.0" spacing="10.0"
      stylesheets="@ResolutionAndBindingExample.css" xmlns="http://javafx.com/javafx/8"
      xmlns:fx="http://javafx.com/fxml/1" fx:controller="ResolutionAndBindingController">
```

The stylesheet sets the background color of the VBox to azure. Resource resolution is used to set the text for three labels in the program:

```
<Label text="%location">
<Label text="%resources">
<Label text="%currentDate">
```

These labels will get their texts from the resource bundle that is supplied to the `FXMLLoader` before the FXML file is loaded. Both the default locale and a French locale translation of the properties file are provided. Variable resolution happens between a defined `java.util.Date` instance and a `Label`:

```
<fx:define>
    <Date fx:id="capturedDate"/>
</fx:define>
<Label fx:id="currentDateLabel" text="$capturedDate"/>
```

The defined `Date` was given the `fx:id` of `capturedDate` and the label used the variable for its text. Finally, the expression binding happens between a `TextField` and a `Label`:

```
<TextField fx:id="textField"/>
<Label text="${textField.text}"/>
```

The `TextField` was given the `fx:id` of `textField` and the label binds to the expression `textField.text`, with a result of the label mimicking what is typed in the text field. When the ResolutionAndBindingExample is run with the French locale, the Resolution and Binding Example window shown in Figure 3-6 is displayed.

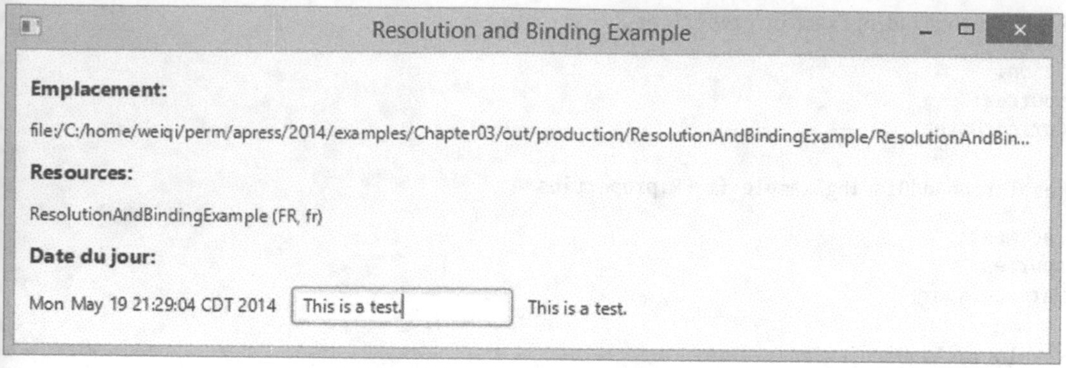

Figure 3-6. The ResolutionAndBindingExample program

Using Multiple FXML Files

Because the result of loading an FXML file is a JavaFX Node that can be used in a Scene, you are not limited to using only one FXML file for any Scene. You can, for example, break your scene into two or more parts and represent each part by its own FXML file. Then you can call one of the load() methods of FXMLLoader on the FXML file of each part, and assemble the resulting nodes programmatically into your scene.

The FXML file format supports another mechanism to combine separately prepared FXML files together. One FXML file can include another with an fx:include element. The fx:include element supports three attributes: the source attribute holds the location of the included FXML file; the resources attribute holds the location of the resource bundle that is used by the included FXML file; and the charset attribute holds the charset for the included FXML file. If the source attribute starts with a "/" character, it is interpreted as a path in the classpath; otherwise it is interpreted as relative to the location of the including FXML file. The resource and the charset attributes are optional. When they are not specified, their values used for loading the including FXML file are used. The builder factory and the controller factory used for loading the including FXML file are also used for loading the included FXML file.

An fx:id can be specified for an fx:include element. When an fx:id is specified, a corresponding field in the controller of the including FXML file can be specified, and the FXMLLoader will inject this field with the result of loading the included FXML file. Moreover, if the included FXML file has an fx:controller specified in its root element, that included FXML file's controller can also be injected into the including FXML file's controller, provided a properly named and typed field is available in the including file's controller to receive the injected included FXML file's controller. In the example application of this section, we use two FXML files to represent the application's UI. The including FXML file has lines like the following:

```
<BorderPane maxHeight="-Infinity"
        ...
        fx:controller="IncludeExampleTreeController">
    <fx:include fx:id="details"
                source="IncludeExampleDetail.fxml" />
```

and the included FXML has lines like the following:

```
<VBox maxHeight="-Infinity"
    ...
    fx:controller="IncludeExampleDetailController">
```

Consequently, loading the included FXML file will result in a root element of type VBox, and a controller of type `IncludeExampleDetailController`. The controller of the including FXML file, `IncludeExampleTreeController` has fields like the following:

```
@FXML
private VBox details;

@FXML
private IncludeExampleDetailController detailsController;
```

These fields will hold the loaded root and controller of the included FXML file when the including FXML file is loaded.

The complete source codes of this section's example are shown in Listings 3-20 to 3-25.

Listing 3-20. `IncludeExampleTree.fxml`

```
<?xml version="1.0" encoding="UTF-8"?>

<?import javafx.geometry.Insets?>
<?import javafx.scene.control.Label?>
<?import javafx.scene.control.TreeTableColumn?>
<?import javafx.scene.control.TreeTableView?>
<?import javafx.scene.layout.BorderPane?>
<?import javafx.scene.layout.VBox?>
<?import javafx.scene.text.Font?>
<BorderPane maxHeight="-Infinity"
            maxWidth="-Infinity"
            minHeight="-Infinity"
            minWidth="-Infinity"
            prefHeight="400.0"
            prefWidth="600.0"
            xmlns="http://javafx.com/javafx/8"
            xmlns:fx="http://javafx.com/fxml/1"
            fx:controller="IncludeExampleTreeController">
    <top>
        <Label text="Product Details"
               BorderPane.alignment="CENTER">
            <font>
                <Font name="System Bold Italic" size="36.0"/>
            </font>
        </Label>
    </top>
    <left>
        <VBox spacing="10.0">
            <children>
                <Label text="List of Products:">
                    <font>
                        <Font name="System Bold" size="12.0"/>
                    </font>
                </Label>
                <TreeTableView fx:id="treeTableView"
                               prefHeight="200.0"
                               prefWidth="200.0"
```

```
                                   BorderPane.alignment="CENTER"
                                   VBox.vgrow="ALWAYS">
                    <columns>
                        <TreeTableColumn fx:id="category"
                                         editable="false"
                                         prefWidth="125.0"
                                         text="Category"/>
                        <TreeTableColumn fx:id="name"
                                         editable="false"
                                         prefWidth="75.0"
                                         text="Name"/>
                    </columns>
                </TreeTableView>
            </children>
            <BorderPane.margin>
                <Insets/>
            </BorderPane.margin>
        </VBox>
    </left>
    <center>
        <fx:include fx:id="details"
                    source="IncludeExampleDetail.fxml"/>
    </center>
    <padding>
        <Insets bottom="10.0" left="10.0" right="10.0" top="10.0"/>
    </padding>
</BorderPane>
```

Listing 3-21. IncludeExampleDetail.fxml

```
<?xml version="1.0" encoding="UTF-8"?>

<?import javafx.geometry.Insets?>
<?import javafx.scene.control.Label?>
<?import javafx.scene.control.TextArea?>
<?import javafx.scene.layout.VBox?>
<?import javafx.scene.text.Font?>
<VBox maxHeight="-Infinity"
      maxWidth="-Infinity"
      minHeight="-Infinity"
      minWidth="-Infinity"
      prefHeight="346.0"
      prefWidth="384.0"
      spacing="10.0"
      xmlns="http://javafx.com/javafx/8"
      xmlns:fx="http://javafx.com/fxml/1"
      fx:controller="IncludeExampleDetailController">
    <children>
        <Label text="Category:">
            <font>
                <Font name="System Bold" size="12.0"/>
            </font>
        </Label>
```

```
        <Label fx:id="category" text="[Category]"/>
        <Label text="Name:">
            <font>
                <Font name="System Bold" size="12.0"/>
            </font>
        </Label>
        <Label fx:id="name" text="[Name]"/>
        <Label text="Description:">
            <font>
                <Font name="System Bold" size="12.0"/>
            </font>
        </Label>
        <TextArea fx:id="description"
                  prefHeight="200.0"
                  prefWidth="200.0"
                  VBox.vgrow="ALWAYS"/>
    </children>
    <padding>
        <Insets bottom="10.0" left="20.0" right="10.0" top="30.0"/>
    </padding>
</VBox>
```

Listing 3-22. IncludeExampleTreeController.java

```
import javafx.beans.property.ReadOnlyStringWrapper;
import javafx.fxml.FXML;
import javafx.scene.control.TreeItem;
import javafx.scene.control.TreeTableColumn;
import javafx.scene.control.TreeTableView;
import javafx.scene.layout.VBox;

public class IncludeExampleTreeController {
    @FXML
    private TreeTableView<Product> treeTableView;

    @FXML
    private TreeTableColumn<Product, String> category;

    @FXML
    private TreeTableColumn<Product, String> name;

    @FXML
    private VBox details;

    @FXML
    private IncludeExampleDetailController detailsController;

    @FXML
    public void initialize() {
        Product[] products = new Product[101];
        for (int i = 0; i <= 100; i++) {
            products[i] = new Product();
            products[i].setCategory("Category" + (i / 10));
```

```
            products[i].setName("Name" + i);
            products[i].setDescription("Description" + i);
        }
        TreeItem<Product> root = new TreeItem<>(products[100]);
        root.setExpanded(true);
        for (int i = 0; i < 10; i++) {
            TreeItem<Product> firstLevel =
                new TreeItem<>(products[i * 10]);
            firstLevel.setExpanded(true);
            for (int j = 1; j < 10; j++) {
                TreeItem<Product> secondLevel =
                    new TreeItem<>(products[i * 10 + j]);
                secondLevel.setExpanded(true);
                firstLevel.getChildren().add(secondLevel);
            }
            root.getChildren().add(firstLevel);
        }

        category.setCellValueFactory(param ->
            new ReadOnlyStringWrapper(param.getValue().getValue().getCategory()));
        name.setCellValueFactory(param ->
            new ReadOnlyStringWrapper(param.getValue().getValue().getName()));

        treeTableView.setRoot(root);

        treeTableView.getSelectionModel().selectedItemProperty()
            .addListener((observable, oldValue, newValue) -> {
                Product product = null;
                if (newValue != null) {
                    product = newValue.getValue();
                }
                detailsController.setProduct(product);
            });
    }
}
```

Listing 3-23. IncludeExampleDetailController.java

```
import javafx.beans.value.ChangeListener;
import javafx.fxml.FXML;
import javafx.scene.control.Label;
import javafx.scene.control.TextArea;

public class IncludeExampleDetailController {
    @FXML
    private Label category;

    @FXML
    private Label name;

    @FXML
    private TextArea description;
```

```
    private Product product;
    private ChangeListener<String> listener;

    public void setProduct(Product product) {
        if (this.product != null) {
            unhookListener();
        }
        this.product = product;
        hookTo(product);
    }

    private void unhookListener() {
        description.textProperty().removeListener(listener);
    }

    private void hookTo(Product product) {
        if (product == null) {
            category.setText("");
            name.setText("");
            description.setText("");
            listener = null;
        } else {
            category.setText(product.getCategory());
            name.setText(product.getName());
            description.setText(product.getDescription());
            listener = (observable, oldValue, newValue) ->
                product.setDescription(newValue);
            description.textProperty().addListener(listener);
        }
    }
}
```

Listing 3-24. IncludeExample.java

```
import javafx.application.Application;
import javafx.fxml.FXMLLoader;
import javafx.scene.Scene;
import javafx.scene.layout.BorderPane;
import javafx.stage.Stage;

public class IncludeExample extends Application {
    @Override
    public void start(Stage primaryStage) throws Exception {
        FXMLLoader fxmlLoader = new FXMLLoader();
        fxmlLoader.setLocation(
            IncludeExample.class.getResource("IncludeExampleTree.fxml"));
        final BorderPane borderPane = fxmlLoader.load();
        Scene scene = new Scene(borderPane, 600, 400);
        primaryStage.setTitle("Include Example");
        primaryStage.setScene(scene);
        primaryStage.show();
    }
```

```
    public static void main(String[] args) {
        launch(args);
    }
}
```

Listing 3-25. Product.java

```
public class Product {
    private String category;
    private String name;
    private String description;

    public String getCategory() {
        return category;
    }

    public void setCategory(String category) {
        this.category = category;
    }

    public String getDescription() {
        return description;
    }

    public void setDescription(String description) {
        this.description = description;
    }

    public String getName() {
        return name;
    }

    public void setName(String name) {
        this.name = name;
    }
}
```

In this IncludeExample program, we build up the UI in two FXML files, each one backed by its own controller. The UI features a `TreeTableView` on the left side, and some `Labels` and a `TextArea` on the right side. The `TreeTableView` is loaded with dummy `Product` data. When a row in the left `TreeTableView` is selected, the corresponding `Product` is shown on the right side. You can edit the `Product`'s description field using the `TextArea` on the right side. As you navigate away from an old row to a new row on the left side, the `Product` on the right side reflects the change. However, all the changes that you made to previously displayed `Products` are retained in the model. When you navigate back to a modified `Product`, your changes will be shown again. The `TreeTableView` class is covered in more detail in Chapter 6.

We used a `ChangeListener<String>` that is attached to the `TextField`'s `textProperty` to synchronize the text in the `TextField` and the `description` in the `Product`. JavaFX properties and change listeners are part of the JavaFX Properties and Bindings API. We cover this API in the next chapter.

When the IncludeExample is run, the Include Example window shown in Figure 3-7 is displayed.

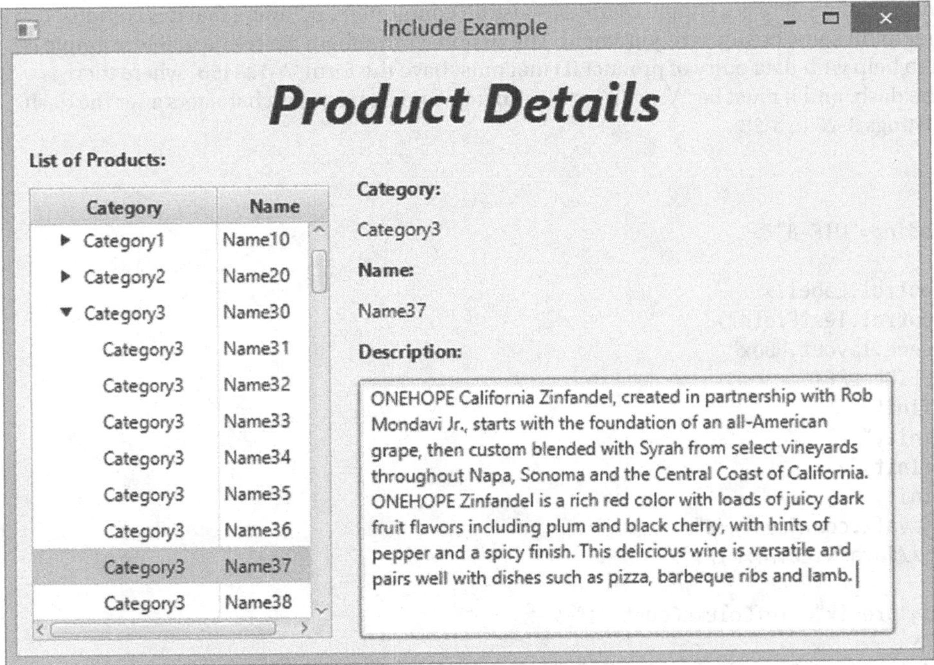

Figure 3-7. *The IncludeExample program*

Creating Custom Components Using fx:root

The `fx:include` element allows us to attach one FXML file into another FXML file. Similarly, the `fx:root` element allows us to attach an FXML file to a `Node` that is provided in code. The `fx:root` element must be the top-level element in an FXML file. It must be supplied with a `type` attribute, which determines the type of the `Node` that needs to be created in code to load this FXML file.

In its simplest form, you can change any one of the earlier FXML files' top-level element from

```
<SomeType ...
```

to

```
<fx:root type="some.package.SomeType" ...
```

and instantiate `SomeType` in code and set it as the root in the `FXMLLoader` before loading the FXML file, like the following:

```
SomeType someType = new SomeType();
fxmlLoader.setRoot(someType);
fxmlLoader.load();
```

The next example goes one step further. It defines a class that extends the `fx:root` type of the FXML file, and serves as both the root and the controller of the FXML file. It loads the FXML file in its constructor, and uses the `initialize()` method to set up the desired relationships between the nodes that are constructed in the FXML file. This class can then be used as if it is a native JavaFX node. Classes that are constructed this way are called *custom components.*

The custom component we define here is a simple *composite* custom component, meaning that it is composed of several nodes that together fulfill some business requirement. The custom component we create in this example is called ProdId. It's designed to help with data entry of product ID that must have the form "A-123456" where there is only one character before the dash, and it must be "A" or "B" or "C." There could be up to six characters after the dash. This program is shown in Listings 3-26 to 3-28.

Listing 3-26. ProdId.fxml

```
<?xml version="1.0" encoding="UTF-8"?>

<?import javafx.scene.control.Label?>
<?import javafx.scene.control.TextField?>
<fx:root type="javafx.scene.layout.HBox"
         alignment="BASELINE_LEFT"
         maxHeight="-Infinity"
         maxWidth="-Infinity"
         minHeight="-Infinity"
         minWidth="-Infinity"
         xmlns="http://javafx.com/javafx/8"
         xmlns:fx="http://javafx.com/fxml/1">
    <children>
        <TextField fx:id="prefix" prefColumnCount="1"/>
        <Label text="-"/>
        <TextField fx:id="prodCode" prefColumnCount="6"/>
    </children>
</fx:root>
```

Listing 3-27. ProdId.java

```
package projavafx.customcomponent;

import javafx.beans.property.SimpleStringProperty;
import javafx.beans.property.StringProperty;
import javafx.fxml.FXML;
import javafx.fxml.FXMLLoader;
import javafx.scene.control.TextField;
import javafx.scene.layout.HBox;

import java.io.IOException;

public class ProdId extends HBox {

    @FXML
    private TextField prefix;

    @FXML
    private TextField prodCode;

    private StringProperty prodId = new SimpleStringProperty();
```

```
    public ProdId() throws IOException {
        FXMLLoader fxmlLoader = new FXMLLoader(ProdId.class.getResource("ProdId.fxml"));
        fxmlLoader.setRoot(this);
        fxmlLoader.setController(this);
        fxmlLoader.load();
    }

    @FXML
    public void initialize() {
        prefix.textProperty().addListener((observable, oldValue, newValue) -> {
            switch (newValue) {
                case "A":
                case "B":
                case "C":
                    prodCode.requestFocus();
                    break;
                default:
                    prefix.setText("");
            }
        });
        prodCode.textProperty().addListener((observable, oldValue, newValue) -> {
            if (newValue.length() > 6) {
                prodCode.setText(newValue.substring(0, 6));
            } else if (newValue.length() == 0) {
                prefix.requestFocus();
            }
        });
        prodId.bind(prefix.textProperty().concat("-").concat(prodCode.textProperty()));
    }

    public String getProdId() {
        return prodId.get();
    }

    public StringProperty prodIdProperty() {
        return prodId;
    }

    public void setProdId(String prodId) {
        this.prodId.set(prodId);
    }
}
```

Listing 3-28. CustomComponent.java

```
package projavafx.customcomponent;

import javafx.application.Application;
import javafx.geometry.Insets;
import javafx.geometry.Pos;
import javafx.scene.Scene;
import javafx.scene.control.Label;
```

```
import javafx.scene.layout.HBox;
import javafx.scene.layout.VBox;
import javafx.scene.text.Font;
import javafx.stage.Stage;

public class CustomComponent extends Application {
    @Override
    public void start(Stage primaryStage) throws Exception {
        VBox vBox = new VBox(10);
        vBox.setPadding(new Insets(10, 10, 10, 10));
        vBox.setAlignment(Pos.BASELINE_CENTER);

        final Label prodIdLabel = new Label("Enter Product Id:");
        final ProdId prodId = new ProdId();

        final Label label = new Label();
        label.setFont(Font.font(48));
        label.textProperty().bind(prodId.prodIdProperty());

        HBox hBox = new HBox(10);
        hBox.setPadding(new Insets(10, 10, 10, 10));
        hBox.setAlignment(Pos.BASELINE_LEFT);
        hBox.getChildren().addAll(prodIdLabel, prodId);

        vBox.getChildren().addAll(hBox, label);
        Scene scene = new Scene(vBox);
        primaryStage.setTitle("Custom Component Example");
        primaryStage.setScene(scene);
        primaryStage.show();
    }

    public static void main(String[] args) {
        launch(args);
    }
}
```

Notice that in the main program `CustomComponent` class, we did not load any FXML files. We simply instantiated `ProdId`, and proceed to use it as if it is a native JavaFX node. The FXML file simply put two `TextFields` and a `Label` in an HBox type `fx:root`. No `fx:controller` is set because we want to set it in the constructor of the `ProdId` class. In addition to the two injected `TextFields`, we have another `StringProperty` field called `prodId`, for which we defined a getter `getProdId()`, a setter `setProdId()`, and a property getter `prodIdProperty()`.

```
private StringProperty prodId = new SimpleStringProperty();

public String getProdId() {
    return prodId.get();
}

public StringProperty prodIdProperty() {
    return prodId;
}
```

```
public void setProdId(String prodId) {
    this.prodId.set(prodId);
}
```

The validation requirement and the convenience functionality are in the `initialize()` method, which will be called by the `FXMLLoader` when it has finished loading the FXML file. We hooked up `ChangeListeners` to the `textProperty` of the two `TextFields`, and allow only valid changes to occur. We also move the cursor to `prodCode` when the `prefix` is filled with the correct data. Likewise, when we back off from the `prodCode` field, the cursor will naturally jump to the `prefix` text field.

```
@FXML
public void initialize() {
    prefix.textProperty().addListener((observable, oldValue, newValue) -> {
        switch (newValue) {
            case "A":
            case "B":
            case "C":
                prodCode.requestFocus();
                break;
            default:
                prefix.setText("");
        }
    });
    prodCode.textProperty().addListener((observable, oldValue, newValue) -> {
        if (newValue.length() > 6) {
            prodCode.setText(newValue.substring(0, 6));
        } else if (newValue.length() == 0) {
            prefix.requestFocus();
        }
    });
    prodId.bind(prefix.textProperty().concat("-").concat(prodCode.textProperty()));
}
```

When the CustomComponent program is run, the Custom Component Example window shown in Figure 3-8 is displayed.

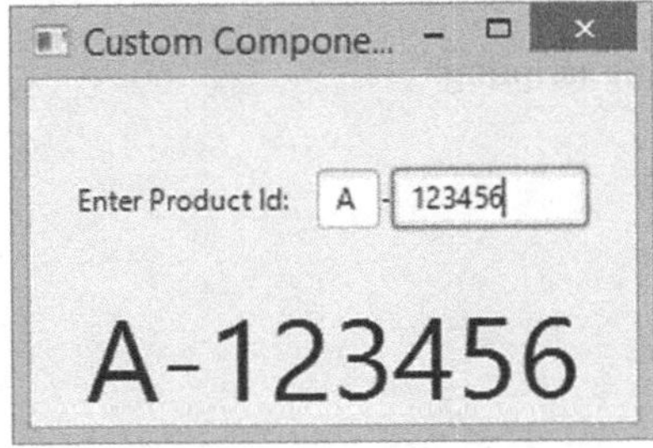

Figure 3-8. *The CustomComponent program*

Event Handling Using Scripting or Controller Properties

In the last section, we introduced you to using a method of the controller as an event handler for a node in an FXML file. JavaFX allows two more ways to set up event handlers in FXML files. One way is to use scripting. Any JSR-223 compatible `javax.script` based scripting engine can be used. The language to be used for scripting must be specified at the top of the FXML file. To use the Nashorn JavaScript engine that ships with Oracle JDK 8, the following processing instruction must be present at the top of the FXML file:

```
<?language javascript?>
```

The `fx:script` element is used to introduce scripts. Both inline scripts and external file scripts are supported. The following is an inline script:

```
<fx:script>
    function actionHandler(event) {
        webView.getEngine().load(address.getText());
    }
</fx:script>
```

The external script takes the following form:

```
<fx:script source="myscript.js"/>
```

Any node in the FXML file that has an `fx:id` can be accessed from the scripting environment by their `fx:id` names. If the FXML file has a controller, then the controller is available as a variable named `controller`. Variables declared in `fx:script` sections are also available for use as variables in attributes in the rest of the FXML file. To use the `actionHandler(event)` function defined in the `fx:script` section as an event handler, it can be specified as follows:

```
<TextField fx:id="address"
           onAction="actionHandler(event)"
```

■ Caution You can use either a function that takes no argument if your event handler does not need to inspect the event object, or a function that takes one argument as the value of the event handler attribute, such as `onAction`. If you call a function with one argument, then you must pass the system-provided event variable into it.

The ScriptingExample in Listings 3-29 and 3-30 illustrates event handling using scripting.

Listing 3-29. `ScriptingExample.fxml`

```
<?xml version="1.0" encoding="UTF-8"?>

<?language javascript?>

<?import javafx.geometry.Insets?>
<?import javafx.scene.control.Button?>
<?import javafx.scene.control.TextField?>
<?import javafx.scene.layout.HBox?>
```

```
<?import javafx.scene.layout.VBox?>
<?import javafx.scene.web.WebView?>
<VBox maxHeight="-Infinity"
      maxWidth="-Infinity"
      minHeight="-Infinity"
      minWidth="-Infinity"
      prefHeight="400.0"
      prefWidth="600.0"
      spacing="10.0"
      xmlns="http://javafx.com/javafx/8"
      xmlns:fx="http://javafx.com/fxml/1">
    <fx:script>
        function actionHandler(event) {
            webView.getEngine().load(address.getText());
        }
         </fx:script>
    <children>
        <HBox spacing="10.0">
            <children>
                <TextField fx:id="address"
                           onAction="actionHandler(event)"
                           HBox.hgrow="ALWAYS">
                    <padding>
                        <Insets bottom="4.0" left="4.0" right="4.0" top="4.0"/>
                    </padding>
                </TextField>
                <Button fx:id="loadButton"
                        mnemonicParsing="false"
                        onAction="actionHandler(event)"
                        text="Load"/>
            </children>
        </HBox>
        <WebView fx:id="webView"
                 prefHeight="200.0"
                 prefWidth="200.0"
                 VBox.vgrow="ALWAYS"/>
    </children>
    <padding>
        <Insets bottom="10.0" left="10.0" right="10.0" top="10.0"/>
    </padding>
</VBox>
```

Listing 3-30. ScriptingExample.java

```
import javafx.application.Application;
import javafx.fxml.FXMLLoader;
import javafx.scene.Scene;
import javafx.scene.layout.VBox;
import javafx.stage.Stage;
```

```
public class ScriptingExample extends Application {
    @Override
    public void start(Stage primaryStage) throws Exception {
        FXMLLoader fxmlLoader = new FXMLLoader();
        fxmlLoader.setLocation(
            ScriptingExample.class.getResource("/ScriptingExample.fxml"));
        final VBox vBox = fxmlLoader.load();
        Scene scene = new Scene(vBox, 600, 400);
        primaryStage.setTitle("Scripting Example");
        primaryStage.setScene(scene);
        primaryStage.show();
    }

    public static void main(String[] args) {
        launch(args);
    }
}
```

When the ScriptingExample is run, the Scripting Example window very similar to Figure 3-4 is displayed.

You can also specify an event handler with the variable syntax:

```
<TextField fx:id="address"
           onAction="$controller.actionHandler"
```

This will set the actionHandler property from the controller as the event handler of the onActionEvent. In the controller, the actionHandler property should have the correct event handler type. For the onAction event, the property should be like the following:

```
@FXML
public EventHandler<ActionEvent> getActionHandler() {
    return event -> {
        // handle the event
    };
}
```

Now that we have a thorough understanding of the FXML file format, we can effectively take advantage of the GUI editing convenience in creating FXML files.

Using JavaFX SceneBuilder

In the previous sections you have learned the fundamentals of the FXML file format. That knowledge should come in very handy when trying to use and comprehend the JavaFX SceneBuilder tool. In this last section of the chapter, we dive into the usages of the JavaFX SceneBuilder.

Because laying out a UI is a highly subjective, sometimes artistic endeavor, a lot depends on the application at hand and the design sensibilities of the UI and user experience teams. We do not pretend to know the best ways of doing UI design. So in this section, we give you a guided tour of the JavaFX SceneBuilder 2.0 itself, point out to you the various parts of the UI designer, and discuss how to turn the knobs and switch the gears to achieve a desired result.

Overview of JavaFX SceneBuilder

When you start JavaFX SceneBuilder, the screen looks like Figure 3-9.

***Figure 3-9.** The JavaFX SceneBuilder program*

When first started, the JavaFX SceneBuilder UI has a menu bar at the top, two accordion containers named Library and Document on the left side of the screen, a Content Panel in the middle of the screen, and an accordion container named Inspector on the right of the screen.

Understanding the Menu Bar and Items

There are nine menus in JavaFX SceneBuilder. Let's examine them one by one.

The File menu is shown in Figure 3-10.

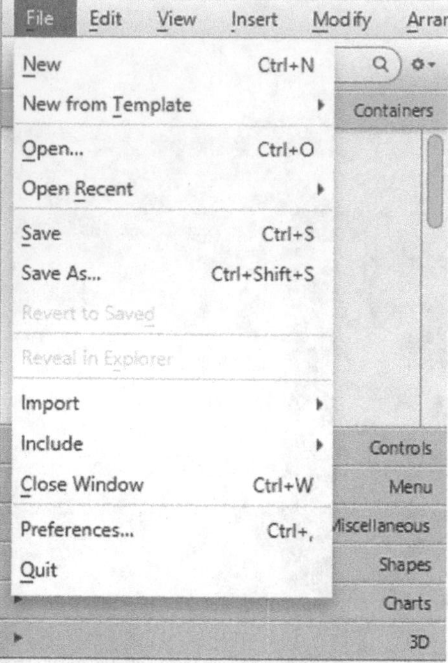

Figure 3-10. The File menu

The New, Open, Save, Save As, Revert to Saved, Reveal in Explorer (or Finder, or Desktop), Close Window, and Exit menu items do pretty much what you think they should do. The New from Template menu item creates a new FXML file from an existing template. The list of templates is shown in Figure 3-11.

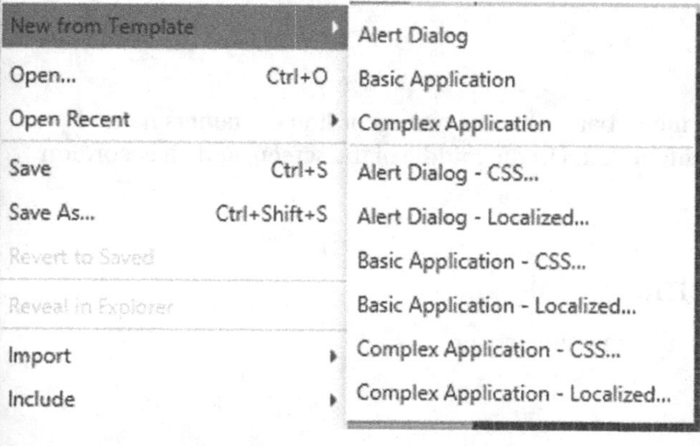

Figure 3-11. The templates

The Import menu item allows you to copy the content of another FXML file into the current FXML file. It also allows you to add image and media files to the current FXML file. Such imported files are wrapped in an `ImageView` or `MediaView` node. The Include menu item allows you to add an `fx:include` element into the current FXML file. The Close Window menu item closes the FXML file being edited in the current window. The Preferences menu item allows you to set certain preferences that control how JavaFX SceneBuilder looks. The Quit menu item allows you to exit the JavaFX SceneBuilder application entirely. It will ask you to save any unsaved files before shutting the application down.

The Edit menu is shown in Figure 3-12.

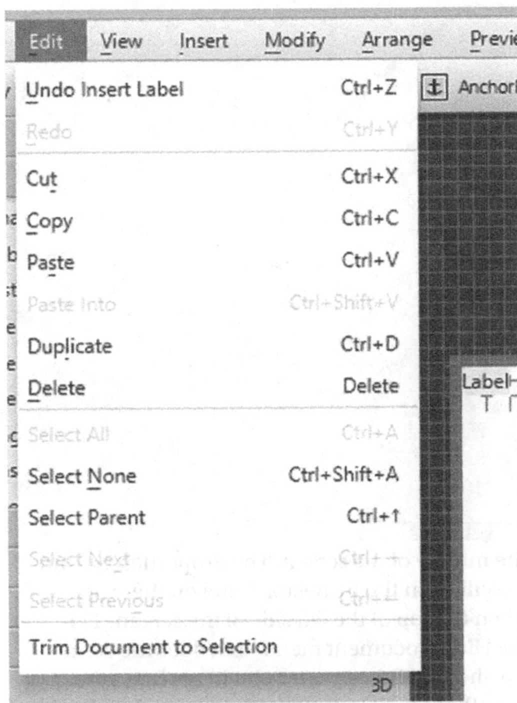

Figure 3-12. *The Edit menu*

The Undo, Redo, Cut, Copy, Paste, Paste Into, Duplicate, Delete, Select All, Select None, Select Parent, Select Next, and Select Previous menu items all perform their normal duties. The Trim Document to Selection menu item deletes everything that is not selected.

The View menu is shown in Figure 3-13.

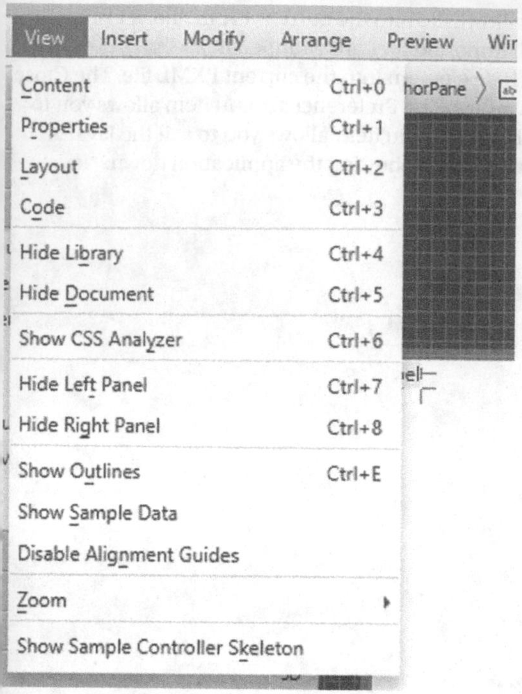

Figure 3-13. *The View menu*

The Content menu item puts the focus on the Content Panel in the middle of the screen. The Properties, Layout, and Code menu items put the focus on the Property, Layout, or Code sections in the Inspector Panel on the right side of the screen. The Hide Library command hides the Library Panel on the top of the left side of the screen. The menu item will change to Show Library once the Library is hidden. The Hide Document menu item does the same to the Document Panel on the bottom of the left side of the screen. The Show CSS Analyzer menu item shows the CSS Analyzer, which is initially not shown. The Hide Left Panel and Hide Right Panel menu items hide the Left Panel (the Library Panel and the Document Panel) or the Right Panel (the Inspector Panel). The Show Outlines menu item shows the outlines of the items. The Show Sample Data menu item will show sample data for `TreeView`, `TableView`, and `TreeTableView` nodes to help you visualize the node at work. The sample data are not saved with the FXML file. The Disable Alignment Guides menu item disables the alignment guidelines that are shown when you move a node around in a container in the Content Panel. These alignment guidelines help you to position the nodes in the right spot on the screen. The Zoom menu item allows you to change the magnification rate of the Content Panel. The Show Sample Controller Skeleton menu item will open a dialog box showing a skeleton controller class declaration based on the controller setting made in the Document Panel and the `fx:ids` declared for the nodes in the FXML file.

Figure 3-14 shows the JavaFX SceneBuilder screen with the CSS Analyzer shown.

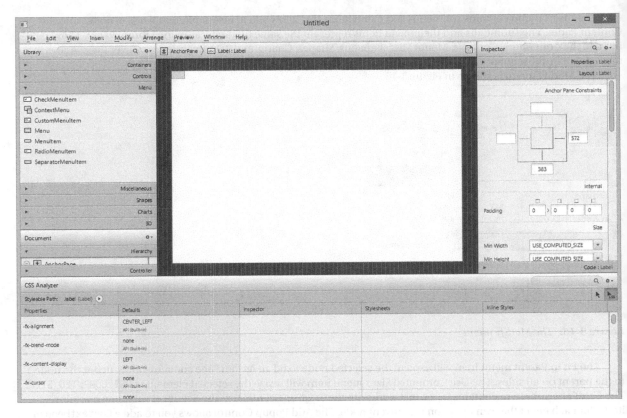

Figure 3-14. The JavaFX SceneBuilder screen with the CSS Analyzer shown

The Insert menu is shown in Figure 3-15.

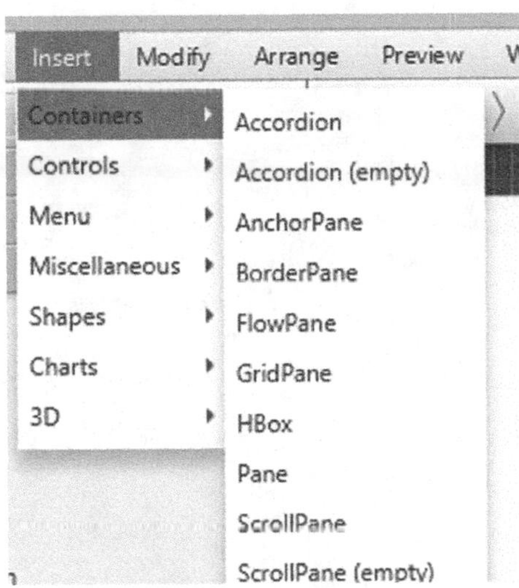

Figure 3-15. The Insert menu

The Insert menu contains submenus and menu items that allow you to insert different kinds of nodes into the Content Panel. The submenus and their menu items represent the same hierarchy as in the Library Panel. They include the Containers, Controls, Menu, Miscellaneous, Shapes, Charts, and 3D categories. We cover these nodes in more detail in subsequent chapters.

The Modify menu is shown in Figure 3-16.

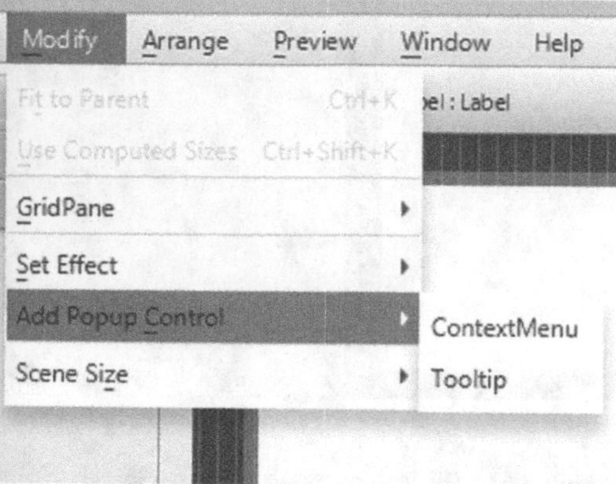

***Figure 3-16.** The Modify menu*

The Fit to Parent menu item will expand the selected node to fill an `AnchorPane` container and anchor the node to the parent on all sides. The Use Computed Sizes menu item will resize the selected element to `USE_COMPUTED_SIZE`. The GridPane submenu contains items that work with the `GridPane` container. The Set Effect submenu contains items for each effect that can be set on the current node. The Add Popup Control allows you to add a `ContextMenu` or a `Tooltip` to the selected node. The Scene Size submenu allows you to change the size of the scene to some popular sizes, including 320x240 (QVGA), 640x480 (VGA), 1280x800, and 1920x1080.

The Arrange menu is shown in Figure 3-17.

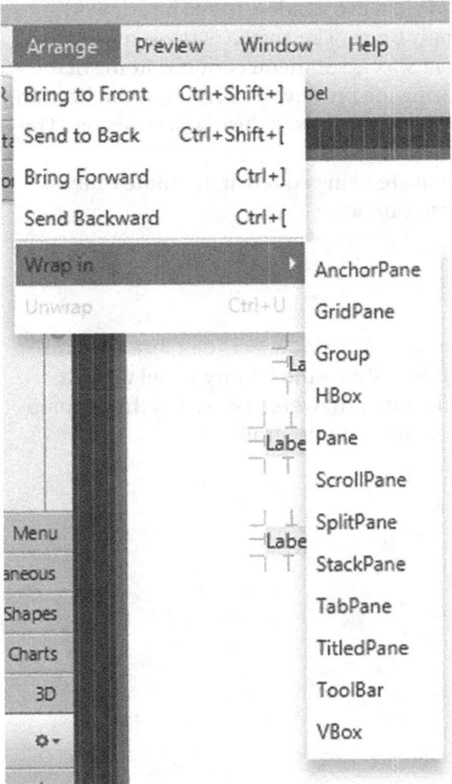

Figure 3-17. *The Arrange menu*

The Bring to Front, Send to Back, Bring Forward, and Send Backward menu items move the selected node to the front, back, up, or down the z-order of overlapping nodes. The Wrap in submenu contains items for each container type and allows you to wrap a group of selected nodes into the container. For example, you can choose to wrap two adjacent `Labels` into an `HBox`. The Unwrap menu item removes the container from the selected node.

The Preview menu is shown in Figure 3-18.

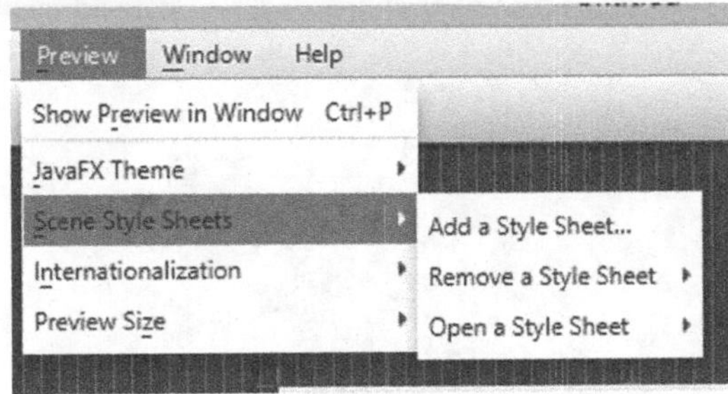

Figure 3-18. *The Preview menu*

The Show Preview in Window menu item allows you to preview the scene in a live window to see how it works in real life. This is the most useful menu item because you will be using it many times. The JavaFX Theme submenu contains various themes that you can preview the scene with. The Scene Style Sheets submenu contains items that allow you to add, remove, or edit a style sheet that is applied to the scene during the preview. The Internationalization submenu contains items that allow you to add, remove, or edit a resource bundle that is used during the preview. The Preview Size submenu contains items for the preferred screen size during the preview.

The Window menu allows you to switch between multiple FXML files that are being edited at the same time.

The Help menu shows the online help and the about box for JavaFX SceneBuilder.

Understanding the Library Panel

The Library Panel lives in the top portion of the Left Panel, and can be hidden using the View ➤ Hide Library menu item. It holds the containers and nodes that you can use to build a UI. Figure 3-19 shows the Library Panel with its Containers drawer open, showing some of the containers. You can click on the other drawers to see what they contain. Figure 3-20 shows the Library Panel with its Controls drawer open, showing some of the controls.

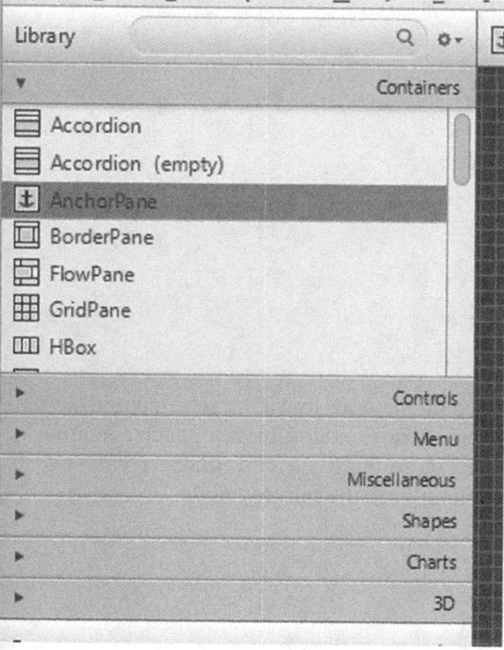

Figure 3-19. *The Library Panel with its Containers drawer open*

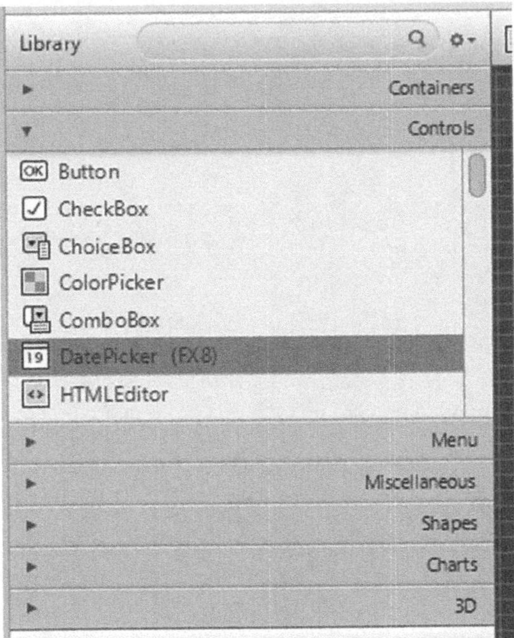

***Figure 3-20.** The Library Panel with its Controls drawer open*

There is a search box at the top of the Library Panel. You can type in the name of a container or a control or something that belongs to one of the other drawers into the search box. As you type, the Library Panel will change its display from the accordion arrangement to a single list with all the nodes whose names match the name entered in the search box. This allows you to find a node by name quickly without having to go through the drawers one by one. Figure 3-21 shows the Library Panel in search mode. To exit search mode, simply click on the x mark on the right end of the search box.

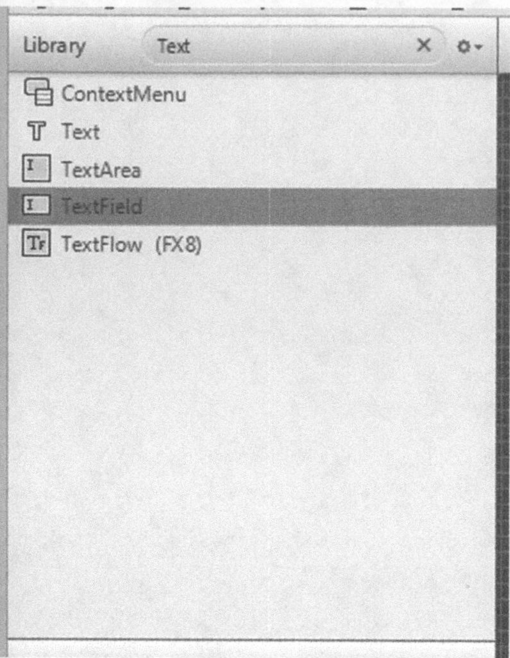

***Figure 3-21.** The Library Panel in search mode*

Once a container or a node is found, you can drag it to the Content Panel, drag it to the Hierarchy tree in the Document Panel, or double-click it. Bringing containers to the Content Panel and then populating the containers with controls and other nodes is how you build up a UI in the JavaFX SceneBuilder.

To the right of the search box is a menu button that contains several menu items and a submenu that alters the Library Panel's behavior. Figure 3-22 shows what is available in this menu button. The View as List menu item changes the Library Panel from displaying its nodes in several sections into displaying its nodes all together without sections. The View as Sections changes the Library Panel from displaying its nodes in one list into displaying its nodes in several sections. The Import JAR/FXML File menu item allows you to import an external jar file or FXML file into JavaFX SceneBuilder as a custom component. The Import Selection menu item allows you to import the currently selected nodes into JavaFX SceneBuilder as custom components. The Custom Library Folder submenu contains two menu items. The Reveal in Explorer menu item opens the folder that holds the custom components in the operating system's File Explorer (or Finder), allowing you to remove any imported custom libraries. The Show JAR Analysis Report menu item displays a report showing JavaFX SceneBuilder's assessment of the imported jar files.

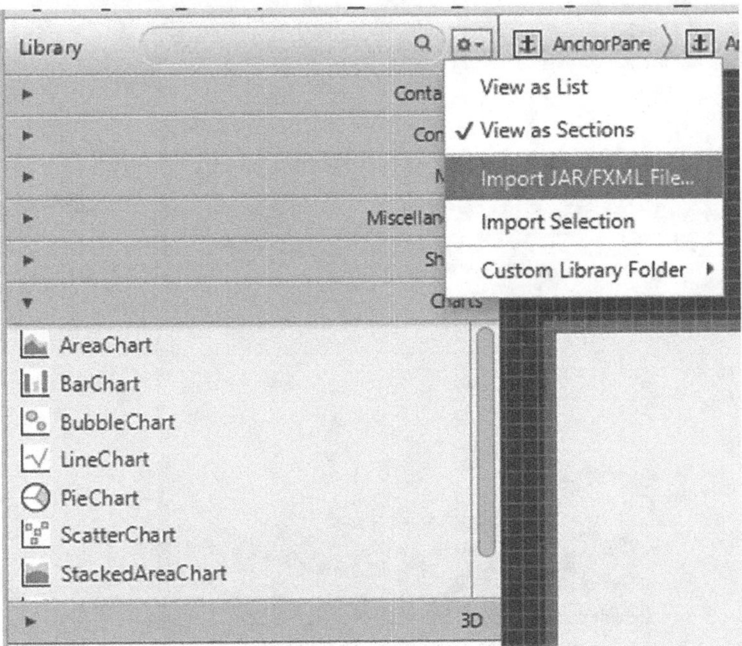

***Figure 3-22.** The Library Panel with its menu open*

To illustrate the importing of a custom component into JavaFX SceneBuilder, we package the class files and the FXML file from the CustomComponent example from the last section into a `CustomComponent.jar` file. We then invoke the Import JAR/FXML File menu item, navigate to the directory, and select the `CustomComponent.jar` file to import. As soon as we click the Open button in the file selection dialog box, JavaFX SceneBuilder opens the Import dialog box, shown in Figure 3-23.

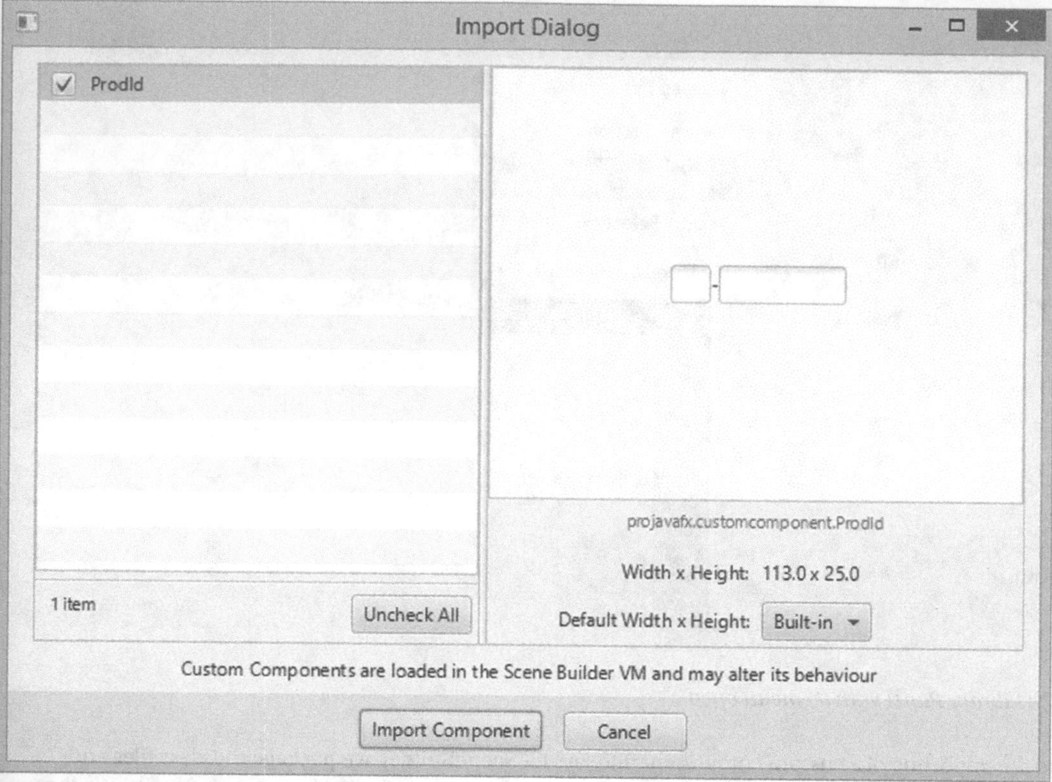

Figure 3-23. *The Import dialog for importing `CustomComponent.jar`*

We can examine each custom component included in the jar file by clicking the custom component name in the list on the left. Information about the selected custom component, including a visual representation of the custom component, is displayed on the right side of the screen. We can select which custom components to import by selecting the check box by the name of the component. We then click the Import Component button to finish the importing process. After importing, the ProdId custom component shows up in the Library Panel's Custom section, and can be added to any further UIs that are built.

Understanding the Document Panel

The Document Panel lives in the bottom portion of the Left Panel, and can be hidden using the View ➤ Hide Document menu item. It holds two sections. The Hierarchy section displays a tree view of all the nodes that are added to the Content Panel, organized by the containment relationship. Because the layout of the nodes in the Content Panel might make it tricky to select a node from the Content Panel, it might be easier to make the selection in the Hierarchy section in the Document Panel.

Figure 3-24 shows the Hierarchy section of the Document Panel for the FXML file in the FXMLLoaderExample in Listing 3-4. You can see the expanded node tree with the WebView node selected.

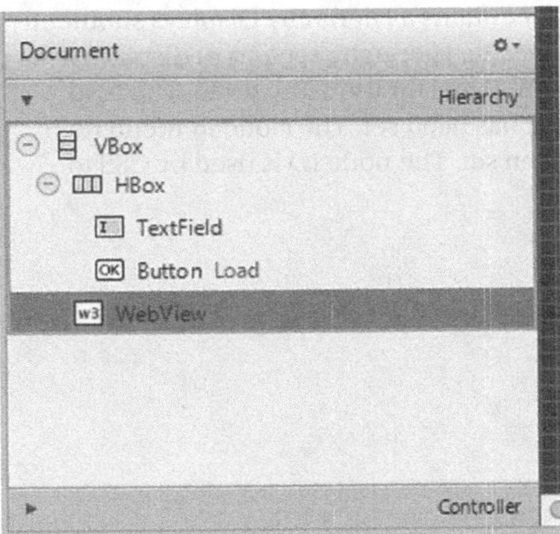

***Figure 3-24.** The Hierarchy section of the Document Panel for `FXMLLoaderExample.fxml`*

The Controller section displays information about the controller of the FXML file. Figure 3-25 shows the Controller section of the Document Panel for the FXML file in the FXMLInjectionExample in Listing 3-7. You can set the name of the controller class in this section. You can also choose to use the `fx:root` construct for the FXML file in this section. You also see a list of nodes with `fx:ids` that are already set, and you can select the nodes by clicking on the row in the Assigned fx:id table.

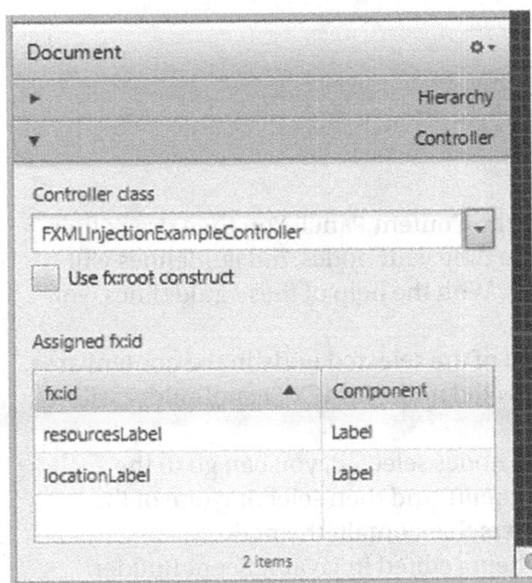

***Figure 3-25.** The Controller section of the Document Panel for `FXMLInjectionExample.fxml`*

There is a menu button in the top right corner of the Document Panel. It contains a Hierarchy Displays submenu that has three menu items, as shown in Figure 3-26. The Info menu item causes the Hierarchy section to display each node with its general information, usually what is also displayed in the Content Panel for the same node. The fx:id menu item causes the Hierarchy section to display each node with its fx:id if it has been set. The Node Id menu item causes the Hierarchy section to display each node with its node ID if it has been set. The node ID is used by CSS to find the node and to manipulate the node's styles.

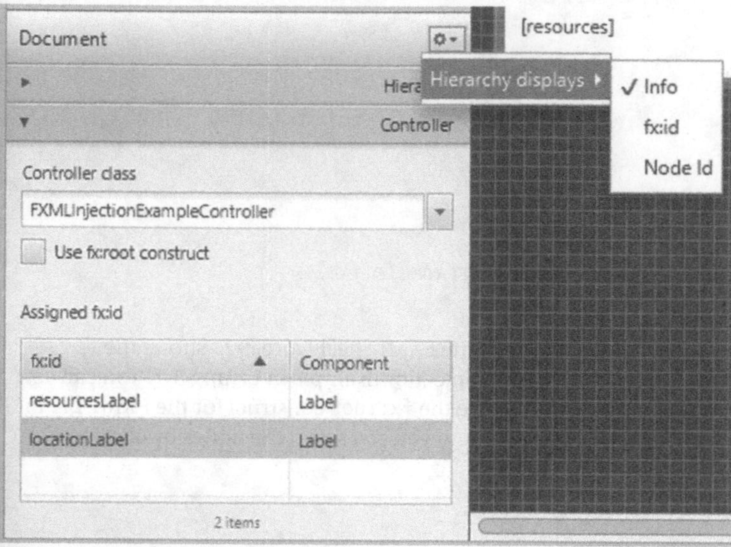

Figure 3-26. The Document Panel with its menu open

Understanding the Content Panel

The Content Panel is where the UI is composed. You first drag a container to the Content Panel. You then drag other nodes to the Content Panel and position then onto the container node. As you drag your nodes, red guidelines will appear as the node you drag reaches certain alignment and spacing positions. With the help of these guidelines, you should be able to create visually pleasing UIs.

Above the Content Panel, there is a bread-crumb bar that shows the path of the selected node in the content area. This allows you to easily navigate to the containing nodes of the currently selected node. JavaFX SceneBuilder will display warning and error messages in this bar when the situation arises.

One handy feature of JavaFX SceneBuilder is that when you have several nodes selected, you can go to the context menu by right-clicking the selected nodes, choosing the Wrap in submenu, and then selecting one of the container types. You can also Unwrap a node this way, removing any containers that contain the node.

Figure 3-27 shows the `IncludeExampleTree.fxml` file from Listing 3-20 being edited in JavaFX SceneBuilder.

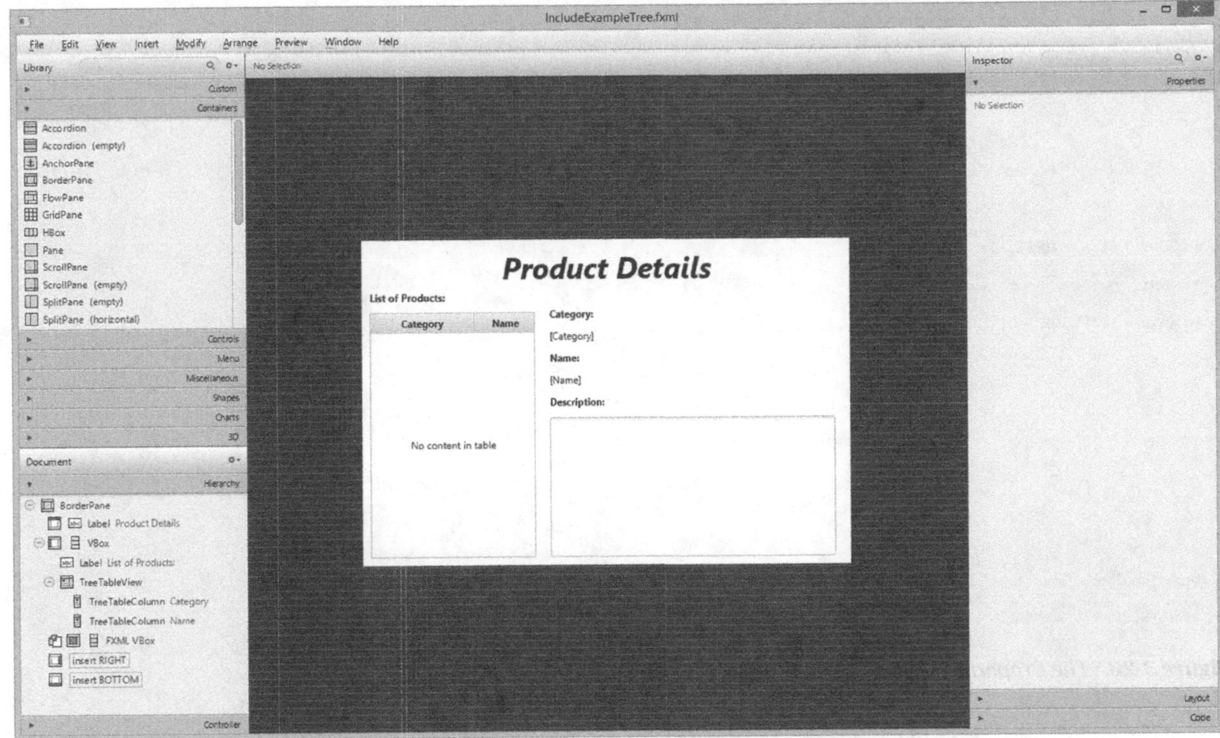

Figure 3-27. *The `IncludeExampleTree.fxml` file being edited in JavaFX SceneBuilder*

Understanding the Inspector Panel

The Inspector Panel lives in the Right Panel and can be hidden using the View ➤ Hide Right Panel menu item. It contains the Properties, Layout, and Code sections. The Properties section lists all the generic properties of the selected node in the Content Panel. You can set the properties by changing the values shown here. You can also change a property back to its default value by invoking the small menu button to the right of the property. You can set the node ID in the ID property editor in the Properties section. Figure 3-28 shows the Properties section of the Inspector Panel.

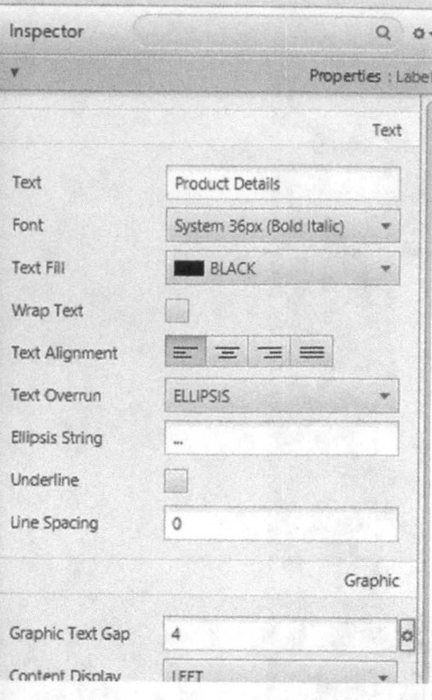

Figure 3-28. *The Properties section of the Inspector Panel*

The Layout section lists all layout-related properties of the currently selected node. Figure 3-29 shows the Layout section of the Inspector Panel.

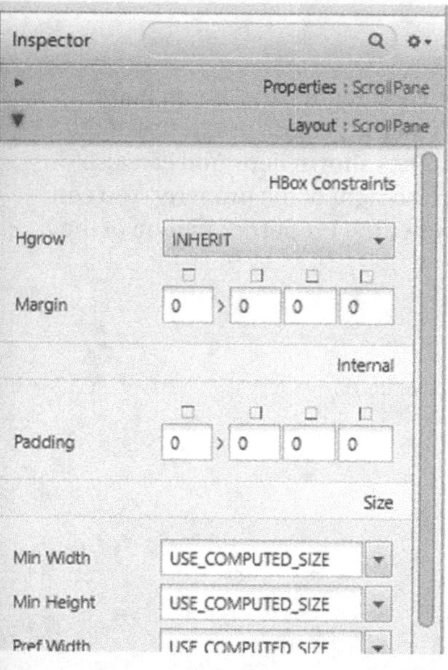

Figure 3-29. *The Layout section of the Inspector Panel*

The Code section lists all the event handlers the selected node in the Content Panel could have. It also allows you to set the fx:id for the selected node. You can hook up the event handlers in the Code section in any way you want, but the most convenient way of providing event handlers is to set them to properly signatured methods in the controller. Figure 3-30 shows the Code section of the Inspector Panel.

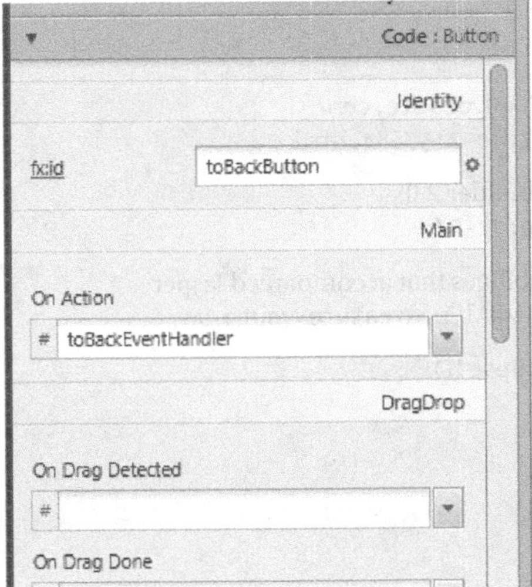

Figure 3-30. *The Code section of the Inspector Panel*

Summary

In this chapter, you learned the declarative way of creating a UI in JavaFX. You learned the following important tools and information:

- FXML files are the carriers of declarative UI information, and are central assets of JavaFX projects.
- FXML files are loaded into JavaFX applications by FXMLLoader. The result of the loading is a node that can be incorporated into a Scene.
- FXML files can have a companion controller class that performs programmatical functions, such as event handling, at runtime on behalf of the nodes declared in the FXML file.
- FXML files can be edited easily in your favorite Java IDEs with smart suggestions and completions.
- FXML files can also be edited in Oracle JavaFX SceneBuilder 2.0, an open source tool for editing FXML files.
- The JavaFX SceneBuilder is a highly productive tool for specifying JavaFX UIs. You can add containers, controls, and other JavaFX nodes into the content of an FXML file.
- You can set up a controller and define the fx:ids of the various nodes in the scene.
- You can organize the hierarchical information in an FXML file by manipulating the containers, controls, and other nodes in the Hierarchy section of the Document Panel.

- You can manipulate the attributes of nodes in an FXML file by using the Properties, Layout, and Code sections in the Inspector Panel.
- You can visually compose your UI in the Content Panel.
- You can analyze the CSS of the UI with the CSS Analyzer.

Resources

- The Oracle JavaFX SceneBuilder 2.0 downloading site: `http://www.oracle.com/technetwork/java/javase/downloads/javafxscenebuilder-info-2157684.html`
- Jasper Pott's blog post announcing the release of JavaFX SceneBuilder 2.0: `http://fxexperience.com/2014/05/announcing-scenebuilder-2-0/`
- A nine-minute video showing off JavaFX SceneBuilder 2.0's capabilities that accompanied Jasper Pott's announcement: `https://www.youtube.com/watch?v=ij0HwRAlCmo&feature=youtu.be`
- The e(fx)clipse Eclipse plug-in to provide JavaFX support for Eclipse IDEs: `http://www.eclipse.org/efxclipse/install.html`

CHAPTER 4

Properties and Bindings

Heaven acts with vitality and persistence.

In correspondence with this

The superior person keeps himself vital without ceasing.

—I Ching

In earlier chapters, we introduced you to the JavaFX 8 platform that is part of Oracle JDK 8. You set up your development environment with your favorite IDE: Eclipse, NetBeans, or IntelliJ IDEA. You wrote and ran your first JavaFX GUI programs. You learned the fundamental building blocks of JavaFX: the `Stage` and `Scene` classes, and the `Nodes` that go into the `Scene`. You have no doubt noticed the use of user-defined model classes to represent the application state and have that state communicated to the UI through properties and bindings.

In this chapter, we give you a guided tour of the JavaFX properties and bindings framework. After recalling a little bit of history and presenting a motivating example that shows various ways that a JavaFX `Property` can be used, we cover key concepts of the framework: `Observable`, `ObservableValue`, `WritableValue`, `ReadOnlyProperty`, `Property`, and `Binding`. We show you the capabilities offered by these fundamental interfaces of the framework. We then show you how `Property` objects are bound together, how `Binding` objects are built out of properties and other bindings—using the factory methods in the `Bindings` utility class, the fluent interface API, or going low level by directly extending abstract classes that implement the `Binding` interface—and how they are used to easily propagate changes in one part of a program to other parts of the program without too much coding. We then introduce the JavaFX Beans naming convention, an extension of the original JavaBeans naming convention that makes organizing your data into encapsulated components an orderly affair. We finish this chapter by showing how to adapt old-style JavaBeans properties into JavaFX properties.

Because the JavaFX properties and bindings framework is a nonvisual part of the JavaFX platform, the example programs in this chapter are also nonvisual in nature. We deal with `Boolean`, `Integer`, `Long`, `Float`, `Double`, `String`, and `Object` type properties and bindings as these are the types in which the JavaFX binding framework specializes. Your GUI building fun resumes in the next and further chapters.

Forerunners of JavaFX Binding

The need for exposing attributes of Java components directly to client code, allowing them to observe and to manipulate such attributes and to take action when their values change, was recognized early in Java's life. The JavaBeans framework in Java 1.1 provided support for properties through the now familiar getter and setter convention. It also supported the propagations of property changes through its `PropertyChangeEvent` and `PropertyChangeListener` mechanism. Although the JavaBeans framework is used in many Swing applications, its use is quite cumbersome and requires quite a bit of boilerplate code. Several higher level data binding frameworks were created over the years with various levels of success. The heritage of the JavaBeans in the JavaFX properties and bindings framework lies mainly in the JavaFX Beans getter, setter, and property getter naming convention when defining JavaFX components. We talk about the JavaFX Beans getter, setter, and property getter naming convention later in this chapter, after we have covered the key concepts and interfaces of the JavaFX properties and bindings framework.

Another strand of heritage of the JavaFX properties and bindings framework comes from the JavaFX Script language that was part of the JavaFX 1.x platform. Although the JavaFX Script language was deprecated in the JavaFX platform in favor of a Java-based API, one of the goals of the transition was to preserve most of the powers of the JavaFX Script's `bind` keyword, the expressive power of which has delighted many JavaFX enthusiasts. As an example, JavaFX Script supports the binding to complex expressions:

```
var a = 1;
var b = 10;
var m = 4;
def c = bind for (x in [a..b] where x < m) { x * x };
```

This code will automatically recalculate the value of `c` whenever the values of `a`, `b`, or `m` are changed.

Although the JavaFX properties and bindings framework does not support all of the binding constructs of JavaFX Script, it supports the binding of many useful expressions. We talk more about constructing compound binding expressions after we cover the key concepts and interfaces of the framework.

A Motivating Example

Let's start with an example in Listing 4-1 that shows off the capabilities of the `Property` interface through the use of a couple of instances of the `SimpleIntegerProperty` class.

Listing 4-1. MotivatingExample.java

```
import javafx.beans.InvalidationListener;
import javafx.beans.property.IntegerProperty;
import javafx.beans.property.SimpleIntegerProperty;
import javafx.beans.value.ChangeListener;
import javafx.beans.value.ObservableValue;

public class MotivatingExample {
    private static IntegerProperty intProperty;

    public static void main(String[] args) {
        createProperty();
        addAndRemoveInvalidationListener();
        addAndRemoveChangeListener();
        bindAndUnbindOnePropertyToAnother();
    }

    private static void createProperty() {
        System.out.println();
        intProperty = new SimpleIntegerProperty(1024);
        System.out.println("intProperty = " + intProperty);
        System.out.println("intProperty.get() = " + intProperty.get());
        System.out.println("intProperty.getValue() = " + intProperty.getValue().intValue());
    }
```

```
private static void addAndRemoveInvalidationListener() {
    System.out.println();
    final InvalidationListener invalidationListener = observable ->
        System.out.println("The observable has been invalidated: " + observable + ".");

    intProperty.addListener(invalidationListener);
    System.out.println("Added invalidation listener.");

    System.out.println("Calling intProperty.set(2048).");
    intProperty.set(2048);

    System.out.println("Calling intProperty.setValue(3072).");
    intProperty.setValue(Integer.valueOf(3072));

    intProperty.removeListener(invalidationListener);
    System.out.println("Removed invalidation listener.");

    System.out.println("Calling intProperty.set(4096).");
    intProperty.set(4096);
}

private static void addAndRemoveChangeListener() {
    System.out.println();
    final ChangeListener changeListener = (ObservableValue observableValue, Object oldValue,
                                           Object newValue) ->
        System.out.println("The observableValue has changed: oldValue = " + oldValue + ",
                           newValue = " + newValue);
    intProperty.addListener(changeListener);
    System.out.println("Added change listener.");

    System.out.println("Calling intProperty.set(5120).");
    intProperty.set(5120);

    intProperty.removeListener(changeListener);
    System.out.println("Removed change listener.");

    System.out.println("Calling intProperty.set(6144).");
    intProperty.set(6144);
}

private static void bindAndUnbindOnePropertyToAnother() {
    System.out.println();
    IntegerProperty otherProperty = new SimpleIntegerProperty(0);
    System.out.println("otherProperty.get() = " + otherProperty.get());

    System.out.println("Binding otherProperty to intProperty.");
    otherProperty.bind(intProperty);
    System.out.println("otherProperty.get() = " + otherProperty.get());

    System.out.println("Calling intProperty.set(7168).");
    intProperty.set(7168);
    System.out.println("otherProperty.get() = " + otherProperty.get());
```

```
        System.out.println("Unbinding otherProperty from intProperty.");
        otherProperty.unbind();
        System.out.println("otherProperty.get() = " + otherProperty.get());

        System.out.println("Calling intProperty.set(8192).");
        intProperty.set(8192);
        System.out.println("otherProperty.get() = " + otherProperty.get());
    }
}
```

In this example we created a `SimpleIntegerProperty` object called `intProperty` with an initial value of `1024`. We then updated its value through a series of different integers while we added and then removed an `InvalidationListener`, added and then removed a `ChangeListener`, and finally created another `SimpleIntegerProperty` named `otherProperty`, bound it to and then unbound it from `intProperty`. We have taken advantage of the Java 8 Lambda syntax in defining our listeners. The sample program used a generous amount of `println` calls to show what is happening inside the program.

When we run the program in Listing 4-1, the following output is printed to the console:

```
intProperty = IntegerProperty [value: 1024]
intProperty.get() = 1024
intProperty.getValue() = 1024

Added invalidation listener.
Calling intProperty.set(2048).
The observable has been invalidated: IntegerProperty [value: 2048].
Calling intProperty.setValue(3072).
The observable has been invalidated: IntegerProperty [value: 3072].
Removed invalidation listener.
Calling intProperty.set(4096).

Added change listener.
Calling intProperty.set(5120).
The observableValue has changed: oldValue = 4096, newValue = 5120
Removed change listener.
Calling intProperty.set(6144).

otherProperty.get() = 0
Binding otherProperty to intProperty.
otherProperty.get() = 6144
Calling intProperty.set(7168).
otherProperty.get() = 7168
Unbinding otherProperty from intProperty.
otherProperty.get() = 7168
Calling intProperty.set(8192).
otherProperty.get() = 7168
```

By correlating the output lines with the program source code (or by stepping through the code in the debugger of your favorite IDE), we can draw the following conclusions.

- A SimpleIntegerProperty object such as intProperty and otherProperty holds an int value. The value can be manipulated with the get(), set(), getValue(), and setValue() methods. The get() and set() methods perform their operation with the primitive int type. The getValue() and setValue() methods use the Integer wrapper type.
- You can add and remove InvalidationListener objects to and from intProperty.
- You can add and remove ChangeListener objects to and from intProperty.
- Another Property object such as otherProperty can bind itself to intProperty. When that happens, otherProperty receives the value of intProperty.
- When a new value is set on intProperty, whatever object that is attached to it is notified. The notification is not sent if the object is removed.
- When notified, InvalidationListener objects are only informed of which object is sending out the notification and that object is only known as an Observable.
- When notified, ChangeListener objects are informed on two more pieces of information—the oldValue and the newValue—in addition to the object sending the notification. The sending object is known as an ObservableValue.
- In the case of a binding property such as otherProperty, we cannot tell from the output when or how it is notified of the change of value in intProperty. However, we can infer that it must have known of the change because when we asked otherProperty for its value we got back the latest value of intProperty.

■ **Note** Even though this motivating example uses an Integer property, similar examples can be made to use properties based on the Boolean, Long, Float, Double, String, and Object types. In the JavaFX properties and bindings framework, when interfaces are extended or implemented for concrete types, they are always done for the Boolean, Integer, Long, Float, Double, String, and Object types.

This example brings to our attention some of the key interfaces and concepts of the JavaFX properties and bindings framework: including the Observable and the associated InvalidationListener interfaces, the ObservableValue and the associated ChangeListener interfaces, the get(), set(), getValue(), and setValue() methods that allow us to manipulate the values of a SimpleIntegerProperty object directly, and the bind() method that allows us to relinquish direct manipulation of the value of a SimpleIntegerProperty object by subordinating it to another SimpleIntegerProperty object.

In the next section we show you these and some other key interfaces and concepts of the JavaFX properties and bindings framework in more detail.

Understanding Key Interfaces and Concepts

Figure 4-1 is a UML diagram showing the key interfaces of the JavaFX properties and bindings framework. It includes some interfaces that you have seen in the last section, and some that you haven't yet seen.

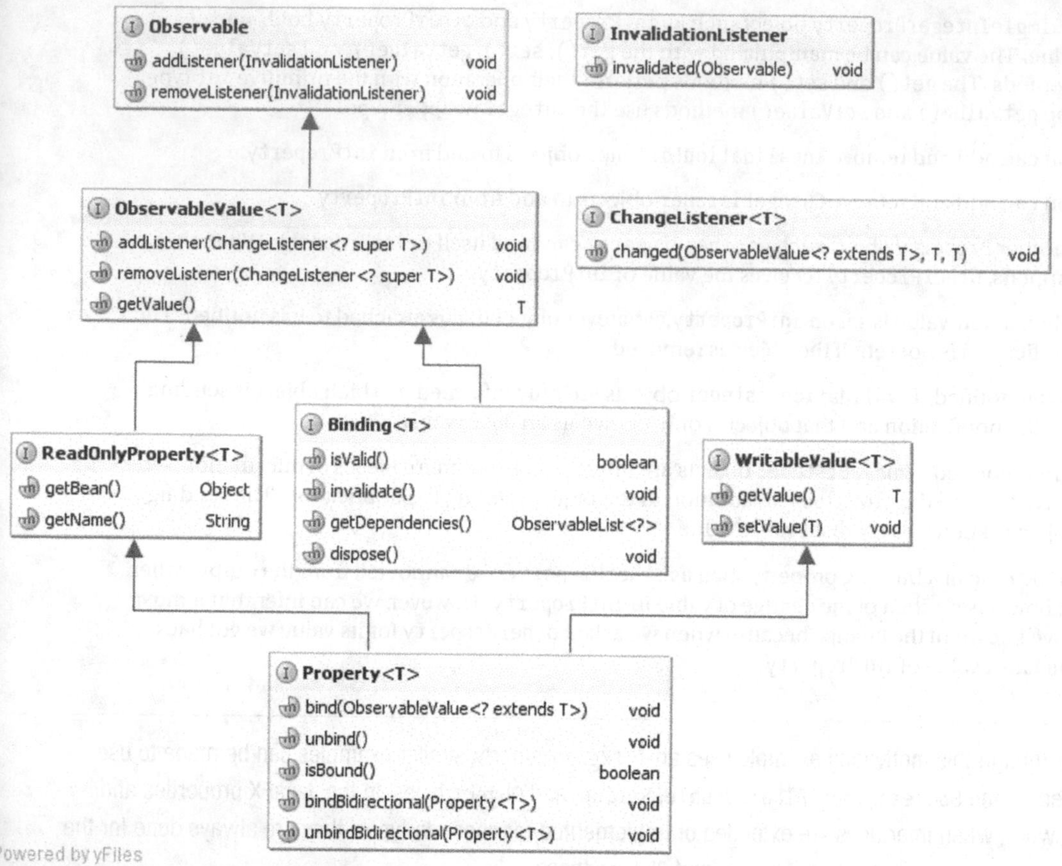

***Figure 4-1.** Key interfaces of the JavaFX properties and bindings framework*

■ **Note** We did not show you the fully qualified names of the interfaces in the UML diagram. These interfaces are spread out in four packages: `javafx.beans`, `javafx.beans.binding`, `javafx.beans.property`, and `javafx.beans.value`. You can easily figure out which interface belongs to which package by examining the JavaFX API documentation or by the "find class" feature of your favorite IDE.

Understanding the Observable Interface

At the root of the hierarchy is the `Observable` interface. You can register `InvalidationListener` objects to an `Observable` object to receive *invalidation* events. You have already seen invalidation events fired from one kind of `Observable` object, the `SimpleIntegerProperty` object `intProperty` in the motivating example in the last section. It is fired when the `set()` or `setValue()` methods are called to change the underlying value from one `int` to a different `int`.

■ **Note** An invalidation event is fired only once by any of the implementations of the `Property` interface in the JavaFX properties and bindings framework if you call the setter with the same value several times in a row.

Another place where invalidation events are fired is from `Binding` objects. You haven't seen an example of a `Binding` object yet, but there are plenty of `Binding` objects in the second half of this chapter. For now we just note that a `Binding` object may become invalid, for example, when its `invalidate()` method is called or, as we show later in this chapter, when one of its dependencies fires an invalidation event.

■ **Note** An invalidation event is fired only once by any of the implementations of the `Binding` interface in the JavaFX properties and bindings framework if it becomes invalid several times in a row.

Understanding the ObservableValue Interface

Next up in the hierarchy is the `ObservableValue` interface. It's simply an `Observable` that has a value. Its `getValue()` method returns its value. The `getValue()` method that we called on the `SimpleIntegerProperty` objects in the motivating example can be considered to have come from this interface. You can register `ChangeListener` objects to an `ObservableValue` object to receive *change* events.

You saw change events being fired in the motivating example in the last section. When the change event fires, the `ChangeListener` receives two more pieces of information: the old value and the new value of the `ObservableValue` object.

■ **Note** A change event is fired only once by any of the implementations of the `ObservableValue` interface in the JavaFX properties and bindings framework if you call the setter with the same value several times in a row.

The distinction between an invalidation event and a change event is made so that the JavaFX properties and bindings framework may support *lazy evaluations*. We show an example of this by looking at three lines of code from the motivating example:

```
otherProperty.bind(intProperty);
intProperty.set(7168);
System.out.println("otherProperty.get() = " + otherProperty.get());
```

When `intProperty.set(7168)` is called, it fires an invalidation event to `otherProperty`. On receiving this invalidation event, `otherProperty` simply makes a note of the fact that its value is no longer valid. It does not immediately perform a recalculation of its value by querying `intProperty` for its value. The recalculation is performed later when `otherProperty.get()` is called. Imagine if instead of calling `intProperty.set()` only once as in the preceding code we call `intProperty.set()` multiple times; `otherProperty` still recalculates its value only once.

■ **Note** The `ObservableValue` interface is not the only direct subinterface of `Observable`. There are four other direct subinterfaces of `Observable` that live in the `javafx.collections` package: `ObservableList`, `ObservableMap`, `ObservableSet`, and `ObservableArray` with corresponding `ListChangeListener`, `MapChangeListener`, `SetChangeListener`, and `ArrayChangeListener` as callback mechanisms. These JavaFX observable collections are covered in Chapter 7, "Collections and Concurrency."

Understanding the WritableValue Interface

This might be the simplest subsection in the entire chapter, for the WritableValue interface is truly as simple as it looks. Its purpose is to inject the getValue() and setValue() methods into implementations of this interface. All implementation classes of WritableValue in the JavaFX properties and bindings framework also implement ObservableValue, therefore you can make an argument that the value of WritableValue is only to provide the setValue() method.

You have seen the setValue() method at work in the motivating example.

Understanding the ReadOnlyProperty Interface

The ReadOnlyProperty interface injects two methods into its implementations. The getBean() method should return the Object that contains the ReadOnlyRroperty or null if it is not contained in an Object. The getName() method should return the name of the ReadOnlyProperty or the empty string if the ReadOnlyProperty does not have a name.

The containing object and the name provide *contextual* information about a ReadOnlyProperty. The contextual information of a property does not play any direct role in the propagation of invalidation events or the recalculation of values. However, if provided, it will be taken into account in some peripheral calculations.

In our motivating example, the intProperty is constructed without any contextual information. Had we used the full constructor to supply it a name:

```
intProperty = new SimpleIntegerProperty(null, "intProperty", 1024);
```

the output would have contained the property name:

```
intProperty = IntegerProperty [name: intProperty, value: 1024]
```

Understanding the Property Interface

Now we come to the bottom of our key interfaces hierarchy. The Property interface has as its superinterfaces all four interfaces we have examined thus far: Observable, ObservableValue, ReadOnlyProperty, and WritableValue. Therefore it inherits all the methods from these interfaces. It also provides five methods of its own:

```
void bind(ObservableValue<? extends T> observableValue);
void unbind();
boolean isBound();
void bindBidirectional(Property<T> tProperty);
void unbindBidirectional(Property<T> tProperty);
```

You have seen two of the methods at work in the motivating example in the last section: bind() and unbind().

Calling bind() creates a *unidirectional binding* or a dependency between the Property object and the ObservableValue argument. Once they enter this relationship, calling the set() or setValue() methods on the Property object will cause a RuntimeException to be thrown. Calling the get() or getValue() methods on the Property object will return the value of the ObservableValue object. And, of course, changing the value of the ObservableValue object will invalidate the Property object. Calling unbind() releases any existing unidirectional binding the Property object may have. If a unidirectional binding is in effect, the isBound() method returns true; otherwise it returns false.

Calling bindBidirectional() creates a *bidirectional binding* between the Property caller and the Property argument. Notice that unlike the bind() method, which takes an ObservableValue argument, the bindBidirectional() method takes a Property argument. Only two Property objects can be bound together bidirectionally. Once they enter this relationship, calling the `set()` or `setValue()` methods on either `Property` object will cause both objects' values to be updated. Calling `unbindBidirectional()` releases any existing bidirectional binding the caller and the argument may have. The program in Listing 4-2 shows a simple bidirectional binding at work.

Listing 4-2. BidirectionalBindingExample.java

```
import javafx.beans.property.SimpleStringProperty;
import javafx.beans.property.StringProperty;

public class BidirectionalBindingExample {
    public static void main(String[] args) {
        System.out.println("Constructing two StringProperty objects.");
        StringProperty prop1 = new SimpleStringProperty("");
        StringProperty prop2 = new SimpleStringProperty("");

        System.out.println("Calling bindBidirectional.");
        prop2.bindBidirectional(prop1);

        System.out.println("prop1.isBound() = " + prop1.isBound());
        System.out.println("prop2.isBound() = " + prop2.isBound());

        System.out.println("Calling prop1.set(\"prop1 says: Hi!\")");
        prop1.set("prop1 says: Hi!");
        System.out.println("prop2.get() returned:");
        System.out.println(prop2.get());

        System.out.println("Calling prop2.set(prop2.get() + \"\\nprop2 says: Bye!\")");
        prop2.set(prop2.get() + "\nprop2 says: Bye!");
        System.out.println("prop1.get() returned:");
        System.out.println(prop1.get());
    }
}
```

In this example we created two `SimpleStringProperty` objects called `prop1` and `prop2`, created a bidirectional binding between them, and then called `set()` and `get()` on both properties.

When we run the program in Listing 4-2, the following output is printed to the console:

```
Constructing two StringProperty objects.
Calling bindBidirectional.
prop1.isBound() = false
prop2.isBound() = false
Calling prop1.set("prop1 says: Hi!")
prop2.get() returned:
prop1 says: Hi!
Calling prop2.set(prop2.get() + "\nprop2 says: Bye!")
prop1.get() returned:
prop1 says: Hi!
prop2 says: Bye!
```

■ **Caution** Each Property object may have at most one active unidirectional binding at a time. It may have as many bidirectional bindings as you want. The isBound() method pertains only to unidirectional bindings. Calling bind() a second time with a different ObservableValue argument while a unidirectional binding is already in effect will unbind the existing one and replace it with the new one.

Understanding the Binding Interface

The Binding interface defines four methods that reveal the intentions of the interface. A Binding object is an ObservableValue whose validity can be queried with the isValid() method and set with the invalidate() method. It has a list of dependencies that can be obtained with the getDependencies() method. And finally a dispose() method signals that the binding will not be used anymore and resources used by it can be cleaned up.

From this brief description of the Binding interface, we can infer that it represents a *unidirectional binding with multiple dependencies*. Each dependency, we imagine, could be an ObservableValue to which the Binding is registered to receive invalidation events. When the get() or getValue() method is called, if the binding is invalidated, its value is recalculated.

The JavaFX properties and bindings framework does not provide any concrete classes that implement the Binding interface. However, it provides multiple ways to create your own Binding objects easily: You can extend the abstract base classes in the framework; you can use a set of static methods in the utility class Bindings to create new bindings out of existing regular Java values (i.e., unobservable values), properties, and bindings; you can also use a set of methods that are provided in the various properties and bindings classes and form a fluent interface API to create new bindings. We go through the utility methods and the fluent interface API in the "Creating Bindings" section later in this chapter. For now, we show you the first example of a binding by extending the DoubleBinding abstract class. The program in Listing 4-3 uses a binding to calculate the area of a rectangle.

Listing 4-3. RectangleAreaExample.java

```
import javafx.beans.binding.DoubleBinding;
import javafx.beans.property.DoubleProperty;
import javafx.beans.property.SimpleDoubleProperty;

public class RectangleAreaExample {
    public static void main(String[] args) {
        System.out.println("Constructing x with initial value of 2.0.");
        final DoubleProperty x = new SimpleDoubleProperty(null, "x", 2.0);
        System.out.println("Constructing y with initial value of 3.0.");
        final DoubleProperty y = new SimpleDoubleProperty(null, "y", 3.0);
        System.out.println("Creating binding area with dependencies x and y.");
        DoubleBinding area = new DoubleBinding() {
            private double value;

            {
                super.bind(x, y);
            }

            @Override
            protected double computeValue() {
                System.out.println("computeValue() is called.");
                return x.get() * y.get();
            }
        };
```

```
        System.out.println("area.get() = " + area.get());
        System.out.println("area.get() = " + area.get());
        System.out.println("Setting x to 5");
        x.set(5);
        System.out.println("Setting y to 7");
        y.set(7);
        System.out.println("area.get() = " + area.get());
    }
}
```

In the anonymous inner class, we called the protected bind() method in the superclass DoubleBinding, informing the superclass that we would like to listen to invalidation events from the DoubleProperty objects x and y. We finally implemented the protected abstract computeValue() method in the superclass DoubleBinding to do the actual calculation when a recalculation is needed.

When we run the program in Listing 4-3, the following output is printed to the console:

```
Constructing x with initial value of 2.0.
Constructing y with initial value of 3.0.
Creating binding area with dependencies x and y.
computeValue() is called.
area.get() = 6.0
area.get() = 6.0
Setting x to 5
Setting y to 7
computeValue() is called.
area.get() = 35.0
```

Notice that computeValue() is called only once when we call area.get() twice in a row.

■ **Caution** The DoubleBinding abstract class contains a default implementation of dispose() that is empty and a default implementation of getDependencies() that returns an empty list. To make this example a correct Binding implementation, we should override these two methods to behave correctly.

Now that you have a firm grasp of the key interfaces and concepts of the JavaFX properties and bindings framework, we show you how these generic interfaces are specialized to type-specific interfaces and implemented in type-specific abstract and concrete classes.

Type-Specific Specializations of Key Interfaces

We did not emphasize this fact in the last section because we believe its omission does not hurt the explanations there, but except for Observable and InvalidationListener, the rest of the interfaces are generic interfaces with a type parameter <T>. In this section we examine how these generic interfaces are specialized to the specific types of interest: Boolean, Integer, Long, Float, Double, String, and Object. We also examine some of the abstract and concrete classes of the framework and explore typical usage scenarios of each class.

■ Note Specializations of these interfaces also exist for `List`, `Map`, and `Set`. They are designed for working with observable collections. We cover observable collections in Chapter 7.

A Common Theme for Type-Specific Interfaces

Although the generic interfaces are not all specialized in exactly the same way, a common theme exists:

- The `Boolean` type is specialized directly.
- The `Integer`, `Long`, `Float`, and `Double` types are specialized through the `Number` supertype.
- The `String` type is specialized through the `Object` type.

This theme exists in the type-specific specializations of all the key interfaces. As an example, we examine the subinterfaces of the `ObservableValue<T>` interface:

- `ObservableBooleanValue` extends `ObservableValue<Boolean>`, and it offers one additional method.
  - `boolean get();`
- `ObservableNumberValue` extends `ObservableValue<Number>`, and it offers four additional methods.
  - `int intValue();`
  - `long longValue();`
  - `float floatValue();`
  - `double doubleValue();`
- `ObservableObjectValue<T>` extends `ObservableValue<t>`, and it offers one additional method.
  - `T get();`
- `ObservableIntegerValue`, `ObservableLongValue`, `ObservableFloatValue`, and `ObservableDoubleValue` extend `ObservableNumberValue` and each offers an additional `get()` method that returns the appropriate primitive type value.
- `ObservableStringValue` extends `ObservableObjectValue<String>` and inherits its `get()` method that returns `String`.

Notice that the `get()` method that we have been using in the examples is defined in the type-specific `ObservableValue` subinterfaces. A similar examination reveals that the `set()` method that we have been using in the examples is defined in the type-specific `WritableValue` subinterfaces.

A practical consequence of this derivation hierarchy is that any numerical property can call `bind()` on any other numerical property or binding. Indeed, the signature of the `bind()` method on any numerical property is

```
void bind(ObservableValue<? extends Number>  observable);
```

and any numerical property and binding is assignable to the generic parameter type. The program in Listing 4-4 shows that any numerical properties of different specific types can be bound to each other.

Listing 4-4. NumericPropertiesExample.java

```
import javafx.beans.property.DoubleProperty;
import javafx.beans.property.FloatProperty;
import javafx.beans.property.IntegerProperty;
import javafx.beans.property.LongProperty;
import javafx.beans.property.SimpleDoubleProperty;
import javafx.beans.property.SimpleFloatProperty;
import javafx.beans.property.SimpleIntegerProperty;
import javafx.beans.property.SimpleLongProperty;

public class NumericPropertiesExample {
    public static void main(String[] args) {
        IntegerProperty i = new SimpleIntegerProperty(null, "i", 1024);
        LongProperty l = new SimpleLongProperty(null, "l", 0L);
        FloatProperty f = new SimpleFloatProperty(null, "f", 0.0F);
        DoubleProperty d = new SimpleDoubleProperty(null, "d", 0.0);
        System.out.println("Constructed numerical properties i, l, f, d.");

        System.out.println("i.get() = " + i.get());
        System.out.println("l.get() = " + l.get());
        System.out.println("f.get() = " + f.get());
        System.out.println("d.get() = " + d.get());

        l.bind(i);
        f.bind(l);
        d.bind(f);
        System.out.println("Bound l to i, f to l, d to f.");

        System.out.println("i.get() = " + i.get());
        System.out.println("l.get() = " + l.get());
        System.out.println("f.get() = " + f.get());
        System.out.println("d.get() = " + d.get());

        System.out.println("Calling i.set(2048).");
        i.set(2048);

        System.out.println("i.get() = " + i.get());
        System.out.println("l.get() = " + l.get());
        System.out.println("f.get() = " + f.get());
        System.out.println("d.get() = " + d.get());

        d.unbind();
        f.unbind();
        l.unbind();
        System.out.println("Unbound l to i, f to l, d to f.");

        f.bind(d);
        l.bind(f);
        i.bind(l);
        System.out.println("Bound f to d, l to f, i to l.");
```

```
        System.out.println("Calling d.set(10000000000L).");
        d.set(10000000000L);

        System.out.println("d.get() = " + d.get());
        System.out.println("f.get() = " + f.get());
        System.out.println("l.get() = " + l.get());
        System.out.println("i.get() = " + i.get());
    }
}
```

In this example we created four numeric properties and bound them into a chain in decreasing size to demonstrate that the bindings work as expected. We then reversed the order of the chain and set the double property's value to a number that would overflow the integer property to highlight the fact that even though you can bind different sizes of numeric properties together, when the value of the dependent property is outside the range of the binding property, normal Java numeric conversion applies.

When we run the program in Listing 4-4, the following is printed to the console:

```
Constructed numerical properties i, l, f, d.
i.get() = 1024
l.get() = 0
f.get() = 0.0
d.get() = 0.0
Bound l to i, f to l, d to f.
i.get() = 1024
l.get() = 1024
f.get() = 1024.0
d.get() = 1024.0
Calling i.set(2048).
i.get() = 2048
l.get() = 2048
f.get() = 2048.0
d.get() = 2048.0
Unbound l to i, f to l, d to f.
Bound f to d, l to f, i to l.
Calling d.set(10000000000L).
d.get() = 1.0E10
f.get() = 1.0E10
l.get() = 10000000000
i.get() = 1410065408
```

Commonly Used Classes

We now give a survey of the content of the four packages `javafx.beans`, `javafx.beans.binding`, `javafx.beans.property`, and `javafx.beans.value`. In this section, "the `SimpleIntegerProperty` series of classes" refers to the classes extrapolated over the `Boolean`, `Integer`, `Long`, `Float`, `Double`, `String`, and `Object` types. Therefore what is said also applies to `SimpleBooleanProperty`, and so on.

- The most often used classes in the JavaFX properties and bindings framework are the `SimpleIntegerProperty` series of classes. They provide all the functionalities of the `Property` interface including lazy evaluation. They are used in all the examples of this chapter up to this point.

- Another set of concrete classes in the JavaFX properties and bindings framework is the ReadOnlyIntegerWrapper series of classes. These classes implement the Property interface but also have a getReadOnlyProperty() method that returns a ReadOnlyProperty that is synchronized with the main Property. They are very handy to use when you need a full-blown Property for the implementation of a component but you only want to hand out a ReadOnlyProperty to the client of the component.
- The IntegerPropertyBase series of abstract classes can be extended to provide implementations of full Property classes, although in practice the SimpleIntegerProperty series of classes is easier to use. The only abstract methods in the IntegerPropertyBase series of classes are getBean() and getName().
- The ReadOnlyIntegerPropertyBase series of abstract classes can be extended to provide implementations of ReadOnlyProperty classes. This is rarely necessary. The only abstract methods in the ReadOnlyIntegerPropertyBase series of classes are get(), getBean(), and getName().
- The WeakInvalidationListener and WeakChangeListener classes can be used to wrap InvalidationListener and ChangeListener instances before addListener() is called. They hold weak references of the wrapped listener instances. As long as you hold a reference to the wrapped listener on your side, the weak references will be kept alive and you will receive events. When you are done with the wrapped listener and have unreferenced it from your side, the weak references will be eligible for garbage collection and later garbage collected. All the JavaFX properties and bindings framework Observable objects know how to clean up a weak listener after its weak reference has been garbage collected. This prevents memory leaks when the listeners are not removed after use. The WeakInvalidationListener and WeakListener classes implement the WeakListener interface, whose wasGarbageCollected() method will return true if the wrapped listener instance was garbage collected.

That covers all the JavaFX properties and bindings APIs that reside in the javafx.beans, javafx.beans.property, and javafx.beans.value packages and some but not all of the APIs in the javafx.beans.binding package. The javafx.beans.property.adapters package provides adapters between old-style JavaBeans properties and JavaFX properties. We will cover these adapters in the "Adapting JavaBeans Properties to JavaFX Properties" section. The remaining classes of the javafx.beans.binding package are APIs that help you to create new bindings out of existing properties and bindings. That is the focus of the next section.

Creating Bindings

We now turn our focus to the creation of new bindings out of existing properties and bindings. You learned in the "Understanding Key Interfaces and Concepts" section earlier in this chapter that a binding is an observable value that has a list of dependencies that are also observable values.

The JavaFX properties and bindings framework offers three ways of creating new bindings:

- Extending the IntegerBinding series of abstract classes.
- Using the bindings-creating static methods in the utilities class Bindings.
- Using the fluent interface API provided by the IntegerExpression series of abstract classes.

You saw the direct extension approach in the "Understanding the Binding Interface" section earlier in this chapter. We explore the Bindings utility class next.

Understanding the Bindings Utility Class

The Bindings class contains 236 factory methods that make new bindings out of existing observable values and regular values. Most of the methods are overloaded to take into account that both observable values and regular Java (unobservable) values can be used to build new bindings. At least one of the parameters must be an observable value. Here are the signatures of the nine overloaded add() methods:

```
public static NumberBinding add(ObservableNumberValue n1, ObservableNumberValue n2)
public static DoubleBinding add(ObservableNumberValue n, double d)
public static DoubleBinding add(double d, ObservableNumberValue n)
public static NumberBinding add(ObservableNumberValue n, float f)
public static NumberBinding add(float f, ObservableNumberValue n)
public static NumberBinding add(ObservableNumberValue n, long l)
public static NumberBinding add(long l, ObservableNumberValue n)
public static NumberBinding add(ObservableNumberValue n, int i)
public static NumberBinding add(int i, ObservableNumberValue n)
```

When the add() method is called, it returns a NumberBinding with dependencies that include all the observable value parameters, and whose value is the sum of the value of its two parameters. Similarly overloaded methods exist for subtract(), multiply(), and divide().

■ **Note** Recall from the last section that ObservableIntegerValue, ObservableLongValue, ObservableFloatValue, and ObservableDoubleValue are subclasses of ObservableNumberValue. Therefore the four arithmetic methods just mentioned can take any combinations of these observable numeric values as well as any unobservable values.

The program in Listing 4-5 uses the arithmetic methods in Bindings to calculate the area of a triangle in the Cartesian plane with vertices (x1, y1), (x2, y2), (x3, y3) using this formula:

```
Area = (x1*y2 + x2*y3 + x3*y1 - x1*y3 - x2*y1 - x3*y2) / 2
```

Listing 4-5. TriangleAreaExample.java

```
import javafx.beans.binding.Bindings;
import javafx.beans.binding.NumberBinding;
import javafx.beans.property.IntegerProperty;
import javafx.beans.property.SimpleIntegerProperty;

public class TriangleAreaExample {
    public static void main(String[] args) {
        IntegerProperty x1 = new SimpleIntegerProperty(0);
        IntegerProperty y1 = new SimpleIntegerProperty(0);
        IntegerProperty x2 = new SimpleIntegerProperty(0);
        IntegerProperty y2 = new SimpleIntegerProperty(0);
        IntegerProperty x3 = new SimpleIntegerProperty(0);
        IntegerProperty y3 = new SimpleIntegerProperty(0);

        final NumberBinding x1y2 = Bindings.multiply(x1, y2);
        final NumberBinding x2y3 = Bindings.multiply(x2, y3);
```

```
        final NumberBinding x3y1 = Bindings.multiply(x3, y1);
        final NumberBinding x1y3 = Bindings.multiply(x1, y3);
        final NumberBinding x2y1 = Bindings.multiply(x2, y1);
        final NumberBinding x3y2 = Bindings.multiply(x3, y2);

        final NumberBinding sum1 = Bindings.add(x1y2, x2y3);
        final NumberBinding sum2 = Bindings.add(sum1, x3y1);
        final NumberBinding sum3 = Bindings.add(sum2, x3y1);
        final NumberBinding diff1 = Bindings.subtract(sum3, x1y3);
        final NumberBinding diff2 = Bindings.subtract(diff1, x2y1);
        final NumberBinding determinant = Bindings.subtract(diff2, x3y2);
        final NumberBinding area = Bindings.divide(determinant, 2.0D);

        x1.set(0); y1.set(0);
        x2.set(6); y2.set(0);
        x3.set(4); y3.set(3);

        printResult(x1, y1, x2, y2, x3, y3, area);

        x1.set(1); y1.set(0);
        x2.set(2); y2.set(2);
        x3.set(0); y3.set(1);

        printResult(x1, y1, x2, y2, x3, y3, area);
    }

    private static void printResult(IntegerProperty x1, IntegerProperty y1,
                                    IntegerProperty x2, IntegerProperty y2,
                                    IntegerProperty x3, IntegerProperty y3,
                                    NumberBinding area) {
        System.out.println("For A(" +
                x1.get() + "," + y1.get() + "), B(" +
                x2.get() + "," + y2.get() + "), C(" +
                x3.get() + "," + y3.get() + "), the area of triangle ABC is " + area.getValue());
    }
}
```

We used IntegerProperty to represent the coordinates. The building up of the NumberBinding area uses all four arithmetic factory methods of Bindings. Because we started with IntegerProperty objects, even though the return type from the arithmetic factory methods of Bindings are NumberBinding, the actual object that is returned, up to determinant, are IntegerBinding objects. We used 2.0D rather than a mere 2 in the divide() call to force the division to be done as a double division, not as int division. All the properties and bindings that we build up form a tree structure with area as the root, the intermediate bindings as internal nodes, and the properties x1, y1, x2, y2, x3, y3 as leaves. This tree is similar to the parse tree we will get if we parse the mathematical expression for the area formula using grammar for the regular arithmetic expressions.

When we run the program in Listing 4-5, the following output is printed to the console:

```
For A(0,0), B(6,0), C(4,3), the area of triangle ABC is 9.0
For A(1,0), B(2,2), C(0,1), the area of triangle ABC is 1.5
```

Aside from the arithmetic methods, the Bindings class also has the following factory methods.

- Logical operators: and, or, not
- Numeric operators: min, max, negate
- Object operators: isNull, isNotNull
- String operators: length, isEmpty, isNotEmpty
- Relational operators:
    - equal
    - equalIgnoreCase
    - greaterThan
    - greaterThanOrEqual
    - lessThan
    - lessThanOrEqual
    - notEqual
    - notEqualIgnoreCase
- Creation operators:
    - createBooleanBinding
    - createIntegerBinding
    - createLongBinding
    - createFloatBinding
    - createDoubleBinding
    - createStringBinding
    - createObjectBinding
- Selection operators:select
    - selectBoolean
    - selectInteger
    - selectLong
    - selectFloat
    - selectDouble
    - selectString

Except for the creation operators and the selection operators, the preceding operators all do what you think they will do. The object operators are meaningful only for observable string values and observable object values. The string operators are meaningful only for observable string values. All relational operators except for the IgnoreCase ones apply to numeric values. There are versions of the equal and notEqual operators for numeric values that have a third double parameter for the tolerance when comparing float or double values. The equal and notEqual operators also apply to boolean, string, and object values. For string and object values, the equal and notEqual operator compares their values using the equals() method.

The creation operators provide a convenient way of creating a binding without directly extending the abstract base class. It takes a Callable and any number of dependencies as an argument. The area double binding in Listing 4-3 can be rewritten as follows, using a lambda expression as the Callable:

```
DoubleBinding area = Bindings.createDoubleBinding(() -> {
    return x.get() * y.get();
}, x, y);
```

The selection operators operate on what are called *JavaFX beans*, Java classes constructed according to the JavaFX Beans specification. We talk about JavaFX Beans in the "Understanding JavaFX Beans Convention" section later in this chapter.

There are a number of methods in Bindings that deal with observable collections. We cover them in Chapter 7.

That covers all methods in Bindings that return a binding object. There are 18 methods in Bindings that do not return a binding object. The various bindBidirectional() and unbindBidirectional() methods create bidirectional bindings. As a matter of fact, the bindBidirectional() and unbindBidirectional() methods in the various properties classes simply call the corresponding ones in the Bindings class. The bindContent() and unbindContent() methods bind an ordinary collection to an observable collection. The convert(), concat(), and a pair of overloaded format() methods return StringExpression objects. And finally the when() method returns a When object.

The When and the StringExpression classes are part of the fluent interface API for creating bindings, which we cover in the next subsection.

Understanding the Fluent Interface API

If you asked the questions "Why would anybody name a method when()? And what kind of information would the When class encapsulate?," welcome to the club. While you were not looking, the object-oriented programming community invented a brand new method of API design that totally disregards the decades-old principles of object-oriented practices. Instead of encapsulating data and distributing business logic into relevant domain objects, this new methodology produces a style of API that encourages method chaining and uses the return type of one method to determine what methods are available for the next car of the choo-choo train. Method names are chosen not to convey complete meaning, but to make the entire method chain read like a fluent sentence. This style of APIs is called *fluent interface APIs*.

■ **Note** You can find a more thorough exposition of fluent interfaces on Martin Fowler's web site, referenced at the end of this chapter.

The fluent interface APIs for creating bindings are defined in the IntegerExpression series of classes. IntegerExpression is a superclass of both IntegerProperty and IntegerBinding, making the methods of IntegerExpression also available in the IntegerProperty and IntegerBinding classes. The four numeric expression classes share a common superinterface NumberExpression, where all the methods are defined. The type-specific expression classes override some of the methods that yield a NumberBinding to return a more appropriate type of binding.

The methods thus made available for the seven kinds of properties and bindings are listed here:

- For BooleanProperty and BooleanBinding
    - BooleanBinding and(ObservableBooleanValue b)
    - BooleanBinding or(ObservableBooleanValue b)
    - BooleanBinding not()
    - BooleanBinding isEqualTo(ObservableBooleanValue b)

    - BooleanBinding isNotEqualTo(ObservableBooleanValue b)
    - StringBinding asString()
- Common for all numeric properties and bindings
    - BooleanBinding isEqualTo(ObservableNumberValue m)
    - BooleanBinding isEqualTo(ObservableNumberValue m, double err)
    - BooleanBinding isEqualTo(double d, double err)
    - BooleanBinding isEqualTo(float f, double err)
    - BooleanBinding isEqualTo(long l)
    - BooleanBinding isEqualTo(long l, double err)
    - BooleanBinding isEqualTo(int i)
    - BooleanBinding isEqualTo(int i, double err)
    - BooleanBinding isNotEqualTo(ObservableNumberValue m)
    - BooleanBinding isNotEqualTo(ObservableNumberValue m, double err)
    - BooleanBinding isNotEqualTo(double d, double err)
    - BooleanBinding isNotEqualTo(float f, double err)
    - BooleanBinding isNotEqualTo(long l)
    - BooleanBinding isNotEqualTo(long l, double err)
    - BooleanBinding isNotEqualTo(int i)
    - BooleanBinding isNotEqualTo(int i, double err)
    - BooleanBinding greaterThan(ObservableNumberValue m)
    - BooleanBinding greaterThan(double d)
    - BooleanBinding greaterThan(float f)
    - BooleanBinding greaterThan(long l)
    - BooleanBinding greaterThan(int i)
    - BooleanBinding lessThan(ObservableNumberValue m)
    - BooleanBinding lessThan(double d)
    - BooleanBinding lessThan(float f)
    - BooleanBinding lessThan(long l)
    - BooleanBinding lessThan(int i)
    - BooleanBinding greaterThanOrEqualTo(ObservableNumberValue m)
    - BooleanBinding greaterThanOrEqualTo(double d)
    - BooleanBinding greaterThanOrEqualTo(float f)
    - BooleanBinding greaterThanOrEqualTo(long l)

- `BooleanBinding greaterThanOrEqualTo(int i)`
- `BooleanBinding lessThanOrEqualTo(ObservableNumberValue m)`
- `BooleanBinding lessThanOrEqualTo(double d)`
- `BooleanBinding lessThanOrEqualTo(float f)`
- `BooleanBinding lessThanOrEqualTo(long l)`
- `BooleanBinding lessThanOrEqualTo(int i)`
- `StringBinding asString()`
- `StringBinding asString(String str)`
- `StringBinding asString(Locale locale, String str)`

- For `IntegerProperty` and `IntegerBinding`
  - `IntegerBinding negate()`
  - `NumberBinding add(ObservableNumberValue n)`
  - `DoubleBinding add(double d)`
  - `FloatBinding add(float f)`
  - `LongBinding add(long l)`
  - `IntegerBinding add(int i)`
  - `NumberBinding subtract(ObservableNumberValue n)`
  - `DoubleBinding subtract(double d)`
  - `FloatBinding subtract(float f)`
  - `LongBinding subtract(long l)`
  - `IntegerBinding subtract(int i)`
  - `NumberBinding multiply(ObservableNumberValue n)`
  - `DoubleBinding multiply(double d)`
  - `FloatBinding multiply(float f)`
  - `LongBinding multiply(long l)`
  - `IntegerBinding multiply(int i)`
  - `NumberBinding divide(ObservableNumberValue n)`
  - `DoubleBinding divide(double d)`
  - `FloatBinding divide(float f)`
  - `LongBinding divide(long l)`
  - `IntegerBinding divide(int i)`
- For `LongProperty` and `LongBinding`
  - `LongBinding negate()`
  - `NumberBinding add(ObservableNumberValue n)`

- DoubleBinding add(double d)
- FloatBinding add(float f)
- LongBinding add(long l)
- LongBinding add(int i)
- NumberBinding subtract(ObservableNumberValue n)
- DoubleBinding subtract(double d)
- FloatBinding subtract(float f)
- LongBinding subtract(long l)
- LongBinding subtract(int i)
- NumberBinding multiply(ObservableNumberValue n)
- DoubleBinding multiply(double d)
- FloatBinding multiply(float f)
- LongBinding multiply(long l)
- LongBinding multiply(int i)
- NumberBinding divide(ObservableNumberValue n)
- DoubleBinding divide(double d)
- FloatBinding divide(float f)
- LongBinding divide(long l)
- LongBinding divide(int i)

- For FloatProperty and FloatBinding
    - FloatBinding negate()
    - NumberBinding add(ObservableNumberValue n)
    - DoubleBinding add(double d)
    - FloatBinding add(float g)
    - FloatBinding add(long l)
    - FloatBinding add(int i)
    - NumberBinding subtract(ObservableNumberValue n)
    - DoubleBinding subtract(double d)
    - FloatBinding subtract(float g)
    - FloatBinding subtract(long l)
    - FloatBinding subtract(int i)
    - NumberBinding multiply(ObservableNumberValue n)
    - DoubleBinding multiply(double d)

    - `FloatBinding multiply(float g)`
    - `FloatBinding multiply(long l)`
    - `FloatBinding multiply(int i)`
    - `NumberBinding divide(ObservableNumberValue n)`
    - `DoubleBinding divide(double d)`
    - `FloatBinding divide(float g)`
    - `FloatBinding divide(long l)`
    - `FloatBinding divide(int i)`
- For `DoubleProperty` and `DoubleBinding`
    - `DoubleBinding negate()`
    - `DoubleBinding add(ObservableNumberValue n)`
    - `DoubleBinding add(double d)`
    - `DoubleBinding add(float f)`
    - `DoubleBinding add(long l)`
    - `DoubleBinding add(int i)`
    - `DoubleBinding subtract(ObservableNumberValue n)`
    - `DoubleBinding subtract(double d)`
    - `DoubleBinding subtract(float f)`
    - `DoubleBinding subtract(long l)`
    - `DoubleBinding subtract(int i)`
    - `DoubleBinding multiply(ObservableNumberValue n)`
    - `DoubleBinding multiply(double d)`
    - `DoubleBinding multiply(float f)`
    - `DoubleBinding multiply(long l)`
    - `DoubleBinding multiply(int i)`
    - `DoubleBinding divide(ObservableNumberValue n)`
    - `DoubleBinding divide(double d)`
    - `DoubleBinding divide(float f)`
    - `DoubleBinding divide(long l)`
    - `DoubleBinding divide(int i)`
- For `StringProperty` and `StringBinding`
    - `StringExpression concat(Object obj)`
    - `BooleanBinding isEqualTo(ObservableStringValue str)`

    - BooleanBinding isEqualTo(String str)
    - BooleanBinding isNotEqualTo(ObservableStringValue str)
    - BooleanBinding isNotEqualTo(String str)
    - BooleanBinding isEqualToIgnoreCase(ObservableStringValue str)
    - BooleanBinding isEqualToIgnoreCase(String str)
    - BooleanBinding isNotEqualToIgnoreCase(ObservableStringValue str)
    - BooleanBinding isNotEqualToIgnoreCase(String str)
    - BooleanBinding greaterThan(ObservableStringValue str)
    - BooleanBinding greaterThan(String str)
    - BooleanBinding lessThan(ObservableStringValue str)
    - BooleanBinding lessThan(String str)
    - BooleanBinding greaterThanOrEqualTo(ObservableStringValue str)
    - BooleanBinding greaterThanOrEqualTo(String str)
    - BooleanBinding lessThanOrEqualTo(ObservableStringValue str)
    - BooleanBinding lessThanOrEqualTo(String str)
    - BooleanBinding isNull()
    - BooleanBinding isNotNull()
    - IntegerBinding length()
    - BooleanExpression isEmpty()
    - BooleanExpression isNotEmpty()
- For ObjectProperty and ObjectBinding
    - BooleanBinding isEqualTo(ObservableObjectValue<?> obj)
    - BooleanBinding isEqualTo(Object obj)
    - BooleanBinding isNotEqualTo(ObservableObjectValue<?> obj)
    - BooleanBinding isNotEqualTo(Object obj)
    - BooleanBinding isNull()
    - BooleanBinding isNotNull()

With these methods, you can create an infinite variety of bindings by starting with a property and calling one of the methods that is appropriate for the type of the property to get a binding, and calling one of the methods that is appropriate for the type of the binding to get another binding, and so on. One fact that is worth pointing out here is that all the methods for the type-specific numeric expressions are defined in the NumberExpression base interface with a return type of NumberBinding, and are overridden in the type-specific expression classes with an identical parameter signature but a more specific return type. This way of overriding a method in a subclass with an identical parameter signature but a more specific return type is called *covariant return-type overriding*, and has been a Java language feature since Java 5. One of the consequences of this fact is that numeric bindings built with the fluent interface API have more specific types than those built with factory methods in the Bindings class.

Sometimes it is necessary to convert a type-specific expression into an object expression holding the same type of value. This can be done with the asObject() method in the type-specific expression class. The conversion back can be done using static methods in the expressions class. For IntegerExpression these static methods are

```
static IntegerExpression integerExpression(ObservableIntegerValue value)
static <T extends java.lang.Number> IntegerExpression integerExpression(ObservableValue<T> value)
```

The program in Listing 4-6 is a modification of the triangle area example in Listing 4-5 that uses the fluent interface API instead of calling factory methods in the Bindings class.

Listing 4-6. TriangleAreaFluentExample.java

```
import javafx.beans.binding.Bindings;
import javafx.beans.binding.NumberBinding;
import javafx.beans.binding.StringExpression;
import javafx.beans.property.IntegerProperty;
import javafx.beans.property.SimpleIntegerProperty;

public class TriangleAreaFluentExample {
    public static void main(String[] args) {
        IntegerProperty x1 = new SimpleIntegerProperty(0);
        IntegerProperty y1 = new SimpleIntegerProperty(0);
        IntegerProperty x2 = new SimpleIntegerProperty(0);
        IntegerProperty y2 = new SimpleIntegerProperty(0);
        IntegerProperty x3 = new SimpleIntegerProperty(0);
        IntegerProperty y3 = new SimpleIntegerProperty(0);

        final NumberBinding area = x1.multiply(y2)
                .add(x2.multiply(y3))
                .add(x3.multiply(y1))
                .subtract(x1.multiply(y3))
                .subtract(x2.multiply(y1))
                .subtract(x3.multiply(y2))
                .divide(2.0D);

        StringExpression output = Bindings.format(
                "For A(%d,%d), B(%d,%d), C(%d,%d), the area of triangle ABC is %3.1f",
                x1, y1, x2, y2, x3, y3, area);

        x1.set(0); y1.set(0);
        x2.set(6); y2.set(0);
        x3.set(4); y3.set(3);

        System.out.println(output.get());

        x1.set(1); y1.set(0);
        x2.set(2); y2.set(2);
        x3.set(0); y3.set(1);

        System.out.println(output.get());
    }
}
```

Notice how the 13 lines of code and 12 intermediate variables used in Listing 4-5 to build up the area binding are reduced to the 7 lines of code with no intermediate variables used in Listing 4-6. We also used the `Bindings.format()` method to build up a `StringExpression` object called `output`. There are two overloaded `Bindings.format()` methods with signatures:

```
StringExpression format(Locale locale, String format, Object... args)
StringExpression format(String format, Object... args)
```

They work similarly to the corresponding `String.format()` methods in that they format the values `args` according to the format specification `format` and the `Locale locale`, or the default `Locale`. If any of the `args` is an `ObservableValue`, its change is reflected in the `StringExpression`.

When we run the program in Listing 4-6, the following output is printed to the console:

```
For A(0,0), B(6,0), C(4,3), the area of triangle ABC is 9.0
For A(1,0), B(2,2), C(0,1), the area of triangle ABC is 1.5
```

Next we unravel the mystery of the `When` class and the role it plays in constructing bindings that are essentially if/then/else expressions. The `When` class has a constructor that takes an `ObservableBooleanValue` argument:

```
public When(ObservableBooleanValue b)
```

It has the following 11 overloaded `then()` methods.

```
When.NumberConditionBuilder then(ObservableNumberValue n)
When.NumberConditionBuilder then(double d)
When.NumberConditionBuilder then(float f)
When.NumberConditionBuilder then(long l)
When.NumberConditionBuilder then(int i)
When.BooleanConditionBuilder then(ObservableBooleanValue b)
When.BooleanConditionBuilder then(boolean b)
When.StringConditionBuilder then(ObservableStringValue str)
When.StringConditionBuilder then(String str)
When.ObjectConditionBuilder<T> then(ObservableObjectValue<T> obj)
When.ObjectConditionBuilder<T> then(T obj)
```

The type of object returned from the `then()` method depends on the type of the argument. If the argument is a numeric type, either observable or unobservable, the return type is a nested class `When.NumberConditionBuilder`. Similarly, for Boolean arguments, the return type is `When.BooleanConditionBuilder`; for string arguments, `When.StringConditionBuilder`; and for object arguments, `When.ObjectConditionBuilder`.

These condition builders in turn have the following `otherwise()` methods.

- For `When.NumberConditionBuilder`
  - `NumberBinding otherwise(ObservableNumberValue n)`
  - `DoubleBinding otherwise(double d)`
  - `NumberBinding otherwise(float f)`
  - `NumberBinding otherwise(long l)`
  - `NumberBinding otherwise(int i)`

- For `When.BooleanConditionBuilder`
  - `BooleanBinding otherwise(ObservableBooleanValue b)`
  - `BooleanBinding otherwise(boolean b)`
- For `When.StringConditionBuilder`
  - `StringBinding otherwise(ObservableStringValue str)`
  - `StringBinding otherwise(String str)`
- For `When.ObjectConditionBuilder`
  - `ObjectBinding<T> otherwise(ObservableObjectValue<T> obj)`
  - `ObjectBinding<T> otherwise(T obj)`

The net effect of these method signatures is that you can build up a binding that resembles an if/then/else expression this way:

```
new When(b).then(x).otherwise(y)
```

where b is an `ObservableBooleanValue`, and x and y are of similar types and can be either observable or unobservable. The resulting binding will be of a type similar to that of x and y.

The program in Listing 4-7 uses the fluent interface API from the `When` class to calculate the area of a triangle with given sides a, b, and c. Recall that to form a triangle, the three sides must satisfy the following conditions:

```
a + b > c, b + c > a, c + a > b.
```

When the preceding conditions are satisfied, the area of the triangle can be calculated using Heron's formula:

```
Area = sqrt(s * (s - a) * (s - b) * (s - c))
```

where s is the semiperimeter:

```
s = (a + b + c) / 2.
```

Listing 4-7. HeronsFormulaExample.java

```
import javafx.beans.binding.DoubleBinding;
import javafx.beans.binding.When;
import javafx.beans.property.DoubleProperty;
import javafx.beans.property.SimpleDoubleProperty;
public class HeronsFormulaExample {
    public static void main(String[] args) {
        DoubleProperty a = new SimpleDoubleProperty(0);
        DoubleProperty b = new SimpleDoubleProperty(0);
        DoubleProperty c = new SimpleDoubleProperty(0);

        DoubleBinding s = a.add(b).add(c).divide(2.0D);

        final DoubleBinding areaSquared = new When(
                        a.add(b).greaterThan(c)
                        .and(b.add(c).greaterThan(a))
```

```
                    .and(c.add(a).greaterThan(b)))
            .then(s.multiply(s.subtract(a))
                    .multiply(s.subtract(b))
                    .multiply(s.subtract(c)))
            .otherwise(0.0D);

        a.set(3);
        b.set(4);
        c.set(5);
        System.out.printf("Given sides a = %1.0f, b = %1.0f, and c = %1.0f," +
                " the area of the triangle is %3.2f\n", a.get(), b.get(), c.get(),
                Math.sqrt(areaSquared.get()));

        a.set(2);
        b.set(2);
        c.set(2);
        System.out.printf("Given sides a = %1.0f, b = %1.0f, and c = %1.0f," +
                " the area of the triangle is %3.2f\n", a.get(), b.get(), c.get(),
                Math.sqrt(areaSquared.get()));
    }
}
```

Inasmuch as there is no ready-made binding method in `DoubleExpression` that calculates the square root, we create a `DoubleBinding` for `areaSquared` instead. The constructor argument for `When()` is a `BooleanBinding` built out of the three conditions on `a`, `b`, and `c`. The argument for the `then()` method is a `DoubleBinding` that calculates the square of the area of the triangle. And because the `then()` argument is numeric, the `otherwise()` argument also has to be numeric. We choose to use `0.0D` to signal that an invalid triangle is encountered.

■ **Note** Instead of using the `When()` constructor, you can also use the factory method `when()` in the `Bindings` utility class to create the `When` object.

When we run the program in Listing 4-7, the following output is printed to the console:

```
Given sides a = 3, b = 4, and c = 5, the area of the triangle is 6.00.
Given sides a = 2, b = 2, and c = 2, the area of the triangle is 1.73.
```

If the binding defined in Listing 4-7 makes your head spin a little, you are not alone. We choose this example simply to illustrate the use of the fluent interface API offered by the `When` class. As a matter of fact, this example might be better served with a direct subclassing approach we first introduced in the "Understanding the Binding Interface" section earlier in this chapter.

The program in Listing 4-8 solves the same problem as Listing 4-7 by using the direct extension method.

Listing 4-8. HeronsFormulaDirectExtensionExample.java

```
import javafx.beans.binding.DoubleBinding;
import javafx.beans.property.DoubleProperty;
import javafx.beans.property.SimpleDoubleProperty;
```

```
public class HeronsFormulaDirectExtensionExample {
    public static void main(String[] args) {
        final DoubleProperty a = new SimpleDoubleProperty(0);
        final DoubleProperty b = new SimpleDoubleProperty(0);
        final DoubleProperty c = new SimpleDoubleProperty(0);

        DoubleBinding area = new DoubleBinding() {
            {
                super.bind(a, b, c);
            }
            @Override
            protected double computeValue() {
                double a0 = a.get();
                double b0 = b.get();
                double c0 = c.get();

                if ((a0 + b0 > c0) && (b0 + c0 > a0) && (c0 + a0 > b0)) {
                    double s = (a0 + b0 + c0) / 2.0D;
                    return Math.sqrt(s * (s - a0) * (s - b0) * (s - c0));
                } else {
                    return 0.0D;
                }
            }
        };

        a.set(3);
        b.set(4);
        c.set(5);
        System.out.printf("Given sides a = %1.0f, b = %1.0f, and c = %1.0f," +
                " the area of the triangle is %3.2f\n", a.get(), b.get(), c.get(),
                area.get());

        a.set(2);
        b.set(2);
        c.set(2);
        System.out.printf("Given sides a = %1.0f, b = %1.0f, and c = %1.0f," +
                " the area of the triangle is %3.2f\n", a.get(), b.get(), c.get(),
                area.get());
    }
}
```

The direct extension method is preferred for complicated expressions and for expressions that go beyond the available operators.

Now that you have mastered all the APIs in the `javafx.beans`, `javafx.beans.binding`, `javafx.beans.property`, and `javafx.beans.value` packages, you are ready to step beyond the details of the JavaFX properties and bindings framework and learn how these properties are organized into bigger components called JavaFX Beans.

Understanding the JavaFX Beans Convention

JavaFX introduces the concept of JavaFX Beans, a set of conventions that provide properties support for Java objects. In this section, we talk about the naming conventions for specifying JavaFX Beans properties, several ways of implementing JavaFX Beans properties, and finally the use of selection bindings.

The JavaFX Beans Specification

For many years Java has used the JavaBeans API to represent a property of an object. A JavaBeans property is represented by a pair of getter and setter methods. Property changes are propagated to property change listeners through the firing of property change events in the setter code.

JavaFX introduces the JavaFX Beans specification that adds properties support to Java objects through the help of the properties classes from the JavaFX properties and bindings framework.

■ **Caution** The word *property* is used here with two distinct meanings. When we say JavaFX Beans properties, it should be understood to mean a higher level concept similar to JavaBeans properties. When we say JavaFX properties and bindings framework properties, it should be understood to mean the various implementations of the `Property` or `ReadOnlyProperty` interfaces, such as `IntegerProperty`, `StringProperty`, and so on. JavaFX Beans properties are specified using JavaFX properties and bindings framework properties.

Like their JavaBeans counterparts, *JavaFX Beans properties* are specified by a set of methods in a Java class. To define a JavaFX Beans property in a Java class, you provide three methods: the getter, the setter, and the property getter. For a property named `height` of type `double`, the three methods are:

```
public final double getHeight();
public final void setHeight(double h);
public DoubleProperty heightProperty();
```

The names of the getter and setter methods follow the JavaBeans convention. They are obtained by concatenating "`get`" and "`set`" with the name of the property with the first character capitalized. For `boolean` type properties, the getter name can also start with "`is`". The name of the property getter is obtained by concatenating the name of the property with "`Property`". To define a *read-only JavaFX Beans property*, you can either remove the setter method or change it to a private method and change the return type of the property getter to be a `ReadOnlyProperty`.

This specification speaks only about the interface of JavaFX Beans properties and does not impose any implementation constraints. Depending on the number of properties a JavaFX Bean may have, and the usage patterns of these properties, there are several implementation strategies. Not surprisingly, all of them use the JavaFX properties and bindings framework properties as the backing store for the values of the JavaFX Beans properties. We show you these strategies in the next two subsections.

Understanding the Eagerly Instantiated Properties Strategy

The *eagerly instantiated properties* strategy is the simplest way to implement JavaFX Beans properties. For every JavaFX Beans property you want to define in an object, you introduce a private field in the class that is of the appropriate JavaFX properties and bindings framework property type. These private fields are instantiated at bean construction time. The getter and setter methods simply call the private field's `get()` and `set()` methods. The property getter simply returns the private field itself.

The program in Listing 4-9 defines a JavaFX Bean with an `int` property `i`, a `String` property `str`, and a `Color` property `color`.

Listing 4-9. JavaFXBeanModelExample.java

```
import javafx.beans.property.IntegerProperty;
import javafx.beans.property.ObjectProperty;
import javafx.beans.property.SimpleIntegerProperty;
import javafx.beans.property.SimpleObjectProperty;
```

```
import javafx.beans.property.SimpleStringProperty;
import javafx.beans.property.StringProperty;
import javafx.scene.paint.Color;

public class JavaFXBeanModelExample {
    private IntegerProperty i = new SimpleIntegerProperty(this, "i", 0);
    private StringProperty str = new SimpleStringProperty(this, "str", "Hello");
    private ObjectProperty<Color> color = new SimpleObjectProperty<Color>(this, "color", Color.BLACK);

    public final int getI() {
        return i.get();
    }

    public final void setI(int i) {
        this.i.set(i);
    }

    public IntegerProperty iProperty() {
        return i;
    }

    public final String getStr() {
        return str.get();
    }

    public final void setStr(String str) {
        this.str.set(str);
    }

    public StringProperty strProperty() {
        return str;
    }

    public final Color getColor() {
        return color.get();
    }

    public final void setColor(Color color) {
        this.color.set(color);
    }

    public ObjectProperty<Color> colorProperty() {
        return color;
    }
}
```

This is a straightforward Java class. There are only two things we want to point out in this implementation. First, the getter and setter methods are declared `final` by convention. Second, when the private fields are initialized, we called the simple properties constructors with the full context information, supplying them with `this` as the first parameter. In all of our previous examples in this chapter, we used `null` as the first parameter for the simple properties constructors because those properties are not part of a higher level JavaFX Bean object.

The program in Listing 4-10 defines a view class that watches over an instance of the JavaFX Bean defined in Listing 4-9. It observes changes to the i, str, and color properties of the bean by hooking up change listeners that print out any changes to the console.

Listing 4-10. JavaFXBeanViewExample.java

```
import javafx.beans.value.ChangeListener;
import javafx.beans.value.ObservableValue;
import javafx.scene.paint.Color;

public class JavaFXBeanViewExample {
    private JavaFXBeanModelExample model;

    public JavaFXBeanViewExample(JavaFXBeanModelExample model) {
        this.model = model;
        hookupChangeListeners();
    }

    private void hookupChangeListeners() {
        model.iProperty().addListener(new ChangeListener<Number>() {
            @Override
            public void changed(ObservableValue<? extends Number> observableValue, Number↩
oldValue, Number newValue) {
                System.out.println("Property i changed: old value = " + oldValue + ", new↩
value = " + newValue);
            }
        });

        model.strProperty().addListener(new ChangeListener<String>() {
            @Override
            public void changed(ObservableValue<? extends String> observableValue, String↩
oldValue, String newValue) {
                System.out.println("Property str changed: old value = " + oldValue + ", new↩
value = " + newValue);
            }
        });

        model.colorProperty().addListener(new ChangeListener<Color>() {
            @Override
            public void changed(ObservableValue<? extends Color> observableValue, Color↩
oldValue, Color newValue) {
                System.out.println("Property color changed: old value = " + oldValue + ",↩
new value = " + newValue);
            }
        });
    }
}
```

The program in Listing 4-11 defines a controller that can modify a model object.

Listing 4-11. JavaFXBeanControllerExample.java

```
import javafx.scene.paint.Color;

public class JavaFXBeanControllerExample {
    private JavaFXBeanModelExample model;
    private JavaFXBeanViewExample view;

    public JavaFXBeanControllerExample(JavaFXBeanModelExample model, JavaFXBeanViewExample↵
 view) {
        this.model = model;
        this.view = view;
    }

    public void incrementIPropertyOnModel() {
        model.setI(model.getI() + 1);
    }

    public void changeStrPropertyOnModel() {
        final String str = model.getStr();
        if (str.equals("Hello")) {
            model.setStr("World");
        } else {
            model.setStr("Hello");
        }
    }

    public void switchColorPropertyOnModel() {
        final Color color = model.getColor();
        if (color.equals(Color.BLACK)) {
            model.setColor(Color.WHITE);
        } else {
            model.setColor(Color.BLACK);
        }
    }
}
```

Notice that this is not a full-blown controller and does not do anything with its reference to the view object. The program in Listing 4-12 provides a main program that assembles and test drives the classes in Listings 4-9 to 4-11 in a typical model–view–controller pattern.

Listing 4-12. JavaFXbeanMainExample.java

```
public class JavaFXBeanMainExample {
    public static void main(String[] args) {
        JavaFXBeanModelExample model = new JavaFXBeanModelExample();
        JavaFXBeanViewExample view = new JavaFXBeanViewExample(model);
        JavaFXBeanControllerExample controller = new JavaFXBeanControllerExample(model, view);

        controller.incrementIPropertyOnModel();
        controller.changeStrPropertyOnModel();
        controller.switchColorPropertyOnModel();
```

```
        controller.incrementIPropertyOnModel();
        controller.changeStrPropertyOnModel();
        controller.switchColorPropertyOnModel();
    }
}
```

When we run the program in Listings 4-9 to 4-12, the following output is printed to the console:

```
Property i changed: old value = 0, new value = 1
Property str changed: old value = Hello, new value = World
Property color changed: old value = 0x000000ff, new value = 0xffffffff
Property i changed: old value = 1, new value = 2
Property str changed: old value = World, new value = Hello
Property color changed: old value = 0xffffffff, new value = 0x000000ff
```

Understanding the Lazily Instantiated Properties Strategy

If your JavaFX Bean has many properties, instantiating all the properties objects up front at bean creation time may be too heavy an approach. The memory for all the properties objects is truly wasted if only a few of the properties are actually used. In such situations, you can use one of several lazily instantiated properties strategies. Two typical such strategies are the *half-lazy instantiation* strategy and the *full-lazy instantiation* strategy.

In the half-lazy strategy, the property object is instantiated only if the setter is called with a value that is different from the default value, or if the property getter is called. The program in Listing 4-13 illustrates how this strategy is implemented.

Listing 4-13. JavaFXBeanModelHalfLazyExample.java

```
import javafx.beans.property.SimpleStringProperty;
import javafx.beans.property.StringProperty;

public class JavaFXBeanModelHalfLazyExample {
    private static final String DEFAULT_STR = "Hello";
    private StringProperty str;

    public final String getStr() {
        if (str != null) {
            return str.get();
        } else {
            return DEFAULT_STR;
        }
    }

    public final void setStr(String str) {
        if ((this.str != null) || !(str.equals(DEFAULT_STR))) {
            strProperty().set(str);
        }
    }
```

```
    public StringProperty strProperty() {
        if (str == null) {
            str = new SimpleStringProperty(this, "str", DEFAULT_STR);
        }
        return str;
    }
}
```

In this strategy, the client code can call the getter many times without the property object being instantiated. If the property object is null, the getter simply returns the default value. As soon as the setter is called with a value that is different from the default value, it will call the property getter, which lazily instantiates the property object. The property object is also instantiated if the client code calls the property getter directly.

In the full-lazy strategy, the property object is instantiated only if the property getter is called. The getter and setter go through the property object only if it is already instantiated. Otherwise they go through a separate field.

The program in Listing 4-14 shows an example of a full-lazy property.

Listing 4-14. JavaFXBeanModelFullLazyExample.java

```
import javafx.beans.property.SimpleStringProperty;
import javafx.beans.property.StringProperty;

public class JavaFXBeanModelFullLazyExample {
    private static final String DEFAULT_STR = "Hello";
    private StringProperty str;
    private String _str = DEFAULT_STR;

    public final String getStr() {
        if (str != null) {
            return str.get();
        } else {
            return _str;
        }
    }

    public final void setStr(String str) {
        if (this.str != null) {
            this.str.set(str);
        } else {
            _str = str;
        }
    }

    public StringProperty strProperty() {
        if (str == null) {
            str = new SimpleStringProperty(this, "str", DEFAULT_STR);
        }
        return str;
    }
}
```

■ **Caution** The full-lazy instantiation strategy incurs the cost of an extra field to stave off the need for property instantiation a little longer. Similarly, both the half-lazy and the full-lazy instantiation strategies incur costs of implementation complexity and runtime performance to gain the benefit of a potentially reduced runtime memory footprint. This is a classical trade-off situation in software engineering. Which strategy you choose will depend on the circumstance of your application. Our advice is to introduce optimization only if there is a need.

Using Selection Bindings

As you saw in the "Understanding the Bindings Utility Class" section earlier, the `Bindings` utility class contains seven selection operators. The method signatures of these operators are:

- `select(Object root, String... steps)`
- `selectBoolean(Object root, String... steps)`
- `selectDouble(Object root, String... steps)`
- `selectFloat(Object root, String... steps)`
- `selectInteger(Object root, String... steps)`
- `selectLong(Object root, String... steps)`
- `selectString(Object root, String... steps)`

These selection operators allow you to create bindings that observe deeply nested JavaFX Beans properties. Suppose that you have a JavaFX bean that has a property, whose type is a JavaFX bean that has a property, whose type is a JavaFX bean that has a property, and so on. Suppose also that you are observing the root of this properties chain through an `ObjectProperty`. You can then create a binding that observes the deeply nested JavaFX Beans property by calling one of the select methods whose type matches the type of the deeply nested JavaFX Beans property with the `ObjectProperty` as the root, and the successive JavaFX Beans property names that reach into the deeply nested JavaFX Beans property as the rest of the arguments.

■ **Note** There is another set of select methods that takes an `ObservableValue` as the first parameter. They were introduced in JavaFX 2.0. The set of select methods that takes an `Object` as the first parameter allows us to use any Java object, not merely JavaFX Beans, as the root of a selection binding.

In the following example, we use a few classes from the `javafx.scene.effect` package—`Lighting` and `Light`—to illustrate how the selection operator works. We teach you how to apply lighting to a JavaFX scene graph in a later chapter of the book. For now, our interest lies in the fact that `Lighting` is a JavaFX bean that has a property named `light` whose type is `Light`, and that `Light` is also a JavaFX bean that has a property named `color` whose type is `Color` (in `javafx.scene.paint`).

The program in Listing 4-15 illustrates how to observe the color of the light of the lighting.

Listing 4-15. SelectBindingExample.java

```
import javafx.beans.binding.Bindings;
import javafx.beans.binding.ObjectBinding;
import javafx.beans.property.ObjectProperty;
import javafx.beans.property.SimpleObjectProperty;
```

```
import javafx.beans.value.ChangeListener;
import javafx.beans.value.ObservableValue;
import javafx.scene.effect.Light;
import javafx.scene.effect.Lighting;
import javafx.scene.paint.Color;

public class SelectBindingExample {
    public static void main(String[] args) {
        ObjectProperty<Lighting> root = new SimpleObjectProperty<>(new Lighting());
        final ObjectBinding<Color> selectBinding = Bindings.select(root, "light", "color");
        selectBinding.addListener(new ChangeListener<Color>() {
            @Override
            public void changed(ObservableValue<? extends Color> observableValue, Color
                oldValue, Color newValue) {
                System.out.println("\tThe color changed:\n\t\told color = " +
                    oldValue + ",\n\t\tnew color = " + newValue);
            }
        });

        System.out.println("firstLight is black.");
        Light firstLight = new Light.Point();
        firstLight.setColor(Color.BLACK);

        System.out.println("secondLight is white.");
        Light secondLight = new Light.Point();
        secondLight.setColor(Color.WHITE);

        System.out.println("firstLighting has firstLight.");
        Lighting firstLighting = new Lighting();
        firstLighting.setLight(firstLight);

        System.out.println("secondLighting has secondLight.");
        Lighting secondLighting = new Lighting();
        secondLighting.setLight(secondLight);

        System.out.println("Making root observe firstLighting.");
        root.set(firstLighting);

        System.out.println("Making root observe secondLighting.");
        root.set(secondLighting);

        System.out.println("Changing secondLighting's light to firstLight");
        secondLighting.setLight(firstLight);

        System.out.println("Changing firstLight's color to red");
        firstLight.setColor(Color.RED);
    }
}
```

In this example, the root is an ObjectProperty that observes Lighting objects. The binding colorBinding observes the color property of the light property of the Lighting object that is the value of root. We then created some Light and Lighting objects and changed their configuration in various ways.

When we run the program in Listing 4-15, the following output is printed to the console:

```
firstLight is black.
secondLight is white.
firstLighting has firstLight.
secondLighting has secondLight.
Making root observe firstLighting.
    The color changed:
        old color = 0xffffffff,
        new color = 0x000000ff
Making root observe secondLighting.
    The color changed:
        old color = 0x000000ff,
        new color = 0xffffffff
Changing secondLighting's light to firstLight
    The color changed:
        old color = 0xffffffff,
        new color = 0x000000ff
Changing firstLight's color to red
    The color changed:
        old color = 0x000000ff,
        new color = 0xff0000ff
```

As expected, a change event is fired for every change in the configuration of the object being observed by root, and the value of colorBinding always reflects the color of the light of the current Lighting object in root.

■ **Caution** The JavaFX properties and bindings framework does not issue any warnings if the supplied property names do not match any property names in a JavaFX bean. It will simply have the default value for the type: null for object type, zero for numeric types, false for boolean type, and the empty string for string type.

Adapting JavaBeans Properties to JavaFX Properties

Over the many years since the JavaBeans specification was published, a lot of JavaBeans were written for various projects, products, and libraries. To better help Java developers leverage these JavaBeans, a set of adapters were provided in the javafx.beans.properties.adapter package to make them useful in the JavaFX world by creating a JavaFX property out of JavaBeans properties.

In this section, we first briefly review the JavaBeans specification definition of properties, bound properties, and constrained properties by way of a simple example. We then show you how to create JavaFX properties out of JavaBeans properties using the adapters.

Understanding JavaBeans Properties

JavaBeans *properties* are defined using the familiar getter and setter naming convention. A property is "read only" if only a getter is provided, and it is "read/write" if both a getter and a setter are provided. A JavaBeans event is made up of the event object, the event listener interface, and listener registration methods on the JavaBean. Two particular kinds of events are available for use by JavaBeans properties: A PropertyChange event can be fired when a JavaBeans property is changed; a VetoableChange event can also be fired when a JavaBeans property is changed; and if the listener throws a PropertyVetoException, the property change should not take effect. A property whose setter fires PropertyChange events is called a *bound property*. A property whose setter fires VetoableChange events is called a *constrained property*. Helper classes PropertyChangeSupport and VetoableChangeSupport allow bound properties and constrained properties to be easily defined in JavaBean classes.

Listing 4-16 defines a JavaBean Person with three properties: name, address, and phoneNumber. The address property is a bound property, and the phoneNumber property is a constrained property.

Listing 4-16. Person.java

```
import java.beans.PropertyChangeListener;
import java.beans.PropertyChangeSupport;
import java.beans.PropertyVetoException;
import java.beans.VetoableChangeListener;
import java.beans.VetoableChangeSupport;

public class Person {
    private PropertyChangeSupport propertyChangeSupport;
    private VetoableChangeSupport vetoableChangeSupport;
    private String name;
    private String address;
    private String phoneNumber;

    public Person() {
        propertyChangeSupport = new PropertyChangeSupport(this);
        vetoableChangeSupport = new VetoableChangeSupport(this);
    }

    public String getName() {
        return name;
    }

    public void setName(String name) {
        this.name = name;
    }

    public String getAddress() {
        return address;
    }

    public void setAddress(String address) {
        String oldAddress = this.address;
        this.address = address;
        propertyChangeSupport.firePropertyChange("address", oldAddress, this.address);
    }

    public String getPhoneNumber() {
        return phoneNumber;
    }
```

```
    public void setPhoneNumber(String phoneNumber) throws PropertyVetoException {
        String oldPhoneNumber = this.phoneNumber;
        vetoableChangeSupport.fireVetoableChange("phoneNumber", oldPhoneNumber, phoneNumber);
        this.phoneNumber = phoneNumber;
        propertyChangeSupport.firePropertyChange("phoneNumber", oldPhoneNumber, this.phoneNumber);
    }

    public void addPropertyChangeListener(PropertyChangeListener l) {
        propertyChangeSupport.addPropertyChangeListener(l);
    }

    public void removePropertyChangeListener(PropertyChangeListener l) {
        propertyChangeSupport.removePropertyChangeListener(l);
    }

    public PropertyChangeListener[] getPropertyChangeListeners() {
        return propertyChangeSupport.getPropertyChangeListeners();
    }

    public void addVetoableChangeListener(VetoableChangeListener l) {
        vetoableChangeSupport.addVetoableChangeListener(l);
    }

    public void removeVetoableChangeListener(VetoableChangeListener l) {
        vetoableChangeSupport.removeVetoableChangeListener(l);
    }

    public VetoableChangeListener[] getVetoableChangeListeners() {
        return vetoableChangeSupport.getVetoableChangeListeners();
    }
}
```

Understanding the JavaFX Property Adapters

The interfaces and classes in the javafx.beans.property.adapter package can be used to easily adapt JavaBeans properties to JavaFX properties. The ReadOnlyJavaBeanProperty interface is a subinterface of ReadOnlyProperty, and adds two methods:

```
void dispose()
void fireValueChangedEvent()
```

The JavaBeanProperty interface extends the ReadOnlyJavaBeanProperty and the Property interfaces. Each of these two interfaces has concrete class specializations for Boolean, Integer, Long, Float, Double, Object, and String types. These classes do not have public constructors. Instead, builder classes are provided to create instances of these types. We use the JavaBeanStringProperty class in the following example code. The same pattern applies to all other JavaFX property adapters. The JavaBeanStringPropertyBuilder supports the following methods:

```
public static JavaBeanStringPropertyBuilder create()
public JavaBeanStringProperty build()
public JavaBeanStringPropertyBuilder name(java.lang.String)
public JavaBeanStringPropertyBuilder bean(java.lang.Object)
```

```
public JavaBeanStringPropertyBuilder beanClass(java.lang.Class<?>)
public JavaBeanStringPropertyBuilder getter(java.lang.String)
public JavaBeanStringPropertyBuilder setter(java.lang.String)
public JavaBeanStringPropertyBuilder getter(java.lang.reflect.Method)
public JavaBeanStringPropertyBuilder setter(java.lang.reflect.Method)
```

To use the builder, start by calling its static method `create()`. Then call a chain of the methods that returns the builder itself. Finally, the `build()` method is called to create the property. For most cases, it suffices to call the `bean()` and the `name()` methods to specify the JavaBean instance and the name of the property. The `getter()` and `setter()` methods can be used to specify a getter and setter that does not follow the naming convention. The `beanClass()` method can be used to specify the JavaBean class. Setting the JavaBean class up front on the builder allows you to more efficiently create adapters for the same JavaBeans property for multiple instances of the same JavaBean class.

■ **Note** Although the builders of the JavaFX scene, control, and so on, classes have been deprecated, the builders in the `javafx.beans.property.adapter` package have not been deprecated. They are required to generate the JavaBeans property adapters.

The program in Listing 4-17 illustrates the adaption of the three JavaBeans properties of the `Person` class into `JavaBeanStringProperty` objects.

Listing 4-17. JavaBeanPropertiesExamples.java

```
import javafx.beans.property.SimpleStringProperty;
import javafx.beans.property.adapter.JavaBeanStringProperty;
import javafx.beans.property.adapter.JavaBeanStringPropertyBuilder;

import java.beans.PropertyVetoException;

public class JavaBeanPropertiesExample {
    public static void main(String[] args) throws NoSuchMethodException {
        adaptJavaBeansProperty();
        adaptBoundProperty();
        adaptConstrainedProperty();
    }

    private static void adaptJavaBeansProperty() throws NoSuchMethodException {
        Person person = new Person();
        JavaBeanStringProperty nameProperty = JavaBeanStringPropertyBuilder.create()
            .bean(person)
            .name("name")
            .build();
        nameProperty.addListener((observable, oldValue, newValue) -> {
            System.out.println("JavaFX property " + observable + " changed:");
            System.out.println("\toldValue = " + oldValue + ", newValue = " + newValue);
        });

        System.out.println("Setting name on the JavaBeans property");
        person.setName("Weiqi Gao");
        System.out.println("Calling fireValueChange");
```

```
        nameProperty.fireValueChangedEvent();
        System.out.println("nameProperty.get() = " + nameProperty.get());

        System.out.println("Setting value on the JavaFX property");
        nameProperty.set("Johan Vos");
        System.out.println("person.getName() = " + person.getName());
    }

    private static void adaptBoundProperty() throws NoSuchMethodException {
        System.out.println();
        Person person = new Person();
        JavaBeanStringProperty addressProperty = JavaBeanStringPropertyBuilder.create()
            .bean(person)
            .name("address")
            .build();
        addressProperty.addListener((observable, oldValue, newValue) -> {
            System.out.println("JavaFX property " + observable + " changed:");
            System.out.println("\toldValue = " + oldValue + ", newValue = " + newValue);
        });

        System.out.println("Setting address on the JavaBeans property");
        person.setAddress("12345 main Street");
    }

    private static void adaptConstrainedProperty() throws NoSuchMethodException {
        System.out.println();
        Person person = new Person();
        JavaBeanStringProperty phoneNumberProperty = JavaBeanStringPropertyBuilder.create()
            .bean(person)
            .name("phoneNumber")
            .build();
        phoneNumberProperty.addListener((observable, oldValue, newValue) -> {
            System.out.println("JavaFX property " + observable + " changed:");
            System.out.println("\toldValue = " + oldValue + ", newValue = " + newValue);
        });

        System.out.println("Setting phoneNumber on the JavaBeans property");
        try {
            person.setPhoneNumber("800-555-1212");
        } catch (PropertyVetoException e) {
            System.out.println("A JavaBeans property change is vetoed.");
        }

        System.out.println("Bind phoneNumberProperty to another property");
        SimpleStringProperty stringProperty = new SimpleStringProperty("866-555-1212");
        phoneNumberProperty.bind(stringProperty);
```

```
        System.out.println("Setting phoneNumber on the JavaBeans property");
        try {
            person.setPhoneNumber("888-555-1212");
        } catch (PropertyVetoException e) {
            System.out.println("A JavaBeans property change is vetoed.");
        }
        System.out.println("person.getPhoneNumber() = " + person.getPhoneNumber());
    }
}
```

In the adaptJavaBeanProperty() method, we instantiated a Person bean and adapted its name JavaBeans property into a JavaFX JavaBeanStringProperty. To help you understand when a ChangeEvent is delivered to the nameProperty, we added a ChangeListener (in the form of a lambda expression) to it. Because name is not a bound property, when we call person.setName(), the nameProperty is not aware of the change. To notify nameProperty of the change, we call its fireValueChangedEvent() method. When we call nameProperty.get(), we get the name that we have set on the person bean. Conversely, after we call nameProperty.set(), a call to person.getName() will return what we have set on nameProperty.

In the adaptBoundProperty() method, we instantiated a Person bean and adapted its address JavaBeans property into a JavaFX JavaBeanStringProperty. To help you understand when a ChangeEvent is delivered to the addressProperty, we added a ChangeListener (in the form of a lambda expression) to it. Because address is a bound property, the addressProperty is registered as a PropertyChangeListener to the person bean; therefore when we call person.setAddress(), the addressProperty is notified immediately without us having to call the fireValuechangedEvent() method.

In the adaptConstrainedProperty() method, we instantiated a Person bean and adapted its phoneNumber JavaBeans property into a JavaBeanStringProperty. Again we added a ChangeListener to it. Because phoneNumber is a constrained property, phoneNumberProperty is capable of vetoing person.setPhoneNumber() calls. When that happens, the person.setPhoneNumber() call throws a PropertyVetoException. The phoneNumberProperty will veto such a change if it is itself bound to another JavaFX property. We call person.setPhoneNumber() twice, once before we bind phoneNumberProperty to another JavaFX property, and once after phoneNumberProperty is bound. The first call succeeds in altering the value of the phoneNumberProperty, and the second call throws a PropertyVetoException.

When we run the program in Listing 4-17, the following output is printed to the console:

```
Setting name on the JavaBeans property
Calling fireValueChange
JavaFX property StringProperty [bean: Person@776ec8df, name: name, value: Weiqi Gao] changed:
        oldValue = null, newValue = Weiqi Gao
nameProperty.get() = Weiqi Gao
Setting value on the JavaFX property
JavaFX property StringProperty [bean: Person@776ec8df, name: name, value: Johan Vos] changed:
        oldValue = Weiqi Gao, newValue = Johan Vos
person.getName() = Johan Vos

Setting address on the JavaBeans property
JavaFX property StringProperty [bean: Person@41629346, name: address, value: 12345 main Street]
changed:
        oldValue = null, newValue = 12345 main Street
```

```
Setting phoneNumber on the JavaBeans property
JavaFX property StringProperty [bean: Person@6d311334, name: phoneNumber, value: 800-555-1212]
changed:
        oldValue = null, newValue = 800-555-1212
Bind phoneNumberProperty to another property
JavaFX property StringProperty [bean: Person@6d311334, name: phoneNumber, value: 866-555-1212]
changed:
        oldValue = 800-555-1212, newValue = 866-555-1212
Setting phoneNumber on the JavaBeans property
A JavaBeans property change is vetoed.
person.getPhoneNumber() = 866-555-1212
```

Summary

In this chapter, you learned the fundamentals of the JavaFX properties and bindings framework and the JavaFX Beans specification. You should now understand the following important principles.

- JavaFX properties and bindings framework properties and bindings are the fundamental workhorses of the framework.
- They conform to the key interfaces of the framework.
- They fire two kinds of events: invalidation event and change event.
- All properties and bindings provided by the JavaFX properties and bindings framework recalculate their values lazily, only when a value is requested. To force them into eager reevaluation, attach a `ChangeListener` to them.
- New bindings are created out of existing properties and bindings in one of three ways: using the factory methods of the `Bindings` utility class, using the fluent interface API, or directly extending the `IntegerBinding` series of abstract classes.
- The JavaFX Beans specification uses three methods to define a property: the getter, the setter, and the property getter.
- JavaFX Beans properties can be implemented through the eager, half-lazy, and full-lazy strategies.
- Old-style JavaBeans properties can be adapted easily to JavaFX properties.

Resources

Here are some useful resources for understanding properties and bindings:

- *Martin Fowler's write-up on fluent interface APIs:* `http://www.martinfowler.com/bliki/FluentInterface.html`
- *The Properties and Binding tutorial at* `Oracle's JavaFX.com` *site:* `http://docs.oracle.com/javase/8/javafx/properties-binding-tutorial/`
- *Michael Heinrichs's blog includes entries on JavaFX properties and bindings:* `http://blog.netopyr.com/`

CHAPTER 5

■ ■ ■

Building Dynamic UI Layouts in JavaFX

When I am working on a problem, I never think about beauty. I think only of how to solve the problem. But when I have finished, if the solution is not beautiful, I know it is wrong.

—Buckminster Fuller

JavaFX has facilities for creating dynamic layouts that allow you to easily create beautiful-looking UIs that scale to any resolution and are backed by clean code. At your disposal you have the simple, yet elegant, binding facility; powerful custom layouts built on top of the `Pane` and `Region` classes; and the built-in layouts that include `HBox`, `VBox`, `AnchorPane`, `BorderPane`, `FlowPane`, `TilePane`, `StackPane`, `GridPane`, and `TextFlow`.

In this chapter we show how you can leverage these dynamic layout mechanisms to build complicated UIs with zero static positioning.

Introducing JavaFX Reversi

To demonstrate the power of dynamic layout in JavaFX, the goal of this chapter is to build a fully functional version of the popular Reversi game. Reversi is a game of strategy where players take turns on an eight-by-eight game board placing black and white pieces. The objective of the game is to have the most pieces on the board by surrounding your opponent's pieces and flipping them over to your color.

Originally invented in 1880 by Lewis Waterman and James Mollett, Reversi gained considerable popularity in nineteenth-century England, and was one of the first titles published by German game manufacturer Ravensburger. It is more commonly known today as Othello, which is trademarked and sold by Pressman.

The rules of Reversi are extremely simple, which lets us focus on the JavaFX layout. To make things a little more challenging, we are going to bring Reversi into the twenty-first century with a modern RIA-style interface and fully resizable layout.

Board Layout and Basic Rules

Reversi is a turn-based game where two players choose white and black sides. Each player gets 32 pieces to play; the first player is black.

The initial board setup has four pieces placed in alternating cells in the center of the board (see Figure 5-1).

Figure 5-1. *This is the starting board position for Reversi*

Black gets the first turn and can place a piece anywhere adjacent to one of white's pieces where there is a matching black piece on the same line (vertical, horizontal, or diagonal). From the starting position, there are only four legal moves, which are highlighted in Figure 5-1. All moves are equal position-wise, so let's assume that black goes in the uppermost position. This allows black to flip the upper white piece, taking that entire column (see Figure 5-2).

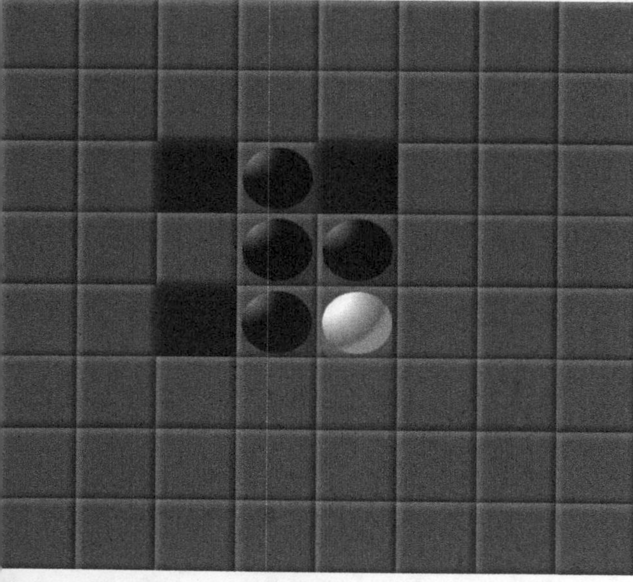

Figure 5-2. *The board position after black's first move*

White gets the second turn and has three available options highlighted in Figure 5-2. Let's assume white goes in the lowermost position, flipping one black piece. Now it is black's turn again with five available positions (shown in Figure 5-3).

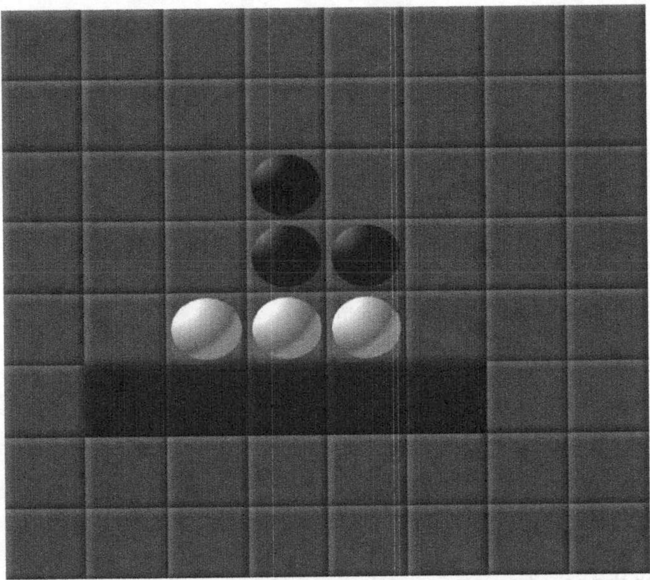

Figure 5-3. *The board position after the next move by white*

Play continues this way, alternating between black and white unless one player has no moves, in which case they pass on that turn. The game is over when both players have no moves, and the winner is the player with the most pieces on the final board.

Building a JavaFX Model for Reversi

Now that you are armed with knowledge of how Reversi works, it is time to translate that into a set of Java classes that represent the game model.

Your `ReversiModel` class needs to contain two primary pieces of information: the current board position and the player whose turn it is. Listing 5-1 shows a basic model class to get you started.

Listing 5-1. `ReversiModel` Class for the Reversi Application

```
public class ReversiModel {
  public static int BOARD_SIZE = 8;

  public ObjectProperty<Owner> turn = new SimpleObjectProperty<>(Owner.BLACK);

  public ObjectProperty<Owner>[][] board = new ObjectProperty[BOARD_SIZE][BOARD_SIZE];

  private ReversiModel() {
    for (int i = 0; i < BOARD_SIZE; i++) {
      for (int j = 0; j < BOARD_SIZE; j++) {
        board[i][j] = new SimpleObjectProperty<>(Owner.NONE);
      }
```

```
    }
    initBoard();
  }

  public static ReversiModel getInstance() {
    return ReversiModelHolder.INSTANCE;
  }

  private static class ReversiModelHolder {
    private static final ReversiModel INSTANCE = new ReversiModel();
  }
}
```

There are a few things to point out about this model.

- It uses the Java singleton pattern for creating and providing access to an instance.
- The board size is defined via a constant, which makes it easy to adjust the dimensions in the future.
- The turn variable is declared as an observable object property so that we can make use of it in bind statements.
- The board is declared as a two-dimensional array containing observable object properties, allowing binding to the current game state.
- The model references an `Owner` class for both the board contents and the current turn.

Next we need to define the `Owner` enumeration that is used in the `ReversiModel`. As shown in the following code, you can define the `Owner` class as a Java enum that contains states for `WHITE`, `BLACK`, and, in the case of empty cells, `NONE`.

```
public enum Owner {
  NONE,
  WHITE,
  BLACK;

  public Owner opposite() {
    return this == WHITE ? BLACK : this == BLACK ? WHITE : NONE;
  }

  public Color getColor() {
    return this == Owner.WHITE ? Color.WHITE : Color.BLACK;
  }

  public String getColorStyle() {
    return this == Owner.WHITE ? "white" : "black";
  }
}
```

This enumeration class contains a few extra helper functions that we make use of later. The first is called `opposite()` and can be used to convert from black to white and vice versa, which is very useful for swapping turns and implementing the game algorithm later. The next two methods return a color as either a JavaFX Color object or a style `String` for use within style properties in the UI.

The final step is to initialize our model to the starting position for a Reversi game. The following implementation of the initBoard() method places the first four pieces in the center of the board.

```
private void initBoard() {
  int center1 = BOARD_SIZE / 2 - 1;
  int center2 = BOARD_SIZE /2;
  board[center1][center1].setValue(Owner.WHITE);
  board[center1][center2].setValue(Owner.BLACK);
  board[center2][center1].setValue(Owner.BLACK);
  board[center2][center2].setValue(Owner.WHITE);
}
```

We come back to the model later, but let's switch over to building out the Reversi UI by using some of the basic dynamic layout mechanisms in JavaFX.

Dynamic Layout Techniques

JavaFX provides a wide variety of layouts that are suitable for different tasks. They range from the versatile bind to the freeform Pane and Region, which allow you to create an entirely new layout on the fly. There is also a large set of built-in layouts, including HBox, VBox, AnchorPane, BorderPane, StackPane, TilePane, FlowPane, and GridPane, that can be composed to accomplish sophisticated layouts.

To demonstrate this, we show how you can build a UI shell for the Reversi application that has absolutely no static positioned components and that supports dynamic resizing.

Centering Text Using Bind

One of the most powerful facilities in JavaFX is the ability to bind variables. Earlier we showed how binding could be used to keep the UI and model in sync with no complicated events or listeners.

Another very powerful use of binding is to keep UI components in alignment by binding to their location and size. This technique can be used to align components to the edges of a window, keep nodes in relative alignment with each other, or center them inside a container, which is what we show in this example.

To accomplish this, you need to make use of several properties and methods of the Node class in combination with bind. The common Node members that you need to use when creating bound layouts are listed in Table 5-1.

To demonstrate, Listing 5-2 is a simple code example that shows how to center the "JavaFX Reversi" title within a Scene.

Table 5-1. *Node Variables Commonly Used in Bind Layouts*

Access	Name	Type/Return	Description
public	layoutXProperty	DoubleProperty	Horizontal offset of the Node for layout positioning
public	layoutYProperty	DoubleProperty	Vertical offset of the Node for layout positioning
public	prefWidth(double)	Double	Preferred width of the Node (when given the passed-in height for nodes with a vertical content bias)
public	prefHeight(double)	Double	Preferred height of the Node (when given the passed-in width for nodes with a horizontal content bias)

Listing 5-2. Example of Centering Text in a Scene

```
public class CenterUsingBind extends Application {

  public static void main(String[] args) {
    launch(args);
  }

  @Override
  public void start(Stage primaryStage) {
    Text text = new Text("JavaFX Reversi");
    text.setTextOrigin(VPos.TOP);
    text.setFont(Font.font(null, FontWeight.BOLD, 18));
    Scene scene = new Scene(new Group(text), 400, 100);
    text.layoutXProperty().bind(scene.widthProperty().subtract(text.prefWidth(-1)).divide(2));
    text.layoutYProperty().bind(scene.heightProperty().subtract(text.prefHeight(-1)).divide(2));
    primaryStage.setScene(scene);
    primaryStage.show();
  }
}
```

Here are some specific points to highlight about Listing 5-2:

- The default value for the `textOrigin` property of `Text` is `BASELINE`, which aligns to the bottom of the letters, not including descenders. We chose to use `TOP` instead, which makes the origin line up with the top of the letters. This makes `Text` behave similarly to most other `Nodes`, and is much easier to center.

- We have to add the `Text` node to a `Group` to add it to the `Scene`, which expects a container of type `Parent`. There are better options than using a `Group`, as we show in the next section, because this disables any automatic resizing.

- When getting the `prefWidth` and `prefHeight` we pass in a parameter of -1 for the counterdimension, because this does not affect the returned dimensions for `Text` nodes. (`Text` nodes have no content bias.)

Running this program produces a window where the title stays centered even if you resize the frame, as shown in Figure 5-4.

Figure 5-4. *A* `Text` *node centered within a* `Scene` *using bind*

Centering Revisited Using a StackPane

In the previous section you saw how to center text using the bind operator. That is one way to center text, but we show you an alternative approach using the StackPane class, which has built-in capabilities for aligning nodes.

The StackPane class is a layout container that allows you to layer nodes on top of each other to create composite effects. For all the nodes in a StackPane to be visible, the upper nodes must be shaped or transparent so that it is possible to see through them. Table 5-2 lists some of the functions that you can use to add and align nodes in a StackPane.

Table 5-2. *Functions on the StackPane Layout Class*

Name	Defined In	Description
setAlignment(Pos)	StackPane	Sets the default alignment of nodes added to a StackPane
setAlignment(Node, Pos)	StackPane	Static function to set the alignment for a given node when added to a StackPane
getChildren():ObservableList<Node>	Pane	A sequence of children that will be stacked from back to front

The order of the children in the content sequence controls the z-order of the StackPane, with the first element (index 0) appearing on the bottom and the last (index size -1) on the top. The setAlignment functions can be used to control the alignment of nodes that do not fill all the available space in the StackPane. When the node alignment is set, that gets precedence; otherwise the default alignment for the StackPane is used. Finally, if neither is set, a default value of CENTER is used to align nodes.

To build on the previous example, we invert the text and background by adding a black Ellipse to the scene that covers most of the background and by changing the color of the Text node to white. Also, to simplify the alignment and allow layering of nodes, we use a StackPane instead of bind to lay out the nodes, as shown in Listing 5-3.

Listing 5-3. Example of Using a StackPane to Overlay and Align Nodes

```
public class CenterUsingStack extends Application {

  public static void main(String[] args) {
    launch(args);
  }

  @Override
  public void start(Stage primaryStage) {
    Text text = new Text("JavaFX Reversi");
    text.setFont(Font.font(null, FontWeight.BOLD, 18));
    text.setFill(Color.WHITE);
    Ellipse ellipse = new Ellipse();
    StackPane stack = new StackPane();
    stack.getChildren().addAll(ellipse, text);
    Scene scene = new Scene(stack, 400, 100);
    ellipse.radiusXProperty().bind(scene.widthProperty().divide(2));
    ellipse.radiusYProperty().bind(scene.heightProperty().divide(2));
    primaryStage.setScene(scene);
    primaryStage.show();
  }
}
```

Notice that there is nothing special that we needed to do to align the Text in the window. The default alignment for nodes in a StackPane is to center them, which is exactly what we wanted to happen. Later we show how you can override this behavior on a per-layout or per-node basis.

Because a StackPane extends Parent, there is no need to wrap it in a Group when adding it to the Scene. Also, when adding a resizable container such as a StackPane to a Scene, it will automatically get resized when the window size changes. Some bindings were still required to keep the Ellipse properly sized. It is common to use bind together with layouts in this fashion.

The completed example is shown running in Figure 5-5.

***Figure 5-5.** Inverted JavaFX Reversi logo using a StackPane*

Aligning to Edges Using StackPanes and TilePanes

Using edge alignment, you can improve the title program to fit in with the Reversi theme. To emphasize the black-and-white contrast of the Reversi pieces, let's create a design where the words are alternating colors on an alternating background.

To accomplish this visual effect, you need to do the following.

1. Create a Scene that has a white background (the default).
2. Add a TilePane to the Scene to split it into a left and right half.
3. On the right side, add a Text node with "Reversi" aligned to the left.
4. On the left side, add a StackPane with a black background.
5. Add a Text node to the StackPane with "JavaFX" in white text aligned to the right.

One way of looking at this problem is that you are creating two equal-size tiles that will contain text aligned toward the center of the window. The right side is simply a Text node that is aligned to the left edge, and the left side can be accomplished using a StackPane with right-aligned Text. Rather than using a Rectangle object, which would require binding to set its dimensions, we make use of the background-color style that is a feature of the Region class that all layouts extend.

To create equal-size tiles, we use the built-in TilePane layout. This layout divides its content into equal-sized areas to fit all of its nodes. The available layout methods on TilePane are shown in Table 5-3.

Table 5-3. *Layout Methods on the TilePane Class*

Name	Default	Description
setPrefRows(int)		Number of rows used to calculate the preferred height of the TilePane
setPrefColumns(int)		Number of columns used to calculate the preferred width of the TilePane
setHGap(double)	0	Horizontal gap between the columns
setVGap(double)	0	Vertical gap between the rows
setAlignment(Pos)	TOP_LEFT	Alignment of the TilePane contents
setAlignment(Node, Pos)		Alignment of nodes added to the TilePane
setMargin(Node, Insets)		Margin used around nodes added to the TilePane
setTileAlignment(Pos)	CENTER	Default alignment of nodes added to the TilePane
setPrefTileWidth(double)	USE_COMPUTED_SIZE	Sets the preferred tile width (can be reset by setting it back to the default)
setPrefTileHeight(double)	USE_COMPUTED_SIZE	Sets the preferred tile height (can be reset by setting it back to the default)
setOrientation(Orientation)	HORIZONTAL	Direction in which the tiles should be laid out; can be either HORIZONTAL or VERTICAL
setSnapToPixel(boolean)	True	Whether or not the layout will align tiles to the pixel boundaries or use fractional tile widths

TilePane is a very versatile class with lots of options for setting the preferred tile width and height, preferred number of rows and columns, gaps between rows and columns, and the horizontal and vertical position. Most of these have reasonable defaults, such as preferredTileWidth and preferredTileHeight, that use the largest preferred width/height of all its children. Similarly, rows and columns are set automatically based on the number of tiles that fit the width and height of the TilePane.

Just like the StackPane class, TilePane also has variables for setting the default alignment and also the alignment of each individual node added. We use the latter, because we want the text aligned to the right on one side and the left on the other.

Rather than using separate horizontal and vertical positions like JavaFX 1.3, JavaFX 8 uses a single Pos enumeration that contains all the combinations. Table 5-4 lists all the possible values you can pass in where a Pos is expected.

Table 5-4. *Different Combinations for the Pos Enumeration*

Name	Description
TOP_LEFT	Aligns to the top-left of the container
TOP_CENTER	Aligns to the top-center of the container
TOP_RIGHT	Aligns to the top-right of the container
CENTER_LEFT	Aligns to the middle of the left side of the container

(*continued*)

Table 5-4. *(continued)*

Name	Description
CENTER	Aligns to the center of the container
CENTER_RIGHT	Aligns to the middle of the right side of the container
BOTTOM_LEFT	Aligns to the bottom-left of the container
BOTTOM_CENTER	Aligns to the bottom-center of the container
BOTTOM_RIGHT	Aligns to the bottom-right of the container
BASELINE_LEFT	Aligns to the left side along the baseline (bottom of text and components)
BASELINE_CENTER	Aligns to the center along the baseline (bottom of text and components)
BASELINE_RIGHT	Aligns to the right along the baseline (bottom of text and components)

We take advantage of the Pos constants of BASELINE_LEFT and BASELINE_RIGHT to align half the text to the right and the other half to the left, as shown in Listing 5-4.

Listing 5-4. Example Showing How to Use a TilePane and StackPane to Align Nodes

```
public class AlignUsingStackAndTile extends Application {

  public static void main(String[] args) {
    launch(args);
  }

  @Override
  public void start(Stage primaryStage) {
    StackPane left = new StackPane();
    left.setStyle("-fx-background-color: black");
    Text text = new Text("JavaFX");
    text.setFont(Font.font(null, FontWeight.BOLD, 18));
    text.setFill(Color.WHITE);
    StackPane.setAlignment(text, Pos.BASELINE_RIGHT);
    left.getChildren().add(text);
    Text right = new Text("Reversi");
    right.setFont(Font.font(null, FontWeight.BOLD, 18));
    TilePane tiles = new TilePane();
    tiles.setSnapToPixel(false);
    TilePane.setAlignment(right, Pos.BASELINE_LEFT);
    tiles.getChildren().addAll(left, right);
    Scene scene = new Scene(tiles, 400, 100);
    left.prefWidthProperty().bind(scene.widthProperty().divide(2));
    left.prefHeightProperty().bind(scene.heightProperty());
    primaryStage.setScene(scene);
    primaryStage.show();
  }
```

The completed layout makes use of a TilePane for splitting the background, a StackPane for layering nodes, and binding to make the contents resize with the Scene. To prevent wrapping artifacts on fractional tile sizes, we set the snapToPixels property to false. This allows fractional tile widths and prevents rounding errors from causing our layout to wrap to the next line.

The end result is that the layout resizes correctly when the size of the Scene is changed, including the StackPane with a black background, which always occupies half the area, as shown in Figure 5-6.

***Figure 5-6.** Result of running the node alignment example*

Using FlowPane and Boxes for Directional Alignment

In the previous sections we showed how you can use StackPane and TilePane to create dynamic nested UIs, but what if you simply want to arrange nodes along a vertical or horizontal line? This is where the directional layouts, HBox, VBox, and FlowPane, come in. They allow you to lay out a string of nodes at their preferred size with or without wrapping.

To demonstrate directional node alignment, we show you how to implement the next piece of the Reversi UI: the player score box. There are two score boxes for the players, each with very similar content:

- *Score:* The number of pieces of the player's color on the board
- *Player Color:* The color of the player's pieces
- *Turns Remaining:* The number of turns remaining

Before starting on the UI, this is a good time to flush out the model with additional methods to capture these requirements. Listing 5-5 shows an example implementation of getScore and getTurnsRemaining that returns exactly what we need to populate the player score box UI.

Listing 5-5. Additional Model Methods to Implement Player Score Back End

```
public NumberExpression getScore(Owner owner) {
  NumberExpression score = new SimpleIntegerProperty();
  for (int i = 0; i < BOARD_SIZE; i++) {
    for (int j = 0; j < BOARD_SIZE; j++) {
      score = score.add(Bindings.when(board[i][j].isEqualTo(owner)).then(1).otherwise(0));
    }
  }
  return score;
}

public NumberBinding getTurnsRemaining(Owner owner) {
  NumberExpression emptyCellCount = getScore(Owner.NONE);
  return Bindings.when(turn.isEqualTo(owner))
    .then(emptyCellCount.add(1).divide(2))
    .otherwise(emptyCellCount.divide(2));
}
```

Some points to highlight about Listing 5-5 include the following:

- Both `getScore` and `getTurnsRemaining` return bindings that will automatically recalculate their values when the turn and board state change.
- The `getScore` method uses a `SimpleIntegerProperty` as a bound aggregator to sum the total number of cells belonging to the owner.
- The `getTurnsRemainingMethod` uses a conditional binding and bound arithmetic to calculate the number of remaining turns for a given owner.

Now that we have the model functions created, we can use them to build a JavaFX UI class that shows each player's score. Because we need to create the same UI components twice, this is a good time to raise the abstraction level of the UI by creating functions that create portions of the UI. This lets us reuse the same score box for both players.

Listing 5-6 has the first half of the code and shows how to set up a simple two-column `TilePane` layout that contains the player score boxes.

Listing 5-6. First Half of Player Score Implementation

```
@Override
public void start(Stage primaryStage) {
    TilePane tiles = new TilePane(createScore(Owner.BLACK), createScore(Owner.WHITE));
    tiles.setSnapToPixel(false);
    Scene scene = new Scene(tiles, 600, 120);
    primaryStage.setScene(scene);
    tiles.prefTileWidthProperty().bind(scene.widthProperty().divide(2));
    tiles.prefTileHeightProperty().bind(scene.heightProperty());
    primaryStage.show();

}
```

Notice that we have explicitly bound the `tileWidth` and `tileHeight`. This ensures that the tiles resize together with the window. Also notice that we have bound against the scene's width and height rather than the tile's dimensions. Binding against the parent's width works properly, because the bind update happens synchronously, whereas binding against your own width and height will happen after layout is complete and produce artifacts.

For the second half, you need to use the `HBox`, `VBox`, and `FlowPane` classes. Table 5-5 shows a list of all the variables available, and to which layouts they apply.

Table 5-5. *List of Variables for HBox, VBox, and FlowPane*

Name	Type	Default	Found in	Description
hpos	HPos	HPos.LEFT	HBox, VBox, FlowPane	Horizontal position of the entire layout
vpos	VPos	VPos.TOP	HBox, VBox, FlowPane	Vertical position of the entire layout
nodeHPos	HPos	HPos.LEFT, HPos.CENTER	VBox, FlowPane	Default horizontal alignment of nodes
nodeVPos	VPos	HPos.TOP, HPos.CENTER	HBox, FlowPane	Default vertical alignment of nodes
spacing	Number	0	HBox, VBox	Space between nodes in the direction of layout
hgap	Number	0	FlowPane	Horizontal gap between the rows
vgap	Number	0	FlowPane	Vertical gap between the columns
vertical	Boolean	false	FlowPane	True if this FlowPane runs top-to-bottom, false for left-to-right

The main difference between HBox/VBox and FlowPane is that the FlowPane layout will wrap when it reaches the container width for horizontal layouts and container height for vertical layouts, whereas HBox and VBox always retain their orientation.

Listing 5-7 shows the implementation of the createScore method, which takes the model functions you wrote earlier and turns them into a visual representation.

Listing 5-7. Implementation of createScore Method Using Directional Alignment

```
private StackPane createScore(Owner owner) {
    Region background;
    Ellipse piece = new Ellipse(32, 20);
    piece.setFill(owner.getColor());
    DropShadow pieceEffect = new DropShadow();
    pieceEffect.setColor(Color.DODGERBLUE);
    pieceEffect.setSpread(.2);
    piece.setEffect(pieceEffect);

    Text score = new Text();
    score.setFont(Font.font(null, FontWeight.BOLD, 100));
    score.setFill(owner.getColor());
    Text remaining = new Text();
    remaining.setFont(Font.font(null, FontWeight.BOLD, 12));
    remaining.setFill(owner.getColor());
    VBox remainingBox = new VBox(10, piece, remaining);
    remainingBox.setAlignment(Pos.CENTER);
    FlowPane flowPane = new FlowPane(20, 10, score, remainingBox);
    flowPane.setAlignment(Pos.CENTER);
    background = new Region();
    background.setStyle("-fx-background-color: " + owner.opposite().getColorStyle());
    ReversiModel model = ReversiModel.getInstance();
    StackPane stack = new StackPane(background, flowPane);
    stack.setPrefHeight(1000);
    InnerShadow innerShadow = new InnerShadow();
    innerShadow.setColor(Color.DODGERBLUE);
    innerShadow.setChoke(.5);
    background.effectProperty().bind(Bindings.when(model.turn.isEqualTo(owner))
            .then(innerShadow)
            .otherwise((InnerShadow) null));
    DropShadow dropShadow = new DropShadow();
    dropShadow.setColor(Color.DODGERBLUE);
    dropShadow.setSpread(.2);

    piece.effectProperty().bind(Bindings.when(model.turn.isEqualTo(owner))
            .then(dropShadow)
            .otherwise((DropShadow) null));
    score.textProperty().bind(model.getScore(owner).asString());
    remaining.textProperty().bind(model.getTurnsRemaining(owner).asString().concat(" turns remaining"));
    return stack;
}
```

Notice that we used a FlowPane as the outer layout and a VBox inside to keep the Ellipse and Text vertically aligned. This ensures that the Ellipse will always stay on top of the Text but still allows the display to wrap into a vertical layout if horizontal screen real estate is limited.

We use binding both to enable and disable the special effects (DropShadow and InnerShadow) that highlight the current player's turn, as well as to dynamically update the text based on the model. This is a very powerful use of binding that keeps the UI in sync with the game state without requiring the use of event listeners or imperative callbacks.

The result of running the program for a horizontal layout is shown in Figure 5-7, and the resized vertical layout is shown in Figure 5-8.

Figure 5-7. Output of running the Player Score Example in a horizontally sized window

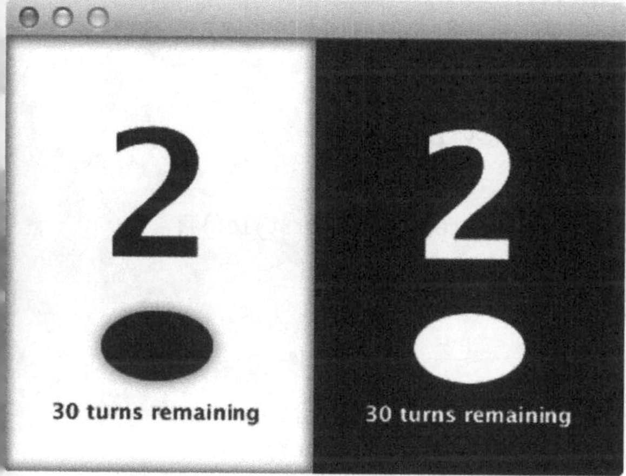

Figure 5-8. Output of running the Player Score Example in a vertically sized window

Although it might be surprising that the starting score is not zero, if you remember the Reversi starting position, there are four pieces in the center of the board, which gives each player two points. Also, the sum of all the scores and turns remaining should always add up to 64, which is true in this case.

The next step is to combine the logo and score using a BorderPane to build the minimal shell for the Reversi application.

Composing a Layout Using BorderPane

We have built up several elements of the Reversi UI, and now we need to tie them together into a single composition. In this section we demonstrate how you can use the BorderPane class to quickly put together other components in a common layout pattern. Unlike the layouts used earlier in this chapter, you should not modify the BorderPane's list of children, but instead use the properties for each of the content areas listed in Table 5-6.

***Table 5-6.** Properties Available in the `BorderPanel` Class*

Name	Type	Description
`top`	`Node`	Element placed at the top edge of the `BorderPane` area; will be resized to its preferred height and extended to fill the full width
`bottom`	`Node`	Element placed at the bottom edge of the `BorderPane` area; will be resized to its preferred height and extended to fill the full width
`left`	`Node`	Element placed at the left edge of the `BorderPane` area; will be resized to its preferred width and extended to fill the full height between the top and bottom nodes
`right`	`Node`	Element placed at the right edge of the `BorderPane` area; will be resized to its preferred width and extended to fill the full height between the top and bottom nodes
`center`	`Node`	Element placed in the center of the `BorderPane` area; will be extended to fill the full space between the top, bottom, right, and left nodes

The `BorderPane`'s top and bottom areas get positioned first, followed by the left and right, which can extend up to the height minus the top and bottom. Finally the center resizes to take any remaining space in the layout.

For our use in the Reversi application, we require only the top, center, and bottom content areas. The layout code to set up the `BorderPane` with these three content areas is shown in Listing 5-8.

Listing 5-8. Reversi Root Stage Declaration Using a `BorderPane` for Layout

```
@Override
public void start(Stage primaryStage) {
        BorderPane root = new BorderPane();
        root.setCenter(createBackground());
        root.setTop(createTitle());
        root.setBottom(createScoreBoxes());
        Scene scene = new Scene(root, 600, 400);
        primaryStage.setScene(scene);
        primaryStage.show();
}
```

We are using this to create a dock-like behavior where the title is aligned to the top with a fixed height and the score boxes are aligned to the bottom, also with a fixed height. All remaining space in the center is occupied by the grid. This could also have been done using bind expressions, but using a `BorderPane` guarantees that the layout function will be called once per layout cycle, yielding higher performance and artifact-free layout.

Listing 5-9 shows a simple abstraction of a `createScoreBoxes()` function from the section "Using `FlowPane` and Boxes for Directional Alignment," earlier in this chapter. Notice that the `tileWidth` is dynamically bound to the parent width using the `Bindings.selectDouble()` function, which breaks the dependency on the scene.

Listing 5-9. Create Score Boxes Function

```
private Node createScoreBoxes() {
        TilePane scoreTiles = new TilePane(createScore(Owner.BLACK), createScore(Owner.WHITE));
        scoreTiles.setSnapToPixel(false);
        scoreTiles.setPrefColumns(2);
        scoreTiles.prefTileWidthProperty().bind(Bindings.selectDouble(tiles.parentProperty(),
        "width").divide(2));
        return scoreTiles;
}
```

Implementing createTitle is a similar modification of the Scene definition from the earlier section "Aligning to Edges Using StackPanes and TilePanes." In this case we have also increased the preferred height of the title to give it a little padding around the text. The additional changes required are highlighted in bold in Listing 5-10.

Listing 5-10. Changes Required to the Title Creation Code to Turn It into a Function

```
private Node createTitle() {
  StackPane left = new StackPane();
    left.setStyle("-fx-background-color: black");
    Text text = new Text("JavaFX");
    text.setFont(Font.font(null, FontWeight.BOLD, 18));
    text.setFill(Color.WHITE);
    StackPane.setAlignment(text, Pos.CENTER_RIGHT);
    left.getChildren().add(text);
    Text right = new Text("Reversi");
    right.setFont(Font.font(null, FontWeight.BOLD, 18));
    titleTiles = new TilePane();
    titleTiles.setSnapToPixel(false);
    TilePane.setAlignment(right, Pos.CENTER_LEFT);
    titleTiles.getChildren().addAll(left, right);
    titleTiles.setPrefTileHeight(40);
    titleTiles.prefTileWidthProperty().bind(Bindings.selectDouble(tiles.parentProperty(),
    "width").divide(2));
    return titleTiles;
}
```

The final task is to create the board background by implementing createBackground(). In the "Laying Out the Tiles Using a GridPane" section later in this chapter, we show you how to use a GridPane to implement the Reversi board, but for now you can simply create a Region and fill it with a RadialGradient. RadialGradients are very similar to the LinearGradients you have created in past exercises, but will render the colors in an ellipse from the center outward. Because we are using the Region to create the background, we need to configure the RadialGradient using the style property, as shown in Listing 5-11.

Listing 5-11. Bound Function to Create the Reversi Board Background

```
private Node createBackground() {
    Region answer = new Region();
    answer.setStyle("-fx-background-color: radial-gradient(radius 100%, white, gray)");
    return answer;
}
```

When you run the complete program, you should see a window that looks like Figure 5-9.

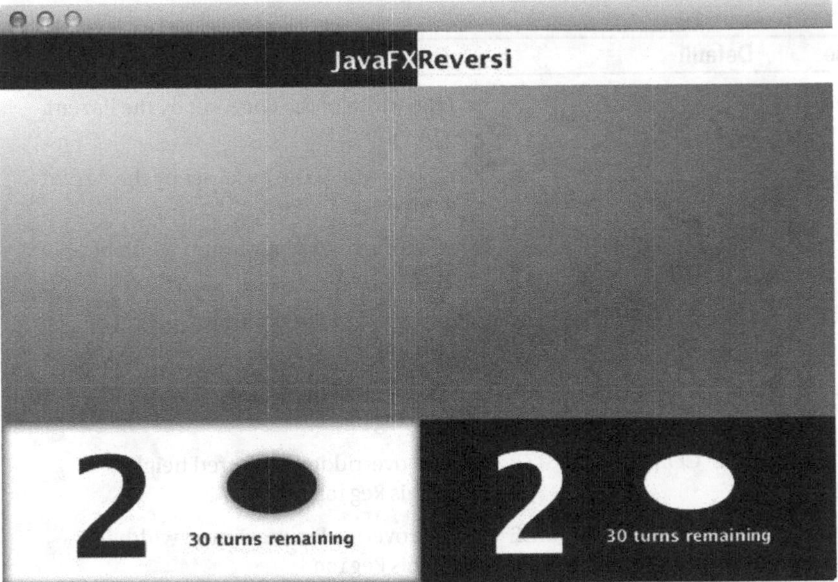

***Figure 5-9.** Reversi user interface with title, background, and scores*

Try resizing the window and notice that the BorderPanel keeps the components' edge aligned and automatically resizes them to fill all available space. This combined example demonstrates how bind and the built-in layouts can be used to compose dynamic layouts in JavaFX easily.

Creating Custom Regions

In previous sections we have made use of the Region class to provide simple styled backgrounds for our application, but the Region class underlies all of the JavaFX layouts and is capable of much more than just this.

In this section we show you how to create custom Regions in JavaFX that are fully resizable to build the Reversi playing pieces and squares that make up the game board. In the following section we show you how to build dynamic containers from scratch to take these resizable nodes and use the final layout, GridPane, to construct a dynamic playing board that resizes both the squares and the playing pieces.

Building a Custom Square Region

The foundation class of all the JavaFX layouts is the Region. It has standard functions on it to get bounds preferences for layout and also variables to set the width and height of the Node. In this section we show you how you can build a Reversi board square that dynamically responds to height and width changes by extending Region. The Region class has ten properties that you can use to control the dimensions and layout, as shown in Table 5-7.

Table 5-7. *Properties of the Region Class*

Name	Access	Type	Default	Description
width	Read-only	Double		The width of the Node, set by the Parent container
height	Read-only	Double		The height of the Node, set by the Parent container
minWidth	Read/write	Double	USE_COMPUTED_SIZE	The overridden minimum width of this Region
minHeight	Read/write	Double	USE_COMPUTED_SIZE	The overridden minimum height of this Region
prefWidth	Read/write	Double	USE_COMPUTED_SIZE	The overridden preferred width of this Region
prefHeight	Read/write	Double	USE_COMPUTED_SIZE	The overridden preferred height of this Region
maxWidth	Read/write	Double	USE_COMPUTED_SIZE	The overridden maximum width of this Region
maxHeight	Read/write	Double	USE_COMPUTED_SIZE	The overridden maximum height of this Region
padding	Read/write	Insets	Insets.EMPTY	The amount of space requested on the top, bottom, left, and right of this Region
snapToPixel	Read/write	Boolean	True	If true, will round off the position and size of the Region to integral values

The width and height of a Region are read-only properties that you can use to get the size after layout is complete. Be careful binding directly to the width and height, because any changes that affect the size of this node or its children will not be updated until the next layout cycle, causing artifacts.

The padding property lets you set the amount of space to surround the content of the region during layout. Again, we use the snapToPixel property before to make sure the TilePane fits within the scene boundaries with no rounding errors. It is defined on the Region class and the default value of true will help reduce artifacts caused by pixel misalignment.

The remaining properties let you override the min, max, and pref width and height of this Region. They are hints to the Parent about how it should allocate space, and default to the calculated value for this Region. Once set, these properties can be reset to their calculated values by giving them a value of Region.USE_COMPUTED_SIZE. Also, the min and max properties can be assigned to the same value as the respective pref property by giving them a value of Region.USE_PREF_SIZE.

To define the calculated values for these, override the calculate* functions defined on the Region class as listed in Table 5-8.

Table 5-8. *Functions of the Region Class*

Name	Access	Returns	Description
computeMinWidth(height)	Protected	Double	Returns the computed minimum width of this Region. The default is the sum of the left and right insets.
computeMinHeight(width)	Protected	Double	Returns the computed minimum height of the Region. The default is the sum of the top and bottom insets.
computePrefWidth(height)	Protected	Double	Returns the computed preferred width of the Region. The default is the sum of the left and right insets plus the width needed to hold the children when given their preferred location and size.
computePrefHeight(width)	Protected	Double	Returns the computed preferred height of this Region. The default is the sum of the top and bottom insets plus the height needed to hold the children when given their preferred location and size.
computeMaxWidth(height)	Protected	Double	Returns the computed maximum width of this Region. The default is Double.MAX_VALUE.
computeMaxHeight(width)	Protected	Double	Returns the computed maximum height of this Region. The default is Double.MAX_VALUE.

The defaults returned by the compute functions are fine, except for the preferred width and height, which both return 0 because we have no children and no insets. To get a nonzero preferred size, we can either override the computePrefWidth/Height methods or simply call one of the setters for the preferredWidth/Height properties. The following implementation does the latter.

```
public class ReversiSquare extends Region {
  public ReversiSquare() {
    setStyle("-fx-background-color: burlywood");
    Light.Distant light = new Light.Distant();
    light.setAzimuth(-135);
    light.setElevation(30);
    setEffect(LightingBuilder.create().light(light).build());
    setPrefSize(200, 200);
  }
}
```

To provide styling to the squares in the preceding code, we set the style property, which accepts CSS properties for the background and borders. Because you cannot specify JavaFX lighting effects in CSS, we use the LightingBuilder to create a distant lighting effect and set it on the Region.

■ **Caution** On platforms without hardware acceleration of effects, the Lighting effect could significantly affect performance.

To exercise this class, we create a quick StackPane wrapper holding a single ReversiSquare that resizes with the scene, as shown in Listing 5-12.

Listing 5-12. Wrapper Script to Show a ReversiSquare That Resizes with the Scene

```
public class ReversiSquareTest extends Application {
  public static void main(String[] args) {
    launch(args);
  }

  @Override
  public void start(Stage primaryStage) {
        Scene scene = new Scene(new StackPane(new ReversiSquare()));
        primaryStage.setScene(scene);
        primaryStage.show();
  }
}
```

Running the completed class produces a distinctive board square that dynamically resizes with the window, as shown in Figure 5-10.

Figure 5-10. *Single Reversi square that resizes with the window*

Building a Resizable Reversi Piece

Creating a Reversi playing piece is done very similarly to how you created a square in the previous section. Your class should extend Region and have a public owner property that can be set to change the color of the playing piece to either WHITE or BLACK:

```
public class ReversiPiece extends Region {
  private ObjectProperty<Owner> ownerProperty = new SimpleObjectProperty<>(this, "owner" , Owner.NONE);
  public ObjectProperty<Owner> ownerProperty() {
    return ownerProperty;
  }
  public Owner getOwner() {
    return ownerProperty.get();
  }
  public void setOwner(Owner owner) {
    ownerProperty.set(owner);
  }
```

We used the simplified property format in this example, with a SimpleObjectProperty of generic type Owner that gets created on object initialization. It has public methods to get the property or get and set the value and default to Owner.NONE, which should show no playing piece.

To create the style of the playing piece, we make use of a conditional bind in the constructor to change the style whenever the owner changes. In the case of a WHITE playing piece, we use a radial gradient that goes from white to gray to black (simulating a shadow). In the case of a BLACK playing piece, we use a radial gradient that goes from white quickly to black (simulating a highlight).

We can also hide the playing piece when the owner is NONE by using a second conditional bind to set the radius to 0. Finally to give the Region a circular shape, we set the background radius to a very large value (1,000 em), which gives us a rounded rectangle with zero length sides (or an oval) as shown in the following code at the beginning of the constructor.

```
public ReversiPiece() {
  styleProperty().bind(Bindings.when(ownerProperty.isEqualTo(Owner.NONE))
    .then("radius 0")
    .otherwise(Bindings.when(ownerProperty.isEqualTo(Owner.WHITE))
      .then("-fx-background-color: radial-gradient(radius 100%, white .4, gray .9, darkgray 1)")
      .otherwise("-fx-background-color: radial-gradient(radius 100%, white 0, black .6)"))
    .concat("; -fx-background-radius: 1000em; -fx-background-insets: 5"));
  ...
```

The constructor code continues on to set up a reflection effect that will make the playing surface seem glossy, and also sets a preferred size with enough room around the edges to match the preferred size of the square minus a five-pixel background inset. The last step is to set the playing piece to be transparent to mouse events, so that the square underneath can pick them up instead:

```
  ...
  Reflection reflection = new Reflection();
  reflection.setFraction(1);
  reflection.topOffsetProperty().bind(heightProperty().multiply(-.75));
  setEffect(reflection);
  setPrefSize(180, 180);
  setMouseTransparent(true);
}
```

For convenience we also include a constructor version that takes an initial value for the owner property:

```
public ReversiPiece(Owner owner) {
  this();
  ownerProperty.setValue(owner);
}
```

To demonstrate the finished product, you need to make a few additions to the previous sample application to overlay the Reversi piece. The easiest way to accomplish this is to refactor the Scene to use a StackPane layout to place the Reversi piece on top of the square, and put it inside an HBox so you can have side-by-side playing pieces.

We also make use of a new constraint on HBox and VBox called grow. Setting hgrow on an element added to an HBox or vgrow on an element added to a VBox lets the element expand from its preferred size to take additional space as it becomes available. For a more detailed discussion of grow and priority, see the next section on the GridPane where it is used heavily.

The completed wrapper code using stacks, boxes, and the grow constraint is shown in Listing 5-13.

Listing 5-13. Wrapper Application That Displays Two Reversi Squares Side by Side with Playing Pieces on Top

```
public class ReversiPieceTest extends Application {
  public static void main(String[] args) {
    launch(args);
  }

  @Override
  public void start(Stage primaryStage) {
    Node white = new StackPane(new ReversiSquare(), new ReversiPiece(Owner.WHITE));
    Node black = new StackPane(new ReversiSquare(), new ReversiPiece(Owner.BLACK));
    HBox hbox = new HBox(white, black);
    hbox.setSnapToPixel(false);
    primaryStage.setScene(new Scene(hbox));
    HBox.setHgrow(white, Priority.ALWAYS);
    HBox.setHgrow(black, Priority.ALWAYS);
    primaryStage.show();
  }
}
```

Figure 5-11 shows the completed application with both white and black pieces displayed side by side.

Figure 5-11. *One Reversi square with a white playing piece on it, and another with a black piece*

Laying Out the Tiles Using a `GridPane`

One of the most flexible and powerful layouts contained in JavaFX is the `GridPane`. It lets you arrange the children in a grid composed of rows and columns, optionally assigning constraints such as `alignment`, `grow`, and `margin` to individual nodes or an entire row or column. You can also do advanced layouts that will span rows or columns, giving you a layout container that is truly a superset of all the other containers discussed so far.

Table 5-9 lists the different properties of `GridPane` that you can set either per `Node` or on an entire column or row (with the exception of `margin`).

Table 5-9. *Properties Available on Nodes in a GridPane Layout*

Name	Type	Description
`halignment`	HPos	Horizontal alignment of nodes in `GridPane` cell; can be one of LEFT, CENTER, or RIGHT
`valignment`	VPos	Vertical alignment of nodes in a `GridPane` cell; can be one of TOP, CENTER, BASELINE, or BOTTOM
`hgrow`	Priority	Priority for the `GridPane` cell growing horizontally beyond its preferred side
`vgrow`	Priority	Priority for the `GridPane` cell growing vertically beyond its preferred size
`margin`	Insets	Margin surrounding the element in the `GridPane` cell, specified as an Inset with a top, left, bottom, and right stand-off
`fillWidth`	Boolean	Specifies if the node should be expanded to fit the column width, or kept at its own width
`fillHeight`	Boolean	Specifies if the node should be expanded to fit the row height, or kept at its own height

Just as with earlier layouts, these constraints can be set via a series of like-named static methods on the `GridPane` class that accept a node and constraint value. The first two constraints for alignment are similar to the `alignment` on `StackPane`, except they are constrained to be in either the horizontal or vertical direction. However, the cross-product of using horizontal and vertical alignment together gives you the same 12 combinations.

`Margin` is similar to the like-name constraint first described in the earlier section entitled, "Aligning to Edges Using `StackPanes` and `TilePanes`." It is also the only constraint that can be applied solely to individual nodes, but not an entire row or column.

Both `hgrow` and `vgrow` take a value of type `Priority`, similar to the like-name constraints on `HBox` and `VBox`, respectively. These can be given one of three possible values:

- NEVER: Will never grow beyond the preferred dimensions of the node.
- SOMETIMES: Will only grow if there is still available space after all nodes with `grow` priority "ALWAYS" are taken into account.
- ALWAYS: Will grow up to the maximum dimensions of the node, sharing space equally with other nodes that have a `grow` priority of "ALWAYS."

Setting the `grow` constraint property can greatly simplify the job of laying out complex UIs. For example, you could use a grow constraint of NEVER on a `button` and ALWAYS on a `TextField` to ensure that the text field fills the form width, and the button is sized perfectly for the contained text.

The `fillWidth` and `fillHeight` properties are useful for nodes with preferred sizes that are smaller than the allocated space in the `GridPane`. If those properties are supplied with a Boolean value of true, the container will rather use the available size instead of the preferred size to layout the node.

We take advantage of the flexible capabilities of the `GridPane` to lay out the grid of squares and pieces for the Reversi application. The default `alignment`, `grow` policy, and `margin` work perfectly for the needs of our playing board, so the only thing we need to update as we add in squares is the x and y position. We don't even need to set the size of the grid, because it will automatically scale to fit the number and position of components that get added in.

To start with, we need to update the `start` method in the Reversi application to put the tiles on top of the background. To accomplish this we make use of a `StackPane` to compose the center region of the `BorderLayout` as shown in Listing 5-14.

Listing 5-14. Changes to the Reversi Application to Overlay a List of Tiles (Highlighted in Bold)

```
@Override
public void start(Stage primaryStage) {
        BorderPane borderPane = new BorderPane();
        borderPane.setTop(createTitle());
        borderPane.setCenter(new StackPane(createBackground(), tiles()));
        borderPane.setBottom(createScoreBoxes());
        Scene scene = new Scene(borderPane, 600, 400);
        primaryStage.setScene(scene);
        primaryStage.show();
}
```

The implementation of the tiles method is a direct application of what we have learned about the GridPane layout. We simply create a new GridPane using the default constructor, and then go in a couple of loops across columns and then rows to populate each of the game cells as shown in Listing 5-15.

Listing 5-15. Implementation of the Tiles Method Using a GridPane

```
private Node tiles() {
  GridPane board = new GridPane();
  for (int i = 0; i < ReversiModel.BOARD_SIZE; i++) {
    for (int j = 0; j < ReversiModel.BOARD_SIZE; j++) {
      ReversiSquare square = new ReversiSquare();
      ReversiPiece piece = new ReversiPiece();
      piece.ownerProperty().bind(model.board[i][j]);
      board.add(new StackPane(square, piece), i, j);
    }
  }
  return board;
}
```

Notice that we are using the GridPane add method that takes a node first, and then the x, y coordinates second for convenience. Also, we are making use of a nested StackPane to hold the ReversiSquare on the bottom and the ReversiPiece on top.

The single binding from model.board to each playing piece is all that is needed to have the UI reflect the current board state and update whenever the model is changed. With these simple changes, the Reversi application shows us our starting position with two black and two white pieces played, as shown in Figure 5-12.

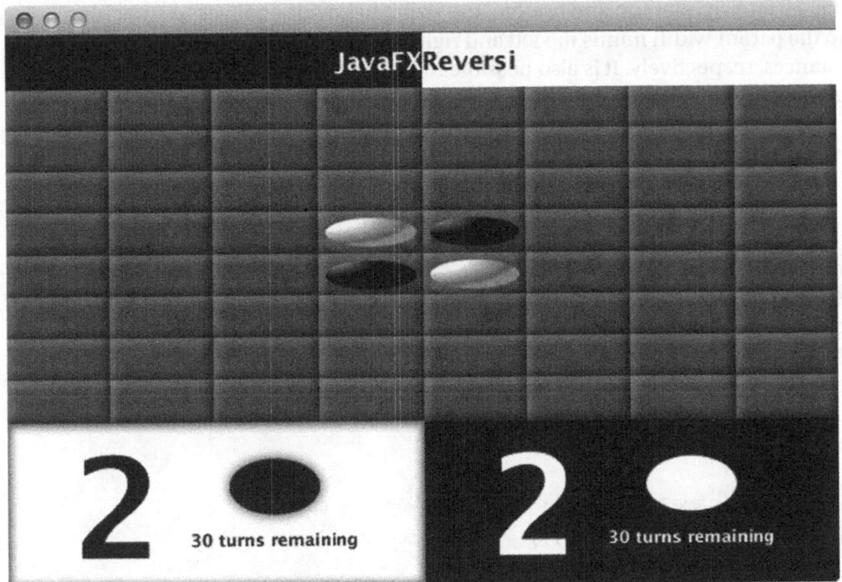

***Figure 5-12.** Reversi application with a `GridPane` to display the board and pieces*

Aligning and Stretching with AnchorPane

The last built-in layout is the AnchorPane. It is a fairly specialized layout that serves two related purposes. When used with one or two nonopposing constraints, it can be used to align the child to a particular corner of the layout with a set stand-off. The other purpose is to stretch the child horizontally, vertically, both by setting opposing constraints, again with an optional stand-off from the parent edges as shown in Figure 5-13.

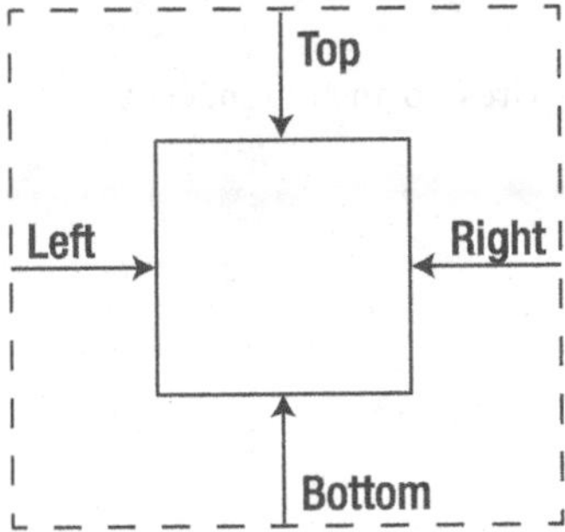

***Figure 5-13.** AnchorPane constraints for a child Node (solid line) in a `Parent` (dashed line)*

The AnchorPane works by accepting a list of children that are displayed in stack order, each of which can optionally specify constraints for left, right, top, and bottom anchors. If no anchors are specified, it will position children at the top left of the container. Once an anchor is set, it will align to a set distance away from that edge and get the minimum of the preferred size and the container size.

If opposing anchors are set on the left and right or top and bottom, the sizing behavior changes to stretching where the child width will be equal to the parent width minus the left and right anchor distances or the parent height minus the top and bottom anchor distances, respectively. It is also possible to set all four anchors, in which case the child will resize both dimensions together with the parent.

With a few modifications to the Reversi application we make use of both the alignment and stretching properties of an AnchorPane to add in a new Restart button to the UI. The first step is to refactor the Reversi constructor to extract the existing game view into a variable and add in an AnchorPane as the root node:

```
@Override
public void start(Stage primaryStage) {
        TilePane title = createTitle();
        TilePane scoreBoxes = createScoreBoxes();
        BorderPane game = new BorderPane();
        game.setTop(title);
        game.setCenter(new StackPane(createBackground(), tiles()));
        game.setBottom(scoreBoxes);
        Node restart = restart();
        AnchorPane root = new AnchorPane(game, restart);
        primaryStage.setScene(new Scene(root, 600, 400));
  ...
```

Notice that we have also added in a second component to the AnchorPane for the Restart button that we define later. The rest of the method goes on to set the AnchorPane constraints for the game and restart nodes so that the former scales together with the scene, and the latter is aligned 10 pixels off the top-right corner:

```
  ...
  AnchorPane.setTopAnchor(game, 0d);
  AnchorPane.setBottomAnchor(game, 0d);
  AnchorPane.setLeftAnchor(game, 0d);
  AnchorPane.setRightAnchor(game, 0d);
  AnchorPane.setRightAnchor(restart, 10d);
  AnchorPane.setTopAnchor(restart, 10d);
}
```

The next step is to create the restart() method that builds the Restart button and wires up an ActionEvent handler that will reset the model:

```
private Node restart() {
  Button button = new Button("Restart");
  button.setOnAction(e -> model.restart());
  return button;
}
```

Finally, you need to implement the restart model function that will restart all the squares to their initial values and set the turn back to black:

```
public void restart() {
  for (int i = 0; i < BOARD_SIZE; i++) {
    for (int j = 0; j < BOARD_SIZE; j++) {
      board[i][j].setValue(Owner.NONE);
    }
```

```
    }
    initBoard();
    turn.setValue(Owner.BLACK);
}
```

After running the completed application you will have a fully functional Restart button that is anchored to the top-right corner, as shown in Figure 5-14.

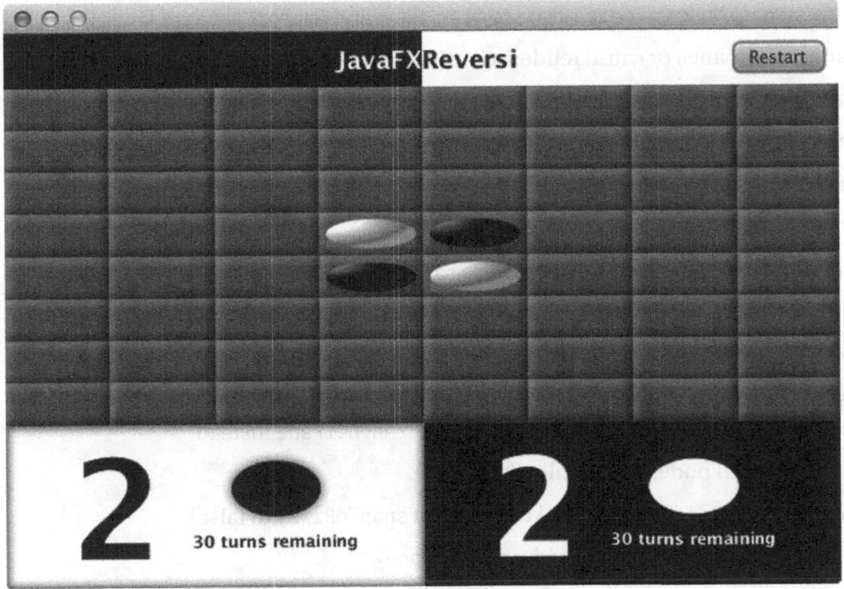

Figure 5-14. *Reversi application with a Restart button anchored to the top-right corner*

When to Use Different Layouts

The combination of different layout techniques discussed throughout this chapter creates a very powerful capability for creating dynamic layouts. However, inasmuch as there are so many ways to accomplish the same results, it can often be confusing as to what the best practice is when creating new layouts. In this section, we discuss the benefits and disadvantages of each layout in different situations to help you more easily ascertain which best suits your application needs.

Binding was the first technique described, and it is powerful enough to construct virtually any dynamic UI you can imagine. However, bind has two primary drawbacks:

- *Complexity*. The more nodes in the UI, the more edges and constraints each one must adhere to to show up in the right location.
- *Performance*. Although JavaFX is very efficient about how it evaluates bind statements, too many bound variables will result in reduced performance, and also display artifacts on resizing.

That is where the built-in layouts, `HBox`, `VBox`, `FlowPane`, `StackPane`, `TilePane`, `GridPane`, and `AnchorPane`, come in. For the common case where a series of `Nodes` are stacked horizontally or vertically, using a box layout will result in less complex code than the equivalent bind. Also, unlike bind, layout containers are evaluated only once per display cycle, so you are guaranteed consistent performance regardless of the complexity of your UI.

In practice, you usually need to use both layouts and bind together to create a dynamic layout. Table 5-10 explains for what situations each type of layout is most suitable.

Table 5-10. *When to Use Bind Versus Layouts*

Technique	Applicability
bind	Use for resizing fixed Shapes, such as Rectangles, Ellipses, and Lines.
	Easy to create layouts where Nodes overlap (also see StackPane and AnchorPane).
	Overuse can reduce performance or cause rendering artifacts.
HBox/VBox	Use for vertical or horizontal alignment of nodes.
	High performance; can be used for large number of Nodes.
	Make use of alignment and grow constraints for more complex use cases.
FlowPane	Similar to HBox/VBox in usage.
	Useful in situations where the layout should wrap lines to fit.
StackPane	Allows composition through overlapping of Nodes.
	Very useful to create layered effects such as placing text over a background.
	Be careful when stacking nodes where mouse events need to pass through. Use the mouseTransparent property on nodes or consider an AnchorPane instead.
TilePane	Creates a tiled effect where all nodes are equally sized.
	Can be forced to fill the parent via binding (make sure to set snapToPixel to false).
	Is not a replacement for a general-purpose Grid (see GridPane).
GridPane	Provides the most flexible layout container available.
	Should be used wherever components need pixel-perfect row and column alignment.
	Cannot be used to overlap components, except in conjunction with another layout.
AnchorPane	Highly specialized layout that can be used either for edge alignment or stretching.
	Best layout for overlapping components (passes through mouse events cleanly).
	Some use cases better accomplished with margins/padding or other constraints.

Bringing Reversi to Life

Up to this point we have been singularly focused on layouts, which is important but doesn't make for a very interesting game. However, the beauty of using dynamic layouts is that with a few enhancements to the game algorithm, we can turn this static application into a dynamic, playable game.

Highlighting Legal Moves

The first step of a playable game algorithm is to make sure that pieces can be placed only on legal squares. Rather than simply implement an algorithm in the back end, we take this as an opportunity to add a feature to the application where it shows you all of the next available moves.

Going back to the Reversi game rules, a move is valid only in the following circumstances.

- There is not already another piece at the same location.
- The piece is placed adjacent to a piece of the opposite color, and on that same line, there is another piece of the same color on the opposite end that would allow a flip of one or more of the opposing player's pieces.

To start with, you need to add a `legalMove` function to the model class that checks whether the cell is empty and then verifies all eight directions around a given `Cell`:

```
public BooleanBinding legalMove(int x, int y) {
  return board[x][y].isEqualTo(Owner.NONE).and(
    canFlip(x, y, 0, -1, turn).or(
    canFlip(x, y, -1, -1, turn).or(
    canFlip(x, y, -1, 0, turn).or(
    canFlip(x, y, -1, 1, turn).or(
    canFlip(x, y, 0, 1, turn).or(
    canFlip(x, y, 1, 1, turn).or(
    canFlip(x, y, 1, 0, turn).or(
    canFlip(x, y, 1, -1, turn))))))))
  );
}
```

■ **Note** We have chosen to make all the public model functions return bindings. This makes it possible to use property binding to update the UI and will efficiently defer updates until the playing board changes.

The `canFlip` method validates the second condition for the given direction indicated by the `cellX`, `cellY` arguments and the player whose turn is indicated. Because it would be more complicated and less efficient to use the fluent binding interface, we chose to create a custom binding instead.

Creating a custom binding involves the following.

- First override the binding class (in this case `BooleanBinding`) with an inner class.
- To set up the bound variables, use a static initializer that calls the bind function for each variable on which the algorithm depends.
- Override the `computeValue` method, and return the new calculated value of the binding.

The basic algorithm for calculating whether this is a legal move is to check the first cell in the given direction to make sure it is a different color, and if it is, continue walking cells until you find one that is the same color. If you do find one that is the same color, it is a legal move with pieces to flip, but if the next cell is the same color or there is no opposite color piece at the other end, it is not a legal move.

This means that the static initializer needs to add a property binding for every cell in the given direction, and the algorithm needs to use a loop to go through all of the cells, checking their owner, as shown in the following code.

```
public BooleanBinding canFlip(final int cellX, final int cellY, final int directionX, final int
directionY, final ObjectProperty<Owner> turn) {
  return new BooleanBinding() {
    {
      bind(turn);
      int x = cellX + directionX;
```

```
      int y = cellY + directionY;
      while (x >=0 && x < BOARD_SIZE && y >=0 && y < BOARD_SIZE) {
        bind(board[x][y]);
        x += directionX;
        y += directionY;
      }
    }
    @Override
    protected boolean computeValue() {
      Owner turnVal = turn.get();
      int x = cellX + directionX;
      int y = cellY + directionY;
      boolean first = true;
      while (x >=0 && x < BOARD_SIZE && y >=0 && y < BOARD_SIZE && board[x][y].get() != Owner.NONE) {
        if (board[x][y].get() == turnVal) {
          return !first;
        }
        first = false;
        x += directionX;
        y += directionY;
      }
      return false;
    }
  };
}
```

The last step in highlighting legal moves is to wire the `legalMove` model function up to the squares. This involves binding the `style` property of the `ReversiSquare` class to the `legalMove` method (changes in bold).

```
public ReversiSquare(final int x, final int y) {
  styleProperty().bind(Bindings.when(model.legalMove(x, y))
    .then("-fx-background-color: derive(dodgerblue, -60%)")
    .otherwise("-fx-background-color: burlywood"));
  Light.Distant light = new Light.Distant();
```

■ **Tip** The `derive` function used is a JavaFX-specific CSS function that lets you create a new color based on an existing one. The second parameter is brightness, which can range from –100% (black) to 100% white.

Also, don't forget to add in the static model variable on which this code depends:

```
private static ReversiModel model = ReversiModel.getInstance();
```

And also to update the `ReversiSquare` construction in the `tiles()` method to pass in the x and y board coordinates:

```
ReversiSquare square = new ReversiSquare(i, j);
```

Now on running the application, it correctly highlights the same four moves for black that were described in the "Board Layout and Basic Rules" section, as shown in Figure 5-15.

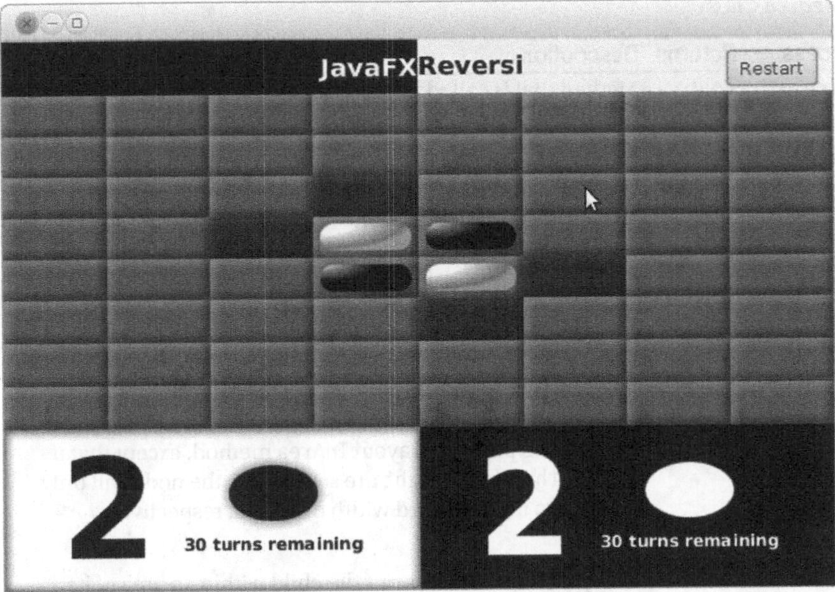

Figure 5-15. *Reversi application highlighting the available moves for black's first turn*

Highlighting the Active Cell

The simplest example of board interaction is to highlight the current cell that the user has moused over. Rather than highlighting cells that are not playable, you can take advantage of the `legalMove()` function you defined in the last section to highlight only cells that are active.

For the highlight, we are going to use a nested `Region` with a blue stroke to outline the cell the cursor is over. Although we could simply add a stroke to our existing `Region`, creating a separate `Region` makes it easier to isolate the highlight and animate it independently.

The highlight region can be quickly created as a variable in the `ReversiSquare` class using CSS styling and the builder pattern shown in Listing 5-16.

Listing 5-16. Additions to the `ReversiSquare create()` Method to Enable Highlighting

```
private Region highlight = RegionBuilder.create()
  .opacity(0)
  .style("-fx-border-width: 3; -fx-border-color: dodgerblue")
  .build();
```

Then to add it in to the scenegraph, you can append the following line in the constructor.

```
getChildren().add(highlight);
```

The default layout of the `Region` class simply sets children to their preferred size, but does not position them or allow them to fill the content area. We want the highlight to match the size of the square, therefore we need to override the layout algorithm and supply our own. Table 5-12 lists several additional functions of `Region` that allow us to override the layout algorithm and help with sizing and positioning of child nodes.

Table 5-11. Layout Functions of the Region Class

Name	Access	Returns	Description
`layoutChildren()`	Protected	Void	Method that is called to perform layout on the child nodes. Can be overridden to supply a custom algorithm.
`layoutInArea(node, x, y, width, height, baseline, halign, valign)`	Protected	Void	Helper method that will position the given `Node` at the specified coordinates and scale resizable nodes to fit the given width and height. If the node is resizable or the node's maximum dimensions prevent it from being resized, it will be positioned according to the given baseline, `halign`, and `valign`.
`layoutInArea(node, x, y, width, height, baseline, margin, halign, valign)`	Protected	Void	Same as the previous `layoutInArea` method, except that the given margin will be applied to the edges of the node.
`layoutInArea(node, x, y, width, height, baseline, margin, fillWidth, fillHeight, halign, valign)`	Protected	Void	Same as the previous `layoutInArea` method, except that if `fillWidth` or `fillHeight` are set to false, the node will only scale up to the preferred width or height, respectively.
`layoutInArea(node, x, y, width, height, baseline, margin, fillWidth, fillHeight, halign, valign, isSnapToPixel)`	Public	Void	Utility method that lays out the child within an area of its parent defined by `areaX,areaY, areaWidth x areaHeight`, with a baseline offset relative to that area.

To make sure the size and position of the contained region match the parent, we are going to override the `layoutChildren` method and supply our own algorithm. The first variant of the `layoutInArea` helper method allows us to position and scale in one shot, which is ideal for our use case:

```
@Override
protected void layoutChildren() {
  layoutInArea(highlight, 0, 0, getWidth(), getHeight(), getBaselineOffset(), HPos.CENTER, VPos.CENTER);
}
```

To create the animation highlight, we make use of a `FadeTransition` that animates the opacity of the highlight created in Listing 5-16 from 0.0 to 1.0. This is used to produce a fade-in effect when the user mouses over the `Node` and a fade-out effect when the user mouses out. The following code shows the `FadeTransition` to accomplish this.

```
private FadeTransition highlightTransition = FadeTransitionBuilder.create()
  .node(highlight)
  .duration(Duration.millis(200))
  .fromValue(0)
  .toValue(1)
  .build();
```

■ **Note** Even though the starting value of the opacity was set to 0, you still need to set the `fromValue` property of the transition to 0 explicitly for it to work correctly in reverse.

The last step is to add in the event listeners that will fire when the user mouses over the `Node`. These can be added by calling the `addEventHandler` method with a lambda expression that accepts `MouseEvents`:

```
addEventHandler(MouseEvent.MOUSE_ENTERED_TARGET, t -> {
    if (model.legalMove(x, y).get()) {
        highlightTransition.setRate(1);
        highlightTransition.play();
    }
});
addEventHandler(MouseEvent.MOUSE_EXITED_TARGET, t -> {
    highlightTransition.setRate(-1);
    highlightTransition.play();
});
```

Notice that the code plays the same animation in either case, but changes the rate of the animation based on whether it should be played forwards (1) or backwards (-1). This ensures that the animation will seamlessly transition even if it is in progress.

When run, the Reversi application now animates a subtle blue outline over the highlighted `Node` under the cursor, as shown in Figure 5-16.

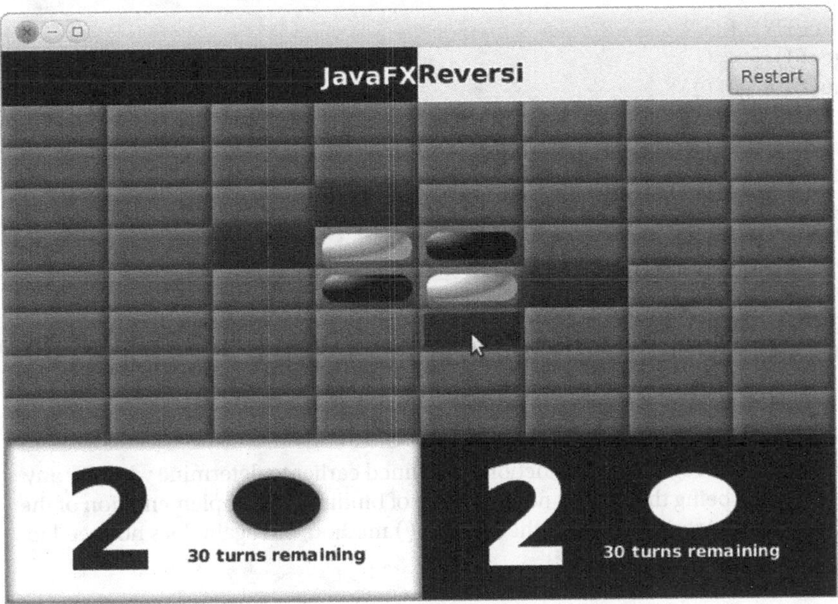

***Figure 5-16.** The Reversi application with a highlight animation over the active cell*

Taking Turns

The last bit of missing functionality in the Reversi application is the ability for players to take turns placing pieces on the board. We already have the infrastructure needed to accept mouse input and display pieces. All that is needed is a little glue code, plus some model enhancements to finish the game play.

Picking up where we left off in the previous section, the first step is to add an `onMouseClicked` event handler to the `ReversiSquare` `init` method:

```
setOnMouseClicked(t -> {
            model.play(x, y);
            highlightTransition.setRate(-1);
            highlightTransition.play();
        });
```

This method both calls the model function to play the current turn and also removes the highlight from the current cell, similar to the mouse exited event handler.

The `play()` function in the model class needs to perform several activities for each legal move:

- Set the clicked cell to be owned by the current player.
- Flip over captured pieces in any of eight possible directions.
- Change the turn to be the opposite player's.

An example implementation of the `play()` method is shown in Listing 5-17.

Listing 5-17. Example `play()` Method That Flips Cells in Eight Directions

```
public void play(int cellX, int cellY) {
  if (legalMove(cellX, cellY).get()) {
    board[cellX][cellY].setValue(turn.get());
    flip(cellX, cellY, 0, -1, turn);
    flip(cellX, cellY, -1, -1, turn);
    flip(cellX, cellY, -1, 0, turn);
    flip(cellX, cellY, -1, 1, turn);
    flip(cellX, cellY, 0, 1, turn);
    flip(cellX, cellY, 1, 1, turn);
    flip(cellX, cellY, 1, 0, turn);
    flip(cellX, cellY, 1, -1, turn);
    turn.setValue(turn.getValue().opposite());
  }
}
```

Notice that it follows the same pattern as the `legalMove()` function we defined earlier to determine whether any pieces can be flipped, with the main difference being that it does not make use of binding. The implementation of the flip method also shares many similarities to the algorithm used in the `canFlip()` method, but again does not need to bother with creating a binding:

```
public void flip(int cellX, int cellY, int directionX, int directionY, ObjectProperty<Owner> turn) {
  if (canFlip(cellX, cellY, directionX, directionY, turn).get()) {
    int x = cellX + directionX;
    int y = cellY + directionY;
    while (x >=0 && x < BOARD_SIZE && y >=0 && y < BOARD_SIZE && board[x][y].get() != turn.get()) {
```

```
      board[x][y].setValue(turn.get());
      x += directionX;
      y += directionY;
    }
  }
}
```

With a completed game algorithm, you can now play a full game with two players at the same computer, as shown in Figure 5-16. Notice that even the turn indicator that you set up at the beginning of the chapter is now properly flipping and indicating the current player.

Declaring the User Interface Using FXML

So far, we have created the complete UI for the Reversi application using the JavaFX APIs. Doing so, we programmatically defined the UI. This approach allows a developer to get a clear insight into the structure and the behavior of the different components of the UI. As we explained in Chapter 3, it is often interesting to declare a UI rather than to program it.

Listing 5-18 provides an FXML file that declares the same UI as the one we developed in the previous sections.

Listing 5-18. The Reversi User Interface Declared in FXML

```
<?xml version="1.0" encoding="UTF-8"?>

<?import java.lang.*?>
<?import javafx.scene.control.*?>
<?import javafx.scene.layout.*?>
<?import javafx.scene.shape.*?>
<?import javafx.scene.text.*?>

<AnchorPane id="AnchorPane" xmlns="http://javafx.com/javafx/8" xmlns:fx="http://javafx.com/fxml/1"
fx:controller="projavafx.reversifxml.BoardController">
    <children>
        <BorderPane AnchorPane.bottomAnchor="0.0" AnchorPane.leftAnchor="0.0"
AnchorPane.rightAnchor="0.0" AnchorPane.topAnchor="0.0">
            <top>
                <TilePane fx:id="titlePane" prefTileHeight="40.0" snapToPixel="false"
BorderPane.alignment="CENTER">
                    <children>
                        <StackPane snapToPixel="false" style="-fx-background-color: black;">
                            <children>
                                <Text fill="WHITE" strokeType="OUTSIDE" strokeWidth="0.0"
text="JavaFX" StackPane.alignment="CENTER_RIGHT">
                                    <font>
                                        <Font name="System Bold" size="18.0" />
                                    </font>
                                </Text>
                            </children>
                        </StackPane>
                        <Text strokeType="OUTSIDE" strokeWidth="0.0" text="Reversi"
TilePane.alignment="CENTER_LEFT">
```

```
                    <font>
                        <Font name="System Bold" size="18.0" />
                    </font>
                </Text>
            </children>
        </TilePane>
    </top>
    <center>
        <StackPane fx:id="centerPane">
            <children>
                <Region style="-fx-background-color:
radial-gradient(radius 100%, white, gray);" />
            </children>
        </StackPane>
    </center>
    <bottom>
        <TilePane fx:id="scorePane" BorderPane.alignment="CENTER">
            <children>
                <StackPane fx:id="leftScore">
                    <children>
                        <Region fx:id="whiteRegion" style="-fx-background-color: white;" />
                        <FlowPane alignment="CENTER" hgap="20.0" vgap="10.0">
                            <children>
                                <Text fx:id="scoreBlack" strokeType="OUTSIDE"
strokeWidth="0.0" text="1">
                                    <font>
                                        <Font name="System Bold" size="100.0" />
                                    </font>
                                </Text>
                                <VBox alignment="CENTER" spacing="10.0">
                                    <children>
                                        <Ellipse fx:id="blackEllipse" radiusX="32.0"
radiusY="20.0" stroke="BLACK" strokeType="INSIDE" />
                                        <Text fx:id="remainingBlack" strokeType="OUTSIDE"
strokeWidth="0.0" text="Text">
                                            <font>
                                                <Font name="System Bold" size="12.0" />
                                            </font>
                                        </Text>
                                    </children>
                                </VBox>
                            </children>
                        </FlowPane>
                    </children>
                </StackPane>
                <StackPane fx:id="rightScore">
                    <children>
                        <Region fx:id="blackRegion" style="-fx-background-color: black;" />
                        <FlowPane alignment="CENTER" hgap="20.0" vgap="10.0">
                            <children>
                                <Text fx:id="scoreWhite" fill="WHITE" strokeType="OUTSIDE"
strokeWidth="0.0" text="2">
```

```
                                                <font>
                                                    <Font name="System Bold" size="100.0" />
                                                </font>
                                            </Text>
                                            <VBox alignment="CENTER"  spacing="10.0">
                                                <children>
                                                    <Ellipse fx:id="whiteEllipse" fill="WHITE"
radiusX="32.0" radiusY="20.0" stroke="BLACK" strokeType="INSIDE" />
                                                    <Text fx:id="remainingWhite" fill="WHITE"
strokeType="OUTSIDE" strokeWidth="0.0" text="turns remaining">
                                                        <font>
                                                            <Font name="System Bold" size="12.0" />
                                                        </font>
                                                    </Text>
                                                </children>
                                            </VBox>
                                        </children>
                                    </FlowPane>
                                </children>
                            </StackPane>
                        </children>
                    </TilePane>
                </bottom>
            </BorderPane>
            <Button layoutX="520.0" layoutY="14.0" mnemonicParsing="false" onAction="#restart"
text="Restart" AnchorPane.rightAnchor="10.0" AnchorPane.topAnchor="10.0" />
    </children>
</AnchorPane>
```

This XML file was not hand-coded, but it is the result of a design process facilitated by ScreenBuilder 2, which was discussed in Chapter 3.

We have the declaration of the UI in an FXML file, but we still need to wire the game logic together. An important part of this wiring is the declaration of the Controller class, which is done near the top of the FXML file:

```
<AnchorPane ... fx:controller="projavafx.reversifxml.BoardController">
```

The BoardController is a new class that provides programmatic access to the components declared in the FXML file. Listing 5-19 shows the content of this controller class.

Listing 5-19. Implementation of the Controller Class

```
public class BoardController  {

    private final ReversiModel model = ReversiModel.getInstance();
    @FXML private TilePane titlePane;
    @FXML private TilePane scorePane;
    @FXML private StackPane centerPane;
    @FXML private Text scoreBlack;
    @FXML private Text scoreWhite;
    @FXML private Text remainingBlack;
    @FXML private Text remainingWhite;
```

```
    @FXML private Region blackRegion;
    @FXML private Region whiteRegion;
    @FXML private Ellipse blackEllipse;
    @FXML private Ellipse whiteEllipse;

    public void initialize() {
        titlePane.prefTileWidthProperty().bind(Bindings.selectDouble(titlePane.parentProperty(),
"width").divide(2));
        scorePane.prefTileWidthProperty().bind(Bindings.selectDouble(scorePane.parentProperty(),
"width").divide(2));
        centerPane.getChildren().add(tiles());
        scoreBlack.textProperty().bind(model.getScore(Owner.BLACK).asString());
        scoreWhite.textProperty().bind(model.getScore(Owner.WHITE).asString());
        remainingBlack.textProperty().bind(model.getTurnsRemaining(Owner.BLACK).asString().concat("
turns remaining"));
        remainingWhite.textProperty().bind(model.getTurnsRemaining(Owner.WHITE).asString().concat("
turns remaining"));

        InnerShadow innerShadow = new InnerShadow();
        innerShadow.setColor(Color.DODGERBLUE);
        innerShadow.setChoke(0.5);
        whiteRegion.effectProperty().bind(Bindings.when(model.turn.isEqualTo(Owner.WHITE))
                .then(innerShadow)
                .otherwise((InnerShadow) null));
        blackRegion.effectProperty().bind(Bindings.when(model.turn.isEqualTo(Owner.BLACK))
                .then(innerShadow)
                .otherwise((InnerShadow) null));
        DropShadow dropShadow = new DropShadow();
        dropShadow.setColor(Color.DODGERBLUE);
        dropShadow.setSpread(0.2);
        blackEllipse.setEffect(dropShadow);
        blackEllipse.effectProperty().bind(Bindings.when(model.turn.isEqualTo(Owner.BLACK))
                .then(dropShadow)
                .otherwise((DropShadow) null));
        whiteEllipse.effectProperty().bind(Bindings.when(model.turn.isEqualTo(Owner.WHITE))
                .then(dropShadow)
                .otherwise((DropShadow) null));

    }

    @FXML
    public void restart() {
        model.restart();
    }

    private Node tiles() {
        GridPane board = new GridPane();
        for (int i = 0; i < ReversiModel.BOARD_SIZE; i++) {
            for (int j = 0; j < ReversiModel.BOARD_SIZE; j++) {
                ReversiSquare square = new ReversiSquare(i, j);
                ReversiPiece piece = new ReversiPiece();
```

```
                piece.ownerProperty().bind(model.board[i][j]);
                board.add(new StackPane(square, piece), i, j);
            }
        }
        return board;
    }

}
```

The BoardController class contains a number of variables that are annotated with the @FXML annotation. As explained in Chapter 3, this technique binds the components defined in the FXML file with JavaFX objects.

When the FXML file is loaded, the initialize() method of the controller will be called. In this method, we create the required bindings and we populate the gridpane with the tiles.

The required bindings are exactly the same as the bindings we created in the previous sections; for example, we bind the preferred width for the tiles in the top part of the borderpane as follows:

```
titlePane.prefTileWidthProperty().bind(Bindings.selectDouble(titlePane.parentProperty(), "width").
divide(2));
```

Creating the tiles is done in exactly the same way as we did it without FXML. This time, we add the tiles to the centerPane variable, which corresponds, due to the @FXML annotation, to the element with id centerPane in the FXML file. Indeed, the FXML file contains the declaration

```
<StackPane fx:id="centerPane">
```

and our code contains this statement:

```
    @FXML private StackPane centerPane;
...
centerPane.getChildren().add(tiles());
```

The combination of these two statements will cause the tiles to be displayed in the StackPane declared in the FXML file.

The code in Listing 5-19 also shows that it is possible to bind actions on FXML-declared components to method calls in the controller class. Clicking the restart button will cause the restart() method to be called. Again, this is achieved by the collaboration between the FXML file and the controller class. The FXML file declares the restart button and its action as follows:

```
<Button layoutX="520.0" layoutY="14.0" mnemonicParsing="false" onAction="#restart" text="Restart"
AnchorPane.rightAnchor="10.0" AnchorPane.topAnchor="10.0" />
```

The onAction attribute that links to the method in the controller class is shown in bold.

In the BoardController class, the restart() function is annotated with @FXML, which provides the binding with the restart action defined in the FXML file:

```
@FXML
public void restart() {
    model.restart();
}
```

In case you wonder when you should use FXML and when you should program the UI in Java, there is no single correct answer. In general, declaring a layout is often easier done in FXML, when you use an appropriate tool (e.g., SceneBuilder). The business logic and wiring is often done in corresponding controller classes. However, the most important factor is that the developers and designers should find a way that allows them to be the most productive!

Additional Game Enhancements

The Reversi application that was developed in this chapter is completely dynamic and flexible both in layout and structure, so it is time to take advantage of this and push the limits of your coding skills.

Here are some coding challenges that you can use to take the Reversi application from a well-designed tutorial to a full-fledged application.

- There is one rule that we neglected to implement, which is skipping turns. If, and only if, a player has no available options to play, the next player can go. Try implementing a facility that automatically detects whether there are no legal moves and skips a turn.
- Playing against another player on the same computer is not nearly as interesting as playing against a remote opponent. After reading some of the later chapters on back-end integration with JavaFX, try implementing a network-capable version of the Reversi application.
- Wouldn't it be great to have a JavaFX AI for playing Reversi? Give it a try, and see if you can create an unbeatable opponent!

Summary

In this chapter you were able to fully leverage the JavaFX layout capabilities to do dynamic layout of a complex application. Along the way, you learned how to

- Align `Nodes` using bind.
- Use `StackPane` to layer `Nodes` and create composite layouts.
- Use `TilePane` to do fixed-size layouts.
- Use `FlowPane`, `HBox`, and `VBox` to do directional layouts with and without wrapping.
- Create a dynamic game board using binding and `GridPane`.
- Use `AnchorPane` to align and stretch overlapping nodes.
- Create custom components using `Regions` and CSS.
- Build a rich UI backed by a game model.
- Apply JavaFX effects and transitions.
- Use FXML to create the UI in a declarative way.

After experiencing the advantages of dynamic layout, you will be hard-pressed to go back to static positioning of components with fixed sizes. In the next chapter we show you how to create custom UI components and charts that you can use to create even more impressive business-centric applications.

Resources

For more information about dynamic layouts, consult the following resources.

- JavaFX 2.0Layout: A Class Tour: `http://amyfowlersblog.wordpress.com/2011/06/02/javafx2-0-layout-a-class-tour/`
- Working with layouts in JavaFX: `http://docs.oracle.com/javase/8/javafx/layout-tutorial/index.html`

To learn more about the game of Reversi, please refer to the following resource.

- Wikipedia, "Reversi." URL: `http://en.wikipedia.org/wiki/Reversi`

CHAPTER 6

Using the JavaFX UI Controls

Miracles are a retelling in small letters of the very same story which is written across the whole world in letters too large for some of us to see.

—C. S. Lewis

In Chapter 2 you learned how to create user interfaces (UIs) in JavaFX by creating a stage, putting a scene on the stage, and putting nodes in the scene. You also learned how to handle mouse and keyboard events, as well as how to animate nodes in the scene.

In this chapter we pick up the UI discussion from Chapter 2 by showing you how to use the UI controls available in JavaFX. The knowledge you've gained about property binding in Chapter 4 and layouts in Chapter 5 will serve you well in this chapter, as it builds on those concepts.

Trying Out the JavaFX UI Controls

JavaFX has a rich set of UI controls for creating your applications. These range from relatively simple controls such as `TextField` to more complex controls such as `WebView`. To get you up to speed quickly on these controls, we've created an example application named StarterApp. This application has an example of most of the UI controls available in JavaFX, and it also serves as a starting point from which you can use modifications to create an application.

Before walking through the behavior of the program, go ahead and open the project and execute it by following the instructions for building and executing the AudioConfig project in Chapter 1. The project file is located in the `Chapter06` directory subordinate to which you extracted the book's code download bundle.

EXAMINING THE BEHAVIOR OF THE STARTERAPP PROGRAM

When the program starts, its appearance should be similar to the screenshot in Figure 6-1.

Starter App

File Edit

TableView | Accordion/TitledPane | SplitPane/TreeView/ListView | TreeTableView | ScrollPane/Miscellaneous | HTMLEditor | WebView

First Name	Last Name	Phone Number
FirstName1	LastName1	Phone1
FirstName2	LastName2	Phone2
FirstName3	LastName3	Phone3
FirstName4	LastName4	Phone4
FirstName5	LastName5	Phone5
FirstName6	LastName6	Phone6
FirstName7	LastName7	Phone7
FirstName8	LastName8	Phone8
FirstName9	LastName9	Phone9
FirstName10	LastName10	Phone10
FirstName11	LastName11	Phone11
FirstName12	LastName12	Phone12
FirstName13	LastName13	Phone13
FirstName14	LastName14	Phone14
FirstName15	LastName15	Phone15
FirstName16	LastName16	Phone16
FirstName17	LastName17	Phone17
FirstName18	LastName18	Phone18
FirstName19	LastName19	Phone19
FirstName20	LastName20	Phone20

Figure 6-1. *The StarterApp program when first invoked*

To fully examine its behavior, perform the following steps.

1. Click the File menu, noticing that the drop-down menu contains a menu item named New, with an image and the Ctrl+N shortcut key combination as shown in Figure 6-2.

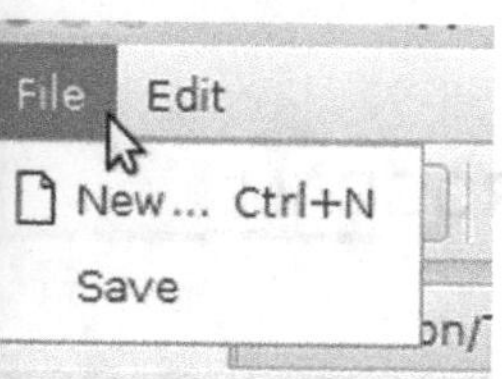

Figure 6-2. *The File menu of the StarterApp program*

2. Select the New menu item by clicking it or pressing the shortcut key combination, noticing that the following message appears in the Java console: “ACTION occurred on MenuItem New”.

3. Examine the toolbar under the menu bar, shown in Figure 6-3, clicking the leftmost button that has the same image that is on the New menu item. Notice that the following message appears in the Java console: “New toolbar button clicked”.

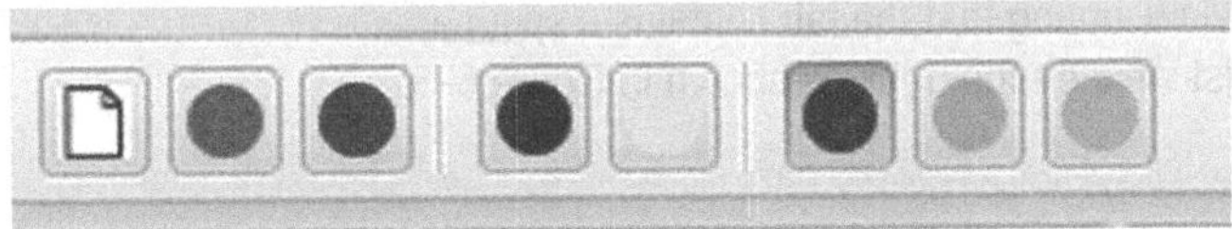

Figure 6-3. The toolbar of the StarterApp program

4. Hover the mouse cursor over the leftmost button in the toolbar, noticing that a tooltip appears with the message: "New Document... Ctrl+N".
5. Click the fourth and fifth buttons on the toolbar, located between the vertical separator bars. Note that the buttons have two states, independent of each other.
6. Click the three rightmost buttons on the toolbar, located to the right of the last vertical separator bar. Note that the buttons have two states, but that only one button at a time is in the selected (depressed) state.
7. Drag the thumb on the vertical scrollbar on the right side of the `TableView`, noting that there are 10,000 rows in the table containing FirstName, LastName, and Phone data in each row. Click on one of the rows, noting that a message like "Person: FirstNameX LastNameX chosen in TableView" prints to the Java console.
8. Drag the TableView column headers horizontally to rearrange them. Drag the right and left sides of the column headers to resize them.
9. Click the tab labeled Accordion/TitledPane, noting that the tab contains an Accordion control with three expandable titled panes as shown in Figure 6-4. Click each `TitledPane`, noting that each one expands and collapses.

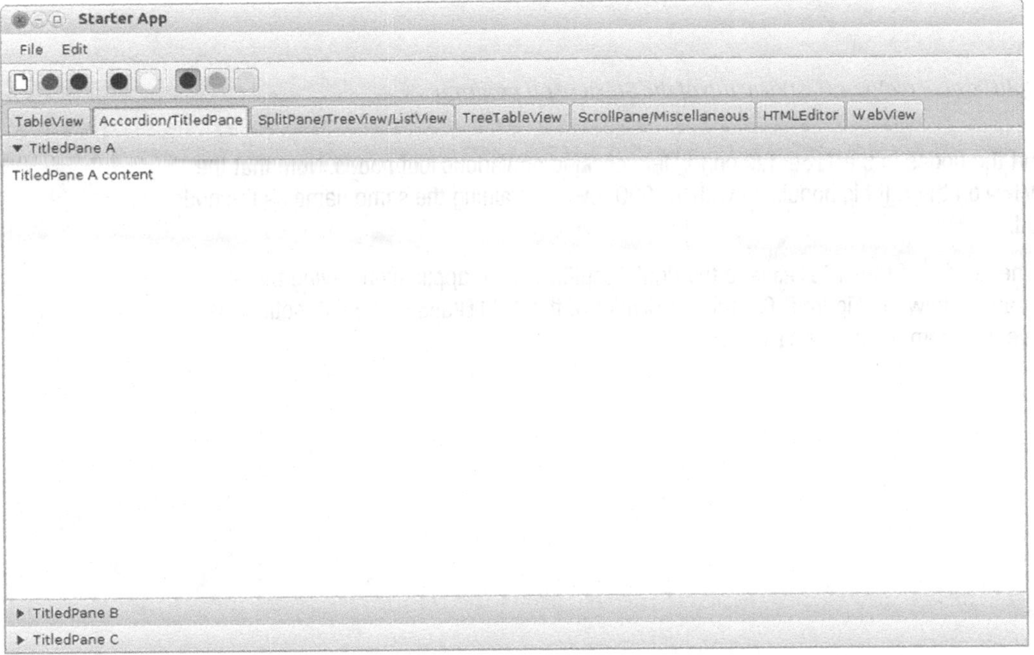

Figure 6-4. The Accordion/TitledPane tab of the StarterApp program

10. Click the tab labeled SplitPane/TreeView/ListView, noting that the tab contains a split pane with a tree control on the left and an empty list view on the right, as shown in Figure 6-5.

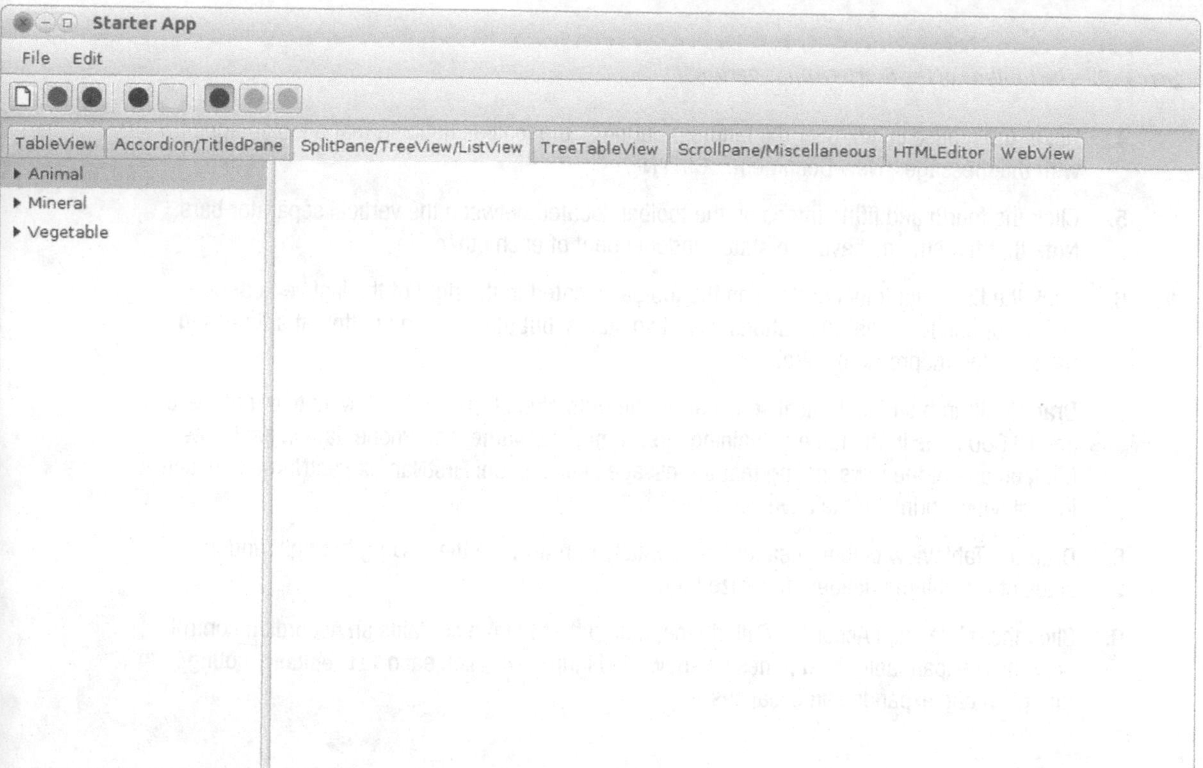

***Figure 6-5.** The SplitPane/TreeView/ListView tab of the StarterApp program*

11. Expand the nodes in the `TreeView` on the left, clicking on various leaf nodes. Note that the `ListView` on the right is populated with 10,000 rows containing the same name as the node clicked.

12. Drag the divider of the `SplitPane` to the right, resulting in the application having the appearance shown in Figure 6-6. Drag the divider of the `SplitPane` to the left, noting that it is prevented from hiding the `TreeView`.

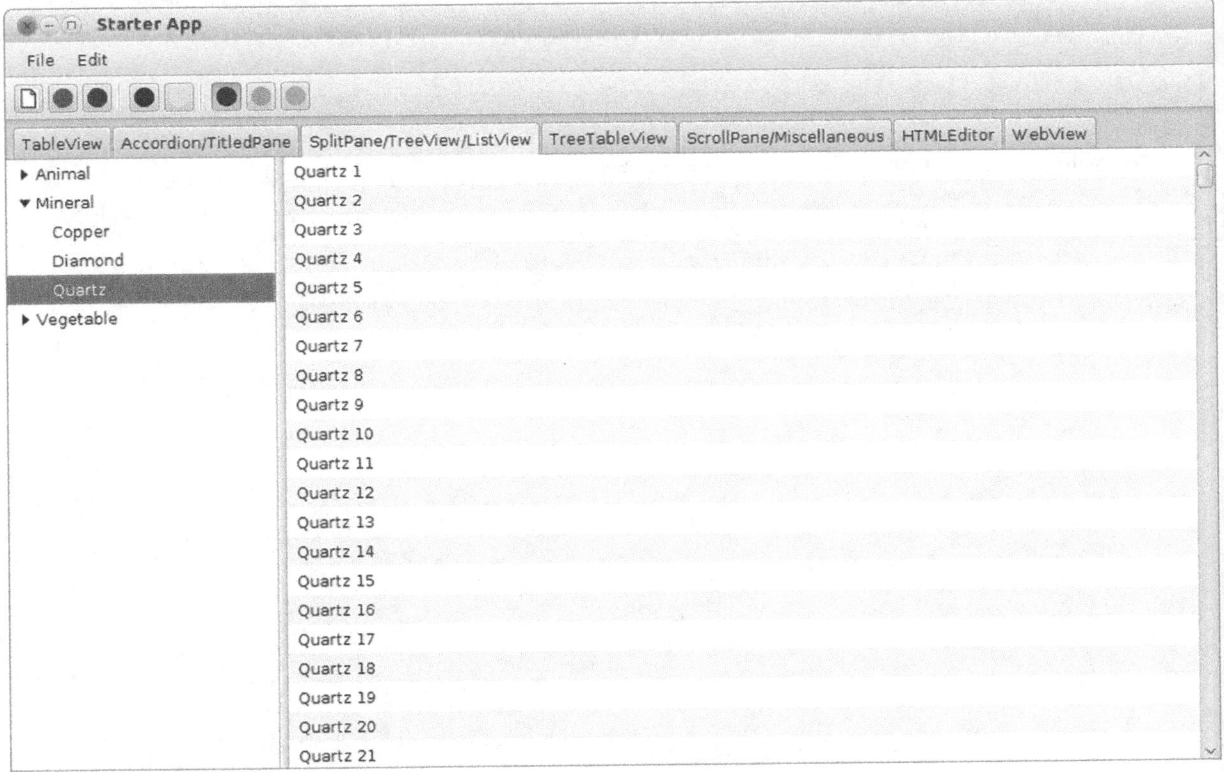

Figure 6-6. *After expanding the nodes on the `TreeView` and selecting one of the leaf nodes*

13. Click the tab labeled TreeTableView, and notice a table with a tree control to the left and with columns describing each person's details as shown in Figure 6-7.

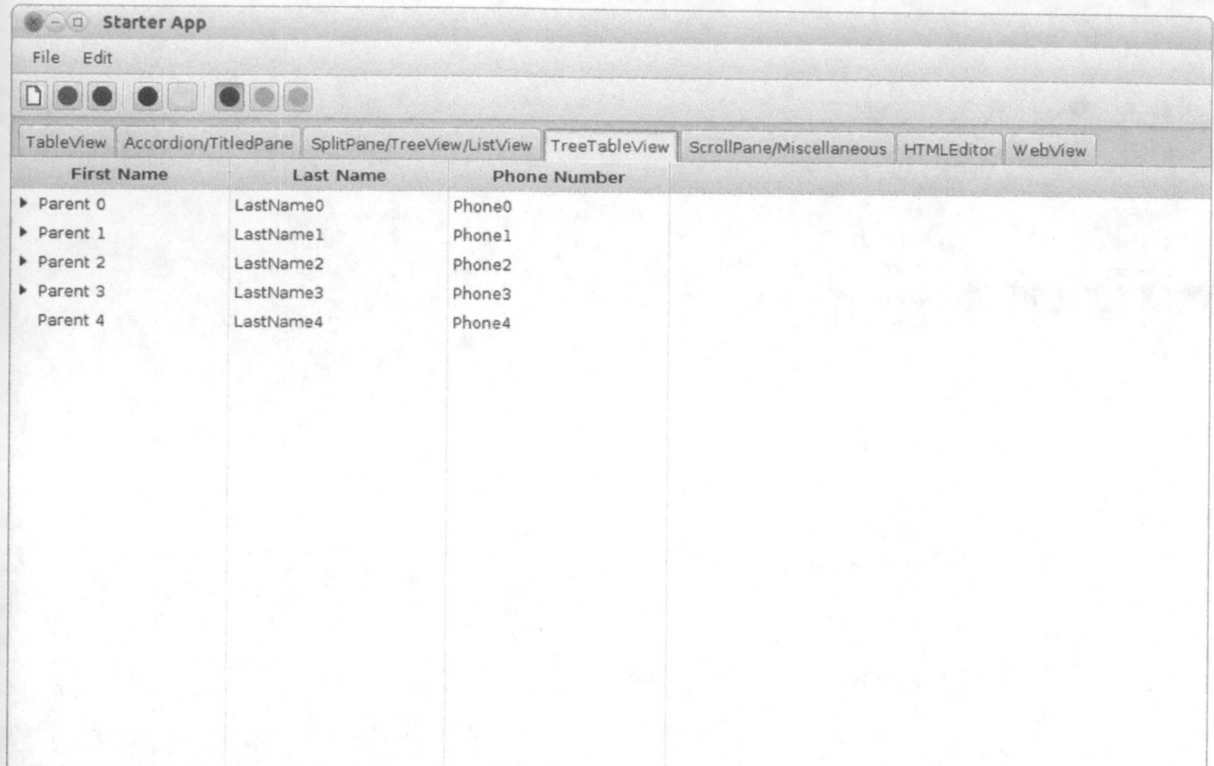

Figure 6-7. *The TreeTableView tab of the StarterApp program*

14. Click on some of the arrows, and browse throughout the tree rendering children and grandchildren. This will result in a view similar to Figure 6-8.

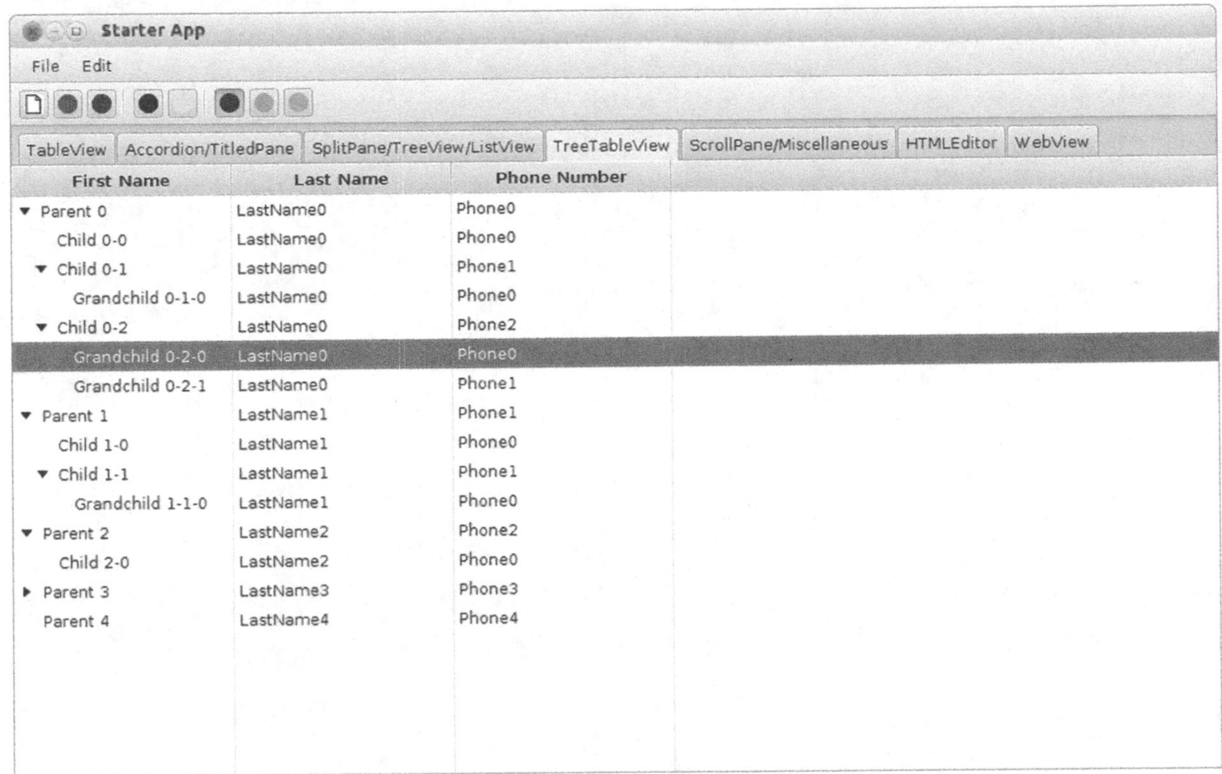

Figure 6-8. *After expanding some of the nodes, a view similar to this one will appear*

15. Click the tab labeled ScrollPane/Miscellaneous, noting that the tab contains a variety of UI controls in a scrollable pane, as shown in Figure 6-9.

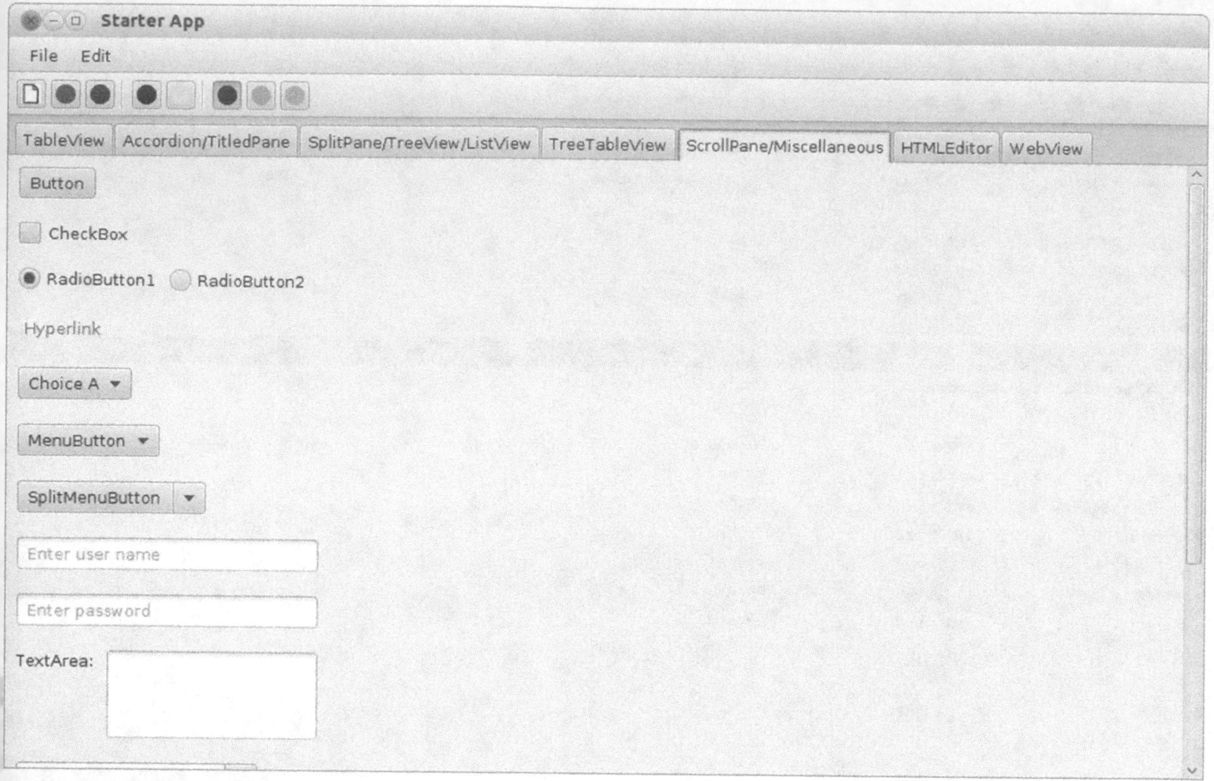

Figure 6-9. The ScrollPane/Miscellaneous tab of the StarterApp program

16. Click the `Button` (labeled "Button"), noting that the following message is output to the Java console: "ACTION occurred on Button".
17. Click the `CheckBox`, noting that the following message is output to the Java console: "ACTION occurred on CheckBox, and selectedProperty is: true".
18. Select each radio button, noting that a message such as "RadioButton2 selected" is output to the Java console when a given `RadioButton` is selected.
19. Click the `Hyperlink` control, noting that the following message is output to the Java console: "ACTION occurred on Hyperlink".
20. Select various items (e.g., "Choice B") in the `ChoiceBox`, noting that a message such as "Choice B chosen in ChoiceBox" is output to the Java console when a given item is selected.
21. Select the "MenuItem A" option in the `MenuButton` (labeled "MenuButton"), noting that the message "ACTION occurred on Menu Item A" is output to the Java console.
22. Click on the text area of the `SplitMenuButton` (labeled "SplitMenuButton"), noting that the following message is output to the Java console: "ACTION occurred on SplitMenuButton".
23. Click the down arrow on the right side of the `SplitMenuButton` and select the "MenuItem A" option, noting that the message "ACTION occurred on Menu Item A" is output to the Java console.

24. Scroll down as necessary in the `ScrollPane` to see the controls shown in Figure 6-10.

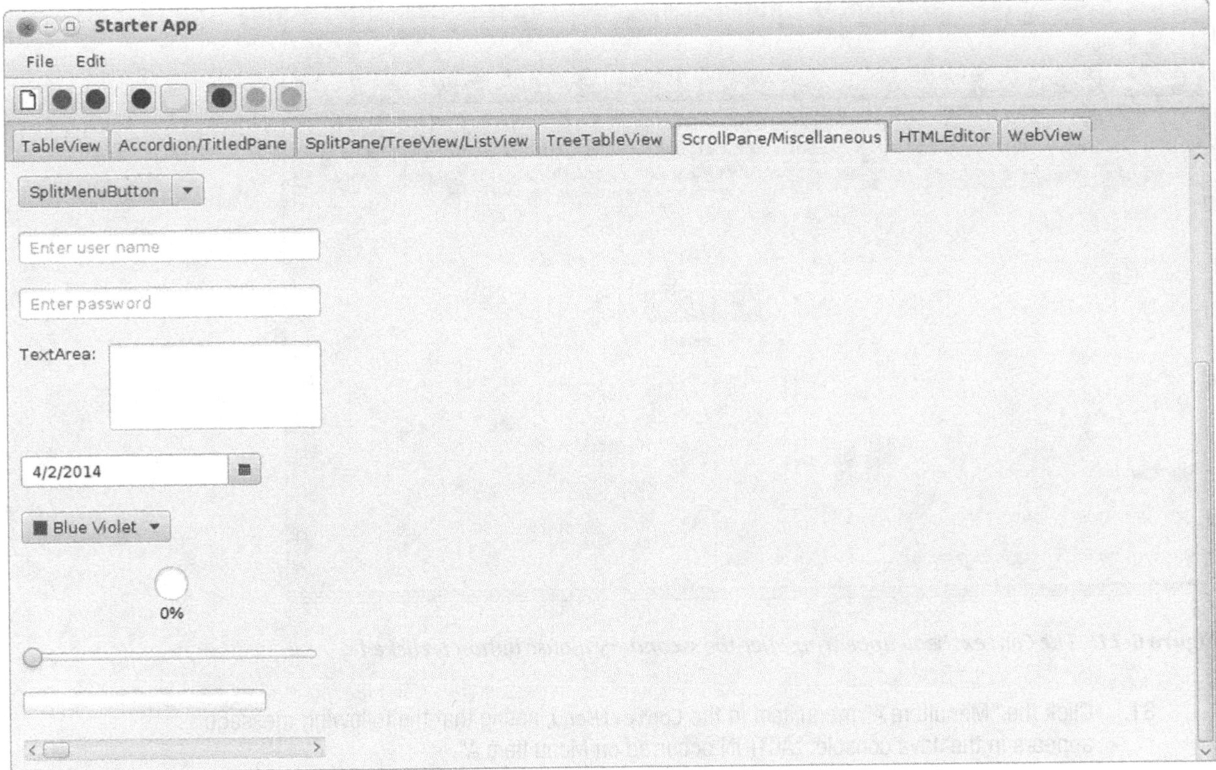

***Figure 6-10.** The ScrollPane/Miscellaneous tab scrolled to the bottom*

25. Enter some text into the `TextField` that has the prompt text "Enter user name," noting that each time the text is modified the contents of the `TextField` are output to the Java console.

26. Enter some text into the `PasswordField` that has the prompt text "Enter password," noting that a mask character is displayed instead of the characters that you typed. Click on anything other than the `PasswordField`, causing it to lose focus, noting that the contents of the `PasswordField` are output to the Java console.

27. Enter some text into the `TextArea` (labeled "TextArea"). Click on anything other than the `TextArea`, causing it to lose focus, noting that the contents of the `TextArea` are output to the Java console.

28. Slide the thumb of the horizontal `Slider` to the right, noticing that the `ProgressIndicator` above it displays from 0% through 99%, and then Done. Slide it all the way to the left, noticing that `ProgressIndicator` changes in appearance to its spinning indeterminate state.

29. Slide the thumb of the horizontal `ScrollBar` to the right, noticing that the `ProgressBar` above it represents the same value. Slide it all the way to the left, noticing that `ProgressBar` changes in appearance to its indeterminate state.

30. Click the secondary (usually the right) button on your mouse somewhere in the blank area of the `ScrollPane`, noting that a `ContextMenu` appears as shown in Figure 6-11.

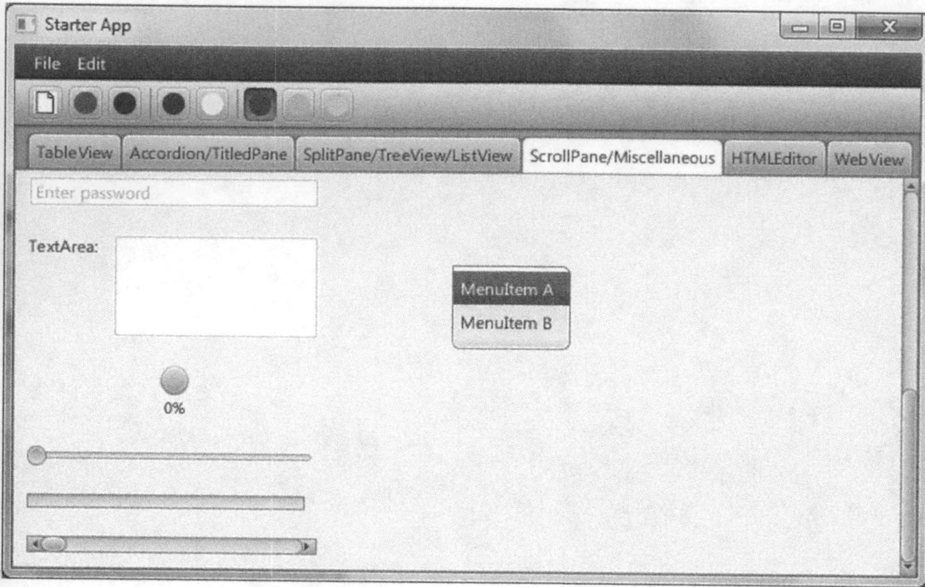

***Figure 6-11.** The `ContextMenu` appearing after the secondary mouse button is clicked*

31. Click the "MenuItem A" menu item in the `ContextMenu`, noting that the following message appears in the Java console: "ACTION occurred on Menu Item A".

32. Click the tab labeled HTMLEditor, noting that the tab contains a rich text editor and a button labeled View HTML, as shown in Figure 6-12.

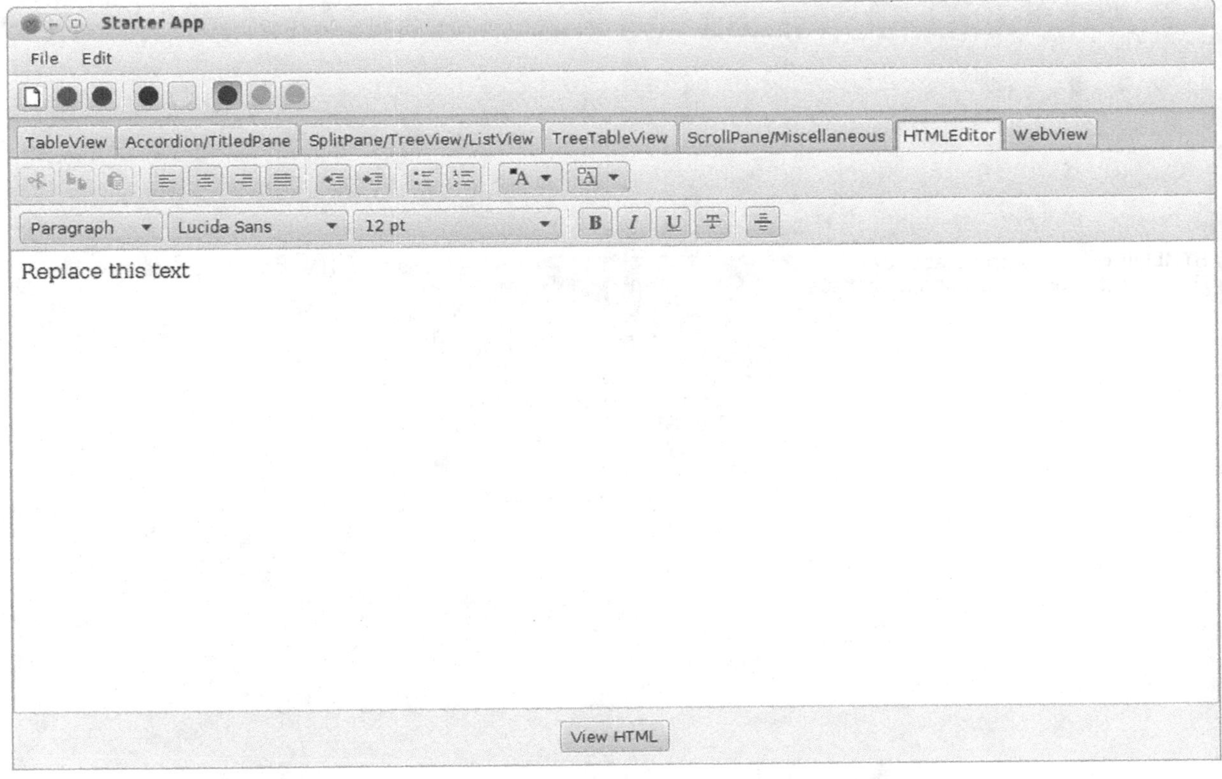

Figure 6-12. *The HTMLEditor tab of the StarterApp program*

33. Type some text into the editing area, using various tools in the editor's toolbars to style the text. When finished, click the View HTML button to see the HTML in the underlying data model displayed in a Popup, as shown in Figure 6-13.

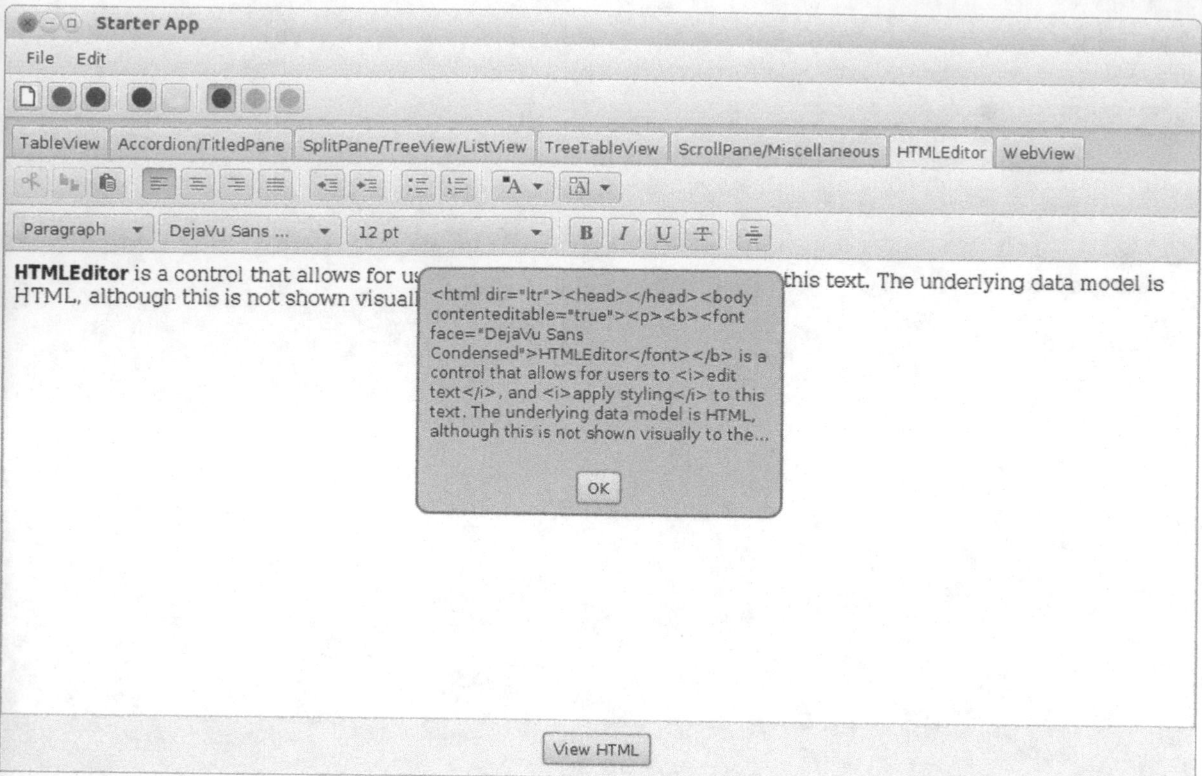

Figure 6-13. *After editing text in the HTMLEditor and clicking View HTML*

34. Click OK to dismiss the popup. Then click the tab labeled WebView, noting that the tab contains a web browser displaying a randomly selected web page (if your computer is connected to the Internet), as shown in Figure 6-14.

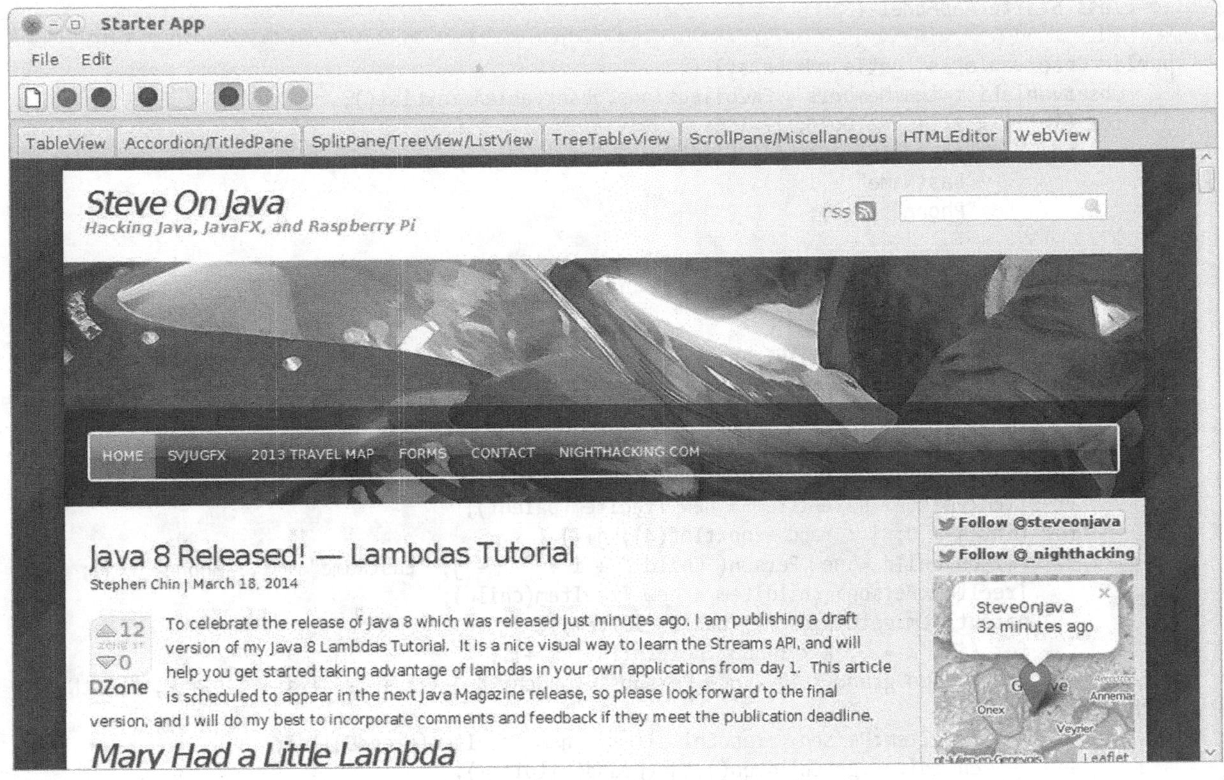

Figure 6-14. *The WebView tab of the StarterApp program*

35. Click on one of the other tabs in the application, and then on the WebView tab, noting that the Java console displays a randomly selected URL that the WebView is attempting to load.

Congratulations on sticking with this 35-step exercise! Performing this exercise has prepared you to relate to the code behind it, which we now walk through together.

Leveraging the JavaFX UI Controls

Similar to the Audio Configuration program in Chapter 1, our StarterApp program contains a model class named `StarterAppModel`, shown in Listing 6-1.

Listing 6-1. The Source Code for `StarterAppModel.java`

```
package projavafx.starterapp.model;

import java.util.Random;
import javafx.beans.property.DoubleProperty;
import javafx.beans.property.SimpleDoubleProperty;
import javafx.collections.FXCollections;
import javafx.collections.ObservableList;
import javafx.scene.control.TreeItem;
```

```
public class StarterAppModel {

    public ObservableList getTeamMembers() {
        ObservableList teamMembers = FXCollections.observableArrayList();
        for (int i = 1; i <= 10000; i++) {
            teamMembers.add(new Person("FirstName" + i,
                    "LastName" + i,
                    "Phone" + i));
        }
        return teamMembers;
    }

    public TreeItem<Person> getFamilyTree() {
        Random random = new Random();
        TreeItem<Person> root = new TreeItem();
        for (int i = 0; i < 5; i++) {
            Person parent = new Person("Parent " + i, "LastName" + i, "Phone" + i);
            TreeItem<Person> parentItem = new TreeItem(parent);
            for (int j = 0; j < random.nextInt(4); j++) {
                Person child = new Person("Child " + i + "-" + j, "LastName" + i, "Phone" + j);
                TreeItem<Person> childItem = new TreeItem(child);
                parentItem.getChildren().add(childItem);
                for (int k = 0; k < random.nextInt(4); k++) {
                    Person grandChild = new Person("Grandchild " + i + "-" + j + "-" + k, "LastName"
+ i, "Phone" + k);
                    TreeItem<Person> grandChildItem = new TreeItem(grandChild);
                    childItem.getChildren().add(grandChildItem);
                }
            }
            root.getChildren().add(parentItem);
        }
        return root;
    }

    public String getRandomWebSite() {
        String[] webSites = {
            "http://javafx.com",
            "http://fxexperience.com",
            "http://steveonjava.com",
            "http://javafxpert.com",
            "http://pleasingsoftware.blogspot.com",
            "http://www.weiqigao.com/blog",
            "http://blogs.lodgon.com/johan",
            "http://google.com"
        };
        int randomIdx = (int) (Math.random() * webSites.length);
        return webSites[randomIdx];
    }

    public ObservableList listViewItems = FXCollections.observableArrayList();
```

```
    public ObservableList choiceBoxItems = FXCollections.observableArrayList(
            "Choice A",
            "Choice B",
            "Choice C",
            "Choice D"
    );

    public double maxRpm = 8000.0;
    public DoubleProperty rpm = new SimpleDoubleProperty(0);

    public double maxKph = 300.0;
    public DoubleProperty kph = new SimpleDoubleProperty(0);
}
```

We refer to snippets from this listing as they apply to relevant UI controls that we walk through in the main Java file of the StarterApp program. This file is named `StarterAppMain.java` and is shown in its entirety one chunk at a time during our discussion of the JavaFX UI controls.

Setting the stage for the StarterApp program, Listing 6-2 shows the first portion of the `StarterAppMain.java` file, in which the `Stage` and `Scene` are received and created. In addition, the root of the `Scene` is assigned a `BorderPane`, which provides the UI structure in which the `MenuBar`, `ToolBar`, and `TabPane` will reside.

Listing 6-2. The First Portion of `StarterAppMain.java`

```
package projavafx.starterapp.ui;

... imports omitted...

public class StarterAppMain extends Application {

    StarterAppModel model = new StarterAppModel();
    Stage stage;

    public static void main(String[] args) {
        Application.launch(args);
    }

    @Override
    public void start(final Stage primaryStage) {
        stage = primaryStage;
        VBox topBox = new VBox(createMenus(), createToolBar());
        BorderPane borderPane = new BorderPane();
        borderPane.setCenter(createTabs());
        borderPane.setTop(topBox);
        Scene scene = new Scene(borderPane, 980, 600);
        scene.getStylesheets().add("/projavafx/starterapp/ui/starterApp.css");
        stage.setScene(scene);
        stage.setTitle("Starter App");
        stage.show();
    }
```

The following items are of particular note in Listing 6-2:

- The top area of the BorderPane will contain the MenuBar and ToolBar shown in Figure 6-1, created by the createMenus() and createToolBar() methods that we walk through soon.
- The center area of the BorderPane will contain the TabPane shown in Figure 6-1, created by the createTabs() method that we walk through soon as well.
- A style sheet named starterApp.css is loaded, which we refer to later when discussing relevant functionality.

Creating a Menu and Defining Menu Items

To create the menu structure, our StarterApp program defines a method that we've arbitrarily named createMenus(), shown in Listing 6-3. This method returns a MenuBar instance that contains the desired menu structure.

Listing 6-3. The createMenus() Method Located in StarterAppMain.java

```
MenuBar createMenus() {
    MenuItem itemNew = new MenuItem("New...", new ImageView(
            new Image(getClass().getResourceAsStream("images/paper.png"))));
    itemNew.setAccelerator(KeyCombination.keyCombination("Ctrl+N"));
    itemNew.setOnAction(e -> System.out.println(e.getEventType()
            + " occurred on MenuItem New"));
    MenuItem itemSave = new MenuItem("Save");
    Menu menuFile = new Menu("File");
    menuFile.getItems().addAll(itemNew, itemSave);
    MenuItem itemCut = new MenuItem("Cut");
    MenuItem itemCopy = new MenuItem("Copy");
    MenuItem itemPaste = new MenuItem("Paste");
    Menu menuEdit = new Menu("Edit");
    menuEdit.getItems().addAll(itemCut, itemCopy, itemPaste);
    MenuBar menuBar = new MenuBar();
    menuBar.getMenus().addAll(menuFile, menuEdit);
    return menuBar;
}
```

As previously shown in Figure 6-2, in addition to a title, menu items often have a graphic and an accelerator key combination. In the following snippet from Listing 5-3, the menu item named New is defined with a title, graphic, and an accelerator key, as well as an action to be performed when the menu item is selected.

```
MenuItem itemNew = new MenuItem("New...", new ImageView(
            new Image(getClass().getResourceAsStream("images/paper.png"))));
    itemNew.setAccelerator(KeyCombination.keyCombination("Ctrl+N"));
    itemNew.setOnAction(e -> System.out.println(e.getEventType()
            + " occurred on MenuItem New"));
```

The recommended size for a menu item graphic is 16 × 16 pixels, which is the size of the graphic used in the New menu item of the StarterApp program. To load the graphic from the file system, the argument supplied to the Image constructor in the preceding snippet causes the same class loader that loaded the StarterAppMain class to load the paper.png file. This paper.png file is loaded from the images directory subordinate to the location of the StartAppMain.class file.

To define the Ctrl+N accelerator key combination, the static keyCombination() method of the KeyCombination class is used to create a KeyCombination instance. This instance is passed into the setAccelerator() method of the MenuItem.

The onAction() event handler in the preceding snippet defines a lambda expression that is invoked when the user selects the New menu item. The resulting message printed to the Java console is the one to which Step 2 of the earlier exercise refers.

Creating a Toolbar

To create the toolbar, our StarterApp program defines a method that we've arbitrarily named createToolBar(), shown in Listing 6-4. This method leverages the Button, Separator, ToggleButton, and ToggleGroup classes, and returns a ToolBar instance that contains the desired toolbar buttons.

Listing 6-4. The createToolBar() Method Located in StarterAppMain.java

```
ToolBar createToolBar() {
    final ToggleGroup alignToggleGroup = new ToggleGroup();
    Button newButton = new Button();
    .setGraphic(new ImageView(new Image(getClass().getResourceAsStream
    ("images/paper.png"))));
    newButton.setId("newButton");
    newButton.setTooltip(new Tooltip("New Document... Ctrl+N"));
    newButton.setOnAction(e -> System.out.println("New toolbar button clicked"));
    Button editButton = new Button();
    editButton.setGraphic(new Circle(8, Color.GREEN));
    editButton.setId("editButton");
    Button deleteButton = new Button();
    deleteButton.setGraphic(new Circle(8, Color.BLUE));
    deleteButton.setId("deleteButton");
    ToggleButton boldButton = new ToggleButton();
    boldButton.setGraphic(new Circle(8, Color.MAROON));
    boldButton.setId("boldButton");
    boldButton.setOnAction(e -> {
        ToggleButton tb = ((ToggleButton) e.getTarget());
        System.out.print(e.getEventType() + " occurred on ToggleButton "
                + tb.getId());
        System.out.print(", and selectedProperty is: ");
        System.out.println(tb.selectedProperty().getValue());
    });
    ToggleButton italicButton = new ToggleButton();
    italicButton.setGraphic(new Circle(8, Color.YELLOW));
    italicButton.setId("italicButton");
    italicButton.setOnAction(e -> {
        ToggleButton tb = ((ToggleButton) e.getTarget());
        System.out.print(e.getEventType() + " occurred on ToggleButton "
                + tb.getId());
        System.out.print(", and selectedProperty is: ");
        System.out.println(tb.selectedProperty().getValue());
    });
    ToggleButton leftAlignButton = new ToggleButton();
    leftAlignButton.setGraphic(new Circle(8, Color.PURPLE));
```

```
    leftAlignButton.setId("leftAlignButton");
    leftAlignButton.setToggleGroup(alignToggleGroup);
    ToggleButton centerAlignButton = new ToggleButton();
    centerAlignButton.setGraphic(new Circle(8, Color.ORANGE));
    centerAlignButton.setId("centerAlignButton");
    centerAlignButton.setToggleGroup(alignToggleGroup);
    ToggleButton rightAlignButton = new ToggleButton();
    rightAlignButton.setGraphic(new Circle(8, Color.CYAN));
    rightAlignButton.setId("rightAlignButton");
    rightAlignButton.setToggleGroup(alignToggleGroup);
    ToolBar toolBar = new ToolBar(
            newButton,
            editButton,
            deleteButton,
            new Separator(Orientation.VERTICAL),
            boldButton,
            italicButton,
            new Separator(Orientation.VERTICAL),
            leftAlignButton,
            centerAlignButton,
            rightAlignButton
    );

    alignToggleGroup.selectToggle(alignToggleGroup.getToggles().get(0));
    alignToggleGroup.selectedToggleProperty().addListener((ov, oldValue, newValue) -> {
        ToggleButton tb = ((ToggleButton) alignToggleGroup.getSelectedToggle());
        if (tb != null) {
            System.out.println(tb.getId() + " selected");
        }
    });

    return toolBar;
}
```

Defining Graphical Buttons

As shown in Figure 6-1, toolbar buttons often have a graphic rather than a title. They also often have a tooltip that pops up when the mouse cursor hovers over the button, as demonstrated in Step 4 of the exercise. In the following snippet from Listing 6-4, the toolbar button that causes a New Document to be created is defined with a graphic and tooltip, as well as an action to be performed when the toolbar button is selected:

```
Button newButton = new Button();
newButton.setGraphic(new ImageView(new Image(getClass().getResourceAsStream
("images/paper.png"))));
newButton.setId("newButton");
newButton.setTooltip(new Tooltip("New Document... Ctrl+N"));
newButton.setOnAction(e -> System.out.println("New toolbar button clicked"));
```

Note that the setId() method of the Button is used in the preceding snippet. This causes the padding in the button to be set to four pixels on all four sides as a result of the following rule in the starterApp.css style sheet.

```
#newButton {
    -fx-padding: 4 4 4 4;
}
```

The toolbar button defined in the previous code snippet is a JavaFX Button, but there are often use cases in which a JavaFX ToggleButton is a more appropriate choice. The following section discusses such cases, and how to implement toggle buttons in a toolbar.

Defining Toggle Buttons

In Steps 5 and 6 of the preceding exercise, you interacted with buttons that have two states: selected and not selected. The buttons in Step 5 are toggle buttons, as are the buttons in Step 6. The buttons in Step 5 operate independently of each other, but only one of the buttons in Step 6 can be in the selected (depressed) state at any given time. The following snippet from Listing 6-4 contains the code behind one of the buttons in Step 5.

```
ToggleButton boldButton = new ToggleButton();
boldButton.setGraphic(new Circle(8, Color.MAROON));
boldButton.setId("boldButton");
boldButton.setOnAction(e -> {
    ToggleButton tb = ((ToggleButton) e.getTarget());
    System.out.print(e.getEventType() + " occurred on ToggleButton "
            + tb.getId());
    System.out.print(", and selectedProperty is: ");
    System.out.println(tb.selectedProperty().getValue());
});
```

This use case is the classic Bold button in many document editing applications, where the Bold button is either selected or not selected. The ToggleButton shown in the preceding snippet contains this dual-state functionality, so it is a natural fit for this use case.

The onAction() event handler in this snippet demonstrates how you can ascertain the state of the ToggleButton as a result of being clicked. As shown in the snippet, use the getTarget() method of the ActionEvent to obtain a reference to the ToggleButton; then use its selectedProperty() method to get a reference to its selected property. Finally, use the getValue() method to get the value (either true or false) of the selected property.

Using Toggle Groups

As pointed out in the previous section, only one of the buttons in Step 6 of the preceding exercise can be in the selected (depressed) state at any given time. The following snippet from Listing 6-4 contains the code behind one of the buttons in Step 6.

```
final ToggleGroup alignToggleGroup = new ToggleGroup();
ToggleButton leftAlignButton = new ToggleButton();
leftAlignButton.setGraphic(new Circle(8, Color.PURPLE));
leftAlignButton.setId("leftAlignButton");
leftAlignButton.setToggleGroup(alignToggleGroup);
...
```

```
    alignToggleGroup.selectToggle(alignToggleGroup.getToggles().get(0));
    alignToggleGroup.selectedToggleProperty().addListener((ov, oldValue, newValue) -> {
    ToggleButton tb = ((ToggleButton) alignToggleGroup.getSelectedToggle());
    if (tb != null) {
        System.out.println(tb.getId() + " selected");
    }
});
```

This use case is the classic Left-Alignment button in many document editing applications, where only one of the Alignment buttons may be selected at any given time. The ToggleGroup instance is passed into the setToggleGroup() method of the ToggleButton shown in the preceding snippet to provide this mutually exclusive behavior.

In addition to providing mutual exclusivity, the ToggleGroup instance is used in this snippet for two purposes:

1. To initially select the first ToggleButton in the group, by using the selectToggle() method of the ToggleGroup instance.
2. To detect when the currently selected ToggleButton changes. This is accomplished by adding a ChangeListener to the selectedToggle property of the ToggleGroup, and then using its getSelectedToggle() method to ascertain which ToggleButton is currently selected. Note that this is generally preferred over putting an onAction event handler in each of the toggle buttons that are participating in a toggle group.

Inserting a Separator into a Toolbar

It is sometimes useful to visually separate toolbar buttons by using the vertical separators shown in Figure 6-3. To accomplish this, use the Separator class as shown in this line from Listing 6-4:

```
new Separator(Orientation.VERTICAL),
```

Although we didn't make use of separators in the menus of this StarterApp program, Separator objects may be used in menus as well. Of course, separators used in menus typically have a HORIZONTAL Orientation.

Creating a TabPane and Defining Tabs

One of the principles of UI design is called *progressive disclosure*, which states that a UI should reveal its functionality progressively rather than inundating the user with all of its functionality at once. The TabPane is a good example of this principle in use, as each tab discloses its functionality while hiding the functionality contained in the other tabs.

To create the TabPane instance, our StarterApp program defines a method that we've arbitrarily named createTabs(), shown in Listing 6-5. This method leverages the TabPane and Tab classes, and returns a TabPane instance that contains the desired Tab objects.

Listing 6-5. The createTabs() Method Located in StarterAppMain.java

```
TabPane createTabs() {
   final WebView webView = new WebView();
   Tab tableTab = new Tab("TableView");
   tableTab.setContent(createTableDemoNode());
   tableTab.setClosable(false);
   Tab accordionTab = new Tab("Accordion/TitledPane");
   accordionTab.setContent(createAccordionTitledDemoNode());
   accordionTab.setClosable(false);
```

```
    Tab splitTab = new Tab("SplitPane/TreeView/ListView");
    splitTab.setContent(createSplitTreeListDemoNode());
    splitTab.setClosable(false);
    Tab scrollTab = new Tab("ScrollPane/Miscellaneous");
    scrollTab.setContent(createScrollMiscDemoNode());
    scrollTab.setClosable(false);
    Tab htmlTab = new Tab("HTMLEditor");
    htmlTab.setContent(createHtmlEditorDemoNode());
    htmlTab.setClosable(false);
    Tab webViewTab = new Tab("WebView");
    webViewTab.setContent(webView);
    webViewTab.setClosable(false);
    webViewTab.setOnSelectionChanged(e -> {
        String randomWebSite = model.getRandomWebSite();
        if (webViewTab.isSelected()) {
            webView.getEngine().load(randomWebSite);
            System.out.println("WebView tab is selected, loading: "
                    + randomWebSite);
        }
    });
    TabPane tabPane = new TabPane();
    tabPane.getTabs().addAll(
            tableTab,
            accordionTab,
            splitTab,
            scrollTab,
            htmlTab,
            webViewTab
    );

    return tabPane;
}
```

To define a tab in its simplest form, you need only supply its text (which appears on the tab), and content (which appears when that tab is selected). The following snippet from Listing 6-5 demonstrates some other features of the TabPane used in the StarterApp program:

```
Tab webViewTab = new Tab("WebView");
webViewTab.setContent(webView);
webViewTab.setClosable(false);
webViewTab.setOnSelectionChanged(e -> {
    String randomWebSite = model.getRandomWebSite();
    if (webViewTab.isSelected()) {
        webView.getEngine().load(randomWebSite);
        System.out.println("WebView tab is selected, loading: "
                + randomWebSite);
    }
});
```

In addition to supplying text and content, we're also specifying that the tab shouldn't be closable, and that some processing should occur when the user chooses the tab. The latter is implemented using the onSelectionChanged() method shown previously, which enables you to implement life cycle functionality when a tab is exposed or hidden (i.e., selected or not selected). In the preceding snippet, we're causing the WebView (which is covered later) to load a randomly selected site when the tab is selected.

Now that you understand how the menus, toolbar, and tabs were created in the StarterApp program, let's examine the UI controls on each tab. We start with the leftmost tab, labeled TableView, and work our way to the right.

Creating a TableView

As you experienced in Steps 7 and 8 of the exercise, the TableView shown in Figure 6-1 contains 10,000 rows of data, and allows its columns to be rearranged and resized. The code that defines and populates the TableView in the StarterApp program is shown in Listing 6-6.

Listing 6-6. The createTableDemoNode() Method Located in StarterAppMain.java

```
Node createTableDemoNode() {
  TableView table = new TableView(model.getTeamMembers());
  TableColumn firstNameColumn = new TableColumn("First Name");
  firstNameColumn.setCellValueFactory(new PropertyValueFactory("firstName"));
  firstNameColumn.setPrefWidth(180);
  TableColumn lastNameColumn = new TableColumn("Last Name");
  lastNameColumn.setCellValueFactory(new PropertyValueFactory("lastName"));
  lastNameColumn.setPrefWidth(180);
  TableColumn phoneColumn = new TableColumn("Phone Number");
  phoneColumn.setCellValueFactory(new PropertyValueFactory("phone"));
  phoneColumn.setPrefWidth(180);
  table.getColumns().addAll(firstNameColumn, lastNameColumn, phoneColumn);
  table.getSelectionModel().selectedItemProperty()
          .addListener((ObservableValue observable, Object oldValue, Object newValue) -> {
              Person selectedPerson = (Person) newValue;
              System.out.println(selectedPerson + " chosen in TableView");
          });
  return table;
}
```

In addition to the code in Listing 6-6, the following code snippet from Listing 6-1 contains a method from our StarterAppModel class that creates the Person instances that will be displayed in the TableView:

```
public ObservableList getTeamMembers() {
  ObservableList teamMembers = FXCollections.observableArrayList();
  for (int i = 1; i <= 10000; i++) {
    teamMembers.add(new Person("FirstName" + i,
                               "LastName" + i,
                               "Phone" + i));
  }
  return teamMembers;
}
```

Assigning Items to a Table

The TableView constructor at the beginning of Listing 6-6 causes the ObservableList containing Person instances (returned from the getTeamMembers() method) to be associated with the TableView. If the contents of the underlying ObservableList change, the TableView is automatically updated to reflect the changes.

Defining TableView Columns

To define the columns in our TableView we use the methods shown in this snippet from Listing 6-6:

```
TableColumn firstNameColumn = new TableColumn("First Name");
firstNameColumn.setCellValueFactory(new PropertyValueFactory("firstName"));
firstNameColumn.setPrefWidth(180);
```

The String parameter we provide to the constructor specifies the text that should appear in the column header, and the setPrefWidth() method specifies the column's preferred width in pixels.

The argument passed into the setCellValueFactory() method specifies a property that will be used to populate this column. In this case, the property is the firstNameProperty defined in the Person model class of our StarterApp program, shown in Listing 6-7.

Listing 6-7. The Source Code for Person.java

```
package projavafx.starterapp.model;

import javafx.beans.property.SimpleStringProperty;
import javafx.beans.property.StringProperty;

public final class Person {
  private StringProperty firstName;
  public void setFirstName(String value) { firstNameProperty().set(value); }
  public String getFirstName() { return firstNameProperty().get(); }
  public StringProperty firstNameProperty() {
    if (firstName == null) firstName = new SimpleStringProperty(this, "firstName");
    return firstName;
  }

  private StringProperty lastName;
  public void setLastName(String value) { lastNameProperty().set(value); }
  public String getLastName() { return lastNameProperty().get(); }
  public StringProperty lastNameProperty() {
    if (lastName == null) lastName = new SimpleStringProperty(this, "lastName");
    return lastName;
  }

  private StringProperty phone;
  public void setPhone(String value) { phoneProperty().set(value); }
  public String getPhone() { return phoneProperty().get(); }
  public StringProperty phoneProperty() {
    if (phone == null) phone = new SimpleStringProperty(this, "phone");
    return phone;
  }
```

```
  public Person(String firstName, String lastName, String phone) {
    setFirstName(firstName);
    setLastName(lastName);
    setPhone(phone);
  }

  public String toString() {
    return "Person: " + firstName.getValue() + " " + lastName.getValue();
  }
}
```

Detecting When a Row Is Selected

To detect when the user selects a row in the `TableView`, the StarterApp program adds a `ChangeListener` to the `selectedItem` property of the table view's selection model. The code for accomplishing this is shown in this snippet from Listing 6-6:

```
table.getSelectionModel().selectedItemProperty()
            .addListener((ObservableValue observable, Object oldValue, Object newValue) -> {
                Person selectedPerson = (Person) newValue;
                System.out.println(selectedPerson + " chosen in TableView");
            });
```

When the user selects a row, the lambda expression is invoked, which prints data from the underlying `Person` instance represented by that row. This is the behavior you observed in Step 7 of the previous exercise.

Now that we've explored some of the capabilities of the `TableView`, let's move on to the next tab, Accordion/TitledPane.

Creating an `Accordion` and Defining a `TitledPane`

As you experienced in Step 9 of the exercise, the `Accordion` shown in Figure 6-4 contains some `TitledPane` instances, each of which contains nodes and may be expanded and collapsed. The code that defines and populates the `Accordion` in the StarterApp program is shown in Listing 6-8.

Listing 6-8. The `createAccordionTitledDemoNode()` Method Located in `StarterAppMain.java`

```
Node createAccordionTitledDemoNode() {
    TitledPane paneA = new TitledPane("TitledPane A", new TextArea("TitledPane A content"));
        TitledPane paneB = new TitledPane("TitledPane B", new TextArea("TitledPane B content"));
        TitledPane paneC = new TitledPane("TitledPane C", new TextArea("TitledPane C content"));
        Accordion accordion = new Accordion();
        accordion.getPanes().addAll(paneA, paneB, paneC);
        accordion.setExpandedPane(paneA);
        return accordion;
}
```

As shown in the following snippet from Listing 6-8, a `TitledPane` is typically given the `text` for its title, and a `Node` subclass (in this case a `TextArea`) for its `content`:

```
TitledPane paneA = new TitledPane("TitledPane A", new TextArea("TitledPane A content"));
...
accordion.setExpandedPane(paneA);
```

In addition, we want the first TitledPane in our example initially to be expanded, so the setExpandedPane() method of the Accordion is used to accomplish this.

Now that you know how to create Accordion and TitledPane controls, we move on to the next tab, SplitPane/TreeView/ListView.

Creating a TreeView

As you experienced in Steps 10 and 11 of the exercise, the TreeView shown in Figure 6-5 contains a hierarchical structure of tree items, each of which may be expanded and collapsed. The code that defines and populates the TreeView in the StarterApp program is shown in Listing 6-9.

Listing 6-9. The createSplitTreeListDemoNode() Method Located in StarterAppMain.java

```
Node createSplitTreeListDemoNode() {
    TreeItem animalTree = new TreeItem("Animal");
        animalTree.getChildren().addAll(new TreeItem("Lion"), new TreeItem("Tiger"), new
        TreeItem("Bear"));
        TreeItem mineralTree = new TreeItem("Mineral");
        mineralTree.getChildren().addAll(new TreeItem("Copper"), new TreeItem("Diamond"), new
        TreeItem("Quartz"));
        TreeItem vegetableTree = new TreeItem("Vegetable");
        vegetableTree.getChildren().addAll(new TreeItem("Arugula"), new TreeItem("Broccoli"),
        new TreeItem("Cabbage"));

        TreeItem root = new TreeItem("Root");
        root.getChildren().addAll(animalTree, mineralTree, vegetableTree);
        TreeView treeView = new TreeView(root);
        treeView.setMinWidth(150);
        treeView.setShowRoot(false);
        treeView.setEditable(false);

        ListView listView = new ListView(model.listViewItems);

        SplitPane splitPane = new SplitPane();
        splitPane.getItems().addAll(treeView, listView);

        treeView.getSelectionModel().setSelectionMode(SelectionMode.SINGLE);
        treeView.getSelectionModel().selectedItemProperty()
                .addListener((ObservableValue observable, Object oldValue, Object newValue) -> {
                    TreeItem treeItem = (TreeItem) newValue;
                    if (newValue != null && treeItem.isLeaf()) {
                        model.listViewItems.clear();
                        for (int i = 1; i <= 10000; i++) {
                            model.listViewItems.add(treeItem.getValue() + " " + i);
                        }
                    }
                });

        return splitPane;
}
```

As shown in the following snippet from Listing 6-9, a TreeView can be supplied with values for several properties, including whether the root TreeItem should show and whether the TreeView is editable. In the StarterApp program we're also setting the minWidth so that the user can't hide the TreeView by dragging the SplitPane divider (as you noticed in Step 12 of the previous exercise).

```
TreeView treeView = new TreeView(root);
treeView.setMinWidth(150);
treeView.setShowRoot(false);
treeView.setEditable(false);
  ...
```

Defining a TreeItem

Taking a look at the following snippet from Listing 6-9, you see that each TreeItem is given the value that it represents, and 0 or more children TreeItem objects:

```
animalTree.getChildren().addAll(new TreeItem("Lion"), new TreeItem("Tiger"), new TreeItem("Bear"));
TreeItem root = new TreeItem("Root");
root.getChildren().addAll(animalTree, mineralTree, vegetableTree);
```

In addition, you can set properties such as

- graphic, which displays a Node in the TreeItem
- expanded, which controls whether the TreeItem is expanded or collapsed

Now that you know how to create a TreeView and its TreeItem instances, let's examine how to detect when a TreeItem has been selected.

Detecting When a TreeItem Is Selected

To detect when the user selects a TreeItem in the TreeView, the StarterApp program adds a ChangeListener to the selectedItem property of the tree view's selection model. The code for accomplishing this is shown in this snippet from Listing 6-9:

```
treeView.getSelectionModel().setSelectionMode(SelectionMode.SINGLE);
    treeView.getSelectionModel().selectedItemProperty()
            .addListener((ObservableValue observable, Object oldValue, Object newValue) -> {
                TreeItem treeItem = (TreeItem) newValue;
                if (newValue != null && treeItem.isLeaf()) {
                    model.listViewItems.clear();
                    for (int i = 1; i <= 10000; i++) {
                        model.listViewItems.add(treeItem.getValue() + " " + i);
                    }
                }
            });
```

A TreeView may allow the user to select a single row, or multiple rows, based on its selection mode. In the first line of the preceding snippet, we're setting the selection mode of the TableView to SINGLE.

In Step 11 of the exercise, when you clicked on a leaf TreeItem in the TreeView, the ListView on the right side of Figure 6-6 was populated. The code in this snippet accomplishes this by first checking to see if the selected TreeItem is a leaf, and then populating the model that backs the ListView.

Creating a ListView and Assigning Items to a ListView

The following code snippet, from Listing 6-9, defines and populates the ListView in the StarterApp program:

```
ListView listView = new ListView(model.listViewItems);
```

In addition to the code in the preceding snippet, the following line from Listing 6-1 contains an instance variable from our StarterAppModel class that contains the objects that will be displayed in the ListView:

```
public ObservableList listViewItems = FXCollections.observableArrayList();
```

Recall that this is the same instance variable that is populated when clicking a leaf TreeItem in the previous section.

The parameter we provide to the ListView constructor causes the ObservableList named listViewItems in the model to be associated with the ListView. As demonstrated in Step 11 of the previous exercise, if contents of the underlying ObservableList change the ListView is automatically updated to reflect the changes.

Creating a SplitPane

As you experienced in Step 12 of the previous exercise, the SplitPane shown in Figure 6-6 contains a TreeView and a ListView, and its divider can be dragged by the user. The following code snippet, from Listing 6-9, defines and populates the SplitPane in the StarterApp program:

```
    SplitPane splitPane = new SplitPane();
splitPane.getItems().addAll(treeView, listView);
```

In this case there are two nodes in the SplitPane, which means that there will be just one divider. Note that a SplitPane may have more than two nodes and therefore more than one divider.

In addition to the functionality shown in the previous snippet, a SplitPane may also have its orientation set to VERTICAL, and its dividerPositions set to given percentages of the pane.

Now that you know how to create TreeView, ListView, and SplitPane controls, we move on to the next tab, ScrollPane/Miscellaneous.

Creating a TreeTableView

Sometimes, it is useful to combine a tree and a table. This is especially important when the data that has to be visualized is hierarchical and each entry contains the same type of properties. In this case, the TreeTableView class provides a great solution. As you can see in Figures 6-7 and 6-8, a TreeTableView provides the functionality offered by a TreeView, but for every entry that is shown, we can also show additional columns in a TreeTableView.

The data in a TreeTableView is created using TreeItem instances. In our StarterApp program, we created data in the getFamily() method of the model, as shown in Listing 6-10.

Listing 6-10. Create Hierarchical Data in StarterAppModel.java

```
public TreeItem<Person> getFamilyTree() {
    Random random = new Random();
    TreeItem<Person> root = new TreeItem();
    for (int i = 0; i < 5; i++) {
        Person parent = new Person("Parent " + i, "LastName" + i, "Phone" + i);
        TreeItem<Person> parentItem = new TreeItem(parent);
        for (int j = 0; j < random.nextInt(4); j++) {
            Person child = new Person("Child " + i + "-" + j, "LastName" + i, "Phone" + j);
```

```
            TreeItem<Person> childItem = new TreeItem(child);
            parentItem.getChildren().add(childItem);
            for (int k = 0; k < random.nextInt(4); k++) {
                Person grandChild = new Person("Grandchild " + i + "-" + j + "-" + k,
                "LastName" + i, "Phone" + k);
                TreeItem<Person> grandChildItem = new TreeItem(grandChild);
                childItem.getChildren().add(grandChildItem);
            }
        }
        root.getChildren().add(parentItem);
    }
    return root;
}
```

In this code, we create a number of persons, starting with five "parents." We then add a random number of children (between zero and three) to each parent, and each of the children can have a random number of children itself—so-called grandchildren. All parents are added to a root node on the TreeItem. Rendering this hierarchical data using a TreeTableView is demonstrated in Listing 6-11.

Listing 6-11. Rendering Hierarchical Data Using a TreeTableView Instance in StarterAppMain.java

```
Node createTreeTableDemoNode() {
        TreeTableView<Person> treeTableView = new TreeTableView(model.getFamilyTree());
        TreeTableColumn<Person, String> firstNameColumn = new TreeTableColumn("First Name");
        firstNameColumn.setCellValueFactory(new TreeItemPropertyValueFactory("firstName"));
        firstNameColumn.setPrefWidth(180);
        TreeTableColumn lastNameColumn = new TreeTableColumn("Last Name");
        lastNameColumn.setCellValueFactory(new TreeItemPropertyValueFactory("lastName"));
        lastNameColumn.setPrefWidth(180);
        TreeTableColumn phoneColumn = new TreeTableColumn("Phone Number");
        phoneColumn.setCellValueFactory(new TreeItemPropertyValueFactory("phone"));
        phoneColumn.setPrefWidth(180);
        treeTableView.getColumns().addAll(firstNameColumn, lastNameColumn, phoneColumn);
        treeTableView.getSelectionModel().selectedItemProperty().addListener((ObservableValue<?
        extends TreeItem<Person>>observable, TreeItem<Person> oldValue, TreeItem<Person> newValue) -> {
            Person selectedPerson = newValue.getValue();
            System.out.println(selectedPerson + " chosen in TreeTableView");
        });
        treeTableView.setShowRoot(false);
        return treeTableView;
}
```

As you can see from this code, the TreeTableView looks rather similar to the TableView. There are some obvious differences, though. Rather than using TableColumn instances to describe the columns, a TreeTableView requires one to use TreeTableColumn instances. Also, if we want to set the CellValueFactory for a specific column, we can use the convenience class TreeItemPropertyValueFactory, which will make sure the value of the property with the supplied name is rendered in the particular call for a specific column. We now move on to the next tab, ScrollPane/ Miscellaneous.

Defining a ScrollPane

As you experienced in Step 22 of the previous exercise, the ScrollPane shown in Figures 6-9 and 6-10 contains several UI controls, and has a vertical scrollbar so that all of the controls may be accessed.

The code from the StarterApp program that defines the ScrollPane and populates it with UI controls is shown in Listing 6-12.

Listing 6-12. The createScrollMiscDemoNode() Method Located in StarterAppMain.java

```
Node createScrollMiscDemoNode() {
      final ToggleGroup radioToggleGroup = new ToggleGroup();
      ChoiceBox choiceBox;
      final TextField textField;
      final PasswordField passwordField;
      final TextArea textArea;
      Slider slider;
      ProgressIndicator progressIndicator;
      ProgressBar progressBar;
      ScrollBar scrollBar;
      Button button = new Button("Button");
      button.setOnAction(e -> System.out.println(e.getEventType() + " occurred on Button"));
      final CheckBox checkBox = new CheckBox("CheckBox");
      checkBox.setOnAction(e -> {
          System.out.print(e.getEventType() + " occurred on CheckBox");
          System.out.print(", and selectedProperty is: ");
          System.out.println(checkBox.selectedProperty().getValue());
      });

      RadioButton radioButton1 = new RadioButton("RadioButton1");
      radioButton1.setToggleGroup(radioToggleGroup);
      RadioButton radioButton2 = new RadioButton("RadioButton2");
      radioButton2.setToggleGroup(radioToggleGroup);
      HBox radioBox = new HBox(10, radioButton1, radioButton2);

      Hyperlink link = new Hyperlink("Hyperlink");
      link.setOnAction(e -> System.out.println(e.getEventType() + " occurred on Hyperlink"));

      choiceBox = new ChoiceBox(model.choiceBoxItems);

      MenuItem menuA = new MenuItem("MenuItem A");
      menuA.setOnAction(e -> System.out.println(e.getEventType() + " occurred on Menu Item A"));
      MenuItem menuB = new MenuItem("MenuItem B");
      MenuButton menuButton = new MenuButton("MenuButton");
      menuButton.getItems().addAll(menuA, menuB);

      MenuItem splitMenuA = new MenuItem("MenuItem A");
      splitMenuA.setOnAction(e -> System.out.println(e.getEventType()
              + " occurred on Menu Item A"));
      MenuItem splitMenuB = new MenuItem("MenuItem B");
      SplitMenuButton splitMenuButton = new SplitMenuButton(splitMenuA, splitMenuB);
      splitMenuButton.setText("SplitMenuButton");
      splitMenuButton.setOnAction(e -> System.out.println(e.getEventType()
              + " occurred on SplitMenuButton"));
```

```
        textField = new TextField();
        textField.setPromptText("Enter user name");
        textField.setPrefColumnCount(16);

        passwordField = new PasswordField();
        passwordField.setPromptText("Enter password");
        passwordField.setPrefColumnCount(16);

        textArea = new TextArea();
        textArea.setPrefColumnCount(12);
        textArea.setPrefRowCount(4);

        LocalDate today = LocalDate.now();
        DatePicker datePicker = new DatePicker(today);
        datePicker.setOnAction(e -> System.out.println("Selected date: " + datePicker.getValue()));

        ColorPicker colorPicker = new ColorPicker(Color.BLUEVIOLET);
        colorPicker.setOnAction(e -> System.out.println("Selected color: " + colorPicker.getValue()));

        progressIndicator = new ProgressIndicator();
        progressIndicator.setPrefWidth(200);

        slider = new Slider(-1, model.maxRpm, 0);
        slider.setPrefWidth(200);

        progressBar = new ProgressBar();
        progressBar.setPrefWidth(200);

        scrollBar = new ScrollBar();
        scrollBar.setPrefWidth(200);
        scrollBar.setMin(-1);
        scrollBar.setMax(model.maxKph);

        VBox variousControls = new VBox(20,
                button,
                checkBox,
                radioBox,
                link,
                choiceBox,
                menuButton,
                splitMenuButton,
                textField,
                passwordField,
                new HBox(10, new Label("TextArea:"), textArea),
                datePicker, colorPicker,
                progressIndicator, slider,
                progressBar, scrollBar);

        variousControls.setPadding(new Insets(10, 10, 10, 10));
        radioToggleGroup.selectToggle(radioToggleGroup.getToggles().get(0));
        radioToggleGroup.selectedToggleProperty().addListener((ov, oldValue, newValue) -> {
            RadioButton rb = ((RadioButton) radioToggleGroup.getSelectedToggle());
```

```
        if (rb != null) {
            System.out.println(rb.getText() + " selected");
        }
    });

    textField.textProperty().addListener((ov, oldValue, newValue) -> {
        System.out.println("TextField text is: " + textField.getText());
    });

    passwordField.focusedProperty().addListener((ov, oldValue, newValue) -> {
        if (!passwordField.isFocused()) {
            System.out.println("PasswordField text is: "
                    + passwordField.getText());
        }
    });

    textArea.focusedProperty().addListener((ov, oldValue, newValue) -> {
        if (!textArea.isFocused()) {
            System.out.println("TextArea text is: " + textArea.getText());
        }
    });

    slider.valueProperty().bindBidirectional(model.rpm);
    progressIndicator.progressProperty().bind(model.rpm.divide(model.maxRpm));

    scrollBar.valueProperty().bindBidirectional(model.kph);
    progressBar.progressProperty().bind(model.kph.divide(model.maxKph));

    choiceBox.getSelectionModel().selectFirst();
    choiceBox.getSelectionModel().selectedItemProperty()
            .addListener((observable, oldValue, newValue) -> {
                System.out.println(newValue + " chosen in ChoiceBox");
            });

    ScrollPane scrollPane = new ScrollPane(variousControls);
    scrollPane.setHbarPolicy(ScrollPane.ScrollBarPolicy.NEVER);
    scrollPane.setVbarPolicy(ScrollPane.ScrollBarPolicy.AS_NEEDED);
    scrollPane.setOnMousePressed((MouseEvent me) -> {
        if (me.getButton() == MouseButton.SECONDARY) {
            contextMenu.show(stage, me.getScreenX(), me.getScreenY());
        }
    });

    MenuItem contextA = new MenuItem("MenuItem A");
    contextA.setOnAction(e -> System.out.println(e.getEventType()
            + " occurred on Menu Item A"));
    MenuItem contextB = new MenuItem("MenuItem B");
    contextMenu = new ContextMenu(contextA, contextB);

    return scrollPane;
}
```

As shown in the following snippet from Listing 6-12, the content of a ScrollPane is a Node subclass, in this case a VBox that contains several nodes. When the contents are larger than the viewable area of the ScrollPane, horizontal and/or vertical scrollbars appear according to the specified hbarPolicy and vbarPolicy.

```
ScrollPane scrollPane = new ScrollPane(variousControls);
scrollPane.setHbarPolicy(ScrollPane.ScrollBarPolicy.NEVER);
scrollPane.setVbarPolicy(ScrollPane.ScrollBarPolicy.AS_NEEDED);
scrollPane.setOnMousePressed((MouseEvent me) -> {
    if (me.getButton() == MouseButton.SECONDARY) {
        contextMenu.show(stage, me.getScreenX(), me.getScreenY());
    }
});
```

Other useful ScrollPane properties include:

- pannable, which enables the user to pan the contents of the ScrollPane by dragging it with the mouse
- fitToWidth/fitToHeight, which causes the content node (if resizable) to be stretched to fit the width/height of the ScrollPane

Note that we're using an onMousePressed() event handler in the previous snippet. We walk through that functionality after discussing some of the UI controls that are contained within our ScrollPane, beginning with the CheckBox.

Using a CheckBox

As you experienced in Step 17 of the exercise, the ScrollPane shown in Figure 6-9 contains a CheckBox. When the CheckBox is clicked, a message is printed to the Java console indicating the state of its selected property. The following code snippet, from Listing 6-12, implements this functionality in the StarterApp program:

```
final CheckBox checkBox = new CheckBox("CheckBox");
checkBox.setOnAction(e -> {
    System.out.print(e.getEventType() + " occurred on CheckBox");
    System.out.print(", and selectedProperty is: ");
    System.out.println(checkBox.selectedProperty().getValue());
});
```

A CheckBox may also represent a third indeterminate state by setting its allowIndeterminate property to true. This third state is typically represented in the CheckBox with a dash, and is useful for indicating that the state represented by the CheckBox is unknown.

Defining a RadioButton

In Step 18 of the previous exercise, you selected each of the RadioButton controls shown in Figure 6-9. As a result, a message was printed to the Java console indicating which RadioButton was selected. The following code snippet, from Listing 6-12, implements this functionality in the StarterApp program:

```
final ToggleGroup radioToggleGroup = new ToggleGroup();
RadioButton radioButton1 = new RadioButton("RadioButton1");
radioButton1.setToggleGroup(radioToggleGroup);
```

```
RadioButton radioButton2 = new RadioButton("RadioButton2");
radioButton2.setToggleGroup(radioToggleGroup);
HBox radioBox = new HBox(10, radioButton1, radioButton2);
...
radioToggleGroup.selectToggle(radioToggleGroup.getToggles().get(0));
radioToggleGroup.selectedToggleProperty().addListener((ov, oldValue, newValue) -> {
    RadioButton rb = ((RadioButton) radioToggleGroup.getSelectedToggle());
    if (rb != null) {
        System.out.println(rb.getText() + " selected");
    }
});
```

Because the `RadioButton` class extends the `ToggleButton` class, the code in the preceding snippet is very similar to the code in the section "Using Toggle Groups" earlier in this chapter. Please review that section if you'd like an explanation of the code in this snippet.

Creating a Hyperlink

The `Hyperlink` control is a button that has the appearance of a link seen in a browser. It can have a graphic, text, or both, and it responds to mouse rollovers and clicks. In Step 19 of the previous exercise, you clicked the `Hyperlink` control shown in Figure 6-9. As a result, a message was printed to the Java console indicating that it was clicked. The following code snippet from Listing 6-12 implements this functionality in the StarterApp program:

```
Hyperlink link = new Hyperlink("Hyperlink");
link.setOnAction(e -> System.out.println(e.getEventType() + " occurred on Hyperlink"));
```

Defining a ChoiceBox

When clicked, a `ChoiceBox` control presents a popup containing a list of items from which to choose. In Step 20 of the previous exercise, you clicked the `ChoiceBox` control shown in Figure 6-9. As a result, a message was printed to the Java console indicating which item you chose. The following code snippet from Listing 6-12 implements this functionality in the StarterApp program:

```
ChoiceBox choiceBox;
choiceBox = new ChoiceBox(model.choiceBoxItems);
choiceBox.getSelectionModel().selectFirst();
choiceBox.getSelectionModel().selectedItemProperty()
        .addListener((observable, oldValue, newValue) -> {
            System.out.println(newValue + " chosen in ChoiceBox");
        });
```

To initially select the first item in the `ChoiceBox`, the preceding snippet invokes the `selectFirst()` method of the choice box's `selectionModel`. To detect when the user chooses an item in the `ChoiceBox`, we add the `ChangeListener` shown in the snippet to the `selectedItem` property of the choice box's selection model.

In addition to the code in the preceding snippet, the following snippet from Listing 6-1 contains an instance variable from our StarterAppModel class that contains the objects that will be displayed in the ChoiceBox:

```
public ObservableList choiceBoxItems = FXCollections.observableArrayList(
    "Choice A",
    "Choice B",
    "Choice C",
    "Choice D"
);
```

Now we move on to a control named MenuButton whose appearance is similar to the ChoiceBox, but whose behavior is similar to a Menu.

Using a MenuButton

When clicked, a MenuButton control pops up a context menu that contains MenuItem instances from which to choose. In Step 21 of the previous exercise, you clicked the MenuButton control shown in Figure 6-9. As a result, a message was printed to the Java console indicating which MenuItem you chose. The following code snippet, from Listing 6-12, implements this functionality in the StarterApp program:

```
MenuItem menuA = new MenuItem("MenuItem A");
menuA.setOnAction(e -> System.out.println(e.getEventType() + " occurred on Menu Item A"));
MenuItem menuB = new MenuItem("MenuItem B");
MenuButton menuButton = new MenuButton("MenuButton");
menuButton.getItems().addAll(menuA, menuB);
```

Because of the similarity between the MenuButton and Menu classes, the concepts in the previous snippet are covered in the section "Creating a Menu and Defining Menu Items" earlier in the chapter. One of the distinguishing features of MenuButton is the popupSide property, which enables you to choose on which side of the MenuButton the ContextMenu should pop up.

Another way to pop up a ContextMenu that doesn't require using a MenuButton is our next topic of discussion.

Creating a ContextMenu

In Step 30 of the previous exercise, you clicked the secondary mouse button in a blank area of the ScrollPane shown in Figure 6-11, and a ContextMenu popped up, from which you chose a MenuItem. The following snippet from Listing 6-12 realizes this behavior:

```
MenuItem contextA = new MenuItem("MenuItem A");
contextA.setOnAction(e -> System.out.println(e.getEventType()
        + " occurred on Menu Item A"));
MenuItem contextB = new MenuItem("MenuItem B");
final ContextMenu contextMenu = new ContextMenu(contextA, contextB);
ScrollPane scrollPane = new ScrollPane(variousControls);
...
scrollPane.setOnMousePressed((MouseEvent me) -> {
    if (me.getButton() == MouseButton.SECONDARY) {
        contextMenu.show(stage, me.getScreenX(), me.getScreenY());
    }
});
```

When the user presses the secondary mouse button, the lambda expression defined in the setOnMousePressed method is invoked. Calling the show() method in the manner used in the snippet causes the ContextMenu to be displayed on the screen at the location in which the mouse was pressed. A ContextMenu must have an owner, either a Node or a Stage, for it to be displayed, which is why the Stage object was passed into the show() method.

Creating a SplitMenuButton

Very similar to the MenuButton, the SplitMenuButton pops up a ContextMenu when the down arrow is clicked. In addition, when the main part of the SplitMenuButton is clicked, the behavior is that of a Button. Both of these behaviors are demonstrated in Steps 22 and 23 of the previous exercise when interacting with the SplitMenuButton shown in Figure 6-9. The following snippet from Listing 6-12 realizes these behaviors:

```
MenuItem splitMenuA = new MenuItem("MenuItem A");
splitMenuA.setOnAction(e -> System.out.println(e.getEventType()
        + " occurred on Menu Item A"));
MenuItem splitMenuB = new MenuItem("MenuItem B");
SplitMenuButton splitMenuButton = new SplitMenuButton(splitMenuA, splitMenuB);
splitMenuButton.setText("SplitMenuButton");
splitMenuButton.setOnAction(e -> System.out.println(e.getEventType()
        + " occurred on SplitMenuButton"));
```

Let's move away from the button-like UI controls and turn our attention to some UI controls that accept text input, starting with the TextField.

Defining a TextField

In Step 25 of the exercise, as you entered text into the TextField shown in Figure 6-9, the contents of the TextField were printed to the Java console each time the contents changed (e.g., as characters were typed into the TextField). The following snippet from Listing 6-12 creates the TextField and implements these behaviors:

```
final TextField textField = new TextField();
textField.setPromptText("Enter user name");
textField.setPrefColumnCount(16);
textField.textProperty().addListener((ov, oldValue, newValue) -> {
    System.out.println("TextField text is: " + textField.getText());
});
```

To detect when the text property of the TextField has changed, the code in this snippet adds a ChangeListener to the text property. The new value of the text property is then printed to the Java console in the body of the lambda expression.

Using a PasswordField

The PasswordField extends the TextField class, and its purpose is to mask the characters that are typed into it. In Step 26 of the exercise, when you entered text into the PasswordField shown in Figure 6-9 and subsequently caused the PasswordField to lose focus, the contents of the PasswordField were printed to the Java console. The following snippet from Listing 6-12 creates the PasswordField and implements these behaviors:

```
final PasswordField passwordField = new PasswordField();
    passwordField.setPromptText("Enter password");
    passwordField.setPrefColumnCount(16);
```

```
passwordField.focusedProperty().addListener((ov, oldValue, newValue) -> {
    if (!passwordField.isFocused()) {
        System.out.println("PasswordField text is: "
            + passwordField.getText());
    }
});
```

To detect when the PasswordField has lost focus, the code in the preceding snippet adds a ChangeListener to the focused property. The value of the text property is then printed to the Java console in the body of the lambda expression if the PasswordField is indeed not focused.

Creating a TextArea

The TextArea control is similar to the TextField control, but allows for multiple lines of text. In Step 27 of the exercise, when you entered text into the TextArea shown in Figure 6-9 and subsequently caused the TextArea to lose focus, the contents of the TextArea were printed to the Java console. The following snippet from Listing 6-12 creates the TextArea and implements these behaviors:

```
final TextArea textArea = new TextArea();
    textArea.setPrefColumnCount(12);
    textArea.setPrefRowCount(4);
    textArea.focusedProperty().addListener((ov, oldValue, newValue) -> {
        if (!textArea.isFocused()) {
            System.out.println("TextArea text is: " + textArea.getText());
        }
    });
```

Some useful TextArea properties not demonstrated in the preceding snippet are:

- wrapText, which controls whether the text will wrap in the TextArea
- scrollLeft/scrollTop, which are the number of pixels by which the content is horizontally or vertically scrolled

Let's move away from the UI controls that accept text input, and briefly talk about two very convenient utilities.

Creating a DatePicker and a ColorPicker

When JavaFX 2 was released with a number of controls, attention was paid to what else was needed in real-world applications. Some new controls have been added in JavaFX 2.2 and JavaFX 8, based on input from the developer community. A particularly useful control is the DatePicker, which allows users to open a calendar view and select a particular date. The following snippet from Listing 6-12 shows how to include this control in a JavaFX application:

```
LocalDate today = LocalDate.now();
DatePicker datePicker = new DatePicker(today);
datePicker.setOnAction(e -> System.out.println("Selected date: " + datePicker.getValue()));
```

When the user clicks the date control shown in Figure 6-10, a calendar will pop up. Selecting a date on the calendar will trigger the onAction event handler on the datePicker instance, and the lambda expression will print the selected date to the standard console.

Similar to the DatePicker class, a ColorPicker allows users to select a color from a palette. The following two lines of code, taken from Listing 6-12, show all that is needed to create the color picker control that is shown in Figure 6-10.

```
ColorPicker colorPicker = new ColorPicker(Color.BLUEVIOLET);
colorPicker.setOnAction(e -> System.out.println("Selected color: " + colorPicker.getValue()));
```

Again, clicking on the control will open a wider control where the user can select a color. When the selection is done, the lambda expression in the onAction event handler on the colorPicker is called, and the selected color is printed to the standard console.

We will now move on toward controls that graphically represent numeric values in various ranges.

Creating a Slider

The Slider control represents a numeric value with its thumb, and enables the user to choose a numeric value by dragging its thumb. In Step 28 of the exercise you interacted with the Slider, shown in Figure 6-10, to control the value of the ProgressIndicator directly above it. The following snippet from Listing 6-12 contains the code that realizes the Slider-related portions of this behavior:

```
final Slider slider = new Slider(-1, model.maxRpm, 0);
slider.setPrefWidth(200);
slider.valueProperty().bindBidirectional(model.rpm);
```

The range of the Slider is set through its min and max properties, which in this case are –1 and the value of the maxRpm instance variable located in the StarterAppModel class. The min and max properties and the initial value are passed via the constructor.

Also, the value property of the Slider is bidirectionally bound to the rpm property in the model, which is used for keeping the ProgressIndicator updated as you experienced in Step 26. The following code snippet from Listing 6-1 contains the relevant instance variables from our StarterAppModel class:

```
public double maxRpm = 8000.0;
public DoubleProperty rpm = new SimpleDoubleProperty(0);
```

Defining a ProgressIndicator

The ProgressIndicator control displays the progress of an operation, either expressed as percent complete or indeterminate. The following snippet contains the code that creates the ProgressIndicator and keeps its progress property updated from the relevant instance variables in the model.

```
final ProgressIndicator progressIndicator = new ProgressIndicator();
progressIndicator.setPrefWidth(200);
progressIndicator.progressProperty().bind(model.rpm.divide(model.maxRpm));
```

As a result of the bind shown in this snippet, when the rpm variable in the StarterAppModel class is negative, the progress property of the ProgressIndicator becomes negative. This causes the ProgressIndicator to assume the indeterminate appearance that you experienced in Step 28 of the exercise. Note that we're using the Fluent API covered in Chapter 4 in the bind expression.

Defining a ScrollBar

The ScrollBar control, like the Slider control discussed earlier, represents a numeric value with its thumb, and enables the user to choose a numeric value by dragging its thumb. The ScrollBar control is typically used in conjunction with other nodes to define a new UI component, the ScrollPane and ListView serving as two examples of this. In Step 29 you interacted with the ScrollBar, shown in Figure 6-10, to control the value of the ProgressBar directly above it. The following snippet from Listing 6-12 contains the code that realizes the ScrollBar-related portions of this behavior:

```
final ScrollBar scrollBar = new ScrollBar();
scrollBar.setPrefWidth(200);
scrollBar.setMin(-1);
scrollBar.setMax(model.maxKph);
scrollBar.valueProperty().bindBidirectional(model.kph);
```

As with the Slider, the range of the ScrollBar is set through its min and max properties, which in this case are -1 and the value of the maxKph instance variable located in the StarterAppModel class. Also, the value property of the ScrollBar is bidirectionally bound to the kph property in the model, which is used for keeping the ProgressBar updated as you experienced in Step 29. The following code snippet from Listing 6-1 contains the relevant instance variables from our StarterAppModel class:

```
public double maxKph = 300.0;
public DoubleProperty kph = new SimpleDoubleProperty(0);
```

Using a ProgressBar

The ProgressBar control is a specialization of the ProgressIndicator that displays the progress of an operation as a bar. The following snippet contains the code that creates the ProgressBar and keeps its progress property updated from the relevant instance variables in the model.

```
final ProgressBar progressBar = new ProgressBar();
progressBar.setPrefWidth(200);
progressBar.progressProperty().bind(model.kph.divide(model.maxKph));
```

As a result of the bind shown in this snippet, when the kph variable in the StarterAppModel class is negative, the progress property of the ProgressBar becomes negative. This causes the ProgressBar to assume the indeterminate appearance that you experienced in Step 29.

Now we move away from the UI controls that graphically represent numeric values in various ranges, toward the controls that deal with HTML and other web-related content.

Creating an HTMLEditor

The HTMLEditor control enables users to edit rich text, with its underlying data represented in HTML. As you experienced in Step 32 of the exercise, the HTMLEditor shown in Figure 6-12 contains several tools for editing text, as well as the editing area itself.

To create the HTMLEditor instance, our StarterApp program defines a method that we've arbitrarily named createHtmlEditorDemoNode(), shown in Listing 6-13. This method leverages the BorderPane, HTMLEditor, and Button classes, returning a BorderPane instance that contains the HTMLEditor and a button labeled View HTML.

Listing 6-13. The createHtmlEditorDemoNode() Method Located in StarterAppMain.java

```
Node createHtmlEditorDemoNode() {
      final BorderPane htmlEditorDemo;
      final HTMLEditor htmlEditor = new HTMLEditor();
      htmlEditor.setHtmlText("<p>Replace this text</p>");
      Button viewHtmlButton = new Button("View HTML");
      viewHtmlButton.setOnAction(e -> {
          Popup alertPopup = createAlertPopup(htmlEditor.getHtmlText());
          alertPopup.show(stage,
                  (stage.getWidth() - alertPopup.getWidth()) / 2 + stage.getX(),
                  (stage.getHeight() - alertPopup.getHeight()) / 2 + stage.getY());
      });
      htmlEditorDemo = new BorderPane();
      htmlEditorDemo.setCenter(htmlEditor);
      htmlEditorDemo.setBottom(viewHtmlButton);

      BorderPane.setAlignment(viewHtmlButton, Pos.CENTER);
      BorderPane.setMargin(viewHtmlButton, new Insets(10, 0, 10, 0));
      return htmlEditorDemo;
}
```

Creating a Popup

As you experienced in Step 33 in the exercise, when the Button is clicked, the Popup shown in Figure 6-13 is created and displayed. This Popup displays the HTML that represents the text in the editing area. The preceding snippet contains the code that calls the show() method of the Popup. The Popup, however, is created by another method in StarterAppMain.java, arbitrarily named createAlertPopup() and shown in Listing 6-14.

Listing 6-14. The createAlertPopup() Method Located in StarterAppMain.java

```
Popup createAlertPopup(String text) {
    Popup alertPopup = new Popup();

    htmlLabel = new Label(text);
    htmlLabel.setWrapText(true);
    htmlLabel.setMaxWidth(280);
    htmlLabel.setMaxHeight(140);

    Button okButton = new Button("OK");
    okButton.setOnAction(e -> alertPopup.hide());

    BorderPane borderPane = new BorderPane();
    borderPane.setCenter(htmlLabel);
    borderPane.setBottom(okButton);

    Rectangle rectangle = new Rectangle(300, 200, Color.LIGHTBLUE);
    rectangle.setArcHeight(20);
    rectangle.setArcWidth(20);
    rectangle.setStroke(Color.GRAY);
    rectangle.setStrokeWidth(2);
    StackPane contentPane = new StackPane(rectangle, borderPane);
```

```
    alertPopup.getContent().add(contentPane);

    BorderPane.setAlignment(okButton, Pos.CENTER);
    BorderPane.setMargin(okButton, new Insets(10, 0, 10, 0));
    return alertPopup;
}
```

Here are some relevant notes about the `createAlertPopup()` method code:

- A `String` argument containing the HTML to be displayed is passed into the method.
- A `Popup` instance is created. A `StackPane`, including a `BorderPane` that has a `Label` containing the HTML, is added to the `Popup`.
- The `onAction` handler in the OK button causes the `Popup` to `hide` from view, as you experienced in Step 34 of the exercise.

Let's move on to the final UI control in the StarterApp program.

Using a `WebView`

The `WebView` control is a web browser that you can embed in JavaFX applications. As you experienced in Steps 34 and 35 of the exercise, the `WebView` control shown in Figure 6-14 automatically displays a randomly selected web page when the tab labeled PasswordField is selected.

In the following snippet from Listing 6-5, the `WebView` created earlier is assigned to the `Tab`'s content and properties are assigned, including the lambda expression that is called when the tab is selected.

```
Tab webViewTab = new Tab("WebView");
webViewTab.setContent(webView);
webViewTab.setClosable(false);
webViewTab.setOnSelectionChanged(e -> {
    String randomWebSite = model.getRandomWebSite();
    if (webViewTab.isSelected()) {
        webView.getEngine().load(randomWebSite);
        System.out.println("WebView tab is selected, loading: "
                + randomWebSite);
    }
});
```

The code in the `onSelectionChanged()` method earlier calls a method in the `StarterAppModel` class to get the URL of a randomly selected web site. The `getEngine()` method of the `WebView` is then invoked to get the `WebEngine` instance associated with the `WebView`. The `load()` method of the `WebEngine` is invoked, passing a `String` that contains the randomly selected URL, which causes the `WebView` to display the web page retrieved from that URL. The following snippet contains the relevant code from the `StarterAppModel` class:

```
public String getRandomWebSite() {
  String[] webSites = {
    "http://javafx.com",
    "http://fxexperience.com",
    "http://steveonjava.com",
    "http://javafxpert.com",
    "http://pleasingsoftware.blogspot.com",
```

```
    "http://weiqigao.blogspot.com/",
    "http://blogs.lodgon.com/johan",
    "http://google.com"
  };
  int randomIdx = (int)(Math.random() * webSites.length);
  return webSites[randomIdx];
}
```

The `WebView` control and its `WebEngine` counterpart have additional capabilities documented in the `javafx.scene.web` package of the API that are worth investigating.

Summary

Congratulations! You gained a lot of experience with the UI controls in JavaFX.

- You tried out most of the JavaFX UI controls in the context of the StarterApp program, which also serves as starting point from which you can modify and create an application.
- You explored code examples and explanations for these JavaFX UI controls.

Resources

For some additional information using JavaFX UI controls, consult the following resource.

- *Using JavaFX UI Controls*, developed by Oracle: `http://docs.oracle.com/javase/8/javafx/user-interface-tutorial/ui_controls.htm`

CHAPTER 7

Collections and Concurrency

When you know a thing, to hold that you know it; and when you do not know a thing, to allow that you do not know it;—this is knowledge.

—Confucius

After the fast-paced exploration of JavaFX layouts in Chapter 5 and JavaFX UI controls in Chapter 6, we refocus our attention on some of the lower level facilities of JavaFX in this chapter.

Recall that in Chapter 4 you learned about the `Observable` interface and one of its subinterfaces `ObservableValue`. In this chapter, we examine four other subinterfaces of `Observable`—`ObservableList`, `ObservableMap`, `ObservableSet`, and `ObservableArray`—rounding out the story of the `Observable` family of interfaces and classes.

We then cover concurrency in JavaFX. We explain the JavaFX threading model, pointing out the most important threads present in a JavaFX application. We look at the rules that you must follow to ensure your JavaFX application is responsive to user inputs and not locked up by event handlers that take too long to execute. We also show you how the `javafx.concurrent` framework can be used to offload long-running routines to background threads.

We conclude this chapter with examples that show how a JavaFX scene graph can be embedded into a Swing application using `JFXPanel`, how it can be embedded into an SWT application using `FXCanvas`, paying attention to how to make the JavaFX event thread play nicely with the Swing event dispatching thread, and how Swing components can be embedded into a JavaFX scene using `SwingNode`.

Understanding Observable Collections and Arrays

As we saw in Chapter 4, the `Observable` interface has five direct subinterfaces—the `ObservableValue` interface, the `ObservableList` interface, the `ObservableMap` interface, the `ObservableSet` interface, and the `ObservableArray` interface. We learned that the `ObservableValue` interface plays a central role in the JavaFX Properties and Bindings framework.

The `ObservableList`, `ObservableMap`, `ObservableSet`, and `ObservableArray` interfaces reside in the `javafx.collections` package, and are referred to as the JavaFX observable collections and arrays. In addition to extending the `Observable` interface, `ObservableList`, `ObservableMap`, and `ObservableSet` also extend the `java.util.List`, `java.util.Map`, and `java.util.Set` interfaces, respectively, making them genuine collections in the eyes of the Java collections framework. You can call all the Java collections framework methods you are familiar with on objects of these interfaces and expect exactly the same results. What the JavaFX observable collections and arrays provide in addition to the stock Java collections framework are notifications to registered listeners. Because they are `Observables`, you can register `InvalidationListeners` with the JavaFX observable collections and arrays objects and be notified when the content of the observable collections and arrays becomes invalid.

Each of the JavaFX observable collections and arrays interfaces supports a change event that conveys more detailed information of the change. We examine the JavaFX observable collections and arrays and the change events that they support in the following sections.

Understanding `ObservableList`

Figure 7-1 is a UML diagram showing the `ObservableList` and supporting interfaces.

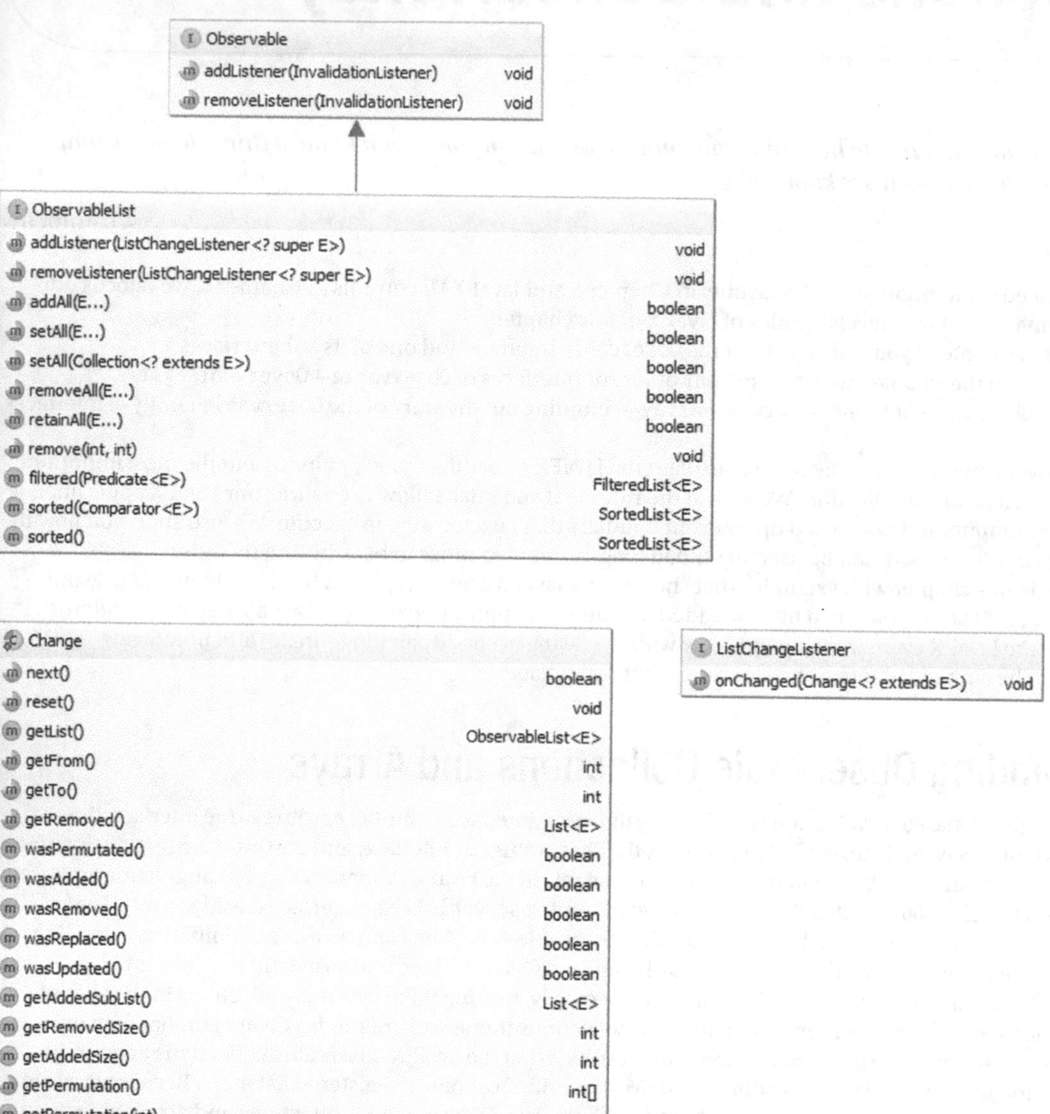

***Figure 7-1.** Key interfaces that support the JavaFX observable list*

To prevent clutter, we omitted the java.util.List interface from the diagram in Figure 7-1. The java.util.List interface is the other super interface of ObservableList. The following two methods on the ObservableList interface allow you to register and unregister ListChangeListeners:

- addListener(ListChangeListener<? super E> listener)
- removeListener(ListChangeListener<? super E> listener)

The following additional methods on ObservableList make working with the interface easier:

- addAll(E... elements)
- setAll(E... elements)
- setAll(Collection<? extends E> col)
- removeAll(E... elements)
- retainAll(E... elements)
- remove(int from, int to)
- filtered(Predicate<E>)
- sorted(Comparator<E>)
- sorted()

The filtered() and the two sorted() methods return a FilteredList or a SortedList that wraps the ObservableList. When the original ObservableList is mutated, the wrapper FilteredList and SortedList reflect the changes.

The ListChangeListener interface has only one method: onChange(ListChangeListener.Change<? extends E> change). This method is called back when the content of the ObservableList is manipulated. Notice that this method's parameter type is the nested class Change that is declared in the ListChangeListener interface. We show you how to use the ListChangeListener.Change class in the next subsection. For now, we look at a simple example in Listing 7-1 illustrating the firing of invalidation and list change events when an ObservableList is manipulated.

Listing 7-1. ObservableListExample.java

```
import javafx.beans.Observable;
import javafx.collections.FXCollections;
import javafx.collections.ObservableList;

import java.util.Arrays;
import java.util.Iterator;
import java.util.List;

import static javafx.collections.ListChangeListener.Change;

public class ObservableListExample {
    public static void main(String[] args) {
        ObservableList<String> strings = FXCollections.observableArrayList();

        strings.addListener((Observable observable) -> {
            System.out.println("\tlist invalidated");
        });
```

```
        strings.addListener((Change<? extends String> change) -> {
            System.out.println("\tstrings = " + change.getList());
        });

        System.out.println("Calling add(\"First\"): ");
        strings.add("First");

        System.out.println("Calling add(0, \"Zeroth\"): ");
        strings.add(0, "Zeroth");

        System.out.println("Calling addAll(\"Second\", \"Third\"): ");
        strings.addAll("Second", "Third");

        System.out.println("Calling set(1, \"New First\"): ");
        strings.set(1, "New First");

        final List<String> list = Arrays.asList("Second_1", "Second_2");
        System.out.println("Calling addAll(3, list): ");
        strings.addAll(3, list);

        System.out.println("Calling remove(2, 4): ");
        strings.remove(2, 4);

        final Iterator<String> iterator = strings.iterator();
        while (iterator.hasNext()) {
            final String next = iterator.next();
            if (next.contains("t")) {
                System.out.println("Calling remove() on iterator: ");
                iterator.remove();
            }
        }

        System.out.println("Calling removeAll(\"Third\", \"Fourth\"): ");
        strings.removeAll("Third", "Fourth");
    }
}
```

Unlike the Java collections framework, where the public API contains both the interfaces, such as `List`, `Map`, and `Set`, and concrete implementations of the interfaces that you can instantiate, such as `ArrayList`, `HashMap`, and `HashSet`, the JavaFX observable collections framework provides only the interfaces `ObservableList`, `ObservableMap`, `ObservableSet`, and `ObservableArray`, but not concrete implementation classes. To obtain an object of a JavaFX observable collections and arrays interface, you use the utility class `FXCollections`. In Listing 7-1, we obtain an `ObservableList<String>` object by calling a factory method on `FXCollections`:

```
ObservableList<String> strings = FXCollections.observableArrayList();
```

We then hooked an `InvalidationListener` and a `ListChangeListener` to the observable list. Because both listeners have a one-argument method and are added using `addListener()`, we have to specify the parameter type in the lambda expressions. The invalidation listener simply prints out a message every time it's called. The list change listener prints out the content of the observable list. The rest of the program simply manipulates the content of the observable list in various ways: by calling methods on the `java.util.List` interface, by calling some of the new convenience methods added to `ObservableList`, and by calling the `remove()` method on an `Iterator` obtained from the observable list.

When we run the program in Listing 7-1, the following output is printed to the console:

```
Calling add("First"):
        list invalidated
        strings = [First]
Calling add(0, "Zeroth"):
        list invalidated
        strings = [Zeroth, First]
Calling addAll("Second", "Third"):
        list invalidated
        strings = [Zeroth, First, Second, Third]
Calling set(1, "New First"):
        list invalidated
        strings = [Zeroth, New First, Second, Third]
Calling addAll(3, list):
        list invalidated
        strings = [Zeroth, New First, Second, Second_1, Second_2, Third]
Calling remove(2, 4):
        list invalidated
        strings = [Zeroth, New First, Second_2, Third]
Calling remove() on iterator:
        list invalidated
        strings = [New First, Second_2, Third]
Calling remove() on iterator:
        list invalidated
        strings = [Second_2, Third]
Calling removeAll("Third", "Fourth"):
        list invalidated
        strings = [Second_2]
```

Indeed, every call that we made in the code to change the content of the observable list triggered a callback on both the invalidation listener and the list change listener.

If an instance of an invalidation listener or a list change listener has already been added as a listener to an observable list, all subsequent addListener() calls with that instance as an argument are ignored. Of course, you can add as many distinct invalidation listeners and list change listeners as you like to an observable list.

Handling Change Events in ListChangeListener

In this section, we take a closer look at the ListChangeListener.Change class and discuss how the onChange() callback method should handle the list change event.

As we saw in the preceding section, for an ObservableList obtained by calling FXCollections.observableArrayList(), each mutator call—that is, each call to a single method that changes the content of the observable list—generates a list change event delivered to each registered observer. The event object, an instance of a class that implements the ListChangeListener.Change interface, can be thought of as representing one or more discrete changes, each of which is of one of four kinds: elements added, elements removed, elements replaced, or elements permuted. The ListChangeListener.Change class provides the following methods that allow you to get at this detailed information about the change:

- boolean next()
- void reset()

- boolean wasAdded()
- boolean wasRemoved()
- boolean wasReplaced()
- boolean wasPermutated()
- int getFrom()
- int getTo()
- int getAddedSize()
- List<E> getAddedSublist()
- int getRemovedSize()
- List<E> getRemoved()
- int getPermutation(int i)
- ObservableList<E> getList()

The next() and reset() methods control a cursor that iterates through all the discrete changes in the event object. On entry to the onChange() method of ListChangeListener, the cursor is positioned before the first discrete change. You must call the next() method to move the cursor to the first discrete change. Succeeding calls to the next() method will move the cursor to the remaining discrete changes. If the next discrete change is reached, the return value will be true. If the cursor is already on the last discrete change, the return value will be false. Once the cursor is positioned on a valid discrete change, the methods wasAdded(), wasRemoved(), wasReplaced(), and wasPermutated() can be called to determine the kind of change the discrete change represents.

■ **Caution** The wasAdded(), wasRemoved(), wasReplaced(), and wasPermutated() methods are not orthogonal. A discrete change is a replacement only if it is both an addition and a removal. The proper order for testing the kind of a discrete change, therefore, is to first determine whether it is a permutation or a replacement and then to determine whether it is an addition or a removal.

Once you have determined the kind of discrete change, you can call the other methods to get more information about it. For addition, the getFrom() method returns the index in the observable list where new elements were added; the getTo() method returns the index of the element that is one past the end of the added elements; the getAddedSize() method returns the number of elements that were added; and the getAddedSublist() method returns a List<E> that contains the added elements. For removal, the getFrom() and getTo() methods both return the index in the observable list where elements were removed; the getRemovedSize() method returns the number of elements that were removed; and the getRemoved() method returns a List<E> that contains the removed elements. For replacement, both the methods that are relevant for addition and the methods that are relevant for removal should be examined, because a replacement can be seen as a removal followed by an addition at the same index. For permutation, the getPermutation(int i) method returns the index of an element in the observable list after the permutation whose index in the observable list before the permutation was i. In all situations, the getList() method always returns the underlying observable list.

In the example shown in Listing 7-2, we perform various list manipulations after attaching a ListChangeListener to an ObservableList. The implementation of ListChangeListener, called MyListener, includes a pretty printer for the ListChangeListener.Change object, and prints out the list change event object when an event is fired.

Listing 7-2. ListChangeEventExample.java

```
import javafx.collections.FXCollections;
import javafx.collections.ListChangeListener;
import javafx.collections.ObservableList;

public class ListChangeEventExample {
    public static void main(String[] args) {
        ObservableList<String> strings = FXCollections.observableArrayList();
        strings.addListener(new MyListener());

        System.out.println("Calling addAll(\"Zero\", \"One\", \"Two\", \"Three\"): ");
        strings.addAll("Zero", "One", "Two", "Three");

        System.out.println("Calling FXCollections.sort(strings): ");
        FXCollections.sort(strings);

        System.out.println("Calling set(1, \"Three_1\"): ");
        strings.set(1, "Three_1");

        System.out.println("Calling setAll(\"One_1\", \"Three_1\", \"Two_1\", \"Zero_1\"): ");
        strings.setAll("One_1", "Three_1", "Two_1", "Zero_1");

        System.out.println("Calling removeAll(\"One_1\", \"Two_1\", \"Zero_1\"): ");
        strings.removeAll("One_1", "Two_1", "Zero_1");
    }

    private static class MyListener implements ListChangeListener<String> {
        @Override
        public void onChanged(Change<? extends String> change) {
            System.out.println("\tlist = " + change.getList());
            System.out.println(prettyPrint(change));
        }

        private String prettyPrint(Change<? extends String> change) {
            StringBuilder sb = new StringBuilder("\tChange event data:\n");
            int i = 0;
            while (change.next()) {
                sb.append("\t\tcursor = ")
                    .append(i++)
                    .append("\n");

                final String kind =
                    change.wasPermutated() ? "permutated" :
                        change.wasReplaced() ? "replaced" :
                            change.wasRemoved() ? "removed" :
                                change.wasAdded() ? "added" : "none";

                sb.append("\t\tKind of change: ")
                    .append(kind)
                    .append("\n");
```

```
            sb.append("\t\tAffected range: [")
                .append(change.getFrom())
                .append(", ")
                .append(change.getTo())
                .append("]\n");

            if (kind.equals("added") || kind.equals("replaced")) {
                sb.append("\t\tAdded size: ")
                    .append(change.getAddedSize())
                    .append("\n");
                sb.append("\t\tAdded sublist: ")
                    .append(change.getAddedSubList())
                    .append("\n");
            }

            if (kind.equals("removed") || kind.equals("replaced")) {
                sb.append("\t\tRemoved size: ")
                    .append(change.getRemovedSize())
                    .append("\n");
                sb.append("\t\tRemoved: ")
                    .append(change.getRemoved())
                    .append("\n");
            }

            if (kind.equals("permutated")) {
                StringBuilder permutationStringBuilder = new StringBuilder("[");
                for (int k = change.getFrom(); k < change.getTo(); k++) {
                    permutationStringBuilder.append(k)
                        .append("->")
                        .append(change.getPermutation(k));
                    if (k < change.getTo() - 1) {
                        permutationStringBuilder.append(", ");
                    }
                }
                permutationStringBuilder.append("]");
                String permutation = permutationStringBuilder.toString();
                sb.append("\t\tPermutation: ").append(permutation).append("\n");
            }
        }
        return sb.toString();
    }
  }
}
```

In the preceding example, we triggered the four kinds of discrete changes in an observable list. Because no methods on an `ObservableList` will trigger a permutation event, we used the `sort()` utility method from the `FXCollections` class to effect a permutation. We have more to say about `FXCollections` in a later section. We triggered the replace event twice, once with `set()`, and once with `setAll()`. The nice thing about `setAll()` is that it effectively does a `clear()` and an `addAll()` in one operation and generates only one change event.

When we run the program in Listing 7-2, the following output is printed to the console:

```
Calling addAll("Zero", "One", "Two", "Three"):
        list = [Zero, One, Two, Three]
        Change event data:
                cursor= 0
                Kind of change: added
                Affected range: [0, 4]
                Added size: 4
                Added sublist: [Zero, One, Two, Three]

Calling FXCollections.sort(strings):
        list = [One, Three, Two, Zero]
        Change event data:
                cursor = 0
                Kind of change: permutated
                Affected range: [0, 4]
                Permutation: [0->3, 1->0, 2->2, 3->1]

Calling set(1, "Three_1"):
        list = [One, Three_1, Two, Zero]
        Change event data:
                cursor = 0
                Kind of change: replaced
                Affected range: [1, 2]
                Added size: 1
                Added sublist: [Three_1]
                Removed size: 1
                Removed: [Three]

Calling setAll("One_1", "Three_1", "Two_1", "Zero_1"):
        list = [One_1, Three_1, Two_1, Zero_1]
        Change event data:
                cursor = 0
                Kind of change: replaced
                Affected range: [0, 4]
                Added size: 4
                Added sublist: [One_1, Three_1, Two_1, Zero_1]
                Removed size: 4
                Removed: [One, Three_1, Two, Zero]

Calling removeAll("One_1", "Two_1", "Zero_1"):
        list = [Three_1]
        Change event data:
                cursor = 0
                Kind of change: removed
                Affected range: [0, 0]
                Removed size: 1
                Removed: [One_1]
                cursor = 1
```

```
Kind of change: removed
Affected range: [1, 1]
Removed size: 2
Removed: [Two_1, Zero_1]
```

In all but the `removeAll()` call, the list change event object contains only one discrete change. The reason that the `removeAll()` call generates a list change event that contains two discrete changes is that the three elements that we wish to remove fall in two disjoint ranges in the list.

In the majority of use cases where we care about list change events, you don't necessarily need to distinguish the kinds of discrete changes. Sometimes you simply want to do something to all added and removed elements. In such a case, your `ListChangeListener` method can be as simple as the following.

```
@Override
public void onChanged(Change<? extends Foo> change) {
    while (change.next()) {
        for (Foo foo : change.getAddedSubList()) {
            // starting up
        }
        for (Foo foo : change.getRemoved()) {
            // cleaning up
        }
    }
}
```

Understanding ObservableMap

Although `ObservableMap` appears equivalent to `ObservableList` in the JavaFX observable collections framework hierarchy, it is actually not as sophisticated as `ObservableList`. Figure 7-2 is a UML diagram showing the `ObservableMap` and supporting interfaces.

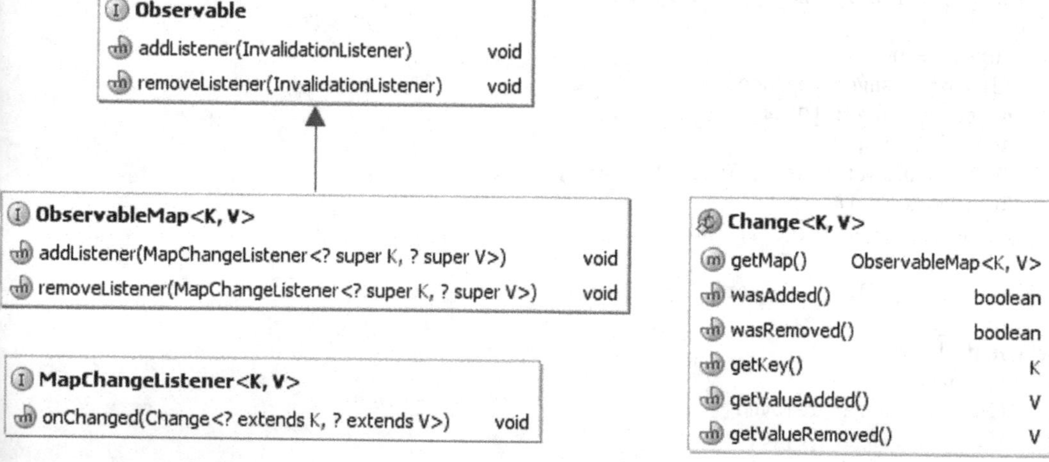

***Figure 7-2.** Key interfaces that support the JavaFX observable map*

To prevent clutter, we omitted the java.util.Map interface from the diagram in Figure 7-2. The java.util.Map interface is the other super interface of ObservableMap. The following methods on the ObservableMap interface allow you to register and unregister MapChangeListeners:

- addListener(MapChangeListener<? super K, ? super V> listener)
- addListener(MapChangeListener<? super K, ? super V> listener)

There are no additional convenience methods on ObservableMap.

The MapChangeListener interface has only one method: onChange(MapChangeListener.Change<? extends K, ? extends V> change). This method is called back when the content of the ObservableMap is manipulated. Notice that this method's parameter type is the nested class Change that is declared in the MapChangeListener interface. Unlike the ListChangeListener.Change class, the MapChangeListener.Change class is geared toward reporting the change of a single key in a map. If a method call on ObservableMap affects multiple keys, as many map change events as the number of affected keys will be fired.

The MapChangeListener.Change class provides the following methods for you to inspect the changes made to a key.

- boolean wasAdded() returns true if a new value was added for the key.
- boolean wasRemoved() returns true if an old value was removed from the key.
- K getKey() returns the affected key.
- V getValueAdded() returns the value that was added for the key.
- V getValueRemoved() returns the value that was removed for the key. (Note that a put() call with an existing key will cause the old value to be removed.)
- ObservableMap<K, V> getMap()

In the example in Listing 7-3, we perform various map manipulations after attaching a MapChangeListener to an ObservableMap. The implementation of MapChangeListener, called MyListener, includes a pretty printer for the MapChangeListener.Change object, and prints out the map change event object when an event is fired.

Listing 7-3. MapChangeEventExample.java

```
import javafx.collections.FXCollections;
import javafx.collections.MapChangeListener;
import javafx.collections.ObservableMap;

import java.util.HashMap;
import java.util.Iterator;
import java.util.Map;

public class MapChangeEventExample {
    public static void main(String[] args) {
        ObservableMap<String, Integer> map = FXCollections.observableHashMap();
        map.addListener(new MyListener());

        System.out.println("Calling put(\"First\", 1): ");
        map.put("First", 1);

        System.out.println("Calling put(\"First\", 100): ");
        map.put("First", 100);
```

```
        Map<String, Integer> anotherMap = new HashMap<>();
        anotherMap.put("Second", 2);
        anotherMap.put("Third", 3);
        System.out.println("Calling putAll(anotherMap): ");
        map.putAll(anotherMap);

        final Iterator<Map.Entry<String, Integer>>entryIterator = map.entrySet().iterator();
        while (entryIterator.hasNext()) {
            final Map.Entry<String, Integer> next = entryIterator.next();
            if (next.getKey().equals("Second")) {
                System.out.println("Calling remove on entryIterator: ");
                entryIterator.remove();
            }
        }

        final Iterator<Integer> valueIterator = map.values().iterator();
        while (valueIterator.hasNext()) {
            final Integer next = valueIterator.next();
            if (next == 3) {
                System.out.println("Calling remove on valueIterator: ");
                valueIterator.remove();
            }
        }
    }

    private static class MyListener implements MapChangeListener<String, Integer> {
        @Override
        public void onChanged(Change<? extends String, ? extends Integer> change) {
            System.out.println("\tmap = " + change.getMap());
            System.out.println(prettyPrint(change));
        }

        private String prettyPrint(Change<? extends String, ? extends Integer> change) {
            StringBuilder sb = new StringBuilder("\tChange event data:\n");
            sb.append("\t\tWas added: ").append(change.wasAdded()).append("\n");
            sb.append("\t\tWas removed: ").append(change.wasRemoved()).append("\n");
            sb.append("\t\tKey: ").append(change.getKey()).append("\n");
            sb.append("\t\tValue added: ").append(change.getValueAdded()).append("\n");
            sb.append("\t\tValue removed: ").append(change.getValueRemoved()).append("\n");
            return sb.toString();
        }
    }
}
```

When we run the program in Listing 7-3, the following output is printed to the console:

```
Calling put("First", 1):
        map = {First=1}
        Change event data:
                Was added: true
                Was removed: false
```

```
                Key: First
                Value added: 1
                Value removed: null

Calling put("First", 100):
        map = {First=100}
        Change event data:
                Was added: true
                Was removed: true
                Key: First
                Value added: 100
                Value removed: 1

Calling putAll(anotherMap):
        map = {Second=2, First=100}
        Change event data:
                Was added: true
                Was removed: false
                Key: Second
                Value added: 2
                Value removed: null

        map = {Second=2, Third=3, First=100}
        Change event data:
                Was added: true
                Was removed: false
                Key: Third
                Value added: 3
                Value removed: null

Calling remove on entryIterator:
        map = {Third=3, First=100}
        Change event data:
                Was added: false
                Was removed: true
                Key: Second
                Value added: null
                Value removed: 2

Calling remove on valueIterator:
        map = {First=100}
        Change event data:
                Was added: false
                Was removed: true
                Key: Third
                Value added: null
                Value removed: 3
```

In the preceding example, notice that the putAll() call generated two map change events because the other map contains two keys.

Understanding ObservableSet

The ObservableSet interface is similar to the ObservableMap interface in that its SetChangeListener.Change object tracks a single element. Figure 7-3 is a UML diagram showing the ObservableSet and supporting interfaces.

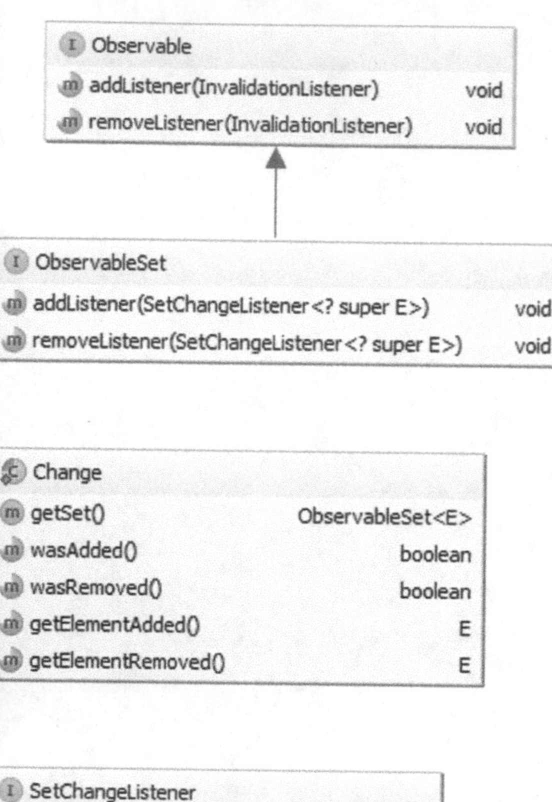

Figure 7-3. *Key interfaces that support the JavaFX observable set*

To prevent clutter, we omitted the java.util.Set interface from the diagram in Figure 7-3. The java.util.Set interface is the other super interface of ObservableSet. The following methods on the ObservableSet interface allow you to register and unregister SetChangeListeners:

- addListener(SetChangeListener<? super E> listener)
- addListener(SetChangeListener<? super E> listener)

There are no additional convenience methods on ObservableSet.

The SetChangeListener interface has only one method: onChange(SetChangeListener.Change<? extends E> change). This method is called back when the content of the ObservableSet is manipulated. Notice that this method's parameter type is the nested class Change that is declared in the SetChangeListener interface. The SetChangeListener.Change class is geared toward reporting the change of a single element in a set. If a method call on ObservableSet affects multiple elements, as many set change events as the number of affected elements will be fired.

The SetChangeListener.Change class provides the following methods for you to inspect the changes made to an element.

- boolean wasAdded() returns true if a new element was added to the set.
- boolean wasRemoved() returns true if an element was removed from the set.
- E getElementAdded() returns the element that was added to the set.
- E getElementRemoved() returns the element that was removed from the set.
- ObservableSet<E> getSet()

In the example in Listing 7-4, we perform various set manipulations after attaching a SetChangeListener to an ObservableSet. The implementation of SetChangeListener, called MyListener, includes a pretty printer for the SetChangeListener.Change object, and prints out the set change event object when an event is fired.

Listing 7-4. SetChangeEventExample.java

```
import javafx.collections.FXCollections;
import javafx.collections.ObservableSet;
import javafx.collections.SetChangeListener;

import java.util.Arrays;

public class SetChangeEventExample {
    public static void main(String[] args) {
        ObservableSet<String> set = FXCollections.observableSet();
        set.addListener(new MyListener());

        System.out.println("Calling add(\"First\"): ");
        set.add("First");

        System.out.println("Calling addAll(Arrays.asList(\"Second\", \"Third\")): ");
        set.addAll(Arrays.asList("Second", "Third"));

        System.out.println("Calling remove(\"Third\"): ");
        set.remove("Third");
    }

    private static class MyListener implements SetChangeListener<String> {
        @Override
        public void onChanged(Change<? extends String> change) {
            System.out.println("\tset = " + change.getSet());
            System.out.println(prettyPrint(change));
        }

        private String prettyPrint(Change<? extends String> change) {
            StringBuilder sb = new StringBuilder("\tChange event data:\n");
            sb.append("\t\tWas added: ").append(change.wasAdded()).append("\n");
            sb.append("\t\tWas removed: ").append(change.wasRemoved()).append("\n");
            sb.append("\t\tElement added: ").append(change.getElementAdded()).append("\n");
            sb.append("\t\tElement removed: ").append(change.getElementRemoved()).append("\n");
            return sb.toString();
        }
    }
}
```

When we run the program in Listing 7-4, the following output is printed to the console:

```
Calling add("First"):
	set = [First]
	Change event data:
		Was added: true
		Was removed: false
		Element added: First
		Element removed: null

Calling addAll(Arrays.asList("Second", "Third")):
	set = [Second, First]
	Change event data:
		Was added: true
		Was removed: false
		Element added: Second
		Element removed: null

	set = [Second, First, Third]
	Change event data:
		Was added: true
		Was removed: false
		Element added: Third
		Element removed: null

Calling remove("Third"):
	set = [Second, First]
	Change event data:
		Was added: false
		Was removed: true
		Element added: null
		Element removed: Third
```

In the preceding example, notice that the addAll() call generated two set change events because the list that was added to the observable set contains two elements.

Understanding ObservableArrays

The ObservableArray interface is introduced for situations where a list of primitive int or float values needs to be observed but the overhead of boxing and unboxing of the primitive values every time they are added or removed from the list is unacceptable for performance reasons. Implementations of ObservableArray and its two subinterfaces, ObservableIntegerArray and ObservableFloatArray, are expected to use primitive arrays as the backing stores of their content. The JavaFX 3D API makes use of ObservableArray, ObservableIntegerArray, and ObservableFloatArray. Figure 7-4 is a UML diagram showing the ObservableArray and supporting interfaces.

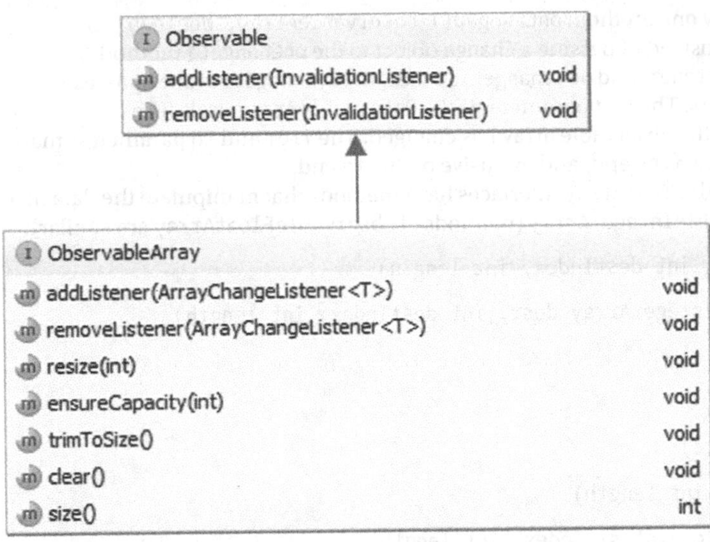

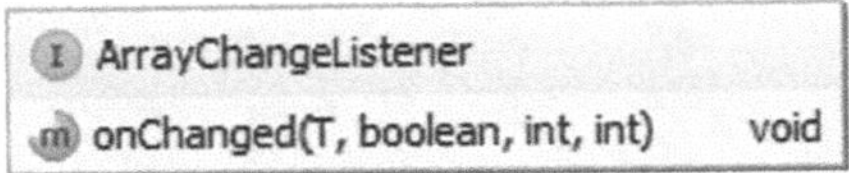

***Figure 7-4.** Key interfaces that support the JavaFX observable array*

Unlike for the ObservableList, ObservableMap, and ObservableSet interfaces, the ObservableArray interface does not implement any Java collections framework interfaces. The following methods on the ObservableArray interface allow you to register and unregister ArrayChangeListeners:

- addListener(ArrayChangeListener<T> listener)
- removeListener(ArrayChangeListener<T> listener)

The following additional methods on ObservableArray give you control of the underlying primitive arrays:

- resize(int size)
- ensureCapacity(int capacity)
- trimToSize()
- clear()
- size()

These methods deal with the capacity and size of an ObservableArray. The *capacity* is the length of the underlying primitive array. The *size* is the number of elements that actually contain application data. The capacity is always greater than or equal to the size. The ensureCapacity() method allocates a new underlying primitive array if the length of the current underlying primitive array is less than the desired new capacity. The resize() method changes the size of ObservableArray. If the new size is greater than the current capacity, the capacity is increased. If the new size is greater than the current size, the additional elements are filled with zero. If the new size is less than the current size, resize() does not actually shrink the array, but the "lost" elements are filled with zero. The trimToSize() method replaces the underlying primitive array with one whose length is the same as the size of the ObservableArray. The clear() method resizes the ObservableArray to size zero. The size() method returns the current size of the ObservableArray.

The ArrayChangeListener interface has only one method: onChanged(T observableArray, boolean sizeChanged, int from, int to). Notice that instead of passing a Change object to the onChange() method, as is done in ListChangeListener, MapChangeListener, and SetChangeListener, ArrayChangeListener passes characteristics of the change directly as parameters. The first parameter is the ObservableArray itself. The sizeChanged parameter will be true if the size of the observable array has changed. The from and to parameters mark the range of the changed elements, inclusive on the from end, and exclusive on the to end.

The ObservableIntegerArray and ObservableFloatArray interfaces have methods that manipulate the data in a type-specific way. We list the methods of ObservableIntegerArray (methods of ObservableFloatArray are similar):

- copyTo(int srcIndex, int[] dest, int destIndex, int length)
- copyTo(int srcIndex, ObservableIntegerArray dest, int destIndex, int length)
- int get(int index)
- addAll(int... elements)
- addAll(ObservableIntegerArray src)
- addAll(int[] src, int srcIndex, int length)
- addAll(ObservableIntegerArray src, int srcIndex, int length)
- setAll(int... elements)
- setAll(int[] src, int srcIndex, int length)
- setAll(ObservableIntegerArray src)
- setAll(ObservableIntegerArray src, int srcIndex, int length)
- set(int destIndex, int[] src, int srcIndex, int length)
- set(int destIndex, ObservableIntegerArray src, int srcIndex, int length)
- set(int index, int value)
- int[] toArray(int[] dest)
- int[] toArray(int srcIndex, int[] dest, int length)

The addAll() methods append to the ObservableIntegerArray. The setAll() methods replace the content of the ObservableIntegerArray. The sources to these two sets of methods can be a vararg array of ints, an ObservableIntegerArray, an int array with a starting index and a length, or an ObservableIntegerArray with a starting index and a length. The get() method returns the value at the specified index. The set() methods replace a portion of the ObservableIntegerArray with new values starting at the index specified in the first parameter. The replacement data can be a single int value, an int array with a starting index and a length, or an ObservableIntegerArray with a starting index and a length. If there is not enough room in the original ObservableIntegerArray to accommodate the replacement data, an ArrayIndexOutOfBoundsException is thrown. The copyTo() methods copy a portion of the ObservableIntegerArray starting at the specified srcIndex into a destination int array or ObservableIntegerArray starting at the specified destIndex. The length parameter dictates the length of the portion copied. If there are not enough elements in the source ObservableIntegerArray to form a portion of the specified length, or if there is not enough room in the destination to accommodate the copied portion, an ArrayIndexOutOfBoundsException is thrown. The toArray() methods copy the content of the ObservableIntegerArray into an int array. If the dest parameter is not null and has enough room, it is filled and returned; otherwise a new int array is allocated, filled, and returned. In the form where the srcIndex and length are specified, if there are not enough elements in the ObservableIntegerArray, an ArrayIndexOutOfBoundsException is thrown.

In the example shown in Listing 7-5, we perform various array manipulations after attaching an ArrayChangeListener to an ObservableIntegerArray. We print out the parameters passed to the onChange() method when an event is fired.

Listing 7-5. ArrayChangeEventExample.java

```
import javafx.collections.FXCollections;
import javafx.collections.ObservableIntegerArray;

public class ArrayChangeEventExample {
    public static void main(String[] args) {
        final ObservableIntegerArray ints = FXCollections.observableIntegerArray(10, 20);
        ints.addListener((array, sizeChanged, from, to) -> {
            StringBuilder sb = new StringBuilder("\tObservable Array = ").append(array).append("\n")
                .append("\t\tsizeChanged = ").append(sizeChanged).append("\n")
                .append("\t\tfrom = ").append(from).append("\n")
                .append("\t\tto = ").append(to).append("\n");
            System.out.println(sb.toString());
        });

        ints.ensureCapacity(20);

        System.out.println("Calling addAll(30, 40):");
        ints.addAll(30, 40);

        final int[] src = {50, 60, 70};
        System.out.println("Calling addAll(src, 1, 2):");
        ints.addAll(src, 1, 2);

        System.out.println("Calling set(0, src, 0, 1):");
        ints.set(0, src, 0, 1);

        System.out.println("Calling setAll(src):");
        ints.setAll(src);

        ints.trimToSize();

        final ObservableIntegerArray ints2 = FXCollections.observableIntegerArray();
        ints2.resize(ints.size());

        System.out.println("Calling copyTo(0, ints2, 0, ints.size()):");
        ints.copyTo(0, ints2, 0, ints.size());

        System.out.println("\tDestination = " + ints2);
    }
}
```

When we run the program in Listing 7-5, the following output is printed to the console:

```
Calling addAll(30, 40):
        Observable Array = [10, 20, 30, 40]
                sizeChanged = true
                from = 2
                to = 4

Calling addAll(src, 1, 2):
        Observable Array = [10, 20, 30, 40, 60, 70]
                sizeChanged = true
                from = 4
                to = 6

Calling set(0, src, 0, 1):
        Observable Array = [50, 20, 30, 40, 60, 70]
                sizeChanged = false
                from = 0
                to = 1

Calling setAll(src):
        Observable Array = [50, 60, 70]
                sizeChanged = true
                from = 0
                to = 3

Calling copyTo(0, ints2, 0, ints.size()):
        Destination = [50, 60, 70]
```

Using Factory and Utility Methods from FXCollections

The FXCollections class plays a similar role in the JavaFX observable collections and arrays framework that the java.util.Collections class plays in the Java collections framework. The FXCollections class contains the following factory methods for ObservableList:

- `ObservableList<E> observableList(List<E> list)`
- `ObservableList<E> observableList(List<E> list, Callback<E, Observable[]> extractor);`
- `ObservableList<E> observableArrayList()`
- `ObservableList<E> observableArrayList(Callback<E, Observable[]> extractor);`
- `ObservableList<E> observableArrayList(E... items)`
- `ObservableList<E> observableArrayList(Collection<? extends E> col)`
- `ObservableList<E> concat(ObservableList<E>... lists)`
- `ObservableList<E> unmodifiableObservableList(ObservableList<E> list)`
- `ObservableList<E> checkedObservableList(ObservableList<E> list, Class<E> type)`

- ObservableList<E> synchronizedObservableList(ObservableList<E> list)
- ObservableList<E> emptyObservableList()
- ObservableList<E> singletonObservableList(E e)

It contains the following factory methods for ObservableMap:

- ObservableMap<K, V> observableMap(Map<K, V> map)
- ObservableMap<K, V> unmodifiableObservableMap(ObservableMap<K, V> map)
- ObservableMap<K, V> checkedObservableMap(ObservableMap<K, V> map, Class<K> keyType, Class<V> valType)
- ObservableMap<K, V> synchronizedObservableMap(ObservableMap<K, V> map)
- ObservableMap<K, V> emptyObservableMap();
- ObservableMap<K, V> observableHashMap()

It contains the following factory methods for ObservableSet:

- ObservableSet<E> observableSet(Set<E> set)
- ObservableSet<E> observableSet(E...)
- ObservableSet<E> unmodifiableObservableSet(ObservableSet<E> set)
- ObservableSet<E> checkedObservableSet(ObservableSet<E> set, Class<E> type)
- ObservableSet<E> synchronizedObservableSet(ObservableSet<E>)
- ObservableSet<E> emptyObservableSet()

It contains the following factory methods for ObservableIntegerArray and ObservableFloatArray:

- ObservableIntegerArray observableIntegerArray()
- ObservableIntegerArray observableIntegerArray(int...)
- ObservableIntegerArray observableIntegerArray(ObservableIntegerArray)
- ObservableFloatArray observableFloatArray()
- ObservableFloatArray observableFloatArray(float...)
- ObservableFloatArray observableFloatArray(ObservableFloatArray)

It also contains nine utility methods that are parallels of methods with the same name in java.util.Collections. They all act on ObservableList objects. And they differ from their java.util.Collections counterparts in that when they act on an ObservableList, care is taken to generate only one list change event, whereas their java.util.Collections counterpart would have generated more than one list change event.

- void copy(ObservableList<? super T> dest, java.util.List<? extends T> src)
- void fill(ObservableList<? super T> list, T obj)
- boolean replaceAll(ObservableList<T> list, T oldVal, T newVal)
- void reverse(ObservableList list)
- void rotate(ObservableList list, int distance)
- void shuffle(ObservableList<?> list)

- void shuffle(ObservableList list, java.util.Random rnd)
- void sort(ObservableList<T> list)
- void sort(ObservableList<T> list, java.util.Comparator<? super T> c)

We illustrate the effects of these utility methods in Listing 7-6.

Listing 7-6. FXCollectionsExample.java

```
import javafx.collections.FXCollections;
import javafx.collections.ListChangeListener;
import javafx.collections.ObservableList;

import java.util.Arrays;
import java.util.Comparator;
import java.util.Random;

public class FXCollectionsExample {
   public static void main(String[] args) {
      ObservableList<String> strings = FXCollections.observableArrayList();
      strings.addListener(new MyListener());

      System.out.println("Calling addAll(\"Zero\", \"One\", \"Two\", \"Three\"): ");
      strings.addAll("Zero", "One", "Two", "Three");

      System.out.println("Calling copy: ");
      FXCollections.copy(strings, Arrays.asList("Four", "Five"));

      System.out.println("Calling replaceAll: ");
      FXCollections.replaceAll(strings, "Two", "Two_1");

      System.out.println("Calling reverse: ");
      FXCollections.reverse(strings);

      System.out.println("Calling rotate(strings, 2): ");
      FXCollections.rotate(strings, 2);

      System.out.println("Calling shuffle(strings): ");
      FXCollections.shuffle(strings);

      System.out.println("Calling shuffle(strings, new Random(0L)): ");
      FXCollections.shuffle(strings, new Random(0L));

      System.out.println("Calling sort(strings): ");
      FXCollections.sort(strings);

      System.out.println("Calling sort(strings, c) with custom comparator: ");
      FXCollections.sort(strings, new Comparator<String>() {
         @Override
         public int compare(String lhs, String rhs) {
            // Reverse the order
            return rhs.compareTo(lhs);
         }
      });
```

```
        System.out.println("Calling fill(strings, \"Ten\"): ");
        FXCollections.fill(strings, "Ten");
    }

    // We omitted the nested class MyListener, which is the same as in Listing 7-2
}
```

When we run the program in Listing 7-6, the following output is printed to the console:

```
Calling addAll("Zero", "One", "Two", "Three"):
        list = [Zero, One, Two, Three]
        Change event data:
                cursor = 0
                Kind of change: added
                Affected range: [0, 4]
                Added size: 4
                Added sublist: [Zero, One, Two, Three]

Calling copy:
        list = [Four, Five, Two, Three]
        Change event data:
                cursor = 0
                Kind of change: replaced
                Affected range: [0, 4]
                Added size: 4
                Added sublist: [Four, Five, Two, Three]
                Removed size: 4
                Removed: [Zero, One, Two, Three]

Calling replaceAll:
        list = [Four, Five, Two_1, Three]
        Change event data:
                cursor = 0
                Kind of change: replaced
                Affected range: [0, 4]
                Added size: 4
                Added sublist: [Four, Five, Two_1, Three]
                Removed size: 4
                Removed: [Four, Five, Two, Three]

Calling reverse:
        list = [Three, Two_1, Five, Four]
        Change event data:
                cursor = 0
                Kind of change: replaced
                Affected range: [0, 4]
                Added size: 4
                Added sublist: [Three, Two_1, Five, Four]
                Removed size: 4
                Removed: [Four, Five, Two_1, Three]
```

```
Calling rotate(strings, 2):
        list = [Five, Four, Three, Two_1]
        Change event data:
                cursor = 0
                Kind of change: replaced
                Affected range: [0, 4]
                Added size: 4
                Added sublist: [Five, Four, Three, Two_1]
                Removed size: 4
                Removed: [Three, Two_1, Five, Four]

Calling shuffle(strings):
        list = [Three, Four, Two_1, Five]
        Change event data:
                cursor = 0
                Kind of change: replaced
                Affected range: [0, 4]
                Added size: 4
                Added sublist: [Three, Four, Two_1, Five]
                Removed size: 4
                Removed: [Five, Four, Three, Two_1]

Calling shuffle(strings, new Random(0L)):
        list = [Five, Three, Four, Two_1]
        Change event data:
                cursor = 0
                Kind of change: replaced
                Affected range: [0, 4]
                Added size: 4
                Added sublist: [Five, Three, Four, Two_1]
                Removed size: 4
                Removed: [Three, Four, Two_1, Five]

Calling sort(strings):
        list = [Five, Four, Three, Two_1]
        Change event data:
                cursor = 0
                Kind of change: permutated
                Affected range: [0, 4]
                Permutation: [0->0, 1->2, 2->1, 3->3]

Calling sort(strings, c) with custom comparator:
        list = [Two_1, Three, Four, Five]
        Change event data:
                cursor = 0
                Kind of change: permutated
                Affected range: [0, 4]
                Permutation: [0->3, 1->2, 2->1, 3->0]
```

```
Calling fill(strings, "Ten"):
        list = [Ten, Ten, Ten, Ten]
        Change event data:
                cursor = 0
                Kind of change: replaced
                Affected range: [0, 4]
                Added size: 4
                Added sublist: [Ten, Ten, Ten, Ten]
                Removed size: 4
                Removed: [Two_1, Three, Four, Five]
```

Notice that each invocation of a utility method in FXCollections generated exactly one list change event.

Using the JavaFX Concurrency Framework

It is common knowledge nowadays that almost all GUI platforms use a single-threaded event dispatching model. JavaFX is no exception, and indeed all UI events in JavaFX are processed in the *JavaFX Application Thread*. However, with multicore desktop machines becoming common in recent years (e.g., I'm writing this chapter on my quad-core PC), it is natural for the designers of JavaFX to take advantage of the full power of the hardware by leveraging the excellent concurrency support of the Java programming language.

In this section, we examine important threads that are present in all JavaFX applications. We explain the role they play in the overall scheme of JavaFX applications. We then turn our attention to the JavaFX Application Thread, explaining why executing long-running code in the JavaFX Application Thread makes your application appear to hang. Finally, we look at the javafx.concurrent framework and show you how to use it to execute long-running code in a worker thread off the JavaFX Application Thread and communicate the result back to the JavaFX Application Thread to update the GUI states.

■ **Note** If you are familiar with Swing programming, the JavaFX Application Thread is similar to Swing's Event Dispatcher Thread (EDT), usually with the name "AWT-EventQueue-0."

Identifying the Threads in a JavaFX Application

The program in Listing 7-7 creates a simple JavaFX GUI with a ListView, a TextArea and a Button, and populates the ListView with the names of all live threads of the application. When you select an item from the ListView, that thread's stack trace is displayed in the TextArea. The original list of threads and stack traces is populated as the application is starting up. You can update the list of threads and stack traces by clicking the Update button.

Listing 7-7. JavaFXThreadsExample.java

```
import javafx.application.Application;
import javafx.beans.value.ChangeListener;
import javafx.beans.value.ObservableValue;
import javafx.collections.FXCollections;
import javafx.collections.ObservableList;
import javafx.event.ActionEvent;
import javafx.event.EventHandler;
```

```
import javafx.geometry.Insets;
import javafx.scene.Scene;
import javafx.scene.control.Button;
import javafx.scene.control.ListView;
import javafx.scene.control.TextArea;
import javafx.scene.layout.VBox;
import javafx.stage.Stage;

import java.util.Map;

public class JavaFXThreadsExample extends Application
    implements EventHandler<ActionEvent>, ChangeListener<Number> {

    private Model model;
    private View view;

    public static void main(String[] args) {
        launch(args);
    }

    public JavaFXThreadsExample() {
        model = new Model();
    }

    @Override
    public void start(Stage stage) throws Exception {
        view = new View(model);
        hookupEvents();
        stage.setTitle("JavaFX Threads Information");
        stage.setScene(view.scene);
        stage.show();
    }

    private void hookupEvents() {
        view.updateButton.setOnAction(this);
        view.threadNames.getSelectionModel().selectedIndexProperty().addListener(this);
    }

    @Override
    public void changed(ObservableValue<? extends Number> observableValue,
                        Number oldValue, Number newValue) {
        int index = (Integer) newValue;
        if (index >=0) {
            view.stackTrace.setText(model.stackTraces.get(index));
        }
    }

    @Override
    public void handle(ActionEvent actionEvent) {
        model.update();
    }
```

```
    public static class Model {
        public ObservableList<String> threadNames;
        public ObservableList<String> stackTraces;

        public Model() {
            threadNames = FXCollections.observableArrayList();
            stackTraces = FXCollections.observableArrayList();
            update();
        }

        public void update() {
            threadNames.clear();
            stackTraces.clear();
            final Map<Thread, StackTraceElement[]> map = Thread.getAllStackTraces();
            for (Map.Entry<Thread, StackTraceElement[]> entry : map.entrySet()) {
                threadNames.add("\"" + entry.getKey().getName() + "\"");
                stackTraces.add(formatStackTrace(entry.getValue()));
            }
        }

        private String formatStackTrace(StackTraceElement[] value) {
            StringBuilder sb = new StringBuilder("StackTrace: \n");
            for (StackTraceElement stackTraceElement : value) {
                sb.append("    at ").append(stackTraceElement.toString()).append("\n");
            }
            return sb.toString();
        }
    }

    private static class View {
        public ListView<String> threadNames;
        public TextArea stackTrace;
        public Button updateButton;
        public Scene scene;

        private View(Model model) {
            threadNames = new ListView<>(model.threadNames);
            stackTrace = new TextArea();
            updateButton = new Button("Update");
            VBox vBox = new VBox(10, threadNames, stackTrace, updateButton);
            vBox.setPadding(new Insets(10, 10, 10, 10));
            scene = new Scene(vBox, 440, 640);
        }
    }
}
```

This is a pretty minimal JavaFX GUI application. Before letting you run this program, we point out several features of the program. First of all, make a mental note of the main() method:

```
public static void main(String[] args) {
    launch(args);
}
```

You have seen this method several times already. This stylized main() method always appears in a class that extends the javafx.application.Application class. There is an overloaded version of the Application.launch() method that takes a Class object as the first parameter that can be called from other classes:

```
launch(Class<? Extends Application> appClass, String[] args)
```

Therefore you can move the main() method to another class:

```
public class Main {
    public static void main(String[] args) {
        Application.launch(JavaFXThreadsExample.class, args);
    }
}
```

to achieve the same result.

Next, notice that the nested class Model builds up its data model, which consists of a list of all live threads and the stack traces of each thread, in its update() method:

```
public void update() {
    threadNames.clear();
    stackTraces.clear();
    final Map<Thread, StackTraceElement[]> map = Thread.getAllStackTraces();
    for (Map.Entry<Thread, StackTraceElement[]> entry : map.entrySet()) {
        threadNames.add("\"" + entry.getKey().getName() + "\"");
        stackTraces.add(formatStackTrace(entry.getValue()));
    }
}
```

This method is called once in the constructor of Model, which is called from the constructor of the JavaFXThreadsExample, and once from the event handler of the Update button.

When we run the program in Listing 7-7, the GUI in Figure 7-5 is displayed on the screen. You can explore the threads in this JavaFX program by clicking on each thread name in the list and seeing the stack trace for that thread in the text area. Here are some interesting observations:

- The "main" thread's call stack includes a call to com.sun.javafx.application.LauncherImpl.launchApplication().
- The "JavaFX-Launcher" thread's call stack includes a call to com.sun.javafx.application.PlatformImpl.runAndWait(). This puts code, including the invocation of the constructor, on the JavaFX Application Thread.
- The "JavaFX Application Thread" thread's call stack includes the native method com.sun.glass.ui.win.WinApplication._runLoop() on a Windows box, and something similar on Mac or Linux boxes.
- The "QuantumRenderer-0" thread's call stack includes the method com.sun.javafx.tk.quantum.QuantumRenderer$PipelineRunnable.run().

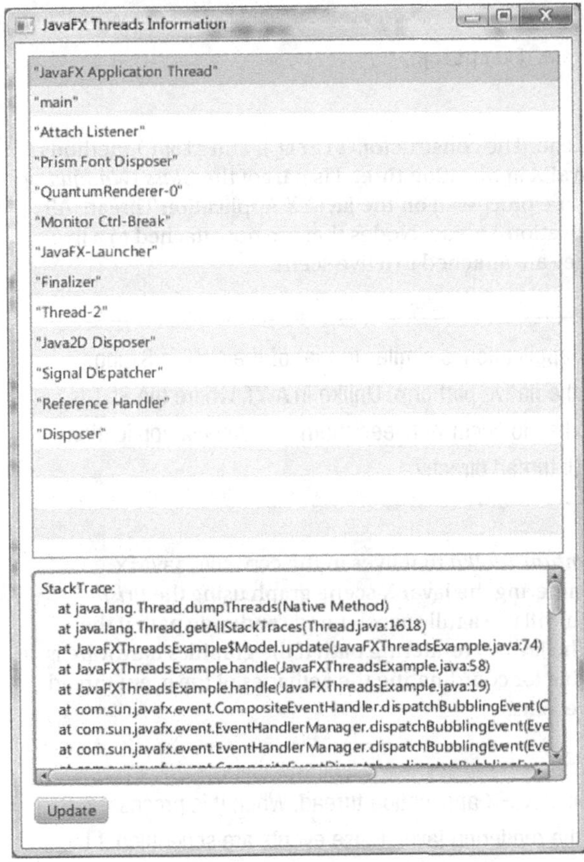

Figure 7-5. *The `JavaFXThreadsExample` program*

Now when you click the Update button and examine the call stack for the "`JavaFX Application Thread`" thread, you will discover that the event handler of the Update button is executed on the JavaFX Application Thread.

This little experiment reveals some of the architectural elements of the JavaFX runtime system. Although parts of this information include implementation details represented by, appropriately, classes in the `com.sun` hierarchy—therefore not to be used in code of normal JavaFX applications—it is nevertheless beneficial to have some knowledge of how the internals work.

■ **Caution** In the discussion that follows, we mention Java classes in packages with names that begin with `com.sun`. These classes are implementation details of the JavaFX runtime system and are not meant to be used in normal JavaFX applications. They might change in future releases of JavaFX.

The `javafx.application.Application` class provides life-cycle support for JavaFX applications. In addition to the two static `launch()` methods we mentioned earlier in this section, it provides the following life-cycle methods.

- `public void init() throws Exception`
- `public abstract void start(Stage stage) throws Exception`
- `public void stop() throws Exception`

The `init()` method is called in the "`JavaFX-Launcher`" thread. The constructor, `start()`, and `stop()` methods are called in the "`JavaFX Application Thread`" thread. The JavaFX application thread is part of the *Glass Windowing Toolkit* in the `com.sun.glass` package hierarchy. JavaFX events are processed on the JavaFX Application Thread. All live scene manipulation must be performed in the JavaFX Application Thread. Nodes that are not attached to a live scene can be created and manipulated in other threads until they are attached to a live scene.

■ **Note** The role the Glass Windowing Toolkit plays in a JavaFX application is similar to that of the AWT in Swing applications. It provides drawing surfaces and input events from the native platform. Unlike in AWT, where the EDT is different from the native platform's UI thread and communication has to occur between them, the JavaFX application thread in the Glass Windowing Toolkit uses the native platform's UI thread directly.

The owner of the "QuantumRenderer-0" thread is the *Quantum Toolkit* that lives in the `com.sun.javafx.tk.quantum` package hierarchy. This thread is responsible for rendering the JavaFX scene graph using the *Prism Graphics Engine* in the `com.sun.prism` package hierarchy. Prism will use a fully accelerated rendering path if the graphics hardware is supported by JavaFX and will fall back to the Java2D rendering path if the graphics hardware is not supported by JavaFX. The Quantum Toolkit is also responsible for coordinating the activities of the event thread and the rendering thread. It does the coordination using `pulse` events.

■ **Note** A *pulse event* is an event that is put on the queue for the JavaFX application thread. When it is processed, it synchronizes the state of the elements of the scene graph down the rendering layer. Pulse events are scheduled if the states of the scene graph change, either through running animation or by modifying the scene graph directly. Pulse events are throttled at 60 frames per second.

Had the `JavaFXThreadsExample` program included media playing, another thread named "`JFXMedia Player EventQueueThread`" would have shown up on the list. This thread is responsible for synchronizing the latest frame through the scene graph by using the JavaFX application thread.

Fixing Unresponsive UIs

Event handlers execute on the JavaFX application thread, thus if an event handler takes too long to finish its work, the whole UI will become unresponsive because any subsequent user actions will simply queue up and won't be handled until the long-running event handler is done.

We illustrate this in Listing 7-8.

Listing 7-8. `UnresponsiveUIExample.java`

```
import javafx.application.Application;
import javafx.beans.property.ObjectProperty;
import javafx.beans.property.SimpleObjectProperty;
import javafx.geometry.Insets;
```

```
import javafx.geometry.Pos;
import javafx.scene.Scene;
import javafx.scene.control.Button;
import javafx.scene.layout.BorderPane;
import javafx.scene.layout.HBox;
import javafx.scene.paint.Color;
import javafx.scene.paint.Paint;
import javafx.scene.shape.Rectangle;
import javafx.stage.Stage;

public class UnresponsiveUIExample extends Application {
    private Model model;
    private View view;

    public static void main(String[] args) {
        launch(args);
    }

    public UnresponsiveUIExample() {
        model = new Model();
    }

    @Override
    public void start(Stage stage) throws Exception {
        view = new View(model);
        hookupEvents();
        stage.setTitle("Unresponsive UI Example");
        stage.setScene(view.scene);
        stage.show();
    }

    private void hookupEvents() {
        view.changeFillButton.setOnAction(actionEvent -> {
            final Paint fillPaint = model.getFillPaint();
            if (fillPaint.equals(Color.LIGHTGRAY)) {
                model.setFillPaint(Color.GRAY);
            } else {
                model.setFillPaint(Color.LIGHTGRAY);
            }
            // Bad code, this will cause the UI to be unresponsive
            try {
                Thread.sleep(Long.MAX_VALUE);
            } catch (InterruptedException e) {
                //  TODO properly handle interruption
            }
        });

        view.changeStrokeButton.setOnAction(actionEvent -> {
            final Paint strokePaint = model.getStrokePaint();
            if (strokePaint.equals(Color.DARKGRAY)) {
                model.setStrokePaint(Color.BLACK);
```

```
            } else {
                model.setStrokePaint(Color.DARKGRAY);
            }
        });
    }

    private static class Model {
        private ObjectProperty<Paint> fillPaint = new SimpleObjectProperty<>();
        private ObjectProperty<Paint> strokePaint = new SimpleObjectProperty<>();

        private Model() {
            fillPaint.set(Color.LIGHTGRAY);
            strokePaint.set(Color.DARKGRAY);
        }

        final public Paint getFillPaint() {
            return fillPaint.get();
        }

        final public void setFillPaint(Paint value) {
            this.fillPaint.set(value);
        }

        final public Paint getStrokePaint() {
            return strokePaint.get();
        }

        final public void setStrokePaint(Paint value) {
            this.strokePaint.set(value);
        }

        final public ObjectProperty<Paint> fillPaintProperty() {
            return fillPaint;
        }

        final public ObjectProperty<Paint> strokePaintProperty() {
            return strokePaint;
        }
    }

    private static class View {
        public Rectangle rectangle;
        public Button changeFillButton;
        public Button changeStrokeButton;
        public HBox buttonHBox;
        public Scene scene;

        private View(Model model) {
            rectangle = new Rectangle(200, 200);
            rectangle.setStrokeWidth(10);
            rectangle.fillProperty().bind(model.fillPaintProperty());
            rectangle.strokeProperty().bind(model.strokePaintProperty());
```

```
        changeFillButton = new Button("Change Fill");
        changeStrokeButton = new Button("Change Stroke");

        buttonHBox = new HBox(10, changeFillButton, changeStrokeButton);
        buttonHBox.setPadding(new Insets(10, 10, 10, 10));
        buttonHBox.setAlignment(Pos.CENTER);

        BorderPane root = new BorderPane(rectangle, null, null, buttonHBox, null);
        root.setPadding(new Insets(10, 10, 10, 10));

        scene = new Scene(root);
    }
  }
}
```

This class stands up a simple UI with a rectangle with a pronounced `Color.DARKGRAY` stroke and a `Color.LIGHTGRAY` fill in the center of a `BorderPane`, and two buttons at the bottom labeled "Change Fill" and "Change Stroke." The "Change Fill" button is supposed to toggle the fill of the rectangle between `Color.LIGHTGRAY` and `Color.GRAY`. The "Change Stroke" button is supposed to toggle the stroke of the rectangle between `Color.DARKGRAY` and `Color.BLACK`. When we run the program in Listing 7-8, the GUI in Figure 7-6 is displayed on the screen.

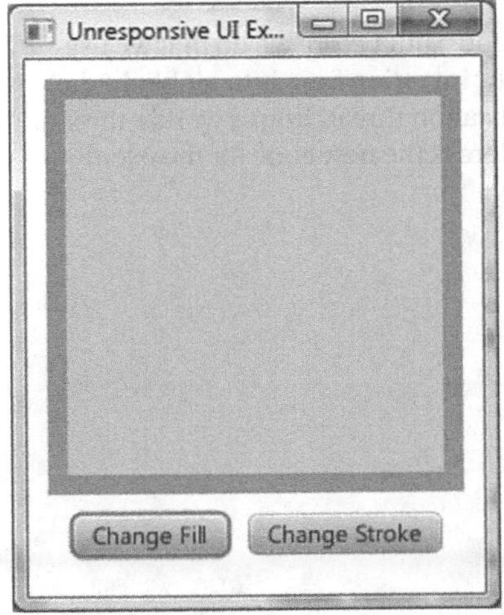

Figure 7-6. *The `UnresponsiveUIExample` program*

However, this program has a bug in the event handler of the "Change Fill" button:

```
@Override
public void handle(ActionEvent actionEvent) {
    final Paint fillPaint = model.getFillPaint();
    if (fillPaint.equals(Color.LIGHTGRAY)) {
        model.setFillPaint(Color.GRAY);
    } else {
        model.setFillPaint(Color.LIGHTGRAY);
    }
```

```
    // Bad code, this will cause the UI to be unresponsive
    try {
        Thread.sleep(Long.MAX_VALUE);
    } catch (InterruptedException e) {
        // TODO properly handle interruption
    }
}
```

The Thread.sleep(Long.MAX_VALUE) simulates code that takes a long time to execute. In real-life applications, this might be a database call, a web service call, or a piece of complicated code. As a result, if you click the "Change Fill" button, the color change is not seen in the rectangle. What is worse, the whole UI appears to be locked up: The "Change Fill" and "Change Stroke" buttons stop working; the close window button that is provided by the operating system will not have the desired effect. The operating system might also mark the program as "Not Responding," and the only way to stop the program is to use the operating system's forced kill functionality.

To fix problems like this, we need to offload long-running code to worker threads and communicate the result of the long computation back to the JavaFX application thread to update the states of the UI so that the user can see the result. Depending on when you learned your Java, your answer to the first question of offloading code to worker threads might be different. If you are a longtime Java programmer your instinctive reaction might be to instantiate a Runnable, wrap it in a Thread, and call start() on it. If you started with Java after Java 5 and learned the java.util.concurrent hierarchy of classes, your reaction might be to stand up a java.util.concurrent.ExecutorService and submit java.util.concurrent.FutureTasks to it. JavaFX includes a worker threading framework based on the latter approach in the javafx.concurrent package.

We examine the interfaces and classes in this framework in the next few sections, but before we do that we use the Runnable and Thread approach to offload computation to a worker thread. Our intention here is to highlight the answer to the second question of how to cause code to be run on the JavaFX application thread from a worker thread. The complete corrected program can be found in ResponsiveUIExample.java. Here is the new code for the event handler of the "Change Fill" button:

```
view.changeFillButton.setOnAction(actionEvent -> {
    final Paint fillPaint = model.getFillPaint();
    if (fillPaint.equals(Color.LIGHTGRAY)) {
        model.setFillPaint(Color.GRAY);
    } else {
        model.setFillPaint(Color.LIGHTGRAY);
    }
    Runnable task = () -> {
        try {
            Thread.sleep(3000);
            Platform.runLater(() -> {
                final Rectangle rect = view.rectangle;
                double newArcSize =
                rect.getArcHeight() < 20 ? 30 : 0;
                rect.setArcWidth(newArcSize);
                rect.setArcHeight(newArcSize);
            });
        } catch (InterruptedException e) {
            // TODO properly handle interruption
        }
    };
    new Thread(task).start();
});
```

We have replaced the long sleep with code that executes in a worker thread. After sleeping for three seconds, the worker thread calls the `runLater()` method of the `javafx.application.Platform` class, passing it another `Runnable` that toggles the rounded corners of the rectangle. Because the long-running computation is done in a worker thread, the event handler is not blocking the JavaFX application thread. The change of fill is now reflected immediately in the UI. Because the `Platform.runLater()` call causes the `Runnable` to be executed on the JavaFX application thread, the change to the rounded corners is reflected in the UI after three seconds. The reason we have to execute the `Runnable` on the JavaFX application thread is that it modifies the state of a live scene.

The `Platform` class includes the following other helpful utility methods:

- `public static boolean isFxApplicationThread()` returns `true` if it is executed on the JavaFX application thread and `false` otherwise.
- `public static boolean isSupported(ConditionalFeature)` tests whether the execution environment supports a `ConditionalFeature`. Testable `ConditionalFeatures` include `GRAPHICS`, `CONTROLS`, `MEDIA`, `WEB`, `SWT`, `SWING`, `FXML`, `SCENE3D`, `EFFECT`, `SHAPE_CLIP`, `INPUT_METHOD`, `TRANSPARENT_WINDOW`, `UNIFIED_WINDOW`, `TWO_LEVEL_FOCUS`, `VIRTUAL_KEYBOARD`, `INPUT_TOUCH`, `INPUT_MULTITOUCH`, and `INPUT_POINTER`.
- `public static void exit()`, if called after the application's `start()` method has been called, causes the application's `stop()` method to be executed on the JavaFX application thread before the JavaFX application thread and other JavaFX platform threads are taken down. If the application's `start()` method has not been called yet, the application's `stop()` method may not be called.
- `public static boolean isImplicitExit()` and `public static void setImplicitExit(boolean)` tests and sets the implicit exit flag. When this flag is true, the JavaFX runtime will shut down when the last application window is closed. Otherwise you have to explicitly call `Platform.exit()` to shut down the JavaFX runtime. The default value of this flag is `true`.

■ **Note** If you are familiar with Swing programming, you should see the similarity between JavaFX's `Platform.runLater()` and Swing's `EventQueue.invokerLater()`, or `SwingUtilities.invokeLater()`.

Now that we have solved our problem with `Runnable` and `Thread` and `Platform.runLater()`, it is time to see how we can use JavaFX's built-in worker threading framework to solve the problem in a more flexible and elegant way.

Understanding the javafx.concurrent Framework

The JavaFX worker threading framework in the `javafx.concurrent` package combines the versatility and flexibility of the Java concurrency framework introduced in Java 5 with the convenience of the JavaFX properties and bindings framework to produce an easy-to-use toolset that is aware of the JavaFX application threading rules and also very easy to use. It consists of one interface, `Worker`, and three abstract base classes, `Task<V>`, `Service<V>`, and `ScheduledService<V>`, that implement the interface.

Understanding the Worker Interface

The Worker interface specifies a JavaFX bean with nine read-only properties, one method named cancel(), and a state model and state transition rules. A Worker represents a unit of work that runs in one or more background threads yet has some of its internal states safely observable to the JavaFX application thread. The nine read-only properties are as follows.

- title is a String property that represents the title of the task.
- message is a String property that represents a more detailed message as the task progresses.
- running is a boolean property that is true only when the Worker is in the Worker.State.SCHEDULED or Worker.State.RUNNING state.
- state is an Object property that represents the Worker.State of the task.
- totalWork is a double property that represents the total amount of work of the task. Its value is -1.0 when the total amount of work is not known.
- workDone is a double property that represents the amount of work that has been done so far in the task. Its value is -1.0 or a number between 0 and totalWork.
- progress is a double property that represents the percentage of the total work that has been done so far in the task. Its value is -1.0 or the ratio between workDone and totalWork.
- value is an Object property that represents the output of the task. Its value is non-null only when the task has finished successfully, that is, has reached the Worker.State.SUCCEEDED state.
- exception is an Object property that represents a Throwable that the implementation of the task has thrown to the JavaFX worker threading framework. Its value is non-null only when the task is in the Worker.State.FAILED state.

The preceding properties are meant to be accessed from the JavaFX application thread. It is safe to bind scene graph properties to them because the invalidation events and change events of these properties are fired on the JavaFX application thread. It is helpful to think of the properties through an imaginary task progress message box that you see in many GUI applications. They usually have a title, a progress bar indicating the percentage of the work that has been done, and a message telling the user how many items it has processed already and how many more to go. All of these properties are set by the JavaFX worker threading framework itself or by the actual implementation of the task.

The running, state, value, and exception properties are controlled by the framework and no user intervention is needed for them to be observed in the JavaFX application thread. When the framework wants to change these properties, it does the heavy lifting of making sure that the change is done on the JavaFX application thread. The title, message, totalWork, workDone, and progress properties are updatable by the implementation code of the task by calling framework-provided protected methods that do the heavy lifting of making sure that the change is done on the JavaFX application thread.

Worker.State is a nested enum that defines the following six states of a Worker:

- READY (initial state)
- SCHEDULED (transitional state)
- RUNNING (transitional state)
- SUCCEEDED (terminal state)
- CANCELLED (terminal state)
- FAILED (terminal state)

The cancel() method will transition the Worker to the CANCELLED state if it is not already in the SUCCEEDED or FAILED state.

Now that you are familiar with the properties and states of the Worker interface, you can proceed to learn the three abstract classes in the JavaFX worker threading framework that implements this interface, Task<V> and Service<V>, and ScheduledService<V>.

Understanding the Task<V> Abstract Class

The Task<V> abstract class is an implementation of the Worker interface that is meant to be used for one-shot tasks. Once its state progresses to SUCCEEDED or FAILED or CANCELLED, it will stay in the terminal state forever. The Task<V> abstract class extends the FutureTask<V> class, and as a consequence supports the Runnable, Future<V>, and RunnableFuture<V> interfaces as well as the Worker interface. The Future<V>, RunnableFuture<V>, and FutureTask<V> interfaces and class are part of the java.util.concurrent package. Because of this heritage, a Task<V> object can be used in various ways that befit its parent class. However, for typical JavaFX usage, it is enough to use just the methods in the Task<V> class itself, a list of which can be found in the Javadoc for the class. Here is a listing of these methods, excluding the read-only properties that were discussed in the preceding section:

- protected abstract V call() throws Exception
- public final boolean cancel()
- public boolean cancel(boolean mayInterruptIfRunning)
- protected void updateTitle(String title)
- protected void updateMessage(String message)
- protected void updateProgress(long workDone, long totalWork)
- protected void updateProgress(double workDone, double totalWork)
- protected void updateValue(V)

The Task<V> abstract class implements the javafx.event.EventTarget interface. The events it supports are represented by the WorkerStateEvent class. There is a WorkerStateEvent for each of the five Worker.States. The events are fired when the Task<V> transitions into a state. There are five object properties of type EventHandler<WorkerStateEvent> as well as five protected methods in Task<V>. These event handlers and protected methods are called when the corresponding event is fired:

- onScheduled property
- onRunning property
- onSucceeded property
- onCancelled property
- onFailed property
- protected void scheduled()
- protected void running()
- protected void succeeded()
- protected void cancelled()
- protected void failed()

Extensions of Task<V> must override the protected abstract call() method to perform the actual work. The implementation of the call() method may call the protected methods updateTitle(), updateMessage(), updateProgress(), and updateValue() to publish its internal state to the JavaFX application thread. The implementation has total control of what the title and message of the task should be. For the updateProgress() call that takes two longs, the workDone and totalWork must either both be -1, indicating indeterminate progress, or satisfy the relations workDone >=0 and workDone <= totalWork, resulting in a progress value of between 0.0 and 1.0 (0% to 100%).

■ **Caution** The updateProgress() API will throw an exception if workDone > totalWork, or if one of them is <-1. However, it allows you to pass in (0, 0), resulting in a progress of NaN.

The two cancel() methods can be called from any thread, and will move the task to the CANCELLED state if it is not already in the SUCCEEDED or FAILED state. If either cancel() method is called before the task is run, it will move to the CANCELLED state and will never be run. The two cancel() methods differ only if the task is in the RUNNING state, and only in their treatment of the running thread. If cancel(true) is called, the thread will receive an interrupt. For this interrupt to have the desired effect of causing the task to finish processing quickly, the implementation of the call() method has to be coded in a way that will detect the interrupt and skip any further processing. The no-argument cancel() method simply forwards to cancel(true).

Listing 7-9 illustrates the creation of a Task, starting it, and observing the properties of the task from a simple GUI that displays all nine of the properties.

Listing 7-9. WorkerAndTaskExample.java

```
import javafx.application.Application;
import javafx.beans.binding.Bindings;
import javafx.beans.property.ReadOnlyObjectProperty;
import javafx.concurrent.Task;
import javafx.concurrent.Worker;
import javafx.geometry.HPos;
import javafx.geometry.Insets;
import javafx.geometry.Pos;
import javafx.scene.Scene;
import javafx.scene.control.Button;
import javafx.scene.control.Label;
import javafx.scene.control.ProgressBar;
import javafx.scene.layout.BorderPane;
import javafx.scene.layout.ColumnConstraints;
import javafx.scene.layout.GridPane;
import javafx.scene.layout.HBox;
import javafx.stage.Stage;

import java.util.concurrent.atomic.AtomicBoolean;

public class WorkerAndTaskExample extends Application {
    private Model model;
    private View view;

    public static void main(String[] args) {
        launch(args);
    }
```

```
    public WorkerAndTaskExample() {
        model = new Model();
    }

    @Override
    public void start(Stage stage) throws Exception {
        view = new View(model);
        hookupEvents();
        stage.setTitle("Worker and Task Example");
        stage.setScene(view.scene);
        stage.show();
    }

    private void hookupEvents() {
        view.startButton.setOnAction(actionEvent -> {
            new Thread((Runnable) model.worker).start();
        });
        view.cancelButton.setOnAction(actionEvent -> {
            model.worker.cancel();
        });
        view.exceptionButton.setOnAction(actionEvent -> {
            model.shouldThrow.getAndSet(true);
        });
    }

    private static class Model {
        public Worker<String> worker;
        public AtomicBoolean shouldThrow = new AtomicBoolean(false);

        private Model() {
            worker = new Task<String>() {
                @Override
                protected String call() throws Exception {
                    updateTitle("Example Task");
                    updateMessage("Starting...");
                    final int total = 250;
                    updateProgress(0, total);
                    for (int i = 1; i <= total; i++) {
                        if (isCancelled()) {
                            updateValue("Canceled at " + System.currentTimeMillis());
                            return null; // ignored
                        }
                        try {
                            Thread.sleep(20);
                        } catch (InterruptedException e) {
                                updateValue("Canceled at " + System.currentTimeMillis());
                                return null; // ignored                         }
                        if (shouldThrow.get()) {
                            throw new RuntimeException("Exception thrown at " +
System.currentTimeMillis());
                        }
```

```
                    updateTitle("Example Task (" + i + ")");
                    updateMessage("Processed " + i + " of " + total + " items.");
                    updateProgress(i, total);
                }
                return "Completed at " + System.currentTimeMillis();
            }

            @Override
            protected void scheduled() {
                System.out.println("The task is scheduled.");
            }

            @Override
            protected void running() {
                System.out.println("The task is running.");
            }
        };
        ((Task<String>) worker).setOnSucceeded(event -> {
            System.out.println("The task succeeded.");
        });
        ((Task<String>) worker).setOnCancelled(event -> {
            System.out.println("The task is canceled.");
        });
        ((Task<String>) worker).setOnFailed(event -> {
            System.out.println("The task failed.");
        });
    }
}

private static class View {
    public ProgressBar progressBar;

    public Label title;
    public Label message;
    public Label running;
    public Label state;
    public Label totalWork;
    public Label workDone;
    public Label progress;
    public Label value;
    public Label exception;

    public Button startButton;
    public Button cancelButton;
    public Button exceptionButton;

    public Scene scene;

    private View(final Model model) {
        progressBar = new ProgressBar();
        progressBar.setMinWidth(250);
```

```
title = new Label();
message = new Label();
running = new Label();
state = new Label();
totalWork = new Label();
workDone = new Label();
progress = new Label();
value = new Label();
exception = new Label();

startButton = new Button("Start");
cancelButton = new Button("Cancel");
exceptionButton = new Button("Exception");

final ReadOnlyObjectProperty<Worker.State> stateProperty =
    model.worker.stateProperty();

progressBar.progressProperty().bind(model.worker.progressProperty());

title.textProperty().bind(
    model.worker.titleProperty());
message.textProperty().bind(
    model.worker.messageProperty());
running.textProperty().bind(
    Bindings.format("%s", model.worker.runningProperty()));
state.textProperty().bind(
    Bindings.format("%s", stateProperty));
totalWork.textProperty().bind(
    model.worker.totalWorkProperty().asString());
workDone.textProperty().bind(
    model.worker.workDoneProperty().asString());
progress.textProperty().bind(
    Bindings.format("%5.2f%%", model.worker.progressProperty().multiply(100)));
value.textProperty().bind(
    model.worker.valueProperty());
exception.textProperty().bind(Bindings.createStringBinding(() -> {
    final Throwable exception = model.worker.getException();
    if (exception == null) return "";
    return exception.getMessage();
}, model.worker.exceptionProperty()));

startButton.disableProperty().bind(
    stateProperty.isNotEqualTo(Worker.State.READY));
cancelButton.disableProperty().bind(
    stateProperty.isNotEqualTo(Worker.State.RUNNING));
exceptionButton.disableProperty().bind(
    stateProperty.isNotEqualTo(Worker.State.RUNNING));

HBox topPane = new HBox(10, progressBar);
topPane.setAlignment(Pos.CENTER);
topPane.setPadding(new Insets(10, 10, 10, 10));
```

```
            ColumnConstraints constraints1 = new ColumnConstraints();
            constraints1.setHalignment(HPos.CENTER);
            constraints1.setMinWidth(65);

            ColumnConstraints constraints2 = new ColumnConstraints();
            constraints2.setHalignment(HPos.LEFT);
            constraints2.setMinWidth(200);

            GridPane centerPane = new GridPane();
            centerPane.setHgap(10);
            centerPane.setVgap(10);
            centerPane.setPadding(new Insets(10, 10, 10, 10));
            centerPane.getColumnConstraints()
                .addAll(constraints1, constraints2);

            centerPane.add(new Label("Title:"), 0, 0);
            centerPane.add(new Label("Message:"), 0, 1);
            centerPane.add(new Label("Running:"), 0, 2);
            centerPane.add(new Label("State:"), 0, 3);
            centerPane.add(new Label("Total Work:"), 0, 4);
            centerPane.add(new Label("Work Done:"), 0, 5);
            centerPane.add(new Label("Progress:"), 0, 6);
            centerPane.add(new Label("Value:"), 0, 7);
            centerPane.add(new Label("Exception:"), 0, 8);

            centerPane.add(title, 1, 0);
            centerPane.add(message, 1, 1);
            centerPane.add(running, 1, 2);
            centerPane.add(state, 1, 3);
            centerPane.add(totalWork, 1, 4);
            centerPane.add(workDone, 1, 5);
            centerPane.add(progress, 1, 6);
            centerPane.add(value, 1, 7);
            centerPane.add(exception, 1, 8);

            HBox buttonPane = new HBox(10,
                startButton, cancelButton, exceptionButton);
            buttonPane.setPadding(new Insets(10, 10, 10, 10));
            buttonPane.setAlignment(Pos.CENTER);

            BorderPane root = new BorderPane(centerPane,
                topPane, null, buttonPane, null);
            scene = new Scene(root);
        }
    }
```

The Model nested class for this program holds a worker field of type Worker, and a shouldThrow field of type AtomicBoolean. The worker field is initialized to an instance of an anonymous subclass of Task<String> that implements its call() method by simulating the processing of 250 items at a 20-milliseconds-per-item pace. It updates the properties of the task at the beginning of the call and in each iteration of the loop. It handles cancellation in two places. It checks the `isCancelled()` flag at the top of each iteration, and it also checks the `isCancelled()` flag in the `InterruptedException` handler of the `Thread.sleep()` call. If the task is cancelled, it calls the `updateValue()`, and gets out of the `loop` and returns quickly. The return value is ignored by the framework. The `shouldThrow` field is controlled by the `View` to communicate to the task that it should throw an exception.

The `View` nested class of this program creates a simple UI that has a `ProgressBar` at the top, a set of `Labels` at the center that display the various properties of the worker, and three buttons at the bottom. The contents of the `Labels` are bound to the various properties of the `worker`. The `disable` properties of the buttons are also bound to the state property of the `worker` so that only the relevant buttons are enabled at any time. For example, the Start button is enabled when the program starts but becomes disabled after it is pressed and the task execution begins. Similarly, the Cancel and Exception buttons are enabled only if the task is running.

When we run the program in Listing 7-9, the GUI in Figure 7-7 is displayed on the screen.

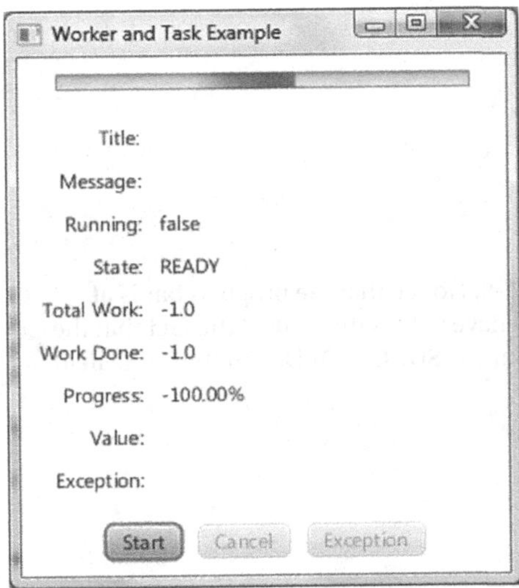

***Figure 7-7.** The `WorkerAndTaskExample` program after starting up*

Notice that the progress bar is in an indeterminate state. The values of Title, Message, Value, and Exception are empty. The value of Running is false. The value of State is READY, the values of Total Work and Work Done are -1.0, and Progress displays -100%. The Start button is enabled, whereas the Cancel and Exception buttons are disabled.

After the Start button is clicked, the task starts to execute and the GUI automatically reflects the values of the properties as the task progresses. Figure 7-8 is a screenshot of the application at this stage. Notice that the progress bar is in a determinate state and reflects the progress of the task. The values of Title and Message reflects what is set to these properties in the implementation of the `call()` method in the task. The value of Running is true. The value of State is RUNNING, and the values of Total Work, Work Done, and Progress reflect the current state of the executing task: 156 of 250 items done. The Value and the Exception fields are empty because neither a value nor an exception is available from the task. The Start button is disabled now. The Cancel and Exception buttons are enabled, indicating that we may attempt to cancel the task or force an exception to be thrown from the task at this moment.

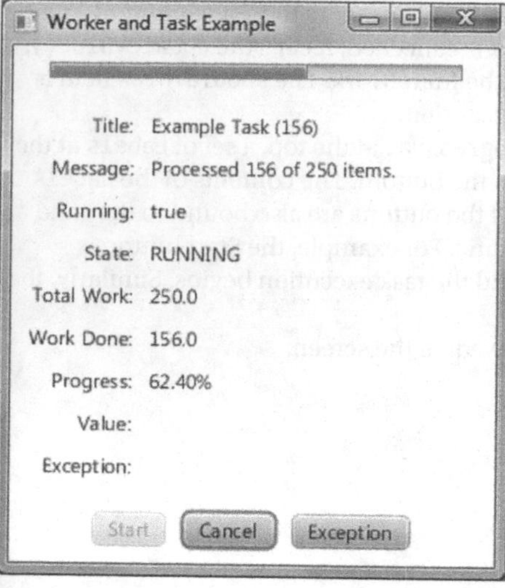

Figure 7-8. The `WorkerAndTaskExample` program while a task is in progress

When the task finishes normally, we arrive at the screenshot in Figure 7-9. Notice that the progress bar is at 100.00%. The Title, Message, Total Work, Work Done, and Progress fields all have values that reflect the fact that the task has finished processing all 250 items. The Running value is false. The State is SUCCEEDED, and the Value field now contains the return value from the `call()` method.

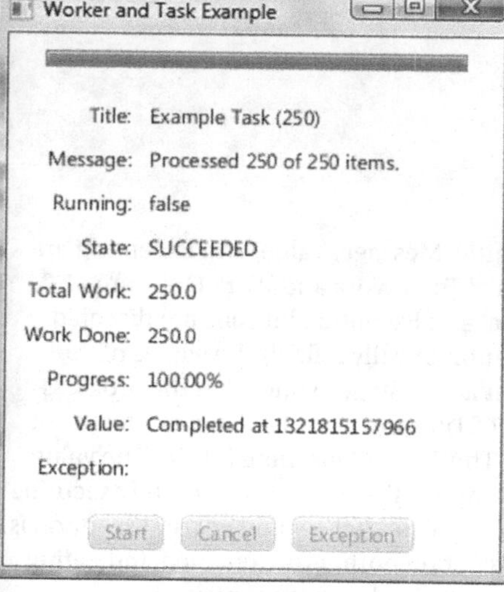

Figure 7-9. The `WorkerAndTaskExample` program after the task succeeded

If, instead of letting the task finish normally, we click the Cancel button, the task will finish immediately and the screenshot in Figure 7-10 results. Notice that the State field has the value CANCELLED now. The Value field contains the string we passed to the `updateValue()` method when the task was cancelled. When we detect that the task is cancelled, we have two choices of exiting from the method body. In the program in Listing 7-7, we chose to update the Value and return from the method. We could also have chosen to exit from the method body by throwing a `RuntimeException`. Had we made that choice, the screenshot would have an empty Value field but with a nonempty Exception field. The state of the worker would have been `CANCELLED` either way.

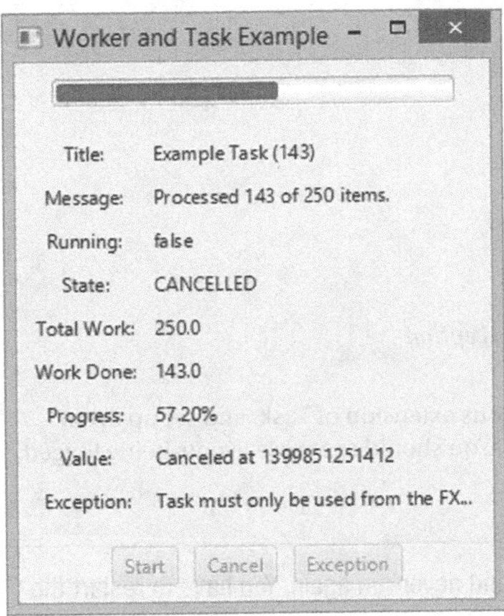

Figure 7-10. *The `WorkerAndTaskExample` program after the task has been cancelled*

■ **Caution** When you return normally in response to cancellation, a bug in the current implementation of `Task` causes an `IllegalStateException` to be recorded as the exception of the `Task`. This will be fixed in the next release.

The final screenshot, Figure 7-11, shows what happens when the Exception button is clicked when the task is executing. We simulate an exception in the task by setting an `AtomicBoolean` flag from the JavaFX application, which the task then picks up in the `worker` thread and throws the exception. Notice that the status field has the value FAILED now. The Value field is empty because the task did not complete successfully. The Exception field is filled with the message of the `RuntimeException` that we threw.

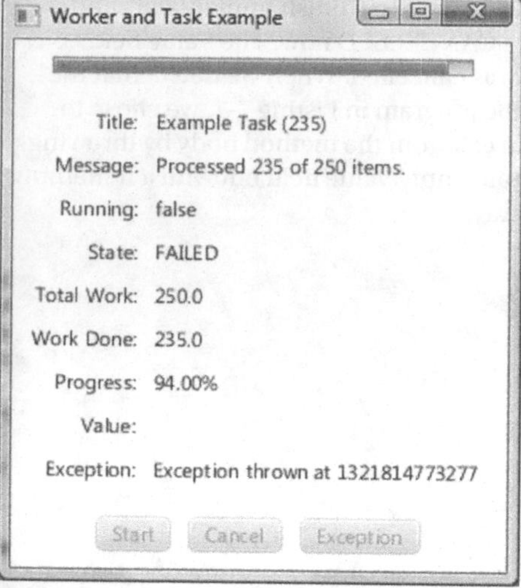

Figure 7-11. *The `WorkerAndTaskExample` program after the task threw an exception*

We overrode the `scheduled()` and `running()` methods in the anonymous extension of `Task`, and set up event handlers for the succeeded, cancelled, and failed events, in the `Model` class. You should see these events being logged onto the console as you work through the scenarios.

■ **Note** The `Task<V>` class defines one-shot tasks that are executed once and never run again. You have to restart the `WorkerAndTaskExample` program after each run of the task.

Understanding the `Service<V>` Abstract Class

The `Service<V>` abstract class is an implementation of the `Worker` interface that is meant to be reused. It extends `Worker`'s state model by allowing its state to be reset to `Worker.State.READY`. The `Service<V>` abstract class does not extend any class and implements the `Worker` and `EventTarget` interfaces. In addition to the nine read-only properties of the `Worker` interface, `Service<V>` has an additional read write property of type `Executor` called `executor`. It also has the event handler properties and the protected event callback methods just like the `Task` class. Here is a listing of the rest of the methods of `Service<V>`:

- `protected abstract Task<V> createTask()`
- `public void start()`
- `public void reset()`
- `public void restart()`
- `public boolean cancel()`

Extensions of `Service<V>` must override the protected abstract `createTask()` method to generate a freshly created `Task`. The `start()` method can only be called when the `Service<V>` object is in the `Worker.State.READY` state. It calls `createTask()` to obtain a freshly minted `Task`, and asks the `executor` property for an `Executor`. If the `executor` property is not set, it creates its own `Executor`. It binds the `Service<V>` object's nine `Worker` properties to that of the `Task`'s. It then transitions the `Task` to the `Worker.State.SCHEDULED` state, and executes the `Task` on the Executor. The reset() method can only be called when the Service<V>'s state is not Worker.State.SCHEDULED or Worker.State.RUNNING. It simply unbinds the nine Service<V> properties from that of the underlying Task and resets their values to fresh startup values: Worker.State.READY for the state property, and null or "" or false or -1 for the other properties. The restart() method simply cancels the currently executing Task, if any, and then does a reset() followed by a start(). The cancel() method will cancel the currently executing Task, if any; otherwise it will transition the Service<V> to the Worker.State.CANCELLED state.

Listing 7-10 illustrates using an instance of an anonymous subclass of the Service<V> abstract class to execute Tasks repeatedly in its own Executor.

Listing 7-10. ServiceExample.java

```
import javafx.application.Application;
import javafx.beans.binding.Bindings;
import javafx.beans.property.IntegerProperty;
import javafx.beans.property.ReadOnlyObjectProperty;
import javafx.beans.property.SimpleIntegerProperty;
import javafx.concurrent.Service;
import javafx.concurrent.Task;
import javafx.concurrent.Worker;
import javafx.geometry.HPos;
import javafx.geometry.Insets;
import javafx.geometry.Pos;
import javafx.scene.Scene;
import javafx.scene.control.Button;
import javafx.scene.control.Label;
import javafx.scene.control.ProgressBar;
import javafx.scene.control.TextField;
import javafx.scene.layout.BorderPane;
import javafx.scene.layout.ColumnConstraints;
import javafx.scene.layout.GridPane;
import javafx.scene.layout.HBox;
import javafx.stage.Stage;

import java.util.concurrent.atomic.AtomicBoolean;

public class ServiceExample extends Application {
    private Model model;
    private View view;

    public static void main(String[] args) {
        launch(args);
    }

    public ServiceExample() {
        model = new Model();
    }

    @Override
    public void start(Stage stage) throws Exception {
        view = new View(model);
        hookupEvents();
```

```
        stage.setTitle("Service Example");
        stage.setScene(view.scene);
        stage.show();
    }

    private void hookupEvents() {
        view.startButton.setOnAction(actionEvent -> {
            model.shouldThrow.getAndSet(false);
            ((Service) model.worker).restart();
        });
        view.cancelButton.setOnAction(actionEvent -> {
            model.worker.cancel();
        });
        view.exceptionButton.setOnAction(actionEvent -> {
            model.shouldThrow.getAndSet(true);
        });
    }

    private static class Model {
        public Worker<String> worker;
        public AtomicBoolean shouldThrow = new AtomicBoolean(false);
        public IntegerProperty numberOfItems = new SimpleIntegerProperty(250);

        private Model() {
            worker = new Service<String>() {
                @Override
                protected Task createTask() {
                    return new Task<String>() {
                        @Override
                        protected String call() throws Exception {
                            updateTitle("Example Service");
                            updateMessage("Starting...");
                            final int total = numberOfItems.get();
                            updateProgress(0, total);
                            for (int i = 1; i <= total; i++) {
                                if (isCancelled()) {
                                    updateValue("Canceled at " + System.currentTimeMillis());
                                    return null; // ignored
                                }
                                try {
                                    Thread.sleep(20);
                                } catch (InterruptedException e) {
                                    if (isCancelled()) {
                                        updateValue("Canceled at " + System.currentTimeMillis());
                                        return null; // ignored
                                    }
                                }
                                if (shouldThrow.get()) {
                                    throw new RuntimeException("Exception thrown at " +
System.currentTimeMillis());
                                }
```

```
                        updateTitle("Example Service (" + i + ")");
                        updateMessage("Processed " + i + " of " + total + " items.");
                        updateProgress(i, total);
                    }
                    return "Completed at " + System.currentTimeMillis();
                }
            };
        }
    };
}
}

private static class View {
    public ProgressBar progressBar;

    public Label title;
    public Label message;
    public Label running;
    public Label state;
    public Label totalWork;
    public Label workDone;
    public Label progress;
    public Label value;
    public Label exception;

    public TextField numberOfItems;
    public Button startButton;
    public Button cancelButton;
    public Button exceptionButton;

    public Scene scene;

    private View(final Model model) {
        progressBar = new ProgressBar();
        progressBar.setMinWidth(250);

        title = new Label();
        message = new Label();
        running = new Label();
        state = new Label();
        totalWork = new Label();
        workDone = new Label();
        progress = new Label();
        value = new Label();
        exception = new Label();
        numberOfItems = new TextField();
        numberOfItems.setMaxWidth(40);

        startButton = new Button("Start");
        cancelButton = new Button("Cancel");
        exceptionButton = new Button("Exception");
```

```
        final ReadOnlyObjectProperty<Worker.State> stateProperty =
            model.worker.stateProperty();

        progressBar.progressProperty().bind(model.worker.progressProperty());

        title.textProperty().bind(
            model.worker.titleProperty());
        message.textProperty().bind(
            model.worker.messageProperty());
        running.textProperty().bind(
            Bindings.format("%s", model.worker.runningProperty()));
        state.textProperty().bind(
            Bindings.format("%s", stateProperty));
        totalWork.textProperty().bind(
            model.worker.totalWorkProperty().asString());
        workDone.textProperty().bind(
            model.worker.workDoneProperty().asString());
        progress.textProperty().bind(
            Bindings.format("%5.2f%%", model.worker.progressProperty().multiply(100)));
        value.textProperty().bind(
            model.worker.valueProperty());
        exception.textProperty().bind(Bindings.createStringBinding(() -> {
            final Throwable exception = model.worker.getException();
            if (exception == null) return "";
            return exception.getMessage();
        }, model.worker.exceptionProperty()));

        model.numberOfItems.bind(Bindings.createIntegerBinding(() -> {
            final String text = numberOfItems.getText();
            int n = 250;
            try {
                n = Integer.parseInt(text);
            } catch (NumberFormatException e) {
            }
            return n;
        }, numberOfItems.textProperty()));

        startButton.disableProperty().bind(
            stateProperty.isEqualTo(Worker.State.RUNNING));
        cancelButton.disableProperty().bind(
            stateProperty.isNotEqualTo(Worker.State.RUNNING));
        exceptionButton.disableProperty().bind(
            stateProperty.isNotEqualTo(Worker.State.RUNNING));

        HBox topPane = new HBox(10, progressBar);
        topPane.setPadding(new Insets(10, 10, 10, 10));
        topPane.setAlignment(Pos.CENTER);

        ColumnConstraints constraints1 = new ColumnConstraints();
        constraints1.setHalignment(HPos.RIGHT);
        constraints1.setMinWidth(65);
```

```
            ColumnConstraints constraints2 = new ColumnConstraints();
            constraints2.setHalignment(HPos.LEFT);
            constraints2.setMinWidth(200);

            GridPane centerPane = new GridPane();
            centerPane.setHgap(10);
            centerPane.setVgap(10);
            centerPane.setPadding(new Insets(10, 10, 10, 10));
            centerPane.getColumnConstraints().addAll(constraints1, constraints2);
            centerPane.add(new Label("Title:"), 0, 0);
            centerPane.add(new Label("Message:"), 0, 1);
            centerPane.add(new Label("Running:"), 0, 2);
            centerPane.add(new Label("State:"), 0, 3);
            centerPane.add(new Label("Total Work:"), 0, 4);
            centerPane.add(new Label("Work Done:"), 0, 5);
            centerPane.add(new Label("Progress:"), 0, 6);
            centerPane.add(new Label("Value:"), 0, 7);
            centerPane.add(new Label("Exception:"), 0, 8);

            centerPane.add(title, 1, 0);
            centerPane.add(message, 1, 1);
            centerPane.add(running, 1, 2);
            centerPane.add(state, 1, 3);
            centerPane.add(totalWork, 1, 4);
            centerPane.add(workDone, 1, 5);
            centerPane.add(progress, 1, 6);
            centerPane.add(value, 1, 7);
            centerPane.add(exception, 1, 8);

            HBox buttonPane = new HBox(10,
                new Label("Process"), numberOfItems, new Label("items"),
                startButton, cancelButton, exceptionButton);
            buttonPane.setPadding(new Insets(10, 10, 10, 10));
            buttonPane.setAlignment(Pos.CENTER);

            BorderPane root = new BorderPane(centerPane, topPane, null, buttonPane, null);
            scene = new Scene(root);
        }
    }
}
```

The preceding program is derived from the WorkerAndTaskExample class that we studied in the previous section. The Model nested class for this program holds a worker field of type Worker, a shouldThrow field of type AtomicBoolean, and a numberOfItems field of type IntegerProperty. The worker field is initialized to an instance of an anonymous subclass of Service<String> that implements its createTask() method to return a Task<String> with a call() method that is implemented almost exactly like the Task<String> implementation in the last section, except that instead of always processing 250 items, it picks up the number of items to process from the numberOfItems property from the Model class.

The View nested class of this program creates a UI that is almost identical to that in the previous section but with some additional controls in the button panel. One of the controls added to the button panel is a TextField named numberOfItems. The model's numberOfItems IntegerProperty is bound to an IntegerBinding created with the textProperty() of the view's numberOfItems field. This effectively controls the number of items each newly created Task will process. The Start button is disabled only if the service is in the Worker.State.RUNNING state. Therefore you can click the Start button after a task has finished.

The action handler of the Start button now resets the shouldThrow flag to false and calls restart() of the service.

The screenshots in Figures 7-12 to 7-16 are taken with the ServiceExample program under situations similar to those for the screenshots in Figures 7-7 to 7-11 for the WorkerAndTaskExample program.

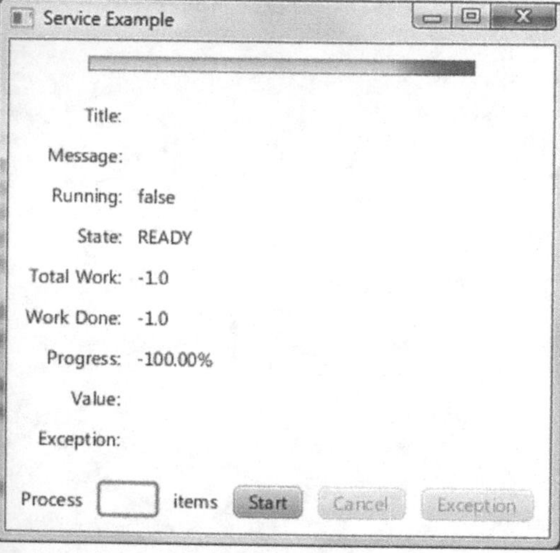

Figure 7-12. *The ServiceExample program after starting up*

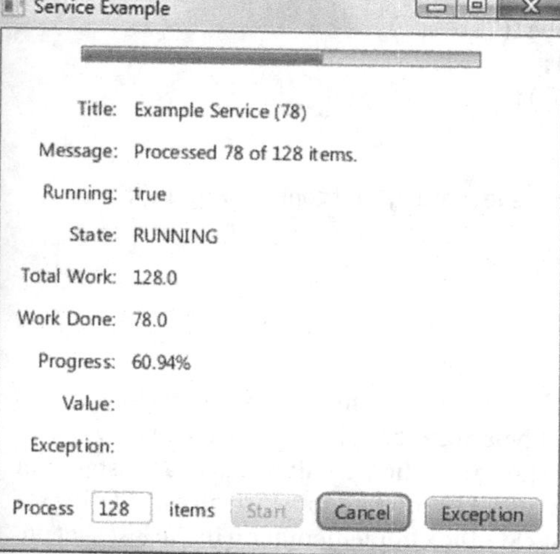

Figure 7-13. *The ServiceExample program while a task is in progress*

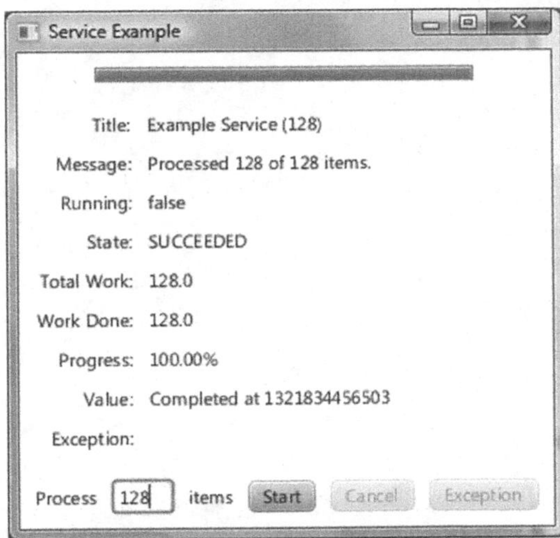

***Figure 7-14.** The `ServiceExample` program after the task succeeded*

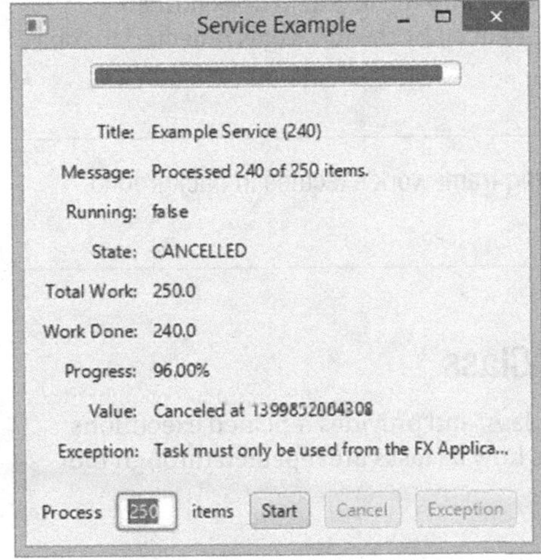

***Figure 7-15.** The `ServiceExample` program after the task has been cancelled*

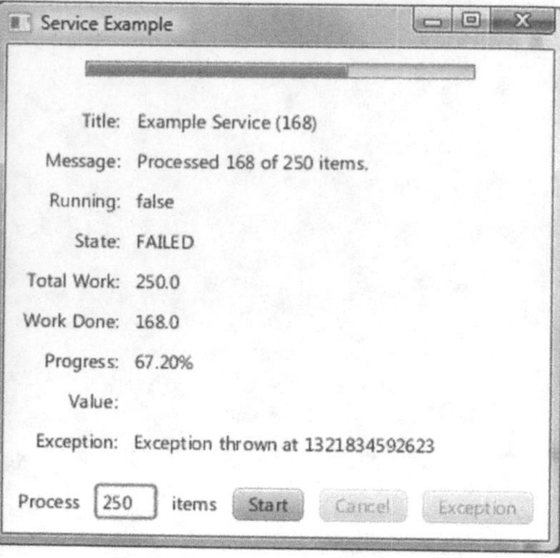

Figure 7-16. *The `ServiceExample` program after the task threw an exception*

As you can see from the preceding screenshots, the number that is entered into the text field does indeed influence the number of items processed in each run of the service, as is evidenced by the messages reflected in the UI in the screenshots.

■ **Caution** Because the task that is started with the JavaFX worker threading framework executes in background threads, it is very important not to access any live scenes in the task code.

Understanding the `ScheduledService<V>` Abstract Class

The `ScheduledService<V>` abstract class extends the `Service<V>` abstract class, and provides repeated executions of the tasks created by the service. The `ScheduledService<V>` class controls how its tasks are repeated through the following properties:

- `delay`
- `period`
- `backOffStrategy`
- `restartOnFailure`
- `maximumFailureCount`
- `currentFailureCount`
- `cumulativePeriod`
- `maximumCumulativePeriod`
- `lastValue`

The delay property controls how much time must elapse after the start() call on the scheduled service before the task starts to run. The period property controls how much time must elapse after one run of the task before the next run of the task can start. The period measures the differences between the start of one run and the start of the next run. The delay and period are object properties of type Duration. If no failure condition occurs while the task is executing, the ScheduledService will keep on repeating the task indefinitely.

If a failure condition occurs while the task is executing, what happens next is controlled by the restartOnFailure property. If this property is false, the ScheduledService will remain in the FAILED state and nothing more will happen. If the restartOnFailure property is true, the ScheduledService will rerun the task again. The rerunning of failed tasks is controlled by the backOffStrategy, maximumFailureCount, and maximumCumulativePeriod properties. The back off strategy is simply a lambda expression that takes the ScheduledService as an argument and returns a Duration, which is set as the value of the cumulativePeriod property. The rerunning of the task will start when the elapsed time since the start of the last failed run of the task reaches cumulativePeriod. In addition to cumulativePeriod, the ScheduledService also keeps track of the currentFailureCount property, which is the number of consecutive failed runs in the current sequence of failed runs. If the rerunning of the task is successful, ScheduledService will go back to its normal behavior of running the task in period time intervals. Otherwise—that is, if the rerun failed again—ScheduledService will ask the backOffStrategy for a new cumulativePeriod, and rerun again. If the currentFailureCount reaches maximumFailureCount, or if the cumulativePeriod becomes greater than or equal to the maximumCumulativePeriod, the ScheduledService will go into the FAILED state and nothing more will happen.

Three back off strategies are provided. They are constants in ScheduledService. The LINEAR_BACKOFF_STRATEGY returns ever longer Durations that grow linearly. The EXPONENTIAL_BACKOFF_STRATEGY returns ever longer Durations that grow exponentially. The LOGARITHMIC_BACKOFF_STRATEGY returns ever longer Durations that grow logarithmically. You can easily define your own back off strategies.

You can reset and restart a ScheduledService by calling reset() and start() methods.

Mixing JavaFX with Other GUI Toolkits

Having examined the threading paradigm of the JavaFX runtime and ways to execute code from the JavaFX application thread, we now look at how to make JavaFX coexist with some other GUI toolkits. JavaFX provides classes and frameworks that make it possible to mix JavaFX with Swing or SWT. You can embed a JavaFX scene in a Swing application. You can embed a JavaFX scene in a SWT application. And you can embed Swing components in a JavaFX application.

Embedding JavaFX Scenes in Swing Applications

JavaFX supports embedding a JavaFX scene into a Swing application through the javafx.embed.swing package of classes. This is a pretty small package that includes one public class for embedding JavaFX scenes into Swing—JFXPanel—and another class—SwingNode—for embedding Swing components into JavaFX applications. The JFXPanel class extends javax.swing.JComponent, and as such can be placed in a Swing program just as any other Swing component. JFXPanel can also host a JavaFX scene, and as such can add a JavaFX scene to a Swing program.

However, this Swing program with a JavaFX scene embedded in it needs both the Swing runtime to make its Swing portion function correctly, and the JavaFX runtime to make the JavaFX portion function correctly. Therefore it has both the Swing Event Dispatching Thread (EDT) and the JavaFX Application Thread. The JFXPanel class does a two-way translation of all the user events between Swing and JavaFX.

Just as JavaFX has the rule that requires all access to live scenes to be done in the JavaFX Application Thread, Swing has the rule that requires all access to Swing GUIs to be done in the EDT. You still need to jump the thread if you want to alter a Swing component from a JavaFX event handler or vice versa. The proper way to execute a piece of code on the JavaFX Application Thread, as we saw earlier, is to use Platform.runLater(). The proper way to execute a piece of code on the Swing EDT is to use EventQueue.invokeLater().

In this section, we convert a pure Swing program into a Swing and JavaFX hybrid program. We start off with the Swing program in Listing 7-11, which is very similar to the ResponsiveUIExample program.

Listing 7-11. NoJavaFXSceneInSwingExample.java

```
import javax.swing.*;
import java.awt.*;
import java.awt.event.ActionEvent;
import java.awt.event.ActionListener;

public class NoJavaFXSceneInSwingExample {
    public static void main(final String[] args) {
        EventQueue.invokeLater(new Runnable() {
            @Override
            public void run() {
                swingMain(args);
            }
        });
    }
    private static void swingMain(String[] args) {
        Model model = new Model();
        View view = new View(model);
        Controller controller = new Controller(model, view);
        controller.mainLoop();
    }

    private static class Model {
        public Color fillColor = Color.LIGHT_GRAY;
        public Color strokeColor = Color.DARK_GRAY;
    }

    private static class View {
        public JFrame frame;
        public JComponent canvas;
        public JButton changeFillButton;
        public JButton changeStrokeButton;

        private View(final Model model) {
            frame = new JFrame("No JavaFX in Swing Example");
            canvas = new JComponent() {
                @Override
                public void paint(Graphics g) {
                    g.setColor(model.strokeColor);
                    g.fillRect(0, 0, 200, 200);
                    g.setColor(model.fillColor);
                    g.fillRect(10, 10, 180, 180);
                }

                @Override
                public Dimension getPreferredSize() {
                    return new Dimension(200, 200);
                }
            };
```

```
            FlowLayout canvasPanelLayout = new FlowLayout(FlowLayout.CENTER, 10, 10);
            JPanel canvasPanel = new JPanel(canvasPanelLayout);
            canvasPanel.add(canvas);

            changeFillButton = new JButton("Change Fill");
            changeStrokeButton = new JButton("Change Stroke");
            FlowLayout buttonPanelLayout = new FlowLayout(FlowLayout.CENTER, 10, 10);
            JPanel buttonPanel = new JPanel(buttonPanelLayout);
            buttonPanel.add(changeFillButton);
            buttonPanel.add(changeStrokeButton);

            frame.add(canvasPanel, BorderLayout.CENTER);
            frame.add(buttonPanel, BorderLayout.SOUTH);
            frame.setDefaultCloseOperation(JFrame.EXIT_ON_CLOSE);
            frame.setLocationByPlatform(true);
            frame.pack();
        }
    }
    private static class Controller {
        private View view;

        private Controller(final Model model, final View view) {
            this.view = view;
            this.view.changeFillButton.addActionListener(new ActionListener() {
                @Override
                public void actionPerformed(ActionEvent e) {
                    if (model.fillColor.equals(Color.LIGHT_GRAY)) {
                        model.fillColor = Color.GRAY;
                    } else {
                        model.fillColor = Color.LIGHT_GRAY;
                    }
                    view.canvas.repaint();
                }
            });
            this.view.changeStrokeButton.addActionListener(new ActionListener() {
                @Override
                public void actionPerformed(ActionEvent e) {
                    if (model.strokeColor.equals(Color.DARK_GRAY)) {
                        model.strokeColor = Color.BLACK;
                    } else {
                        model.strokeColor = Color.DARK_GRAY;
                    }
                    view.canvas.repaint();
                }
            });
        }

        public void mainLoop() {
            view.frame.setVisible(true);
        }
    }
}
```

When the program in Listing 7-11 is run, the UI in Figure 7-17 is displayed. It is a JFrame holding three Swing components, a JComponent with overridden paint()and getPreferredSize() methods that makes it look like the rectangle we saw in the earlier program, and two JButtons that will change the fill and the stroke of the rectangle.

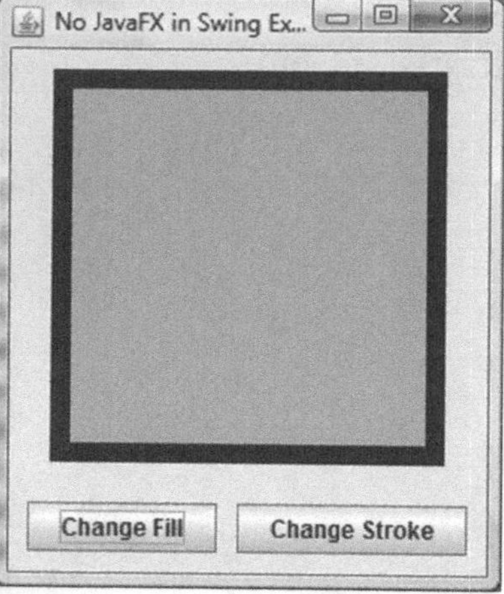

Figure 7-17. The NoJavaFXSceneInSwingExample program

Inasmuch as the custom-painted JComponent in NoJavaFXSceneInSwingExample is hard to maintain over the long run, we replace it with the JavaFX Rectangle. This is done by replacing the Swing code with the equivalent JFXPanel code. Here is the Swing code:

```
canvas = new JComponent() {
    @Override
    public void paint(Graphics g) {
        g.setColor(model.strokeColor);
        g.fillRect(0, 0, 200, 200);
        g.setColor(model.fillColor);
        g.fillRect(10, 10, 180, 180);
    }

    @Override
    public Dimension getPreferredSize() {
        return new Dimension(200, 200);
    }
};
```

And here is the JFXPanel code:

```
canvas = new JFXPanel();
canvas.setPreferredSize(new Dimension(210, 210));
Platform.runLater(new Runnable() {
    @Override
    public void run() {
        final Rectangle rectangle = new Rectangle(200, 200);
        rectangle.setStrokeWidth(10);
        rectangle.fillProperty().bind(model.fillProperty());
```

```
        rectangle.strokeProperty().bind(model.strokeProperty());
        final VBox vBox = new VBox(rectangle);
        final Scene scene = new Scene(vBox);
        canvas.setScene(scene);
    }
});
```

The JFXPanel constructor bootstraps the JavaFX runtime system. We set the preferred size to the JFXPanel for it to be laid out correctly in Swing containers. We then constructed the scene graph on the JavaFX application thread and bound it to the model, which we changed into a JavaFX bean. Another set of changes that need to be made are in the ActionListeners of the two JButtons. Modifying the model triggers a change to the JavaFX rectangle, so the following code needs to be run on the JavaFX application thread:

```
this.view.changeFillButton.addActionListener(e -> {
    Platform.runLater(() -> {
        final Paint fillPaint = model.getFill();
        if (fillPaint.equals(Color.LIGHTGRAY)) {
            model.setFill(Color.GRAY);
        } else {
            model.setFill(Color.LIGHTGRAY);
        }
    });
});
```

The completed Swing JavaFX hybrid program is shown in Listing 7-12.

Listing 7-12. JavaFXSceneInSwingExample.java

```
import javafx.application.Platform;
import javafx.beans.property.ObjectProperty;
import javafx.beans.property.SimpleObjectProperty;
import javafx.embed.swing.JFXPanel;
import javafx.scene.Scene;
import javafx.scene.layout.VBox;
import javafx.scene.paint.Color;
import javafx.scene.paint.Paint;
import javafx.scene.shape.Rectangle;

import javax.swing.*;
import java.awt.*;

public class JavaFXSceneInSwingExample {
    public static void main(final String[] args) {
        EventQueue.invokeLater(() -> {
            swingMain(args);
        });
    }
```

```
    private static void swingMain(String[] args) {
        Model model = new Model();
        View view = new View(model);
        Controller controller = new Controller(model, view);
        controller.mainLoop();
    }

    private static class Model {
        private ObjectProperty<Color> fill = new SimpleObjectProperty<>(Color.LIGHTGRAY);
        private ObjectProperty<Color> stroke = new SimpleObjectProperty<>(Color.DARKGRAY);

        public final Color getFill() {
            return fill.get();
        }

        public final void setFill(Color value) {
            this.fill.set(value);
        }

        public final Color getStroke() {
            return stroke.get();
        }

        public final void setStroke(Color value) {
            this.stroke.set(value);
        }

        public final ObjectProperty<Color> fillProperty() {
            return fill;
        }

        public final ObjectProperty<Color> strokeProperty() {
            return stroke;
        }
    }

    private static class View {
        public JFrame frame;
        public JFXPanel canvas;
        public JButton changeFillButton;
        public JButton changeStrokeButton;

        private View(final Model model) {
            frame = new JFrame("JavaFX in Swing Example");
            canvas = new JFXPanel();
            canvas.setPreferredSize(new Dimension(210, 210));
            Platform.runLater(new Runnable() {
                @Override
                public void run() {
                    final Rectangle rectangle = new Rectangle(200, 200);
                    rectangle.setStrokeWidth(10);
                    rectangle.fillProperty().bind(model.fillProperty());
```

```
                rectangle.strokeProperty().bind(model.strokeProperty());
                final VBox vBox = new VBox(rectangle);
                final Scene scene = new Scene(vBox);
                canvas.setScene(scene);
            }
        });
        FlowLayout canvasPanelLayout = new FlowLayout(FlowLayout.CENTER, 10, 10);
        JPanel canvasPanel = new JPanel(canvasPanelLayout);
        canvasPanel.add(canvas);

        changeFillButton = new JButton("Change Fill");
        changeStrokeButton = new JButton("Change Stroke");
        FlowLayout buttonPanelLayout = new FlowLayout(FlowLayout.CENTER, 10, 10);
        JPanel buttonPanel = new JPanel(buttonPanelLayout);
        buttonPanel.add(changeFillButton);
        buttonPanel.add(changeStrokeButton);

        frame.add(canvasPanel, BorderLayout.CENTER);
        frame.add(buttonPanel, BorderLayout.SOUTH);
        frame.setDefaultCloseOperation(JFrame.EXIT_ON_CLOSE);
        frame.setLocationByPlatform(true);
        frame.pack();
    }
}

private static class Controller {
    private View view;

    private Controller(final Model model, final View view) {
        this.view = view;
        this.view.changeFillButton.addActionListener(e -> {
            Platform.runLater(() -> {
                final Paint fillPaint = model.getFill();
                if (fillPaint.equals(Color.LIGHTGRAY)) {
                    model.setFill(Color.GRAY);
                } else {
                    model.setFill(Color.LIGHTGRAY);
                }
            });
        });
        this.view.changeStrokeButton.addActionListener(e -> {
            Platform.runLater(() -> {
                final Paint strokePaint = model.getStroke();
                if (strokePaint.equals(Color.DARKGRAY)) {
                    model.setStroke(Color.BLACK);
                } else {
                    model.setStroke(Color.DARKGRAY);
                }
            });
        });
    }
```

```
        public void mainLoop() {
            view.frame.setVisible(true);
        }
    }
}
```

When the program in Listing 7-12 is run, the GUI in Figure 7-18 is displayed. You can't tell from the screenshot, but the rectangle in the center of the JFrame is a JavaFX rectangle.

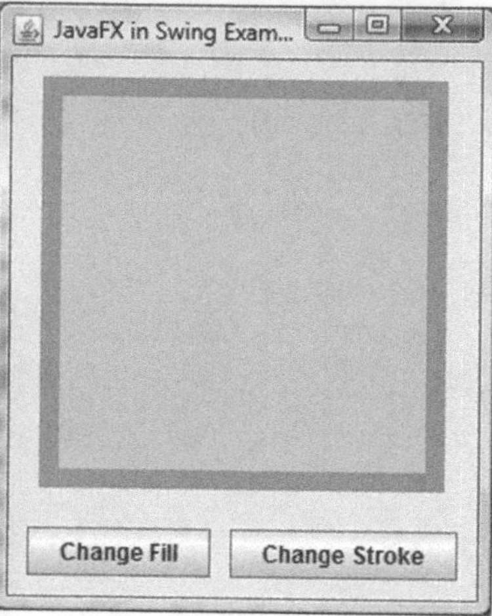

Figure 7-18. The JavaFXSceneInSwingExample program

Embedding JavaFX Scenes in SWT Applications

JavaFX is capable of embedding a JavaFX scene into an SWT application through the `javafx.embed.swt` package of classes. It contains two public classes, `FXCanvas` and `SWTFXUtils`. The `FXCanvas` class extends `org.eclipse.swt.widgets.Canvas`, and can be placed in an SWT program just like any other SWT widget. `FXCanvas` can also host a JavaFX scene, and can add a JavaFX scene to an SWT program.

Because both SWT and JavaFX use the native platform's UI thread as their own event dispatching thread, the SWT UI thread (where a Display object is instantiated and where the main loop is started and where all other UI widgets must be created and accessed) and the JavaFX application thread are one and the same. Therefore there is no need to use `Platform.runLater()` or its SWT equivalent `display.asyncExec()` in your SWT and JavaFX event handlers.

The SWT program in Listing 7-13 is an SWT port of the Swing program in Listing 7-11.

Listing 7-13. NoJavaFXSceneInSWTExample.java

```
import org.eclipse.swt.SWT;
import org.eclipse.swt.events.MouseEvent;
import org.eclipse.swt.events.MouseMoveListener;
import org.eclipse.swt.events.MouseTrackAdapter;
import org.eclipse.swt.events.PaintEvent;
import org.eclipse.swt.events.PaintListener;
import org.eclipse.swt.events.SelectionAdapter;
import org.eclipse.swt.events.SelectionEvent;
import org.eclipse.swt.graphics.Color;
```

```
import org.eclipse.swt.graphics.GC;
import org.eclipse.swt.graphics.RGB;
import org.eclipse.swt.layout.RowData;
import org.eclipse.swt.layout.RowLayout;
import org.eclipse.swt.widgets.Button;
import org.eclipse.swt.widgets.Canvas;
import org.eclipse.swt.widgets.Composite;
import org.eclipse.swt.widgets.Display;
import org.eclipse.swt.widgets.Label;
import org.eclipse.swt.widgets.Shell;

public class NoJavaFXSceneInSWTExample {
    public static void main(final String[] args) {
        Model model = new Model();
        View view = new View(model);
        Controller controller = new Controller(model, view);
        controller.mainLoop();
    }

    private static class Model {
        public static final RGB LIGHT_GRAY = new RGB(0xd3, 0xd3, 0xd3);
        public static final RGB GRAY = new RGB(0x80, 0x80, 0x80);
        public static final RGB DARK_GRAY = new RGB(0xa9, 0xa9, 0xa9);
        public static final RGB BLACK = new RGB(0x0, 0x0, 0x0);
        public RGB fillColor = LIGHT_GRAY;
        public RGB strokeColor = DARK_GRAY;
    }

    private static class View {
        public Display display;
        public Shell frame;
        public Canvas canvas;
        public Button changeFillButton;
        public Button changeStrokeButton;
        public Label mouseLocation;
        public boolean mouseInCanvas;

        private View(final Model model) {
            this.display = new Display();
            frame = new Shell(display);
            frame.setText("No JavaFX in SWT Example");
            RowLayout frameLayout = new RowLayout(SWT.VERTICAL);
            frameLayout.spacing = 10;
            frameLayout.center = true;
            frame.setLayout(frameLayout);

            Composite canvasPanel = new Composite(frame, SWT.NONE);
            RowLayout canvasPanelLayout = new RowLayout(SWT.VERTICAL);
            canvasPanelLayout.spacing = 10;
            canvasPanel.setLayout(canvasPanelLayout);
```

```
            canvas = new Canvas(canvasPanel, SWT.NONE);
            canvas.setLayoutData(new RowData(200, 200));
            canvas.addPaintListener(new PaintListener() {
                @Override
                public void paintControl(PaintEvent paintEvent) {
                    final GC gc = paintEvent.gc;
                    final Color strokeColor = new Color(display, model.strokeColor);
                    gc.setBackground(strokeColor);
                    gc.fillRectangle(0, 0, 200, 200);
                    final Color fillColor = new Color(display, model.fillColor);
                    gc.setBackground(fillColor);
                    gc.fillRectangle(10, 10, 180, 180);
                    strokeColor.dispose();
                    fillColor.dispose();
                }
            });

            Composite buttonPanel = new Composite(frame, SWT.NONE);
            RowLayout buttonPanelLayout = new RowLayout(SWT.HORIZONTAL);
            buttonPanelLayout.spacing = 10;
            buttonPanelLayout.center = true;
            buttonPanel.setLayout(buttonPanelLayout);

            changeFillButton = new Button(buttonPanel, SWT.NONE);
            changeFillButton.setText("Change Fill");
            changeStrokeButton = new Button(buttonPanel, SWT.NONE);
            changeStrokeButton.setText("Change Stroke");
            mouseLocation = new Label(buttonPanel, SWT.NONE);
            mouseLocation.setLayoutData(new RowData(50, 15));

            frame.pack();
        }
    }

    private static class Controller {
        private View view;

        private Controller(final Model model, final View view) {
            this.view = view;
            view.changeFillButton.addSelectionListener(new SelectionAdapter() {
                @Override
                public void widgetSelected(SelectionEvent e) {
                    if (model.fillColor.equals(model.LIGHT_GRAY)) {
                        model.fillColor = model.GRAY;
                    } else {
                        model.fillColor = model.LIGHT_GRAY;
                    }
                    view.canvas.redraw();
                }
            });
```

```
            view.changeStrokeButton.addSelectionListener(new SelectionAdapter() {
                @Override
                public void widgetSelected(SelectionEvent e) {
                    if (model.strokeColor.equals(model.DARK_GRAY)) {
                        model.strokeColor = model.BLACK;
                    } else {
                        model.strokeColor = model.DARK_GRAY;
                    }
                    view.canvas.redraw();
                }
            });
            view.canvas.addMouseMoveListener(new MouseMoveListener() {
                @Override
                public void mouseMove(MouseEvent mouseEvent) {
                    if (view.mouseInCanvas) {
                        view.mouseLocation.setText("(" + mouseEvent.x + ", " + mouseEvent.y + ")");
                    }
                }
            });
            this.view.canvas.addMouseTrackListener(new MouseTrackAdapter() {
                @Override
                public void mouseEnter(MouseEvent e) {
                    view.mouseInCanvas = true;
                }

                @Override
                public void mouseExit(MouseEvent e) {
                    view.mouseInCanvas = false;
                    view.mouseLocation.setText("");
                }
            });

        }

        public void mainLoop() {
            view.frame.open();
            while (!view.frame.isDisposed()) {
                if (!view.display.readAndDispatch()) {
                    view.display.sleep();
                }
            }
            view.display.dispose();
        }
    }
}
```

■ **Note** You need to add the jar file that contains the SWT classes to your classpath to compile the programs in Listings 7-13 and 7-14. On my development machine the SWT jar is located in `%ECLIPSE_HOME%\plugins\ org.eclipse.swt.win32.win32.x86_64_3.102.1.v20140206-1358.jar`, where `%ECLIPSE_HOME%` is my Eclipse (Kepler SR2) installation directory.

When the program in Listing 7-13 is run, the UI in Figure 7-19 is displayed. It is an SWT `Shell` holding four SWT widgets, a `Canvas` with a `PaintListener` that makes it look like the rectangle we saw earlier, two `Buttons` that will change the fill and the stroke of the rectangle, and a `Label` widget that will show the location of the mouse pointer when the mouse is inside the rectangle.

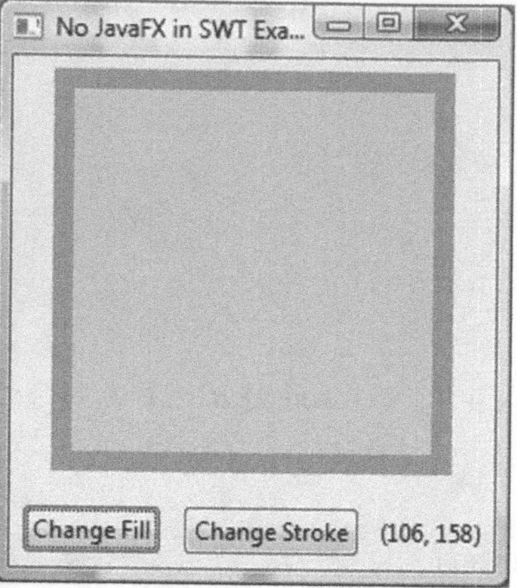

Figure 7-19. *The `NoJavaFXSceneInSWTExample` program*

As we did with the Swing example, we replace the custom painted `Canvas` widget in the program `NoJavaFXSceneInSWTExample` with a JavaFX `Rectangle`. This is done by replacing the SWT code with the equivalent FXCanvas code. Here is the SWT code:

```
canvas = new Canvas(canvasPanel, SWT.NONE);
canvas.setLayoutData(new RowData(200, 200));
canvas.addPaintListener(new PaintListener() {
    @Override
    public void paintControl(PaintEvent paintEvent) {
        final GC gc = paintEvent.gc;
        final Color strokeColor = new Color(display, model.strokeColor);
        gc.setBackground(strokeColor);
        gc.fillRectangle(0, 0, 200, 200);
        final Color fillColor = new Color(display, model.fillColor);
        gc.setBackground(fillColor);
        gc.fillRectangle(10, 10, 180, 180);
        strokeColor.dispose();
        fillColor.dispose();
    }
});
```

And here is the FXCanvas code:

```
canvas = new FXCanvas(canvasPanel, SWT.NONE);
rectangle = new Rectangle(200, 200);
rectangle.setStrokeWidth(10);
VBox vBox = new VBox(rectangle);
```

```
Scene scene = new Scene(vBox, 210, 210);
canvas.setScene(scene);
rectangle.fillProperty().bind(model.fillProperty());
rectangle.strokeProperty().bind(model.strokeProperty());
```

We also changed the model into a JavaFX bean. The event listeners are changed in a natural way. The complete SWT JavaFX hybrid program is shown in Listing 7-14.

Listing 7-14. `JavaFXSceneInSWTExample.java`

```
import javafx.beans.property.ObjectProperty;
import javafx.beans.property.SimpleObjectProperty;
import javafx.embed.swt.FXCanvas;
import javafx.event.EventHandler;
import javafx.scene.Scene;
import javafx.scene.input.MouseEvent;
import javafx.scene.layout.VBox;
import javafx.scene.paint.Color;
import javafx.scene.paint.Paint;
import javafx.scene.shape.Rectangle;
import org.eclipse.swt.SWT;
import org.eclipse.swt.events.SelectionAdapter;
import org.eclipse.swt.events.SelectionEvent;
import org.eclipse.swt.layout.RowData;
import org.eclipse.swt.layout.RowLayout;
import org.eclipse.swt.widgets.Button;
import org.eclipse.swt.widgets.Composite;
import org.eclipse.swt.widgets.Display;
import org.eclipse.swt.widgets.Label;
import org.eclipse.swt.widgets.Shell;

public class JavaFXSceneInSWTExample {
    public static void main(final String[] args) {
        Model model = new Model();
        View view = new View(model);
        Controller controller = new Controller(model, view);
        controller.mainLoop();
    }

    private static class Model {
        private ObjectProperty<Color> fill = new SimpleObjectProperty<>(Color.LIGHTGRAY);
        private ObjectProperty<Color> stroke = new SimpleObjectProperty<>(Color.DARKGRAY);

        public Color getFill() {
            return fill.get();
        }

        public void setFill(Color value) {
            this.fill.set(value);
        }
```

```
        public Color getStroke() {
            return stroke.get();
        }

        public void setStroke(Color value) {
            this.stroke.set(value);
        }

        public ObjectProperty<Color> fillProperty() {
            return fill;
        }

        public ObjectProperty<Color> strokeProperty() {
            return stroke;
        }
    }

    private static class View {
        public Display display;
        public Shell frame;
        public FXCanvas canvas;
        public Button changeFillButton;
        public Button changeStrokeButton;
        public Label mouseLocation;
        public boolean mouseInCanvas;
        public Rectangle rectangle;

        private View(final Model model) {
            this.display = new Display();
            frame = new Shell(display);
            frame.setText("JavaFX in SWT Example");
            RowLayout frameLayout = new RowLayout(SWT.VERTICAL);
            frameLayout.spacing = 10;
            frameLayout.center = true;
            frame.setLayout(frameLayout);

            Composite canvasPanel = new Composite(frame, SWT.NONE);
            RowLayout canvasPanelLayout = new RowLayout(SWT.VERTICAL);
            canvasPanelLayout.spacing = 10;
            canvasPanel.setLayout(canvasPanelLayout);
            canvas = new FXCanvas(canvasPanel, SWT.NONE);
            rectangle = new Rectangle(200, 200);
            rectangle.setStrokeWidth(10);
            VBox vBox = new VBox(rectangle);
            Scene scene = new Scene(vBox, 210, 210);
            canvas.setScene(scene);
            rectangle.fillProperty().bind(model.fillProperty());
            rectangle.strokeProperty().bind(model.strokeProperty());
```

```
            Composite buttonPanel = new Composite(frame, SWT.NONE);
            RowLayout buttonPanelLayout = new RowLayout(SWT.HORIZONTAL);
            buttonPanelLayout.spacing = 10;
            buttonPanelLayout.center = true;
            buttonPanel.setLayout(buttonPanelLayout);

            changeFillButton = new Button(buttonPanel, SWT.NONE);
            changeFillButton.setText("Change Fill");
            changeStrokeButton = new Button(buttonPanel, SWT.NONE);
            changeStrokeButton.setText("Change Stroke");
            mouseLocation = new Label(buttonPanel, SWT.NONE);
            mouseLocation.setLayoutData(new RowData(50, 15));

            frame.pack();
        }
    }

    private static class Controller {
        private View view;

        private Controller(final Model model, final View view) {
            this.view = view;
            view.changeFillButton.addSelectionListener(new SelectionAdapter() {
                @Override
                public void widgetSelected(SelectionEvent e) {
                    final Paint fillPaint = model.getFill();
                    if (fillPaint.equals(Color.LIGHTGRAY)) {
                        model.setFill(Color.GRAY);
                    } else {
                        model.setFill(Color.LIGHTGRAY);
                    }
                }
            });
            view.changeStrokeButton.addSelectionListener(new SelectionAdapter() {
                @Override
                public void widgetSelected(SelectionEvent e) {
                    final Paint strokePaint = model.getStroke();
                    if (strokePaint.equals(Color.DARKGRAY)) {
                        model.setStroke(Color.BLACK);
                    } else {
                        model.setStroke(Color.DARKGRAY);
                    }
                }
            });
            view.rectangle.setOnMouseEntered(new EventHandler<MouseEvent>() {
                @Override
                public void handle(MouseEvent mouseEvent) {
                    view.mouseInCanvas = true;
                }
            });
```

```
            view.rectangle.setOnMouseExited(new EventHandler<MouseEvent>() {
                @Override
                public void handle(final MouseEvent mouseEvent) {
                    view.mouseInCanvas = false;
                    view.mouseLocation.setText("");
                }
            });
            view.rectangle.setOnMouseMoved(new EventHandler<MouseEvent>() {
                @Override
                public void handle(final MouseEvent mouseEvent) {
                    if (view.mouseInCanvas) {
                        view.mouseLocation.setText("(" + (int) mouseEvent.getSceneX() + ", " +
(int) mouseEvent.getSceneY() + ")");
                    }
                }
            });
        }

        public void mainLoop() {
            view.frame.open();
            while (!view.frame.isDisposed()) {
                if (!view.display.readAndDispatch()) view.display.sleep();
            }
            view.display.dispose();
        }
    }
}
```

When the program in Listing 7-14 is run, the GUI in Figure 7-20 is displayed. The rectangle in the center of the SWT Shell is a JavaFX rectangle.

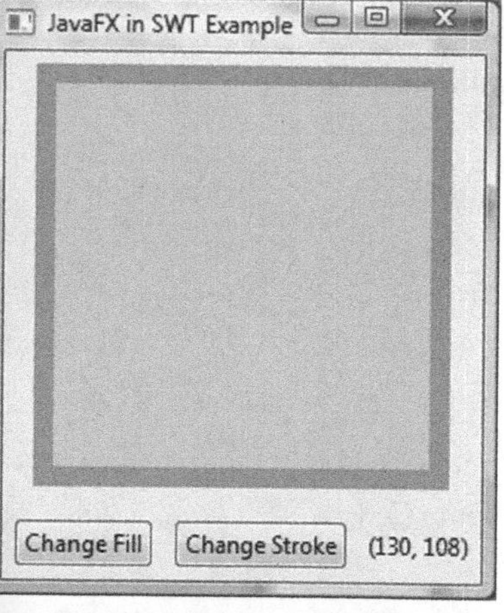

Figure 7-20. *The* `JavaFXSceneInSWTExample` *program*

Embedding Swing Components in JavaFX Applications

The SwingNode class in the javafx.embed.swing package is a JavaFX Node that can host a Swing JComponent, and therefore allows you to embed a Swing component in your JavaFX application. This gives legacy Swing applications a piecemeal way of migrating to JavaFX. Aside from the default constructor, the only other public methods designed for use by application developers are a pair of getter and setter methods for the embedded JComponent:

- public void setContent(JComponent)
- public JComponent getContent()

When a SwingNode that contains a JComponent is attached to a live JavaFX scene, the SwingNode class takes care of forwarding all JavaFX input and focus events to the embedded JComponent. Only lightweight Swing components are allowed to be embedded in JavaFX applications. Just like in the case for a JavaFX scene embedded in a Swing application, the presence of the two event dispatching threads in a JavaFX application with an embedded Swing component, the JavaFX Application Thread and the Swing EDT, warrants our attention. In particular, the requirement of performing JavaFX live scene manipulation in the JavaFX Application Thread and the requirement of performing Swing UI manipulations in the Swing EDT should be honored. In practical terms, this means that if you want to manipulate the Swing UI in a JavaFX event handler, you should send it to the Swing EDT with EventQueue.invokeLater(); and if you want to manipulate JavaFX Nodes in a Swing event listener method, you should send it to the JavaFX Application Thread with Platform.runLater().

In this section, we turn the sample program that we have been using for this chapter into a JavaFX application with an embedded custom Swing component. The custom Swing component is a simple subclass of JComponent that draws a rectangle with a thick border in two different colors.

```
private static class MyRectangle extends JComponent {
    private final Model model;

    public MyRectangle(Model model) {
        this.model = model;
    }

    @Override
    public void paint(Graphics g) {
        g.setColor(model.getStrokeColor());
        g.fillRect(0, 0, 200, 200);
        g.setColor(model.getFillColor());
        g.fillRect(10, 10, 180, 180);
    }

    @Override
    public Dimension getMaximumSize() {
        return new Dimension(200, 200);
    }
}
```

The current implementation of SwingNode lacks the ability to respond well to its JavaFX container Nodes layout requests. We extend it so that the layout of the application is improved:

```
private static class MySwingNode extends SwingNode {
    @Override
    public double minWidth(double height) {
        return 250;
    }
```

```
    @Override
    public double minHeight(double width) {
        return 200;
    }
}
```

When the two JavaFX buttons are clicked, we invoke code that alters the state of the Swing component `MyRectangle` in a `Runnable` represented as a lambda expression through `EventQueue.invokeLater()`:

```
view.changeFillButton.setOnAction(actionEvent -> {
    EventQueue.invokeLater(() -> {
        final java.awt.Color fillColor = model.getFillColor();
        if (fillColor.equals(java.awt.Color.LIGHT_GRAY)) {
            model.setFillColor(java.awt.Color.GRAY);
        } else {
            model.setFillColor(java.awt.Color.LIGHT_GRAY);
        }
        view.canvas.repaint();
    });
});
```

■ **Note** The `repaint()` method is actually one of the rare Swing UI methods that can be called from any thread, not just the Swing EDT. Our use of `EventQueue.invokeLater()` is for illustration purposes only.

When the mouse hovers over the `MyRectangle`, we update a JavaFX Label by updating a `StringProperty` named `mouseLocation` in our `Model` class that the `textProperty` of the `Label` binds to:

```
canvas.addMouseMotionListener(new MouseMotionListener() {
    @Override
    public void mouseDragged(MouseEvent e) {
    }

    @Override
    public void mouseMoved(MouseEvent e) {
        Platform.runLater(() -> {
            model.setMouseLocation("(" + e.getX() + ", " + e.getY() + ")");
        });
    }
});
swingNode.setContent(canvas);
```

The complete Swing component in JavaFX example application is shown in Listing 7-15.

Listing 7-15. SwingComponentInJavaFXExample.java

```
import javafx.application.Application;
import javafx.application.Platform;
import javafx.beans.property.SimpleStringProperty;
import javafx.beans.property.StringProperty;
```

```
import javafx.embed.swing.SwingNode;
import javafx.geometry.Insets;
import javafx.geometry.Pos;
import javafx.scene.Scene;
import javafx.scene.control.Button;
import javafx.scene.control.Label;
import javafx.scene.layout.HBox;
import javafx.scene.layout.VBox;
import javafx.stage.Stage;

import javax.swing.*;
import java.awt.*;
import java.awt.event.MouseAdapter;
import java.awt.event.MouseEvent;
import java.awt.event.MouseMotionListener;

public class SwingComponentInJavaFXExample extends Application {
    private Model model;
    private View view;

    public static void main(String[] args) {
        launch(args);
    }

    public SwingComponentInJavaFXExample() {
        model = new Model();
    }

    @Override
    public void start(Stage stage) throws Exception {
        view = new View(model);
        hookupEvents();
        stage.setTitle("Swing in JavaFX Example");
        stage.setScene(view.scene);
        stage.show();
    }

    private void hookupEvents() {
        view.changeFillButton.setOnAction(actionEvent -> {
            EventQueue.invokeLater(() -> {
                final java.awt.Color fillColor = model.getFillColor();
                if (fillColor.equals(java.awt.Color.LIGHT_GRAY)) {
                    model.setFillColor(java.awt.Color.GRAY);
                } else {
                    model.setFillColor(java.awt.Color.LIGHT_GRAY);
                }
                view.canvas.repaint();
            });
        });
```

```
        view.changeStrokeButton.setOnAction(actionEvent -> {
            EventQueue.invokeLater(() -> {
                final java.awt.Color strokeColor = model.getStrokeColor();
                if (strokeColor.equals(java.awt.Color.GRAY)) {
                    model.setStrokeColor(java.awt.Color.BLACK);
                } else {
                    model.setStrokeColor(java.awt.Color.GRAY);
                }
                view.canvas.repaint();
            });
        });
    }

    private static class Model {
        private java.awt.Color fillColor;
        private java.awt.Color strokeColor;
        final private StringProperty mouseLocation = new SimpleStringProperty(this, "mouseLocation", "");

        private Model() {
            fillColor = java.awt.Color.LIGHT_GRAY;
            strokeColor = java.awt.Color.GRAY;
        }

        public java.awt.Color getFillColor() {
            return fillColor;
        }

        public void setFillColor(java.awt.Color fillColor) {
            this.fillColor = fillColor;
        }

        public java.awt.Color getStrokeColor() {
            return strokeColor;
        }

        public void setStrokeColor(java.awt.Color strokeColor) {
            this.strokeColor = strokeColor;
        }

        public final void setMouseLocation(String mouseLocation) {
            this.mouseLocation.set(mouseLocation);
        }

        public final StringProperty mouseLocationProperty() {
            return mouseLocation;
        }
    }

    private static class View {
        public JComponent canvas;
        public Button changeFillButton;
        public Button changeStrokeButton;
```

```
    public Label mouseLocation;
    public HBox buttonHBox;
    public Scene scene;

    private View(Model model) {
        SwingNode swingNode = new MySwingNode();

        EventQueue.invokeLater(() -> {
            canvas = new MyRectangle(model);
            canvas.addMouseListener(new MouseAdapter() {
                @Override
                public void mouseExited(MouseEvent e) {
                    Platform.runLater(() -> {
                        model.setMouseLocation("");
                    });
                }
            });
            canvas.addMouseMotionListener(new MouseMotionListener() {
                @Override
                public void mouseDragged(MouseEvent e) {
                }

                @Override
                public void mouseMoved(MouseEvent e) {
                    Platform.runLater(() -> {
                        model.setMouseLocation("(" + e.getX() + ", " + e.getY() + ")");
                    });
                }
            });
            swingNode.setContent(canvas);
        });

        changeFillButton = new Button("Change Fill");
        changeStrokeButton = new Button("Change Stroke");
        mouseLocation = new Label("(100, 100)");
        mouseLocation.setPrefSize(60, 15);
        mouseLocation.textProperty().bind(model.mouseLocationProperty());

        buttonHBox = new HBox(10, changeFillButton, changeStrokeButton, mouseLocation);
        buttonHBox.setPadding(new Insets(10, 0, 10, 0));
        buttonHBox.setAlignment(Pos.CENTER);

        VBox root = new VBox(10, swingNode, buttonHBox);
        root.setPadding(new Insets(10, 10, 10, 10));

        scene = new Scene(root);
    }
}
```

```
    private static class MySwingNode extends SwingNode {
        @Override
        public double minWidth(double height) {
            return 250;
        }

        @Override
        public double minHeight(double width) {
            return 200;
        }
    }

    private static class MyRectangle extends JComponent {
        private final Model model;

        public MyRectangle(Model model) {
            this.model = model;
        }

        @Override
        public void paint(Graphics g) {
            g.setColor(model.getStrokeColor());
            g.fillRect(0, 0, 200, 200);
            g.setColor(model.getFillColor());
            g.fillRect(10, 10, 180, 180);
        }

        @Override
        public Dimension getMaximumSize() {
            return new Dimension(200, 200);
        }
    }
}
```

When the program in Listing 7-15 is run, the GUI in Figure 7-21 is displayed. The rectangle in the center of the JavaFX application is a Swing `JComponent`.

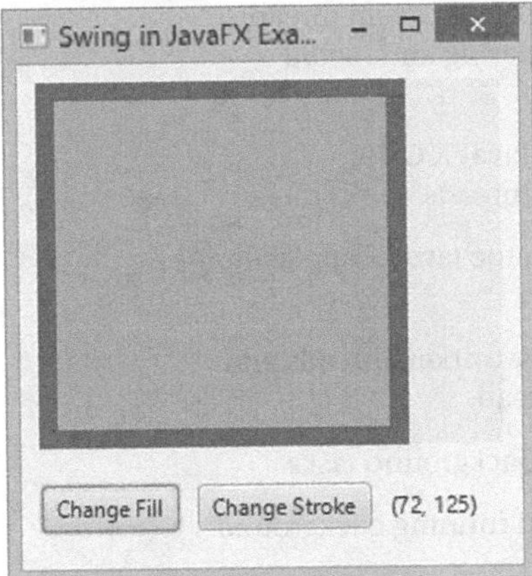

Figure 7-21. *The `SwingComponentInJavaFXExample` program*

■ **Tip** In case you are wondering if there is a way to embed an SWT widget into a JavaFX application, the answer is no. The reason is that SWT widgets are heavyweight components and thus harder to integrate into a lightweight GUI toolkit like JavaFX.

Summary

In this chapter, we looked at JavaFX observable collections, the JavaFX worker threading framework, embedding a JavaFX scene in Swing and SWT applications, and embedding Swing components in JavaFX applications to help you understand the following principles and techniques.

- JavaFX supports observable collections and arrays: `ObservableList`, `ObservableMap`, `ObservableSet`, and `ObservableArray`, with subinterfaces `ObservableIntegerArray` and `ObservableFloatArray`.
- `ObservableList` fires `Change` events through `ListChangeListener`. `ListChangeListener.Change` may contain one or more discrete changes.
- `ObservableMap` fires `Change` events through `MapChangeListener`. `MapChangeListener.Change` represents the change of only one key.
- `ObservableSet` fires `Change` events through `SetChangeListener`. `SetChangeListener.Change` represents the change of only one element.
- `ObservableArray` and its subinterfaces fire change events through `ArrayChangeListener`.
- The `FXCollections` class contains factory methods to create observable collections and arrays, and utility methods to work on them.
- The main event processing thread in JavaFX applications is the JavaFX application thread. All access to live scenes must be done through the JavaFX application thread.

- Other important threads such as the prism rendering thread and the media event thread collaborate with the JavaFX application thread to make graphics rendering and media playback possible.
- Long-running computations on the JavaFX application thread make JavaFX GUIs unresponsive. They should be farmed out to background, or worker, threads.
- The Worker interface defines nine properties that can be observed on the JavaFX application thread. It also defines a cancel() method.
- Task<V> defines a one-time task for offloading work to background, or worker, threads and communicates the results or exceptions to the JavaFX application thread.
- Service<V> defines a reusable mechanism for creating and running background tasks.
- ScheduledService<V> defines a reusable mechanism for creating and running background tasks in a recurring fashion.
- The JFXPanel class is a JComponent that can put a JavaFX scene into a Swing application.
- In a Swing JavaFX hybrid program, use Platform.runLater() in Swing event listeners to access the JavaFX scene, and use EventQueue.invokeLater() or SwingUtilities.invokeLater() in JavaFX event handlers to access Swing widgets.
- The FXCanvas class is an SWT widget that can put a JavaFX scene into an SWT application.
- In an SWT JavaFX hybrid program, the SWT UI thread and the JavaFX application thread are one and the same.
- The SwingNode class is a JavaFX Node that can put a Swing component into a JavaFX application.

Resources

Here are some useful resources for understanding this chapter's material:

- *The JavaFX architecture page on the JavaFX tutorials site:* http://docs.oracle.com/javase/8/javafx/get-started-tutorial/jfx-architecture.htm#JFXST788
- *The original JavaFX worker threading framework write-up on FX Experience:* http://fxexperience.com/2011/07/worker-threading-in-javafx-2-0/
- *The original JavaFX and SWT interoperability write-up on FX Experience:* http://fxexperience.com/2011/12/swt-interop/

CHAPTER 8

Creating Charts in JavaFX

Any sufficiently advanced technology is indistinguishable from magic.

—Arthur C. Clarke

Reporting is an important aspect in many business applications. The JavaFX Platform contains an API for creating charts. Because a `Chart` is basically a `Node`, integrating charts with other parts of a JavaFX application is straightforward. As a consequence, reporting is an integral part of the typical JavaFX Business Application.

Designing an API is often a compromise among a number of requirements. Two of the most common requirements are "make it easy" and "make it easy to extend." The JavaFX Chart API fulfills both of these. The Chart API contains a number of methods that allow developers to change the look and feel as well as the data of the chart, making it a flexible API that can be easily extended. The default values for the settings are very reasonable, though, and make it easy to integrate a chart with a custom application, with only a few lines of code.

The JavaFX Chart API in JavaFX 8 has eight concrete implementations that are ready to be used by developers. Apart from those, developers can add their own implementations by extending one of the abstract classes.

Structure of the JavaFX Chart API

Different types of charts exist, and there are a number of ways to categorize them. The JavaFX Chart API distinguishes between two axis charts and charts without an axis. The JavaFX 8 release contains one implementation of a no-axis chart, which is the `PieChart`. There are a number of two-axis charts, which all extend the abstract class `XYChart`, as shown in Figure 8-1.

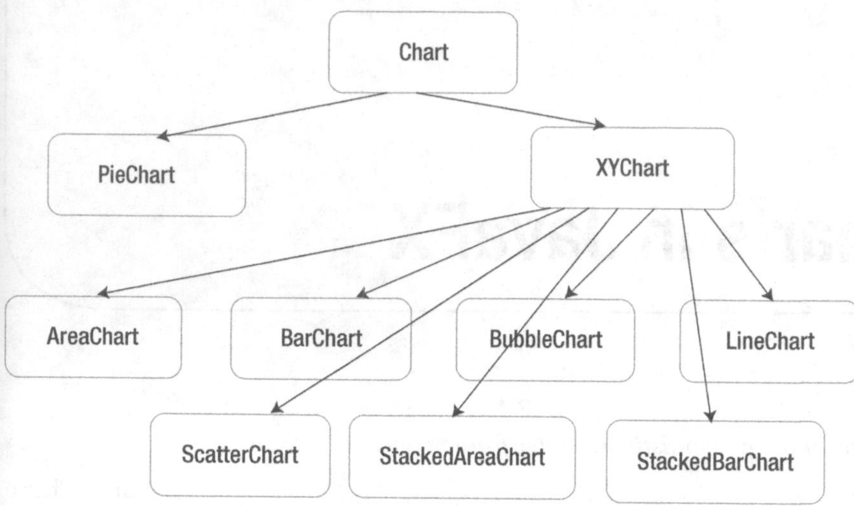

***Figure 8-1.** Overview of the charts in the JavaFX Chart API*

The abstract Chart class defines the setup for all charts. Basically, a chart consists of three parts: the title, legend, and content. The content is specific for each implementation of the chart, but the legend and the title concepts are similar across the implementations. Therefore, the Chart class has a number of properties with corresponding getter and setter methods that allow the manipulation of those concepts. The javadoc of the Chart class mentions the following properties.

```
BooleanProperty animated
ObjectProperty<Node> legend
BooleanProperty legendVisible
ObjectProperty<Side> legendSide
StringProperty title
ObjectProperty<Side> titleSide
```

We use some of these properties in the upcoming examples, but we also show that even without setting values for these properties, the Chart API allows you to create nice charts.

Because Chart extends Region, Parent, and Node, all of the properties and methods available on these classes can be used on a Chart as well. One of the benefits is that the same CSS styling techniques that are used to add style information to JavaFX Nodes also apply to JavaFX Charts.

The *JavaFX CSS Reference Guide*, available at http://download.java.net/jdk8/jfxdocs/javafx/scene/doc-files/cssref.html, contains an overview of CSS properties that can be altered by designers and developers. By default, the modena style sheet that comes with the JavaFX 8.0 Runtime is used to skin JavaFX Charts. For more information on using CSS styles in JavaFX Chart, refer to the Oracle Chart tutorial at http://docs.oracle.com/javase/8/javafx/user-interface-tutorial/css-styles.htm.

Using the JavaFX PieChart

A PieChart renders information in a typical pie structure, where the sizes of the slices are proportional to the values of the data. Before diving into the details, we show a small application that renders a PieChart.

The Simple Example

Our example shows the "market share" of a number of programming languages, based on the TIOBE index in December 2011. The TIOBE Programming Community Index is available at `www.tiobe.com/index.php/content/paperinfo/tpci/index.html`, and it provides an indication of the popularity of programming languages based on search engine traffic. A screenshot of the ranking in December 2011 is shown in Figure 8-2.

Position Dec 2011	Position Dec 2010	Delta in Position	Programming Language	Ratings Dec 2011	Delta Dec 2010	Status
1	1	=	Java	17.561%	-0.44%	A
2	2	=	C	17.057%	+0.98%	A
3	3	=	C++	8.252%	-0.76%	A
4	5	↑	C#	8.205%	+1.52%	A
5	8	↑↑↑	Objective-C	6.805%	+3.56%	A
6	4	↓↓	PHP	6.001%	-1.51%	A
7	7	=	(Visual) Basic	4.757%	-0.36%	A
8	6	↓↓	Python	3.492%	-2.99%	A
9	9	=	Perl	2.472%	+0.14%	A
10	12	↑↑	JavaScript	2.199%	+0.69%	A
11	11	=	Ruby	1.494%	-0.29%	A
12	10	↓↓	Delphi/Object Pascal	1.245%	-0.93%	A
13	13	=	Lisp	1.175%	+0.11%	A
14	23	↑↑↑↑↑↑↑↑↑	PL/SQL	0.803%	+0.24%	A
15	14	↓	Transact-SQL	0.746%	-0.03%	A
16	16	=	Pascal	0.734%	-0.03%	A
17	18	↑	Ada	0.632%	-0.02%	B
18	35	↑↑↑↑↑↑↑↑↑↑	Logo	0.619%	+0.26%	B
19	17	↓↓	Assembly	0.563%	-0.10%	B
20	25	↑↑↑↑↑	ABAP	0.560%	+0.01%	B

Figure 8-2. *Screenshot of the TIOBE index in December 2011, taken from* `www.tiobe.com/index.php/content/paperinfo/tpci/index.html`

■ **Note** The algorithm used by TIOBE is described at `www.tiobe.com/index.php/content/paperinfo/tpci/tpci_definition.htm`.

The scientific value of the numbers is out of scope for our examples.

Listing 8-1 contains the code for the example.

Listing 8-1. Rendering the TIOBE Index in a PieChart

```
package projavafx ;

import javafx.application.Application;
import javafx.collections.FXCollections;
import javafx.collections.ObservableList;
import javafx.scene.Scene;
import javafx.scene.chart.PieChart;
import javafx.scene.layout.StackPane;
import javafx.stage.Stage;

public class ChartApp1 extends Application {

    public static void main(String[] args) {
        launch(args);
    }

    @Override
    public void start(Stage primaryStage) {
        PieChart pieChart = new PieChart();
        pieChart.setData(getChartData());

        primaryStage.setTitle("PieChart");
        StackPane root = new StackPane();
        root.getChildren().add(pieChart);
        primaryStage.setScene(new Scene(root, 400, 250));
        primaryStage.show();
    }

    private ObservableList<PieChart.Data> getChartData() {
        ObservableList<PieChart.Data> answer = FXCollections.observableArrayList();
        answer.addAll(new PieChart.Data("java", 17.56),
                new PieChart.Data("C", 17.06),
                new PieChart.Data("C++", 8.25),
                new PieChart.Data("C#", 8.20),
                new PieChart.Data("ObjectiveC", 6.8),
                new PieChart.Data("PHP", 6.0),
                new PieChart.Data("(Visual)Basic", 4.76),
                new PieChart.Data("Other", 31.37));
        return answer;
    }
}
```

The result of running this example is shown in Figure 8-3.

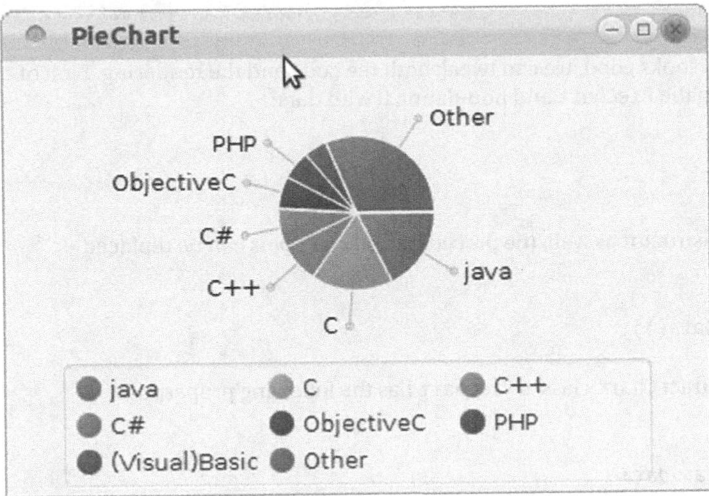

Figure 8-3. Rendering the TIOBE index in a PieChart

With only a limited amount of code, we can render data in a PieChart. Before we make modifications to this example, we explain the different parts.

The code required for setting up the Application, the Stage, and the Scene is covered in Chapter 1. A PieChart extends a Node, so we can easily add it to the scene graph. The first two lines of code in the start method create the PieChart, and add the required data to it:

```
PieChart pieChart = new PieChart();
pieChart.setData(getChartData());
```

The data, which are of type ObservableList<PieChart.Data> are obtained from the getChartData() method and for our example, it contains static data. As the return type of the getChartData() method specifies, the returned data are an ObservableList of PieChart.Data.

An instance of PieChart.Data, which is a nested class of PieChart, contains the information required to draw one slice of the pie. PieChart.Data has a constructor that takes the name of the slice and its value:

```
PieChart.Data(String name, double value)
```

We use this constructor to create data elements containing the name of a programming language and its score in the TIOBE index.

```
new PieChart.Data("java", 17.56)
```

We then add those elements to the ObservableList<PieChart.Data> we need to return.

Some Modifications

Although the result of the simple example already looks good, we can tweak both the code and the rendering. First of all, the example uses two lines of code for creating the PieChart and populating it with data:

```
PieChart pieChart = new PieChart();
pieChart.setData(getChartData());
```

Because PieChart has a single argument constructor as well, the preceding code snippets can be replaced as follows.

```
PieChart pieChart = new PieChart(getChartData());
```

Apart from the properties defined on the abstract Chart class, a PieChart has the following properties.

```
BooleanProperty clockwise
ObjectProperty<ObservableList<PieChart.Data>>data
DoubleProperty labelLineLength
BooleanProperty labelsVisible
DoubleProperty startAngle
```

We covered the data property in the previous section. Some of the other properties are demonstrated in the next code snippet. Listing 8-2 contains a modified version of the start() method.

Listing 8-2. Modified Version of the PieChart Example

```
public void start(Stage primaryStage) {
  PieChart pieChart = new PieChart();
  pieChart.setData(getChartData());
  pieChart.setTitle("Tiobe index");
  pieChart.setLegendSide(Side.LEFT);
  pieChart.setClockwise(false);
  pieChart.setLabelsVisible(false);

  primaryStage.setTitle("PieChart");

  StackPane root = new StackPane();
  root.getChildren().add(pieChart);
  primaryStage.setScene(new Scene(root, 400, 250));
  primaryStage.show();
}
```

Because we used the Side.LEFT field in the new code, we have to import the Side class in our application as well. This is done by adding the line

```
import javafx.geometry.Side
```

in the import block of the code.

Running this modified version results in the modified output shown in Figure 8-4.

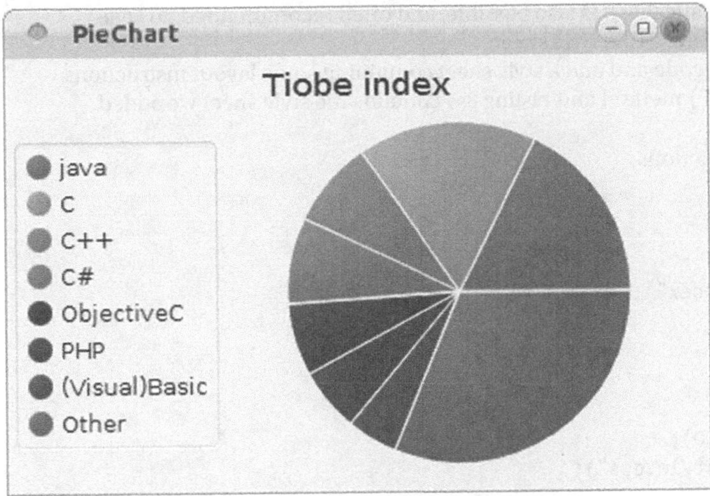

***Figure 8-4.** The output of the modified PieChart example*

Changing a few lines of code results in output that looks very different. We go over the changes we made in a bit more detail. First, we added a title to the chart. That was done using the call

```
pieChart.setTitle("Tiobe index");
```

We could also have used the `titleProperty`:

```
pieChart.titleProperty().set("Tiobe index");
```

Both approaches result in the same output.

■ **Note** The upcoming modifications could also be done using the same patterns. We only document the approach with setter methods, but it is easy to replace this with a property-based approach.

The next line of code in our modified example changes the location of the legend:

```
pieChart.setLegendSide(Side.LEFT);
```

When the `legendSide` is not specified, the legend is shown at the default location, which is below the chart. The `title` and the `legendSide` are both properties that belong to the abstract `Chart` class. As a consequence, they can be set on any chart. The next line in our modified example modifies a property that is specific to a `PieChart`:

```
pieChart.setClockwise(false);
```

By default, the slices in a `PieChart` are rendered clockwise. By setting this property to false, the slices are rendered counterclockwise. We also disabled showing the labels in the `PieChart`. The labels are still shown in the legend, but they do not point to the individual slices anymore. This is achieved by the following line of code:

```
pieChart.setLabelsVisible(false);
```

All layout changes so far are done programmatically. It is also possible, and often recommended, to style applications in general and charts in particular using a CSS style sheet.

We remove the layout changes from the Java code and add a style sheet containing some layout instructions. Listing 8-3 shows the modified code of the `start()` method and Listing 8-4 contains the style sheet we added.

Listing 8-3. Remove Programmatic Layout Instructions

```
public void start(Stage primaryStage) {
    PieChart pieChart = new PieChart();
    pieChart.setData(getChartData());
    pieChart.titleProperty().set("Tiobe index");

    primaryStage.setTitle("PieChart");
    StackPane root = new StackPane();
    root.getChildren().add(pieChart);
    Scene scene = new Scene (root, 400, 250);
    scene.getStylesheets().add("/chartappstyle.css");
    primaryStage.setScene(scene);
    primaryStage.show();
}
```

Listing 8-4. Style Sheet for PieChart Example

```
.chart {
    -fx-clockwise: false;
    -fx-pie-label-visible: true;
    -fx-label-line-length: 5;
    -fx-start-angle: 90;
    -fx-legend-side: right;
}

.chart-pie-label {
    -fx-font-size:9px;
}
.chart-content {
    -fx-padding:1;
}

.default-color0.chart-pie {
    -fx-pie-color:blue;
}

.chart-legend {
    -fx-background-color: #f0e68c;
    -fx-border-color: #696969;
    -fx-border-width:1;
}
```

Running this code results in the output shown in Figure 8-5.

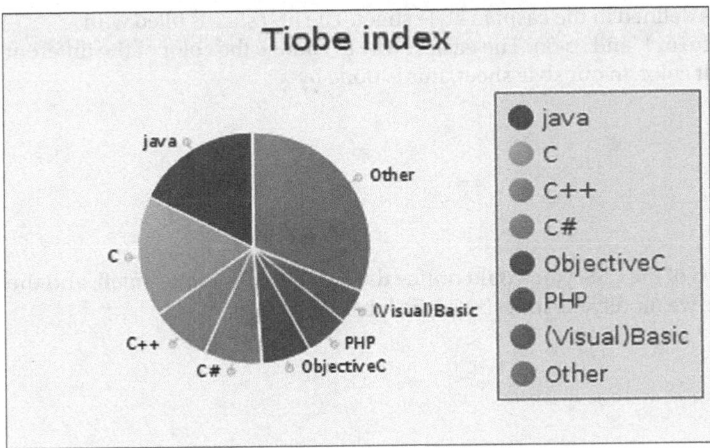

Figure 8-5. *Using CSS to style the PieChart*

We now go over the changes we made. Before we go over the individual changes in detail, we show how we include the CSS with our application. This is achieved by adding the style sheet to the scene, which is done as follows.

```
scene.getStylesheets().add("/chartappstyle.css");
```

The file containing the style sheet, `chartappstyle.css`, must be in the classpath when the application is running. In Listing 8-2, we set the clockwise configuration using

```
pieChart.setClockwise(false)
```

We removed that line from the code in Listing 8-3, and instead defined the `-fx-clockwise` property on the `chart` class in the style sheet:

```
.chart {
    -fx-clockwise: false;
    -fx-pie-label-visible: true;
    -fx-label-line-length: 5;
    -fx-start-angle: 90;
    -fx-legend-side: right;
}
```

In that same `.chart` class definition, we make the labels on the pie visible by setting the `-fx-pie-label-visible` property to true, and we specify the length of the lines for each label to be 5.

Also, we rotate the whole pie by 90 degrees, which is achieved by defining the `-fx-start-angle` property. The labels are now defined in the style sheet, and we remove the corresponding definition from the code by omitting the following line.

```
pieChart.setLabelsVisible(false)
```

To make sure the legend will appear at the right side of the chart, we specify the `-fx-legend-side` property.

By default, a PieChart uses the default colors defined in the caspian style sheet. The first slice is filled with default-color0, the second slice with default-color1, and so on. The easiest way to change the color of the different slices is by overriding the definitions of the default color. In our style sheet, this is done by

```
.default-color0.chart-pie {
    -fx-pie-color: blue;
}
```

The same can be done for the other slices.

If you run the example without the other parts of the CSS, you would notice the chart itself is rather small, and the size of the labels takes too much space. Therefore, we modify the font size of the labels as follows:

```
.chart-pie-label {
    -fx-font-size:9px;
}
```

Also, we decrease the padding in the chart area:

```
.chart-content {
    -fx-padding:1;
}
```

Finally, we change the background and the stroke of the legend. This is achieved by overriding the chart-legend class as follows.

```
.chart-legend {
   -fx-background-color: #f0e68c;
    -fx-border-color: #696969;
    -fx-border-width:1;
}
```

Again, we refer the reader to http://docs.oracle.com/javase/8/javafx/user-interface-tutorial/css-styles.htm for more information about using CSS with JavaFX charts.

Using the XYChart

The XYChart class is an abstract class with seven direct known subclasses. The difference between these classes and the PieChart class is that an XYChart has two axes and an optional alternativeColumn or alternativeRow. This translates to the following list of additional properties on an XYChart.

```
BooleanProperty alternativeColumnFillVisible
BooleanProperty alternativeRowFillVisible
ObjectProperty<ObservableList<XYChart.Series<X,Y>>>data
BooleanProperty horizontalGridLinesVisible
BooleanProperty horizontalZeroLineVisible
BooleanProperty verticalGridLinesVisible
BooleanProperty verticalZeroLineVisible
```

Data in an XYChart are ordered in series. How these series are rendered is specific to the implementation of the subclass of XYChart. In general, a single element in a series contains a number of pairs. The following examples use a hypothetical projection of market share of three programming languages in the future. We start with the TIOBE index for Java, C, and C++ in 2011, and add random values (between -2 and +2) to them for each year until 2020. The resulting (year, number) pairs for Java constitute the Java Series, and the same holds for C and C++. As a result, we have three series, each containing 10 pairs.

A major difference between a PieChart and an XYChart is the presence of an x axis and a y axis in the XYChart. These axes are required when creating an XYChart, as can be observed from the following constructor.

```
XYChart (Axis<X> xAxis, Axis<Y> yAxis)
```

The Axis class is an abstract class extending Region (hence also extending Parent and Node) with two subclasses: CategoryAxis and ValueAxis. The CategoryAxis is used to render labels that are in the String format, as can be observed from the class definition:

```
public class CategoryAxis extends Axis<java.lang.String>
```

The ValueAxis is used to render data entries that represent a Number. It is an abstract class itself, defined as follows.

```
public abstract class ValueAxis <T extends java.lang.Number> extends Axis<T>
```

The ValueAxis class has one concrete subclass, which is the NumberAxis:

```
public final class NumberAxis extends ValueAxis<java.lang.Number>
```

The differences between those Axis classes will become clear throughout the examples. We now show some examples of the different XYChart implementations, starting with the ScatterChart. Some features common to all XYCharts are also explained in the section on ScatterChart.

Note Because the Axis classes extend Region, they allow for applying the same CSS elements as any other Regions. This allows for highly customized Axis instances.

Using the ScatterChart

An instance of the ScatterChart class is used to render data where each data item is represented as a symbol in a two-dimensional area. As mentioned in the previous section, we will render a chart containing three series of data, representing the hypothetical evolution of the TIOBE index for Java, C, and C++. We first show the code of a naive implementation, and refine that to something more useful.

A Simple Implementation

A first implementation of our application using a ScatterChart is shown in Listing 8-5.

Listing 8-5. First Implementation of Rendering Data in a ScatterChart

```
package projavafx ;

import javafx.application.Application;
import javafx.collections.FXCollections;
import javafx.collections.ObservableList;
import javafx.scene.Scene;
```

```
import javafx.scene.chart.NumberAxis;
import javafx.scene.chart.ScatterChart;
import javafx.scene.chart.XYChart;
import javafx.scene.chart.XYChart.Series;
import javafx.scene.layout.StackPane;
import javafx.stage.Stage;

public class ChartApp3 extends Application {
    public static void main(String[] args) {
        launch(args);
    }

    @Override
    public void start(Stage primaryStage) {
        NumberAxis xAxis = new NumberAxis();
        NumberAxis yAxis = new NumberAxis();
        ScatterChart scatterChart = new ScatterChart(xAxis, yAxis);
        scatterChart.setData(getChartData());
        primaryStage.setTitle("ScatterChart");

        StackPane root = new StackPane();
        root.getChildren().add(scatterChart);
        primaryStage.setScene(new Scene(root, 400, 250));
        primaryStage.show();
    }

    private ObservableList<XYChart.Series<Integer, Double>>getChartData() {
        double javaValue = 17.56;
        double cValue = 17.06;
        double cppValue = 8.25;
        ObservableList<XYChart.Series<Integer, Double>>answer = FXCollections.observableArrayList();
        Series<Integer, Double> java = new Series<>();
        Series<Integer, Double> c = new Series<>();
        Series<Integer, Double> cpp = new Series<>();
        for (int i = 2011; i < 2021; i++) {
            java.getData().add(new XYChart.Data(i, javaValue));
            javaValue = javaValue + 4 * Math.random() - 2;
            c.getData().add(new XYChart.Data(i, cValue));
            cValue = cValue + Math.random() - .5;
            cpp.getData().add(new XYChart.Data(i, cppValue));
            cppValue = cppValue + 4 * Math.random() - 2;
        }
        answer.addAll(java, c, cpp);
        return answer;
    }
}
```

Executing this application results in a graph similar to the image shown in Figure 8-6.

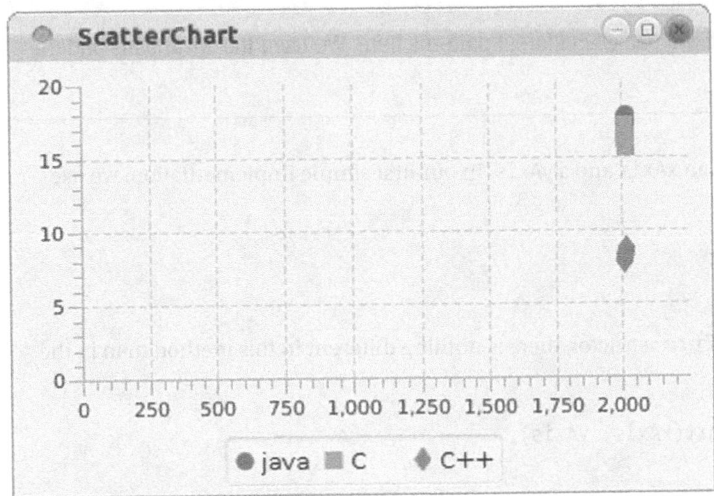

Figure 8-6. *The result of the naive implementation of the* `ScatterChart`

Although the chart shows the required information, it is not very readable. We add a number of enhancements, but first let's have a deeper look at the different parts of the code.

Similar to the `PieChart` example, we created a separate method for obtaining the data. One of the reasons for this is that in real-world applications, it is unlikely to have static data. By isolating the data retrieval in a separate method, it becomes easier to change the way data are obtained.

A single data point is defined by an instance of `XYChart.Data<Integer, Double>`, created with the constructor `XYChart.Data(Integer i, Double d)` where the parameters have the following definitions.

```
i: Integer, representing a specific year (between 2011 and 2020)
d: Double, representing the hypothetical TIOBE index for the particular series in the year
specified by I
```

The local variables `javaValue`, `cValue`, and `cppValue` are used for keeping track of the scores for the different programming languages. They are initialized with the real values from 2011. Each year, an individual score is incremented or decremented by a random value between -2 and +2. Data points are stacked into a series. In our examples, we have three series each containing 10 instances of `XYChart.Data<Integer, Double>`. Those series are of type `XYChart.Series<Integer, Double>`.

The data entries are added to the respective series by calling

```
java.getData().add (...)
c.getData().add(...)
```

and

```
cpp.getData().add(...)
```

Finally, all series are added to the `ObservableList<XYChart.Series<Integer, Double>>`and returned.

The `start()` method of the application contains the functionality required for creating and rendering the `ScatterChart`, and for populating it with the data obtained from the `getChartData` method.

■ **Note** As discussed earlier regarding `PieChart`, we can use different patterns here. We used the JavaBeans pattern in the examples, but we could also use properties.

To create a `ScatterChart`, we need to create an `xAxis` and a `yAxis`. In our first simple implementation, we use two instances of `NumberAxis` for this:

```
NumberAxis xAxis = new NumberAxis();
NumberAxis yAxis = new NumberAxis();
```

Apart from calling the following `ScatterChart` constructor, there is nothing different in this method than in the case of the `PieChart`.

```
ScatterChart scatterChart = new ScatterChart(xAxis, yAxis);
```

Improving the Simple Implementation

One of the first observations when looking at Figure 8-5 is that all data plots in a series are almost rendered on top of each other. The reason for this is clear: the `x-Axis` starts at 0 and ends at 2250. By default, the `NumberAxis` determines its range automatically. We can overrule this behavior by setting the `autoRanging` property to false, and by providing values for the `lowerBound` and the `upperBound`. If we replace the constructor for the `xAxis` in the original example by the following code snippet,

```
NumberAxis xAxis = new NumberAxis();
xAxis.setAutoRanging(false);
xAxis.setLowerBound(2011);
xAxis.setUpperBound(2021);
```

the resulting output will look similar to that shown in Figure 8-7.

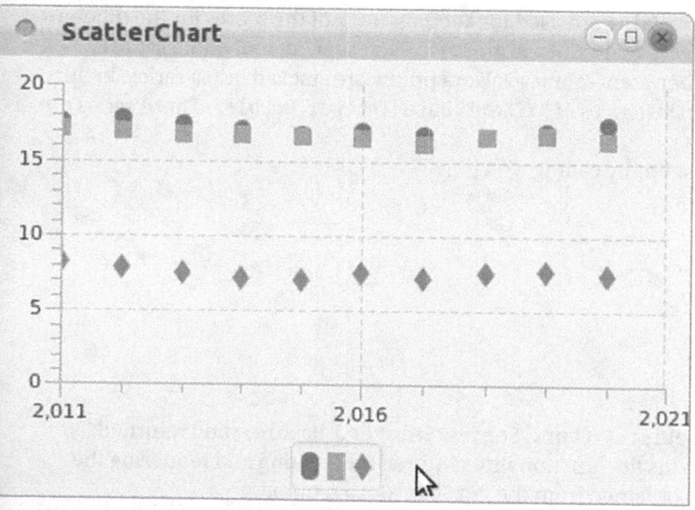

Figure 8-7. Defining the behavior of the `xAxis`

Next, we want to add a title to the chart, and we want to have names near the symbols in the legend node. Adding a title to the chart is no different from adding a title to the PieChart and is achieved by the code:

```
scatterChart.setTitle("Speculations");
```

By adding a name to the three instances of XYChart.Series, we add labels to the symbols in the legend node. The relevant part of the getChartData method becomes

```
Series<Integer, Double> java = new Series<>();
Series<Integer, Double> c = new Series<>();
Series<Integer, Double> cpp = new Series<>();
java.setName("java");
c.setName("C");
cpp.setName("C++");
```

Running the application again after applying both changes results in output similar to that shown in Figure 8-8.

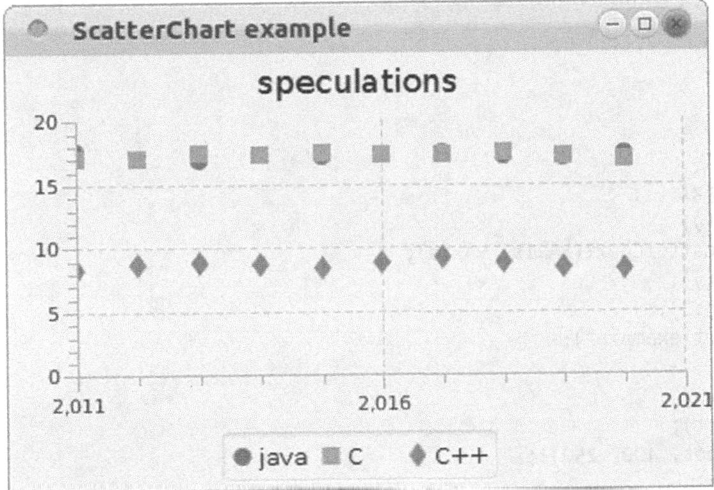

Figure 8-8. *ScatterChart with a title and named symbols*

Until now, we used a NumberAxis for the xAxis. Inasmuch as years can be represented as Number instances, that works. However, because we don't do any numerical operation on the years, and because the distance between consecutive data entries is always one year, we can also use a String value to represent this information.

We now modify the code to work with a CategoryAxis for the xAxis. Changing the xAxis from a NumberAxis to a CategoryAxis also implies that the getChartData() method should return an instance of ObservableList<XYChart.Series<String, Double>>and that implies that the different elements in a single Series should have the type XYChart.Data<String, Double>.

In Listing 8-6, the original code has been modified to use the CategoryAxis.

Listing 8-6. Using CategoryAxis Instead of NumberAxis for the xAxis

```
package projavafx ;

import javafx.application.Application;
import javafx.collections.FXCollections;
import javafx.collections.ObservableList;
import javafx.scene.Scene;
import javafx.scene.chart.CategoryAxis;
import javafx.scene.chart.NumberAxis;
import javafx.scene.chart.ScatterChart;
import javafx.scene.chart.XYChart;
import javafx.scene.chart.XYChart.Series;
import javafx.scene.layout.StackPane;
import javafx.stage.Stage;

public class ChartApp6 extends Application {

    public static void main(String[] args) {
        launch(args);
    }

    @Override
    public void start(Stage primaryStage) {
        CategoryAxis xAxis = new CategoryAxis();
        NumberAxis yAxis = new NumberAxis();
        ScatterChart scatterChart = new ScatterChart(xAxis, yAxis);
        scatterChart.setData(getChartData());
        scatterChart.setTitle("speculations");
        primaryStage.setTitle("ScatterChart example");

        StackPane root = new StackPane();
        root.getChildren().add(scatterChart);
        primaryStage.setScene(new Scene(root, 400, 250));
        primaryStage.show();
    }

    private ObservableList<XYChart.Series<String, Double>>getChartData() {
        double javaValue = 17.56;
        double cValue = 17.06;
        double cppValue = 8.25;
        ObservableList<XYChart.Series<String, Double>>answer = FXCollections.observableArrayList();
        Series<String, Double> java = new Series<>();
        Series<String, Double> c = new Series<>();
        Series<String, Double> cpp = new Series<>();
        java.setName("java");
        c.setName("C");
        cpp.setName("C++");

        for (int i = 2011; i < 2021; i++) {
            java.getData().add(new XYChart.Data(Integer.toString(i), javaValue));
            javaValue = javaValue + 4 * Math.random() - .2;
```

```
            c.getData().add(new XYChart.Data(Integer.toString(i), cValue));
            cValue = cValue + 4 * Math.random() - 2;
            cpp.getData().add(new XYChart.Data(Integer.toString(i), cppValue));
            cppValue = cppValue + 4 * Math.random() - 2;
        }
        answer.addAll(java, c, cpp);
        return answer;
    }
}
```

Running the modified application results in output similar to Figure 8-9.

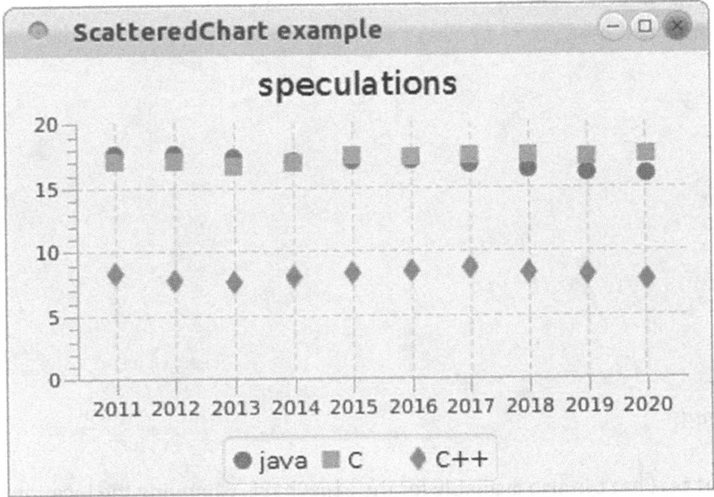

Figure 8-9. *Using a ScatterChart with a CategoryAxis on the xAxis*

Using the LineChart

The example in the previous section resulted in data entries being represented by single dots or symbols. Often, it is desirable to have the dots connected by a line because this helps in seeing trends. The JavaFX LineChart is well suited for this.

The API for the LineChart has many methods in common with the API for the ScatterChart. In fact, we can reuse most of the code in Listing 8-6, and just replace the ScatterChart occurrences with LineChart and the import for javafx.scene.chart.ScatterChart with javafx.scene.chart.LineChart. The data stay exactly the same, so we only show the new start() method in Listing 8-7.

Listing 8-7. Using a LineChart Instead of a ScatterChart

```
public void start(Stage primaryStage) {
    CategoryAxis xAxis = new CategoryAxis();
    NumberAxis yAxis = new NumberAxis();
    LineChart lineChart = new LineChart(xAxis, yAxis);
    lineChart.setData(getChartData());
    lineChart.setTitle("speculations");
    primaryStage.setTitle("LineChart example");
```

```
    StackPane root = new StackPane();
    root.getChildren().add(lineChart);
    primaryStage.setScene(new Scene(root, 400, 250));
    primaryStage.show();
}
```

Running this application gives output like that shown in Figure 8-10.

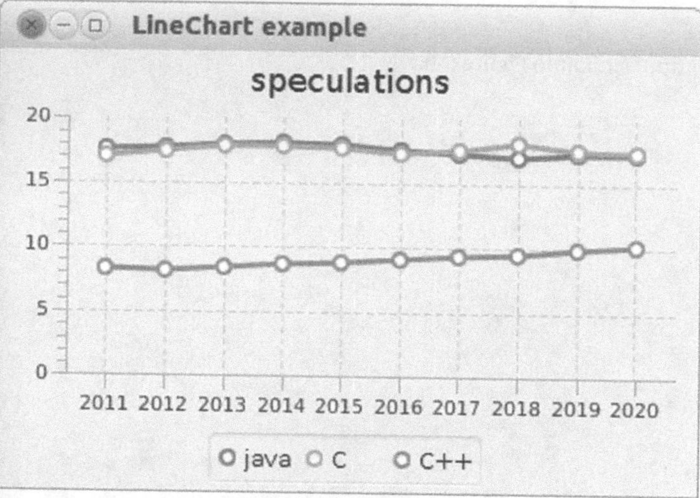

Figure 8-10. *Using a* `LineChart` *for displaying trends*

Most of the functionality available for the `ScatterChart` is also available for the `LineChart`. Changing the location of the legend, adding or removing a title, and using a `NumberAxis` instead of a `CategoryAxis` are possible using the `LineChart`.

Using the BarChart

A `BarChart` is capable of rendering the same data as a `ScatterChart` and a `LineChart`, but it looks different. In a `BarChart`, the focus is often more on showing the relative differences between the different series for a given category. In our case, that means that we focus on the differences between the values for Java, C, and C++.

Again, we do not need to modify the method that returns our data. Indeed, a `BarChart` requires a `CategoryAxis` for its `xAxis`, and we already modified the `getChartData()` method to return an `ObservableList` containing `XYChart.Series<String, double>`. Starting from Listing 8-6, we change only the occurrences of `ScatterChart` to `BarChart` and we obtain Listing 8-8.

Listing 8-8. Using a `BarChart` Instead of a `ScatterChart`

```
public void start(Stage primaryStage) {
    CategoryAxis xAxis = new CategoryAxis();
    NumberAxis yAxis = new NumberAxis();
    BarChart barChart = new BarChart(xAxis, yAxis);
    barChart.setData(getChartData());
    barChart.setTitle("speculations");
    primaryStage.setTitle("BarChart example");
```

```
        StackPane root = new StackPane();
        root.getChildren().add(barChart);
        primaryStage.setScene(new Scene(root, 400, 250));
        primaryStage.show();
    }
```

Once we replace the import for `javafx.scene.chart.ScatterChart` with one for `javafx.scene.chart.BarChart`, we can build the application and run it. The result is a `BarChart` similar to that shown in Figure 8-11.

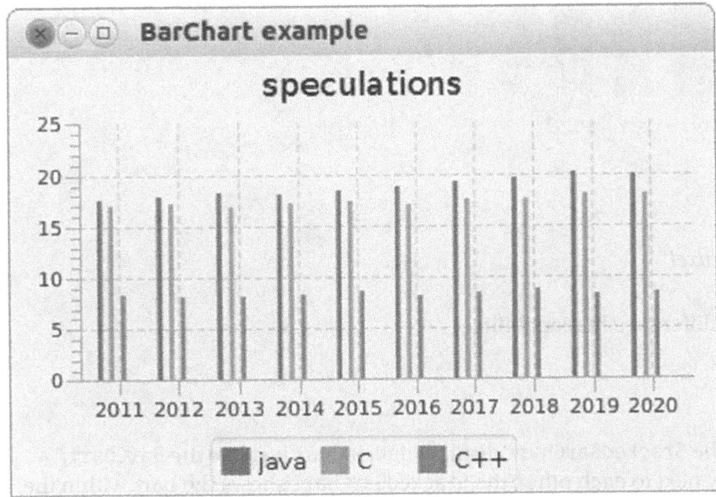

Figure 8-11. *Using BarChart for highlighting differences between the values*

Although the result indeed shows the differences between the values for each year, it is not very clear because the bars are rather small. With a total scene width at 400 pixels, there is not much space to render large bars. However, the `BarChart` API contains methods to define the inner gap between bars and the gap between categories. In our case, we want a smaller gap between the bars, for example, one pixel. This is done by calling

```
barChart.setBarGap(1);
```

Adding this single line of code to the start method and rerunning the application results in the output shown in Figure 8-12.

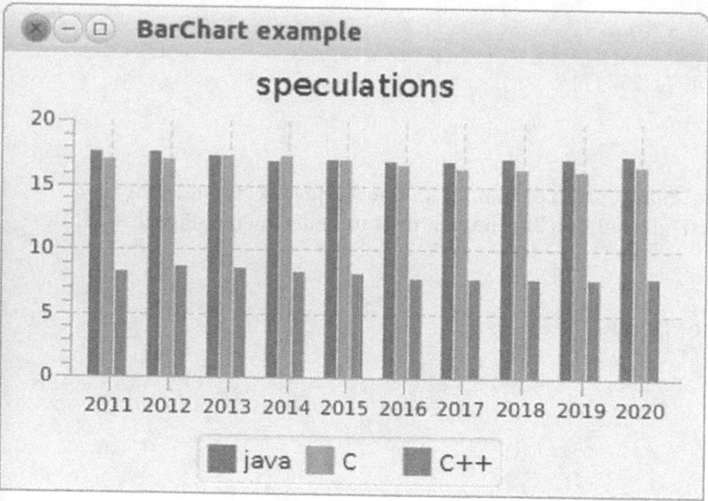

Figure 8-12. *Setting the gap between bars to one pixel*

Clearly, this one line of code leads to a huge difference in readability.

Using the StackedBarChart

The `StackedBarChart` was added in JavaFX 2.1. The `StackedBarChart` displays data in bars just like the `BarChart`, but instead of rendering bars in the same category next to each other, the `StackedBarChart` shows the bars within the same category on top of each other. This often makes it easier to inspect totals.

Typically, categories correspond with the common key values in the data series. As a consequence, in our example the different years (2011, 2012, ... 2020) can be considered as categories. We can add these categories to the `xAxis`, as follows:

```
IntStream.range(2011,2020).forEach(t -> xAxis.getCategories().add(String.valueOf(t)));
```

Apart from this, the only code change is replacing the `BarChart` with the `StackedBarChart` in code and in the import statement. This leads to the code snippet in Listing 8-9.

Listing 8-9. Using a `StackedBarChart` Instead of a `ScatterChart`

```
public void start(Stage primaryStage) {
    CategoryAxis xAxis = new CategoryAxis();
    IntStream.range(2011,2020).forEach(t -> xAxis.getCategories().add(String.valueOf(t)));
    NumberAxis yAxis = new NumberAxis();
    StackedBarChart stackedBarChart = new StackedBarChart(xAxis, yAxis, getChartData());
    stackedBarChart.setTitle("speculations");
    primaryStage.setTitle("StackedBarChart example");

    StackPane root = new StackPane();
    root.getChildren().add(stackedBarChart);
    Scene scene = new Scene(root, 400, 250);
    primaryStage.setScene(scene);
    primaryStage.show();
```

Running the application now produces output like that shown in Figure 8-13.

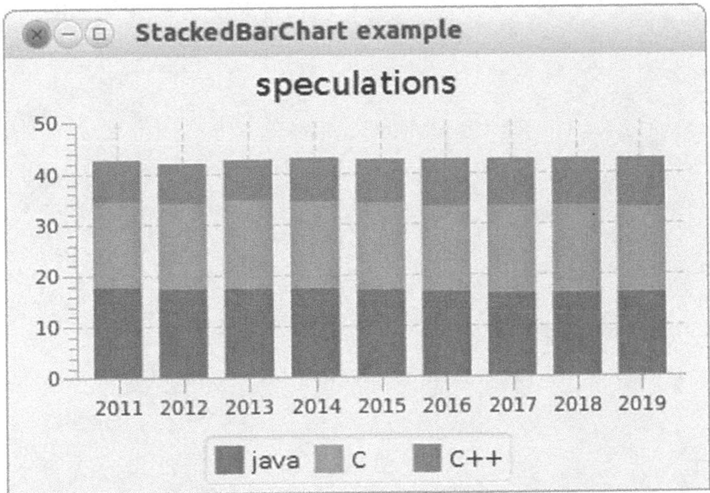

Figure 8-13. *Rendering stacked bar chart plots using* `StackedBarChart`

Using the AreaChart

In some cases, it makes sense to fill the area under the line connecting the dots. Although the same data are rendered as in the case of a `LineChart`, the result looks different. Listing 8-10 contains the modified `start()` method that uses an `AreaChart` instead of the original `ScatterChart`. As in the previous modifications, we didn't change the `getChartData()` method.

Listing 8-10. Using an `AreaChart` Instead of a `ScatterChart`

```
public void start(Stage primaryStage) {
    CategoryAxis xAxis = new CategoryAxis();
    NumberAxis yAxis = new NumberAxis();
    AreaChart areaChart = new AreaChart(xAxis, yAxis);
    areaChart.setData(getChartData());
    areaChart.setTitle("speculations");
    primaryStage.setTitle("AreaChart example");
    StackPane root = new StackPane();
    root.getChildren().add(areaChart);
    primaryStage.setScene(new Scene(root, 400, 250));
    primaryStage.show();
}
```

Running this application results in output like that shown in Figure 8-14.

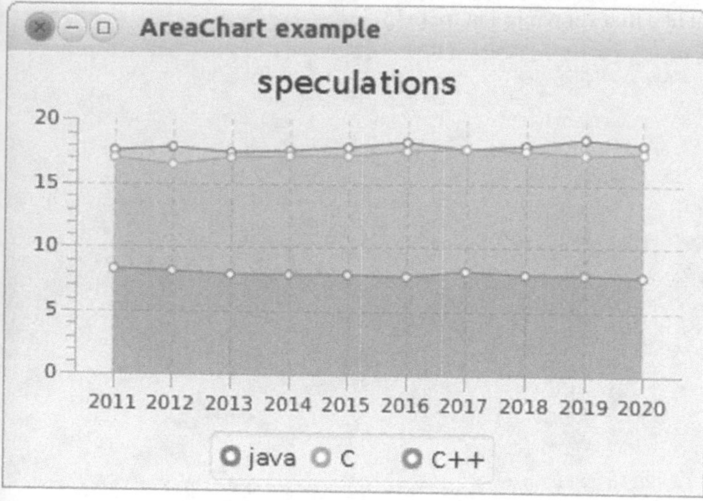

***Figure 8-14.** Rendering area plots using AreaChart*

Using the StackedAreaChart

The `StackedAreaChart` is to the `AreaChart` what the `StackedBarChart` is to the `BarChart`. Rather than showing individual areas, the `StackedAreaChart` always shows the sum of the values in a specific category.

Changing an `AreaChart` into a `StackedAreaChart` only requires the change of one line of code and the appropriate import statement.

```
AreaChart areaChart = new AreaChart(xAxis, yAxis);
```

must be replaced with

```
StackedAreaChart areaChart = new StackedAreaChart(xAxis, yAxis);
```

Applying this change and running the application results in a graph like the one in Figure 8-15.

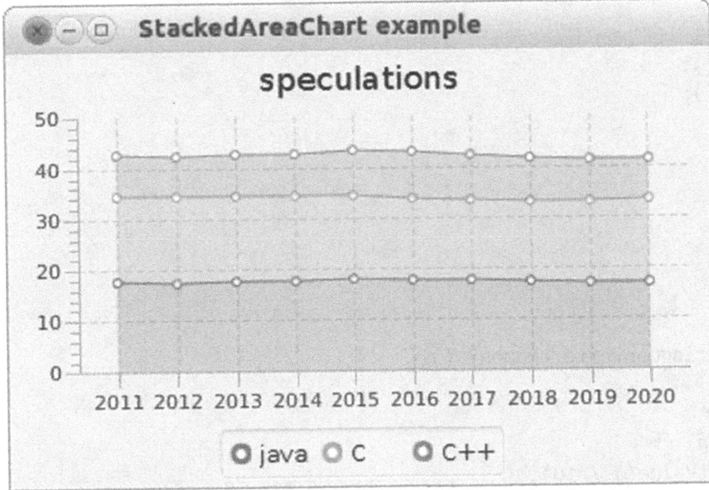

Figure 8-15. *Rendering area plots using* `AreaChart`

Using the BubbleChart

The last implementation of the `XYChart` is a special one. The `BubbleChart` does not contain properties that are not already on the `XYChart` class, but it is the only direct implementation in the current JavaFX `Chart` API that uses the additional parameter on the `XYChart.Data` class.

We first modify the code in Listing 8-6 to use the `BubbleChart` instead of the `ScatterChart`. Because by default, bubbles are stretched when the span on the `xAxis` is much different from the span on the `yAxis`, we do not use years, but a tenth of a year as the value on the `xAxis`. Doing so, we have a span of 100 units on the `xAxis` (10 years) compared with a span of about 30 units on the `yAxis`. This is also more or less the ratio between the width and the height of our chart. As a consequence, the bubbles are relatively circular.

Listing 8-11 contains the code for rendering a `BubbleChart`.

Listing 8-11. Using the `BubbleChart`

```
package projavafx;

import javafx.application.Application;
import javafx.collections.FXCollections;
import javafx.collections.ObservableList;
import javafx.scene.Scene;
import javafx.scene.chart.*;
import javafx.scene.chart.XYChart.Series;
import javafx.scene.layout.StackPane;
import javafx.stage.Stage;
import javafx.util.StringConverter;

public class ChartApp10 extends Application {

    public static void main(String[] args) {
        launch(args);
    }
```

```
    @Override
    public void start(Stage primaryStage) {
        NumberAxis xAxis = new NumberAxis();
        NumberAxis yAxis = new NumberAxis();
        yAxis.setAutoRanging(false);
        yAxis.setLowerBound(0);
        yAxis.setUpperBound(30);
        xAxis.setAutoRanging(false);
        xAxis.setAutoRanging(false);
        xAxis.setLowerBound(20110);
        xAxis.setUpperBound(20201);
        xAxis.setTickUnit(10);
        xAxis.setTickLabelFormatter(new StringConverter<Number>() {

            @Override
            public String toString(Number n) {
                return String.valueOf(n.intValue() / 10);
            }

            @Override
            public Number fromString(String s) {
                return Integer.valueOf(s) * 10;
            }
        });
        BubbleChart bubbleChart = new BubbleChart(xAxis, yAxis);
        bubbleChart.setData(getChartData());
        bubbleChart.setTitle("Speculations");
        primaryStage.setTitle("BubbleChart example");

        StackPane root = new StackPane();
        root.getChildren().add(bubbleChart);
        primaryStage.setScene(new Scene(root, 400, 250));
        primaryStage.show();
    }

    private ObservableList<XYChart.Series<Integer, Double>>getChartData() {
        double javaValue = 17.56;
        double cValue = 17.06;
        double cppValue = 8.25;
        ObservableList<XYChart.Series<Integer, Double>>answer = FXCollections.observableArrayList();
        Series<Integer, Double> java = new Series<>();
        Series<Integer, Double> c = new Series<>();
        Series<Integer, Double> cpp = new Series<>();
        java.setName("java");
        c.setName("C");
        cpp.setName("C++");
        for (int i = 20110; i < 20210; i = i + 10) {
            double diff = Math.random();
            java.getData().add(new XYChart.Data(i, javaValue));
            javaValue = Math.max(javaValue + 4 * diff - 2, 0);
            diff = Math.random();
```

```
            c.getData().add(new XYChart.Data(i, cValue));
            cValue = Math.max(cValue + 4 * diff - 2, 0);
            diff = Math.random();
            cpp.getData().add(new XYChart.Data(i, cppValue));
            cppValue = Math.max(cppValue + 4 * diff - 2, 0);
        }
        answer.addAll(java, c, cpp);
        return answer;
    }

}
```

The xAxis ranges from 20110 to 20201, but of course we want to show the years at the axis. This can be achieved by calling

```
xAxis.setTickLabelFormatter(new StringConverter<Number>() {
  ...
}
```

where the StringConverter we supply converts the numbers we use (e.g., 20150) to Strings (e.g., 2015) and vice versa. Doing so, we are able to use whatever quantity we want for calculating the bubbles and still have a nice way of formatting the labels. Running this example results in the chart shown in Figure 8-16.

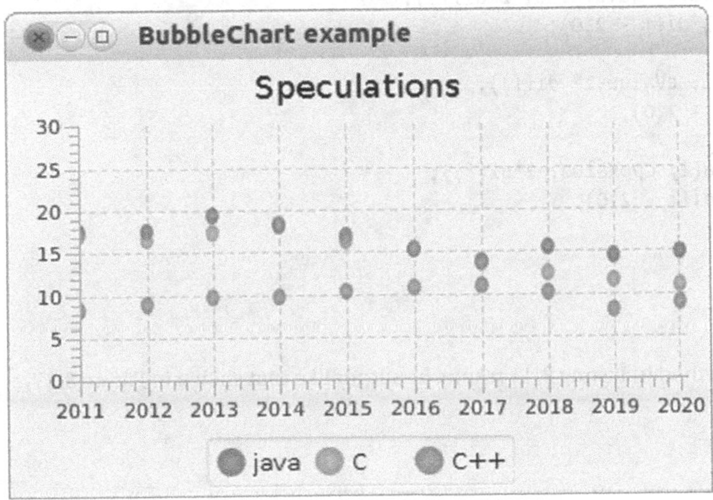

***Figure 8-16.** Using a BubbleChart with fixed radius*

Until now, we didn't leverage the three-argument constructor of XYChart.Data. Apart from the two-argument constructor that we are already familiar with,

```
XYChart.Data (X xValue, Y yValue)
```

XYChart.Data also has a three-argument constructor:

```
XYChart.Data (X xValue, Y yValue, Object extraValue)
```

The extraValue argument can be of any type. This allows for developers to implement their own subclasses of XYChart that take advantage of additional information that can be enclosed inside a single data element. The BubbleChart implementation uses this extraValue for deciding how large the bubbles should be rendered.

We now modify the getChartData() method to use the three-argument constructor. The xValue and yValue parameters are still the same as in the previous listing, but we now add a third parameter that indicates an upcoming trend. The larger this parameter is, the bigger the rise in the next year. The smaller the parameter is, the bigger the drop in the next year. The modified getChartData() method is shown in Listing 8-12.

Listing 8-12. Using a Three-Argument Constructor for XYChart.Data Instances

```
private ObservableList<XYChart.Series<Integer, Double>>getChartData() {
    double javaValue = 17.56;
    double cValue = 17.06;
    double cppValue = 8.25;
    ObservableList<XYChart.Series<Integer, Double>>answer = FXCollections.observableArrayList();
    Series<Integer, Double> java = new Series<>();
    Series<Integer, Double> c = new Series<>();
    Series<Integer, Double> cpp = new Series<>();
    java.setName("java");
    c.setName("C");
    cpp.setName("C++");
    for (int i = 20110; i < 20210; i =  i+10) {
        double diff = Math.random();
        java.getData().add(new XYChart.Data(i, javaValue, 2*diff));
        javaValue = Math.max(javaValue + 4*diff - 2,0);
        diff = Math.random();
        c.getData().add(new XYChart.Data(i, cValue,2* diff));
        cValue = Math.max(cValue + 4*diff - 2,0);
        diff = Math.random();
        cpp.getData().add(new XYChart.Data(i, cppValue, 2*diff));
        cppValue = Math.max(cppValue + 4*diff - 2,0);
    }
    answer.addAll(java, c, cpp);
    return answer;
}
```

Integrating this method with the start() method in Listing 8-11 results in output like that shown in Figure 8-17.

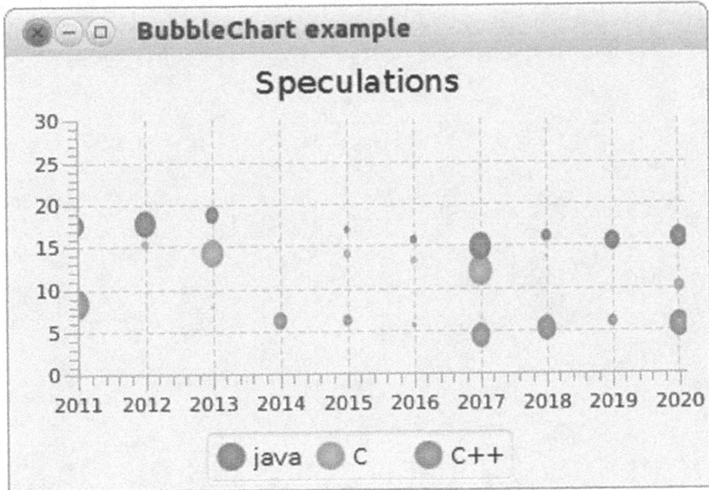

Figure 8-17. *Adding variations in the size of the Bubbles*

Summary

The JavaFX Chart API provides a number of ready-to-use implementations for different chart types. Each of these implementations serves a different purpose, and it is up to the developer to choose the most appropriate Chart.

Modifying a Chart and tuning it for a specific application can be done by applying CSS rules or by using Chart-specific methods or properties.

In case you need a more customized Chart, you can extend the abstract Chart class and take advantage of the existing properties on that class, or you can extend the abstract XYChart class if your chart requires two axes.

Resources

For more information on the JavaFX Chart API, consult the following resources:

- http://docs.oracle.com/javase/8/javafx/user-interface-tutorial/charts.htm
- http://docs.oracle.com/javase/8/javafx/user-interface-tutorial/css-styles.htm

CHAPTER 9

Using the Media Classes

We keep moving forward, opening new doors, and doing new things, because we're curious and curiosity keeps leading us down new paths.

—Walt Disney

In the previous chapters you have learned how to create applications using the JavaFX library. Now we make good use of that knowledge while creating applications that explore the audio and video capabilities of the JavaFX platform.

The Foundation

Since JavaFX 2.0, the media classes in JavaFX are based on an open source multimedia framework named GStreamer.[1] This is a big change from the media library in the early versions of JavaFX, where the native media capabilities of the various supported platforms were used directly. In comparison, the GStreamer-based library provides better stability and more consistency across platforms. The latter should be seen in the light of the "Write Once, Run Anywhere" paradigm of Java. In JavaFX 1, there were large differences between JavaFX Media applications on different platforms. Today, the consistency has the drawback that in some cases, fewer features are provided, but the different platforms provide the same functionality.

Supported Media Formats

Table 9-1 shows the file formats that are supported by the JavaFX media classes. Four audio formats and three video formats are supported. The four audio formats supported in JavaFX (MP3, WAV, AIFF, and AAC) are very common and are all well supported by most audio tools on the market. You should have no trouble obtaining your source audio files in, or converting them to, one of the formats supported by JavaFX.

[1]`http://gstreamer.freedesktop.org/`

Table 9-1. Media Formats Supported by JavaFX

File Extension	Type	Format	Mime Type
.mp3	Audio	MP3: MPEG-1, 2, 2.5 audio with ID3 v2.3, v2.4 metadata	audio/mpeg
.aif, .aiff	Audio	Audio Interchange File Format: uncompressed audio	audio/x-aiff
.wav	Audio	Waveform Audio Format: uncompressed audio	audio/x-wav
.aac, .m4a	Audio	MPEG-4 multimedia container with Advanced Audio Coding (AAC) audio	audio/aac
.fxm	Video	FX Media: VP6 video with MP3 audio	video/x-javafx
.flv	Video	Flash Video: VP6 video with MP3 audio	video/x-flv
.mp4	Video	MPEG-4 multimedia container with H.264/AVC (Advanced Video Coding) video compression	video/mp4

FXM is the "native" JavaFX video format. It consists of VP6 encoded video and MP3 audio, a combination that is also used in Flash Video (FLV) files. An FLV container can host several different options for video and audio encoding other than VP6 and MP3. Therefore, it is not correct to say that JavaFX can play any FLV file. However, the VP6/MP3 combination is very common, so it is fair to say that JavaFX should be able to play most FLV files that can be found on the Internet. FLV video is widely supported by tools from Adobe and others, so you should have no trouble converting or authoring video in this format.

As of JavaFX 2.1, support for H.264 is available. JavaFX now supports MPEG-4 multimedia with H.264 video and AAC audio.

Working with Audio Clips

In the earliest versions of JavaFX, there was no way to play low-latency audio. This much-needed feature became available in version 2.0 using the new `AudioClip` class. Audio clips are not suitable for large or lengthy sounds because the audio data associated with these sounds are decompressed and stored completely in memory. If you need to play a song or other lengthy audio file, you should use a `Media` object instead, which is discussed in the next section.

An `AudioClip` is ideal for playing short sounds in response to user actions in a game or other rich-media application. An `AudioClip` instance is constructed by passing a URI string as the only parameter to the constructor. This URI can point to a resource on the Internet, the local file system, or within the jar file by using the `http:`, `file:`, and `jar:` schemes, respectively. Once an `AudioClip` is constructed, you can adjust several properties that affect the playback of the clip, such as the volume, playback rate, panning, and balance. Calling its `play` method will begin playback of an `AudioClip`. You can call the `play` method repeatedly to begin multiple overlapping playbacks of a given clip.

There are actually three overloaded versions of the `play` method in the `AudioClip` class. Calling the method with no arguments will use the current properties of the `AudioClip` instance for the playback. There is also a variant of the `play` method that takes a volume argument, which allows you to override the volume of the clip for that playback only. The final variant of the `play` method allows you to specify the volume, balance, rate, pan, and priority of that playback. Specifying these parameters as arguments of the `play` methods does not cause them to be saved permanently; they are a one-time-only override of the `AudioClip`'s instance data. There is also a `stop` method that stops all playback of the `AudioClip`.

Listing 9-1 illustrates the simple steps required to create and play an `AudioClip`. This source code is part of the BasicAudioClip example project in the Chapter09 directory of the book's source code.

Listing 9-1. Playing an Audio Clip

```
public class BasicAudioClip extends Application {

    public static void main(String[] args) {
        launch(args);
    }

    @Override
    public void start(Stage primaryStage) {
        final URL resource = getClass().getResource("resources/beep.wav");
        final AudioClip clip = new AudioClip(resource.toString());

        final Button button = new Button("Bing Zzzzt!");
        button.setOnAction((ActionEvent event) -> {
            clip.play(1.0);
        });

        final StackPane stackPane = new StackPane();
        stackPane.setPadding(new Insets(10));
        stackPane.getChildren().add(button);

        final Scene scene = new Scene(stackPane, 200, 200);
        final URL stylesheet = getClass().getResource("media.css");
        scene.getStylesheets().add(stylesheet.toString());

        primaryStage.setTitle("Basic AudioClip Example");
        primaryStage.setScene(scene);
        primaryStage.show();
    }
}
```

The prerequisite to creating an `AudioClip` is to create the URI string for the resource to be loaded. In Listing 9-1, we use the `getResource` method to return the URI for an audio file embedded in the jar file. The URI is converted to a `String` and then passed to the `AudioClip` constructor. As previously mentioned, the `AudioClip` constructor loads the entire sound into memory, decoding it if necessary. If your sound effect files are small, you can store them in an uncompressed format such as the .wav file we use in this example to avoid the overhead of decoding them. Once a sound file grows larger than 100 KB or so, you should consider storing it as a compressed MP3 file instead because the smaller size of the file can more than make up for the overhead of decoding the sound. This is especially true if you are loading your sound files from a server on the Internet. You should also keep in mind that the `AudioClip` constructor will block the current thread until the sound is completely loaded. For this reason, you should consider loading your sound effects on a background thread if you are loading a lot of files or if the files are large. See the Chapter 7 for details on using JavaFX's concurrency classes.

Once the `AudioClip` is constructed, you simply need to call one of its `play` methods to start a playback. The sound in Listing 9-1 is played in response to a button click by calling the `play` method and passing it a volume parameter of 1.0, which causes the sound to be played at maximum volume. The `Button` is then added to a `StackPane` so that it will automatically remain centered in the `Scene`. Finally, the `Scene` is added to the `Stage` and shown to the user. Note that the `media.css` style sheet is applied to the scene. This style sheet is used by all of the sample applications in this chapter. The style sheet is shown in Listing 9-2.

Listing 9-2. The First Version of the Style Sheet Used by the Applications in This Chapter

```
.root {
  -fx-base: #606060;
  -fx-background-color: radial-gradient(center 50% 50%, radius 60%,
                                         #666a6b, #2b2f32);
  -fx-background-image: url("resources/cross.png");
  -fx-background-position: left top;
}

.button {
  -fx-text-fill: #E0E0E0;
  -fx-font-size: 20pt;
  -fx-pref-width: 300px;
}

.label {
  -fx-text-fill: #E0E0E0;
}

#clipLabel {
  -fx-font-size: 24pt;
}

.hyperlink {
  -fx-text-fill: #808080;
}
```

Figure 9-1 shows how this simple AudioClip example should look when it is running. A new playback of the AudioClip is started each time the button is clicked. If you're very quick, you might get two or three playing at a time.

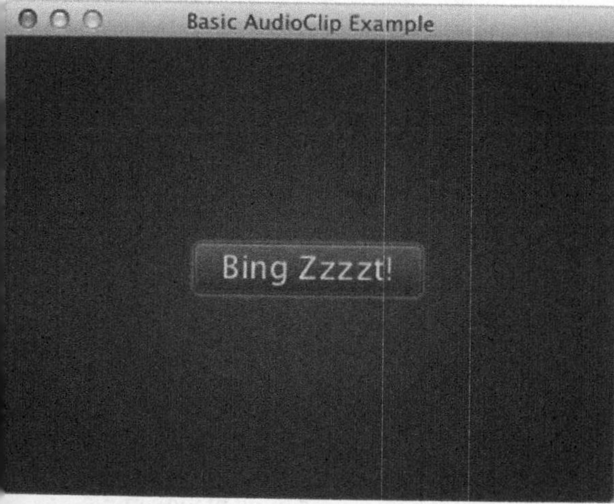

Figure 9-1. *The BasicAudioClip application*

Controlling the Playback Parameters of an AudioClip

We now build on the preceding example to show how AudioClip allows a sound effect to be played at differing volumes and rates. We also show how the balance of an audio clip can be adjusted to control the volume of the left and right channels. This can be useful when you want to achieve a bit of 2D spatialization in your sound effects. The application we end up with is shown in Figure 9-2.

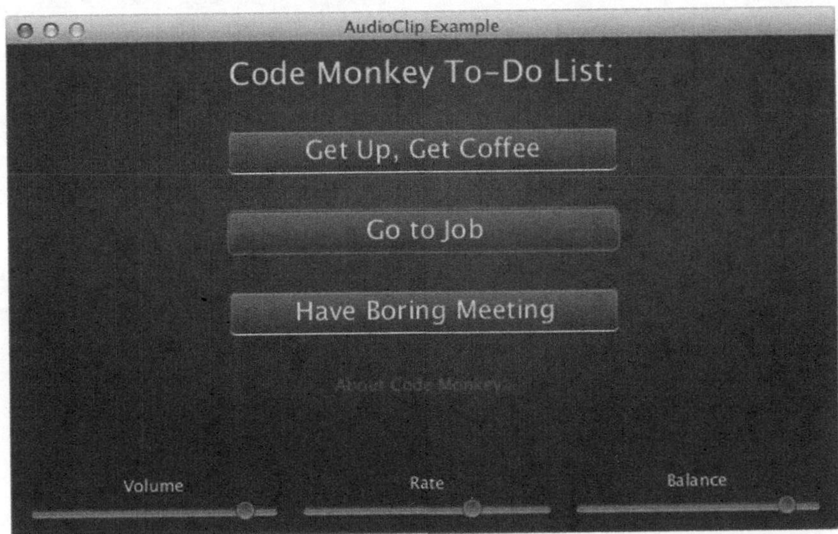

Figure 9-2. *The CodeMonkeyToDo application*

We start by examining the Application class and looking at how the sounds are loaded. Listing 9-3 shows the application with the scene construction code removed. This allows you to see more easily that we are loading MP3 files from the jar file using the getResource method again. In this case, our sound effects are in a different location relative to our application class. Therefore we use a path such as resources/coffee.mp3 to locate them. These clips are a little longer, so the decision was made to use MP3 files to keep the size of the jar file to a minimum at the expense of a little extra decoding time during startup.

The audio clips are all loaded in the constructor of the CodeMonkeyToDo class. Loading them in the constructor guarantees that they are loaded at the very start of the program before the start method is called. Alternatively, we could have overridden the init method of the Application class and loaded our clips there. Notice that the three AudioClips and the three Slider controls are declared as fields in the Application class. This allows convenient access later when the AudioClip is played using the current values from the Slider controls shown in Figure 9-2.

Listing 9-3. The Application Class of the CodeMonkeyToDo Example Program

```
public class CodeMonkeyToDo extends Application {

  private final AudioClip coffeeClip;
  private final AudioClip jobClip;
  private final AudioClip meetingClip;

  private Slider volumeSlider;
  private Slider rateSlider;
  private Slider balanceSlider;
```

```
  public static void main(String[] args) {
    CodeMonkeyToDo.launch(args);
  }

  public CodeMonkeyToDo() {
    coffeeClip = new AudioClip(getClipResourceString("resources/coffee.mp3"));
    jobClip = new AudioClip(getClipResourceString("resources/job.mp3"));
    meetingClip =
        new AudioClip(getClipResourceString("resources/meeting.mp3"));
  }

  // Scene construction code removed for now...

  private String getClipResourceString(String clipName) {
    return getClass().getResource(clipName).toString();
  }
}
```

Constructing the Scene

We now take a brief look at the scene construction code for the application shown in Figure 9-2. The application is organized as a vertical column of buttons that play the audio clips with a row of controls at the bottom of the window. We use a `GridPane` as the top-level layout container for the application. You can see the `GridPane` created in the application's `start` method, which is shown in Listing 9-4. Once the `GridPane` is created and configured, it is passed as an argument to the `createControls` and `createClipList` methods. The `createClipList` method is responsible for creating the vertical column of buttons and is shown and discussed later in this section. The `createControls` method creates `Labels` and the corresponding `Slider` controls that allow the user to set the volume, rate, and balance of the next clip to be played. The `Sliders` and their `Labels` are then added to the `GridPane` before the method returns. After the `grid` has been populated with its controls, it is used as the root node of a new `Scene`. The `Scene` is then styled with our `media.css` style sheet and added to the `primaryStage`, which is then shown to the user.

Listing 9-4. Constructing the Scene and the Volume, Balance, and Rate Controls

```
@Override
public void start(Stage primaryStage) {
  final GridPane grid = new GridPane();
  grid.setPadding(new Insets(10));
  grid.setHgap(10);
  grid.setVgap(5);

  createControls(grid);
  createClipList(grid);  // Shown later...

  final Scene scene = new Scene(grid, 640, 380);
  scene.getStylesheets()
      .add(getClass().getResource("media.css").toString());

  primaryStage.setTitle("AudioClip Example");
  primaryStage.setScene(scene);
  primaryStage.show();
```

```
  private void createControls(GridPane grid) {
    final Label volumeLabel = new Label("Volume");
    final Label rateLabel = new Label("Rate");
    final Label balanceLabel = new Label("Balance");

    GridPane.setHalignment(volumeLabel, HPos.CENTER);
    GridPane.setHalignment(rateLabel, HPos.CENTER);
    GridPane.setHalignment(balanceLabel, HPos.CENTER);

    volumeSlider = new Slider(0.0, 1.0, 1.0);
    rateSlider = new Slider(0.25, 2.5, 1.0);
    balanceSlider = new Slider(-1.0, 1.0, 0.0);

    GridPane.setHgrow(volumeSlider, Priority.ALWAYS);
    GridPane.setHgrow(rateSlider, Priority.ALWAYS);
    GridPane.setHgrow(balanceSlider, Priority.ALWAYS);

    grid.add(volumeLabel, 0, 2);
    grid.add(volumeSlider, 0, 3);
    grid.add(rateLabel, 1, 2);
    grid.add(rateSlider, 1, 3);
    grid.add(balanceLabel, 2, 2);
    grid.add(balanceSlider, 2, 3);
  }
```

Listing 9-5 shows the createClipList method. This method creates a VBox to hold a Label, the three Buttons that play the AudioClips, and a Hyperlink that triggers the display of the Code Monkey web page at jonathancoulton.com in a separate window. The VBox is then added to the GridPane such that it spans all remaining columns in the first row. The VBox is always centered horizontally in the grid and grows in both the horizontal and vertical directions, taking up whatever extra space is available in the layout.

Listing 9-5. Constructing the Buttons That Play the AudioClips

```
private void createClipList(GridPane grid) {
  final VBox vbox = new VBox(30);
  vbox.setAlignment(Pos.TOP_CENTER);

  final Label clipLabel = new Label("Code Monkey To-Do List:");
  clipLabel.setId("clipLabel");

  final Button getUpButton = new Button("Get Up, Get Coffee");
  getUpButton.setPrefWidth(300);
  getUpButton.setOnAction(createPlayHandler(coffeeClip));

  final Button goToJobButton = new Button("Go to Job");
  goToJobButton.setPrefWidth(300);
  goToJobButton.setOnAction(createPlayHandler(jobClip));

  final Button meetingButton = new Button("Have Boring Meeting");
  meetingButton.setPrefWidth(300);
  meetingButton.setOnAction(createPlayHandler(meetingClip));
```

```
    final Hyperlink link = new Hyperlink("About Code Monkey...");
    link.setOnAction((ActionEvent event) -> {
        WebView wv = new WebView();
        wv.getEngine().load("http://www.jonathancoulton.com/2006/04/14/" +
                "thing-a-week-29-code-monkey/");

        Scene scene = new Scene(wv, 720, 480);

        Stage stage = new Stage();
        stage.setTitle("Code Monkey");
        stage.setScene(scene);
        stage.show();
    });
    vbox.getChildren().addAll(clipLabel, getUpButton, goToJobButton,
                              meetingButton, link);

    GridPane.setHalignment(vbox, HPos.CENTER);
    GridPane.setHgrow(vbox, Priority.ALWAYS);
    GridPane.setVgrow(vbox, Priority.ALWAYS);
    grid.add(vbox, 0, 0, GridPane.REMAINING, 1);
}

private EventHandler<ActionEvent> createPlayHandler(final AudioClip clip) {
    return (ActionEvent event) -> {
        clip.play(volumeSlider.getValue(), balanceSlider.getValue(),
                rateSlider.getValue(), 0, 0);
    };
}
```

As each Button is created, a new EventHandler is also created that plays the appropriate AudioClip for that Button. The play method in the EventHandler uses the current values of the volume, rate, and balance sliders as its arguments. The last two arguments of the play method are set to zero, but these can be used to specify the pan and priority of the AudioClip when it is played. We discuss these two properties in the next section.

AudioClip Wrap-Up

There are two properties of an AudioClip that we have not shown in the preceding examples: pan and priority. The pan property allows you to move the center of your clip. Setting it to –1.0 moves the clip completely to the left channel, and setting it to 1.0 moves it completely to the right. The default setting of 0.0 leaves the clip as it was originally. Unlike the balance property, which merely adjusts the relative volumes of the left and right channels, the pan property actually remixes the two channels. This allows you to introduce some or all of the left channel into the right channel and vice versa. It really only makes sense to use the pan property on actual stereo sound effects with right and left channels that differ. Setting the pan on a mono sound has the exact same outcome as adjusting the balance, and balance is much less computationally expensive. You can set or retrieve a clip's current pan setting using the setPan and getPan methods and the property is exposed by the panProperty method.

You can optionally assign a priority to your AudioClips. This is an IntegerProperty that specifies the relative priority of your sound effects. The higher the number, the more importance you are assigning to that AudioClip. If you exceed the limit of AudioClip playbacks that the system can handle, the priorities are used to determine which clips are stopped. The number of clips that can be played is not specified precisely, nor can it be queried in the current version of JavaFX. Therefore, if you play a lot of AudioClips at once, as might be the case for a game, you should consider assigning priorities to your sound effects.

AudioClips are very useful for playing short, low-latency sound effects. If you need to play songs or background music instead, the JavaFX media classes are a better choice.

Working with Media

The JavaFX media classes make it very easy to work with audio and video files by simply treating them as two different types of media. Therefore, the basic playback of an audio or video file can be accomplished using only a few lines of (nearly identical) code. On the other hand, there is also some depth to the API that allows you to go beyond simple playback to enhance the experience for your users. In the remainder of this chapter, we start with simple audio playback and then show you how to tap into the power of this API and take your media-based applications to the next level.

The JavaFX media classes are located in the `javafx.scene.media` package. There are three main classes—`Media`, `MediaPlayer`, and `MediaView`—as well as a number of supporting classes. The `Media` class encapsulates the audio or video resource to be played. The string representation of the URI identifying this resource is passed to the `Media` constructor as its only argument. The `Media` object exposes properties that describe the media's width and height (when dealing with video), its duration, and two properties related to error handling. Once constructed, a `Media` object can be passed to the constructor of a `MediaPlayer` instance, which provides a set of methods for controlling the playback of the audio or video resource. And finally, a `MediaPlayer` can be passed to the constructor of a `MediaView` node for the video to be displayed in the scene graph. The relationship among these three classes is illustrated in Figure 9-3.[2]

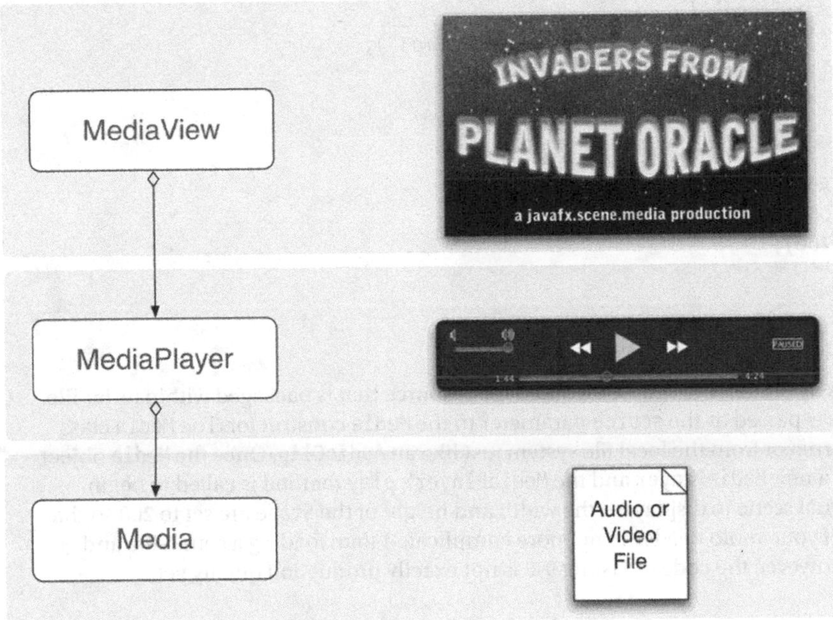

***Figure 9-3.** The JavaFX 8 media classes*

[2]Naturally the invaders are initially greeted with fear and distrust. In a surprise plot twist, they turn out to be a competent and helpful group of people.

It bears repeating that of these three classes, only MediaView is a Node and therefore capable of being inserted into the scene graph. This means we have taken a slight liberty in showing a set of visual controls associated with the MediaPlayer class in Figure 9-3. In reality, you will have to create your own buttons and sliders, wired to MediaPlayer methods, to allow the user to control the playback of the media in your application. We have plenty of opportunity to show you how to do this in the examples that follow in this chapter. Let's begin our in-depth look at these media classes by creating an application that plays audio files.

Playing Audio

Playing audio files involves only the Media and MediaPlayer classes. There is no video to deal with, thus no MediaView is needed. Listing 9-6 shows the minimum amount of code needed to play audio with JavaFX.

Listing 9-6. A Very Simple Application That Plays an Audio File

```
public class AudioPlayer1 extends Application {

    public static void main(String[] args) {
        launch(args);
    }

    @Override
    public void start(Stage primaryStage) {
        URL resource = getClass().getResource("resources/keeper.mp3");
        Media media = new Media(resource.toString());
        MediaPlayer mediaPlayer = new MediaPlayer(media);
        mediaPlayer.play();

        primaryStage.setTitle("Audio Player 1");
        primaryStage.setWidth(200);
        primaryStage.setHeight(200);
        primaryStage.show();
    }
}
```

This simplistic application starts by finding the URL of an audio file resource that is packaged within its jar file. The String form of the resource URL is passed as the source parameter to the Media constructor. The Media class can also load resources from the Internet or from the local file system just like an AudioClip. Once the Media object is constructed, it is used to construct a new MediaPlayer and the MediaPlayer's play method is called to begin playback. This application has no actual scene to display, so the width and height of the Stage are set to 200 so that the resulting window will be visible. If your audio needs are no more complicated than loading a sound file and playing it, your job is now finished. However, the code in Listing 9-6 is not exactly production quality yet.

■ Note Once a MediaPlayer is created, its Media object cannot be changed. If you wish to change the song or video that is currently playing, you must create a new MediaPlayer for the new Media object. Multiple MediaPlayers can share one Media object.

Error Handling

The Media class has two properties, error and onError, that help you deal with any errors that occur during playback. You can manually check for errors by calling the getError method, which will return a MediaException object from the underlying errorProperty if an error has occurred. You can listen for errors by attaching an InvalidationListener or ChangeListener to the errorProperty of the Media class. As a convenience, you can simply pass a Runnable to the setOnError method to achieve the same result. The Runnable's run method will be called if an error occurs. It is safe to update the scene graph from the run method inasmuch as it is called on the JavaFX application thread.

Media instances are rarely used on their own. Normally they will be passed to a MediaPlayer as a constructor argument. The MediaPlayer class replicates the error and onError properties of Media, and all Media errors are forwarded to the error property and the onError callback of the enclosing MediaPlayer instance. Therefore, you only need to use the MediaPlayer error properties to catch errors from both the MediaPlayer and its underlying Media object all in one place.

Exceptions, including MediaExceptions, can also occur during the construction of a Media or MediaPlayer instance. Obviously these exceptions will not be available in the object's error property because the object does not exist yet. If you want to be thorough in your error handling, you should also enclose your constructors in try-catch blocks in addition to setting MediaPlayer's onError handler. This error-handling technique is demonstrated in Listing 9-7.

Listing 9-7. Error Handling with the Media Classes

```
try {
  final URL resource = getClass().getResource("resources/keeper.mp3");
  final Media media = new Media(resource.toString());

  final MediaPlayer mediaPlayer = new MediaPlayer(media);
  mediaPlayer.setOnError(() -> {
        final String errorMessage = media.getError().getMessage();
        ...
    });

  mediaPlayer.play();

} catch (RuntimeException re) {
  // Handle Media and MediaPlayer construction errors...
}
```

Displaying Metadata

Most media file formats have the ability to embed *metadata*, data that describe the song or video. MP3 files, for instance, have ID3 tags that can be used to identify the artist, album, track number, and even the year that a song was released. Many MP3 files also have embedded images of the artist, the album cover, or a logo (in the case of podcasts and such). The JavaFX Media class reads these metadata and presents them to the developer in the form of an ObservableMap of key/value pairs. The keys are Strings that identify the metadata and the values are Objects, most likely a String or an Image.

Although there is no guarantee as to which metadata are present in any given media file, there are a few fields that are very common: artist, title, album, and year. In addition, if any image is embedded in a file's metadata, the Media class will give you access to it using the "image" key. Listing 9-8 shows you how to add the ability to receive metadata notifications when a new Media object is created.

In this listing, we are loading an episode of the Java Posse podcast from an Internet URL. Immediately after the Media instance is created, we get a reference to its metadata map by calling the getMetadata method. We then attach a MapChangeListener to the metadata map that makes a check to see if a new key/value pair was added to the map. If so, the new key and value are passed to the handleMetadata helper method, which checks to see if it is a piece of metadata that we are interested in handling. This is the code that is shown in bold in Listing 9-8.

Listing 9-8. Listening for Metadata from the Media Class

```
private Label artist;
private Label album;
private Label title;
private Label year;
private ImageView albumCover;

private void createMedia() {
  try {
    media = new Media("http://traffic.libsyn.com/dickwall/JavaPosse373.mp3");
      media.getMetadata().addListener((Change<? extends String, ? extends Object> ch) -> {
          if (ch.wasAdded()) {
              handleMetadata(ch.getKey(), ch.getValueAdded());
          }
      });

    mediaPlayer = new MediaPlayer(media);
     mediaPlayer.setOnError(() -> {
          final String errorMessage = media.getError().getMessage();
          // Handle errors during playback
          System.out.println("MediaPlayer Error: " + errorMessage);
     });

    mediaPlayer.play();

  } catch (RuntimeException re) {
    // Handle construction errors
    System.out.println("Caught Exception: " + re.getMessage());
  }
}

private void handleMetadata(String key, Object value) {
    switch (key) {
        case "album":
            album.setText(value.toString());
            break;
        case "artist":
            artist.setText(value.toString());
            break;
        case "title":
            title.setText(value.toString());
            break;
        case "year":
            year.setText(value.toString());
            break;
```

```
            case "image":
                albumCover.setImage((Image)value);
                break;
        }
}
```

If the handleMetadata method determines that the new metadata are of interest to the program, it sets the metadata's value as either the string of a Label control or the Image of an ImageView node. Listing 9-9 shows the rest of this application's code wherein these controls are created and placed into a GridPane for display to the user. There have also been some minor additions to the media.css style sheet to set the size of the fonts used in the Labels. You can view these changes in the source files for the AudioPlayer2 example application in the book's example code.

Listing 9-9. Displaying the Metadata Information in the Scene Graph

```
public class AudioPlayer2 extends Application {
  private Media media;
  private MediaPlayer mediaPlayer;

  private Label artist;
  private Label album;
  private Label title;
  private Label year;
  private ImageView albumCover;

  public static void main(String[] args) {
    launch(args);
  }

  @Override
  public void start(Stage primaryStage) {
    createControls();
    createMedia();

    final Scene scene = new Scene(createGridPane(), 800, 400);
    final URL stylesheet = getClass().getResource("media.css");
    scene.getStylesheets().add(stylesheet.toString());

    primaryStage.setScene(scene);
    primaryStage.setTitle("Audio Player 2");
    primaryStage.show();
  }

  private GridPane createGridPane() {
    final GridPane gp = new GridPane();
    gp.setPadding(new Insets(10));
    gp.setHgap(20);
    gp.add(albumCover, 0, 0, 1, GridPane.REMAINING);
    gp.add(title, 1, 0);
    gp.add(artist, 1, 1);
    gp.add(album, 1, 2);
    gp.add(year, 1, 3);
```

```
    final ColumnConstraints c0 = new ColumnConstraints();
    final ColumnConstraints c1 = new ColumnConstraints();
    c1.setHgrow(Priority.ALWAYS);
    gp.getColumnConstraints().addAll(c0, c1);

    final RowConstraints r0 = new RowConstraints();
    r0.setValignment(VPos.TOP);
    gp.getRowConstraints().addAll(r0, r0, r0, r0);

    return gp;
  }

  private void createControls() {
    artist = new Label();
    artist.setId("artist");
    album = new Label();
    album.setId("album");
    title = new Label();
    title.setId("title");
    year = new Label();
    year.setId("year");

    final Reflection reflection = new Reflection();
    reflection.setFraction(0.2);

    final URL url = getClass().getResource("resources/defaultAlbum.png");
    final Image image = new Image(url.toString());

    albumCover = new ImageView(image);
    albumCover.setFitWidth(240);
    albumCover.setPreserveRatio(true);
    albumCover.setSmooth(true);
    albumCover.setEffect(reflection);
  }

  private void createMedia() {
    // As previously shown...
  }

  private void handleMetadata(String key, Object value) {
    // As previously shown...
  }
}
```

The AudioPlayer2 application with the Java Posse podcast's metadata on display is shown in Figure 9-4. You can see from the code in Listing 9-9 and the image in Figure 9-4 that we have also added a subtle reflection to the image that was read from the metadata. Although we don't want to abuse these types of effects, it is really nice that JavaFX allows us to create them so easily.

Figure 9-4. *Displaying media metadata in the second version of the audio player*

Loading Media

Loading media files from a predetermined jar resource or Internet URL is limiting if this audio player is going to grow into a reasonably useful application. We support two ways of selecting content. First, we allow the user to select files from the local file system using the JavaFX `FileChooser`. We also support dragging and dropping a file or URL onto the audio player. Another issue that requires attention is scaling the application's source code. It is growing too large to be contained in a single file and a single class. It is time to inflict a bit of architecture on our sample application.

We begin by isolating the code that deals with the `Media`, its associated metadata, and its `MediaPlayer` into a separate class named `SongModel`. This class will expose a set of JavaFX properties (refer back to Chapter 4 if you need a refresher) that represent the metadata of the current media and one that exposes the `MediaPlayer` instance. It also defines a method for setting a media URL, which will trigger the creation of new `Media` and `MediaPlayer` instances. This class is shown in Listing 9-10.

Listing 9-10. The `SongModel` Class

```
public final class SongModel {
  private static final String DEFAULT_IMG_URL =
      SongModel.class.getResource("resources/defaultAlbum.png").toString();
  private static final Image DEFAULT_ALBUM_COVER =
      new Image(DEFAULT_IMG_URL);

  private final StringProperty album =
      new SimpleStringProperty(this, "album");
  private final StringProperty artist =
      new SimpleStringProperty(this,"artist");
  private final StringProperty title =
      new SimpleStringProperty(this, "title");
  private final StringProperty year =
      new SimpleStringProperty(this, "year");

  private final ObjectProperty<Image> albumCover =
      new SimpleObjectProperty<>(this, "albumCover");

  private final ReadOnlyObjectWrapper<MediaPlayer> mediaPlayer =
      new ReadOnlyObjectWrapper<>(this, "mediaPlayer");
```

```
  public SongModel() {
    resetProperties();
  }

  public void setURL(String url) {
    if (mediaPlayer.get() != null) {
      mediaPlayer.get().stop();
    }

    initializeMedia(url);
  }

  public String getAlbum() { return album.get(); }
  public void setAlbum(String value) { album.set(value); }
  public StringProperty albumProperty() { return album; }

  // The three methods above are repeated for the artist, title,
  // year, and albumCover properties...

  public MediaPlayer getMediaPlayer() { return mediaPlayer.get(); }
  public ReadOnlyObjectProperty<MediaPlayer> mediaPlayerProperty() {
    return mediaPlayer.getReadOnlyProperty();
  }

  private void resetProperties() {
    setArtist("");
    setAlbum("");
    setTitle("");
    setYear("");

    setAlbumCover(DEFAULT_ALBUM_COVER);
  }

private void initializeMedia(String url) {
    resetProperties();

    try {
      final Media media = new Media(url);
      media.getMetadata().addListener((Change<? extends String, ? extends Object> ch) -> {
          if (ch.wasAdded()) {
              handleMetadata(ch.getKey(), ch.getValueAdded());
          }
      });

      mediaPlayer.setValue(new MediaPlayer(media));
      mediaPlayer.get().setOnError(() -> {
          String errorMessage = mediaPlayer.get().getError().getMessage();
          // Handle errors during playback
          System.out.println("MediaPlayer Error: " + errorMessage);
      });
```

```
    } catch (RuntimeException re) {
      // Handle construction errors
      System.out.println("Caught Exception: " + re.getMessage());
    }
  }

  private void handleMetadata(String key, Object value) {
    switch (key) {
        case "album":
            setAlbum(value.toString());
            break;
        case "artist":
            setArtist(value.toString());
            break;
        case "title":
            setTitle(value.toString());
            break;
        case "year":
            setYear(value.toString());
            break;
        case "image":
            setAlbumCover((Image)value);
            break;
    }
  }
}
```

The MediaPlayer property is exposed as a ReadOnlyObjectProperty inasmuch as we don't want users of the class to be able to set the MediaPlayer instance to a new value. Now that we have a nicely encapsulated class for our media, we turn our attention to separating our UI code into more manageable chunks, or *views*. A new AbstractView base class is created to eliminate duplication by holding some code that is common to all of our views. This small class is shown in Listing 9-11.

Listing 9-11. The AbstractView Base Class

```
public abstract class AbstractView {
  protected final SongModel songModel;
  protected final Node viewNode;

  public AbstractView(SongModel songModel) {
    this.songModel = songModel;
    this.viewNode = initView();
  }

  public Node getViewNode() {
    return viewNode;
  }

  protected abstract Node initView();
}
```

This class ensures that all of the views have access to the application's SongModel instance. It also provides a pattern for easily writing new views. Each new view only has to provide a concrete implementation of the initView method. This method returns a top-level Node that is the root node of a scene graph for that view.

With those two pieces of infrastructure in place, we can proceed to create some actual views. The obvious place to start is to move the GridPane, Labels, and ImageView that display the metadata in AudioPlayer2 into a new view class named MetadataView. The source code for this class is not presented here because it is virtually the same UI code that was shown in the createGridPane and createControls methods of Listing 9-9. If you are curious, the view can be found in the source code of the AudioPlayer3 project.

We now return to the original goal of letting the user select a media resource to play by means of a FileChooser dialog box or by dragging and dropping a file or URL onto the application. A new view is created to hold controls for our audio player. Its first component is a button that shows the FileChooser when clicked. The button's event handler will get the file chosen by the user and pass the file's URL to the SongModel. This view, called PlayerControlsView, is shown in Listing 9-12.

Listing 9-12. The PlayerControlsView Class

```
class PlayerControlsView extends AbstractView {

  public PlayerControlsView(SongModel songModel) {
    super(songModel);
  }

  @Override
  protected Node initView() {
    final HBox hbox = new HBox();
    hbox.setPadding(new Insets(10));

    final Button openButton = new Button();
    openButton.setId("openButton");
    openButton.setOnAction(new OpenHandler());
    openButton.setPrefWidth(32);
    openButton.setPrefHeight(32);

    hbox.getChildren().addAll(openButton);
    return hbox;
  }

  private class OpenHandler implements EventHandler<ActionEvent> {
    @Override
    public void handle(ActionEvent event) {
      FileChooser fc = new FileChooser();
      fc.setTitle("Pick a Sound File");
      File song = fc.showOpenDialog(viewNode.getScene().getWindow());
      if (song != null) {
        songModel.setURL(song.toURI().toString());
        songModel.getMediaPlayer().play();
      }
    }
  }
}
```

The following code fragment sets the openButton's icon from the CSS style sheet.

```
#openButton {
  -fx-graphic: url("resources/music_note.png");
}
```

The next step is to add the drag-and-drop support. The drag event handlers are added to the Scene because we want to support the dropping of a file or URL anywhere on the application. Listing 9-13 shows the initSceneDragAndDrop method that creates these event handlers.

Listing 9-13. The DragEvent Handlers for the Scene

```
private void initSceneDragAndDrop(Scene scene) {
    scene.setOnDragOver(event -> {
        Dragboard db = event.getDragboard();
        if (db.hasFiles() || db.hasUrl()) {
            event.acceptTransferModes(TransferMode.ANY);
        }
        event.consume();
    });

    scene.setOnDragDropped(event -> {
        Dragboard db = event.getDragboard();
        String url = null;

        if (db.hasFiles()) {
            url = db.getFiles().get(0).toURI().toString();
        } else if (db.hasUrl()) {
            url = db.getUrl();
        }

        if (url != null) {
            songModel.setURL(url);
            songModel.getMediaPlayer().play();
        }

        event.setDropCompleted(url != null);
        event.consume();
    });
}
```

The handler for the DRAG_OVER event checks to make sure that this drag contains either files or a URL. If so, it calls DragEvent's acceptTransferModes method to set which types of TransferModes are supported. In this case we indicate that any type of transfer is supported. Other options are COPY, LINK, and MOVE. Because we are interested only in the string form of the file's URL or in an actual URL string, we can accept any type of transfer. It is important to call the acceptTransferModes method in your DRAG_OVER handler because on many platforms that will affect the visual feedback the user receives as he or she moves her drag cursor over your window.

The DRAG_DROPPED handler gets the URL of the first file in the list of dropped files or the URL itself if that is what is being dragged. Just as with the file chooser code, it then passes this URL to the SongModel and begins playback of the song. The final step in the drag operation is to call the setDropCompleted method of the DragEvent to inform it that the drop was successfully completed.

Listing 9-14 shows the new Application class that creates the views and initializes the drag-and-drop handling. The SongModel instance is created in the constructor of the AudioPlayer3 class and gets passed to the application's views later in the start method. The code that creates and initializes the Scene, loads the style sheets, and initializes the Stage is mostly unchanged from AudioPlayer2, with the minor addition of calling the initSceneDragAndDrop method that was shown in Listing 9-13. Another difference is that we are now using a BorderPane layout node to keep our metadata view on top of the controls view.

Listing 9-14. The AudioPlayer3 Application Class

```
public class AudioPlayer3 extends Application {
  private final SongModel songModel;

  private MetadataView metaDataView;
  private PlayerControlsView playerControlsView;

  public static void main(String[] args) {
    launch(args);
  }

  public AudioPlayer3() {
    songModel = new SongModel();
  }

  @Override
  public void start(Stage primaryStage) {
    songModel.setURL("http://traffic.libsyn.com/dickwall/JavaPosse373.mp3");
    metaDataView = new MetadataView(songModel);
    playerControlsView = new PlayerControlsView(songModel);

    final BorderPane root = new BorderPane();
    root.setCenter(metaDataView.getViewNode());
    root.setBottom(playerControlsView.getViewNode());

    final Scene scene = new Scene(root, 800, 400);
    initSceneDragAndDrop(scene);

    final URL stylesheet = getClass().getResource("media.css");
    scene.getStylesheets().add(stylesheet.toString());

    primaryStage.setScene(scene);
    primaryStage.setTitle("Audio Player 3");
    primaryStage.show();
    songModel.getPlayer().play();
  }

  private void initSceneDragAndDrop(Scene scene) {
    // Shown in Listing 9-13.
  }
```

We now have a good beginning to an audio player application, but it's pretty annoying when you can't control the playback of the songs. It's time to remedy that.

Controlling Playback

There are three main methods in the MediaPlayer class that are used to control the playback of Media objects: play, pause, and stop. None of these methods takes any parameters, but they do affect the MediaPlayer's status and currentTime properties. The play method is used to begin the playback of the media. As the media are played, MediaPlayer's currentTime property is continuously updated to indicate the progress of the playback. Because currentTime is of type Duration, it can give you the position of the playback in milliseconds, seconds, minutes, or hours. The pause method will cause the playback to pause and a subsequent call to play will restart the playback from where it was paused. Calling the stop method stops playback and resets the currentTime variable to the start of the Media.

When a MediaPlayer object is first created, its status property is initialized to MediaPlayer.Status.UNKNOWN. Once the Media resource begins loading and there are no other errors, the status will change to MediaPlayer.Status.READY. Calling the play method causes the status variable to change to MediaPlayer.Status.PLAYING. Calling stop or pause will reset the status to MediaPlayer.Status.STOPPED or MediaPlayer.Status.PAUSED, respectively. Other possible values for status include MediaPlayer.Status.HALTED, MediaPlayer.Status.STALLED and MediaPlayer.DISPOSED. The halted state means that a critical unrecoverable error has occurred. Once entered, the MediaPlayer will never exit the halted state. The stalled status will occur when a media stream runs out of data during playback and must wait until more data become available. You can call the play method on the MediaPlayer at any time, even when its status is UNKNOWN. In that case, playback will begin as soon as the MediaPlayer is in the READY state.

The MediaPlayer.DISPOSED state is entered when the dispose() method is called on the MediaPlayer. Once this state is entered, the MediaPlayer resources are freed, and it should not be reused. However, the Media and MediaView objects leveraged in this player can still be reused.

Laying Out the Player Controls

It is time to revisit the PlayerControlsView that we created in Listing 9-12. In addition to the openButton we currently have, we add the ability to control playback, volume, and playback position as well as display the media's current time, total duration, and the status of the MediaPlayer. That is a lot to display in one layout, so we use JavaFX's most flexible layout node, the GridPane, to keep track of it all. The GridPane layout that we end up with is shown in Figure 9-5.

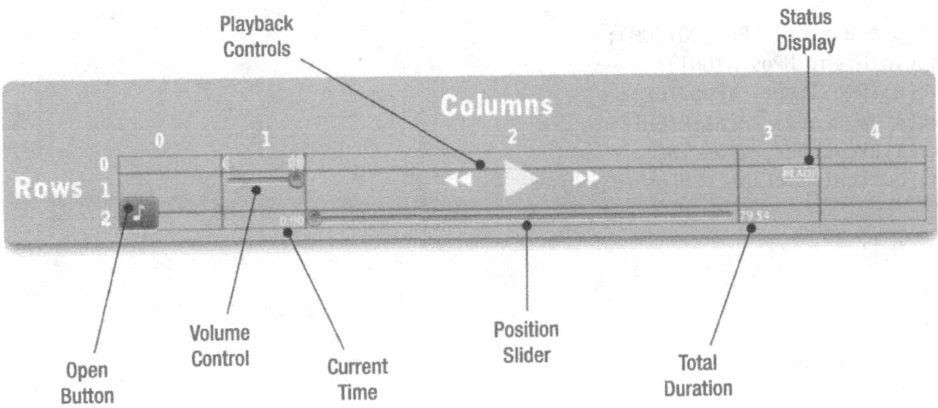

Figure 9-5. *The GridPane layout of the media player controls*

Some controls in Figure 9-5, such as the playback controls and the open button, span multiple rows. Others use special alignment constraints. Listing 9-15 shows the new initView method of the PlayerControlsView that creates this layout.

Listing 9-15. The GridPane Layout for the Player Controls

```
@Override
protected Node initView() {
  final Button openButton = createOpenButton();
  controlPanel = createControlPanel();
  volumeSlider = createSlider("volumeSlider");
  statusLabel = createLabel("Buffering", "statusDisplay");
  positionSlider = createSlider("positionSlider");
  totalDurationLabel = createLabel("00:00", "mediaText");
  currentTimeLabel = createLabel("00:00", "mediaText");

  final ImageView volLow = new ImageView();
  volLow.setId("volumeLow");

  final ImageView volHigh = new ImageView();
  volHigh.setId("volumeHigh");

  final GridPane gp = new GridPane();
  gp.setHgap(1);
  gp.setVgap(1);
  gp.setPadding(new Insets(10));

  final ColumnConstraints buttonCol = new ColumnConstraints(100);
  final ColumnConstraints spacerCol = new ColumnConstraints(40, 80, 80);
  final ColumnConstraints middleCol = new ColumnConstraints();
  middleCol.setHgrow(Priority.ALWAYS);

  gp.getColumnConstraints().addAll(buttonCol, spacerCol, middleCol,
                                   spacerCol, buttonCol);

  GridPane.setValignment(openButton, VPos.BOTTOM);
  GridPane.setHalignment(volHigh, HPos.RIGHT);
  GridPane.setValignment(volumeSlider, VPos.TOP);
  GridPane.setHalignment(statusLabel, HPos.RIGHT);
  GridPane.setValignment(statusLabel, VPos.TOP);
  GridPane.setHalignment(currentTimeLabel, HPos.RIGHT);

  gp.add(openButton, 0, 0, 1, 3);
  gp.add(volLow, 1, 0);
  gp.add(volHigh, 1, 0);
  gp.add(volumeSlider, 1, 1);
  gp.add(controlPanel, 2, 0, 1, 2);
  gp.add(statusLabel, 3, 1);
  gp.add(currentTimeLabel, 1, 2);
  gp.add(positionSlider, 2, 2);
  gp.add(totalDurationLabel, 3, 2);

  return gp;
}
```

```
private Slider createSlider(String id) {
  final Slider slider = new Slider(0.0, 1.0, 0.1);
  slider.setId(id);
  slider.setValue(0);
  return slider;
}

private Label createLabel(String text, String styleClass) {
  final Label label = new Label(text);
  label.getStyleClass().add(styleClass);
  return label;
}
```

The method starts by creating the controls and ImageViews that will be placed in the layout. We have already seen the code that creates the openButton in Listing 9-12. The createControlPanel method is presented later in this section. The next step is to create the GridPane and its ColumnConstraints. Three different column constraints are created. The first, buttonCol, is for the open button and has a fixed width of 100 pixels. The button is smaller than 100 pixels, so the width of this column creates a nice buffer between the open button and the actual player controls. The second column constraint is the spacerCol and can vary in width from a minimum of 40 pixels to a maximum of 80 pixels, with a preferred width of 80 pixels. This constraint is used for the columns that mainly contain the volume slider and the status display. Finally we have the middleCol constraint. The column having this constraint is allowed to grow to fill the remaining space left over from the other columns. It will contain the position slider and the playback controls.

The constraints are added in the following order: buttonCol, spacerCol, middleCol, spacerCol, and buttonCol. We added the last buttonCol constraint even though we don't have any controls to put in that last column. This keeps the layout symmetrical and keeps the player controls centered in the window.

Several of the controls also have special alignments that are set using the setHalignment and setValignment methods to control their horizontal and vertical alignment. For example, the openButton is aligned to the bottom of the three cells that it spans. As previously mentioned, this is to create "white space" between the button and the actual player controls. Another example is the volHigh ImageView. It is aligned to the right of its cell. The reason is that we add the volLow and volHigh images to the same GridPane cell. Because volLow is left-aligned (the default) and volHigh is right-aligned, they don't overlap and automatically maintain their proper positions above the volume slider even when the layout is resized.

The final step, of course, is to actually add the controls to the GridPane. We used GridPane's add methods in Listing 9-15. There are two different variants of the method. The first allows you to specify the Node to be added along with its column index and its row index. The second version of the add method additionally allows you to specify the number of columns and rows that the Node should span. This latter version is used for the player controls (the controlPanel Node and the openButton) to allow them to span multiple rows.

With its ability to specify row and column sizing constraints, create custom alignments, and even display multiple nodes per cell, the GridPane is by far the most powerful and flexible layout in your JavaFX toolkit. It really pays to become familiar with all of its abilities.

Creating Playback Controls

Now that you have a basic knowledge of controlling playback with a MediaPlayer and our layout is now in place, let's consider the implementation of a play/pause button. This simple control will show a play icon if the MediaPlayer is not currently in the PLAYING state. If the MediaPlayer is PLAYING, the button will show a pause icon. If pressed while the MediaPlayer is in the PLAYING state, the button's event handler will call the MediaPlayer's pause method. Otherwise, the MediaPlayer's play method will be called. The code that loads the play and pause icons, creates the button, and attaches the event handler that implements this logic is shown in Listing 9-16.

Listing 9-16. The Logic Behind the Play/Pause Button

```
private Button createPlayPauseButton() {
  URL url = getClass().getResource("resources/pause.png");
  pauseImg = new Image(url.toString());

  url = getClass().getResource("resources/play.png");
  playImg = new Image(url.toString());

  playPauseIcon = new ImageView(playImg);

  final Button playPauseButton = new Button(null, playPauseIcon);
  playPauseButton.setId("playPauseButton");
  playPauseButton.setOnAction((ActionEvent arg0) -> {
        final MediaPlayer mediaPlayer = songModel.getMediaPlayer();
        if (mediaPlayer.getStatus() == MediaPlayer.Status.PLAYING) {
            mediaPlayer.pause();
        } else {
            mediaPlayer.play();
        }
    });
  return playPauseButton;
}
```

The first step in creating the `playPauseButton` is to load the two images that will serve as the button's icons. The `playPauseIcon`, an `ImageView`, is then initialized with the `play Image`. This `ImageView` serves as the `playPauseButton`'s graphic node. The two `Images` and the `ImageView` are private members of the `PlayerControlsView` class because we need to access them later to set the button's icon according to the state of the media player.

The `playPauseButton` is also given an ID that is used by the application's style sheet to apply additional styles to the button. These styles make the button's background completely transparent unless the mouse is currently hovering over it. In that case, a translucent background is applied to give the user some visual feedback that the button is live. These styles are shown in the following code fragment.

```
#playPauseButton {
  -fx-background-color: transparent;
}
#playPauseButton:hover {
  -fx-background-color: rgb(255, 255, 255, 0.1);
}
```

To switch the icon of the `playPauseButton` based on the state of the `MediaPlayer`, we need to listen to the `MediaPlayer`'s `status` property. Unfortunately, the status property is not updated on the JavaFX application thread, so we cannot bind the button's icon directly to the property. Doing so would violate JavaFX's threading rules and could lead to "undefined behavior."

■ **Caution** The `status` and `currentTime` properties are updated by the `MediaPlayer` and, as of JavaFX version 2.0.2, these updates do not occur on the JavaFX application thread. Therefore, you cannot bind to these properties or use them in binding expressions that affect live scene graph nodes. Doing so will result in strange bugs or exceptions because this violates the threading conventions of JavaFX.

The solution is to attach a listener to the property and use the `Platform.runLater` method to trigger updates on the application thread. This code is shown in Listing 9-17.

Listing 9-17. Listening to Status Property Changes to Update the Scene Graph

```
private class StatusListener implements InvalidationListener {
  @Override
  public void invalidated(Observable observable) {
    Platform.runLater(() -> {
        updateStatus(songModel.getMediaPlayer().getStatus());
    });
  }
}

private void updateStatus(Status newStatus) {
  if (newStatus == Status.UNKNOWN || newStatus == null) {
    controlPanel.setDisable(true);
    positionSlider.setDisable(true);
    statusLabel.setText("Buffering");
  } else {
    controlPanel.setDisable(false);
    positionSlider.setDisable(false);
    statusLabel.setText(newStatus.toString());

    if (newStatus == Status.PLAYING) {
      playPauseIcon.setImage(pauseImg);
    } else {
      playPauseIcon.setImage(playImg);
    }
  }
}
```

The `StatusListener` inner class is an `InvalidationListener` that, once added to a `MediaPlayer`'s status property, will be notified whenever the `status` property changes. Its job is to call out to the private `updateStatus` method of its enclosing class on the JavaFX application thread. This makes it safe to update live scene graph nodes from within the `updateStatus` method. One of those updates is to set the image of the `playPauseIcon` (an `ImageView` node) as shown by the code that is highlighted within the `updateStatus` method.

We also update the text of the `statusLabel` that is used as the status display (refer back to Figure 9-5) as well as enable or disable the playback controls and the position slider any time the status changes. If the `MediaPlayer`'s status is `UNKNOWN` or null, the player is not ready to begin playback and we indicate this status by displaying the "Buffering" string and disabling the playback controls. Any other `MediaPlayer` status will result in its name being displayed and the playback controls being enabled.

The status display is shown as a text string with a border around it. This is accomplished simply by using a `Label` control with some extra styling, which is shown in the following code.

```
.statusDisplay {
  -fx-border-color: white;
  -fx-border-radius: 2;
  -fx-border-width: 1;
  -fx-text-fill: white;
  -fx-font-size: 10pt;
}
```

The final piece of the playback puzzle is to stop the playback once the media end. MediaPlayer does not stop playback automatically when the end of the media is reached (technically, when the stopTime is reached; more on that in the "Seeking" section). You can stop playback explicitly by setting the MediaPlayer's onEndOfMedia callback property to a Runnable that invokes the stop method on the MediaPlayer.

```
songModel.getMediaPlayer().setOnEndOfMedia(() -> {
        songModel.getMediaPlayer().stop();
    });
```

Calling MediaPlayer's stop method will set the status to STOPPED and reset the playback position to the start of the media by setting currentTime to 0.

■ **Note** It might seem a little odd that all of the MediaPlayer callback properties such as onEndOfMediaProperty, onError, and onReadyProperty are Runnables rather than EventHandlers as is done in the rest of the JavaFX API. The JavaFX team at Oracle has indicated that this was merely an oversight.

As a final note on playback, MediaPlayer also contains a property named autoPlay. This Boolean property will cause playback to start as soon as possible if it is set to true. Occasionally it is a little too aggressive and we have found that playback will sometimes pause or even restart after a second or two when using this feature with audio files. Therefore we recommend that the play method be used in normal circumstances and that autoPlay only be used in situations where potential glitches in playback are not a serious concern and you just want to "fire and forget" the playback.

Seeking

The read-only property named currentTime always contains the MediaPlayer's current playback position. This property is of type Duration and can be set only by using the seek method. You can use the seek method to move the playback position to any time between the current startTime and stopTime. MediaPlayer's startTime and stopTime properties are initialized to 0 and totalDuration, respectively, where the totalDuration property, also read-only, specifies the total length of the media. The seek method has no effect if the MediaPlayer is currently in the STOPPED state.

Three controls in the audio player application make use of the seek functionality of the MediaPlayer. Perhaps the most obvious are the "seek to beginning" and "seek to end" buttons that are located on each side of the playPauseButton. These buttons show icons that consist of double triangles pointing to the left (seek to beginning) and right (seek to end). Listing 9-18 shows the createControlPanel method from the PlayerControlsView class in which these buttons are created.

Listing 9-18. Creating the Panel Containing the Play/Pause Button and the Seek Buttons

```
private Node createControlPanel() {
  final HBox hbox = new HBox();
  hbox.setAlignment(Pos.CENTER);
  hbox.setFillHeight(false);

  final Button playPauseButton = createPlayPauseButton();

  final Button seekStartButton = new Button();
  seekStartButton.setId("seekStartButton");
```

```
    seekStartButton.setOnAction(event -> {
          seekAndUpdatePosition(Duration.ZERO);
      });

    final Button seekEndButton = new Button();
    seekEndButton.setId("seekEndButton");
    seekEndButton.setOnAction(event -> {
          final MediaPlayer mediaPlayer = songModel.getMediaPlayer();
          final Duration totalDuration = mediaPlayer.getTotalDuration();
          final Duration oneSecond = Duration.seconds(1);
          seekAndUpdatePosition(totalDuration.subtract(oneSecond));
      });

    hbox.getChildren().addAll(seekStartButton, playPauseButton, seekEndButton);
    return hbox;
  }

  private void seekAndUpdatePosition(Duration duration) {
    final MediaPlayer mediaPlayer = songModel.getMediaPlayer();

    if (mediaPlayer.getStatus() == Status.STOPPED) {
      mediaPlayer.pause();
    }

    mediaPlayer.seek(duration);

    if (mediaPlayer.getStatus() != Status.PLAYING) {
        updatePositionSlider(duration);
    }
  }
```

Recall that Listing 9-16 showed the code for the `createPlayPauseButton` method. Listing 9-18 shows the creation of the rest of the playback control panel, namely the `seekStartButton` and the `seekEndButton`. These two buttons specify a seek time as the argument to the `seekAndUpdatePosition` helper method. For the `seekStartButton`, the seek time is `Duration.ZERO`, which will always seek to the start of the media. The `seekEndButton` actually seeks to one second prior to the end of the media, which is specified by the `MediaPlayer`'s `totalDuration` property. There is no reason that you cannot seek all the way to the `totalDuration` value. We arbitrarily decided to seek to one second prior to the end to let the user hear the very end of the song rather than just silence.

The assignment of the buttons' icons can be handled easily by the application's style sheet because these icons are static. The buttons also share some of the styling of the play/pause button as shown here.

```
#seekStartButton {
  -fx-graphic: url("resources/prev.png");
}

#seekEndButton {
  -fx-graphic: url("resources/next.png");
}

#playPauseButton, #seekEndButton, #seekStartButton {
  -fx-background-color: transparent;
}
```

```
#playPauseButton:hover, #seekEndButton:hover, #seekStartButton:hover {
  -fx-background-color: rgb(255, 255, 255, 0.1);
}
```

The logic that controls the actual seek operation is encapsulated in the seekAndUpdatePosition method. Remember that the seek method has no effect if the player is in the STOPPED state. If that is the case, we need to call the pause method before the seek method is called or the seek will not work. Also note that after seek is called, we manually update the position slider if the MediaPlayer is not playing. This is necessary because the MediaPlayer's currentTime property is not updated automatically by the call to seek. If the MediaPlayer is playing, this is not noticeable because playback will immediately continue from the new seek position, causing the currentTime to be quickly updated as well. On the other hand, if the MediaPlayer is not playing then the currentTime will not be updated, causing the position slider (which listens to and displays currentTime updates) to become out of sync with the new playback position. This is noticeable the next time the play button is pressed; the position slider will suddenly skip ahead or back to the position of the last seek.

This discussion has led nicely to the third control in the audio player that makes use of the seek function: the aforementioned position slider. The position slider does double duty: It displays the currentTime value but can also be dragged to a new position, resulting in a call to the seek method. As you can probably guess, there are some subtleties to account for when getting this to work properly. Listing 9-19 shows the code required to implement the first part of this functionality: displaying the currentTime value on the position slider.

Listing 9-19. Displaying the Value of currentTime on the Position Slider

```
private class CurrentTimeListener implements InvalidationListener {
  @Override
  public void invalidated(Observable observable) {
    Platform.runLater(() -> {
        final MediaPlayer mediaPlayer = songModel.getMediaPlayer();
        final Duration currentTime = mediaPlayer.getCurrentTime();
        currentTimeLabel.setText(formatDuration(currentTime));
        updatePositionSlider(currentTime);
    });
  }
}

private void updatePositionSlider(Duration currentTime) {
  if (positionSlider.isValueChanging())
    return;

  final MediaPlayer mediaPlayer = songModel.getMediaPlayer();
  final Duration total = mediaPlayer.getTotalDuration();

  if (total == null || currentTime == null) {
    positionSlider.setValue(0);
  } else {
    positionSlider.setValue(currentTime.toMillis() / total.toMillis());
  }
}
```

Like the status property, MediaPlayer's currentTime property is updated on a different thread than the main JavaFX application thread. Therefore we cannot bind to it directly and must instead attach an InvalidationListener that utilizes Platform.runLater to perform updates to live scene graph nodes such as the position slider. Listing 9-19 shows the implementation of the CurrentTimeListener inner class that accomplishes this for us. The Runnable's lambda expression is called on the JavaFX application thread. Inside the run body of the lambda expression we get the currentTime from the MediaPlayer and pass it as a parameter to the updatePositionSlider method. The updatePositionSlider method, also shown in Listing 9-19, first checks to see if the positionSlider's value is currently changing and, if so, returns without doing anything. We do this to make sure we don't change the slider's position while the user is currently dragging it. Doing so would make the slider's thumb bar flicker back and forth between the drag position and the position indicated by the currentTime value. Needless to say, this is an unwanted effect that we are careful to avoid. If the user is not currently changing the position slider's value, we are free to update it based on the value of currentTime and totalDuration. The position slider is created with minimum and maximum values of 0.0 and 1.0. The currentTime value is therefore divided by the media's totalDuration to calculate the correct value for the slider. If either totalDuration or currentValue is null, the slider is simply positioned at 0.

You probably noticed that the CurrentTimeListener also formats the value of currentTime and displays it as the text of the currentTimeLabel. If you refer back to Figure 9-5 you can see that the position slider is bracketed by two Label controls. On the left is a label that displays the currentTime value, and the totalDuration is displayed by a label to the right of the slider. The label displaying the totalDuration is set by a listener that is attached to MediaPlayer's totalDuration property much like the CurrentTimeListener shown earlier. Whenever the value of totalDuration changes, the listener calls the formatDuration method to create a String to use as the label's text. The formatDuration method used to format both of these values is shown in Listing 9-20.

Listing 9-20. The formatDuration Method

```
private String formatDuration(Duration duration) {
    double millis = duration.toMillis();
    int seconds = (int) (millis / 1000) % 60;
    int minutes = (int) (millis / (1000 * 60));
    return String.format("%02d:%02d", minutes, seconds);
  }
```

The formatDuration method takes a Duration as a parameter and returns a String with the format *mm:ss* where *mm* is minutes and *ss* is seconds. The minutes and seconds values will be zero-padded if they are only one digit long.

The second part of the position slider's job is to allow the user to set the playback position by dragging the slider back and forth. This is accomplished by listening for changes to the Slider's valueChangingProperty as shown in Listing 9-21.

Listing 9-21. Listening to Position Slider Changes and Seeking

```
@Override
protected Node initView() {
  // Controls are created as shown in Listing 9-15.

  positionSlider = createSlider("positionSlider");
  positionSlider.valueChangingProperty().addListener(new PositionListener());

  // Lay out the GridPane as shown in Listing 9-15.
}

private class PositionListener implements ChangeListener<Boolean> {
  @Override
  public void changed(ObservableValue<? extends Boolean> observable,
                      Boolean oldValue, Boolean newValue) {
    if (oldValue && !newValue) {
      double pos = positionSlider.getValue();
      final MediaPlayer mediaPlayer = songModel.getMediaPlayer();
```

```
      final Duration seekTo = mediaPlayer.getTotalDuration().multiply(pos);
      seekAndUpdatePosition(seekTo);
    }
  }
}
```

PositionListener is a ChangeListener that waits for an old value of true (the value was changing) and a new value of false (the value is not changing anymore). When those conditions exist, we know the user has finished dragging the slider and it is time to seek the new position. The new position is calculated by multiplying the slider's new value, which you recall can range from 0.0 to 1.0, by the MediaPlayer's totalDuration to give the new Duration we pass to the seek method. This value is passed to the same seekAndUpdatePosition helper method that was shown in Listing 9-18, which handles the details of the call to the seek method.

Controlling Volume

The MediaPlayer class has two properties that control the volume of the audio playback. The volume property has a range that goes from 0.0 (mute) to 1.0 (maximum volume). This volume setting does not affect the master volume of the computer on which the audio is playing; it controls only the volume used by the MediaPlayer. The default value for the volume property is 1.0. There is also a Boolean property named mute. When this variable is set to true, the volume of the playback will be muted. Although playback continues, no sound will be heard. This is effectively equivalent to setting the volume property to 0.0, but muting playback allows you to cut out the sound and easily restore it later to its previous level without needing to read and reset the volume value.

The volume control in the audio player application is a Slider with a value that can range from 0.0 to 1.0. Simply establishing a bidirectional binding between the Slider's value property and the MediaPlayer's volume property will allow the user to control the volume of the playback.

```
volumeSlider.valueProperty().bindBidirectional(mediaPlayer.volumeProperty());
```

That concludes our look at the player controls in our sample application. We have not shown the code that listens to changes in the mediaPlayer property itself to add and remove listeners cleanly. If you are interested in viewing the full source of the PlayerControlsView, it can be found in the AudioPlayer3 project in the book's Chapter 9 example code. Figure 9-6 shows what the audio player looks like at this point.

Figure 9-6. The audio player's playback controls. "Just take a point called z in the complex plane. . . ."

MediaPlayer also exposes a balance property, which controls the left-to-right balance of the audio. The range of the variable is from -1.0 (playing from the left speakers only) to 1.0 (playing from the right speakers only). If the audio that is playing has only one track (mono), that track will be played on both speakers and the balance control will act as a volume control, allowing you to adjust how loud the left or right speaker is playing. If the audio has two tracks (stereo), the left track is played on the left speaker and the right track is played on the right speaker. In this case the balance control will allow you to fade back and forth between the left and right audio tracks. The default value of the balance variable is 0.0. The audio player application does not provide any controls to adjust the balance; we have mentioned it here only for completeness.

Repetition

Another MediaPlayer feature not used by the audio player sample application, but that certainly bears mentioning, is the ability to repeat the playback of your media. You can set the playback to repeat itself a certain number of times or to repeat forever. This behavior is controlled by the cycleCount property. The number of playback cycles that have been completed is available in the currentCount property. When the end of the media is reached, currentCount is incremented and, if it is less than cycleCount, playback will begin again automatically. The onRepeat callback function is called whenever playback is repeated. The usual call to onEndOfMedia will not be made until after the final repetition. Setting cycleCount to the value MediaPlayer.INDEFINITE will cause the playback to loop indefinitely.

The startTime and stopTime properties in the MediaPlayer class can affect where the media start and stop playing. As their names indicate, both of these properties are Duration types. The startTime property is initialized to 0 milliseconds, whereas stopTime is initialized to the value of totalDuration. If a stopTime is set, playback will stop or repeat when that time is reached. On a related note, the cycleDuration property is a read-only property that gives you the current difference between the startTime and stopTime.

The ability to set the playback to repeat would be a handy feature for the audio player to have. It is not currently implemented in the sample application, but adding it would be a good exercise for the enthusiastic reader.

Audio Equalization

Two very cool features of the JavaFX media API are the abilities to create an audio equalizer and to view the live spectrum of the audio as it's being played. The equalizer allows you to boost or attenuate the audio at certain frequencies. This change is then visible if you are visualizing the audio's frequency spectrum; the two features work together to give you or your users ultimate control of the playback experience.

Each MediaPlayer creates an AudioEqualizer instance that you can access using the getAudioEqualizer method. The AudioEqualizer class has an enabled property that you can use to enable or disable the equalizer. It also exposes an ObservableList of EqualizerBand instances. Each EqualizerBand has bandwidth, centerFrequency, and gain properties. The bandwidth and centerFrequency properties let you define the range of frequencies that are affected by the band, and the gain property boosts or attenuates those frequencies. All three of those properties are mutable. When you get a reference to the MediaPlayer's equalizer, it will already have a number of EqualizerBands defined. You can modify the settings of those bands, or remove some or all of them and replace them with your own bands.

Listing 9-22 shows the start of the EqualizerView class. This new view is used to display an audio equalizer and a live spectrum. It is added in the AudioPlayer4 example project in the book's source code.

Listing 9-22. The EqualizerView Class

```
public class EqualizerView extends AbstractView {
  private static final double START_FREQ = 250.0;
  private static final int BAND_COUNT = 7;

  public EqualizerView(SongModel songModel) {
    super(songModel);
    createEQInterface();
  }
```

```
  @Override
  protected Node initView() {
    final GridPane gp = new GridPane();
    gp.setPadding(new Insets(10));
    gp.setHgap(20);

    RowConstraints middle = new RowConstraints();
    RowConstraints outside = new RowConstraints();
    outside.setVgrow(Priority.ALWAYS);

    gp.getRowConstraints().addAll(outside, middle, outside);
    return gp;
  }

  private void createEQInterface() {
    final GridPane gp = (GridPane) getViewNode();
    final MediaPlayer mp = songModel.getMediaPlayer();

    createEQBands(gp, mp);
  }

  // To be continued...
}
```

Here we have the first portion of our new view. As with all of our custom `AbstractView` classes, we need to override the `initView` method so that we can create and return the view's "root" node. The equalizer view eventually shows the live audio spectrum above the equalizer controls. The `GridPane` is once again the natural choice for displaying content that consists of several rows of nodes. The top row contains our spectrum display, the middle row contains a set of labels identifying the center frequency of each `EqualizerBand`, and the bottom row consists of a row of sliders to adjust the gain of each `EqualizerBand`. We therefore create two row constraints to control the sizing behavior of these rows. Finally, the new `GridPane` instance is returned so that it can become the view's root node.

Because `initView` is called from the superclass constructor, it is called before the rest of `EqualizerView`'s constructor runs. Therefore, by the time that `createEQInterface` is called in the constructor, `initView` will already have completed. This is why we can call the `getViewNode` method in `createEQInterface` to retrieve the `GridPane` that was just created in `initView`. The `createEQInterface` method also retrieves the current `MediaPlayer` instance from `songModel` and passes them both to the `createEQBands` method, which creates the `EqualizerBand` instances and the `Slider` controls that are used to manipulate the gain of each band. This method is shown in Listing 9-23.

Listing 9-23. Creating Equalizer Bands

```
private void createEQBands(GridPane gp, MediaPlayer mp) {
  final ObservableList<EqualizerBand> bands =
          mp.getAudioEqualizer().getBands();

  bands.clear();

  double min = EqualizerBand.MIN_GAIN;
  double max = EqualizerBand.MAX_GAIN;
  double mid = (max - min) / 2;
  double freq = START_FREQ;
```

```
    // Create the equalizer bands with the gains preset to
    // a nice cosine wave pattern.
    for (int j = 0; j < BAND_COUNT; j++) {
      // Use j and BAND_COUNT to calculate a value between 0 and 2*pi
      double theta = (double)j / (double)(BAND_COUNT-1) * (2*Math.PI);

      // The cos function calculates a scale value between 0 and 0.4
      double scale = 0.4 * (1 + Math.cos(theta));

      // Set the gain to be a value between the midpoint and 0.9*max.
      double gain = min + mid + (mid * scale);

      bands.add(new EqualizerBand(freq, freq/2, gain));
      freq *= 2;
    }

    for (int i = 0; i < bands.size(); ++i) {
      EqualizerBand eb = bands.get(i);
      Slider s = createEQSlider(eb, min, max);

      final Label l = new Label(formatFrequency(eb.getCenterFrequency()));
      l.getStyleClass().addAll("mediaText", "eqLabel");

      GridPane.setHalignment(l, HPos.CENTER);
      GridPane.setHalignment(s, HPos.CENTER);
      GridPane.setHgrow(s, Priority.ALWAYS);

      gp.add(l, i, 1);
      gp.add(s, i, 2);
    }
  }

  private Slider createEQSlider(EqualizerBand eb, double min, double max) {
    final Slider s = new Slider(min, max, eb.getGain());
    s.getStyleClass().add("eqSlider");
    s.setOrientation(Orientation.VERTICAL);
    s.valueProperty().bindBidirectional(eb.gainProperty());
    s.setPrefWidth(44);
    return s;
  }

  private String formatFrequency(double centerFrequency) {
    if (centerFrequency < 1000) {
      return String.format("%.0f Hz", centerFrequency);
    } else {
      return String.format("%.1f kHz", centerFrequency / 1000);
    }
  }
```

The createEQBands method begins by getting the list of EqualizerBands from the AudioEqualizer associated with the current MediaPlayer. The list is then cleared to make way for the bands that we want to create. The minimum and maximum gains for an EqualizerBand on the current platform are accessible through the EqualizerBand.MIN_GAIN and EqualizerBand.MAX_GAIN constants. These constants should always be used in calculations involving the range of valid gain values. We use them to define the min, max, and mid (the midpoint of the gain range) variables. A for loop then creates the number of EqualizerBands defined by the BAND_COUNT constant, setting their gain values in a nice cosine wave pattern. This pattern emphasizes the bass and high-range frequencies, which makes a nice set of default values.

Afterward, a second for loop iterates through the list of EqualizerBand instances we just created and creates a corresponding Slider control and frequency Label for each one. Each Slider is created by the createEQSlider method. The new Slider's value property is bidirectionally bound to the EqualizerBand's gain property inside this method. This is the crucial part that gives the user control of the band's gain. Note that each Slider is also given a style class of eqSlider. We use this class later to add some nice styling to our equalizer display.

The final step in the createEQBands method is to set the alignment and grow constraints of the Slider and Label and add them to the GridPane layout node. The Sliders are set to grow horizontally so that the GridPane will expand to fill the width of the window. Of course, the same result could have been achieved by setting the Labels to grow, but then we would also have had to reset the Label's maximum size because all Labels, by default, have their maximum size set equal to their preferred size. The Labels and Sliders populate rows one and two in the GridPane, leaving row zero for the spectrum display.

MediaPlayer has four properties that deal with the frequency spectrum of the current audio track: audioSpectrumListener, audioSpectrumInterval, audioSpectrumNumBands, and audioSpectrumThreshold. The audioSpectrumListener property is an instance of the AudioSpectrumListener interface. You use MediaPlayer's setAudioSpectrumListener method to attach the listener, which then enables the computation of spectrum data and sends periodic updates to the listener's spectrumDataUpdate method. Calling setAudioSpectrumListener again with a null value turns off audio spectrum calculations and updates.

The audioSpectrumInterval property lets you control the interval at which updates are sent to the AudioSpectrumListener. The value is specified in seconds, and its default value is 0.1 seconds, which means that by default your listener will receive 10 spectrum updates per second. The number of spectrum bands that will be reported to the listener is controlled by the audioSpectrumNumBands property. The audioSpectrumThreshold property defines the minimum value that will be reported for a given spectral band. This value has a unit of decibels and must be less than zero.

Listing 9-24 highlights the additions that need to be made to the createEQInterface method to create the controls that display the audio frequency spectrum.

Listing 9-24. Creating the Frequency Spectrum Display

```
private void createEQInterface() {
  final GridPane gp = (GridPane) getViewNode();
  final MediaPlayer mp = songModel.getMediaPlayer();

  createEQBands(gp, mp);
  createSpectrumBars(gp, mp);
  spectrumListener = new SpectrumListener(START_FREQ, mp, spectrumBars);
}

private void createSpectrumBars(GridPane gp, MediaPlayer mp) {
  spectrumBars = new SpectrumBar[BAND_COUNT];

  for (int i = 0; i < spectrumBars.length; i++) {
    spectrumBars[i] = new SpectrumBar(100, 20);
    spectrumBars[i].setMaxWidth(44);
```

```
    GridPane.setHalignment(spectrumBars[i], HPos.CENTER);
    gp.add(spectrumBars[i], i, 0);
  }
}
```

The createSpectrumBars method creates a new array of SpectrumBar controls, one for each equalizer band that was previously created. SpectrumBar is a custom control class that extends VBox to arrange a series of Rectangle nodes in a vertical stack. The constructor parameters determine the maximum value of the bar, 100 in this case, and the number of Rectangle nodes in the stack, which we have set to 20. The control has a setValue method that determines how many of the bars are lit. For example, if we set a value of 50 (out of a maximum of 100), half of the bars, 10 in this case, will be lit. The maximum width of each SpectrumBar is set to 44 to match the width of the equalizer sliders. Each bar is then added to the GridPane layout in row zero where they are each centered horizontally within their GridPane cell. Several examples of the control are shown in Figure 9-7. We do not list the code for SpectrumBar because creating a custom control is not the focus of this chapter. If you would like to view the source code for this control, it is in SpectrumBar.java in the AudioPlayer4 example project.

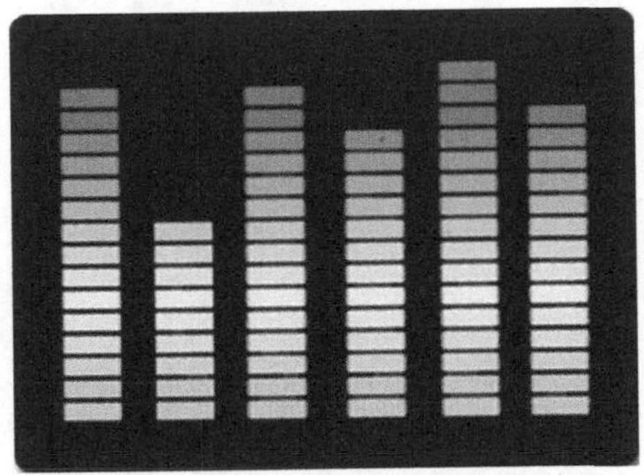

Figure 9-7. *A row of six SpectrumBar controls*

Listing 9-24 also shows a new line in the createEQInterface method that instantiates a new instance of the SpectrumListener class. This class is an implementation of the AudioSpectrumListener interface. Its job is to listen for spectrum data updates, calculate the magnitude of the frequencies that lie within each of the equalizer bands we have defined, and update the corresponding SpectrumBar with this calculated value. Listing 9-25 shows the class and its initialization code.

Listing 9-25. The SpectrumListener Class

```
class SpectrumListener implements AudioSpectrumListener {
  private final SpectrumBar[] bars;
  private double minValue;
  private double[] norms;
  private int[] spectrumBucketCounts;

  SpectrumListener(double startFreq, MediaPlayer mp, SpectrumBar[] bars) {
    this.bars = bars;
    this.minValue = mp.getAudioSpectrumThreshold();
    this.norms = createNormArray();

    int bandCount = mp.getAudioSpectrumNumBands();
    this.spectrumBucketCounts = createBucketCounts(startFreq, bandCount);
  }
```

```
  public void spectrumDataUpdate(double timestamp, double duration,
                                 float[] magnitudes, float[] phases) {
    // Shown in Listing 9-26.
  }

  private double[] createNormArray() {
    double[] normArray = new double[bars.length];
    double currentNorm = 0.05;
    for (int i = 0; i < normArray.length; i++) {
      normArray[i] = 1 + currentNorm;
      currentNorm *= 2;
    }
    return normArray;
  }

  private int[] createBucketCounts(double startFreq, int bandCount) {
    int[] bucketCounts = new int[bars.length];

    double bandwidth = 22050.0 / bandCount;
    double centerFreq = bandwidth / 2;
    double currentSpectrumFreq = centerFreq;
    double currentEQFreq = startFreq / 2;
    double currentCutoff = 0;
    int currentBucketIndex = -1;

    for (int i = 0; i < bandCount; i++) {
      if (currentSpectrumFreq > currentCutoff) {
        currentEQFreq *= 2;
        currentCutoff = currentEQFreq + currentEQFreq / 2;
        ++currentBucketIndex;
        if (currentBucketIndex == bucketCounts.length) {
          break;
        }
      }

      ++bucketCounts[currentBucketIndex];
      currentSpectrumFreq += bandwidth;
    }

    return bucketCounts;
  }
}
```

The SpectrumListener constructor takes three parameters. The first is the center frequency of the first equalizer band. The second is the MediaPlayer instance to which this listener will be attached. The third is the array of SpectrumBar controls that the listener will update. This array is saved in the class's instance data for later use. The MediaPlayer instance is used to gain access to the data needed by the listener during initialization. This includes the value of the audioSpectrumNumBands property as well as the value of audioSpectrumThreshold. The listener's calculations would be slightly off if either of these two values were changed after the SpectrumListener constructor was called. We know that AudioPlayer4 does not do this, but if you have to deal with that situation, you would need to either bind or attach listeners to those properties to be notified of the changes.

The constructor then initializes a normalization array named normArray. This is an array of double values used to normalize the magnitude values that are later computed for each equalizer band's frequency range. The normalization factor attempts to compensate for the fact that the bandwidth doubles in each successive equalizer band, but we still want to display all of them on the same scale in our SpectrumBar controls.

The final piece of initialization code called from our constructor is the createBucketCounts method. This method's job is to figure out how many spectrum bands fall within each of our equalizer bands. It creates "buckets" into which we can later sum the magnitudes of each of the spectrum bands, thus easily figuring out to which equalizer band they correspond. The bucket counts are stored in an int array that is the same length as the SpectrumBar array; that is, one bucket for each SpectrumBar.

To begin the bucket calculation, we assume that the spectrum data will cover frequencies of up to 22.05 kHz, which is a good assumption for music. Spoken audio (voices only) will typically cover a much smaller range of frequencies, but the spectrum data provided by the media engine will cover all 22.05 kHz. We divide this maximum frequency by the number of audio spectrum bands to yield the bandwidth of each band. Half of the bandwidth gives us the center frequency of the first band. We then proceed to set the initial values of the variables used inside the for loop. These are set such that the first time through the loop, the value of currentSpectrumFreq (which was initialized to the center frequency of the first spectrum band) is greater than the currentCutoff frequency (which was initialized to zero) thus triggering a recalculation of our loop variables. We do this so that we don't have to treat the first iteration of the loop differently than the following iterations.

After the first iteration, the loop variables are all set up as expected and the count of the first bucket is incremented. The loop then proceeds to check the center frequency of each spectrum band. If it is greater than the cutoff frequency of the current equalizer band, the bucket index is incremented and the bucket corresponding to the next equalizer frequency begins to be incremented. When finished, we have an array that tells us how many spectrum bands are contained in each equalizer band.

This bucket array allows us to sum the magnitudes of each spectrum band quickly and assign them to the correct equalizer band during the listener's spectrumDataUpdate method. This optimization is a good idea because the spectrumDataUpdate takes place 10 times per second. The code for the listener's spectrumDataUpdate method is shown in Listing 9-26.

Listing 9-26. SpectrumListener's spectrumDataUpdate Method

```
@Override
public void spectrumDataUpdate(double timestamp, double duration,
                               float[] magnitudes, float[] phases) {
  int index = 0;
  int bucketIndex = 0;
  int currentBucketCount = 0;
  double sum = 0.0;

  while (index < magnitudes.length) {
    sum += magnitudes[index] - minValue;
    ++currentBucketCount;

    if (currentBucketCount >=spectrumBucketCounts[bucketIndex]) {
      bars[bucketIndex].setValue(sum / norms[bucketIndex]);
      currentBucketCount = 0;
      sum = 0.0;
      ++bucketIndex;
    }

    ++index;
  }
}
```

The spectrumDataUpdate method takes four parameters. The timestamp parameter gives the time of the update in seconds. The duration is the number of seconds for which the spectrum was computed. The duration should normally be approximately equal to the value of MediaPlayer's audioSpectrumInterval property. The magnitudes array will hold the floating-point values corresponding to the magnitude of each spectrum band. The array length will always equal the value of MediaPlayer's audioSpectrumNumBands property. The value is in decibels and will be between audioSpectrumThreshold and zero. It is always less than zero. Similarly, the phases array contains the phase offset of each spectrum band. These arrays should be treated as read-only by the listener because the MediaPlayer may reuse them between updates.

For our purposes, we are only trying to give the user a general idea of the spectrum content in each of the equalizer bands. Therefore we need to be concerned only with the magnitudes array. We iterate through the array and use the bucket counts to sum the magnitudes of the bands that correspond to each equalizer band. When we reach the count for each bucket, the current sum is divided by the normalization factor and then passed as the value to the corresponding SpectrumBar. Then the values are reset and the sum for the next band is calculated.

We now have the ability to create a custom set of EqualizerBands and to display the magnitude of the frequencies in each band as calculated from the audio signal that is currently being played. This gives a pretty nice equalizer interface for the users of the application. We do need to ensure that we reinitialize our equalizer interface whenever a new MediaPlayer is created (a new song is loaded). A listener attached to SongModel's mediaPlayer property handles this, as shown in Listing 9-27.

Listing 9-27. EqualizerView's MediaPlayer Listener

```
private class MediaPlayerListener implements ChangeListener<MediaPlayer> {
  @Override
  public void changed(ObservableValue<? extends MediaPlayer> observable,
                      MediaPlayer oldValue, MediaPlayer newValue) {
    if (oldValue != null) {
      oldValue.setAudioSpectrumListener(null);
      clearGridPane();
    }

    createEQInterface();
  }

  private void clearGridPane() {
    for (Node node : ((GridPane)getViewNode()).getChildren()) {
      GridPane.clearConstraints(node);
    }
    ((GridPane)getViewNode()).getChildren().clear();
  }
}
```

This inner class resides in EqualizerView. If the oldValue is not null, we set its spectrum listener to null to turn off the spectrum calculations. Then we clear the GridPane and re-create the equalizer interface. This is necessary because each MediaPlayer has its own AudioEqualizer instance that cannot be initialized or set from the outside. It would also be wasteful to have the MediaPlayer compute the audio spectrum when it is not visible, such as when the metadata view is being shown. We can attach another listener to our GridPane's scene property to ensure that this does not happen. Listing 9-28 shows the final version of the EqualizerView constructor with this addition highlighted.

Listing 9-28. The EqualizerView Constructor with the Scene Listener Declared

```
public EqualizerView(SongModel songModel) {
  super(songModel);
```

```
    songModel.mediaPlayerProperty().addListener(new MediaPlayerListener());
    createEQInterface();
    getViewNode().sceneProperty().addListener((observable, oldValue, newValue) -> {
          final MediaPlayer mp = EqualizerView.this.songModel.getMediaPlayer();
          if (newValue != null) {
              mp.setAudioSpectrumListener(spectrumListener);
          } else {
              mp.setAudioSpectrumListener(null);
          }
      });
}
```

Whenever EqualizerView's GridPane is not part of the scene (whenever newValue is null), we make sure to set MediaPlayer's audioSpectrumListener to null to disable the spectrum calculations, which begs the question of how and when to add the equalizer view to the application. We created an EQ button and added it to the far right side of the player controls view. Whenever this button is clicked, the metadata and controls views are hidden and the equalizer view is shown. We have also added a "Back" button to the equalizer view that returns the application to the metadata and controls views. To facilitate the changing of views, a new listener field has been added to the AbstractView class. It lets us specify one event handler per view that can be used to indicate that the "next" view should be shown. The new version of the AbstractView class is shown in Listing 9-29.

Listing 9-29. Adding the setNextHandler Method to AbstractView

```
public abstract class AbstractView {
  protected final SongModel songModel;
  protected final Node viewNode;

  public AbstractView(SongModel songModel) {
    this.songModel = songModel;
    this.viewNode = initView();
  }

  // other methods removed...

  public void setNextHandler(EventHandler<ActionEvent> nextHandler) {
  }
}
```

As you can see, the setNextHandler does nothing by default, so existing views are free to ignore it. Any view that needs to support this new functionality can override the method and pass along the nextHandler argument to whichever control is the source of the next action. In our case, this is the "EQ" button in the player controls view and the "Back" button in the equalizer view. Naturally, the AudioPlayer4 application class also needs to be modified to create the event handlers that are capable of switching between the two "pages" of our final application. We do not detail those changes here, but you can consult the AudioPlayer4 example code if you are curious.

The final version of the audio player application is shown in Figure 9-8. The top image shows the "page" containing the metadata and controls views, and the bottom image shows the final version of the equalizer view.

Figure 9-8. *The final version of AudioPlayer 4 with the metadata/controls view (top) and equalizer view (bottom)*

The bottom image of Figure 9-8 shows the special styling that was applied to the `Slider` and `SpectrumBar` controls of the `EqualizerView`. You might also have noticed that the Back and EQ buttons are shaped like arrows. This was also done via the application's style sheet. Those styles are shown in Listing 9-30.

Listing 9-30. Styling the Equalizer and Buttons

```
#eqButton {
  -fx-shape: "M 1,0 L 10,0 13,5 10,10 1,10 Q 0 10 0 9 L 0,1 Q 0 0 1 0";
  -fx-font-size: 12pt;
  -fx-alignment: center-left;
}
```

```
#backButton {
  -fx-shape: "M 3,0 L 12,0 Q 13,0 13,1 L 13,9 Q 13,10 12,10 L 3,10 1,5";
  -fx-font-size: 12pt;
  -fx-alignment: center-right;
}

.eqSlider {
  -fx-background-radius: 5;
  -fx-background-color: #222, #888, black;
  -fx-background-insets: 0, 1 0 0 1, 1;
  -fx-padding: 2 10;
}

.eqSlider .thumb {
  -fx-background-image: url("resources/thumb.png");
  -fx-padding: 12;
}

.eqSlider:vertical .track{
  -fx-padding: 5;
}

.spectrumBar {
  -fx-background-radius: 5;
  -fx-background-color: #222, #888, black;
  -fx-background-insets: 0, 1 0 0 1, 1;
  -fx-padding: 2 10;
}
```

MediaPlayer Wrap-Up

Playing media files over the Internet happens automatically with the JavaFX media API. All you have to do is point a `Media` object to an HTTP resource and attach it to a `MediaPlayer` with `autoPlay` set to true. If, however, you are interested in monitoring the progress of the download buffer, you can use the `bufferProgressTime` property in the `MediaPlayer` class. When data are loaded from a stream or from disk, the amount of time those data will take to play is calculated and this time is regularly updated as the value of `bufferProgressTime`. By binding to this property, you can receive these updates and effectively monitor the media's buffer.

The final two `MediaPlayer` properties we discuss are the `rate` and `currentRate` properties. Calling `setRate` allows you to control the rate of the playback. Passing a parameter of 1.0 will cause playback to proceed at the normal rate. A parameter of 2.0 would cause your media to be played at twice the normal rate. You can pass any value between 0.0 and 8.0. The `currentRate` property always reflects the actual rate of playback, regardless of the value of the rate property. For example, if playback is currently stalled, `currentRate` will be 0.0 even though `rate` may be set to 4.0.

Playing Video

From an API standpoint, playing video instead of audio is as simple as wrapping a `MediaPlayer` with a `MediaView` and adding the `MediaView` to the scene graph. Listing 9-31 shows how this is done. You simply point a `Media` object at a valid source (a Flash movie in this case) and wrap it with an auto-playing `MediaPlayer`, which, in turn, is wrapped with a `MediaView`. The final step is to add the `MediaView` to the scene and set the size of the scene to match the size of the movie.

Listing 9-31. A Minimalist but Functional Movie Player

```
public class VideoPlayer1 extends Application {

  public static void main(String[] args) {
    launch(args);
  }

  @Override
  public void start(Stage primaryStage) {
    String workingDir = System.getProperty("user.dir");
    File f = new File(workingDir, "../media/omgrobots.flv");

    Media m = new Media(f.toURI().toString());
    MediaPlayer mp = new MediaPlayer(m);
    MediaView mv = new MediaView(mp);

    StackPane root = new StackPane();
    root.getChildren().add(mv);

    primaryStage.setScene(new Scene(root, 960, 540));
    primaryStage.setTitle("Video Player 1");
    primaryStage.show();

    mp.play();
  }
}
```

This example loads the video file from the file system. Loading video from the Internet using an HTTP URL will work just as well, but it is not advisable to package movies of any significant size inside your jar file because that will drastically increase the size of your application. Once we have our file URL, everything becomes familiar. You use the URL to create the `Media` object and wrap that `Media` object in a `MediaPlayer`. The only new step is to construct a `MediaView` node using the `MediaPlayer` as the constructor argument and add it to the root of our scene graph, a `StackPane` in this case. We create a Scene that is sized to fit the dimensions of our movie, then pass it to the stage and show it. The final step is to start the movie playing with the same familiar call to `MediaPlayer`'s `play` method. Figure 9-9 shows this simple movie player in action.

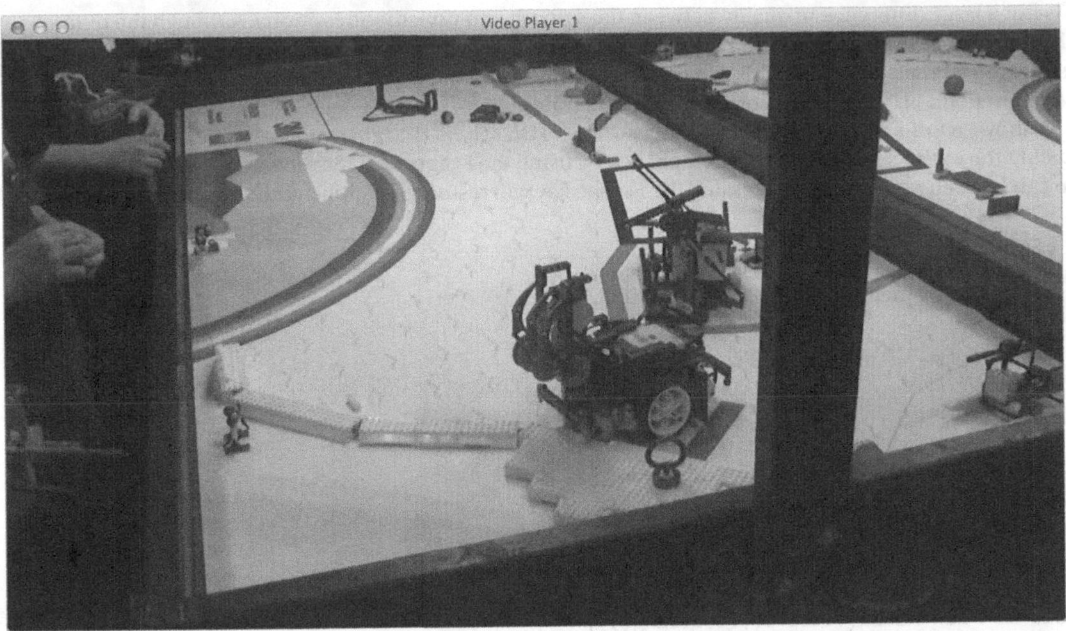

Figure 9-9. Playing a robot movie in JavaFX

Everything you've learned up to this point about playing audio with `Media` and `MediaPlayer` also applies to playing video with `MediaView`. There are only a few extra concepts that you need to know.

Controlling the Size of a `MediaView`

`MediaView` is just another node in the scene graph, so it is possible to scale its content using the usual transforms or the `scaleX` and `scaleY` properties of the `Node` class. There are more convenient ways to get the job done when dealing with `MediaView`s, however. The properties `fitWidth` and `fitHeight` can be used to make the `MediaView` stretch or shrink to the desired size. Using only one of them at a time will make the `MediaView` scale only in that dimension while the size in the other dimension remains unchanged.

If you want to maintain the movie's original aspect ratio as you scale it to fit your application, you can set the `preserveRatio` property to true. If you specify a fit size in one dimension along with setting `preserveRatio` to true, the other dimension will be automatically scaled to match the movie's original aspect ratio as it's being fit along your specified dimension. For example, let's say our movie's size is originally 640 × 352 pixels, which gives an aspect ratio of 640 ÷ 352, or approximately 1.82. If you specify a `fitWidth` of 400 and enable `preserveRatio`, the final height of the movie will be changed from 352 pixels to 400 ÷ 1.82 = 220 pixels. Note that the aspect ratio is preserved because 400 ÷ 220 is also 1.82.

You can also choose to scale in both dimensions by specifying both a `fitWidth` and a `fitHeight` value along with enabling `preserveRatio`. In this case the best fit for the movie will be calculated and the other dimension will be scaled to preserve the original aspect ratio. For example, if the fit area and the movie are both wider than they are tall (the common case), the movie will be scaled to fit horizontally and the height will be determined by using the aspect ratio to calculate the height needed to match the new width.

One last property that is worth knowing about in relation to resizing a movie is the `smooth` property. This is a `Boolean` property that controls the quality of the resulting image after the scale. If `smooth` is true, the scaling algorithm will produce a higher quality image at the cost of some extra computation time. If false, the scaling will be done faster but the result will not look as good. This lets the developer make a time versus quality trade-off. When making a movie smaller, there is not a large difference in quality between the smooth and nonsmooth options. Although the difference in quality while upscaling is noticeable, it still may be acceptable for some applications. Therefore, if you need to generate and show thumbnails of movies, this can be a worthwhile option to consider. By default, `smooth` is usually set to true but this can depend on the platform on which you are running.

Listing 9-32 shows a full-screen movie player that uses the `fitWidth`, `fitHeight`, and `preserveRatio` to scale a movie to play using the entire screen. This is accomplished by using the `Stage`'s `fullScreen` property to ensure that only the movie can be seen on the screen. Pressing the Escape key will restore the application to its normal window.

Listing 9-32. A Full-Screen Movie Player

```
public class FullScreenVideoPlayer extends Application {

  public static void main(String[] args) {
    launch(args);
  }

  @Override
  public void start(Stage primaryStage) {
    String workingDir = System.getProperty("user.dir");
    final File f = new File(workingDir, "../media/omgrobots.flv");

    final Media m = new Media(f.toURI().toString());
    final MediaPlayer mp = new MediaPlayer(m);
    final MediaView mv = new MediaView(mp);

    final DoubleProperty width = mv.fitWidthProperty();
    final DoubleProperty height = mv.fitHeightProperty();

    width.bind(Bindings.selectDouble(mv.sceneProperty(), "width"));
    height.bind(Bindings.selectDouble(mv.sceneProperty(), "height"));

    mv.setPreserveRatio(true);

    StackPane root = new StackPane();
    root.getChildren().add(mv);

    final Scene scene = new Scene(root, 960, 540);
    scene.setFill(Color.BLACK);

    primaryStage.setScene(scene);
    primaryStage.setTitle("Full Screen Video Player");
    primaryStage.setFullScreen(true);
    primaryStage.show();

    mp.play();
  }
}
```

The highlighted code in Listing 9-32 shows that `MediaView`'s `fitWidth` and `fitHeight` properties are bound to the width and height properties of the `MediaView`'s `Scene` object. `Bindings.selectDouble` is used to make sure `fitWidth` and `fitHeight` are updated when the `MediaView` is added to the active scene graph. For the movie to scale properly, the `preserveRatio` property must be set to true.

MediaView and Effects

All of the normal effects that can be applied to a Node can also be applied to a MediaView. Some care must be taken to ensure that the effects are not so expensive as to interfere with the smooth playback of the movie. With that caveat in place, we go over some of the effects that are commonly in use with media player applications. Reflections (see javafx.scene.effect.Reflection) are a popular effect, specifically in demos that are meant to show off a platform's graphical horsepower. A reflection can make the movie look as if it is sitting on a shiny surface. The effect is very compelling because the reflection is updated in real time to match the movie. JavaFX's ColorAdjust effect can be used to alter the colors in the movie for a fun and visually interesting effect. If you're in a more artsy kind of mood, the SepiaTone effect might be just the thing. And, of course, there is the old reliable DropShadow effect to make the movie look as if it is floating over the background. We encourage you to use the example programs and experiment with the different effects in the javafx.scene.effect package. It is a fun and interesting way to learn about them.

Using Markers

The JavaFX 2.0 media API also includes support for media markers. These markers can be used to trigger events during media playback. Every Media object contains an ObservableMap whose keys are Strings and whose values are Durations. During playback, these markers trigger MediaMarkerEvents at the Duration specified by the marker. These events can be caught by passing an EventHandler to the MediaPlayer's setOnMarker method. Listing 9-33 contains the code for the VideoPlayer2 application that sets and then displays the text of these markers during video playback. Although we show them here during video playback, the marker functionality is available during audio playback as well.

Listing 9-33. Displaying Media Markers in a Movie

```
public class VideoPlayer2 extends Application {

  public static void main(String[] args) {
    launch(args);
  }

  @Override
  public void start(Stage primaryStage) {
    final Label markerText = new Label();
    StackPane.setAlignment(markerText, Pos.TOP_CENTER);

    String workingDir = System.getProperty("user.dir");
    final File f = new File(workingDir, "../media/omgrobots.flv");

    final Media m = new Media(f.toURI().toString());

    final ObservableMap<String, Duration> markers = m.getMarkers();
    markers.put("Robot Finds Wall", Duration.millis(3100));
    markers.put("Then Finds the Green Line", Duration.millis(5600));
    markers.put("Robot Grabs Sled", Duration.millis(8000));
    markers.put("And Heads for Home", Duration.millis(11500));
    final MediaPlayer mp = new MediaPlayer(m);
    mp.setOnMarker((event) -> {
        Platform.runLater(() -> {
            markerText.setText(event.getMarker().getKey());
        });
    });

    final MediaView mv = new MediaView(mp);
```

```
        final StackPane root = new StackPane();
        root.getChildren().addAll(mv, markerText);
        root.setOnMouseClicked((event) -> {
            mp.seek(Duration.ZERO);
            markerText.setText("");
        });
        final Scene scene = new Scene(root, 960, 540);
        final URL stylesheet = getClass().getResource("media.css");
        scene.getStylesheets().add(stylesheet.toString());

        primaryStage.setScene(scene);
        primaryStage.setTitle("Video Player 1");
        primaryStage.show();

        mp.play();
    }
}
```

A Label is used to display the text of each marker centered at the top of the screen by setting its alignment to be Pos.TOP_CENTER. Then, after creating the Media object, four markers are inserted into the ObservableMap starting with the message “Robot Finds Wall” at 3.1 seconds and ending with “And Heads for Home” at 11.5 seconds. Once the MediaPlayer is instantiated, a new MediaMarkerEvent handler is created and passed to the setOnMarker method. This event will occur on the JavaFX media thread, so we must use Platform.runLater to set the text of the markerText label on the JavaFX application thread. One other change we've made to this version of the video player is to add an onMouseClicked handler, which seeks back to the beginning of the media and clears the markerText label. This lets you simply click on the window to restart playback. The running application displaying the “And Heads for Home” marker text is shown in Figure 9-10. The styling of the messageLabel text is included in the media.css style sheet that is loaded by the Scene after it is created.

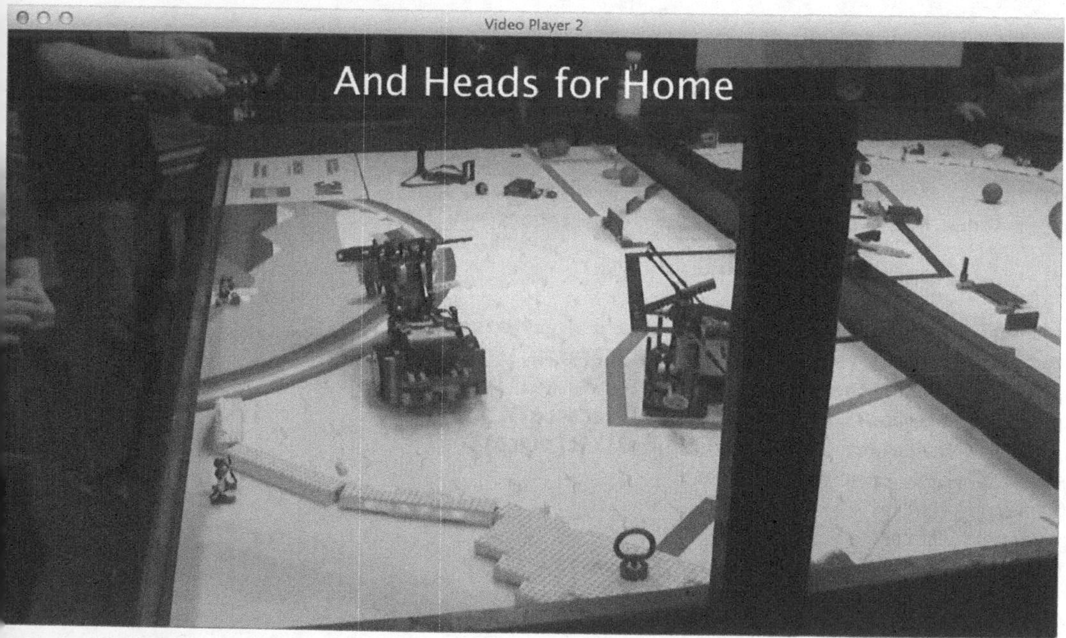

Figure 9-10. Displaying markers during movie playback

One Player, Multiple Views

Each MediaView supports the concept of a viewport. This is a Rectangle2D that defines which part of the movie to view. Multiple MediaViews can share the same MediaPlayer, and through the use of viewports, they can all be displaying different views of the same media. Because they all share the same player, all views will be showing the same frame of video at the same time. The viewport will become your view of the player's content. If you specify a fitWidth or fitHeight, any transforms or effects, they will be applied to the viewport just as they would have been applied to the view as a whole. The code in Listing 9-34 shows how to define multiple MediaViews and viewports for a single MediaPlayer.

The listing starts by defining a Label to hold a "secret" message, which is initially set invisible. After the Media object is created, two markers are defined that will tell us when it is time to split and join the two viewports that we create. Next, two MediaViews are created and each is given one half of the video to view. The arguments to the Rectangle2D constructor specify, in order, the minimum x coordinate, the minimum y coordinate, the width, and the height of the viewport's rectangle. Therefore, you can see that the first MediaView will contain a viewport into the left side of the movie and the second MediaView will view the right side of the movie. A StackPane is created to hold the message behind the two MediaViews; the message is added as the first child. When the "split" marker is triggered, the two viewports will slide apart revealing our message. The "join" marker will trigger the two viewports to slide back together, hiding the message once again.

Listing 9-34. Defining Viewports for MediaViews

```
public class VideoPlayer3 extends Application {
  public static void main(String[] args) {
    launch(args);
  }

  @Override
  public void start(Stage primaryStage) {
    final Label message = new Label("I \u2764 Robots");
    message.setVisible(false);

    String workingDir = System.getProperty("user.dir");
    final File f = new File(workingDir, "../media/omgrobots.flv");

    final Media m = new Media(f.toURI().toString());
    m.getMarkers().put("Split", Duration.millis(3000));
    m.getMarkers().put("Join", Duration.millis(9000));

    final MediaPlayer mp = new MediaPlayer(m);

    final MediaView mv1 = new MediaView(mp);
    mv1.setViewport(new Rectangle2D(0, 0, 960 / 2, 540));
    StackPane.setAlignment(mv1, Pos.CENTER_LEFT);

    final MediaView mv2 = new MediaView(mp);
    mv2.setViewport(new Rectangle2D(960 / 2, 0, 960 / 2, 540));
    StackPane.setAlignment(mv2, Pos.CENTER_RIGHT);

    StackPane root = new StackPane();
    root.getChildren().addAll(message, mv1, mv2);
    root.setOnMouseClicked((event) -> {
        mp.seek(Duration.ZERO);
```

```
            message.setVisible(false);
        });
        final Scene scene = new Scene(root, 960, 540);
        final URL stylesheet = getClass().getResource("media.css");
        scene.getStylesheets().add(stylesheet.toString());

        primaryStage.setScene(scene);
        primaryStage.setTitle("Video Player 3");
        primaryStage.show();
        mp.setOnMarker((event) -> {
            Platform.runLater(() -> {
                if (event.getMarker().getKey().equals("Split")) {
                    message.setVisible(true);
                    buildSplitTransition(mv1, mv2).play();
                } else {
                    buildJoinTransition(mv1, mv2).play();
                }
            });
        });

        mp.play();
    }
}
```

The last step in showing our hidden message is to set a handler for the MediaMarkerEvents that lets us know when it is time to split the two viewports and when it is time to rejoin them. As in the last example, the Platform.runLater method is required because we manipulate the visibility of the message Label as well as apply translations to the two MediaView nodes. The methods that build and return the two transitions are shown in Listing 9-35.

Listing 9-35. Building the Split and Join Transitions

```
private ParallelTransition buildJoinTransition(Node one, Node two) {
    TranslateTransition translate1 = new TranslateTransition(Duration.millis(1000), one);
    translate1.setByX(200);
    TranslateTransition translate2 = new TranslateTransition(Duration.millis(1000), two);
    translate2.setByX(-200);
    ParallelTransition answer = new ParallelTransition(translate1, translate2);
    return answer;
}
private ParallelTransition buildSplitTransition(Node one, Node two) {
    TranslateTransition translate1 = new TranslateTransition(Duration.millis(1000), one);
    translate1.setByX(-200);
    TranslateTransition translate2 = new TranslateTransition(Duration.millis(1000), two);
    translate2.setByX(200);
    ParallelTransition answer = new ParallelTransition(translate1, translate2);
    return answer;

}
```

This example demonstrates that there are many uses for media markers other than simply displaying captions. They can be used to trigger all kinds of events in your applications. A screen shot of the running application with our hidden message revealed is shown in Figure 9-11.

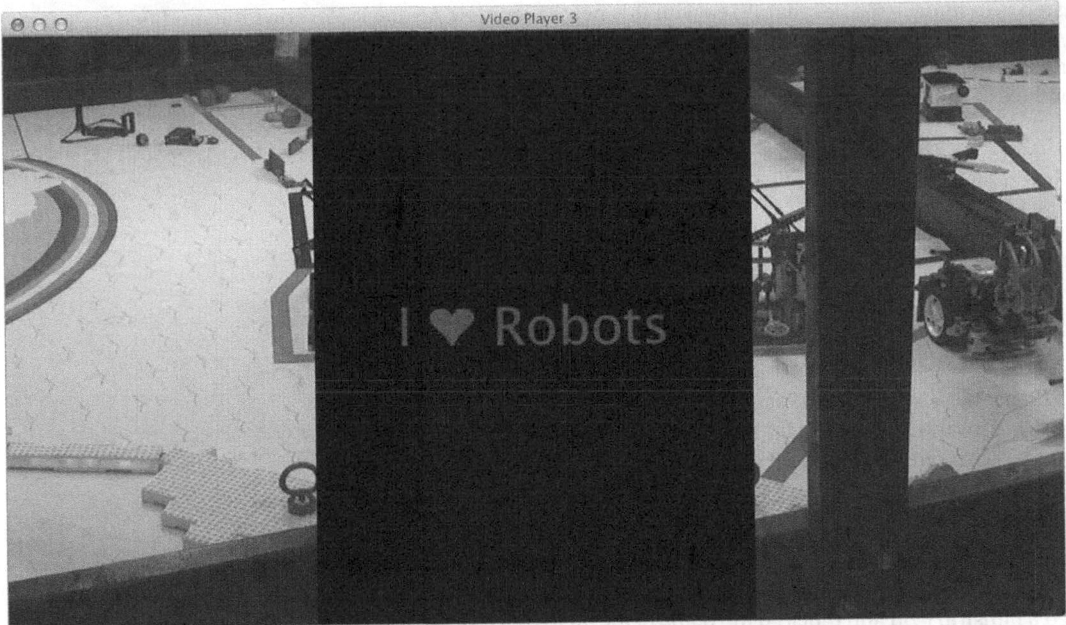

Figure 9-11. The MediaViews slide apart to reveal the hidden message

Converting AudioPlayer into a VideoPlayer

Based on what you have learned so far, you might think that converting the AudioPlayer application to play video is a straightforward task, and you would be right. The first step is simply to rename the SongModel class to the more appropriate MediaModel. No code changes are required. Although movies do not typically contain metadata, it does not hurt to leave in the code that looks for them. Rather than display metadata, we create a new view that displays the MediaView instead. This VideoView class is shown in Listing 9-36.

Listing 9-36. A View That Displays the MediaView Node

```
public class VideoView extends AbstractView {

  public VideoView(MediaModel mediaModel) {
    super(mediaModel);
  }

  @Override
  protected Node initView() {
    MediaView mv = new MediaView();
    mv.mediaPlayerProperty().bind(mediaModel.mediaPlayerProperty());
    return mv;
  }
}
```

This simple class uses its initView method to create a MediaView and bind the MediaView's mediaPlayerProperty to the mediaPlayerProperty we created in our MediaModel (formerly SongModel) class.

The next step is to replace the MetadataView with this new VideoView. Listing 9-37 shows the modified code from the VideoPlayer4 class (formerly AudioPlayer4). Instead of creating the MetadataView, we now create the VideoView, passing it the mediaModel instance. The VideoView's view node is then retrieved and set as the center node of the BorderPane in place of the MetadataView's view node. That is literally all there is to it!

Listing 9-37. Creating the VideoView and Adding It to the Application's First Page

```
private Parent createPageOne() {
  videoView = new VideoView(mediaModel);
  playerControlsView = new PlayerControlsView(mediaModel);
playerControlsView.setNextHandler((ActionEvent arg0) -> {
        rootNode.getChildren().setAll(page2);
    });

  final BorderPane bp = new BorderPane();
  bp.setCenter(videoView.getViewNode());
  bp.setBottom(playerControlsView.getViewNode());

  return bp;
}
```

One final finishing touch is to change the music note icon on the open button to something more appropriate. We therefore created a filmstrip icon and replaced the name of the image file used by the button in the application's style sheet.

```
#openButton {
  -fx-graphic: url("resources/filmstrip.png");
}
```

The final result of our conversion is shown in Figure 9-12 playing a promotional video from Oracle's web site. All of the controls work exactly the same as they did in the version that played audio files, right down to the equalizer. You just have to love JavaFX, don't you?

Figure 9-12. *The converted video player in action*

Summary

In this chapter, you learned about a very important aspect of the JavaFX platform: the media classes. We showed you how to accomplish the following.

- Use the `AudioClip` class to play low-latency sound effects.
- Load the various media types supported by JavaFX into a `Media` object.
- Use the `MediaPlayer` class to play audio files from `.jar` files, from disk, and by loading them over the Internet.
- Build a simple media player that contains a graphical user interface that can be used to control playback of the audio files.
- Take advantage of the `MediaPlayer`'s equalizer and audio frequency spectrum capabilities.
- Play video files using the `MediaView` class.
- Use media markers to trigger events during media playback.
- Split your video playback into multiple viewports.

Resources

For more information on the JavaFX Media API, consult the following resource:

- `http://docs.oracle.com/javase/8/javafx/media-tutorial/overview.htm`

CHAPTER 10

JavaFX 3D

Now I do not know whether I was then a man dreaming I was a butterfly, or whether I am now a butterfly, dreaming I am a man.

—Chuang Tze

After learning about JavaFX's media capabilities, we now put our focus on the 3D capabilities of JavaFX. The JavaFX 3D graphics API provides access to accelerated graphics hardware that is prevalent in modern personal computers and devices through a well-thought-out, very regular Java API that works seamlessly with the rest of the JavaFX APIs. The JavaFX 3D capability makes the JavaFX platform a suitable development platform for more kinds of applications, including scientific, engineering, and industrial visualization; medical and scientific imaging; enhanced user experience; entertainment; and many other innovative applications.

In this chapter, we cover the JavaFX 3D graphics API classes and methods. You will learn about putting JavaFX 3D shapes into a scene, illuminating them with lights, giving them material textures, and creating a view of the scene using cameras. You will also learn how to manipulate them using transformations and animations and how to interact with them using events. Although not part of the JavaFX 3D graphics API, the Canvas and Image Ops APIs are also covered in this chapter.

Overview

The JavaFX 3D graphics API is available only if your computer is equipped with a graphics card that is listed under the system requirements for JavaFX. Table 10-1 lists the supported graphics cards.

Table 10-1. *Graphics Cards Support*

NVIDIA	Mobile GPUs: GeForce 8M and 100M series or higher, NVS 2100M series or higher, and Mobility Quadro FX 300M series or higher
	Desktop GPUs: GeForce 8 and 100 series or higher
	Workstation GPUs: Quadro FX 300 series or higher
ATI	Mobile GPUs: Mobility Radeon HD 3000, 4000, and 5000 series
	Desktop GPUs: Radeon HD 2400, 3000, 4000, 5000, and 6000 series
Intel	Mobile GPUs: GMA 4500MHD and GMA HD
	Desktop GPUs: GMA 4500 and GMA HD

You can test if the system supports the JavaFX 3D graphics API using the `Platform.isSupported()` method for `ConditionalFeature.SCENE3D`:

```
boolean supported = Platform.isSupported(ConditionalFeature.SCENE3D);
```

The rest of the examples in this chapter will work only if this test results in `true`.

As our first foray into the JavaFX 3D world, we consider a first JavaFX 3D example in Listing 10-1.

Listing 10-1. `First3DExample.java`

```
import javafx.application.Application;
import javafx.scene.Group;
import javafx.scene.Scene;
import javafx.scene.shape.Sphere;
import javafx.stage.Stage;

public class First3DExample extends Application {
    @Override
    public void start(Stage stage) throws Exception {
        stage.setTitle("First 3D Example");
        stage.setScene(makeScene());
        stage.show();
    }

    private Scene makeScene() {
        Sphere sphere = new Sphere(100);
        Group root = new Group(sphere);
        root.setTranslateX(320);
        root.setTranslateY(240);
        Scene scene = new Scene(root, 640, 480);

        return scene;
    }

    public static void main(String[] args) {
        launch(args);
    }
}
```

Although the only 3D element in this very simple program is the `Sphere` class, which represents a sphere in the three-dimensional space, its presence in the scene triggers several responses from the JavaFX runtime system. It adds a camera and a light to the scene. It also gives the sphere a material quality. The camera, the light, the 3D object, and the material quality of the 3D object are the basic ingredients of a *3D model*. They work together to bring the 3D model to our two-dimensional screen.

When the program in Listing 10-1 is run, the First 3D Example window in Figure 10-1 is displayed.

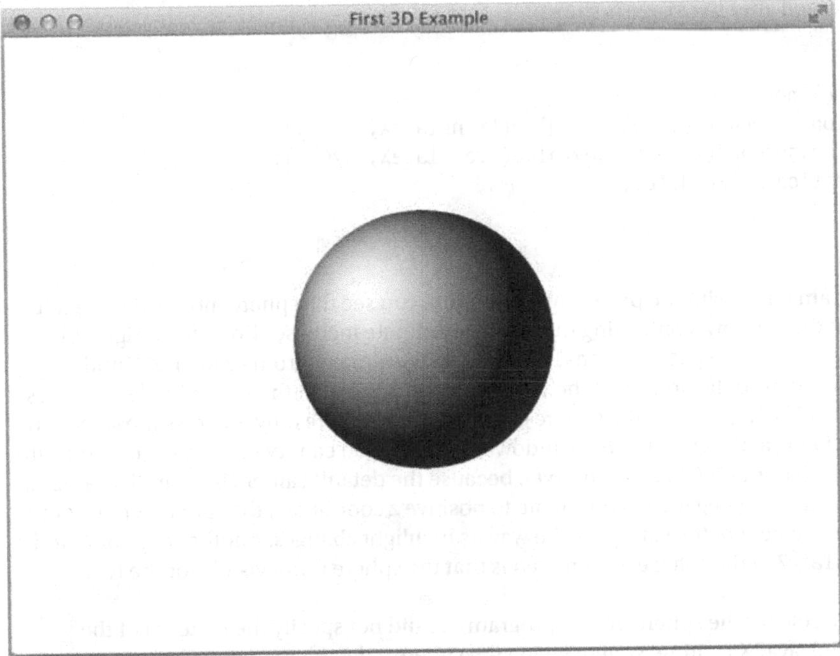

Figure 10-1. *The First3DExample program*

3D objects, lights, and cameras live in a three-dimensional space in which every point is represented by a tuple of three floating point numbers (*x*, *y*, *z*). The three-dimensional space is right-handed, which means if you stretch out the first three fingers of your right hand so that the thumb points to the positive *x* direction and the index finger points to the positive *y* direction, then the third finger points to the positive *z* direction.

The sphere we created in the program is centered at the origin (0, 0, 0) and has a radius of 100. The camera that the JavaFX runtime system added for us is a parallel camera located in negative *z* axis looking into the *xy* plane in such a way that the positive *x* direction points to the right; consequently the positive *y* direction points down and the positive *z* direction points into the screen. The light that the JavaFX runtime system added for us is at the same location as the camera, and it radiates light equally in all directions.

What is shown in the First 3D Example window is a two-dimensional representation of the 3D model. Not everything in the 3D model is shown in the window. For example, the back side of the sphere is not visible. Any part of the 3D model that lies outside the scene's bounds is also not visible. The process of determining what is shown in the two-dimensional representation is called *rendering*.

In this rendered scene, the top left corner has (0, 0) as its *xy* coordinates, and the bottom right corner has (640, 480) as its *xy* coordinates. To have the sphere appear in the middle of the screen, we translated the container `root` by half the screen width in the *x* direction, and by half the screen height in the *y* direction. Notice that the sphere seems to be illuminated from a light source located at (0, 0, *z*) for some negative *z*.

To get a sense of how the coordinate system is oriented in this 3D scene with default camera and light, we can animate the position of the sphere in the *x* direction by introducing a field:

```
DoubleProperty translateX = new SimpleDoubleProperty();
```

Bind the `translateX` property of the `sphere` to it after we create the `sphere`:

```
sphere.translateXProperty().bind(translateX);
```

Call the following animate() method after the stage is shown:

```
private void animate() {
    Timeline timeline = new Timeline(
            new KeyFrame(Duration.seconds(0), new KeyValue(translateX, -320)),
            new KeyFrame(Duration.seconds(2), new KeyValue(translateX, 320)));
    timeline.setCycleCount(Animation.INDEFINITE);
    timeline.play();
}
```

When the First3DExample program is run with the preceding animation, you see the sphere move from the left side of the window to the right side of the window, confirming that the *x* coordinate increases from left to right. In the same manner, you can run the program with the sphere's translateY property animated from -240 to 240, and see the sphere move from the top of the window to the bottom of the window, confirming that the *y* coordinate increases from top to bottom. In both animations, the highlight of the sphere changes as the sphere moves across the screen in a way that is consistent with the light being at the center of the window. In theory, you can try to run the program with the sphere's translateZ being animated from -500 to 500. However, because the default camera is a parallel camera, even though the sphere is indeed moving from negative *z* coordinate to positive *z* coordinate, the sphere remains the same size. You can only discern the movement of the sphere by the way its highlight changes. Another phenomenon that can be observed when the translateZ of the sphere is animated is that the sphere is not visible for the two extremes of the *z* coordinate range.

Finally, turn your attention to the color of the sphere. In our program, we did not specify the material of the sphere. What you see is the result of the JavaFX runtime system giving the sphere a default material.

In the next few sections, we will teach you all about the 3D objects, cameras, lights, and materials that are available in the JavaFX 3D graphics API.

Understanding JavaFX 3D Objects

The JavaFX 3D graphics API provides several Nodes that represent 3D objects. These classes reside in the javafx.scene.shape package, along with their 2D siblings. There is a common base class Shape3D, and four concrete subclasses: Sphere, Box, Cylinder, and MeshView. The Sphere, Box, and Cylinder are predefined 3D shapes, also called 3D primitives. The MeshView is a user-defined shape.

Understanding the Shape3D Base Class

The Shape3D class is a subclass of Node. It includes the following public methods:

- void setMaterial(Material)
- Material getMaterial()
- ObjectProperty<Material> materialProperty()
- void setDrawMode(DrawMode)
- DrawMode getDrawMode()
- ObjectProperty<DrawMode> drawModeProperty()
- void setCullFace(CullFace)
- CullFace getCullFace()
- ObjectProperty<CullFace> cullFaceProperty()

They define three read-write object properties: material, drawMode, and cullFace. They control the surface material, the drawing mode, and the face culling setting for the Shape3D. The object type of the material property is the class javafx.scene.paint.Material. The type of the drawMode property is the enum javafx.scene.shape.DrawMode. The type of the cullFace property is the enum javafx.scene.shape.CullFace.

The Material class contains a set of rendering properties that control how the 3D shape reacts to lights. It gives the 3D shape its unique look. We cover the Material class hierarchy in a later section. For now, it is sufficient to know that there is one concrete class in the hierarchy called PhongMaterial, and that it has a constructor that takes a single Color parameter for its diffuse color. The DrawMode enum has two declarators: LINE and FILL. A drawMode property of DrawMode.LINE will cause the JavaFX runtime to render the 3D shape as a wireframe. A drawMode property of DrawMode.FILL will cause the JavaFX runtime to render the 3D shape as a solid. The CullFace enum has three declarators: NONE, BACK, and FRONT. It controls how the JavaFX runtime renders each constituent polygon (also called a *face*) of the 3D shape. Through a process called *face culling*, the JavaFX runtime might remove some of the faces in a 3D shape from being rendered, thus improving the performance of the 3D model. A cullFace property of CullFace.NONE will cause the JavaFX runtime to not perform any face culling. A cullFace property of CullFace.BACK will cause the JavaFX runtime to cull all back side faces. A cullFace property of CullFace.FRONT will cause the JavaFX runtime to cull all front side faces. We discuss faces of 3D shapes in more detail in the section about user-defined 3D shapes.

The program in Listing 10-2 allows you to experiment with the effects of altering the material, drawMode, and cullFace properties.

Listing 10-2. Shape3DPropertiesExample.java

```
import javafx.application.Application;
import javafx.beans.property.ObjectProperty;
import javafx.beans.property.SimpleObjectProperty;
import javafx.collections.FXCollections;
import javafx.geometry.Insets;
import javafx.geometry.Pos;
import javafx.scene.Scene;
import javafx.scene.control.ColorPicker;
import javafx.scene.control.ComboBox;
import javafx.scene.control.Label;
import javafx.scene.layout.BorderPane;
import javafx.scene.layout.HBox;
import javafx.scene.paint.Color;
import javafx.scene.paint.Material;
import javafx.scene.paint.PhongMaterial;
import javafx.scene.shape.CullFace;
import javafx.scene.shape.DrawMode;
import javafx.scene.shape.Sphere;
import javafx.stage.Stage;

public class Shape3DPropertiesExample extends Application {
    private Model model;
    private View view;

    public Shape3DPropertiesExample() {
        model = new Model();
    }

    @Override
    public void start(Stage stage) throws Exception {
        view = new View(model);
        hookupEvents();
```

```
        stage.setTitle("Shape3D Properties Example");
        stage.setScene(view.scene);
        stage.show();
    }

    private void hookupEvents() {
        view.colorPicker.setOnAction(event -> {
            ColorPicker colorPicker = (ColorPicker) event.getSource();
            model.setMaterial(new PhongMaterial(colorPicker.getValue()));
        });

        view.drawModeComboBox.setOnAction(event -> {
            ComboBox<DrawMode> drawModeComboBox = (ComboBox<DrawMode>) event.getSource();
            model.setDrawMode(drawModeComboBox.getValue());
        });

        view.cullFaceComboBox.setOnAction(event -> {
            ComboBox<CullFace> cullFaceComboBox = (ComboBox<CullFace>) event.getSource();
            model.setCullFace(cullFaceComboBox.getValue());
        });
    }

    public static void main(String[] args) {
        launch(args);
    }

    private static class Model {
        private ObjectProperty<Material> material = new SimpleObjectProperty<>(
                this, "material", new PhongMaterial(Color.BLUE));
        private ObjectProperty<DrawMode> drawMode = new SimpleObjectProperty<>(
                this, "drawMode", DrawMode.FILL);
        private ObjectProperty<CullFace> cullFace = new SimpleObjectProperty<>(
                this, "cullFace", CullFace.BACK);

        public final Material getMaterial() {
            return material.get();
        }

        public final void setMaterial(Material material) {
            this.material.set(material);
        }

        public final ObjectProperty<Material> materialProperty() {
            return material;
        }

        public final DrawMode getDrawMode() {
            return drawMode.getValue();
        }
```

```
        public final void setDrawMode(DrawMode drawMode) {
            this.drawMode.set(drawMode);
        }

        public final ObjectProperty<DrawMode> drawModeProperty() {
            return drawMode;
        }

        public final CullFace getCullFace() {
            return cullFace.get();
        }

        public final void setCullFace(CullFace cullFace) {
            this.cullFace.set(cullFace);
        }

        public final ObjectProperty<CullFace> cullFaceProperty() {
            return cullFace;
        }
    }

    private static class View {
        public Scene scene;
        public Sphere sphere;
        public ColorPicker colorPicker;
        public ComboBox<DrawMode> drawModeComboBox;
        public ComboBox<CullFace> cullFaceComboBox;

        public View(Model model) {
            sphere = new Sphere(100);
            sphere.materialProperty().bind(model.materialProperty());
            sphere.drawModeProperty().bind(model.drawModeProperty());
            sphere.cullFaceProperty().bind(model.cullFaceProperty());

            colorPicker = new ColorPicker(Color.BLUE);

            drawModeComboBox = new ComboBox<>();
            drawModeComboBox.setItems(FXCollections.observableArrayList(
                    DrawMode.FILL, DrawMode.LINE));
            drawModeComboBox.setValue(DrawMode.FILL);

            cullFaceComboBox = new ComboBox<>();
            cullFaceComboBox.setItems(FXCollections.observableArrayList(
                    CullFace.BACK, CullFace.FRONT, CullFace.NONE));
            cullFaceComboBox.setValue(CullFace.BACK);

            HBox hbox = new HBox(10, new Label("Color:"), colorPicker,
                    new Label("DrawMode:"), drawModeComboBox,
                    new Label("CullFace:"), cullFaceComboBox);
            hbox.setPadding(new Insets(10, 10, 10, 10));
            hbox.setAlignment(Pos.CENTER);
```

```
            BorderPane root = new BorderPane(sphere, null, null, hbox, null);
            scene = new Scene(root, 640, 480);
        }
    }
}
```

In this example, we added a color picker and two combo boxes to the bottom of the GUI, allowing you to change the material, drawMode, and cullFace properties in the model. The sphere is shown in the middle of the GUI. The sphere's material, drawMode, and cullFace properties are bound to a similar property in model. Therefore the user's choice is reflected in the sphere.

When the program in Listing 10-2 is run, the Shape3D Properties Example window in Figure 10-2 is displayed. A wireframe of the sphere is shown.

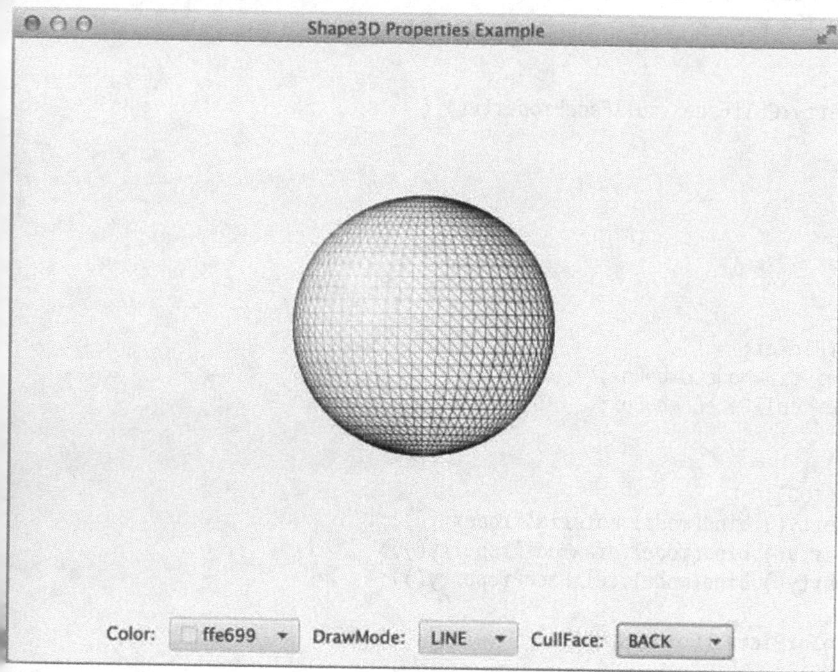

Figure 10-2. The Shape3DPropertiesExample program

Creating Predefined 3D Shapes

The three predefined 3D shapes—Sphere, Cylinder, and Box—can be constructed and put into a JavaFX scene very easily, as we saw for the Sphere class in the last section. In this section, we describe these classes in more detail.

The Sphere class has the following constructors:

- Sphere()
- Sphere(double radius)
- Sphere(double radius, int divisions)

The default constructor creates a sphere of radius 1. The one-parameter constructor creates a sphere with the specified radius. The two-parameter constructor creates a sphere with the specified radius and the number of division points to use along the equator of the sphere to approximate the sphere shape with a set of triangles. The greater the division, the smoother the resulting sphere is. The division number defaults to 64. The center of newly constructed `Spheres` is always at the origin of the three-dimensional space (0, 0, 0).

The `radius` of the sphere is available as a read-write double property. The `divisions` can only be set at construction time, and can be gotten using `getDivisions()`.

The `Cylinder` class has the following constructors:

- `Cylinder()`
- `Cylinder(double radius, double height)`
- `Cylinder(double radius, double height, int divisions)`

The default constructor creates a cylinder with base radius of 1 and height of 2. The two-parameter constructor creates a cylinder with the specified base radius and height. The three-parameter constructor creates a cylinder with the specified base radius and height and the number of division points to use along the circumference of the base to approximate the cylinder shape with a set of triangles. The greater the division number, the smoother the resulting cylinder is. The division number defaults to 64. The base of a newly constructed `Cylinder` is parallel to the *xz* plane, and the height is parallel to the *y* axis. The center of newly constructed `Cylinders` is always at the origin of the three-dimensional space (0, 0, 0).

The `radius` and `height` of the cylinder are available as read-write double properties. The divisions can only be set at construction time, and can be gotten using `getDivisions()`.

The Box class has the following constructors:

- `Box()`
- `Box(double width, double height, double depth)`

The default constructor creates a box with a size of 2 in all three directions. The three-parameter constructor creates a box with the specified width, height, and depth. The width is parallel to the *x* axis, the height is parallel to the *y* axis, and the depth is parallel to the *z* axis. The center of newly constructed Boxes is always at the origin of the three-dimensional space (0, 0, 0).

The `width`, `height`, and depth of the box are available as read-write double properties.

The program in Listing 10-3 illustrates the three predefined 3D shapes in JavaFX.

Listing 10-3. `Predefined3DShapesExample.java`

```
import javafx.application.Application;
import javafx.beans.property.DoubleProperty;
import javafx.beans.property.ObjectProperty;
import javafx.beans.property.SimpleDoubleProperty;
import javafx.beans.property.SimpleObjectProperty;
import javafx.collections.FXCollections;
import javafx.geometry.Insets;
import javafx.geometry.Point3D;
import javafx.geometry.Pos;
import javafx.scene.Group;
import javafx.scene.Scene;
import javafx.scene.control.ComboBox;
import javafx.scene.control.Label;
import javafx.scene.control.Slider;
import javafx.scene.layout.BorderPane;
import javafx.scene.layout.HBox;
```

```
import javafx.scene.layout.VBox;
import javafx.scene.paint.Color;
import javafx.scene.paint.PhongMaterial;
import javafx.scene.shape.Box;
import javafx.scene.shape.CullFace;
import javafx.scene.shape.Cylinder;
import javafx.scene.shape.DrawMode;
import javafx.scene.shape.Shape3D;
import javafx.scene.shape.Sphere;
import javafx.stage.Stage;

public class Predefined3DShapesExample extends Application {
    private Model model;
    private View view;

    public Predefined3DShapesExample() {
        model = new Model();
    }

    @Override
    public void start(Stage stage) throws Exception {
        view = new View(model);
        hookupEvents();
        stage.setTitle("Pre-defined 3D Shapes Example");
        stage.setScene(view.scene);
        stage.show();
    }

    private void hookupEvents() {
        view.drawModeComboBox.setOnAction(event -> {
            ComboBox<DrawMode> drawModeComboBox = (ComboBox<DrawMode>) event.getSource();
            model.setDrawMode(drawModeComboBox.getValue());
        });

        view.cullFaceComboBox.setOnAction(event -> {
            ComboBox<CullFace> cullFaceComboBox = (ComboBox<CullFace>) event.getSource();
            model.setCullFace(cullFaceComboBox.getValue());
        });
    }

    public static void main(String[] args) {
        launch(args);
    }

    private static class Model {
        private DoubleProperty rotate = new SimpleDoubleProperty(
            this, "rotate", 60.0d);
        private ObjectProperty<DrawMode> drawMode = new SimpleObjectProperty<>(
            this, "drawMode", DrawMode.FILL);
        private ObjectProperty<CullFace> cullFace = new SimpleObjectProperty<>(
            this, "cullFace", CullFace.BACK);
```

```
        public final double getRotate() {
            return rotate.doubleValue();
        }

        public final void setRotate(double rotate) {
            this.rotate.set(rotate);
        }

        public final DoubleProperty rotateProperty() {
            return rotate;
        }

        public final DrawMode getDrawMode() {
            return drawMode.getValue();
        }

        public final void setDrawMode(DrawMode drawMode) {
            this.drawMode.set(drawMode);
        }

        public final ObjectProperty<DrawMode> drawModeProperty() {
            return drawMode;
        }

        public final CullFace getCullFace() {
            return cullFace.get();
        }

        public final void setCullFace(CullFace cullFace) {
            this.cullFace.set(cullFace);
        }

        public final ObjectProperty<CullFace> cullFaceProperty() {
            return cullFace;
        }
    }

    private static class View {
        public Scene scene;

        public Sphere sphere;
        public Cylinder cylinder;
        public Box box;

        public ComboBox<DrawMode> drawModeComboBox;
        public ComboBox<CullFace> cullFaceComboBox;
        public Slider rotateSlider;

        public View(Model model) {
            sphere = new Sphere(50);
            cylinder = new Cylinder(50, 100);
            box = new Box(100, 100, 100);
```

```
        sphere.setTranslateX(-200);
        cylinder.setTranslateX(0);
        box.setTranslateX(200);

        sphere.setMaterial(new PhongMaterial(Color.RED));
        cylinder.setMaterial(new PhongMaterial(Color.BLUE));
        box.setMaterial(new PhongMaterial(Color.GREEN));

        setupShape3D(sphere, model);
        setupShape3D(cylinder, model);
        setupShape3D(box, model);

        Group shapesGroup = new Group(sphere, cylinder, box);

        drawModeComboBox = new ComboBox<>();
        drawModeComboBox.setItems(FXCollections.observableArrayList(
            DrawMode.FILL, DrawMode.LINE));
        drawModeComboBox.setValue(DrawMode.FILL);

        cullFaceComboBox = new ComboBox<>();
        cullFaceComboBox.setItems(FXCollections.observableArrayList(
            CullFace.BACK, CullFace.FRONT, CullFace.NONE));
        cullFaceComboBox.setValue(CullFace.BACK);

        HBox hbox1 = new HBox(10, new Label("DrawMode:"), drawModeComboBox,
            new Label("CullFace:"), cullFaceComboBox);
        hbox1.setPadding(new Insets(10, 10, 10, 10));
        hbox1.setAlignment(Pos.CENTER_LEFT);

        rotateSlider = new Slider(-180.0d, 180.0d, 60.0d);
        rotateSlider.setMinWidth(400.0d);
        rotateSlider.setMajorTickUnit(10.0d);
        rotateSlider.setMinorTickCount(5);
        rotateSlider.setShowTickMarks(true);
        rotateSlider.setShowTickLabels(true);

        rotateSlider.valueProperty().bindBidirectional(model.rotateProperty());

        HBox hbox2 = new HBox(10, new Label("Rotate Around (1, 1, 1) Axis:"),
            rotateSlider);
        hbox2.setPadding(new Insets(10, 10, 10, 10));
        hbox2.setAlignment(Pos.CENTER_LEFT);

        VBox controlPanel = new VBox(10, hbox1, hbox2);
        controlPanel.setPadding(new Insets(10, 10, 10, 10));

        BorderPane root = new BorderPane(shapesGroup, null, null, controlPanel, null);
        scene = new Scene(root, 640, 480);
    }
```

```
        private void setupShape3D(Shape3D shape3D, Model model) {
            shape3D.setTranslateY(240.0d);
            shape3D.setRotationAxis(new Point3D(1.0d, 1.0d, 1.0d));

            shape3D.drawModeProperty().bind(model.drawModeProperty());
            shape3D.cullFaceProperty().bind(model.cullFaceProperty());
            shape3D.rotateProperty().bind(model.rotateProperty());
        }
    }
}
```

We create a sphere, a cylinder, and a box, give them distinct colors, and position them side by side. Because our camera is looking into the screen from a negative *z* position, the projected view of the cylinder and the box are not very interesting. So we rotate the 3D shapes around the (1, 1, 1) axis by 60 degrees. The control panel at the bottom of the GUI allows you to change the drawing mode and face culling policies. It also allows you to change the rotation angle.

When the program in Listing 10-3 is run, the Predefined 3D Shapes Example window in Figure 10-3 is displayed.

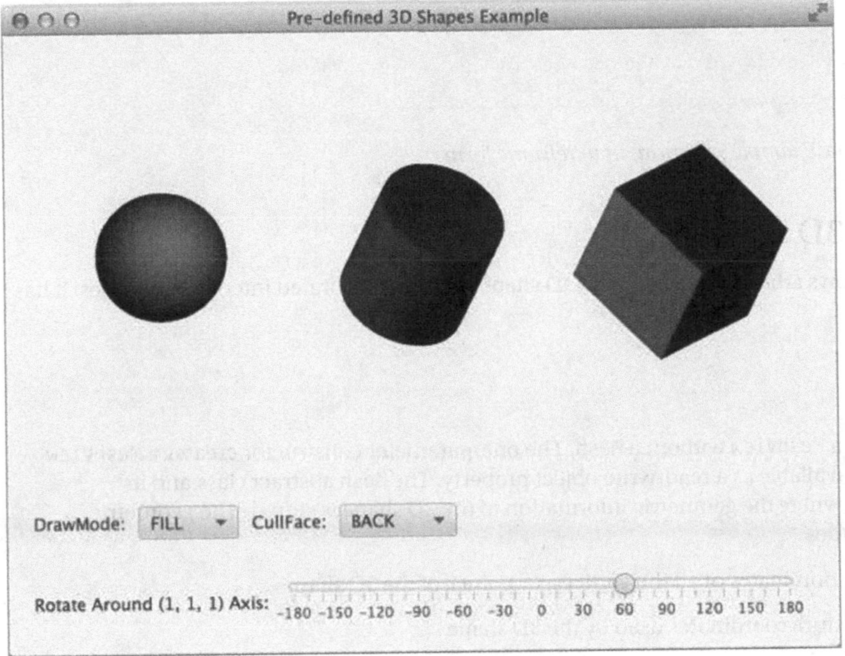

***Figure 10-3.** The Predefined3DShapesExample program*

Figure 10-4 shows the three 3D shapes in wireframe form, with a different rotation angle.

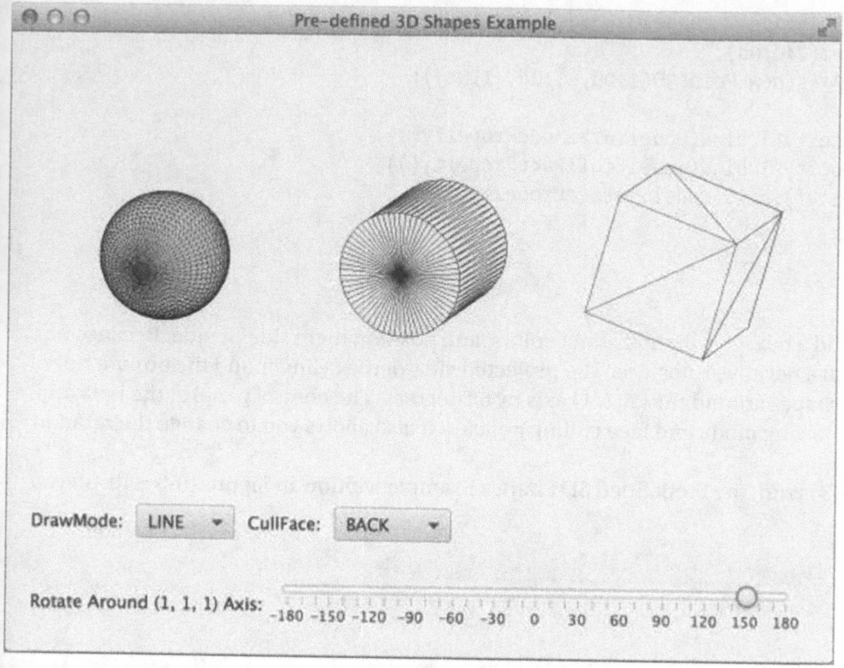

Figure 10-4. *The Predefined3DShapesExample program, in wireframe form*

Creating User-Defined 3D Shapes

The `MeshView` class is a `Node` that allows arbitrary user-defined 3D shapes to be incorporated into JavaFX scenes. It has the following constructors:

- `MeshView()`
- `MeshView(Mesh mesh)`

The default constructor creates a `MeshView` without a `Mesh`. The one-parameter constructor creates a `MeshView` with the specified `mesh`. The `mesh` is available as a read-write object property. The `Mesh` abstract class and its `TriangleMesh` concrete subclass are where the geometric information of the 3D shape is stored. The geometric information in a `TriangleMesh` includes

- The three-dimensional coordinates of all the vertices, or points, of the 3D shape
- The two-dimensional texture coordinates used by the 3D shape
- The faces of the 3D shape, each one a triangle with vertices that are from the vertices list and texture coordinates that are from the texture coordinates list
- The face smoothing groups, which cause the JavaFX runtime to connect faces in the same smoothing group smoothly across their common edges, and to leave the edges between faces not in the same smoothing group as hard edges

For efficiency reasons, the `TriangleMesh` class stores this information in observable arrays. The following public methods allow you to access these observable arrays and their sizes:

- `ObservableFloatArray getPoints()`
- `ObservableFloatArray getTexCoords()`

- `ObservableFaceArray getFaces()`
- `ObservableIntegerArray getFaceSmoothingGroups()`
- `int getPointElementSize()`
- `int getTexCoordElementSize()`
- `int getFaceElementSize()`

The `getPoints()` method returns an `ObservableFloatArray`, which you can use to add three-dimensional vertex coordinates. This observable float array's size must be a multiple of 3, and the elements of the array are interpreted as *x0, y0, z0, x1, y1, z1, …* , where *(x0, y0, z0)* are the coordinates of the first vertex *p0*, *(x1, y1, z1)* are the coordinates of the second vertex *p1*, and so on.

The `getTexCoords()` method returns an `ObservableFloatArray`, which you can use to add two-dimensional texture coordinates. This observable float array's size must be a multiple of 2, and the elements of the array are interpreted as *u0, v0, u1, v1, …* , where *(u0, v0)* is the first texture point, *(u1, v1)* is the second texture point, and so on. We cover texture coordinates in more detail in the materials section. For now it is sufficient to understand the texture coordinates as points in a two-dimensional image with a top left point that has coordinates (0, 0) and a bottom right point that has coordinates (1, 1).

The `getFaces()` method returns an `ObservableFaceArray`, which you can use to add faces to the 3D shape. The `ObservableFaceArray` is a subinterface of the `ObservableIntegerArray` interface. This array's size must be a multiple of 6, and the elements of the array are interpreted as *p0, t0, p1, t1, p2, t2, p3, t3, p4, t4, p5, t5, . . .* , where *p0, t0, p1, t1, p2, t2* defines the first face, *p3, t3, p4, t4, p5, t5* defines the second face, and so on. Of the six ints that define a face, the *p* values are indices into the conceptual points array, which is one-third the length of the actual points array because we consider three float elements from the actual points array as constituting one conceptual point; and the *t* values are indices into the conceptual texture coordinates array, which is one-half the length of the actual texture coordinates array because we consider two float elements from the actual texture coordinates array as constituting one conceptual texture coordinates pair.

The `getFaceSmoothingGroups()` method returns an `ObservableIntegerArray`, which you can use to define smoothing groups for the faces of the 3D shape. You can leave this array empty, in which case the JavaFX runtime will consider all faces of the 3D shape as belonging to one and the same smoothing group, resulting in a 3D shape with a surface that is smooth everywhere. Such is the case for the underlying `TriangleMesh` of the `Sphere` predefined 3D shape. If you fill this array, then you must fill it with the same number of elements as there are conceptual faces, which is one-sixth of the length of the actual faces array because we consider six int elements from the actual faces array as constituting one conceptual face. Each element in the face smoothing group array represents one face of the 3D shape, and two faces belong to the same smoothing group if and only if their representations share a common on bit when each int value is viewed as 32 individual bits. There could be at most 32 face smoothing groups in a `TriangleMesh`.

The `getPointElementSize()` method always returns 3. The `getTexCoordElementSize()` method always returns 2. The `getFaceElementSize()` method always returns 6.

Each face in a 3D shape has two sides. In 3D graphics programming, it is important to distinguish these two sides as either the front side or the back side. JavaFX 3D uses the counterclockwise winding order to define the front side. Imagine yourself standing on one side of the triangle, and trace the edges of the triangle according to the order in which each vertex appears in the definition of the face. If it appears that you are tracing the edges in a counterclockwise fashion, then you are standing on the front side of the face. This concept of front side and back side of faces is what `CullFace.FRONT` and `CullFace.BACK` enum declarators refer to. By default, `Shape3D` uses the `CullFace.BACK` setting, which means the back sides of faces are not rendered.

The program in Listing 10-4 illustrates the use of a user-defined 3D shape in JavaFX.

Listing 10-4. The MeshViewExample.java

```
import javafx.application.Application;
import javafx.beans.property.DoubleProperty;
import javafx.beans.property.ObjectProperty;
import javafx.beans.property.SimpleDoubleProperty;
import javafx.beans.property.SimpleObjectProperty;
import javafx.collections.FXCollections;
import javafx.geometry.Insets;
import javafx.geometry.Point3D;
import javafx.geometry.Pos;
import javafx.scene.Scene;
import javafx.scene.control.ColorPicker;
import javafx.scene.control.ComboBox;
import javafx.scene.control.Label;
import javafx.scene.control.Slider;
import javafx.scene.layout.BorderPane;
import javafx.scene.layout.HBox;
import javafx.scene.layout.VBox;
import javafx.scene.paint.Color;
import javafx.scene.paint.Material;
import javafx.scene.paint.PhongMaterial;
import javafx.scene.shape.*;
import javafx.stage.Stage;

public class MeshViewExample extends Application {
    private Model model;
    private View view;

    public MeshViewExample() {
        model = new Model();
    }

    @Override
    public void start(Stage stage) throws Exception {
        view = new View(model);
        hookupEvents();
        stage.setTitle("MeshView Example");
        stage.setScene(view.scene);
        stage.show();
    }

    private void hookupEvents() {
        view.colorPicker.setOnAction(event -> {
            ColorPicker colorPicker = (ColorPicker) event.getSource();
            model.setMaterial(new PhongMaterial(colorPicker.getValue()));
        });

        view.drawModeComboBox.setOnAction(event -> {
            ComboBox<DrawMode> drawModeComboBox = (ComboBox<DrawMode>) event.getSource();
            model.setDrawMode(drawModeComboBox.getValue());
        });
```

```
        view.cullFaceComboBox.setOnAction(event -> {
            ComboBox<CullFace> cullFaceComboBox = (ComboBox<CullFace>) event.getSource();
            model.setCullFace(cullFaceComboBox.getValue());
        });
    }

    public static void main(String[] args) {
        launch(args);
    }

    private static class Model {
        private DoubleProperty rotate = new SimpleDoubleProperty(
                this, "rotate", 60.0d);
        private ObjectProperty<Material> material = new SimpleObjectProperty<>(
                this, "material", new PhongMaterial(Color.BLUE));
        private ObjectProperty<DrawMode> drawMode = new SimpleObjectProperty<>(
                this, "drawMode", DrawMode.FILL);
        private ObjectProperty<CullFace> cullFace = new SimpleObjectProperty<>(
                this, "cullFace", CullFace.BACK);

        public final double getRotate() {
            return rotate.get();
        }

        public final void setRotate(double rotate) {
            this.rotate.set(rotate);
        }

        public final DoubleProperty rotateProperty() {
            return rotate;
        }

        public final Material getMaterial() {
            return material.get();
        }

        public final void setMaterial(Material material) {
            this.material.set(material);
        }

        public final ObjectProperty<Material> materialProperty() {
            return material;
        }

        public final DrawMode getDrawMode() {
            return drawMode.getValue();
        }

        public final void setDrawMode(DrawMode drawMode) {
            this.drawMode.set(drawMode);
        }
```

```
        public final ObjectProperty<DrawMode> drawModeProperty() {
            return drawMode;
        }

        public final CullFace getCullFace() {
            return cullFace.get();
        }

        public final void setCullFace(CullFace cullFace) {
            this.cullFace.set(cullFace);
        }

        public final ObjectProperty<CullFace> cullFaceProperty() {
            return cullFace;
        }
    }

    private static class View {
        public Scene scene;

        public MeshView meshView;

        public ColorPicker colorPicker;
        public ComboBox<DrawMode> drawModeComboBox;
        public ComboBox<CullFace> cullFaceComboBox;
        public Slider rotateSlider;


        public View(Model model) {
            meshView = new MeshView(createSimplex(200.0f));
            meshView.materialProperty().bind(model.materialProperty());
            meshView.drawModeProperty().bind(model.drawModeProperty());
            meshView.cullFaceProperty().bind(model.cullFaceProperty());
            meshView.setRotationAxis(new Point3D(1, 1, 1));
            meshView.rotateProperty().bind(model.rotateProperty());

            colorPicker = new ColorPicker(Color.BLUE);

            drawModeComboBox = new ComboBox<>();
            drawModeComboBox.setItems(FXCollections.observableArrayList(
                    DrawMode.FILL, DrawMode.LINE));
            drawModeComboBox.setValue(DrawMode.FILL);

            cullFaceComboBox = new ComboBox<>();
            cullFaceComboBox.setItems(FXCollections.observableArrayList(
                    CullFace.BACK, CullFace.FRONT, CullFace.NONE));
            cullFaceComboBox.setValue(CullFace.BACK);

            HBox hbox1 = new HBox(10, new Label("Color:"), colorPicker,
                    new Label("DrawMode:"), drawModeComboBox,
                    new Label("CullFace:"), cullFaceComboBox);
```

```
        hbox1.setPadding(new Insets(10, 10, 10, 10));
        hbox1.setAlignment(Pos.CENTER);

        rotateSlider = new Slider(-180.0d, 180.0d, 60.0d);
        rotateSlider.setMinWidth(400.0d);
        rotateSlider.setMajorTickUnit(10.0d);
        rotateSlider.setMinorTickCount(5);
        rotateSlider.setShowTickMarks(true);
        rotateSlider.setShowTickLabels(true);

        rotateSlider.valueProperty().bindBidirectional(model.rotateProperty());

        HBox hbox2 = new HBox(10, new Label("Rotate Around (1, 1, 1) Axis:"),
                rotateSlider);
        hbox2.setPadding(new Insets(10, 10, 10, 10));
        hbox2.setAlignment(Pos.CENTER_LEFT);

        VBox controlPanel = new VBox(10, hbox1, hbox2);
        controlPanel.setPadding(new Insets(10, 10, 10, 10));


        BorderPane root = new BorderPane(meshView, null, null, controlPanel, null);

        scene = new Scene(root, 640, 480);
    }

    private Mesh createSimplex(float length) {
        TriangleMesh mesh = new TriangleMesh();

        mesh.getPoints().addAll(
                0.0f, 0.0f, 0.0f,   // O
                length, 0.0f, 0.0f, // A
                0.0f, length, 0.0f, // B
                0.0f, 0.0f, length  // C
        );

        mesh.getTexCoords().addAll(
                0.0f, 0.0f,
                0.0f, 1.0f,
                1.0f, 0.0f,
                1.0f, 1.0f
        );

        mesh.getFaces().addAll(
                0, 0, 2, 1, 1, 2, // OBA
                0, 0, 3, 1, 2, 2, // OCB
                0, 0, 1, 1, 3, 2, // OAC
                1, 0, 2, 1, 3, 2  // ABC
        );
```

```
            mesh.getFaceSmoothingGroups().addAll(0, 0, 0, 0);

            return mesh;
        }
    }
}
```

The `createSimplex()` method of the `View` class constructs a very simple `TriangleMesh` called a *simplex*. It has four vertices at *O(0, 0, 0)*, *A(length, 0, 0)*, *B(0, length, 0)*, and *C(0, 0, length)*, and four faces, *OBA*, *OCB*, *OAC*, and *ABC*. No face smoothing groups are defined for this `TriangleMesh`.

When the program in Listing 10-4 is run, the MeshView Example window in Figure 10-5 is displayed. You can change the `material`, `drawMode`, and `cullFace` properties from the control panel. You can also rotate around the (1, 1, 1) axis to see different faces of the simplex.

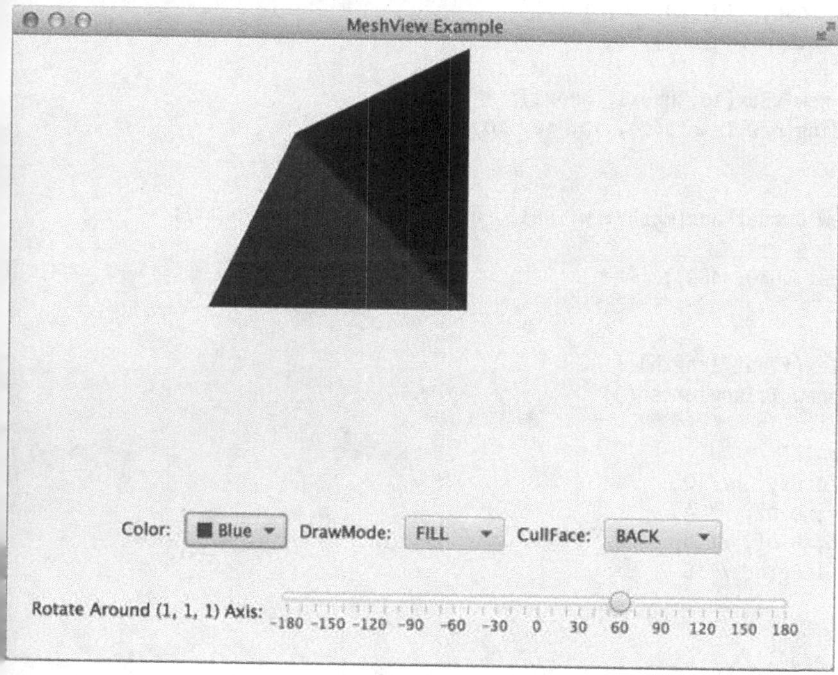

Figure 10-5. *The MeshViewExample program*

Now that we understand the predefined and user-defined 3D shapes, we move on to the other important classes in the JavaFX 3D graphics API.

Adding Cameras to JavaFX 3D Scenes

So far in this chapter, we have not added our own cameras to our JavaFX 3D scenes. We have been relying on the default camera that the JavaFX runtime supplies to the scenes. It allows us to look at our scene from a negative *z* position. To look at our scenes from any other angle, we need to supply our own camera.

The class hierarchy for cameras consists of a `Camera` abstract base class, and its concrete subclasses `ParallelCamera` and `PerspectiveCamera`. They belong to the `javafx.scene` package. The `ParallelCamera` is the camera that the JavaFX runtime supplies when we do not set our own camera. It always displays objects at the same size regardless of distance to the camera. This is called *orthographic projection,* and although much easier to calculate, it does not look realistic. The `PerspectiveCamera` is more interesting for 3D modeling. When using a `PerspectiveCamera`, objects in the distance are smaller than objects in the foreground.

Understanding the PerspectiveCamera

The `PerspectiveCamera` class has the following public constructors:

- `PerspectiveCamera()`
- `PerspectiveCamera(boolean fixedEyeAtCameraZero)`

The default constructor creates a `PerspectiveCamera` with the `fixedEyeAtCameraZero` set to false. The one-parameter constructor creates a `PerspectiveCamera` with the specified `fixedEyeAtCameraZero.` `Cameras` are `Nodes`, and can be placed in a JavaFX scene. A newly created `PerspectiveCamera`, like a newly created `Sphere` or `Cylinder` or `Box`, has its center or eye located in the origin (0, 0, 0) of the three-dimensional space. The eye looks into the positive *z* direction. As a `Node`, the `PerspectiveCamera` itself can be transformed by 3D transformations such as `Rotate`, `Translate`, `Scale`, or even the generic `Affine`. A `fixedEyeAtCameraZero` setting of `true` guarantees that after such transforms, the eye of the `PerspectiveCamera` moves along with it, and remains at the camera's zero position. A `fixedEyeAtCameraZero` setting of `false` allows the eye to drift away from the camera's zero position to accommodate what is in the scene. This is useful for rendering 2D scenes and only makes sense when the camera itself is not transformed in any way. Therefore for use with a 3D model, you should always use the one-parameter constructor, passing in a `fixedEyeAtCameraZero` of `true`.

The `PerspectiveCamera` class has the following public methods:

- `void setFieldOfView(double)`
- `double getFieldOfView()`
- `DoubleProperty fieldOfViewProperty()`
- `void setVerticalFieldOfView(boolean)`
- `boolean isVerticalFieldOfView()`
- `BooleanProperty verticalFieldOfViewProperty()`
- `boolean isFixedEyeAtCameraZero()`

These methods define two properties, `fieldOfView` and `verticalFieldOfView`, for the `PerspectiveCamera` class. The `fieldOfView` is a double property and represents the field of view of the perspective camera in degrees. The default value is 30 degrees. The `verticalFieldOfView` is a boolean property that determines if the field of view property applies to the vertical dimension of the projection plane. The `isFixedEyeAtCameraZero()` method returns the `fixedEyeAtCameraZero` flag the `PerspectiveCamera` is constructed with.

The `PerspectiveCamera` also inherits two double properties from the `Camera` abstract class: `nearClip` and `farClip`. Objects closer to the eye than `nearClip` and objects farther from the eye than `farClip` are not rendered in the scene.

In the program in Listing 10-5, we create a `Box` and a `PerspectiveCamera`. Unlike in previous examples where we transform the 3D objects themselves like the `Box`, in this program we keep the `Box` fixed and transform the `PerspectiveCamera` with a combination of rotating around the *x* axis, rotating around the *y* axis, and a translation along the *z* axis. We animate the rotation degrees from 90 to –90 and the *z* translation from –20 to –80 in a five-second `Timeline`.

Listing 10-5. PerspectiveCameraExample.java

```
import javafx.animation.Animation;
import javafx.animation.KeyFrame;
import javafx.animation.KeyValue;
import javafx.animation.Timeline;
import javafx.application.Application;
import javafx.scene.Group;
import javafx.scene.PerspectiveCamera;
import javafx.scene.Scene;
import javafx.scene.shape.Box;
import javafx.scene.transform.Rotate;
import javafx.scene.transform.Translate;
import javafx.stage.Stage;
import javafx.util.Duration;

public class PerspectiveCameraExample extends Application {
    private View view;

    @Override
    public void start(Stage stage) throws Exception {
        view = new View();
        stage.setTitle("PerspectiveCamera Example");
        stage.setScene(view.scene);
        stage.show();
        view.animate();
    }

    public static void main(String[] args) {
        launch(args);
    }

    private static class View {
        public Scene scene;

        public Box box;
        public PerspectiveCamera camera;

        private final Rotate rotateX;
        private final Rotate rotateY;
        private final Rotate rotateZ;
        private final Translate translateZ;

        private View() {
            box = new Box(10, 10, 10);
            camera = new PerspectiveCamera(true);

            rotateX = new Rotate(-20, Rotate.X_AXIS);
            rotateY = new Rotate(-20, Rotate.Y_AXIS);
            rotateZ = new Rotate(-20, Rotate.Z_AXIS);
            translateZ = new Translate(0, 0, -100);

            camera.getTransforms().addAll(rotateX, rotateY, rotateZ, translateZ);
```

```
            Group group = new Group(box, camera);
            scene = new Scene(group, 640, 480);
            scene.setCamera(camera);
        }

        public void animate() {
            Timeline timeline = new Timeline(
                    new KeyFrame(Duration.seconds(0),
                            new KeyValue(translateZ.zProperty(), -20),
                            new KeyValue(rotateX.angleProperty(), 90),
                            new KeyValue(rotateY.angleProperty(), 90),
                            new KeyValue(rotateZ.angleProperty(), 90)),
                    new KeyFrame(Duration.seconds(5),
                            new KeyValue(translateZ.zProperty(), -80),
                            new KeyValue(rotateX.angleProperty(), -90),
                            new KeyValue(rotateY.angleProperty(), -90),
                            new KeyValue(rotateZ.angleProperty(), -90))
            );
            timeline.setCycleCount(Animation.INDEFINITE);
            timeline.play();
        }
    }
}
```

Notice that the camera needs to be added as a Node to the scene so that we can apply transforms to it. It also needs to be set as the camera to be used by the scene for rendering the 3D model.

When the program in Listing 10-5 is run, the PerspectiveCamera Example window in Figure 10-6 is displayed. We can see the box being viewed from different angles and at different distances from the eye. The box becomes smaller as the camera moves away from it.

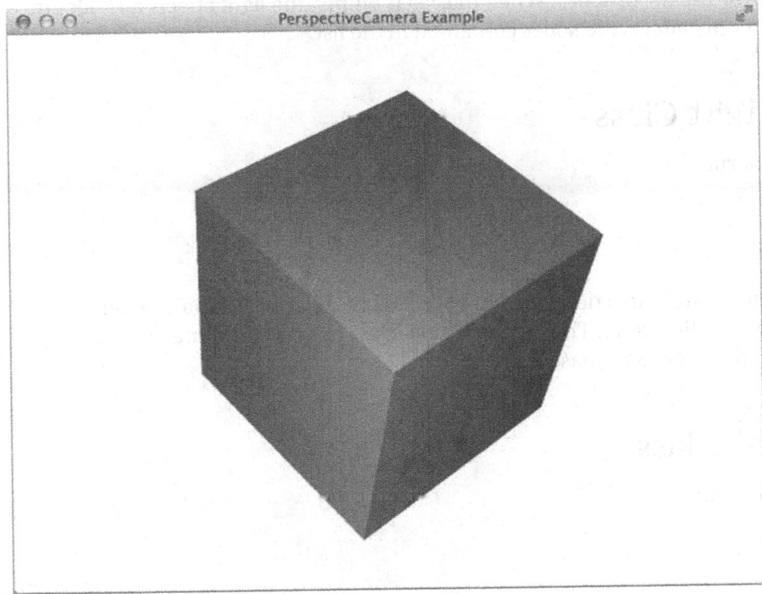

Figure 10-6. *The PerspectiveCameraExample program*

Notice also that when you resize the window, the content of the scene is resized along with the window. This is a consequence of setting `fixedEyeAtCameraZero` to `true` when we created the `PerspectiveCamera`.

Adding Lights to JavaFX Scenes

The lighting class hierarchy for the JavaFX 3D graphics API consists of the `LightBase` abstract class and its concrete subclasses `AmbientLight` and `PointLight`. They belong to the `javafx.scene` package. An `AmbientLight` is a light source that seems to come from all directions. A `PointLight` is a light that has a fixed point in space and radiates light equally in all directions away from itself. They are `Nodes`, so they can be added to a JavaFX scene to provide lighting to the scene. They can also be moved to the desired locations using the `Translate` transform. If they are added to a container, then they move along with the container when the container is transformed.

Understanding the LightBase Class

The `LightBase` abstract class has the following public methods:

- `void setColor(Color)`
- `Color getColor()`
- `ObjectProperty<Color> colorProperty()`
- `void setLightOn(boolean)`
- `boolean isLightOn()`
- `BooleanProperty lightOnProperty()`
- `ObservableList<Node> getScope()`

These methods define two properties, `color` and `lightOn`, for the `LightBase` class. The `color` property is of type `Color` and defines the color of the light. The `lightOn` property is a boolean property and controls whether the light is on. The `getScope()` method returns an `ObservableList` of `Nodes`. When this list is empty, the light affects all `Nodes` in the scene. When this list is not empty, the light only affects the `Nodes` contained in the list.

Understanding the `AmbientLight` Class

The `AmbientLight` class has the following constructors:

- `AmbientLight()`
- `AmbientLight(Color color)`

The default constructor creates an `AmbientLight` with a default color of `Color.WHITE`. The one-parameter constructor creates an `AmbientLight` with the specified color. The `AmbientLight` class has no additional public methods aside from the ones it inherited from the `LightBase` base class.

Understanding the `PointLight` Class

The `PointLight` class has the following constructors:

- `PointLight()`
- `PointLight(Color color)`

The default constructor creates a PointLight with a default color of Color.WHITE. The one-parameter constructor creates a PointLight with the specified color. The PointLight class has no additional public methods aside from the ones it inherited from the LightBase class.

The program in Listing 10-6 illustrates the use of lights in a JavaFX 3D scene. Two PointLights, one red and one blue, are added to a scene that already has a Box and a PerspectiveCamera. A control panel with sliders that can alter the coordinates of the two lights is added at the bottom of the window to allow you to see the effect of the lights being located at various locations.

Listing 10-6. LightExample.java

```
import javafx.application.Application;
import javafx.beans.property.DoubleProperty;
import javafx.beans.property.SimpleDoubleProperty;
import javafx.geometry.Insets;
import javafx.geometry.Pos;
import javafx.scene.*;
import javafx.scene.control.Label;
import javafx.scene.control.Slider;
import javafx.scene.layout.BorderPane;
import javafx.scene.layout.HBox;
import javafx.scene.layout.VBox;
import javafx.scene.paint.Color;
import javafx.scene.shape.Box;
import javafx.scene.transform.Rotate;
import javafx.scene.transform.Translate;
import javafx.stage.Stage;

public class LightExample extends Application {
    private Model model;
    private View view;

    public LightExample() {
        model = new Model();
    }

    @Override
    public void start(Stage stage) throws Exception {
        view = new View(model);
        stage.setTitle("Light Example");
        stage.setScene(view.scene);
        stage.show();
    }

    public static void main(String[] args) {
        launch(args);
    }

    private static class Model {
        private DoubleProperty redLightX = new SimpleDoubleProperty(this, "redLightX", 20.0d);
        private DoubleProperty redLightY = new SimpleDoubleProperty(this, "redLightY", -15.0d);
        private DoubleProperty redLightZ = new SimpleDoubleProperty(this, "redLightZ", -20.0d);
        private DoubleProperty blueLightX = new SimpleDoubleProperty(this, "blueLightX", 15.0d);
```

```
    private DoubleProperty blueLightY = new SimpleDoubleProperty(this, "blueLightY", -15.0d);
    private DoubleProperty blueLightZ = new SimpleDoubleProperty(this, "blueLightZ", -5.0d);

    public double getRedLightX() {
        return redLightX.get();
    }

    public DoubleProperty redLightXProperty() {
        return redLightX;
    }

    public void setRedLightX(double redLightX) {
        this.redLightX.set(redLightX);
    }

    public double getRedLightY() {
        return redLightY.get();
    }

    public DoubleProperty redLightYProperty() {
        return redLightY;
    }

    public void setRedLightY(double redLightY) {
        this.redLightY.set(redLightY);
    }

    public double getRedLightZ() {
        return redLightZ.get();
    }

    public DoubleProperty redLightZProperty() {
        return redLightZ;
    }

    public void setRedLightZ(double redLightZ) {
        this.redLightZ.set(redLightZ);
    }

    public double getBlueLightX() {
        return blueLightX.get();
    }

    public DoubleProperty blueLightXProperty() {
        return blueLightX;
    }

    public void setBlueLightX(double blueLightX) {
        this.blueLightX.set(blueLightX);
    }
```

```
        public double getBlueLightY() {
            return blueLightY.get();
        }

        public DoubleProperty blueLightYProperty() {
            return blueLightY;
        }

        public void setBlueLightY(double blueLightY) {
            this.blueLightY.set(blueLightY);
        }

        public double getBlueLightZ() {
            return blueLightZ.get();
        }

        public DoubleProperty blueLightZProperty() {
            return blueLightZ;
        }

        public void setBlueLightZ(double blueLightZ) {
            this.blueLightZ.set(blueLightZ);
        }
    }

    private static class View {
        public Scene scene;

        public Box box;
        public PerspectiveCamera camera;
        public PointLight redLight;
        public PointLight blueLight;

        private final Rotate rotateX;
        private final Rotate rotateY;
        private final Rotate rotateZ;
        private final Translate translateZ;

        private View(Model model) {
            box = new Box(10, 10, 10);

            camera = new PerspectiveCamera(true);

            rotateX = new Rotate(-20, Rotate.X_AXIS);
            rotateY = new Rotate(-20, Rotate.Y_AXIS);
            rotateZ = new Rotate(-20, Rotate.Z_AXIS);
            translateZ = new Translate(0, 0, -50);

            camera.getTransforms().addAll(rotateX, rotateY, rotateZ, translateZ);
```

```
        redLight = new PointLight(Color.RED);
        redLight.translateXProperty().bind(model.redLightXProperty());
        redLight.translateYProperty().bind(model.redLightYProperty());
        redLight.translateZProperty().bind(model.redLightZProperty());

        blueLight = new PointLight(Color.BLUE);
        blueLight.translateXProperty().bind(model.blueLightXProperty());
        blueLight.translateYProperty().bind(model.blueLightYProperty());
        blueLight.translateZProperty().bind(model.blueLightZProperty());

        Group group = new Group(box, camera, redLight, blueLight);
        SubScene subScene = new SubScene(group, 640, 480, true, SceneAntialiasing.BALANCED);
        subScene.setCamera(camera);

        Slider redLightXSlider = createSlider(20);
        Slider redLightYSlider = createSlider(-20);
        Slider redLightZSlider = createSlider(-20);

        redLightXSlider.valueProperty().bindBidirectional(model.redLightXProperty());

        redLightYSlider.valueProperty().bindBidirectional(model.redLightYProperty());

        redLightZSlider.valueProperty().bindBidirectional(model.redLightZProperty());

        HBox hbox1 = new HBox(10, new Label("Red light x:"), redLightXSlider,
                new Label("y:"), redLightYSlider,
                new Label("z:"), redLightZSlider);
        hbox1.setPadding(new Insets(10, 10, 10, 10));
        hbox1.setAlignment(Pos.CENTER);

        Slider blueLightXSlider = createSlider(15);
        Slider blueLightYSlider = createSlider(-15);
        Slider blueLightZSlider = createSlider(-15);

        blueLightXSlider.valueProperty().bindBidirectional(model.blueLightXProperty());

        blueLightYSlider.valueProperty().bindBidirectional(model.blueLightYProperty());

        blueLightZSlider.valueProperty().bindBidirectional(model.blueLightZProperty());

        HBox hbox2 = new HBox(10, new Label("Blue light x:"), blueLightXSlider,
                new Label("y:"), blueLightYSlider,
                new Label("z:"), blueLightZSlider);
        hbox2.setPadding(new Insets(10, 10, 10, 10));
        hbox2.setAlignment(Pos.CENTER);

        VBox controlPanel = new VBox(10, hbox1, hbox2);
        controlPanel.setPadding(new Insets(10, 10, 10, 10));
        controlPanel.setAlignment(Pos.CENTER);
        BorderPane borderPane = new BorderPane(subScene, null, null, controlPanel, null);
        scene = new Scene(borderPane);
    }

    private Slider createSlider(double value) {
        Slider slider = new Slider(-30, 30, value);
        slider.setShowTickMarks(true);
```

```
            slider.setShowTickLabels(true);
            return slider;
        }
    }
}
```

When the program in Listing 10-6 is run, the Light Example window in Figure 10-7 is displayed.

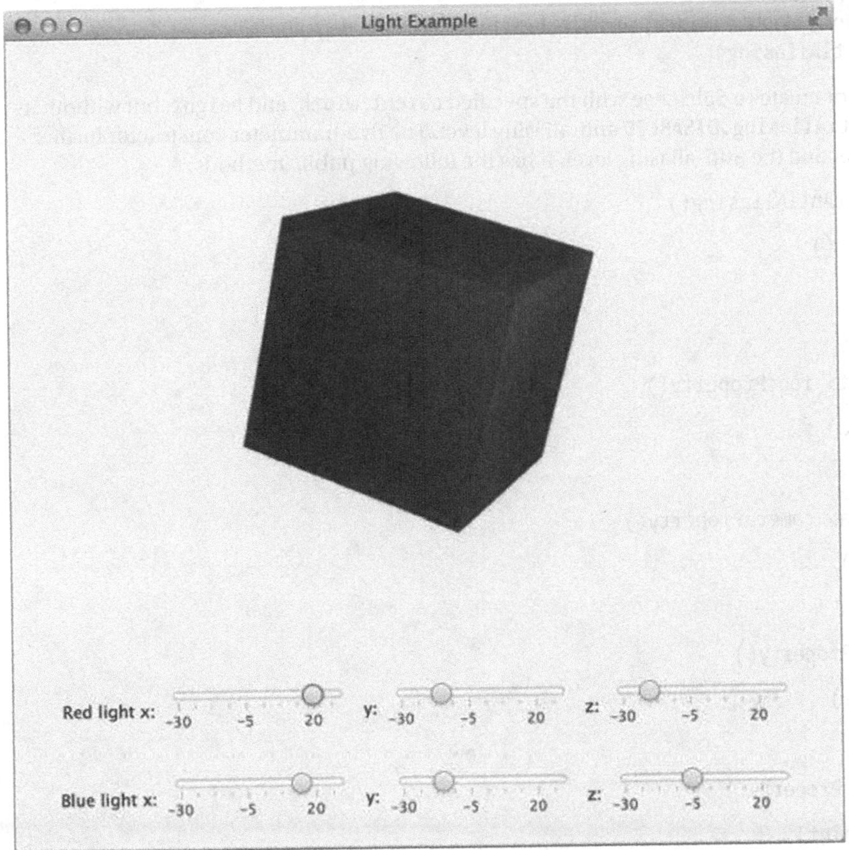

Figure 10-7. *The LightExample program*

As you experiment with different (*x*, *y*, *z*) coordinates of the red light and the blue light, keep in mind that the perspective camera that is rendering the screen is slightly rotated away from the default position, and translated to the negative *z* direction. Therefore the face of the box that is facing us is the face with negative *z* coordinates; the face of the box that is facing right is the face with positive *x* coordinates; and the face of the box that is facing upward is the face with negative *y* coordinates.

Understanding SubScenes

In the LightExample in the last section, we used a JavaFX 3D graphics API that we have not covered yet, the SubScene class. It belongs to the javafx.scene package. A SubScene is a container Node that can add contents to a bigger scene, yet it can have its own camera, depth buffer, and anti-aliasing policy and can render its own content separately from the rest of the scene.

The SubScene class has the following constructors:

- SubScene(Parent parent, double width, double height)
- SubScene(Parent parent, double width, double height, boolean depthBuffer, SceneAntialiasing antiAliasing)

The three-parameter constructor creates a SubScene with the specified parent, width, and height, but without its own depth buffer and with SceneAntiAliasing.DISABLED anti-aliasing level. The five-parameter constructor further allows you to specify the depth buffer and the anti-aliasing level. It has the following public methods:

- SceneAntialiasing getAntiAliasing()
- boolean isDepthBuffer()
- void setRoot(Parent)
- Parent getRoot()
- ObjectProperty<Parent> rootProperty()
- void setCamera(Camera)
- Camera getCamera()
- ObjectProperty<Camera> cameraProperty()
- void setWidth(double)
- double getWidth()
- DoubleProperty widthProperty()
- void setHeight(double)
- double getHeight()
- DoubleProperty heightProperty()
- void setFill(paint.Paint)
- paint.Paint getFill()
- ObjectProperty< Paint> fillProperty()

The getAntiAliasing() and the isDepthBuffer() methods return the anti-aliasing level and the depth buffer parameters passed into the constructor. The other methods define five read-write properties for the SubScene class. These are the root, camera, width, height, and fill properties. They behave the same way as the like-named properties of the Scene class.

The major use of SubScene is to separate 2D and 3D contents in a JavaFX program where both are needed. That is how we used it in the LightExample. We placed the 3D portion of our program into a SubScene to separate it from the rest of the program, which consists of JavaFX controls.

Specifying the Material of 3D Shapes

Now that we have covered the 3D shapes, both predefined and user-defined, the cameras, and the lights, in this section, we deal with the last remaining topic in the JavaFX 3D graphics API. The material API consists of the `Material` abstract class and its concrete subclass `PhongMaterial`. The `Material` class is an abstract base class without any public methods. In all practical situations, it is the `PhongMaterial` class that is used. The material class describes the physical properties of a 3D surface and how they interact with lights.

Understanding the PhongMaterial Class

The `PhongMaterial` class has the following constructors:

- `PhongMaterial()`
- `PhongMaterial(Color diffuseColor)`
- `PhongMaterial(Color diffuseColor, Image diffuseMap, Image specularMap, Image bumpMap, Image selfIlluminationMap)`

The default constructor creates a `PhongMaterial` with the default `diffuseColor` of `Color.WHITE`. The one-parameter constructor creates a `PhongMaterial` with the specified `diffuseColor`. The third constructor creates a `PhongMaterial` with the specified `diffuseColor`, `diffuseMap`, `specularMap`, `bumpMap`, and `selfIlluminationMap`. We discuss what these parameters mean after we cover the properties of the `PhongMaterial` class.

The `PhongMaterial` class has the following public methods:

- `void setDiffuseColor(Color)`
- `Color getDiffuseColor()`
- `ObjectProperty<Color> diffuseColorProperty()`
- `void setSpecularColor(Color)`
- `Color getSpecularColor()`
- `ObjectProperty<Color> specularColorProperty()`
- `void setSpecularPower(double)`
- `double getSpecularPower()`
- `DoubleProperty specularPowerProperty()`
- `void setDiffuseMap(Image)`
- `Image getDiffuseMap()`
- `ObjectProperty<Image> diffuseMapProperty()`
- `void setSpecularMap(Image)`
- `Image getSpecularMap()`
- `ObjectProperty<Image> specularMapProperty()`
- `void setBumpMap(Image)`
- `Image getBumpMap()`
- `ObjectProperty<Image> bumpMapProperty()`

- `void setSelfIlluminationMap(Image)`
- `Image getSelfIlluminationMap()`
- `ObjectProperty<Image> selfIlluminationMapProperty()`

These methods define seven read-write properties for the `PhongMaterial` class. The `diffuseColor` and `specularColor` are object properties of type `Color`. The `specularPower` is a double property. The `diffuseMap`, `specularMap`, `bumpMap`, and `selfIlluminationMap` properties are object properties of type `Image`. Five of the seven properties can be specified in the third constructor. However, once a `PhongMaterial` is constructed, its properties can also be altered.

In several of our earlier examples, we have used the one-parameter `PhongMaterial` constructor, in which we specify the diffuse color of the 3D shapes. The diffuse color is what we normally think of as the color of an object.

The specular color is the color of the highlights reflected off of shiny surfaces, such as a mirror or another well-polished surface.

In the program in Listing 10-7, we add a specular color to the material of a sphere.

Listing 10-7. `SpecularColorExample.java`

```
import javafx.application.Application;
import javafx.scene.Group;
import javafx.scene.PointLight;
import javafx.scene.Scene;
import javafx.scene.paint.Color;
import javafx.scene.paint.PhongMaterial;
import javafx.scene.shape.Sphere;
import javafx.stage.Stage;

public class SpecularColorExample extends Application {
    private View view;

    @Override
    public void start(Stage stage) throws Exception {
        view = new View();
        stage.setTitle("Specular Color Example");
        stage.setScene(view.scene);
        stage.show();
    }

    public static void main(String[] args) {
        launch(args);
    }

    private static class View {
        public Scene scene;
        public Sphere sphere;
        public PointLight light;

        private View() {
            sphere = new Sphere(100);
            PhongMaterial material = new PhongMaterial(Color.BLUE);
            material.setSpecularColor(Color.LIGHTBLUE);
            material.setSpecularPower(10.0d);
            sphere.setMaterial(material);
            sphere.setTranslateZ(300);
```

```
            light = new PointLight(Color.WHITE);

            Group group = new Group(sphere, light);
            group.setTranslateY(240);
            group.setTranslateX(320);
            scene = new Scene(group, 640, 480);
        }
    }
}
```

In this program, we let a white light shine on a sphere with a diffuse color of blue and a specular color of light blue with a specular power of 10. The default specular power in PhongMaterial is 32.0. Therefore our sphere does not have as focused a highlight as the default. When the program in Listing 10-7 is run, the Specular Color Example window shown in Figure 10-8 is displayed.

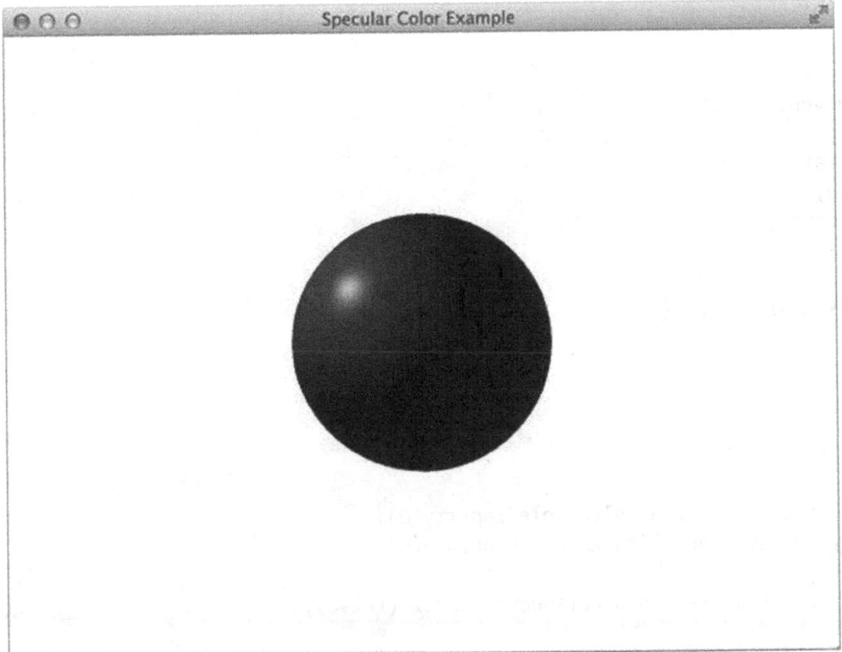

Figure 10-8. *The SpecularColorExample program*

Adding Texture to 3D Shapes

The `diffuseMap` and the `specularMap` serve the same purpose as the `diffuseColor` and `specularColor`, except that the maps provide different color values for different points on the surface of a 3D shape. The `bumpMap` and the `selfIlluminationMap` are similarly mapped to the points on the surface of a 3D shape. The `selfIlluminationMap` provides colors that will shine through even if no light is illuminating the 3D object. The `bumpMap` does not contain color information at all. It contains normal vector information (which just happens to be three numbers, which can be encoded as an RGB color) for each point of the surface, which, when taken into account during the color rendering calculation, will result in a bumped look.

The mapping of the points on the surface to a point on the images is the job of the `TriangleMesh`. We built a `MeshView` with a user-defined `TriangleMesh` earlier in this chapter. In fact, the predefined 3D shapes are also based on `TriangleMeshes` internally. Therefore they are also capable of being texturized. Recall that in `TriangleMesh`, each face is defined by six indices: *p0, t0, p1, t1, p2, t2*, where *p0, p1, p2* are indices into the points array, and *t0, t1, t2* are indices into the `texCoords` array. Looking up the `texCoords` array with *t0, t1, t2* we get the (*u0, v0*), (*u1, v1*), and (*u2, v2*) coordinates. The triangular portion of the image determined by these three coordinates is mapped to the face of the 3D shape.

In the program in Listing 10-8, we use a world map image as the `diffuseMap` of a sphere to make a globe.

Listing 10-8. `EarthSphere.java`

```
import javafx.application.Application;
import javafx.beans.property.DoubleProperty;
import javafx.beans.property.SimpleDoubleProperty;
import javafx.scene.Group;
import javafx.scene.PerspectiveCamera;
import javafx.scene.PointLight;
import javafx.scene.Scene;
import javafx.scene.image.Image;
import javafx.scene.input.MouseEvent;
import javafx.scene.paint.Color;
import javafx.scene.paint.PhongMaterial;
import javafx.scene.shape.Sphere;
import javafx.scene.transform.Rotate;
import javafx.stage.Stage;

public class EarthSphere extends Application {

    double anchorX, anchorY;

    private double anchorAngleX = 0;
    private double anchorAngleY = 0;

    private final DoubleProperty angleX = new SimpleDoubleProperty(0);
    private final DoubleProperty angleY = new SimpleDoubleProperty(0);

    PerspectiveCamera scenePerspectiveCamera = new PerspectiveCamera(false);

    public static void main(String[] args) {
        launch(args);
    }

    @Override
    public void start(Stage stage) {
        stage.setTitle("EarthSphere");

        Image diffuseMap = new Image(EarthSphere.class
                .getResource("earth-mercator.jpg")
                .toExternalForm());

        PhongMaterial earthMaterial = new PhongMaterial();
        earthMaterial.setDiffuseMap(diffuseMap);
```

```
        final Sphere earth = new Sphere(400);
        earth.setMaterial(earthMaterial);

        final Group parent = new Group(earth);
        parent.setTranslateX(450);
        parent.setTranslateY(450);
        parent.setTranslateZ(100);

        Rotate xRotate;
        Rotate yRotate;
        parent.getTransforms().setAll(
                xRotate = new Rotate(0, Rotate.X_AXIS),
                yRotate = new Rotate(0, Rotate.Y_AXIS)
        );
        xRotate.angleProperty().bind(angleX);
        yRotate.angleProperty().bind(angleY);

        final Group root = new Group();
        root.getChildren().add(parent);

        final Scene scene = new Scene(root, 900, 900, true);
        scene.setFill(Color.BLACK);

        scene.setOnMousePressed((MouseEvent event) -> {
            anchorX = event.getSceneX();
            anchorY = event.getSceneY();

            anchorAngleX = angleX.get();
            anchorAngleY = angleY.get();
        });

        scene.setOnMouseDragged((MouseEvent event) -> {
            angleY.set(anchorAngleY + anchorX - event.getSceneX());
        });

        PointLight pointLight = new PointLight(Color.WHITE);
        pointLight.setTranslateX(400);
        pointLight.setTranslateY(400);
        pointLight.setTranslateZ(-3000);

        scene.setCamera(scenePerspectiveCamera);

        root.getChildren().addAll(pointLight, scenePerspectiveCamera);

        stage.setScene(scene);

        stage.show();
    }
}
```

The code that maps the image of the world map onto the sphere is pretty straightforward:

```
Image diffuseMap = new Image(EarthSphere.class
        .getResource("earth-mercator.jpg")
        .toExternalForm());

PhongMaterial earthMaterial = new PhongMaterial();
earthMaterial.setDiffuseMap(diffuseMap);

final Sphere earth = new Sphere(400);
earth.setMaterial(earthMaterial);
```

Note that the image is a world map in Mercator projection, which is required by the internal `TriangleMesh` of `Sphere`. When the program in Listing 10-8 is run, the EarthSphere window in Figure 10-9 is displayed.

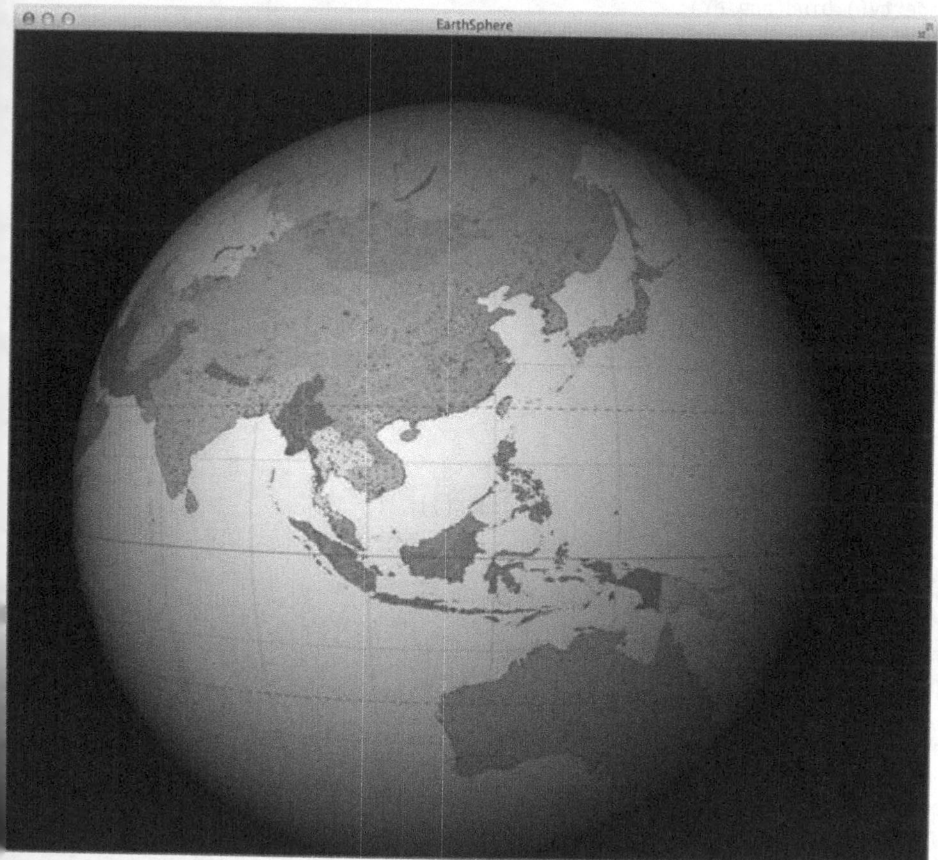

Figure 10-9. *The EarthSphere program*

We can map the image onto a cylinder and a box just as easily. We do not show you the code here, as it is very similar to the code for the sphere. You can look up the code in the downloaded code bundle for this book. We show you the outcome of these programs in Figures 10-10 and 10-11.

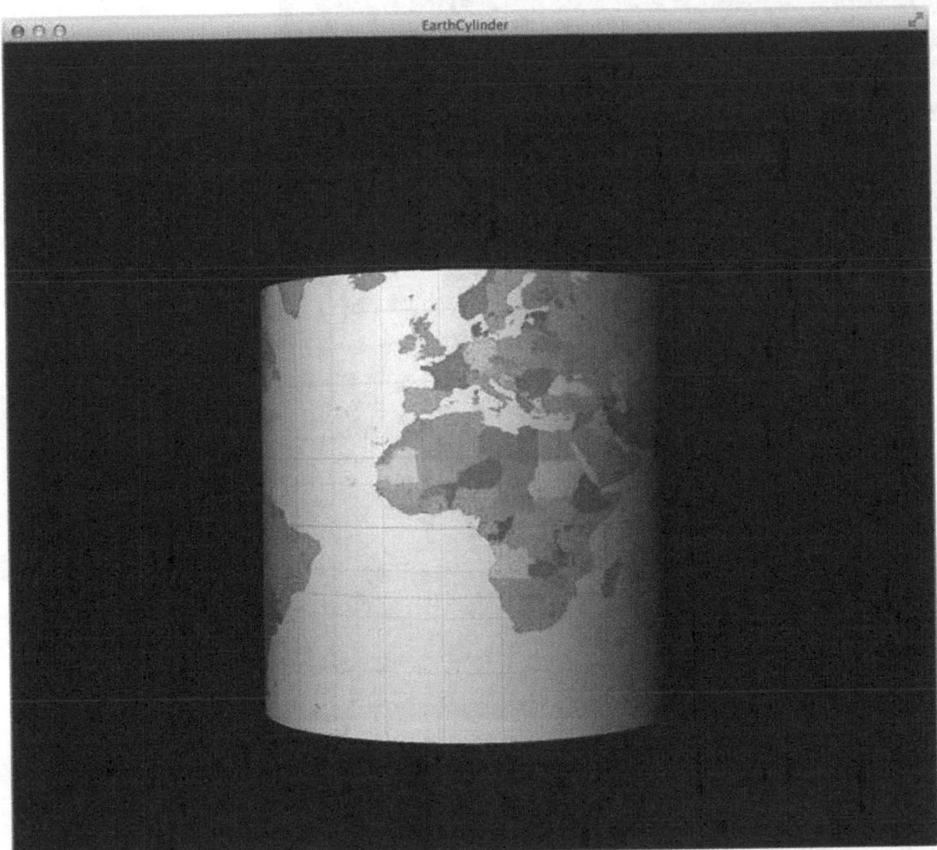

Figure 10-10. *The EarthCylinder program*

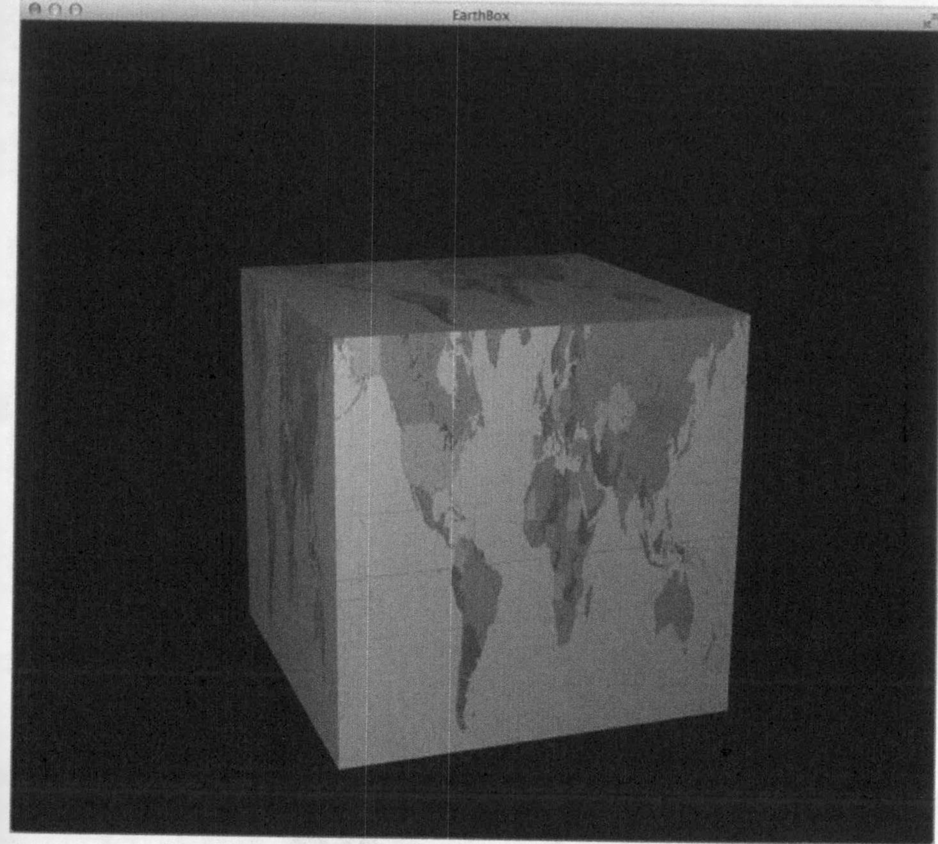

Figure 10-11. *The EarthBox program*

If you pay attention to Figure 10-11, you will notice that all six sides of the box are mapped to the same image. This is a consequence of how the predefined Box class implements its TriangleMesh. We can easily create a user-defined MeshCube with sides that are mapped to different parts of the diffuseMap image file.

In Listing 10-9, we create a MeshCube and then texturize it with an earth-in-a-box image file with an image that looks like an actual spread-out box, resulting in a world map on a cube.

Listing 10-9. MeshCube.java

```
import javafx.application.Application;
import javafx.beans.property.DoubleProperty;
import javafx.beans.property.SimpleDoubleProperty;
import javafx.scene.Group;
import javafx.scene.PerspectiveCamera;
import javafx.scene.PointLight;
import javafx.scene.Scene;
import javafx.scene.image.Image;
import javafx.scene.paint.Color;
import javafx.scene.paint.PhongMaterial;
import javafx.scene.shape.MeshView;
import javafx.scene.shape.TriangleMesh;
```

```
import javafx.scene.transform.Rotate;
import javafx.stage.Stage;

/**
 * @author Jim
 */
public class MeshCube extends Application {

    double anchorX, anchorY;

    private static final float EDGE_LENGTH = 380;

    private double anchorAngleX = 0;
    private double anchorAngleY = 0;

    private final DoubleProperty angleX = new SimpleDoubleProperty(25);
    private final DoubleProperty angleY = new SimpleDoubleProperty(40);

    PerspectiveCamera camera = new PerspectiveCamera(false);

    static TriangleMesh createMesh(float w, float h, float d) {

        if (w * h * d == 0) {
            return null;
        }

        float hw = w / 2f;
        float hh = h / 2f;
        float hd = d / 2f;

        float x0 = 0f;
        float x1 = 1f / 4f;
        float x2 = 2f / 4f;
        float x3 = 3f / 4f;
        float x4 = 1f;
        float y0 = 0f;
        float y1 = 1f / 3f;
        float y2 = 2f / 3f;
        float y3 = 1f;

        TriangleMesh mesh = new TriangleMesh();
        mesh.getPoints().addAll(
            hw, hh, hd,   //point A
            hw, hh, -hd,  //point B
            hw, -hh, hd,  //point C
            hw, -hh, -hd, //point D
            -hw, hh, hd,  //point E
            -hw, hh, -hd, //point F
            -hw, -hh, hd, //point G
            -hw, -hh, -hd //point H
        );
```

```
        mesh.getTexCoords().addAll(
            x1, y0,
            x2, y0,
            x0, y1,
            x1, y1,
            x2, y1,
            x3, y1,
            x4, y1,
            x0, y2,
            x1, y2,
            x2, y2,
            x3, y2,
            x4, y2,
            x1, y3,
            x2, y3
        );
        mesh.getFaces().addAll(
            0, 10, 2, 5, 1, 9,     //triangle A-C-B
            2, 5, 3, 4, 1, 9,      //triangle C-D-B
            4, 7, 5, 8, 6, 2,      //triangle E-F-G
            6, 2, 5, 8, 7, 3,      //triangle G-F-H
            0, 13, 1, 9, 4, 12,    //triangle A-B-E
            4, 12, 1, 9, 5, 8,     //triangle E-B-F
            2, 1, 6, 0, 3, 4,      //triangle C-G-D
            3, 4, 6, 0, 7, 3,      //triangle D-G-H
            0, 10, 4, 11, 2, 5,    //triangle A-E-C
            2, 5, 4, 11, 6, 6,     //triangle C-E-G
            1, 9, 3, 4, 5, 8,      //triangle B-D-F
            5, 8, 3, 4, 7, 3       //triangle F-D-H
        );
        mesh.getFaceSmoothingGroups().addAll(
            0, 0, 1, 1, 2, 2, 3, 3, 4, 4, 5, 5
        );
        return mesh;
    }

    @Override
    public void start(Stage primaryStage) {
        primaryStage.setTitle("MeshCube");

        Image diffuseMap =
            new Image(MeshCube.class
                .getResource("cbGn_pof-bm.png")
                .toExternalForm());

        PhongMaterial earthMaterial = new PhongMaterial();
        earthMaterial.setDiffuseMap(diffuseMap);

        MeshView cube =
            new MeshView(createMesh(EDGE_LENGTH, EDGE_LENGTH, EDGE_LENGTH));
        cube.setMaterial(earthMaterial);
```

```
        final Group parent = new Group(cube);
        parent.setTranslateX(450);
        parent.setTranslateY(400);
        parent.setTranslateZ(0);

        Rotate xRotate;
        Rotate yRotate;
        parent.getTransforms().setAll(
            xRotate = new Rotate(0, Rotate.X_AXIS),
            yRotate = new Rotate(0, Rotate.Y_AXIS)
        );
        xRotate.angleProperty().bind(angleX);
        yRotate.angleProperty().bind(angleY);

        final Group root = new Group(parent);

        final Scene scene = new Scene(root, 900, 900, true);
        scene.setFill(Color.WHITE);

        scene.setOnMousePressed(event -> {
            anchorX = event.getSceneX();
            anchorY = event.getSceneY();
            anchorAngleX = angleX.get();
            anchorAngleY = angleY.get();
        });

        scene.setOnMouseDragged(event -> {
            angleX.set(anchorAngleX - (anchorY - event.getSceneY()));
            angleY.set(anchorAngleY + anchorX - event.getSceneX());
        });

        PointLight pointLight = new PointLight(Color.WHITE);
        pointLight.setTranslateX(300);
        pointLight.setTranslateY(200);
        pointLight.setTranslateZ(-2000);

        root.getChildren().add(pointLight);

        scene.setCamera(camera);
        primaryStage.setScene(scene);

        primaryStage.show();
    }

    public static void main(String[] args) {
        launch(args);
    }
}
```

When the program in Listing 10-9 is run, the MeshCube window of Figure 10-12 is displayed.

Figure 10-12. *The MeshCube program*

Interacting with JavaFX 3D Scenes

The 3D shapes in the JavaFX 3D graphics API support the full range of JavaFX mouse and touch events. Your JavaFX 3D program can take full advantage of these events to implement interactive behaviors. In fact, we have implemented mouse interactions in the EarthSphere, EarthCylinder, EarthBox, and MeshCube programs. In the EarthSphere we set event handlers on the scene:

```
        scene.setOnMousePressed((MouseEvent event) -> {
            anchorX = event.getSceneX();
            anchorY = event.getSceneY();

            anchorAngleX = angleX.get();
            anchorAngleY = angleY.get();
        });

        scene.setOnMouseDragged((MouseEvent event) -> {
            angleY.set(anchorAngleY + anchorX - event.getSceneX());
        });
```

In this code, anchorX and anchorY are double fields of the class, and angleX and angleY are double properties that are bound to the degrees of rotations of the parent node that contains the sphere around the *x* and *y* axis. Here we capture the screen coordinates of the mouse pointer as anchorX and anchorY when the mouse is pressed on the screen. We also query for the degree of rotation about the *x* and *y* axes of the parent node that contains the sphere. When the mouse is dragged, we alter the degree of rotation of the parent node that contains the sphere about the *y* axis by adding the difference between anchorX and the screen *x* coordinate of the new mouse location. Therefore, if you click on the screen and drag the mouse to the right, anchorX - event.getScreenX() is a negative number, hence we decrease the angle of rotation about the *y* axis. Because in this program, the *y* axis is pointing down, a decrease of the rotation about the *y* axis actually makes the sphere to appear to be rotating to the right, matching the direction of the mouse drag.

Understanding the PickResult Class

The JavaFX 3D runtime provides enhanced information about the interplay of the mouse pointer with the 3D scene. This information is provided in terms of an object of class PickResult in the relevant event objects. It is contained in the javafx.scene.input package. The following event objects provide a getPickResult() method that allows you to retrieve this PickResult object:

- ContextMenuEvent
- DragEvent
- GestureEvent
    - RotateEvent
    - ScrollEvent
    - SwipeEvent
    - ZoomEvent
- MouseEvent
    - MouseDragEvent
- TouchPoint

The PickResult class provides the following public constructors:

- PickResult(EventTarget, double, double)
- PickResult(Node, Point3D, double)
- PickResult(Node, Point3D, double, int, Point2D)

The first two constructors are used to create PickResults to work with 2D scenes, and the third constructor creates a PickResult that contains 3D information. The PickResults are usually created by the JavaFX 3D runtime. JavaFX application code usually obtains PickResults by calling the accessor method on the event object.

The PickResult class provides the following public methods:

- Node getIntersectedNode()
- Point3D getIntersectedPoint()
- double getIntersectedDistance()
- int getIntersectedFace()
- Point2D getIntersectedTexCoord()

When the user clicks the mouse on a 3D shape, it touches the 3D shape in a particular point in a particular face. The line segment starting from the eye of the camera in effect for the Scene or SubScene and ending at the point on the 3D shape is called the *pick ray*. The point on the 3D shape is called the *intersected point*. The PickResult provides information about this intersected point. The getIntersectedNode() method returns the 3D shape itself, either a Sphere, a Cylinder, a Box, or a MeshView. The getIntersectedPoint() method returns the 3D coordinates of the intersected point. The coordinates are relative to the 3D shape's local coordinate system. For a Sphere of radius 100, the coordinates (x, y, z) of the returned Point3D will satisfy $x^2 + y^2 + z^2 = 100^2$, regardless of the transforms applied to itself or any of its containing nodes. The getIntersectedDistance() method returns the distance from the eye of the camera to the intersected point. This is the length of the pick ray in the 3D model's world coordinate system. The getIntersectedFace() method returns the face number of the face that contains the intersected point for a MeshView, which has user-defined faces. It returns FACE_UNDEFINED for the predefined 3D shapes Sphere, Cylinder, and Box. The getIntersectedTexCoord() method returns the texture coordinates of the intersected point. Unlike the getIntersectedFace() method, this method will return the texture coordinates for both user-defined and predefined 3D shapes.

The program in Listing 10-10 sets an event handler for the mouse clicked and the mouse dragged event for a sphere, and changes the color of the sphere based on the intersected point's coordinates when you click on or drag the mouse over the sphere.

Listing 10-10. SphereWithEvents.java

```
import javafx.application.Application;
import javafx.beans.property.ObjectProperty;
import javafx.beans.property.SimpleObjectProperty;
import javafx.event.EventHandler;
import javafx.geometry.Point3D;
import javafx.scene.Group;
import javafx.scene.Scene;
import javafx.scene.input.PickResult;
import javafx.scene.paint.Color;
import javafx.scene.paint.Material;
import javafx.scene.paint.PhongMaterial;
import javafx.scene.shape.Sphere;
import javafx.stage.Stage;

import static java.lang.Math.abs;
import static java.lang.Math.min;

public class SphereWithEvents extends Application {
    private Model model;
    private View view;

    public SphereWithEvents() {
        model = new Model();
    }

    @Override
    public void start(Stage primaryStage) throws Exception {
        view = new View(model);
        primaryStage.setTitle("Sphere with MouseEvents");
        primaryStage.setScene(view.scene);
        primaryStage.show();
    }
```

```
public static void main(String[] args) {
    launch(args);
}

private static class Model {
    private ObjectProperty<Material> material = new SimpleObjectProperty<>(
            this, "material", new PhongMaterial());

    public Material getMaterial() {
        return material.get();
    }

    public ObjectProperty<Material> materialProperty() {
        return material;
    }

    public void setMaterial(Material material) {
        this.material.set(material);
    }
}

private static class View {
    public static final int SPHERE_RADIUS = 200;
    public Scene scene;
    public Sphere sphere;

    private View(Model model) {
        sphere = new Sphere(SPHERE_RADIUS);
        sphere.materialProperty().bind(model.materialProperty());

        EventHandler<javafx.scene.input.MouseEvent> handler = event -> {
            PickResult pickResult = event.getPickResult();
            Point3D point = pickResult.getIntersectedPoint();
            model.setMaterial(new PhongMaterial(makeColorOutOfPoint3D(point)));
        };

        sphere.setOnMouseClicked(handler);
        sphere.setOnMouseDragged(handler);
        Group group = new Group(sphere);
        group.setTranslateX(320);
        group.setTranslateY(240);
        scene = new Scene(group, 640, 480);
    }

    private Color makeColorOutOfPoint3D(Point3D point) {
        double x = point.getX();
        double y = point.getY();
        double z = point.getZ();
        return Color.color(normalize(x), normalize(y), normalize(z));
    }
```

```
        private double normalize(double x) {
            return min(abs(x) / SPHERE_RADIUS, 1);
        }
    }
}
```

When the program in Listing 10-10 is run, the Sphere with MouseEvents window in Figure 10-13 is displayed. You can click on or drag the mouse over the sphere to see the sphere changing color.

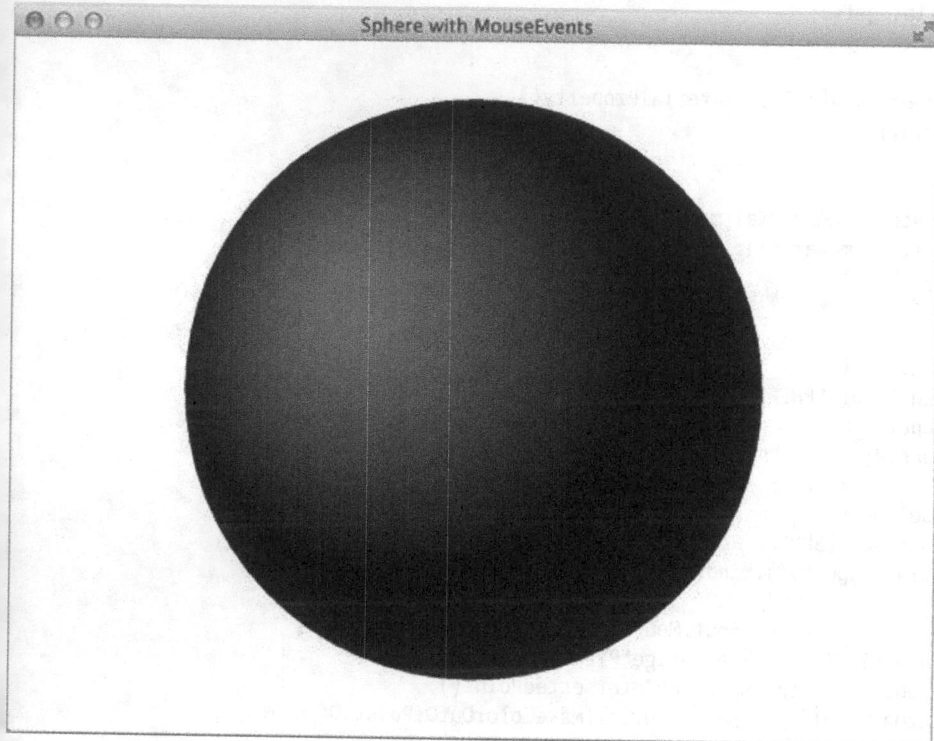

Figure 10-13. *The SphereWithEvents program*

The program in Listing 10-11 displays a user-defined `MeshView` of a cube and contains a control panel that allows the user to control the *z* coordinate of the cube, change the drawing mode between `DrawMode.LINE` and `DrawMode.FILL`, and shows the face number of the intersected face.

Listing 10-11. `MeshCubePickDemo.java`

```
import javafx.application.Application;
import javafx.beans.binding.When;
import javafx.beans.property.BooleanProperty;
import javafx.beans.property.DoubleProperty;
import javafx.beans.property.SimpleBooleanProperty;
import javafx.beans.property.SimpleDoubleProperty;
import javafx.geometry.Insets;
import javafx.scene.Group;
```

```
import javafx.scene.PerspectiveCamera;
import javafx.scene.PointLight;
import javafx.scene.Scene;
import javafx.scene.SubScene;
import javafx.scene.control.CheckBox;
import javafx.scene.control.Label;
import javafx.scene.control.Slider;
import javafx.scene.image.Image;
import javafx.scene.input.MouseEvent;
import javafx.scene.input.PickResult;
import javafx.scene.layout.HBox;
import javafx.scene.paint.Color;
import javafx.scene.paint.PhongMaterial;
import javafx.scene.shape.DrawMode;
import javafx.scene.shape.MeshView;
import javafx.scene.shape.TriangleMesh;
import javafx.scene.transform.Rotate;
import javafx.stage.Stage;

public class MeshCubePickDemo extends Application {

    double anchorX, anchorY;

    private static final float EDGE_LENGTH = 200;

    private double anchorAngleX = 0;
    private double anchorAngleY = 0;

    private final DoubleProperty angleX = new SimpleDoubleProperty(25);
    private final DoubleProperty angleY = new SimpleDoubleProperty(40);

    PerspectiveCamera camera = new PerspectiveCamera(false);

    private Slider zSlider;
    private final DoubleProperty zPos = new SimpleDoubleProperty(-200);

    private CheckBox meshCheckBox;

    private final BooleanProperty showWireframe = new SimpleBooleanProperty(false);

    private Label facePickedLabel = new Label();

    static TriangleMesh createMesh(float w, float h, float d) {

        if (w * h * d == 0) {
            return null;
        }

        float hw = w / 2f;
        float hh = h / 2f;
        float hd = d / 2f;
```

```
    float x0 = 0f;
    float x1 = 1f / 4f;
    float x2 = 2f / 4f;
    float x3 = 3f / 4f;
    float x4 = 1f;
    float y0 = 0f;
    float y1 = 1f / 3f;
    float y2 = 2f / 3f;
    float y3 = 1f;

    TriangleMesh mesh = new TriangleMesh();
    mesh.getPoints().addAll(
        hw, hh, hd,   //point A
        hw, hh, -hd,  //point B
        hw, -hh, hd,  //point C
        hw, -hh, -hd, //point D
        -hw, hh, hd,  //point E
        -hw, hh, -hd, //point F
        -hw, -hh, hd, //point G
        -hw, -hh, -hd //point H
    );
    mesh.getTexCoords().addAll(
        x1, y0,
        x2, y0,
        x0, y1,
        x1, y1,
        x2, y1,
        x3, y1,
        x4, y1,
        x0, y2,
        x1, y2,
        x2, y2,
        x3, y2,
        x4, y2,
        x1, y3,
        x2, y3
    );
    mesh.getFaces().addAll(
        0, 10, 2, 5, 1, 9,    //triangle A-C-B
        2, 5, 3, 4, 1, 9,     //triangle C-D-B
        4, 7, 5, 8, 6, 2,     //triangle E-F-G
        6, 2, 5, 8, 7, 3,     //triangle G-F-H
        0, 13, 1, 9, 4, 12,   //triangle A-B-E
        4, 12, 1, 9, 5, 8,    //triangle E-B-F
        2, 1, 6, 0, 3, 4,     //triangle C-G-D
        3, 4, 6, 0, 7, 3,     //triangle D-G-H
        0, 10, 4, 11, 2, 5,   //triangle A-E-C
        2, 5, 4, 11, 6, 6,    //triangle C-E-G
        1, 9, 3, 4, 5, 8,     //triangle B-D-F
        5, 8, 3, 4, 7, 3      //triangle F-D-H
    );
```

```
        mesh.getFaceSmoothingGroups().addAll(
            0, 0, 1, 1, 2, 2, 3, 3, 4, 4, 5, 5
        );
        return mesh;
    }

    @Override
    public void start(Stage stage) {
        stage.setTitle("MeshCubePickDemo");

        Image diffuseMap = new Image(MeshCubePickDemo.class
            .getResource("cbGn_pof-bm.png").toExternalForm());

        PhongMaterial earthMaterial = new PhongMaterial();
        earthMaterial.setDiffuseMap(diffuseMap);

        MeshView cube =
            new MeshView(createMesh(EDGE_LENGTH, EDGE_LENGTH, EDGE_LENGTH));
        cube.setMaterial(earthMaterial);

        final Group parent = new Group(cube);
        parent.setTranslateX(320);
        parent.setTranslateY(240);
        parent.setTranslateZ(0);

        Rotate xRotate;
        Rotate yRotate;
        parent.getTransforms().setAll(
            xRotate = new Rotate(0, Rotate.X_AXIS),
            yRotate = new Rotate(0, Rotate.Y_AXIS)
        );
        xRotate.angleProperty().bind(angleX);
        yRotate.angleProperty().bind(angleY);

        final Group root = new Group(parent);

        final Scene scene = new Scene(root, 640, 480, true);
        scene.setFill(Color.WHITE);

        scene.setOnMousePressed((MouseEvent event) -> {
            anchorX = event.getSceneX();
            anchorY = event.getSceneY();
            anchorAngleX = angleX.get();
            anchorAngleY = angleY.get();

            PickResult pr = event.getPickResult();

            facePickedLabel.setText("Face picked: "
                + pr.getIntersectedFace());
        });
```

```
        scene.setOnMouseDragged((MouseEvent event) -> {
            angleX.set(anchorAngleX - (anchorY - event.getSceneY()));
            angleY.set(anchorAngleY + anchorX - event.getSceneX());
        });

        PointLight pointLight = new PointLight(Color.WHITE);
        pointLight.setTranslateX(300);
        pointLight.setTranslateY(200);
        pointLight.setTranslateZ(-2000);

        root.getChildren().add(pointLight);

        scene.setCamera(camera);
        stage.setScene(scene);

        // SubScene code
        Label zLabel = new Label("Z");
        zSlider = new Slider(-200, 3000, -200);
        meshCheckBox = new CheckBox("Wireframe");
        HBox subSceneGroup = new HBox(70, new HBox(10, zLabel, zSlider),
            meshCheckBox, facePickedLabel);
        subSceneGroup.setPadding(new Insets(10, 10, 10, 10));
        SubScene subScene = new SubScene(subSceneGroup, 640, 50);

        root.getChildren().add(subScene);

        // Setup binding
        zSlider.valueProperty().bindBidirectional(zPos);
        parent.translateZProperty().bind(zPos);

        meshCheckBox.selectedProperty().bindBidirectional(showWireframe);
        cube.drawModeProperty().bind(new When(showWireframe)
            .then(DrawMode.LINE).otherwise(DrawMode.FILL));

        stage.show();
    }

    public static void main(String[] args) {
        launch(args);
    }
}
```

The user can control the rotation about the *x* and *y* axis by dragging the mouse on the screen. When the user clicks on the scene, the face number of the intersected face is displayed in the control panel. Notice that if you click on the part of the screen outside of the MeshView cube, the face number displayed will be -1, which is the numerical value of the `FACE_UNDEFINED` constant in `PickResult`. Otherwise it will show the face number of one of the 12 faces. The cube has six sides, each of which is represented by two triangles in the `TriangleMesh`.

When the program in Listing 10-11 is run, the MeshCubePickDemo window in Figure 10-14 is displayed. You can click on or drag the mouse over the cube to see the faces of the cube.

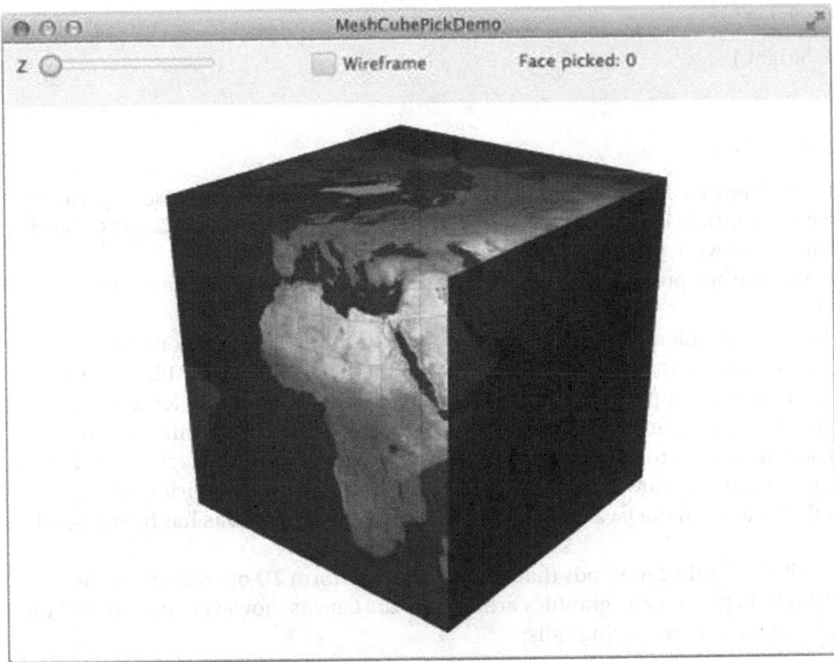

Figure 10-14. *The MeshCubePickDemo program*

Understanding the Canvas and Image Ops APIs

The Canvas and Image Ops APIs allow you to manipulate the 2D graphical content of an on-screen canvas or an off-screen image.

Understanding the Canvas API

The Canvas API consists of two public classes, `Canvas` and `GraphicsContext` in the `javafx.scene.canvas` package. `Canvas` is a `Node` that can be added to a `Scene`.

The `Canvas` class includes two public constructors:

- `Canvas()`
- `Canvas(double width, double height)`

The default constructor creates a `Canvas` with zero `width` and zero `height`. The two-parameter constructor creates a `Canvas` with the specified `width` and `height`.

The `Canvas` class includes the following public methods:

- `GraphicsContext getGraphicsContext2D()`
- `void setWidth(double width)`
- `double getWidth()`

- DoubleProperty widthProperty()
- void setHeight(double height)
- double getHeight()
- DoubleProperty heightProperty()

The getGraphicsContext2D() method returns the GraphicsContext for the Canvas that you can use to perform 2D graphics operations. The same object is returned if you call getGraphicsContext2D() on the same Canvas object multiple times. The other methods define read-write properties width and height for the Canvas.

The GraphicsContext class does not have any public constructors. The only way to obtain an instance of GraphicsContext is from a Canvas object.

GraphicsContext supports a style of 2D operations that is similar to immediate mode 2D operations found in other graphics toolkits such as java.awt.Canvas, javax.swing.Component, and the HTML 5 Canvas API. Unlike in AWT or Java2D, where the drawing on the surface happens in the paint() callback method, the JavaFX Canvas's typical usage scenario is to create the Canvas, get the GraphicsContext from it, draw on the Canvas with calls to GraphicsContext methods, and then add the Canvas to the scene graph. You can continue calling GraphicsContext methods after adding the Canvas to the scene graph. However, all GraphicsContext methods are considered UI manipulating methods, and should only be called in the JavaFX Application thread after the Canvas has been added to the scene graph.

The GraphicsContext class has a full set of public methods that allows you to perform 2D operations on the Canvas that owns it. The following methods do not put any graphics artifacts on the Canvas; however, they control the state of the GraphicsContext and affect subsequent rendering calls:

- void save()
- void restore()
- void translate(double x, double y)
- void scale(double x, double y)
- void rotate(double degrees)
- void transform(double mxx, double myx, double mxy, double myy, double mxt, double myt)
- void transform(Affine xform)
- void setTransform(double mxx, double myx, double mxy, double myy, double mxt, double myt)
- void setTransform(Affine xform)
- Affine getTransform(Affine xform)
- Affine getTransform()
- void setGlobalAlpha(double alpha)
- double getGlobalAlpha()
- void setGlobalBlendMode(BlendMode op)
- BlendMode getGlobalBlendMode()
- void setFill(Paint p)
- Paint getFill()

- `void setStroke(Paint p)`
- `Paint getStroke()`
- `void setLineWidth(double lw)`
- `double getLineWidth()`
- `void setLineCap(StrokeLineCap cap)`
- `StrokeLineCap getLineCap()`
- `void setLineJoin(StrokeLineJoin join)`
- `StrokeLineJoin getLineJoin()`
- `void setMiterLimit(double ml)`
- `double getMiterLimit()`
- `void setFont(Font f)`
- `Font getFont()`
- `void setTextAlign(TextAlignment align)`
- `TextAlignment getTextAlign()`
- `void setTextBaseline(VPos baseline)`
- `VPos getTextBaseline()`
- `void setFillRule(FillRule fillRule)`
- `FillRule getFillRule()`
- `void setEffect(Effect e)`
- `Effect getEffect(Effect e)`
- `void applyEffect(Effect e)`

The various setters and getters alter the characteristics of the `GraphicsContext`. They affect the coordinate transformation, global alpha, global blend mode, fill paint, stroke paint, line width, line cap, line join, miter limit, font, text alignment, text baseline, fill rule, and effect that will be used when the next rendering method call is issued. The `save()` method will push the current settings of these characteristics onto a stack. The `restore()` method will pop the saved settings back onto the `GraphicsContext`.

The following methods put graphics artifacts on the `Canvas`:

- `void fillText(String text, double x, double y)`
- `void strokeText(String text, double x, double y)`
- `void fillText(String text, double x, double y, double maxWidth)`
- `void strokeText(String text, double x, double y, double maxWidth)`
- `void beginPath()`
- `void moveTo(double x0, double y0)`
- `void lineTo(double x1, double y1)`
- `void quadraticCurveTo(double xc, double yc, double x1, double y1)`

- `void bezierCurveTo(double xc1, double yc1, double xc2, double yc2, double x1, double y1)`
- `void arcTo(double x1, double y1, double x2, double y2, double radius)`
- `void arc(double centerX, double centerY, double radiusX, double radiusY, double startAngle, double length)`
- `void rect(double x, double y, double w, double h)`
- `void appendSVGPath(String svgPath)`
- `void closePath()`
- `void fill()`
- `void stroke()`
- `void clip()`
- `void clearRect(double x, double y, double w, double h)`
- `void fillRect(double x, double y, double w, double h)`
- `void strokeRect(double x, double y, double w, double h)`
- `void fillOval(double x, double y, double w, double h)`
- `void strokeOval(double x, double y, double w, double h)`
- `void fillArc(double x, double y, double w, double h, double startAngle, double arcExtent, ArcType closure)`
- `void strokeArc(double x, double y, double w, double h, double startAngle, double arcExtent, ArcType closure)`
- `void fillRoundRect(double x, double y, double w, double h, double arcWidth, double arcHeight)`
- `void strokeRoundRect(double x, double y, double w, double h, double arcWidth, double arcHeight)`
- `void strokeLine(double x1, double y1, double x2, double y2)`
- `void fillPolygon(double[] xPoints, double[] yPoints, int nPoints)`
- `void strokePolygon(double[] xPoints, double[] yPoints, int nPoints)`
- `void strokePolyline(double[] xPoints, double[] yPoints, int nPoints)`
- `void drawImage(Image img, double x, double y)`
- `void drawImage(Image img, double x, double y, double w, double h)`
- `void drawImage(Image img, double sx, double sy, double sw, double sh, double dx, double dy, double dw, double dh)`

The `fillXXX` methods put a shape onto the Canvas with a filled interior. The `strokeXXX` methods put a shape onto the Canvas with a hollow interior. The three `drawImage()` methods draw a `javafx.scene.image.Image` onto the Canvas, with possible scaling and subsetting. The `beginPath()` method starts the building of a path that can be rendered onto the Canvas or used as a clip mask. The `moveTo()`, `lineTo()`, `quadraticCurveTo()`, `bezierCurveTo()`, `arcTo()`, `arc()`, `rect()`, `appendSVGPath()`, and `closePath()` methods add to the path. The `fill()` method renders the path onto the Canvas with a filled interior. The `stroke()` method renders the path onto the Canvas with a hollow interior. The `clip()` method clips the Canvas by the path, so that future rendering method calls won't have any effect outside of the path. The `clearRect()` method will clear a rectangular region of the Canvas with a transparent color value. To clear the entire Canvas, you can call `clearRect(0, 0, width, height)`.

The following methods serve to provide additional information about the GraphicsContext:

- `Canvas getCanvas()`
- `PixelWriter getPixelWriter()`
- `boolean isPointInPath(double x, double y)`

The `getCanvas()` method returns the Canvas object. The `getPixelWriter()` method returns a `PixelWriter` that can be used to manipulate the Canvas on a pixel-by-pixel basis. The `PixelWriter` class is part of the JavaFX Image Ops API, which we cover in the next subsection. The `isPointInPath()` method returns true if the point `(x, y)` is within the current path of the GraphicsContext.

The program in Listing 10-12 displays a Canvas and allows the user to drag the mouse across the screen to draw an oval. The location and size of the oval is also shown on the Canvas.

Listing 10-12. CanvasExample.java

```
import javafx.application.Application;
import javafx.geometry.Point2D;
import javafx.scene.Group;
import javafx.scene.Scene;
import javafx.scene.canvas.Canvas;
import javafx.scene.canvas.GraphicsContext;
import javafx.scene.paint.Color;
import javafx.scene.text.Font;
import javafx.stage.Stage;

import static java.lang.Math.abs;
import static java.lang.Math.min;

public class CanvasExample extends Application {
    private Point2D p0;

    public static void main(String[] args) {
        launch(args);
    }

    @Override
    public void start(Stage stage) {
        stage.setTitle("Canvas Example");
        stage.setScene(makeScene());
        stage.show();
    }

    private Scene makeScene() {
        Canvas canvas = new Canvas(640, 480);

        GraphicsContext graphicsContext = canvas.getGraphicsContext2D();
        graphicsContext.setFill(Color.BLUE);
        graphicsContext.setStroke(Color.RED);
        graphicsContext.setFont(Font.font(14));
        graphicsContext.strokeText("Click and drag mouse to draw ovals", 20, 20);
```

```
        canvas.setOnMousePressed(event -> {
            graphicsContext.clearRect(0, 0, 640, 480);
            p0 = new Point2D(event.getX(), event.getY());
        });

        canvas.setOnMouseDragged(event -> {
            Point2D p1 = new Point2D(event.getX(), event.getY());
            graphicsContext.clearRect(0, 0, 640, 480);
            double x = min(p0.getX(), p1.getX());
            double y = min(p0.getY(), p1.getY());
            double width = abs(p1.getX() - p0.getX());
            double height = abs(p1.getY() - p0.getY());
            graphicsContext.fillOval(x, y, width, height);
            graphicsContext.strokeText("Oval(" + x + ", " + y + ", " +
                width + ", " + height + ")", x, y - 10);
        });
        Group group = new Group(canvas);
        return new Scene(group, 640, 480);
    }
}
```

When the program in Listing 10-12 is run, and after some user interaction, the Canvas Example window in Figure 10-15 is displayed.

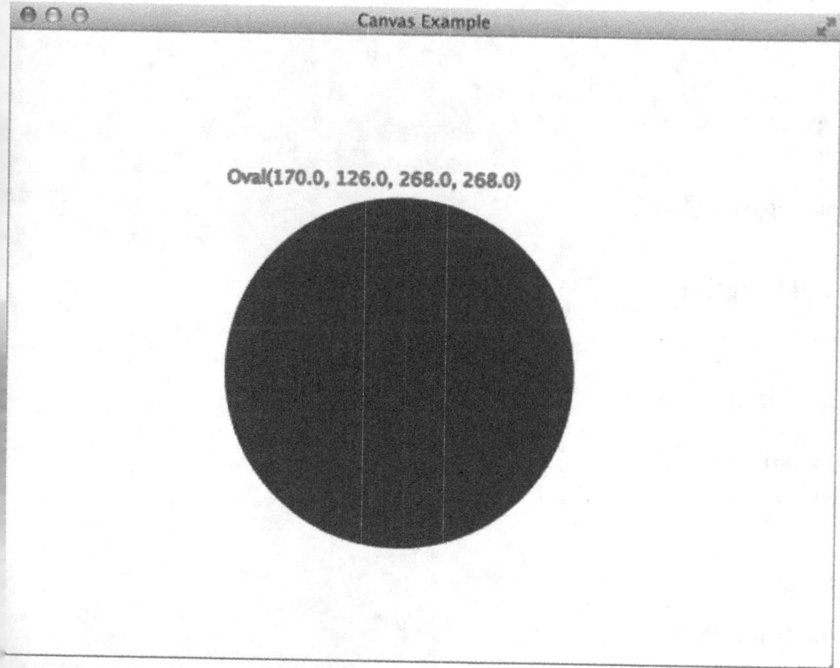

Figure 10-15. The CanvasExample program

Understanding the Image Ops API

The JavaFX Image Ops API allows JavaFX programs to manipulate images at the pixel level. The key to the JavaFX Image Ops API is a pair of interfaces in the javafx.scene.image package: PixelReader and PixelWriter. You can obtain a PixelReader from a javafx.scene.image.Image object. And you can obtain a PixelWriter from a javafx.scene.image.WritableImage object. WritableImage is a subclass of Image.

The PixelReader interface includes the following public methods:

- PixelFormat getPixelFormat()
- int getArgb(int x, int y)
- Color getColor(int x, int y)
- <T extends Buffer> void getPixels(int x, int y, int w, int h, WritablePixelFormat<T> pixelFormat, T buffer, int scanlineStride)
- void getPixels(int x, int y, int w, int h, WritablePixelFormat<ByteBuffer> pixelFormat, byte[] buffer, int offset, int scanlineStride)
- void getPixels(int x, int y, int w, int h, WritablePixelFormat<IntBuffer> pixelFormat, int[] buffer, int offset, int scanlineStride)

The getPixelFormat() method returns the pixel format of the underlying image. The getArgb() method returns the color of the pixel as an 32-bit integer whose 4 bytes from the most significant to the least significant contains the ARGB components of the color at the specified pixel. The getColor() method returns the color at the specified pixel as a Color object. The getPixels() methods take the area of the image specified by the first four parameters (x, y, w, h), read the color of these pixels, and write them to the buffer according to the WritablePixelFormat, the buffer type, offset, and scanlineStride.

The PixelWriter interface includes the following public methods:

- PixelFormat getPixelFormat()
- void setArgb(int x, int y, int argb)
- void setColor(int x, int y, Color color)
- <T extends Buffer> void setPixels(int x, int y, int w, int h, PixelFormat<T> pixelFormat, T buffer, int scanlineStride)
- void setPixels(int x, int y, int w, int h, PixelFormat<ByteBuffer> pixelFormat, byte[] buffer, int offset, int scanlineStride)
- void setPixels(int x, int y, int w, int h, PixelFormat<IntBuffer> pixelFormat, int[] buffer, int offset, int scanlineStride)
- void setPixels(int dstx, int dsty, int w, int h, PixelReader reader, int srcx, int srcy)

The getPixelFormat() method returns the pixel format of the underlying WritableImage. The setArgb() method sets the color of the pixel (x, y) to argb. The setColor() method sets the color of the pixel (x, y) to color. The setPixels() methods that take a pixelFormat parameter set the colors of the pixels in the area (x, y, w, h) to the values specified in buffer, according to the PixelFormat, the buffer type, offset, and scanlineStride. The setPixels() method that takes a PixelReader sets the colors of the pixels in the area (dstx, dsty, w, h) according to what is available from the PixelReader, starting at the pixel (srcx, srcy).

The PixelFormat and WritablePixelFormat describe how the color information of each pixel is stored. Possible types of PixelFormat are described by the enum PixelFormat.Type, which has the following declarators: INT_ARGB_PRE, INT_ARGB, BYTE_BGRA_PRE, BYTE_BGRA, BYTE_RGB, BYTE_INDEXED.

The program in Listing 10-13 demostrate the reading of the pixel colors from the EarthRise image that you saw in Chapter 1.

Listing 10-13. The ImageOpsExample.java

```
import javafx.application.Application;
import javafx.geometry.BoundingBox;
import javafx.scene.Scene;
import javafx.scene.control.ScrollPane;
import javafx.scene.control.TextArea;
import javafx.scene.image.Image;
import javafx.scene.image.ImageView;
import javafx.scene.image.PixelReader;
import javafx.scene.layout.HBox;
import javafx.scene.paint.Color;
import javafx.stage.Stage;

public class ImageOpsExample extends Application {
    @Override
    public void start(Stage stage) throws Exception {
        stage.setTitle("Image Ops Example");
        stage.setScene(makeScene());
        stage.show();
    }

    private Scene makeScene() {
        final String imageUrl = "http://projavafx.com/images/earthrise.jpg";
        Image image = new Image(imageUrl);
        final PixelReader pixelReader = image.getPixelReader();
        ImageView imageView = new ImageView(image);
        TextArea textArea = new TextArea();
        textArea.setPrefSize(image.getWidth(), image.getHeight());
        textArea.setText("Examining: " + imageUrl + "\n" +
            "\tPixelFormat: " + pixelReader.getPixelFormat().getType() + "\n");
        imageView.setOnMouseClicked(event -> {
            final int x = (int) event.getX();
            final int y = (int) event.getY();
            final Color color = pixelReader.getColor(x, y);
            final int argb = pixelReader.getArgb(x, y);
            String pixelDescription = String.format(
                "Pixel[%d, %d]:\n" +
                    "\t argb: %x\n" +
                    "\tcolor: %s (%5.4f, %5.4f, %5.4f, %5.4f)\n",
                x, y, argb, color, color.getOpacity(),
                color.getRed(), color.getGreen(), color.getBlue()
            );
            textArea.setText(textArea.getText() + pixelDescription);

        });
        HBox root = new HBox(10, imageView, textArea);
```

```
        Scene scene = new Scene(root);
        return scene;

    }

    public static void main(String[] args) {
        launch(args);
    }
}
```

This program loads the EarthRise Image from a URL, and puts it and a TextArea into the scene, and then obtains a PixelReader from it. Every time the mouse is clicked on the image, the color of the pixel is appended to the text in the TextArea. When the program in Listing 10-13 is run, after a few clicks on the image, the ImageOps Example window in Figure 10-16 is displayed.

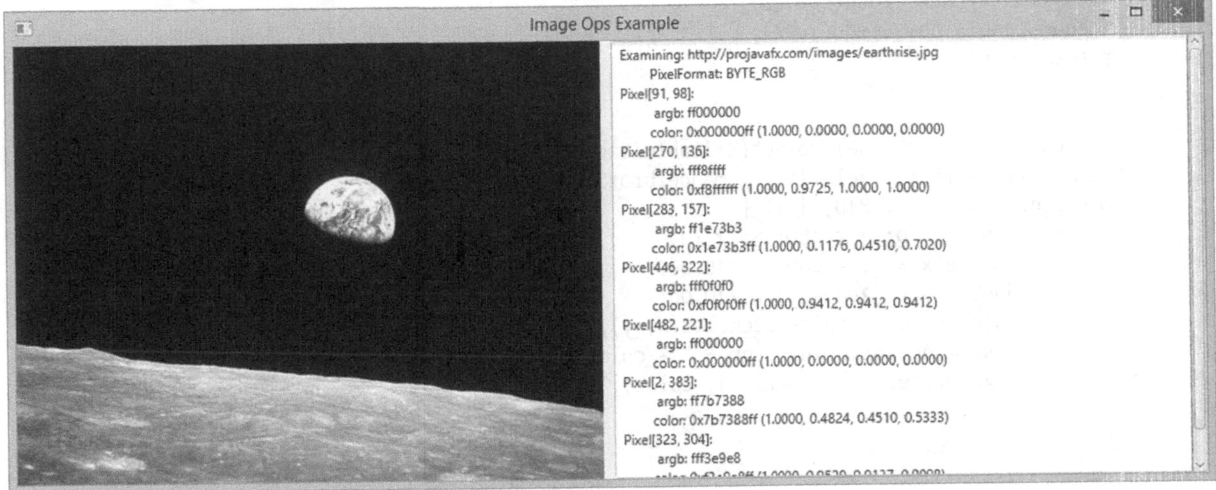

Figure 10-16. *The ImageOpsExample program*

The program in Listing 10-14 creates a WritableImage, draws the Mandelbrot set on it, then draws the image onto a Canvas, and finally puts the Canvas in a scene. The drawing of the Mandelbrot set is done by calculating the color of each pixel and setting the color for the pixel.

Listing 10-14. MandelbrotSetExample.java

```
import javafx.application.Application;
import javafx.scene.Group;
import javafx.scene.Scene;
import javafx.scene.canvas.Canvas;
import javafx.scene.canvas.GraphicsContext;
import javafx.scene.image.PixelWriter;
import javafx.scene.image.WritableImage;
import javafx.scene.paint.Color;
import javafx.stage.Stage;
```

```
public class MandelbrotSetExample extends Application {
    @Override
    public void start(Stage primaryStage) throws Exception {
        primaryStage.setTitle("Mandelbrot iSet Example");
        primaryStage.setScene(makeScene());
        primaryStage.show();
    }

    private Scene makeScene() {
        WritableImage mandelbrotSet = new WritableImage(840, 480);
        populateMandelbrotSet(mandelbrotSet);
        Canvas canvas = new Canvas(840, 480);
        final GraphicsContext graphicsContext =
            canvas.getGraphicsContext2D();
        graphicsContext.drawImage(mandelbrotSet, 0, 0);
        Group root = new Group(canvas);
        Scene scene = new Scene(root);
        return scene;
    }

    private void populateMandelbrotSet(WritableImage mandelbrotSet) {
        final PixelWriter pixelWriter = mandelbrotSet.getPixelWriter();
        for (int i = 0; i < 840; i++) {
            for (int j = 0; j < 480; j++) {
                double x = (i - 600) / 240.0d;
                double y = (240 - j) / 240.0d;
                Color color = calculateColor(x, y);
                System.out.println("argb = " + color);
                pixelWriter.setColor(i, j, color);
            }
        }
    }

    private Color calculateColor(double x0, double y0) {
        double x = 0.0;
        double y = 0.0;
        int iteration = 0;
        int max_iteration = 1000;
        while (x * x + y * y < 2 * 2 && iteration < max_iteration) {
            double xtemp = x * x - y * y + x0;
            y = 2 * x * y + y0;
            x = xtemp;
            iteration = iteration + 1;
        }
        double r = (iteration % 10) / 10.0d;
        double g = ((iteration / 10) % 10) / 10.0d;
        double b = ((iteration / 100) % 10) / 10.0d;
        return Color.color(r, g, b);
    }
```

```
    public static void main(String[] args) {
        launch(args);
    }
}
```

When the program in Listing 10-14 is run, the Mandelbrot Set Example window in Figure 10-17 is displayed.

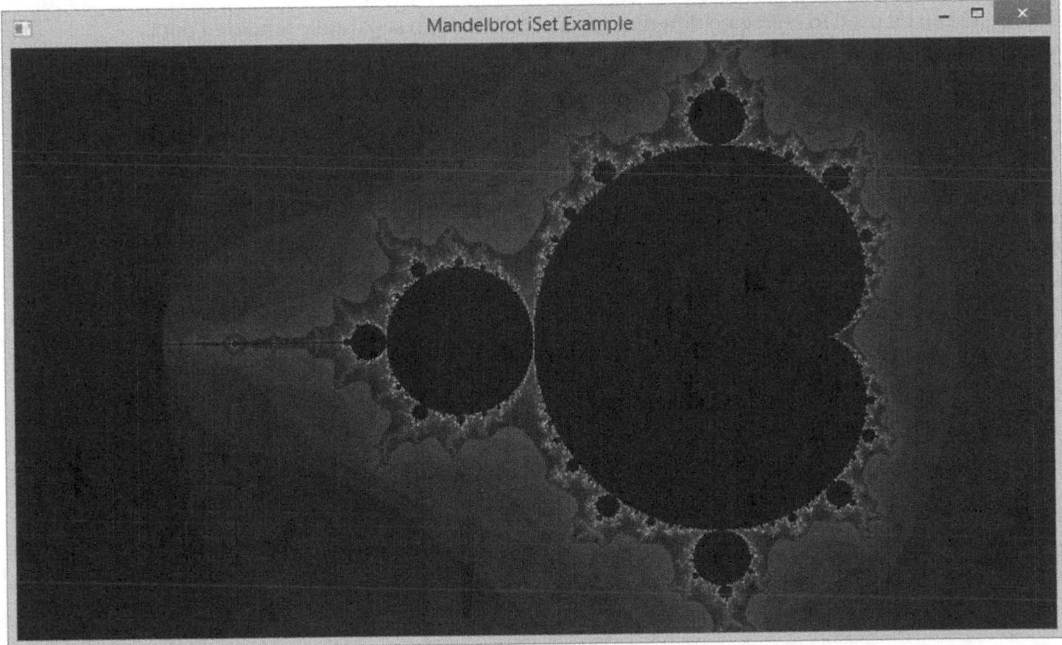

Figure 10-17. The MandelbrotSetExample program

Summary

In this chapter, you learned about the JavaFX 3D graphics API. You should now understand the following 3D modeling concepts:

- 3D modeling involves the creating of 3D shapes, positioning the camera, placing lights, and providing material for the 3D shapes.
- The JavaFX 3D graphics API provides three predefined 3D shapes: `Sphere`, `Cylinder`, and `Box`.
- The `MeshView` class represents user-defined 3D shapes. You create a new `MeshView` by giving it a `TriangleMesh`.
- The `ParallelCamera` gives you a view of the 3D model that is not realistic—objects in the foreground appear to have the same size as objects in the background.
- The `PerspectiveCamera` gives you a more realistic view of the 3D model, with objects farther away appearing to be smaller. The `fieldOfView` controls how wide a view of the 3D model is rendered.
- The `AmbientLight` is a light source that appears to come from all directions.

- The `PointLight` is a light source that emanates from one point and radiates equally in all directions.
- The `PhongMaterial` controls the color and texture of the surface of the 3D shapes we create. The `diffuseColor` is what we usually consider as the color of the 3D shape object. The `specularColor` is the highlight.
- You can map an image onto a 3D shape very easily with the help of `PhongMaterial`.
- A `SubScene` can be used to segregate different parts of a scene into separately rendered parts, each with their own camera, depthBuffer, and anti-aliasing settings.
- You can interact with the 3D scene using the normal JavaFX events. A `PickResult` object can be obtained from certain event objects. It contains information about the node, the face, and the point of intersection with the pick ray.
- You can use the `Canvas` API to perform 2D operations on an on-screen surface.
- You can use the Image Ops API to read pixels from `Images` and write pixels to `WritableImages`.

Resources

Here are some useful resources for understanding the JavaFX 3D graphics APIs:

- *Getting Started with JavaFX 3D Graphics, a tutorial on Oracle's web site:* `http://docs.oracle.com/javase/8/javafx/graphics-tutorial/javafx-3d-graphics.htm`
- *A video of Jim Weaver's Java 8 Intro presentation with JavaFX 3D demos:* `http://bit.ly/1nib0ek`

CHAPTER 11

Accessing Web Services

An expert is a man who has made all the mistakes which can be made, in a narrow field.

—Niels Bohr

The modern application paradigm is clear: Nothing lives in an isolated environment. Client applications interact with data obtained from a wide array of resources, both physical and logical. Whether data are retrieved from a hard disk, a remote database, or an exposed network resource, we expect our applications to be flexible, provide a wide array of data retrieval options, and, in general, work well with others.

So far, we've explained how the JavaFX Platform can be used both for rendering information and for interactively manipulating data. In this chapter, we provide a brief overview of the options available for integrating JavaFX applications with enterprise systems, and then continue with some specific examples of that process.

Our examples are constructed to demonstrate how easily a JavaFX application can access a REST resource and then translate the response (from either JSON or XML format) into a format understandable by JavaFX Controls. As our example external data source, the `StackExchange` APIs are ideal, as they are publicly available, easy to understand, and widely used on the Internet.

Front-End and Back-End Platforms

JavaFX is often considered a front-end platform. Although that statement does not do justice to the APIs in the JavaFX platform that are not related to a UI, it is true that most JavaFX applications focus on the rich and interactive visualization of "content."

One of the great things about Java is the fact that a single language can be used within a wide range of devices, desktops, and servers. The same Java language that creates the core of JavaFX is also the fundamental core of the Java Platform, Enterprise Edition (Java EE).

The Java Platform is the number one development platform for enterprise applications. The combination of the JavaFX platform providing a rich and interactive UI with enterprise applications running on the Java Platform creates huge possibilities. To achieve this, JavaFX applications and Java enterprise applications must be exchanging data.

Exchanging data can happen in a number of ways, and depending on the requirements (from the front end as well as from the back end), one way might be more suited than another.

Basically, there are two different approaches:

- The JavaFX application can leverage the fact that it runs on the same infrastructure as typical enterprise applications, and can deeply integrate with these enterprise components. This is illustrated in Figure 11-1.

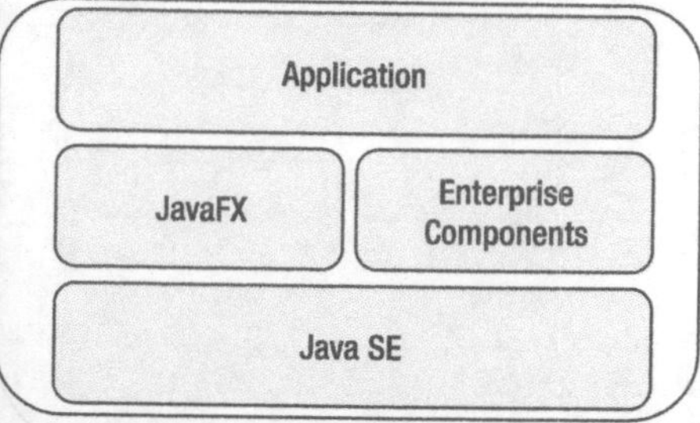

Figure 11-1. JavaFX and enterprise components on a single system

- JavaFX applications live in a relatively simple Java Platform, and exchange data with enterprise servers using standard protocols that are already supported by Java enterprise components. This is shown in Figure 11-2.

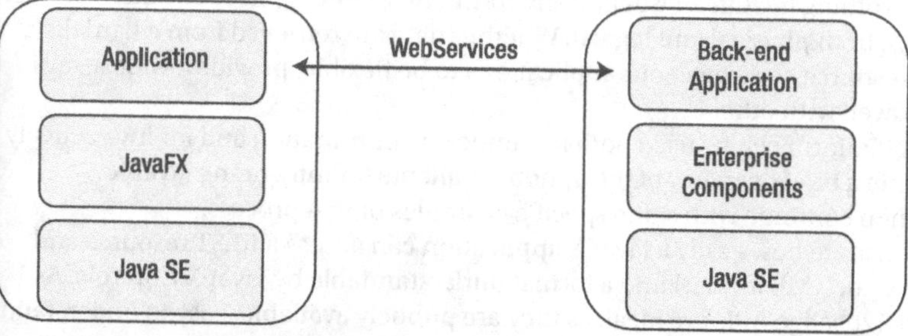

Figure 11-2. JavaFX application communicates with enterprise components on a remote server

The first approach is mentioned and briefly touched on, but the focus of this chapter is on the second approach, where the JavaFX client communicates with Java enterprise components on a remote server.

It should also be stressed here that as long as a standard, well-defined protocol (e.g., SOAP/REST) is used, it is very possible to connect a JavaFX application to a non-Java back-end application. The decoupling between client and server indeed allows for different programming languages to be used on the client and on the server.

Merging JavaFX and Java Enterprise Modules in the Same Environment

JavaFX 8 is built on top of the Java Platform, Standard Edition. As a consequence, all functionality provided by this platform can be leveraged in JavaFX 8. The Java Platform, Enterprise Edition, is also built on top of the Java Platform, Standard Edition. As a consequence, JavaFX applications can live in the same environment as applications using the Java Platform, Enterprise Edition.

The JavaFX developer can thus use his or her favorite enterprise tools to create applications. There are a number of advantages in doing so. Enterprise components offer tools that allow developers to focus on a specific domain layer, while shielding them from, for example, database resources and transactions.

Java is a popular platform in the enterprise environment, and a number of enterprise components and libraries have been developed by companies, organizations, and individuals.

The Java Platform, Enterprise Edition, is defined by specifications that are standardized via the Java Community Process (JCP) program. For the different constituting parts, individual Java Specification Requests (JSRs) are filed. The current version of the Java Platform, Enterprise Edition, Java Enterprise Edition 7, contains the following JSRs.

- Java Servlet 3.1 (JSR 340)
- JavaServer Faces 2.2 (JSR 344)
- Java API for WebSocket 1.0 (JSR 356)
- Java API for JSON Processing 1.0 (JSR 353)
- Expression Language 3.0 (JSR 341)
- JavaServer Pages 2.3 (JSR 245)
- Standard Tag Library for JavaServer Pages (JSTL) 1.2 (JSR 52)
- Debugging Support for Other Languages 1.0 (JSR 45)
- Java API for RESTful Web Services (JAX-RS) 2.0 (JSR 339)
- Java API for XML-Based Web Services (JAX-WS) 2.2 (JSR 224)
- Java Architecture for XML Binding (JAXB) 2.2 (JSR 222)
- Implementing Enterprise Web Services 1.4 (JSR 109)
- Web Services Metadata for the Java Platform (JSR 181)
- Java API for XML-Based RPC (JAX-RPC) 1.1 (JSR 101)
- Java API for XML Registries (JAXR) 1.0 (JSR 93)
- Java Message Service 2.0 (JSR 343)
- Batch Applications for the Java Platform 1.0 (JSR 352)
- Concurrency Utilities for Java EE 1.0 (JSR 236)
- Enterprise JavaBeans 3.2 (JSR 345)
- Bean Validation 1.1 (JSR 349)
- Java Persistence 2.1 (JSR 338)
- Contexts and Dependency Injection (CDI) for Java 1.1 (JSR 346)
- Dependency Injection for Java 1.0 (JSR 330)
- Java EE Connector Architecture 1.7 (JSR 322)
- Java Transaction API (JTA) 1.2 (JSR 907)
- Common Annotations for the Java Platform 1.2 (JSR 250)
- JavaMail 1.5 (JSR 919)
- Java Authentication Service Provider Interface for Containers 1.1 (JSR 196)
- Java Authorization Contract for Containers 1.5 (JSR 115)
- Java APIs for XML Messaging 1.3 (JSR 67)
- J2EE Management 1.1 (JSR 77)
- Java EE Application Deployment 1.2 (JSR 88)

Most of these individual JSRs are implemented by a number of companies, and implementations are often grouped into a product. Typical enterprise components implement one or more JSRs, and they might include additional product-specific functionality. Among the most popular enterprise components we count the Spring Framework, Tomcat/TomEE, Hibernate, JBoss/WildFly, RestEasy, and GlassFish. A number of products implement all JSRs, and those products are then called implementations of the Java Platform, Enterprise Edition, often referred to as Java EE Platforms.

Technically, there are no restrictions in the JavaFX platform that prevent Java enterprise components from being used. However, enterprise development differs from client development in a number of ways:

- Enterprise infrastructure is shifting toward the cloud. Specific tasks (e.g., storage, mail, etc.) are outsourced to components in a "cloud" that offer specific functionality. Enterprise servers are often located in a cloud environment, allowing fast and seamless interaction with cloud components.
- In terms of resource requirements, enterprise systems focus on computing resources (CPU, cache, and memory) where desktop computers and laptops focus instead on visual resources (e.g., graphical hardware acceleration).
- Startup time is hardly an issue in servers, but is critical in many desktop applications. Also, servers are supposed to be up and running 24/7, which is not the case with most clients.
- Deployment and life cycle management are often specific to a server product or a client product. Upgrading servers or server software is often a tedious process. Downtime has to be minimized because client applications might have open connections to the server. Deploying a client application can happen in a number of ways, such as via stand-alone, self-contained applications or Java Network Launch Protocol (JNLP).
- Enterprise development uses a number of patterns (e.g., Inversion of Control, container-based initialization) that can be useful in client development, but that often require a different architecture than traditional clients.

Using JavaFX to Call Remote (Web) Services

Enterprise components are often accessed via web resources. Some specifications clearly describe how web-based frameworks should interact with enterprise components for rendering information. However, there are other specifications that allow enterprise components (written in Java or in another language) to be accessed from non-web resources as well. Because those specifications allow for a decoupling between enterprise development and any other development, they have been defined by a number of stakeholders.

In 1998, Simple Object Access Protocol (SOAP) was invented by Microsoft and subsequently used as "the" exchange format between Java applications and .NET applications. SOAP is based on XML, and the current version 1.2 became a W3C recommendation in 2003. Java provides a number of tools that allow developers to exchange data with SOAP.

Although powerful and relatively readable, SOAP is often considered to be rather verbose. With the rise of mashups and simple services offering specific functionality, a new architectural style emerged: the representational state transfer (REST). REST allows server and client developers to exchange data in a loosely coupled and more streamlined way, where the protocol can be XML, JSON, Atom, or any other format.

SOAP

A number of Enterprise applications use SOAP at the back end, and thus require SOAP to be supported on the client as well. Fortunately, SOAP is supported in Java. The examples in this chapter use the REST protocol inasmuch as this is more comprehensive, but using the `javax.xml.soap` package is perfectly possible in JavaFX applications, because this package is available in the Java Platform, Standard Edition 8.

REST

The remainder of this chapter is about calling REST-based web services. Plenty of resources and documentation about REST and REST-based web services can be found on the Internet. REST-based web services expose a number of URIs that can be accessed using the HTTP protocol. Typically, different HTTP `request` methods (get, post, put, delete) are used to indicate different operations on resources.

REST-based web services can be accessed using standard HTTP technologies, and the Java Platform comes with a number of APIs (mainly in `java.io` and `java.net`) that facilitate access to REST-based web services.

One of the major advantages of JavaFX being written on top of the Java Platform, Standard Edition 8, is the ability to use all of these APIs in JavaFX applications. This is what we do in the first examples in this chapter. We show how we can use Java APIs for consuming REST-based web services and how we can integrate the result in a JavaFX application.

Next, we show how to leverage the JavaFX APIs to avoid common pitfalls (e.g., unresponsive applications, no dynamic update, etc.). Finally, we give a brief overview of third-party libraries that make it easy for JavaFX developers to access REST-based web services.

Setting Up the Application

First of all, we create the framework for our samples. We will use the APIs provided by Stack Exchange. The Stack Exchange network is a cluster of forums, each in a specific domain, where questions and answers are combined in such a way that the "best" answers from the most trusted users bubble to the top. Java developers are probably familiar with StackOverflow, which was the first site in Stack Exchange and provides an incredible number of questions and related answers for IT-related issues.

■ **Note** In the previous edition of this book, *Pro JavaFX 2*, we used the Twitter API in the examples for this chapter. The Twitter API is still available, and it is very good example of how to use REST services. However, all requests to the Twitter API now need to be authenticated. Although this is fully understandable, it makes it a bit harder to get started with a simple example. As you will see in this chapter, we start by making a simple `HTTPConnection` to a REST endpoint, and we don't worry about authentication. The frameworks we introduce near the end of the chapter, are capable of using OAuth-based authentication, and the connection to the Twitter API is left as an exercise for the interested developer.

The REST APIs provided by StackExchange are very well described at `https://api.stackexchange.com`. It is not our goal to explore all the possibilities offered by StackExchange and the corresponding APIs, so the interested reader is referred to the documentation available on the web site.

In the samples in this chapter, we want to visualize the author of a question, the title of the question, and the day the question was asked.

Initially, we represent a question by a Java Object with getters and setters. This is shown in Listing 11-1.

Listing 11-1. `Question` Class

```
package projavafx;

public class Question {

    private String owner;
    private String question;
    private long timestamp;
```

```
    public Question () {
    }
    public Question (String o, String q, long t) {
        this.owner = o;
        this.question = q;
        this.timestamp = t;
    }

    public String getOwner() {
        return owner;
    }

    public void setOwner(String owner) {
        this.owner = owner;
    }

    public String getQuestion() {
        return question;
    }

    public void setQuestion(String question) {
        this.question = question;
    }

    public long getTimestamp() {
        return timestamp;
    }

    public void setTimestamp(long timestamp) {
        this.timestamp = timestamp;
    }

}
```

Our `Question` class has two constructors. The zero-arg constructor is needed in one of the following examples and we come back to this later. The constructor that takes three arguments is used for convenience in other examples.

In Listing 11-2, we show how to display questions. In this first example, the questions are not obtained via the StackExchange API, but they are hard-coded in the example.

Listing 11-2. Framework for Rendering Questions in a `ListView`

```
package projavafx;

import javafx.application.Application;
import javafx.collections.FXCollections;
import javafx.collections.ObservableList;
import javafx.scene.Scene;
import javafx.scene.control.ListView;
import javafx.scene.layout.StackPane;
import javafx.stage.Stage;
```

```
public class StackOverflowApp1 extends Application {

    public static void main(String[] args) {
        launch(args);
    }

    @Override
    public void start(Stage primaryStage) {
        ListView<Question> listView = new ListView<>();
        listView.setItems(getObservableList());
        StackPane root = new StackPane();
        root.getChildren().add(listView);

        Scene scene = new Scene(root, 500, 300);
        primaryStage.setTitle("StackOverflow List");
        primaryStage.setScene(scene);
        primaryStage.show();
    }

    ObservableList<Question> getObservableList() {
        ObservableList<Question> answer = FXCollections.observableArrayList();
        long now = System.currentTimeMillis();
        long yesterday = now - 1000 * 60 * 60 * 24;
        Question q1 = new Question("James", "How can I call a REST service?", now);
        Question q2 = new Question("Stephen", "Does JavaFX work on Android?", yesterday);
        answer.addAll(q1, q2);
        return answer;
    }

}
```

If you have read the previous chapters, this code does not contain anything new. We create a `ListView`, add it to a `StackPane`, create a `Scene`, and render the `Stage`.

The `ListView` is populated with an `ObservableList` containing `Questions`. This `ObservableList` is obtained by calling the `getObservableList()` method. In the following samples, we modify this method and show how to retrieve `Questions` from the StackExchange API.

■ **Note** The `getObservableList` returns an `ObservableList`. The `ListView` automatically observes this `ObservableList`. As a consequence, changes in the `ObservableList` are immediately rendered in the `ListView` control. In a later sample, we leverage this functionality.

Running this example results in the window shown in Figure 11-3.

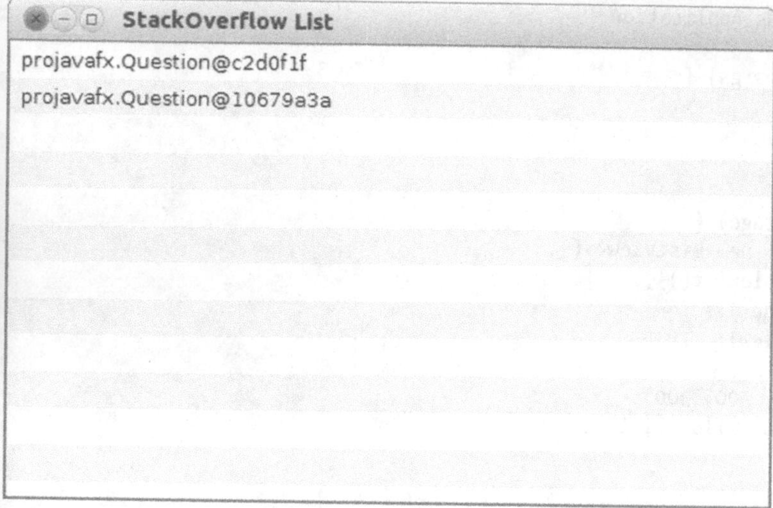

Figure 11-3. The result of the first example

The resulting window contains a ListView with two entries. Those entries correspond to the two questions that are created in the getObservableList() method at the bottom of Listing 11-2.

The information about the questions that is shown in the window is not very useful. Indeed, we told the ListView that it should display some instances of Question, but we did not tell how those should be displayed. The latter can be achieved by specifying a CellFactory. In this chapter, our goal is not to create a fancy UI; rather, we want to show how to retrieve data and render these data in the UI. Hence, we briefly show how the developer can alter the visualization of data by using the CellFactory concept. For an overview of the UI Controls that we use in our examples (ListView and TableView), refer to Chapter 6.

In Listing 11-3, we create a QuestionCell class that extends ListCell and defines how to lay out a cell.

Listing 11-3. Define QuestionCell

```
package projavafx;

import java.text.SimpleDateFormat;
import java.util.Date;
import javafx.scene.control.ListCell;

public class QuestionCell extends ListCell<Question> {

    static final SimpleDateFormat sdf = new SimpleDateFormat ("dd-MM-YY");
    @Override
    protected void updateItem(Question question, boolean empty){
        super.updateItem(question, empty);
        if (empty) {
            setText("");
        } else {
            StringBuilder sb= new StringBuilder();
```

```
            sb.append("[").append(sdf.format(new Date(question.getTimestamp()))).append("]")
                    .append(" ").append(question.getOwner()+": "+question.getQuestion());
            setText(sb.toString());
        }
    }
}
```

When a cell item has to be updated, we tell it to show some text containing the timestamp between square brackets, followed by the author and the title of the question. Next, the `ListView` needs to be told that it should render `QuestionCells`. We do this by calling the `ListView.setCellFactory()` method and provide a lambda expression that creates a new `QuestionCell` when called. In Listing 11-4, we show the modified version of the start method of our `StackOverflowApplication`.

Listing 11-4. Use `CellFactory` on the `ListView`

```
public void start(Stage primaryStage) {
    ListView<Question> listView = new ListView<>();
    listView.setItems(getObservableList());
    listView.setCellFactory(l -> new QuestionCell());
    StackPane root = new StackPane();
    root.getChildren().add(listView);

    Scene scene = new Scene(root, 500, 300);

    primaryStage.setTitle("StackOverflow List");
    primaryStage.setScene(scene);
    primaryStage.show();
}
```

If we now run the application, the output appears as in Figure 11-4.

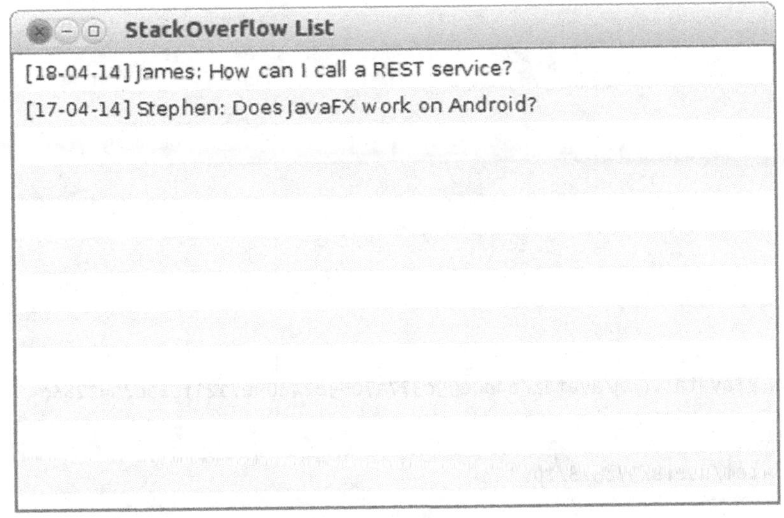

Figure 11-4. *The result of adding a* `QuestionCell`

For every question that is in the items of the ListView, the output is now what we expected it to be. We can do a lot more with CellFactories (e.g., we can use graphics instead of just text), but that is beyond the scope of this chapter.

We now replace the hard-coded questions with real information obtained via the StackExchange API.

Using the StackExchange API

The Stack Exchange Network (http://stackexchange.com) allows third-party developers to browse and access questions and answers using a REST-based interface. StackExchange maintains a number of REST-based APIs, but for our examples we limit ourselves to the Search API. Detailed information on the Search API is obtained from http://api.stackexchange.com/docs.

The resource URL—the endpoint for the REST service—is very simple:

```
http://api.stackexchange.com/2.2/search
```

A number of query parameters can be supplied here. We will only use two parameters, and the interested reader is referred to the StackExchange documentation for information about the other parameters.;

- Site: Specify the domain you want to search, in our case this is "stackoverflow."
- tagged: A semicolon delimited list of tags. We want to search all questions tagged with "javafx."

Combining both parameters leads to the following REST call:

```
http://api.stackexchange.com/2.2/search?tagged=javafx&site=stackoverflow
```

When executing this REST call in a browser, or using a command tool (e.g., curl), the result is something like the JSON-text in Listing 11-5.

Listing 11-5. JSON Response Obtained from the StackExchange Search API


```
{
  "items": [
    {
      "tags": [
        "java",
        "sorting",
        "javafx",
        "tableview"
      ],
      "owner": {
        "reputation": 132,
        "user_id": 578518,
        "user_type": "registered",
        "accept_rate": 84,
        "profile_image": "https://www.gravatar.com/avatar/bdbee99c377a7063b24e09e7121fb1ab?s=128&d=
        identicon&r=PG",
        "display_name": "Rps",
        "link": "http://stackoverflow.com/users/578518/rps"
      },
      "is_answered": false,
      "view_count": 7,
```

```
    "answer_count": 1,
    "score": 0,
    "last_activity_date": 1397845222,
    "creation_date": 1397844823,
    "last_edit_date": 1397845143,
    "question_id": 23159737,
    "link": "http://stackoverflow.com/questions/23159737/javafx-tableview-ordered-by-date",
    "title": "javafx Tableview ordered by date"
  },

...
,"has_more":true
,"quota_max":300,
"quota_remaining":290
}
```

The StackExchange API only provides JSON-based responses. A number of web services deliver information in XML, and others provide both JSON and XML. Because we want to show how to process XML responses as well, we create our own XML-based output for the StackExchange REST Service. Rather than calling an external REST endpoint, this XML response will be obtained by reading a local file.

Our self-defined XML response is shown in Listing 11-6.

Listing 11-6. Artificial XML Response Obtained from the StackExchange Search API

```
<?xml version="1.0" encoding="UTF-8"?>

<items>

  <item>

    <tags>

      <tag>java</tag>

      <tag>sorting</tag>

      <tag>javafx</tag>

      <tag>tableview</tag>

    </tags>

    <owner>Rps</owner>

    <creation_date>1397844823</creation_date>

    <title>javafx Tableview ordered by date</title>

  <item>

</items>
```

Although the data in the JSON response contain the same information as the data in the XML response, the format is, of course, very different. JSON and XML are both widely used on the Internet, and a large number of web services offer responses in both formats.

Depending on the use case and the developer, one format might be preferred over the other. In general, JavaFX applications should be able to work with both formats, because they have to connect with third-party data, and the JavaFX developer cannot always influence the data format used by the back end.

■ **Note** Many applications allow a number of formats, and by specifying the HTTP "Accept" Header, the client can choose between the different formats.

In the next example, we show how to retrieve and parse the JSON response used in the StackExchange Search API.

JSON Response Format

JSON is a very popular format on the Internet, especially in web applications where incoming data are parsed with JavaScript. JSON data are rather compact and more or less human readable.

A number of tools exist in Java for reading and writing JSON data. As of June 2013, when Java Enterprise Edition 7 was released, there is a standard specification in Java that describes how to read and write JSON data. This Java specification is defined as JSR 353, and more information can be obtained at `http://www.jcp.org/en/jsr/detail?id=353`.

JSR 353 only defines a specification, and an implementation is still needed to do the actual work. In our examples, we will use jsonp, which is the Reference Implementation of JSR 353. This Reference Implementation can be found at `https://jsonp.java.net/`. Readers are encouraged to try out their favorite implementation of JSR 353, though.

Although JSR 353 is a specification that is part of the Java Enterprise Edition umbrella, the reference implementation also works in a Java Standard Edition environment. There are no external dependencies.

We now replace the hard-coded list containing two fake questions with real questions obtained via the StackExchange REST API. We keep the existing code, but we modify the `getObservableList()` method as shown in Listing 11-7.

Listing 11-7. Obtain Questions Via the StackExchange REST API, JSON Format and Parse the JSON

```
ObservableList<Question> getObservableList() throws IOException {
    String url = "http://api.stackexchange.com/2.2/search?tagged=javafx&site=stackoverflow";
    URL host = new URL(url);
    JsonReader jr = Json.createReader(new GZIPInputStream(host.openConnection().getInputStream()));

    JsonObject jsonObject = jr.readObject();
    JsonArray jsonArray = jsonObject.getJsonArray("items");
    ObservableList<Question> answer = FXCollections.observableArrayList();

    jsonArray.iterator().forEachRemaining((JsonValue e) -> {
        JsonObject obj = (JsonObject) e;
        JsonString name = obj.getJsonObject("owner").getJsonString("display_name");
        JsonString quest = obj.getJsonString("title");
        JsonNumber jsonNumber = obj.getJsonNumber("creation_date");
        Question q = new Question(name.getString(), quest.getString(), jsonNumber.longValue() * 1000);
        answer.add(q);
    });
    return answer;
```

Before we dive into the code, we show the result of the modified application in Figure 11-5.

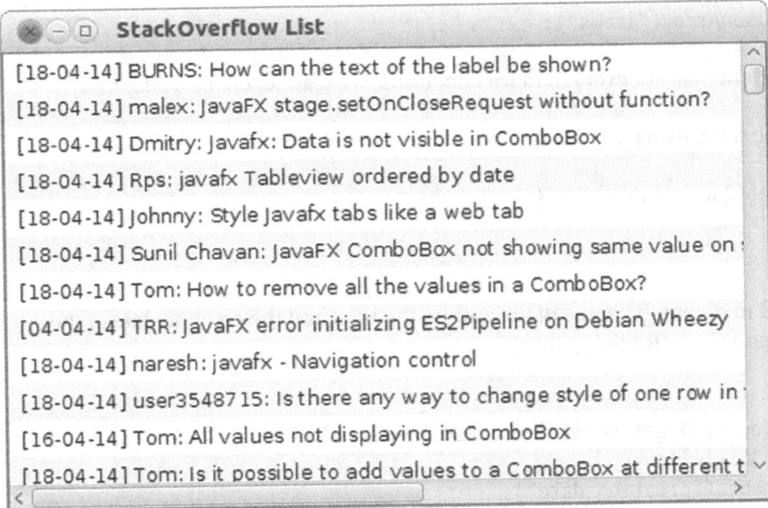

Figure 11-5. *The result of the* `StackOverflowApplication` *retrieving JSON data*

The code in Listing 11-7 can be divided into four parts:

1. Call the REST endpoint.
2. Obtain the raw JSON data.
3. Convert each item into a question.
4. Add the `Questions` to the result.

Calling the REST endpoint is very straightforward:

```
String url = "http://api.stackexchange.com/2.2/search?tagged=javafx&site=stackoverflow";
URL host = new URL(url);
JsonReader jr = Json.createReader(new GZIPInputStream(host.openConnection().getInputStream()));
```

First, we create a URL Object that refers to the desired location. Next, we open the connection to the location. Because StackExchange is sending its data as zipped data, we open a `GZIPInputStream` using the `InputStream` obtained from the connection. We pass this `GZIPInputStream` as the `InputStream` argument in the `Json.createReader()` method.

We now have a JSON reader that consumes the data we want to have. Extracting Java Objects from this JSON reader manually requires specific code for a specific case.

■ **Note** We could also have used a JSON parser instead of a JSON reader. It is not our intention to deliver an exhaustive JSON parsing guide. We only try to show how JSON data can be converted into Java Objects for our specific use case. You can easily find a number of tutorials on JSON on the Internet.

In Listing 11-5, we observe that the questions are in an array named items, starting with the left square bracket ([). We can obtain this JSON array using the following statement:

```
JsonArray jsonArray = jsonObject.getJsonArray("items");
```

Next, we need to iterate over all these elements. For every item we encounter, we want to create a `Question` instance.

Iterating over the array elements can be done using

```
jsonArray.iterator().forEachRemaining((JsonValue e) -> {
    ...
}
```

To create a `Question` instance, we need to obtain the name of the author, the title, and the creation date of the question. The Java JSON API provides a standard way for doing this:

```
JsonObject obj = (JsonObject) e;
JsonString name = obj.getJsonObject("owner").getJsonString("display_name");
JsonString quest = obj.getJsonString("title");
JsonNumber jsonNumber = obj.getJsonNumber("creation_date");
```

Finally, we need to create a `Question` instance based on this information, and add it to the `ObservableList` instance we will return:

```
Question q = new Question(name.getString(), quest.getString(), jsonNumber.longValue() * 1000);
answer.add(q);
```

This example shows that it is very easy to retrieve and read JSON data obtained from a REST endpoint, and convert the result into a `ListView`. In the next section, we demonstrate a similar process for XML responses.

XML Response Format

The XML format is widely used in the Java platform. As a consequence, standardization of XML-based operations in Java happened years ago. There are a number of XML tools built into the Java Platform, Standard Edition, and we can use these APIs and tools in JavaFX without any external dependency. In this section, we first use a DOM processor for parsing the XML response that we artificially built. Next, we use the JAXB standard to automatically obtain Java Objects.

Changing our application from JSON input to XML input requires only the `getObservableList` method to be changed. The new implementation is shown in Listing 11-8.

Listing 11-8. Obtaining Questions from the XML-Based Response

```
ObservableList<Question> getObservableList() throws IOException, ParserConfigurationException,
SAXException {
        ObservableList<Question> answer = FXCollections.observableArrayList();
        InputStream inputStream = this.getClass().getResourceAsStream("/stackoverflow.xml");
        DocumentBuilderFactory dbf = DocumentBuilderFactory.newInstance();
        DocumentBuilder db = dbf.newDocumentBuilder();
        Document doc = db.parse(inputStream);
        NodeList questionNodes = doc.getElementsByTagName("item");
        int count = questionNodes.getLength();
```

```
        for (int i = 0; i < count; i++) {
            Question question = new Question();
            Element questionNode = (Element) questionNodes.item(i);

            NodeList childNodes = questionNode.getChildNodes();
            int cnt2 = childNodes.getLength();
            for (int j = 0; j < cnt2; j++) {
                Node me = childNodes.item(j);
                String nodeName = me.getNodeName();
                if ("creation_date".equals(nodeName)) {
                    question.setTimestamp(Long.parseLong(me.getTextContent()));
                }
                if ("owner".equals(nodeName)) {
                    question.setOwner(me.getTextContent());
                }
                if ("title".equals(nodeName)) {
                    question.setQuestion(me.getTextContent());
                }
        }
        answer.add(question);
    }
    return answer;
}
```

Again, the goal of this section is not to give a comprehensive overview of the DOM APIs. There are a large number of resources available on the Internet that provide information about XML in general, or DOM in particular.

To be able to compile the code in Listing 11-8, the following import statements had to be added.

```
import javax.xml.parsers.DocumentBuilder;
import javax.xml.parsers.DocumentBuilderFactory;
import javax.xml.parsers.ParserConfigurationException;
import org.w3c.dom.Document;
import org.w3c.dom.Node;
import org.w3c.dom.NodeList;
import org.xml.sax.SAXException;
```

Before we go into detail about the code, we show the output of this example in Figure 11-6.

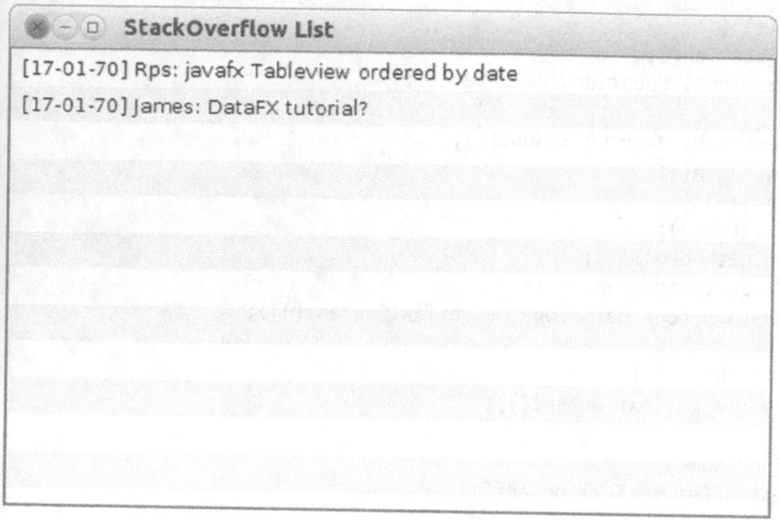

StackOverflow List

[17-01-70] Rps: javafx Tableview ordered by date

[17-01-70] James: DataFX tutorial?

Figure 11-6. *The result of the question application using XML response*

The code in Listing 11-8 shows some similarities to the code in Listing 11-7. In both cases, we process data available in a text format (JSON or XML) and convert the data into Question instances. In Listing 11-8, the DOM approach is used to inspect the received response.

An `org.w3c.dom.Document` instance is obtained using the following code.

```
InputStream inputStream = this.getClass().getResourceAsStream("/stackoverflow.xml");
DocumentBuilderFactory dbf = DocumentBuilderFactory.newInstance();
DocumentBuilder db = dbf.newDocumentBuilder();
Document doc = db.parse(inputStream);
```

In this case, we create a `Document` based on an `InputStream`. The `InputStream` is obtained from the artificially created file. We can also create an `InputStream` from a `URLConnection`, and pass this `InputStream` to the `db.parse()` method. Even easier, the `DocumentBuilder.parse` method also accepts a `String` parameter that contains the URL of a (REST) endpoint.

This shows that although we are using a static file containing questions in this case, we can easily use the same code when using a real REST endpoint.

The resulting `Document` can now be queried. From the XML response shown in Listing 11-6, we learn that the individual questions are enclosed in XML Elements named "item". We use the following to obtain a list of those XML Elements.

```
NodeList questionNodes = doc.getElementsByTagName("item");
```

We then iterate over this list, and obtain the question-specific fields by inspecting the `childNodes` in the respective XML Elements. Finally, we add the resulting question to the `ObservableList` of `Question` objects named answer.

This approach is rather simple, but we still have to do some manual XML parsing. Although this allows for flexibility, parsing becomes harder and more error prone with increasing complexity of the data structure.

Fortunately, the Java Standard Edition APIs contain tools for converting XML directly into Java Objects. The specification for these APIs is defined by the JAXB standard, and is available in the `javax.xml.bind` package. The process of converting XML data into Java Objects is called unmarshalling.

We now modify our example and make it use a mix of DOM parsing and JAXB unmarshalling. Again, we only change the `getObservableList()` method. The modified implementation is shown in Listing 11-9.

Listing 11-9. Combining XML Parsing and JAXB

```
ObservableList<Question> getObservableList() throws IOException, ParserConfigurationException,
SAXException {
    ObservableList<Question> answer = FXCollections.observableArrayList();
    InputStream inputStream = this.getClass().getResourceAsStream("/stackoverflow.xml");
    DocumentBuilderFactory dbf = DocumentBuilderFactory.newInstance();
    DocumentBuilder db = dbf.newDocumentBuilder();
    Document doc = db.parse(inputStream);
    NodeList questionNodes = doc.getElementsByTagName("item");
    int count = questionNodes.getLength();
    for (int i = 0; i < count; i++) {
        Element questionNode = (Element) questionNodes.item(i);
        DOMSource source = new DOMSource(questionNode);
        final Question question = (Question) JAXB.unmarshal(source, Question.class);

        answer.add(question);
    }
    return answer;

}
```

The only difference between this approach and the approach used in Listing 11-8 is the parsing of the individual questions. Instead of using DOM parsing for obtaining the specific fields of the individual questions, we use the unmarshal method in JAXB. The JAXB specifications allow for lots of flexibility and configuration, and the `JAXB.unmarshal` method is only a convenience method. However, in many cases, this method is sufficient. The `JAXB.unmarshal` method takes two parameters: the input source and the class that is the result of the conversion.

We want to convert the XML source into instances of our `Question` class, but how does the JAXB framework know how to map the fields? In many cases, the mapping is straightforward and does not require changes to existing code, but in other cases, the mapping is a bit more complex. Good enough, a whole package with annotations exists that we can use to help JAXB determine the conversion between XML and the Java Object.

To make the code in Listing 11-9 work, we made some minor modifications to the `Question` class. The new code for the `Question` class is shown in Listing 11-10.

Listing 11-10. Question Class with JAXB Annotations

```
package projavafx;

import javax.xml.bind.annotation.XmlAccessType;
import javax.xml.bind.annotation.XmlAccessorType;
import javax.xml.bind.annotation.XmlElement;

@XmlAccessorType(XmlAccessType.FIELD)
public class Question {

    private String owner;
    @XmlElement(name = "title")
    private String question;
    @XmlElement(name = "creation_date")
    private long timestamp;
```

```
    public Question(String o, String q, long t) {
        this.owner = o;
        this.question = q;
        this.timestamp = t;
    }

    public Question() {
    }

    /**
     * @return the owner
     */
    public String getOwner() {
        return owner;
    }

    /**
     * @param owner the owner to set
     */
    public void setOwner(String owner) {
        this.owner = owner;
    }

    /**
     * @return the question
     */
    public String getQuestion() {
        return question;
    }

    /**
     * @param question the question to set
     */
    public void setQuestion(String question) {
        this.question = question;
    }

    /**
     * @return the timestamp
     */
    public long getTimestamp() {
        return timestamp;
    }

    /**
     * @param timestamp the timestamp to set
     */
    public void setTimestamp(long timestamp) {
        this.timestamp = timestamp;
    }

}
```

We added three annotations to the original Question class. First, we annotated the class itself with

```
@XmlAccessorType(XmlAccessType.FIELD)
```

This annotation tells the JAXB framework to map XML data on the fields of this class, as opposed to on the JavaBean properties (getter/setter methods) of this class. The second and third annotations are added to the question field and the timeStamp field:

```
@XmlElement(name = "title")
private String question;
@XmlElement(name = "creation_date")
private long timestamp;
```

This indicates that the question field corresponds to an XML element named "title" and that the timestamp field corresponds to an XML element named "creation_date." Indeed, if we look at Listing 11-6, it shows that the question is in an element with the name "title" and that the timestamp is in an element with the name "creation_date." We have to instruct the JAXB runtime to map this element with our timestamp field, and this is what we do with the @XmlElement annotation.

Using the JAXB annotations made it easy to convert the XML question elements into individual Question instances, but we still had some manual XML processing in our main class. However, we can completely remove the manual XMLParsing and convert the whole XML response into a Java Object. Doing so, the getObservableList() method becomes very simple, as shown in Listing 11-11.

Listing 11-11. Parsing Incoming XML Data Using JAXB

```
ObservableList<Question> getObservableList() {
    InputStream inputStream = this.getClass().getResourceAsStream("/stackoverflow.xml");
    QuestionResponse response = JAXB.unmarshal(inputStream, QuestionResponse.class);
    return FXCollections.observableArrayList(response.getItem());
}
```

In this example, we use JAXB to convert the XML response into an instance of QuestionResponse, and the questions are then obtained via this QuestionResponse instance. Note that we convert the questions from a regular List object into an ObservableList object, as required by the method signature. We later show an example where we don't have to do that additional conversion.

The QuestionResponse class has two goals: map the XML response onto a Java Object and make the question items available as a List of Question instances. This is achieved by the code in Listing 11-12.

Listing 11-12. QuestionResponse Class, Enabling Conversion Between XML Response and Java Objects

```
package projavafx;

import java.util.List;
import javax.xml.bind.annotation.XmlAccessType;
import javax.xml.bind.annotation.XmlAccessorType;
import javax.xml.bind.annotation.XmlRootElement;

@XmlRootElement(name="items")
@XmlAccessorType(XmlAccessType.FIELD)
public class QuestionResponse {

    private List<Question> item;
```

```
    public List<Question> getItem() {
        return item;
    }

    public void setItem(List<Question> item) {
        this.item = item;
    }
}
```

The QuestionResponse class itself has two annotations:

```
@XmlAccessorType(XmlAccessType.FIELD)
```

was already discussed before and

```
@XmlRootElement(name="items")
```

indicates that this class corresponds to a root object in the XML structure, with the name "items." This indeed corresponds to the syntax of the XML response we created in Listing 11-6.

The previous examples show how existing technologies available in the Java 2 Platform, Standard Edition, can be used to obtain data from web services and inject these data in JavaFX controls. We now modify the example code to take advantage of some specific features of the JavaFX Platform.

Asynchronous Processing

A major problem with the examples so far is that they block the UI during the process of data retrieval and parsing. In many real-world situations, this is unacceptable. Calls to external web services might take longer than expected due to network or server issues. Even when the external calls are fast, a temporarily unresponsive UI decreases the overall quality of the application.

Fortunately, the JavaFX Platform allows for concurrency and asynchronous tasks. The concepts of Task, Worker, and Service have already been discussed in Chapter 7. In this section, we show how to leverage the `javafx.concurrent` package when accessing web services. We also leverage the fact that the `ListView` watches the `ObservableList` that contains its items.

The basic idea is that, when creating the `ListView`, we immediately return an empty `ObservableList`, while retrieving the data in a background `Thread`. Once we retrieve and parse the data, we add it to the `ObservableList` and the result will immediately be visible in the `ListView`.

The main class for this example is shown in Listing 11-13. We started with the code in Listing 11-7, where we obtained the questions in JSON format using a REST request to the StackExchange API. With some minor modifications, we could use the XML response as well, though.

Listing 11-13. Use a Background Thread for Retrieving Question `ListView`.

```
package projavafx;

import java.io.IOException;
import javafx.application.Application;
import static javafx.application.Application.launch;
import javafx.beans.InvalidationListener;
import javafx.beans.Observable;
import javafx.collections.FXCollections;
import javafx.collections.ObservableList;
import javafx.concurrent.Service;
```

```
import javafx.concurrent.Worker;
import javafx.scene.Scene;
import javafx.scene.control.ListView;
import javafx.scene.layout.StackPane;
import javafx.stage.Stage;

public class StackOverflow4 extends Application {

    @Override
    public void start(Stage primaryStage) throws IOException {
        ListView<Question> listView = new ListView<>();
        listView.setItems(getObservableList());
        listView.setCellFactory(l -> new QuestionCell());
        StackPane root = new StackPane();
        root.getChildren().add(listView);

        Scene scene = new Scene(root, 500, 300);

        primaryStage.setTitle("StackOverflow List");
        primaryStage.setScene(scene);
        primaryStage.show();
        System.out.println (« Done with the setup ») ;
    }

    ObservableList<Question> getObservableList() throws IOException {
        String url = "http://api.stackexchange.com/2.2/search?order=desc&sort=activity&tagged=javafx
&site=stackoverflow";
        Service<ObservableList<Question>>service = new QuestionRetrievalService(url);

        ObservableList<Question> answer = FXCollections.observableArrayList();
        service.stateProperty().addListener(new InvalidationListener() {

            @Override
            public void invalidated(Observable observable) {
                System.out.println("value is now "+service.getState());
                if (service.getState().equals(Worker.State.SUCCEEDED)) {
                    answer.addAll(service.getValue());
                }
            }
        });
        System.out.println("START SERVICE = "+service.getTitle());
        service.start();
        return answer;
    }

    /**
     * @param args the command line arguments
     */
    public static void main(String[] args) {
        launch(args);
    }
}
```

The main method is not different from the previous example, apart from the addition of a `System.out` log message that will print a message when we are done with the setup.

The `getObservableList` method will first create an instance of `ObservableList`, and this instance is returned on method completion. Initially, this instance will be an empty list. In this method, an instance of `QuestionRetrievalService` is created and the location of the REST endpoint is passed in the constructor. The `QuestionRetrievalService`, which extends `javafx.concurrent.Service`, is started, and we listen for changes in the `State` of the Service. When the state of the Service changes to `State.SUCCEEDED`, we add the retrieved questions to the `ObservableList`. Note that on every state change in the instance of the `QuestionRetrievalService`, we log a message to `System.out`.

We now take a closer look at the `QuestionRetrievalService` to understand how it starts a new `Thread`, and how it makes sure that the retrieved questions are added to the `ListView` control using the JavaFX `Thread`. The code of the `QuestionRetrievalService` is shown in Listing 11-14.

Listing 11-14. `QuestionRetrievalService`

```
package projavafx;

import java.net.URL;
import java.util.zip.GZIPInputStream;
import javafx.collections.FXCollections;
import javafx.collections.ObservableList;
import javafx.concurrent.Service;
import javafx.concurrent.Task;
import javax.json.Json;
import javax.json.JsonArray;
import javax.json.JsonNumber;
import javax.json.JsonObject;
import javax.json.JsonReader;
import javax.json.JsonString;
import javax.json.JsonValue;

public class QuestionRetrievalService extends Service<ObservableList<Question>> {

    private String loc;

    public QuestionRetrievalService(String loc) {
        this.loc = loc;
    }

    @Override
    protected Task<ObservableList<Question>>createTask() {
        return new Task<ObservableList<Question>>() {

            @Override
            protected ObservableList<Question> call() throws Exception {
                URL host = new URL(loc);
                JsonReader jr = Json.createReader(new GZIPInputStream(host.openConnection().
getInputStream()));
```

```
                JsonObject jsonObject = jr.readObject();
                JsonArray jsonArray = jsonObject.getJsonArray("items");
                ObservableList<Question> answer = FXCollections.observableArrayList();

                jsonArray.iterator().forEachRemaining((JsonValue e) -> {
                    JsonObject obj = (JsonObject) e;
                    JsonString name = obj.getJsonObject("owner").getJsonString("display_name");
                    JsonString quest = obj.getJsonString("title");
                    JsonNumber jsonNumber = obj.getJsonNumber("creation_date");
                    Question q = new Question(name.getString(), quest.getString(),
                    jsonNumber.longValue() * 1000);
                    System.out.println("Adding question "+q);
                    answer.add(q);
                });
                return answer;
            }
        };
    }

}
```

The QuestionRetrievalService extends Service and thus has to implement a createTask method. When the Service is started, this task is executed in a separate Thread. The createTask method on the QuestionRetrievalService creates a new Task and returns it. The signature of this method,

```
Task<ObservableList<Question>>createTask(),
```

ensures that the Task creates an ObservableList of questions. The generic type parameter ObservableList<Question> is the same as the type parameter in the declaration of the Service. As a consequence, the getValue() method of the Service will also return an ObservableList of Questions.

Indeed, the following code snippet states that the questionRetrievalService.getValue() should return an ObservableList<Question>.

```
ObservableList<Question> answer = FXCollections.observableArrayList();
...
    if (now == State.SUCCEEDED) {
        answer.addAll(service.getValue());
    }
```

The Task instance that we created in the QuestionRetrievalService has to implement the call method. This method is actually doing what the getObservableList method in the previous examples was doing: retrieving the data and parsing them.

Although the real work in a Service (the Task created by createTask) is done in a background Thread, all methods on the Service, including the getValue() call, should be accessed from the JavaFX Thread. The internal implementation makes sure that all changes to the available properties in the Service are executed on the JavaFX application Thread.

Running the example gives the exact same visual output as running the previous example. However, we added some System.out messages for clarity. If we run the example, the following messages can be seen on the console.

```
State of service is READY
State of service is SCHEDULED
```

```
Done with the setup
State of service is RUNNING
Adding question projavafx.Question@482fb3d5
...
Adding question projavafx.Question@2d622bf7
State of service is SUCCEEDED
```

This shows that the getObservableList method returns before the questions are obtained and added to the list.

Note In theory, you could notice a different behavior inasmuch as the background thread might be completed before the other initialization has been done. In practice, however, this behavior is unlikely when network calls are involved.

Converting Web Services Data to TableView

So far, all our examples showed questions in a ListView. The ListView is an easy and powerful JavaFX Control, however, there are other controls that are in some cases more suitable to render information.

We can show the Question data in a TableView as well, and that is what we do in this section. The retrieval and parsing of the data stay the same as in the previous example. However, we now use a TableView to render the data, and we have to define which columns we want to see. For each column, we have to specify the origination of the data. The code in Listing 11-15 shows the start method used in the example.

Listing 11-15. The Start Method in the Application Rendering Questions in a TableView

```
@Override
  public void start(Stage primaryStage) throws IOException {
     TableView<Question> tableView = new TableView<>();
     tableView.setItems(getObservableList());
     TableColumn<Question, String> dateColumn = new TableColumn<>("Date");
     TableColumn<Question, String> ownerColumn = new TableColumn<>("Owner");
     TableColumn<Question, String> questionColumn = new TableColumn<>("Question");
     dateColumn.setCellValueFactory((CellDataFeatures<Question, String> cdf) -> {
         Question q = cdf.getValue();
         return new SimpleStringProperty(getTimeStampString(q.getTimestamp()));
     });
     ownerColumn.setCellValueFactory((CellDataFeatures<Question, String> cdf) -> {
         Question q = cdf.getValue();
         return new SimpleStringProperty(q.getOwner());
     });
     questionColumn.setCellValueFactory((CellDataFeatures<Question, String> cdf) -> {
         Question q = cdf.getValue();
         return new SimpleStringProperty(q.getQuestion());
     });
     questionColumn.setPrefWidth(350);
     tableView.getColumns().addAll(dateColumn, ownerColumn, questionColumn);
     StackPane root = new StackPane();
     root.getChildren().add(tableView);

     Scene scene = new Scene(root, 500, 300);
```

```
        primaryStage.setTitle("StackOverflow Table");
        primaryStage.setScene(scene);
        primaryStage.show();
    }
```

Clearly, this example requires more code than the example showing a `ListView`. Setting up a table is slightly more complex, due to the different columns that are involved. There is not much difference between setting the contents of the `ListView` and setting the contents of the `TableView`. This is achieved doing

```
tableView.setItems(getObservableList());
```

where the `getObservableList()` method is the same implementation as in the previous example. Note that we could also use the convenient constructor

```
TableView<Question> tableView = new TableView<>(getObservableList());
```

When using a `TableView`, we have to define a number of `TableColumns`. This is done in the following code snippet.

```
TableColumn<Question, String> dateColumn = new TableColumn<>("Date");
TableColumn<Question, String> ownerColumn = new TableColumn<>("Owner");
TableColumn<Question, String> questionColumn = new TableColumn<>("Question");
```

Using the `TableColumn` constructor, we create one `TableColumn` with title "Date," one with title "Owner," and a third one titled "Question." The Generics `<Question, String>` indicate that each entry in a row represents a `Question`, and the individual cells in the specified column are of type `String`.

Next, the instances of `TableColumn` that we created need to know what data they should render. This is done using `CellFactories`, as shown in the following snippet.

```
dateColumn.setCellValueFactory((CellDataFeatures<Question, String> cdf) -> {
    Question q = cdf.getValue();
    return new SimpleStringProperty(getTimeStampString(q.getTimestamp()));
});
```

A detailed description of the `setCellValueFactory` method is beyond the scope of this chapter. The reader is encouraged to have a look at the JavaDoc of the `TableView` and `TableColumn` classes while working with tables. The JavaDoc explains that we have to specify a `Callback` class with a call method that returns an `ObservableValue` containing the content of the specific cell. Fortunately, we can use a lambda expression for this.

The question we are displaying in this row can be obtained via the `CellDataFeatures` instance that is passed as the single parameter in this lambda expression. Because we want to show the timestamp, we return a `SimpleStringProperty` whose content is set to the timestamp of the specified `Question`.

The same technique has to be used for the other `TableColumns` (containing the owner and the question contained within the applicable `Question` object).

Finally, we have to add the columns to the `TableView`:

```
tableView.getColumns().addAll(dateColumn, ownerColumn, questionColumn);
```

Running this example results in the visual output shown in Figure 11-7.

StackOverflow Table

Date	Owner	Question
17-04-14	user332...	JavaFx change background color of disabled texta...
19-04-14	user320...	Null FXML variables
19-04-14	Laambi	Easy way of creating executable JavaFX?
19-04-14	user324...	Java user interface with SWING vs JavaFX
19-04-14	Cheok Y...	JavaFX SimpleSwingBrowser auto fit web page
19-04-14	Tom	Is it possible to make a Java project to executable...
19-04-14	malex	JavaFX load text with more lines in to javafx conta...
11-04-14	ymene	Where should I validate JavaFX Property changes?
19-04-14	Tom	Values not getting edited in MySQL database
18-04-14	ceklock	JavaFX - How to set same width for all buttons bef...
19-04-14	Tom	setMaxHeight() method not working for TextField ...
19-04-14	user354...	newbie toggle button event in javafx
19-04-14	user320...	KeyListener JavaFX

Figure 11-7. *Using a* `TableView` *for rendering questions*

This sample requires lots of boilerplate code for a simple table, but fortunately the JavaFX Platform contains a way to reduce the amount of code. Manually setting the `CellValueFactory` instances for each column is cumbersome, but we can use another method for doing this, by using JavaFX Properties. Listing 11-16 contains a modified version of the start method of the main class, where we leverage the JavaFX Properties concept.

Listing 11-16. Rendering Data in Columns Based on JavaFX Properties

```
@Override
public void start(Stage primaryStage) throws IOException {
    TableView<Question> tableView = new TableView<>();
    tableView.setItems(getObservableList());
    TableColumn<Question, String> dateColumn = new TableColumn<>("Date");
    TableColumn<Question, String> ownerColumn = new TableColumn<>("Owner");
    TableColumn<Question, String> questionColumn = new TableColumn<>("Question");
    dateColumn.setCellValueFactory(new PropertyValueFactory<>("timestampString"));
    ownerColumn.setCellValueFactory(new PropertyValueFactory<>("owner"));
    questionColumn.setCellValueFactory(new PropertyValueFactory<>("question"));
    questionColumn.setPrefWidth(350);
    tableView.getColumns().addAll(dateColumn, ownerColumn, questionColumn);
    StackPane root = new StackPane();
    root.getChildren().add(tableView);

    Scene scene = new Scene(root, 500, 300);

    primaryStage.setTitle("StackOverflow Table");
    primaryStage.setScene(scene);
    primaryStage.show();
}
```

This code is clearly shorter than the code in the previous sample. We actually replaced

```
dateColumn.setCellValueFactory((CellDataFeatures<Question, String> cdf) -> {
    Question q = cdf.getValue();
    return new SimpleStringProperty(getTimeStampString(q.getTimestamp()));
});
```

by

```
dateColumn.setCellValueFactory(new PropertyValueFactory<>("timestampString"));
```

The same holds for the `ownerColumn` and the `questionColumn`.

We are using instances of `javafx.scene.control.cell.PropertyValueFactory<S,T>(String name)` for defining what specific data should be rendered in which cell.

The `PropertyValueFactory` searches for a JavaFX property with the specified name and returns the `ObservableValue` of this property when called. In case no property with such a name can be found, the JavaDoc says the following.

> *In this example, the "firstName" string is used as a reference to an assumed `firstNameProperty()` method in the Person class type (which is the class type of the TableView `items` list). Additionally, this method must return a Property instance. If a method meeting these requirements is found, then the `TableCell` is populated with this ObservableValue. In addition, the TableView will automatically add an observer to the returned value, such that any changes fired will be observed by the TableView, resulting in the cell immediately updating.*
>
> *If no method matching this pattern exists, there is fall-through support for attempting to call get<property>() or is<property>() (that is, `getFirstName()` or is `FirstName()` in the example above). If a method matching this pattern exists, the value returned from this method is wrapped in a `ReadOnlyObjectWrapper` and returned to the TableCell. However, in this situation, this means that the TableCell will not be able to observe the ObservableValue for changes (as is the case in the first approach above).*

From this, it is clear that JavaFX Properties are the preferred way for rendering information in a `TableView`. So far, we used the POJO `Question` class with JavaBean getter and setter methods as the value object for being displayed in both a `ListView` and a `TableView`.

Although the preceding example also works without using JavaFX Properties, as stated by the JavaDoc, we now modify the `Question` class to use a JavaFX Property for the owner information. The `timeStamp` and the text fields could have been modified to use JavaFX Properties as well, but the mixed example shows that the fall-through scenario described in the JavaDoc really works. The modified `Question` class is shown in Listing 11-17.

Listing 11-17. Implementation of `Question` Class Using JavaFX Properties for the Author Field

```
package projavafx;

import java.text.SimpleDateFormat;
import java.util.Date;
import javafx.beans.property.SimpleStringProperty;
import javafx.beans.property.StringProperty;
import javax.xml.bind.annotation.XmlAccessType;
import javax.xml.bind.annotation.XmlAccessorType;
```

```
@XmlAccessorType(XmlAccessType.PROPERTY)
public class Question {

    static final SimpleDateFormat sdf = new SimpleDateFormat ("dd-MM-YY");

    private StringProperty ownerProperty = new SimpleStringProperty();
    private String question;
    private long timestamp;

    public Question (String o, String q, long t) {
        this.ownerProperty.set(o);
        this.question = q;
        this.timestamp = t;
    }

    public String getOwner() {
        return ownerProperty.get();
    }

    public void setOwner(String owner) {
        this.ownerProperty.set(owner);
    }

    public String getQuestion() {
        return question;
    }

    public void setQuestion(String question) {
        this.question = question;
    }

    public long getTimestamp() {
        return timestamp;
    }

    public void setTimestamp(long timestamp) {
        this.timestamp = timestamp;
    }

    public String getTimestampString() {
        return sdf.format(new Date(timestamp));
    }

}
```

There are a few things to note about this implementation. The ownerProperty follows the standard JavaFX Convention, as explained in Chapter 3.

Apart from the introduction of JavaFX Properties, there is another major change in the implementation of the Question class. The class is now annotated with

```
@XmlAccessorType(XmlAccessType.PROPERTY)
```

The reason for this is that when doing so, the setter methods will be called by the JAXB.unmarshal method when it creates an instance of the Question with some specific information. Now that we are using JavaFX Properties instead of primitive types, this is required. The JAXB framework could easily assign the value of the XML Element "owner" to the owner String field, but it cannot assign a value to a JavaFX Property object by default.

By using XmlAccessType.PROPERTY, the setOwner(String v) method will be called by the JAXB framework, supplying the value of the XML Element to the setOwner method. The implementation of this method

```
ownerProperty.set(owner);
```

will then update the JavaFX Property that is subsequently being used by the TableColumn and the TableView.

The other important change in the Question implementation is that we added a method

```
String getTimestampString()
```

This method will return the timestamp in a human-readable format. You might have noticed in Listing 11-16 that we set the CellValueFactory for the dateColumn to a PropertyValueFactory that points to "timestampString" rather than "timeStamp":

```
dateColumn.setCellValueFactory(new PropertyValueFactory<>("timestampString"));
```

The reason for this is that the getTimestamp() method returns a long, whereas we prefer to visualize the timestamp in a more readable format. By adding a getTimestampString() method and pointing the CellValueFactory to this method, the content of the cells in this column will be readable time indications.

The examples we have shown so far in this chapter demonstrate that the Java Platform, Standard Edition, already contains a number of APIs that are very useful when accessing web services. We also showed how to use the JavaFX Concurrent Framework, the ObservableList pattern, JavaFX Properties, and the PropertyValueFactory class to enhance the flow between calling the web service and rendering the data in the JavaFX Controls.

Although there is no rocket science involved in the examples, additional requirements will make things more complex, and more boilerplate code will be required. Fortunately, a number of initiatives have already popped up in the JavaFX community, with the goal of making our lives easier.

Using External Libraries

All our examples so far did not require any additional external library. The Java 2 Platform, Standard Edition, and the JavaFX Platform offer a great environment that can be used for accessing web services. In this section, we use two external libraries and show how they make accessing web services easier.

DataFX

The DataFX library is described at http://datafx.io and it provides an end-to-end toolkit for retrieving, parsing, massaging, populating, viewing, and rendering data. These data might be obtained using web services that communicate with well-known protocols such as REST, SSE, or WebSockets, but can also be obtained from a local file system, a database, or a number of other data sources. DataFX 2 was released in late 2013, and DataFX 8 is expected to be released in September 2014.

DataFX 8 consists of a number of modules:

- Cell Factories, providing a number of useful CellFactories and hence reducing the boilerplate code that is often required in projects
- DataSources, providing a level of abstraction about the origin of the data, both regarding the physical location (file, network resources) and the format (JSON, XML, JDBC, etc.)
- DataFlow API, providing developers a convenient way to manage data across workflows, and to use injection

In the next example, we integrate DataFX with our StackExchange example. Once again, the only change is in the getObservableList method, but for clarity, we show the whole main class in Listing 11-18.

Listing 11-18. Obtaining Questions Using DataFX

```
import java.io.IOException;
import javafx.application.Application;
import static javafx.application.Application.launch;
import javafx.collections.ObservableList;
import javafx.concurrent.Worker;
import javafx.scene.Scene;
import javafx.scene.control.ListView;
import javafx.scene.layout.StackPane;
import javafx.stage.Stage;
import org.datafx.provider.ListDataProvider;
import org.datafx.provider.ListDataProviderBuilder;
import org.datafx.io.RestSource;
import org.datafx.io.RestSourceBuilder;
import org.datafx.io.converter.InputStreamConverter;
import org.datafx.io.converter.JsonConverter;

public class StackOverflowDataFX extends Application {

    @Override
    public void start(Stage primaryStage) throws IOException {
        ListView<Question> listView = new ListView<>();
        listView.setItems(getObservableList());
        listView.setCellFactory(l -> new QuestionCell());
        StackPane root = new StackPane();
        root.getChildren().add(listView);

        Scene scene = new Scene(root, 500, 300);

        primaryStage.setTitle("StackOverflow List");
        primaryStage.setScene(scene);
        primaryStage.show();
        System.out.println ("Done with the setup");
    }

    ObservableList<Question> getObservableList() throws IOException {
        InputStreamConverter converter = new JsonConverter("item", Question.class);

        RestSource restSource = RestSourceBuilder.create()
                .converter(converter)
                .host("http://api.stackexchange.com")
                .path("2.2").path("search")
                .queryParam("order", "desc")
                .queryParam("sort", "activity")
                .queryParam("tagged", "javafx")
                .queryParam("site", "stackoverflow").build();
```

```
        ListDataProvider<Question> ldp = ListDataProviderBuilder.create()
                .dataReader(restSource)
                .build();
        Worker<ObservableList<Question>>retrieve = ldp.retrieve();
        return retrieve.getValue();
    }

public static void main(String[] args) {
        launch(args);
    }
}
```

The relevant part, the implementation of the `getObservableList` method, is very simple. We first construct a `JsonConverter` that will convert JSON objects named "item" to `Question` instances.

Next, we create a `RestSource`, and assign the converter to it. We also supply information on the REST endpoint. We then create a `ListDataSource` that will use the `RestSource` and retrieve the data.

Calling the `ListDataSource.retrieve` method starts an asynchronous Service. Instead of waiting for the result, we can immediately return the result object to our visual controls. The DataFX framework will update the result object while it reads and parses incoming data. For large chunks of data, this is very useful, because this approach allows developers to render parts of the data while other parts are still coming in or are still being processed.

■ **Note** At the time of writing, the DataFX 8 APIs are not final. Developers are encouraged to visit `http://datafx.io` and check the documentation for the latest API documentation.

JAX-RS

The release of Java Enterprise Edition 7 includes the release of JAX-RS 2.0. This specification not only defines how Java developers can provide REST endpoints, but also how Java code can consume REST endpoints.

In the next example, we modify the `QuestionRetrievalService` of Listing 11-14 to use the JAX-RS API. This is shown in Listing 11-19.

Listing 11-19. Using JAX-RS for Retrieving Questions

```
package projavafx.jerseystackoverflow;

import javafx.collections.FXCollections;
import javafx.collections.ObservableList;
import javafx.concurrent.Service;
import javafx.concurrent.Task;
import javax.ws.rs.client.Client;
import javax.ws.rs.client.ClientBuilder;
import javax.ws.rs.client.WebTarget;
import javax.ws.rs.core.MediaType;

public class QuestionRetrievalService extends Service<ObservableList<Question>> {

    private String loc;
    private String path;
    private String search;
```

```
    public QuestionRetrievalService(String loc, String path, String search) {
        this.loc = loc;
        this.path = path;
        this.search = search;
    }

    @Override
    protected Task<ObservableList<Question>>createTask() {
        return new Task<ObservableList<Question>>() {
            @Override
            protected ObservableList<Question> call() throws Exception {
                Client client = ClientBuilder.newClient();
                WebTarget target = client.target(loc).path(path).queryParam("tagged", search).
queryParam("site", "stackoverflow");
                QuestionResponse response = target.request(MediaType.APPLICATION_JSON).
get(QuestionResponse.class);
                return FXCollections.observableArrayList(response.getItem());
            }
        };
    }

}
```

To show one of the nice tools of JAX-RS, we slightly modified the constructor of the `QuestionRetrievalService` to take three parameters:

```
public QuestionRetrievalService(String host, String path, String search);
```

This is because JAX-RS allows us to use the `Builder` pattern to construct REST resources, allowing a distinction among hostname, path, query parameters, and others.

As a consequence, we have to make a slight modification in Listing 11-13:

```
String url = "http://api.stackexchange.com/2.2/search?order=desc&sort=activity&tagged=
javafx&site=stackoverflow";
Service<ObservableList<Question>>service = new QuestionRetrievalService(url);
```

is replaced by

```
String url = "http://api.stackexchange.com/";
String path = "2.2/search";
String search = "javafx";
Service<ObservableList<Question>>service = new QuestionRetrievalService(url, path, search);
```

The hostname, path, and search parameter are used to create a JAX-RS `WebTarget`:

```
Client client = ClientBuilder.newClient();
WebTarget target = client.target(loc).path(path).queryParam("tagged", search)
        .queryParam("site", "stackoverflow");
```

On this WebResource, we can call the request method to execute the request, followed by the get(Class clazz) method, and supply a class parameter. The result of the REST call will then be parsed into an instance of the supplied class, which is also what we did using JAXB in our example in Listing 11-11.

```
QuestionResponse response = target.request(MediaType.APPLICATION_JSON).get(QuestionResponse.class);
```

The response now contains a list of Questions, and we can use the exact same code as in Listing 11-4 to render the questions.

Summary

In this chapter, we explained briefly two options for integrating JavaFX applications and enterprise applications. We demonstrated a number of techniques for retrieving data available via web services, and also showed how to render the data in typical JavaFX controls such as ListView and TableView.

We used a number of third-party tools that facilitate the process of retrieving, parsing, and rendering data. We demonstrated some JavaFX-specific issues related to remote web services (i.e., updating the UI should happen on the JavaFX application thread).

It is important to realize that the decoupling between JavaFX client applications and web services allows for a large degree of freedom. There are different tools and techniques for dealing with web services, and developers are encouraged to use their favorite tools in their JavaFX application.

CHAPTER 12

JavaFX on Embedded and Mobile

It's simple—you read the protocol and write the code.

—Bill Joy

Desktop systems and laptops have a prominent place in many environments. Both business applications and end-user applications written in JavaFX can run on these systems. Although desktops and laptops remain big target markets, there are other, emerging environments for client applications. In this chapter, we show how you can use your existing JavaFX code to create applications for mobile and embedded systems.

OpenJFX, the Origin of the Code

At the JavaOne conference in 2011, Oracle announced that at some point, JavaFX would be completely open source. It took a few years before all technical and legal issues were sorted out, but today, the whole JavaFX platform that you use in your application development is based on open source code. The code for JavaFX is being developed in the OpenJFX project which is a subproject of OpenJDK (see `http://openjdk.org`).

OpenJDK is the place where the Java Platform, Standard Edition itself is being developed as an open source project. The OpenJDK project contains a number of projects, OpenJFX being one of them. It is important to realize that although most contributors to OpenJDK are Oracle employees, the process is open to anyone. Apart from Oracle, a number of large companies (e.g., IBM, Twitter, Apple) contribute code to OpenJDK, as well as a number of individuals. Although reading the code is very easy, there is an intense process before anyone gets commit access to the code base. Given the importance and the usage of the Java Platform, this is a reassuring thought.

The OpenJFX project inside OpenJDK contains all the code required to create the JavaFX Platform. Not only the code is public, but the mailing lists and documentation parts are open as well. As a consequence, every developer is allowed to read the discussions on architecture and implementation of the JavaFX Platform. One of the advantages of this open character is that if you wonder why something in the JavaFX platform is the way it is, you can search for it in the discussion lists. An important resource for information on OpenJFX is the OpenJFX wiki, which is located at `https://wiki.openjdk.java.net/display/OpenJFX/Main`. A screenshot of the landing page for this wiki is shown in Figure 12-1.

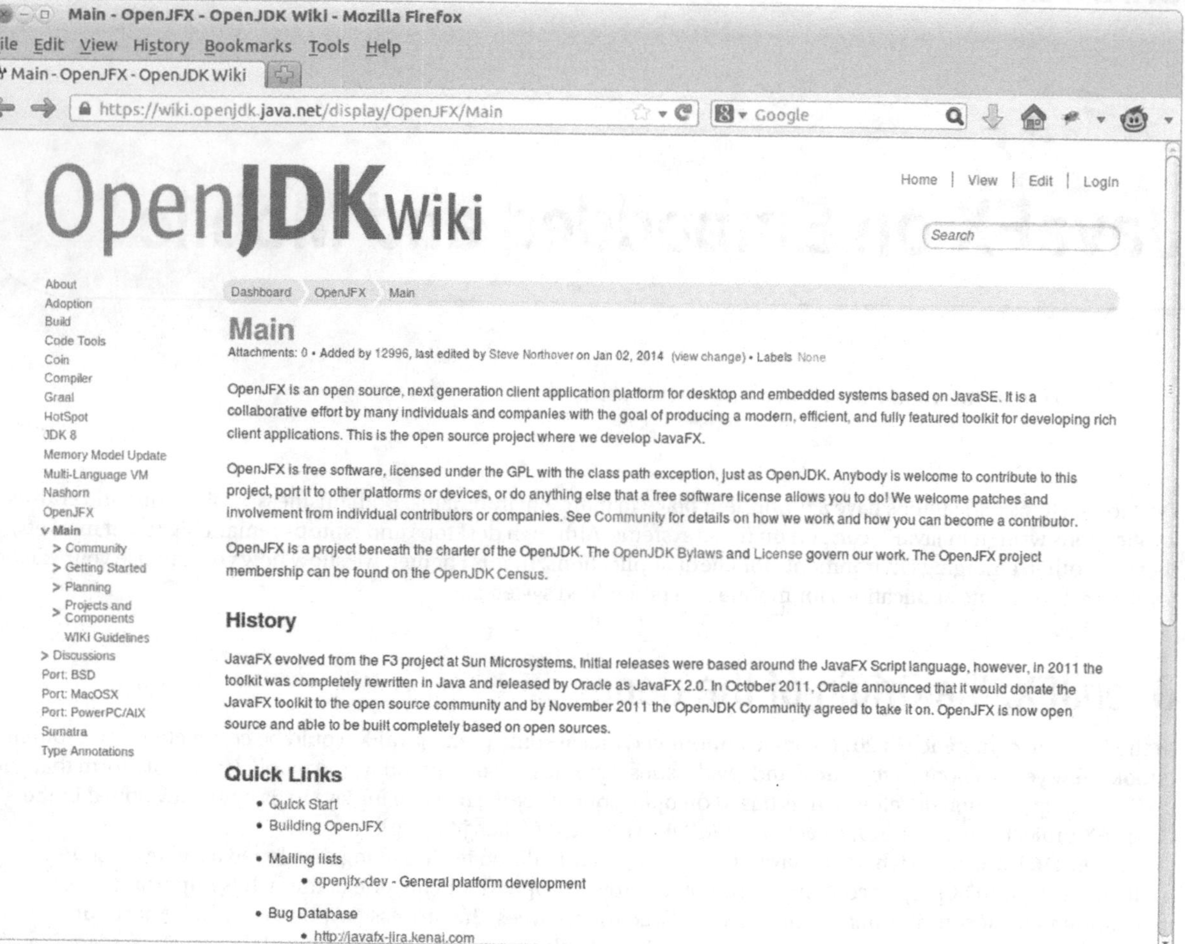

***Figure 12-1.** The OpenJFX wiki on the OpenJDK web site*

The OpenJFX wiki contains useful information on the structure of the JavaFX Platform. It provides links to the issue tracker and mailing lists, which makes it possible to follow up on features and bug fixes.

It is also the starting point for the different JavaFX runtime packages that are created by Oracle and by the community.

The OpenJFX project contains the code for the JavaFX Platform, but not the binary runtime or the SDK. Based on the code, a number of implementations are created. As Figure 12-2 shows, a number of implementations leverage the code in OpenJFX.

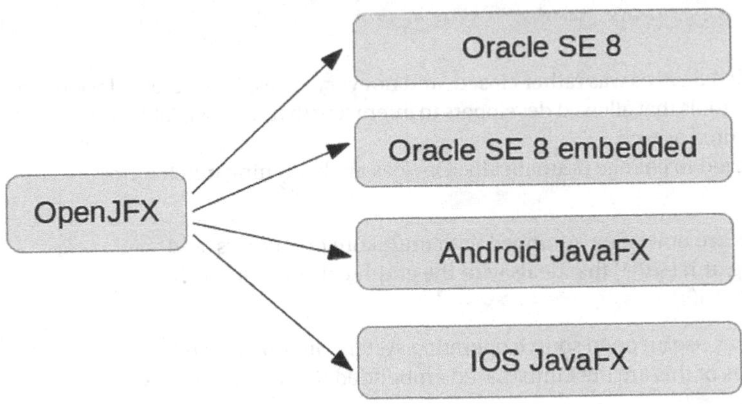

Figure 12-2. *Implementations that leverage the OpenJFX code base*

As the OpenJFX code is completely open source and licensed under the GPL license, it is possible for developers to create their own runtime, as long as they adhere to the license terms.

Oracle uses the code in OpenJFX and the code in OpenJDK to create the Oracle SE 8 SDK and the Oracle SE 8 runtime. These binaries are distributed with the Oracle Binary Code License.

In addition, Oracle creates the Oracle SE 8 embedded system that allows applications to run on embedded devices using a number of compact profiles. The Oracle SE 8 embedded system contains a number of tools that allow application providers to define the most suitable profile. Java SE Embedded is available as a free download for evaluation and development, and requires a commercial license for use in production. We do not discuss Java SE Embedded in this chapter. Developers interested in this product are encouraged to read the Oracle documentation at `http://docs.oracle.com/javase/8/javase-embedded.htm`.

Oracle delivers the SE 8 SDK and runtime for a number of platforms, including the ARM platform. The ARM version of the Java SE Development Kit 8 can be downloaded at `http://www.oracle.com/technetwork/java/javase/downloads/jdk8-arm-downloads-2187472.html`.

■ **Note** The download locations of the Java SE development kit and runtime might change in the future and the link given here might not be valid anymore.

We will talk about JavaFX 8 on ARM in the following section. Next, we will talk about JavaFX on iOS and JavaFX on Android. The runtime for both these ports is based on exactly the same code that Oracle SE 8 is based on, namely the OpenJFX source code. This is extremely important, as it allows developers to write portable applications.

One of the major advantages of JavaFX is the portability of code. It is a huge productivity boost if you can write your application in one language and have it deployed on a number of platforms (desktop, laptop, embedded, mobile).

The availability of the Java 8 platform, and by extension the JavaFX 8 platform for a number of different environments, brings a competitive advantage to Java developers compared to developers that use a specific language for each platform.

It is still possible to leverage features provided by a specific platform in your JavaFX Application. Of course, features that are only available in, for example, iOS cannot be used in an Android environment and vice versa. Therefore, developers who have to create applications that are supposed to have the exact same behavior across different platforms should stick with JavaFX features where possible.

JavaFX on ARM

In the not so distant past, the world of embedded devices was rather closed, and not very accessible for Java developers. Each device had its own, often proprietary set of tools that allowed developers to interact with it. The available resources on a device (processor, memory) were very limited as well.

Over the past couple of years, this has started to change dramatically. Devices are becoming much more powerful, more open, and less expensive.

- *Powerful:* Even embedded devices are now often equipped with multicore processors, and with a specific graphics processing unit (GPU) that deals with the graphical computations, thereby reducing the load on the CPU(s).
- *Open:* Many new embedded devices use an open source operating system on top of a well-known processor. Typical examples of this are the Linux-based embedded devices using ARM processors.
- *Cheaper:* Prices for electronic components have decreased, and assembly is cheaper as well, with Internet users being encouraged to develop and assemble their own boards.

These evolutions have led to a big shift in embedded computing. The tipping point has been reached where it is possible to use the same Java platform on a number of embedded devices as the Java platform that runs on desktop systems.

For smaller systems, the Java Platform, Micro Edition 8 is still the best solution. The starting point for developers who want to know more about the Java Micro Edition is the Oracle web site at `http://docs.oracle.com/javame/8.0/index.html`. Although the Java Platform, Micro Edition 8 is a powerful platform with some interesting APIs allowing a direct link to native interfaces, in this book we focus on the Java Platform, Standard Edition.

A comparison between the Java Platform, Micro Edition 8 and the Java Platform, Standard Edition 8 can be found in Figure 12-3, which is taken from a blog entry by Terence Barr, who is a Senior Technologist, Mobile & Embedded at Oracle.

Feature	Oracle Java ME Embedded	Oracle Java SE Embedded
Java SE 7 and 8 compatibility	Java SE 8 alignment: Coming with Java ME 8	Full compatibility with Java SE
Target hardware	Low-end to mid-range embedded devices • From ~130 KB RAM (micro-controller, RTOS or minimal OS) • To 32 MB RAM (full CPU/OS supported) • Variety of I/O (GPIO, I2C, SPI, ADC/DAC, UART, GPS, ...)	Mid-range to high-end general purpose devices • From ~32/64 MB RAM (full OS required) • Limited set of default supported I/O
Graphics/UI support	Headless focus. Graphics/UI considered for future release.	Optional (JavaFX)
Robust, multi-tasking application model with remote provisioning and management	Standard part of platform	Not part of standard platform (requires additional components & integration, such as OSGi)
Flexible connectivity/networking	Support for wired and wireless connectivity (incl. cellular), multiple access points	Not part of standard platform
Dedicated embedded functionality	VM optimizations, configurability, I/O access, remote operation, auto-start/recovery	Limited (memory management, power management, size optimizations)
Dedicated embedded tooling	Yes: Java ME SDK, plug-ins for NetBeans, Eclipse	No
Platform porting and customization	Portable, extensible, configurable to adapt to a variety of H/W and S/W requirements	Focus on general-purpose hardware. Porting/customization is more specialized/involved.
Suitability for compute/data-intensive apps	Low to moderate (not a focus)	Excellent (with appropriate H/W, including multi-processor/multi-core)
Target use cases	Wireless modules, smart sensors/meters, eHealth devices, industrial control, intelligent network nodes, general IoT/M2M	ATMs, kiosks, gateways, advanced networking equipment, high-end medical, industrial control systems, solutions requiring Java SE compatibility
Single development architecture - Covering the entire embedded space with two Java platforms		

Figure 12-3. *Comparison between Java Micro Edition 8 and Java Standard Edition 8*

As mentioned in the previous section, Oracle delivers a Java Standard Edition 8 development kit and runtime for ARM-based Linux systems. The JavaFX for ARM bundle has been reported to work great with a number of embedded devices, including the Raspberry Pi.

The Raspberry Pi

The Raspberry Pi is a computer that fits on a board the size of a credit card. It was developed by the Raspberry Pi Foundation (see `http://www.raspberrypi.org`) and manufactured by a number of licensed companies. It is often used for educational targets and for demonstrations of technologies.

A picture of a Raspberry Pi board is shown in Figure 12-4.

***Figure 12-4.** The Raspberry Pi board*

Currently, there are two versions of the Raspberry Pi, priced at $25 and $35, respectively. Both versions come with an ARM11 32-bit RISC processor. The lower priced model has 256 MB of memory, and the higher priced model has 512 MB of memory. The Raspberry Pi has no internal hard drive, but is booted from an SD card.

The recommended operating system for the Raspberry Pi is Raspbian Wheezy, which is based on the open source Debian Linux operating system. Raspbian Wheezy is using an ARM hard-float architecture. Good enough, as the JDK 8 for ARM, as delivered by Oracle, is built for an ARM hard-float architecture as well.

The Raspberry Pi comes with a decent GPU, which makes it a perfect candidate for showcasing JavaFX applications. The Raspberry Pi board itself has no output screen, but it contains a number of interfaces (e.g., HDMI, Composite RCA, DSI) to interact with standard displays. Because the Raspberry Pi has an Ethernet connection, it is very convenient to use SSH (secure shell) to log in on the Raspberry Pi from a workstation.

JavaFX on the Raspberry Pi

As mentioned before, the JavaFX platform that you can use to develop JavaFX applications on the Raspberry Pi (and on ARM-based Linux systems in general) is based on the code available in OpenJFX.

The wiki part of the OpenJFX project contains detailed and up-to-date instructions on how to set up a Raspberry Pi with JavaFX. You can read these instructions at the following web site: `https://wiki.openjdk.java.net/display/OpenJFX/OpenJFX+on+the+Raspberry+Pi`. Because the JavaFX runtime on the Raspberry Pi provides the same API as the JavaFX runtime on Desktop, we can leverage all the nice features of JavaFX 8—and Java 8 in general—in our applications. In particular, support for Lambda expressions and streams that was added in Java 8 works very well using the JavaFX runtime on the Raspberry Pi.

A nice example of this is the Mary Had a Little Lambda project. This project, which is a JavaFX answer on the popular "Mary Had a Little Lamb" song, is a typical showcase for Lambda expressions and the stream API in a JavaFX application. The code is maintained by Stephen Chin in GitHub at `https://github.com/steveonjava/MaryHadALittleLambda/tree/master/src/sample`.

The code contains the necessary files to open it as a NetBeans project, but it can also be compiled, packaged, and executed using the command-line ant tool. You can get a local copy of the code by executing

```
git clone https://github.com/steveonjava/MaryHadALittleLambda.git
```

■ **Note** You need a git client on your system to retrieve the code. In case you don't have a git client, you can easily install this. On Linux, this is done using `sudo apt-get install git`. On Windows, the download URL is `http://git-scm.com/download/win`. On MacOS, the download URL is `http://git-scm.com/download/mac`.

After you retrieve the code, you can build and run it on the desktop with a single command:

```
ant
```

■ **Note** If you don't have the ant build tool, you can download it for your operating system at `http://ant.apache.org/bindownload.cgi`.

Alternatively, you can open the project in NetBeans, and run it there similarly to the other NetBeans projects in the previous chapters of this book.

Running the code on a desktop system results in the output shown in Figure 12-5.

Figure 12-5. *Desktop version of the MaryHadALittleLambda project*

Deploying JavaFX Applications on the Embedded ARM Systems

There are a number of ways to deploy JavaFX Applications on embedded systems. Specific embedded systems often have specific requirements, limitations, and options. In this section, we describe two approaches for the generic case where we have SSH access to an embedded ARM system. In both approaches, we assume that the embedded system is already equipped with a Java 8 Runtime, Standard Edition.

Using Command-Line Tools

This approach is very similar to deploying JavaFX applications on Linux systems in general. Using your favorite build tools, you create a JAR containing your application and all dependencies on your local development system. Next, you use SCP (secure copy) to transfer that JAR file to the embedded system where you can also execute it. Typically, you have to log in to the embedded system using SSH, execute the Java command, and supply the location of the JAR file.

Using NetBeans

NetBeans 8 contains built-in support for running Java and JavaFX applications on remote platforms (including embedded systems). Using this feature allows you to not only create the application on your local development system, but also to push it to the embedded system, execute it there, and inspect the system output locally. Under the hood, NetBeans is doing the same as we did in the previous approach using command-line tools. Everything is nicely integrated in the IDE, though, and the switch between testing on your local development system or running on an embedded system is very easy. To use this feature, we first have to tell NetBeans where our embedded system is running, and how NetBeans can access it. This is done by selecting the Tools ➤ Java Platforms menu, and clicking the Add Platform button. The screenshot in Figure 12-6 will be shown.

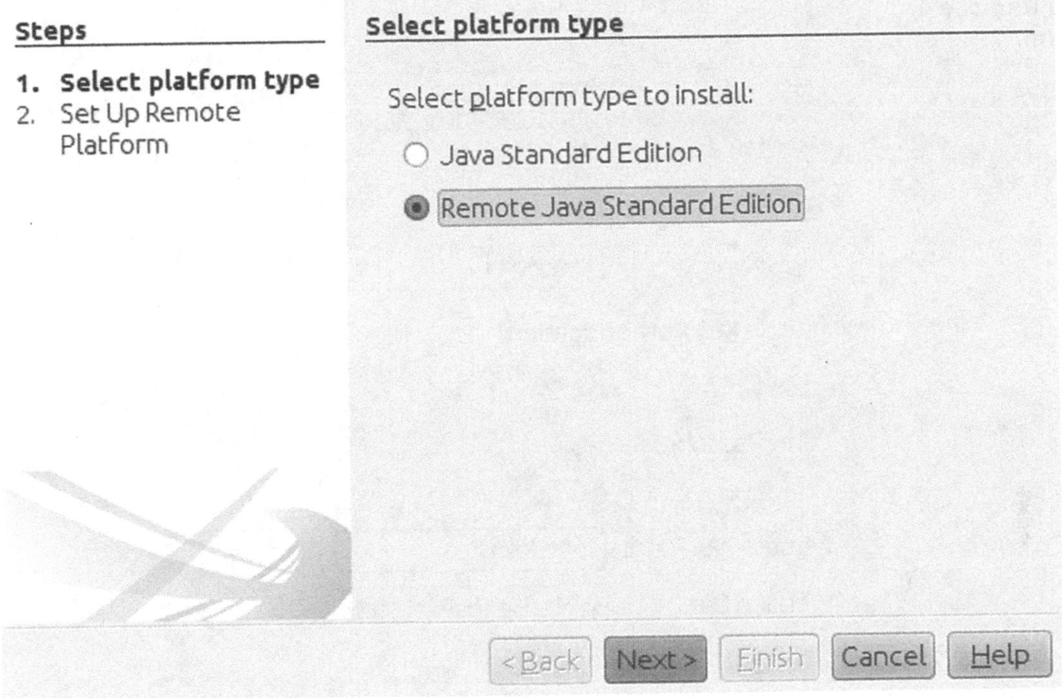

Figure 12-6. *NetBeans wizard for adding a Remote Java Platform*

Select Remote Java Standard Edition and click Next. The next screen, shown in Figure 12-7, shows a number of configuration parameters that will be used by NetBeans to transfer your application to the remote system, and to execute the Java process.

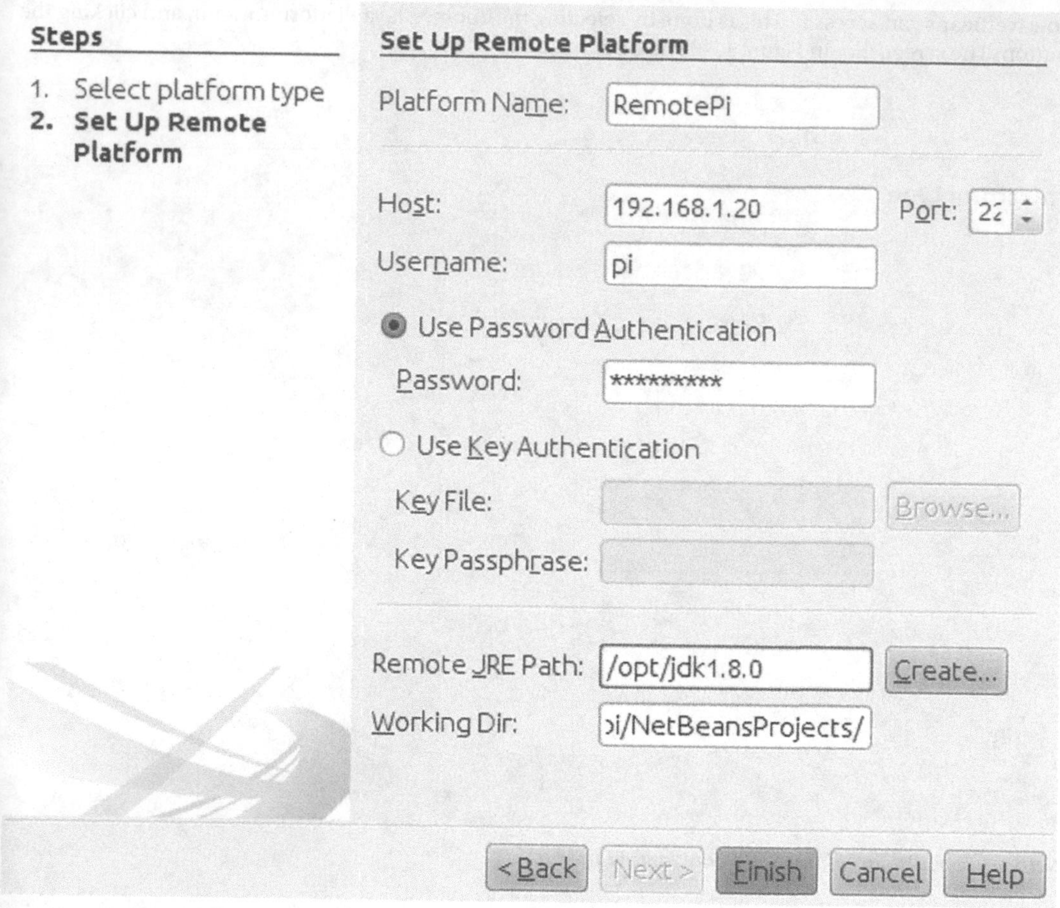

Figure 12-7. Configuration of a remote Java platform in NetBeans

The Platform name can be chosen freely. The Host and Port parameters have to correspond with the IP address of the embedded system. In this case, we assume that the embedded system is running on our local intranet at address 192.168.1.20, using the standard SSH port 22. Because NetBeans will transfer files to the embedded system and execute commands on it, it needs to be able to authenticate itself. This can be done by providing a password, or a key with a passphrase. In this case, we provide the typical username that comes standard with Raspberry Pi systems, which is "pi". The corresponding password is "raspberry" by default.

Next, we have to point NetBeans to the location of the JRE, which we assume to be installed at `/opt/jdk1.8.0`.

■ **Note** You can also use NetBeans in combination with Java Standard Edition Embedded to create a JRE installation on your embedded system.

Finally, we have to specify the working directory for NetBeans. Accepting the default directory is fine here. Click Finish to confirm the configuration information.

As a result of these configuration steps, a new Remote Java Platform has been created. If you now open a Java or JavaFX project, right-click the Project, select Project Properties, and select the Run tab, you will be able to specify the new Remote Java Platform, as shown in Figure 12-8.

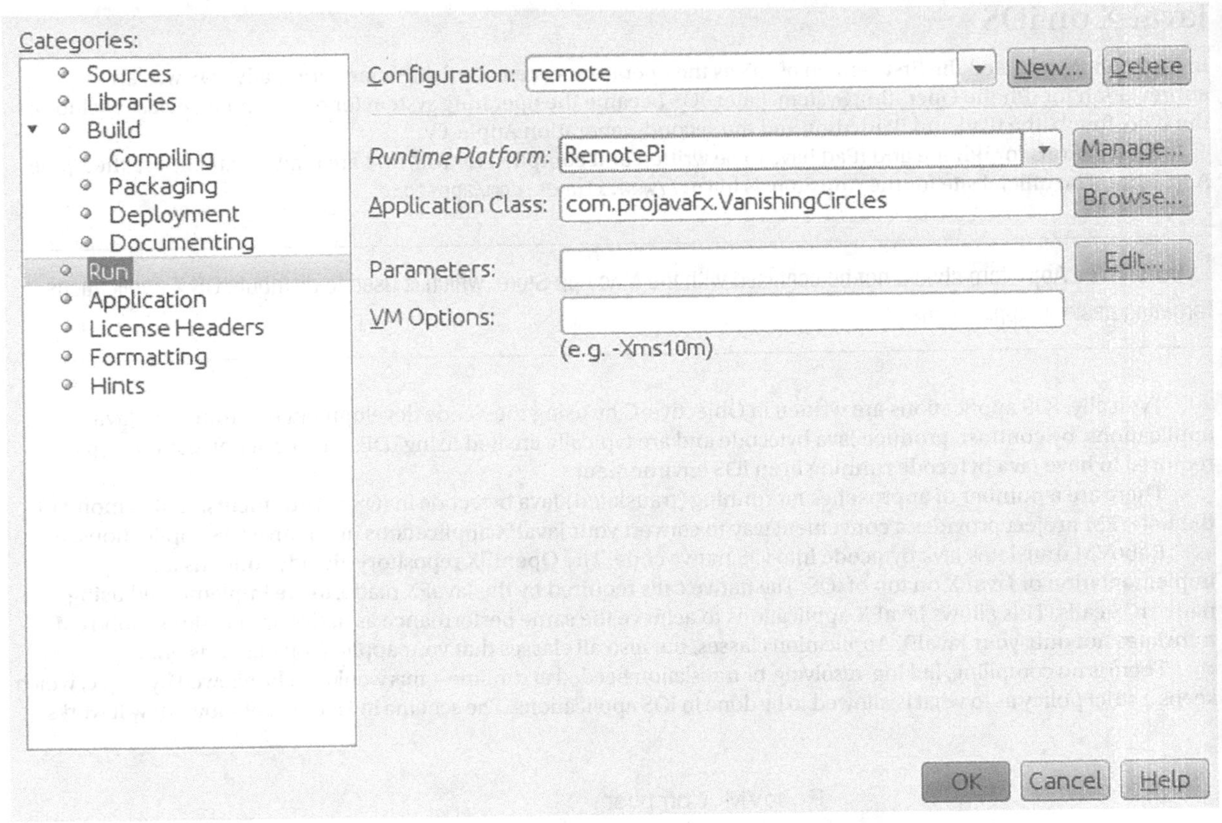

***Figure 12-8.** Project properties showing the Runtime Platform option*

The Runtime Platform option in the Run settings shows the platforms that you can choose to execute your Java or JavaFX application. Switching between your local development system and the remote embedded system (which we named RemotePi) will cause the application to either run on your local system or on the embedded system.

JavaFX on Mobile

Currently, more mobile devices (phones and tablets) are sold than desktop systems. It is estimated that in 2014, more people will use mobile devices to access the Internet than desktop systems. This fact alone is a game-changer in the IT industry. One of the consequences is that information and services should be accessible via a mobile interface to reach the majority of Internet users. There are more changes, though. Where the majority of the information on desktop systems is consumed using a web browser, this is not true on mobile devices. Users of mobile devices prefer to use native applications, or so-called apps, rather than a web browser. This means that companies and organizations that want to reach their mobile users should create applications instead of (mobile) web pages. This is a huge opportunity for JavaFX developers, as it is possible to create mobile applications using JavaFX. Rather than creating a mobile web site with HTML, CSS, and JavaScript, Java developers can now create JavaFX applications and package them as mobile applications.

JavaFX on iOS

In 2007, Apple released the first version of iOS as the operating system for the iPhone. Originally, iOS was an abbreviation for iPhone Operating System. Later, iOS became the operating system for other Apple devices including the iPod Touch, the iPad and iPad Mini, and the second-generation Apple TV.

Applications for iPhone and iPad have to be written and compiled for iOS, and are made available via the Apple App Store. The official site for the App Store is `http://www.itunes.com/appstore`.

■ **Note** The App Store should not be confused with the Mac App Store, which is used to distribute OS X applications, targeting desktop applications.

Typically, iOS applications are written in Objective-C by using the Xcode development environment. Java applications, by contrast, produce Java bytecode and are typically created using IDEs. Hence, a translation step is required to have Java bytecode running in an iOS environment.

There are a number of approaches for running (translated) Java bytecode in iOS environments. At this moment, the RoboVM project provides a convenient way to convert your JavaFX applications into native iOS applications.

RoboVM translates Java bytecode into iOS native code. The OpenJFX repository already contains an implementation of JavaFX on top of iOS. The native calls required by the JavaFX platform are implemented using native iOS calls. This allows JavaFX applications to achieve the same performance as native applications. RoboVM translates not only your JavaFX Application classes, but also all classes that your application depends on.

There is no compiling, linking, resolving, or translation needed at runtime—this would not be allowed by Apple, which keeps a strict policy as to what is allowed to be done in iOS applications. The schema in Figure 12-9 shows how it works.

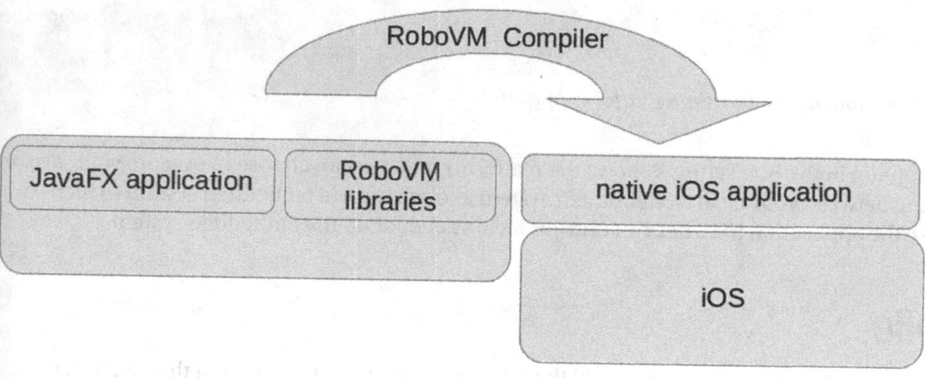

Figure 12-9. *Running JavaFX applications on top of RoboVM*

As you can see from the schema, the RoboVM project contains both libraries as well as a compiler. The RoboVM compiler compiles your JavaFX application file and all the required class files, and links it together with the required libraries. RoboVM can produce executables for MacOS and for iOS.

The steps required to convert a JavaFX application into a native iOS application are described in the RoboVM documentation pages. Currently, there are a number of options a developer can follow:

- Use eclipse with the RoboVM plug-in.
- Use maven with the RoboVM maven plug-in.
- Directly execute the RoboVM compiler using a command-line approach.

As an example, we will write a very simple JavaFX Application and explain the steps required to create an iOS application. The code for this simple application is shown in Listing 12-1.

Listing 12-1. Simple JavaFX Application That Will Be Ported to iOS and Android

```
package projavafx;

import java.util.Random;
import javafx.application.Application;
import javafx.event.ActionEvent;
import javafx.event.EventHandler;
import javafx.scene.Scene;
import javafx.scene.control.Button;
import javafx.scene.control.Label;
import javafx.scene.layout.StackPane;
import javafx.stage.Stage;

public class SimplePort extends Application {

    final String[] days = new String[]{"Monday", "Tuesday", "Wednesday", "Thursday", "Friday",
"Saturday", "Sunday"};
    @Override
    public void start(Stage primaryStage) {
        Random random = new Random();
        Button btn = new Button();
        btn.setText("Guess a day");
        Label answer = new Label("no input received");
        answer.setTranslateY(50);
        btn.setOnAction(new EventHandler<ActionEvent>() {

            @Override
            public void handle(ActionEvent event) {
                int day = random.nextInt(7);
                answer.setText(days[day]);
            }
        });

        StackPane root = new StackPane();
        root.getChildren().addAll(btn, answer);

        Scene scene = new Scene(root, 300, 250);

        primaryStage.setTitle("JavaFX Porting");
        primaryStage.setScene(scene);
        primaryStage.show();
    }

    public static void main(String[] args) {
        launch(args);
    }

}
```

Compiling the code and running it on a desktop environment produces the output shown in Figure 12-10.

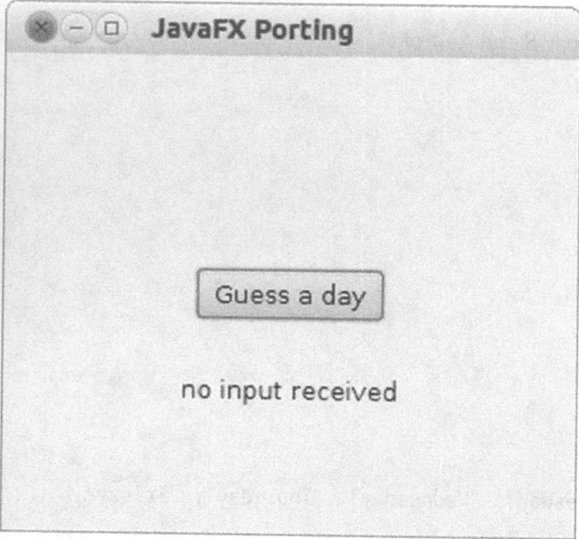

***Figure 12-10.** Desktop output for our SimplePort application*

If you click the Guess a day button, the text below the button will change into a random day. The output will then look similar to that shown in Figure 12-11.

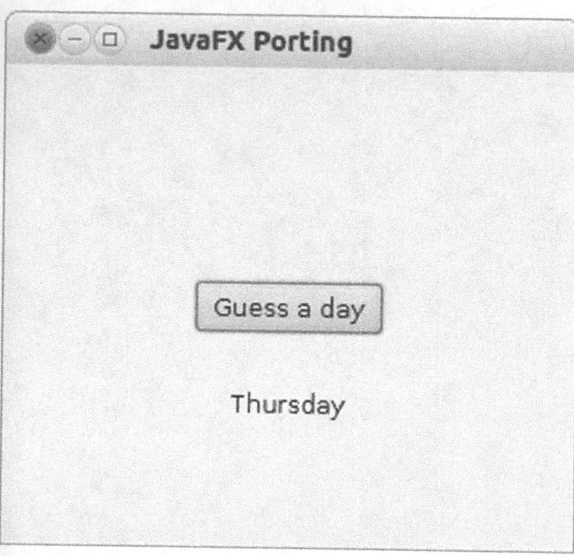

***Figure 12-11.** Desktop output of the SimplePort application after clicking the button*

If you have read the previous chapters in this book, the code of this application has no secrets anymore. We create a StackPane containing a button and a label. The label is positioned below the button. An EventHandler is added to the button. When the button is clicked, the code in the EventHandler will cause the text of the label to be changed to a random day.

As mentioned before, converting this JavaFX Application into a native iOS application can be done in a number of ways. We will use the maven approach here, as it turns out to be a simple way to create and run iOS applications.

Before we can create the iOS application, we need a launcher class. The code in Listing 12-2 shows what a launcher for a RoboVM iOS application looks like.

Listing 12-2. Launcher Class for iOS Application

```
package projavafx;
import javafx.application.Application;
import org.robovm.cocoatouch.foundation.NSAutoreleasePool;
import org.robovm.cocoatouch.foundation.NSDictionary;
import org.robovm.cocoatouch.uikit.UIApplication;
import org.robovm.cocoatouch.uikit.UIApplicationDelegate;

public class SimplePortJFXLauncher extends UIApplicationDelegate.Adapter {

    @Override
    public boolean didFinishLaunching(UIApplication application, NSDictionary launchOptions) {

        Thread launchThread = new Thread() {
            @Override
            public void run() {
                Application.launch(SimplePort.class);
            }
        };
        launchThread.setDaemon(true);
        launchThread.start();

        return true;
    }

    public static void main(String[] args) throws Exception {
        System.setProperty("glass.platform", "ios");
        System.setProperty("prism.text", "native");

        NSAutoreleasePool pool = new NSAutoreleasePool();
        UIApplication.main(args, null, SimplePortJFXLauncher.class);
        pool.drain();
    }
}
```

The main method of this launcher class contains some iOS-specific code. Note that we could add even more iOS-specific code, but this is outside the scope of what we want to address here.

The didFinishLaunching callback handler will launch the JavaFX Application by calling the static launch method on the javafx.application.Application class, thereby providing the classname of the JavaFX Application.

Now we have all the required code we need to build, test, and run the application. The RoboVM maven plug-in is a nice tool for doing this. We need a pom file that will get the RoboVM maven plug-in and configure the goals. The code for this pom file is shown in Listing 12-3.

Listing 12-3. The pom File for Building and Running Our JavaFX Application on iOS

```
<?xml version="1.0"?>

<project xmlns="http://maven.apache.org/POM/4.0.0"
xmlns:xsi="http://www.w3.org/2001/XMLSchema-instance"

         xsi:schemaLocation="http://maven.apache.org/POM/4.0.0
http://maven.apache.org/xsd/maven-4.0.0.xsd">

  <modelVersion>4.0.0</modelVersion>

  <groupId>projavafx</groupId>
  <artifactId>simpleport</artifactId>
  <name>ProJavaFX SimplePort</name>

  <packaging>jar</packaging>

  <version>1.0-SNAPSHOT</version>

  <dependencies>
    <dependency>
      <groupId>org.robovm</groupId>
      <artifactId>robovm-rt</artifactId>
      <version>0.0.11</version>
    </dependency>
    <dependency>
      <groupId>org.robovm</groupId>
      <artifactId>robovm-cocoatouch</artifactId>
      <version>0.0.11</version>
    </dependency>
  </dependencies>
  <build>
    <plugins>
      <plugin>
        <groupId>org.robovm</groupId>
        <artifactId>robovm-maven-plugin</artifactId>
        <version>0.0.11.1</version>
        <configuration>
          <config>
            <mainClass>projavafx.SimplePortJFXLauncher</mainClass>
          </config>
          <includeJFX>true</includeJFX>
        </configuration>
      </plugin>
    </plugins>
  </build>
</project>
```

The dependencies section in this pom file indicates that our project requires two artifacts in the `org.robovm` space. The configuration for the robovm-maven-plug-in can be used to provide information on the JavaFX

Application. At the very least, we need to provide the name of the class that will launch the JavaFX Application. This is done by the following line of configuration:

```
<mainClass>projavafx.SimplePortJFXLauncher</mainClass>
```

An important part of the pom file is the following entry:

```
<includeJFX>true</includeJFX>
```

This tells the plug-in that the JavaFX runtime needs to be included in the iOS application that we are about to create.

Once the pom file is ready, building the iOS application is straightforward. Building and running the application on the iPhone Simulator is done by the following maven command:

```
mvn robovm:iphone-sim
```

The result of this command is the iPhone Simulator showing our application, as shown in Figure 12-12.

Figure 12-12. *iPhone simulator showing the SimplePort application. Clicking the Guess a day button on the simulator triggers the event handler and the output will change, as shown in Figure 12-13*

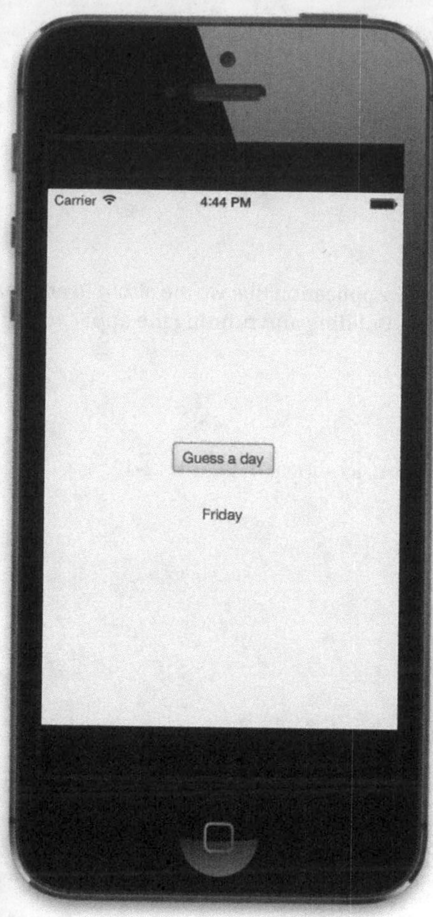

Figure 12-13. *The iPhone simulator showing our application after we clicked the button. To show the application on a real device, you need to set up a Mac with a complete iOS development environment. Setting up such an environment is outside the scope of this book*

On a Mac with an iOS development environment connected to a real device, installing the application on the device is done using the following maven command:

```
mvn robovm:ios-device
```

The application will now be installed on the device. The picture in Figure 12-14 shows a screenshot of a real iPhone running our application.

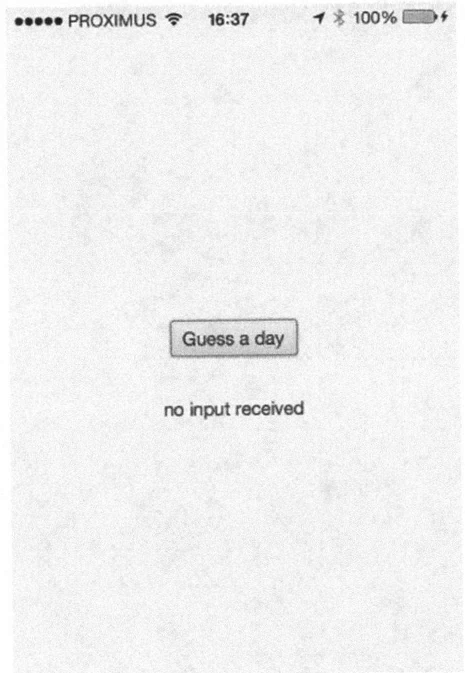

Figure 12-14. *Screenshot of a real iPhone running our SimplePort application*

The event handling works on the real iPhone as well, which can be proven by clicking the Guess a day button. The resulting screenshot is shown in Figure 12-15.

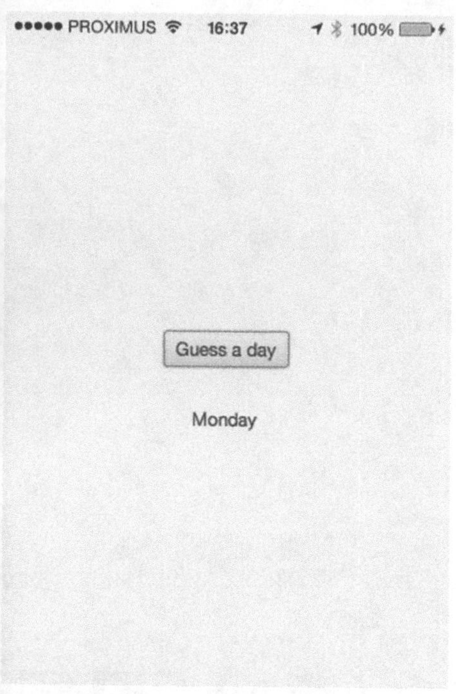

Figure 12-15. *Screenshot from a real iPhone running the SimplePort application after the Guess a day button was clicked*

JavaFX on Android

The Android platform is Google's operating system for mobile devices and tablets. It is expanding to more and more devices, ranging from wearable devices to televisions and car computers. Android is a Linux-based system, using the Dalvik VM. There are many similarities between the Dalvik VM and the Java VM, but they are not exactly the same. Most of the standard Java packages are also available in Dalvik, but not all of them.

The JavaFX Android porting project is based on the OpenJFX project. The code and documentation for this project is available at `http://bitbucket.org/javafxports/android`.

Most of the native code required to build the JavaFX platform and to execute JavaFX Applications on the Android platform is available in the OpenJFX repository. The Java classes that are needed by the JavaFX Platform and that are not available in Dalvik are added in the JavaFX Android porting project.

At the time of this writing, creating an Android application (or an APK bundle) is achieved using command-line tools that are provided by the JavaFX Android porting project.

The following steps have to be performed:

1. Download and install the latest Android SDK, which can be found at `http://developer.android.com/sdk/index.html`.

2. Download the JavaFX Dalvik SDK. Make sure you have the latest version of the JavaFX Dalvik SDK, available at `https://bitbucket.org/javafxports/android/downloads`.

3. Create a regular JavaFX application. This can be any JavaFX application you also use for desktop purposes. However, at this moment the JavaFX Android project does not support Java 8 code.

4. Use the JavaFX Dalvik SDK to create a JavaFX-Dalvik project. The JavaFX Dalvik SDK contains a directory `android-tools` with a Gradle build script that requires some parameters and that will produce the Android Application Project directory.

5. Build the Android application. The Android Application Project directory contains an ant structure that allows us to build the Android application.

6. Install the application on an Android device, run it in an emulator, or submit it to the Play store.

We demonstrate these steps next, again using the SimplePort application we introduced in the previous section.

Building JavaFX Android applications is a bit different from building JavaFX iOS applications. However, the same source tree and even the same `pom.xml` file can be used as the starting point for both target environments. Because it is at this time not possible to use Java 8 APIs (e.g., Stream API) on top of Dalvik, we need to tell the Java compiler that we want to generate bytecode compatible with Java 7. The following additions to the `pom.xml` file will do this:

```
<properties>

   <maven.compiler.source>1.7</maven.compiler.source>

   <maven.compiler.target>1.7</maven.compiler.target>

</properties>
```

The first step in the JavaFX Android build sequence is similar to building regular JavaFX desktop applications. You just create an application with JavaFX and Java code. As opposed to the RoboVM approach for generating iOS applications, no launcher class is created in the source code of the application. However, because meta-information is also required for creating Android applications, this implies that we need an additional step in the Android build sequence that is not needed in the iOS build sequence.

The result of

```
mvn clean install
```

is a target directory containing

```
simpleport-1.0-SNAPSHOT.jar
```

In Step 4 of the sequence, we have to create a JavaFX Dalvik project using the Gradle build script provided with the javafx-dalvik SDK. The `android-tools` directory in the javafx-dalvik SDK contains a `build.gradle` file that requires a number of parameters. Typically, a build script is created that sets these parameters.

The following build script will create the SimplePort Android project, based on the JavaFX application we created in the previous step.

```
#!/bin/bash

# this is an example script. Change the parameters according to your local setup

export ANDROID_SDK=/opt/android-sdk

export PATH=$ANDROID_SDK/tools:$PATH

export CURRENT_DIR=`pwd`
```

```
export WORKDIR=$CURRENT_DIR/work

export APPDIR=/home/johan/javafx/ProJavaFX/projavafx8/ch12/SimplePort/target

gradlew --info createProject -PDEBUG -PDIR=$WORKDIR -PPACKAGE=org.javafxports
-P
NAME=SimplePort -PANDROID_SDK=$ANDROID_SDK -PJFX_SDK=$CURRENT_DIR/../build/dalvik-sdk

-PJFX_APP=$APPDIR -PJFX_MAIN=projavafx.SimplePort
```

The result of executing this build script is the creation of a directory in the WORKDIR directory with the name SimplePort (the value of the NAME parameter). In this directory, the required Android project structure is created for you, along with a build.xml file allowing an ant task to create the package. To create an Android package, you have to change to the new directory and execute

```
ant clean debug
```

This will create a debug-version (not signed) of the Android application in the bin subdirectory of the directory.

The Android application can now be transferred to a real Android device connected to your development system, by calling $ANDROID_SDK/platform-tools/adb install -r bin/SimplePort-debug.apk. The application is now available on your Android device. Clicking the icon will execute it, and the screenshot in Figure 12-16 shows the result.

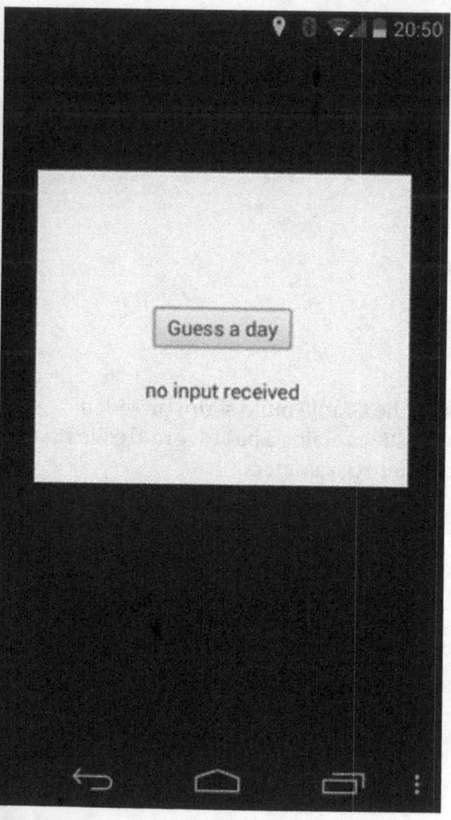

Figure 12-16. Screenshot of the application on a Nexus 5 Android device

Again, clicking the Guess a day button triggers the event handler and the screenshot shown in Figure 12-17 is generated.

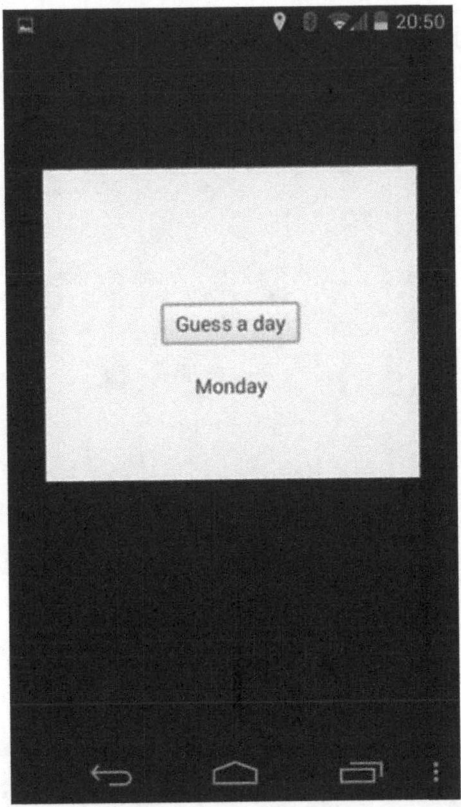

Figure 12-17. *Screenshot of a Nexus 5 Android device after clicking the Guess a day button*

JavaFXPorts, Putting It All Together

The embedded and mobile worlds are in a constant and fast evolution. The JavaFX platform itself is still evolving. The web site `http://javafxports.org` is dedicated to keeping track of the status of environments that are capable of running JavaFX applications.

The JavaFXPorts web site is maintained by the JavaFX community. Although the content is independent from Oracle, it contains links to both Oracle products (open as well as commercial) and third-party products.

Summary

The market potential of JavaFX is huge, and it is too big for a single company to control it. Over the past years, there has been a very good collaboration between Oracle and the JavaFX community. The JavaFX team at Oracle has been very open and transparent on the architecture and technical discussions, and the community has provided great feedback. Also, a number of open source projects have been created. The mix of Oracle input and community input has led to the JavaFX 8 Platform being available on a growing list of environments.

Resources

Here are some useful resources for understanding JavaFX on embedded and mobile:

- *JavaFX on Raspberry Pi, a HOWTO*: `http://javafx.steveonjava.com/javafx-on-raspberry-pi-3-easy-steps/`
- *JavaFXPorts*: `http://javafxports.org`
- *RoboVM*: `http://www.robovm.org`

CHAPTER 13

JavaFX Languages and Markup

Computer programming is tremendous fun. Like music, it is a skill that derives from an unknown blend of innate talent and constant practice. Like drawing, it can be shaped to a variety of ends—commercial, artistic, and pure entertainment. Programmers have a well-deserved reputation for working long hours, but are rarely credited with being driven by creative fevers. Programmers talk about software development on weekends, vacations, and over meals not because they lack imagination, but because their imagination reveals worlds that others cannot see.

—Larry O'Brien and Bruce Eckel

JavaFX provides a rich set of capabilities for building applications that lets you create immersive UIs that go beyond what you can accomplish with traditional UI toolkits. However, it does not stop there, because JavaFX sits on top of the Java language, so you can also take full advantage of all the languages and tools that have been developed for the Java platform. Also, JavaFX comes with FXML, its own UI declaration language written in XML, which is quite powerful in its own right.

In this chapter we show how you can leverage different languages and markup to create great-looking JavaFX UIs with less code. The wonderful thing about all the languages and capabilities discussed in this chapter is that it is your choice. You can continue to build JavaFX applications in pure Java using the imperative style, or you can take advantage of your favorite JVM language. Who knows? You might even become a convert to one of the languages discussed in this chapter based on its usage for JavaFX alone.

A Quick Comparison of Alternative Languages

To give you an idea of the power and expressiveness of using different JVM languages, we start out by taking a simple example and showing it in six different representations. The example is an extension of the Colorful Circles application designed by Jasper Potts from the JavaFX team. It is a great example of shapes, animation, and effects in a very small amount of code, and we have adapted it to show binding and interactivity as well. The running Vanishing Circles application is shown in Figure 13-1.

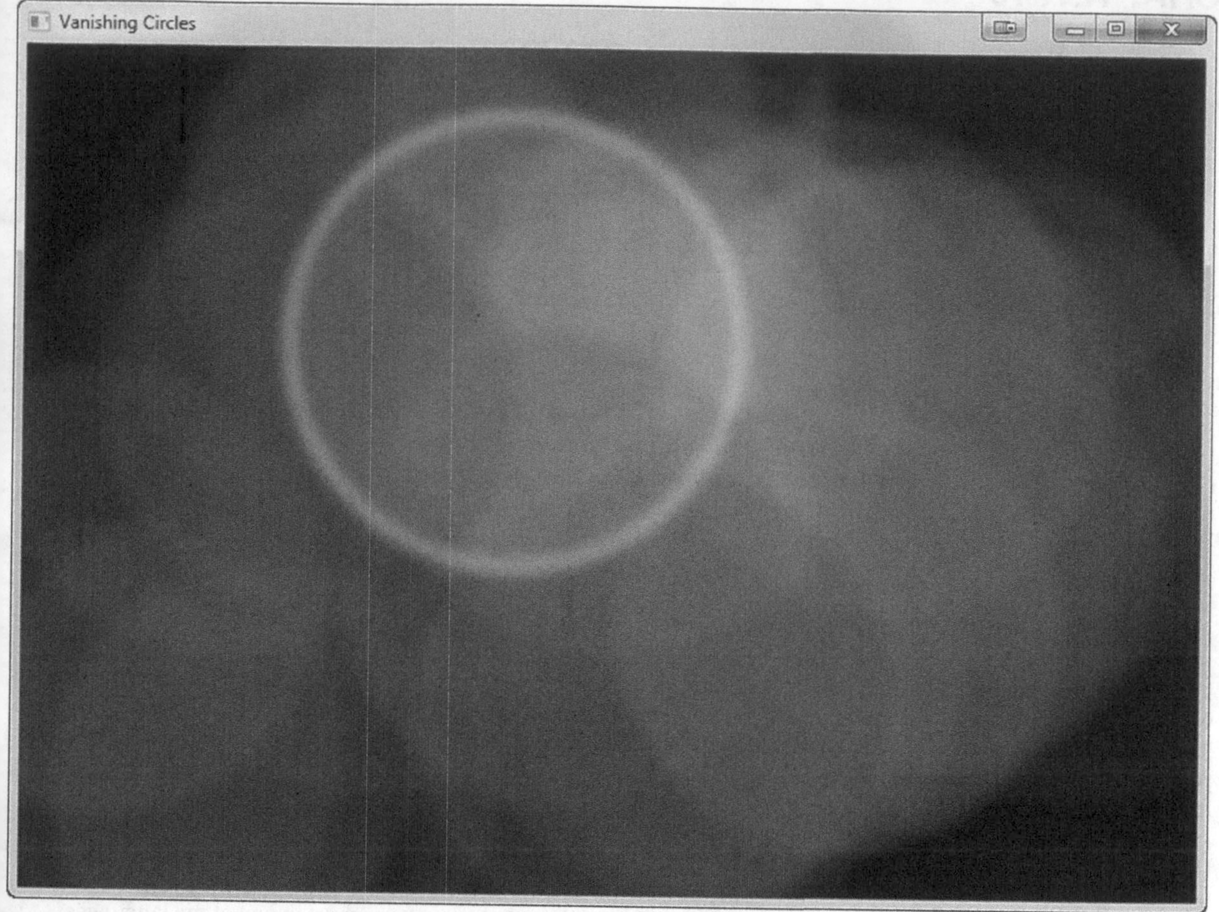

Figure 13-1. The Vanishing Circles application demonstrating JavaFX effects, animation, and interaction

Vanishing Circles in Java

To start with, let's show the code in standard Java imperative style. This is the most verbose way of writing JavaFX code, but it is also the most straightforward for anyone familiar with the Java programming language and earlier UI toolkits such as Swing. The full code listing for writing this example is shown in Listing 13-1.

Listing 13-1. Vanishing Circles Application Written in Imperative Java Style

```
public class VanishingCircles extends Application {

  public static void main(String[] args) {
    launch(args);
  }

  @Override
  public void start(Stage primaryStage) {
    primaryStage.setTitle("Vanishing Circles");
    Group root = new Group();
```

```
    Scene scene = new Scene(root, 800, 600, Color.BLACK);
    List<Circle> circles = new ArrayList<>();
    for (int i = 0; i < 50; i++) {
      final Circle circle = new Circle(150);
      circle.setCenterX(Math.random() * 800);
      circle.setCenterY(Math.random() * 600);
      circle.setFill(new Color(Math.random(), Math.random(), Math.random(), .2));
      circle.setEffect(new BoxBlur(10, 10, 3));
      circle.addEventHandler(MouseEvent.MOUSE_CLICKED, e -> {
          KeyValue collapse = new KeyValue(circle.radiusProperty(), 0);
          new Timeline(new KeyFrame(Duration.seconds(3), collapse)).play();
      });
      circle.setStroke(Color.WHITE);
      circle.strokeWidthProperty().bind(Bindings
        .when(circle.hoverProperty())
        .then(4)
        .otherwise(0));
      circles.add(circle);
    }
    root.getChildren().addAll(circles);
    primaryStage.setScene(scene);
    primaryStage.show();

    Timeline moveCircles = new Timeline();
    circles.stream().forEach(circle -> {
          KeyValue moveX = new KeyValue(circle.centerXProperty(), Math.random() * 800);
          KeyValue moveY = new KeyValue(circle.centerYProperty(), Math.random() * 600);
          moveCircles.getKeyFrames().add(new KeyFrame(Duration.seconds(40), moveX, moveY));
      });
    moveCircles.play();
  }
}
```

Although the code is fairly easy to understand, it is also quite verbose. The basic functionality can be summarized as follows.

- Fifty circles of varying colors are overlaid with a transparent fill.
- Those circles are animated in a semirandom pattern around the window.
- When the mouse hovers over a circle, the circle gets surrounded by a white border.
- Upon clicking a circle, it slowly shrinks and vanishes.

In a very short amount of code this lets us demonstrate many different JavaFX features, including shapes, effects, animation, binding, streams, and event listeners using lambda expressions. In the next few examples we convert this exact application to several different languages and representations, letting you see how these features vary in each of the choices available to you.

Vanishing Circles in Alternative JVM Languages

Now we move on to different JVM languages and show what is possible by using Groovy and Scala. These both make use of an inner domain-specific language (DSL) written on top of the JavaFX APIs.

Groovy is a great choice for those getting started with JVM languages, because its syntax most closely matches the Java language. In fact, with a few minor changes all Java programs are also valid Groovy programs! However, to get the full advantage of the language features in Groovy you need to make use of a DSL written for your target use case, such as GroovyFX. GroovyFX is an open source project that lets you write JavaFX code in the Groovy language that looks like the code in Listing 13-2.

Listing 13-2. Vanishing Circles Application Written in Groovy Using the GroovyFX DSL

```
GroovyFX.start { primaryStage ->
  def sg = new SceneGraphBuilder()
  def rand = new Random().&nextInt
  def circles = []

  sg.stage(title: 'Vanishing Circles', show: true) {
    scene(fill: black, width: 800, height: 600) {
      50.times {
        circles << circle(centerX: rand(800), centerY: rand(600), radius: 150, stroke: white,
                strokeWidth: bind('hover', converter: {val -> val ? 4 : 0})) {
          fill rgb(rand(255), rand(255), rand(255), 0.2)
          effect boxBlur(width: 10, height: 10, iterations: 3)
          onMouseClicked { e ->
            timeline {
              at(3.s) { change e.source.radiusProperty() to 0 }
            }.play()
          }
        }
      }
    }

    timeline(cycleCount: Timeline.INDEFINITE, autoReverse: true) {
      circles.each { circle ->
        at (40.s) {
          change circle.centerXProperty() to rand(800)
          change circle.centerYProperty() to rand(600)
        }
      }
    }.play()
  }
}
```

This GroovyFX code has the same functionality as the earlier JavaFX examples, but is significantly shorter and more expressive. Also, as your application grows you will get even more benefit from using a DSL such as this, allowing you to write more complex and feature-rich applications with less code.

Some of the Groovy language features that this code takes advantage of include the following:

- *Groovy builder pattern*: Groovy makes it particularly easy to build powerful and concise builder code, as demonstrated with the GroovyFX SceneGraphBuilder.
- *Named parameters*: Remembering the order of arguments to methods and constructors with long argument lists is hard, but named parameters allow you to be explicit and change the order for your convenience.

- *Class extension*: Groovy allows you to add new methods and functionality to existing classes, as demonstrated by the creation of duration objects with syntax 40.s where "s" is a method on integers.
- *Closures*: The event handlers are greatly simplified by creating anonymous single method interface extensions via closures.

All of this contributes to a very concise and readable syntax with very little boilerplate code. We dig into the features of how each of the JavaFX features translates to Groovy syntax in the later section entitled "Making Your JavaFX Groovy."

The second JVM language we cover is Scala. It provides a lot of the same benefits as Groovy, but has the additional benefit of being fully type safe. This means that the compiler will catch bugs and type errors before you even run your application, which can be a huge boon to productivity, and shorten your development and testing cycle.

Again, we take advantage of an inner DSL written in the Scala language called ScalaFX, which is another open source project that provides a full wrapper library for the JavaFX APIs. The code listing for the Vanishing Circles application written using ScalaFX is shown in Listing 13-3.

Listing 13-3. Vanishing Circles Application Written in Scala Using the ScalaFX DSL

```
object VanishingCircles extends JFXApp {
  var circles: Seq[Circle] = null
  stage = new PrimaryStage {
    title = "Vanishing Circles"
    width = 800
    height = 600
    scene = new Scene {
      fill = BLACK
      circles = for (i <- 0 until 50) yield new Circle {
        centerX = random * 800
        centerY = random * 600
        radius = 150
        fill = color(random, random, random, .2)
        effect = new BoxBlur(10, 10, 3)
        strokeWidth <== when (hover) then 4 otherwise 0
        stroke = White
        onMouseClicked = {
          Timeline(at (3 s) {radius -> 0}).play()
        }
      }
      content = circles
    }
  }

  new Timeline {
    cycleCount = INDEFINITE
    autoReverse = true
    keyFrames = for (circle <- circles) yield at (40 s) {
      Set(
        circle.centerX -> random * stage.width,
        circle.centerY -> random * stage.height
      )
    }
  }.play();
}
```

The Scala example makes use of an object literal pattern for constructing the scene graph, which gives the same benefits as the Java and Groovy builders. It also benefits from the powerful binding support that is built into the ScalaFX libraries. Some of the Scala language features that this code takes advantage of include the following:

- *Operator overloading*: Scala lets you overload the existing operators and create entirely new ones. This is used in several places, including the bind and animation syntax.
- *Implicits*: Scala's answer to class extension is via the implicit conversions. This makes it possible to extend the JavaFX API classes with convenience methods for object literal construction, giving you all the power of builders with the core classes.
- *Closures*: Scala also supports closures, which makes event handlers much more concise, and allows powerful looping constructs such as the for...yield syntax.
- *DSL-friendly syntax*: The usual code punctuation, such as dots and parentheses, is optional in most situations, making it possible to build fluent APIs that read like language keywords.

Although the code ends up being fairly short and easy to understand, there is quite a bit of depth to the Scala language. We show how you can take advantage of some of the built-in features of Scala to further improve your applications in the section later in this chapter entitled "Scala and JavaFX."

As you have seen, using a DSL to write your JavaFX code can produce significant benefits over what you would have to write in Java using either the imperative or builder styles. Also, because all of these languages sit on top of the same underlying JavaFX APIs, they have the same functionality as applications written in pure Java. Therefore, the choice is yours as to which language you want to use to write your JavaFX applications.

In the next few sections we go into each of these languages in more detail to help you get started with developing your JavaFX applications using them. Also, it is possible to use virtually any JVM language to write JavaFX applications with, so if you have a favorite language that is not listed here, it is worth a try!

Making Your JavaFX Groovy

According to job trends, Groovy is the most popular language that runs on the JVM other than Java.[1] This is helped by the fact that Groovy is extremely easy to get started with; other than a few minor differences,[2] any Java program is also a valid Groovy application. This makes it very easy for Java developers to start using it, even before they appreciate all the power and convenience that Groovy brings to the Java ecosystem.

Groovy source files compile directly to Java bytecodes and can run anywhere you have a JVM. As a result, you can access any Java libraries directly, including the JavaFX APIs. A well-written Groovy application will almost always be shorter than the equivalent Java version, because of all the conveniences built into the language. Some of the features of the Groovy language that make it attractive as a replacement for Java and JavaFX code include the following:

- *Closures*: Recently introduced in Java 8, closures are particularly important for GUI programming, because they make it much simpler to write code that gets called when an event happens.
- *Operator overloading*: Groovy lets you overload existing operators or define new ones, which is important for writing a readable DSL.
- *Dynamic typing*: Types are optional in Groovy code, which makes it easier to write succinct code.
- *Getter/setter access*: Groovy will automatically convert direct field access to getters and setters, which shortens this very common pattern for accessing Java APIs.

[1]Scala, Groovy, Clojure, Jython, JRuby, and Java: Jobs by Language, `http://bloodredsun.com/2011/10/04/scala-groovy-clojure-jython-jruby-java-jobs/`, October 2011.

[2]Differences from Java, `http://groovy.codehaus.org/Differences+from+Java`, 2011.

- *Named constructor parameters*: When initializing an object with a constructor, you can also set fields on the class by referring to them by name. This pattern is used quite a bit in our GroovyFX code later.
- *Built-in data structure syntax*: Many commonly used data structures, such as Lists and Maps, have a built-in syntax in Groovy, which makes it much more convenient to work with them and build them dynamically.

Using JavaFX directly from Groovy is possible; however, you are missing out on a lot of the benefits of Groovy without using a dedicated DSL library, such as GroovyFX. In the next few sections we show you some of the benefits of writing JavaFX code using the Groovy language and GroovyFX library.

Introduction to GroovyFX

GroovyFX is a library for developing JavaFX applications in Groovy that lets you build your application in a more Groovy-like fashion. It was started by Jim Clarke and Dean Iverson, one of the coauthors of this title, and is being developed as an open source Groovy module. Russel Winder, who is a well-known expert on Groovy, has updated it for Java 8. The main landing page for GroovyFX is on GitHub at `http://groovyfx-project.github.com/`.

Some of the benefits of writing code using GroovyFX, rather than simply coding directly against the JavaFX APIs include the following:

- *Builder pattern*: GroovyFX has Groovy builders for all the major JavaFX classes, making it easy and convenient to declaratively construct a scene graph.
- *Property generation*: The JavaFX property pattern for writing your own properties is quite long-winded, but is replaced with a one-line annotation in GroovyFX.
- *Timeline DSL*: GroovyFX has a convenient shorthand syntax for animation.
- *Convenient bind syntax*: GroovyFX makes creating bindings much more terse and readable than the equivalent Java code.
- *API improvements*: A lot of the JavaFX APIs have been tweaked and enhanced to make them easier to use.

To get you started using GroovyFX, we walk you through setting up a small GroovyFX project from scratch. These directions assume that you already have a current Java and JavaFX 8 SDK installed on your system. Also, we have chosen to tailor the instructions for the IntelliJ Community Edition, which is a free, open source IDE with a long track record of excellent Groovy support. There is also Groovy support for Eclipse, NetBeans, and many other IDEs, so if you have a preference for a different IDE, you can easily adapt these instructions to work with your IDE of choice.

To start with, download and install the latest version of IntelliJ IDEA. The community edition comes with Groovy support, so there is no need to purchase the Ultimate Edition. The IntelliJ web site can be found at `http://www.jetbrains.com/idea`.

After installing and launching IntelliJ, you need to create a new Java project with Groovy language support enabled. On the landing page you can click Create New Project, or if you are on a different screen you can get to the same wizard by selecting New Project... from the File menu. This will present you with the New Project Wizard shown in Figure 13-2.

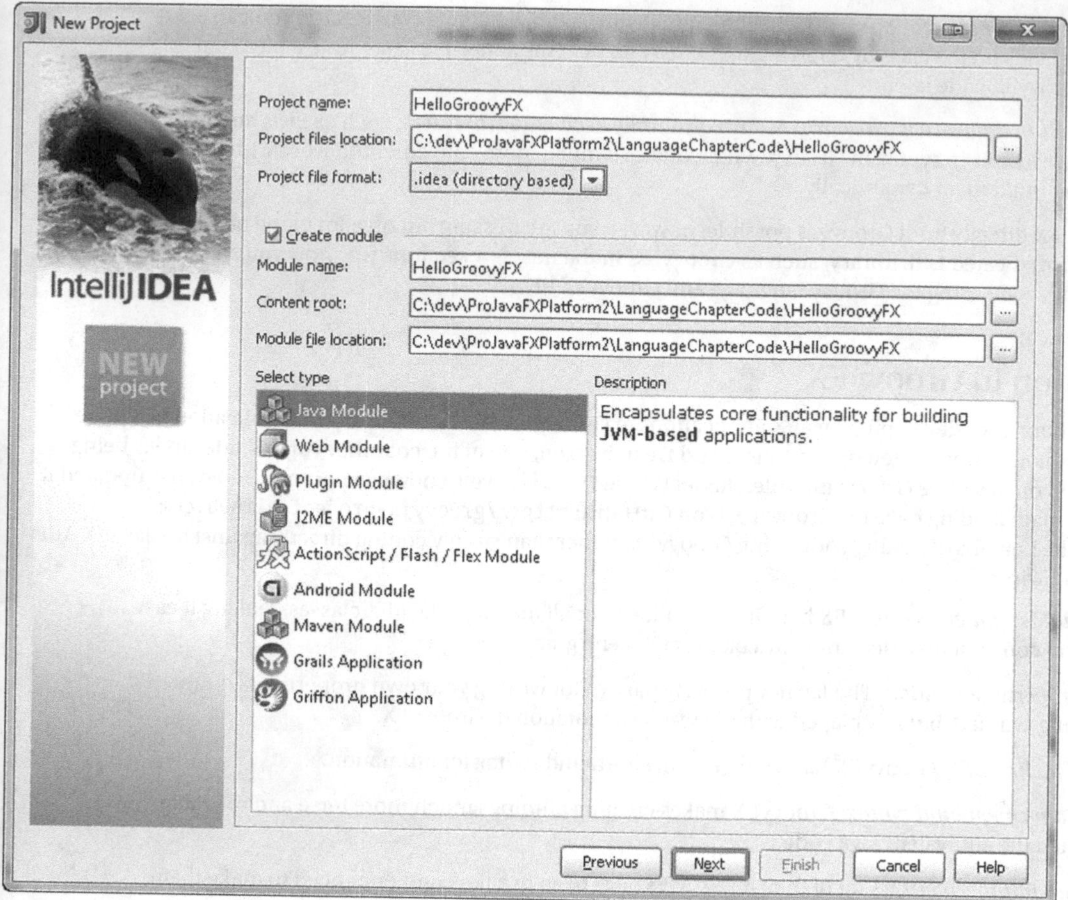

Figure 13-2. *IntelliJ New Project Wizard dialog box*

Name your project HelloGroovyFX, make sure that the project type is set to Java Module, and then click Next. For the next page of the wizard, you can simply accept the default src folder location and continue, which will take you to the extension screen shown in Figure 13-3.

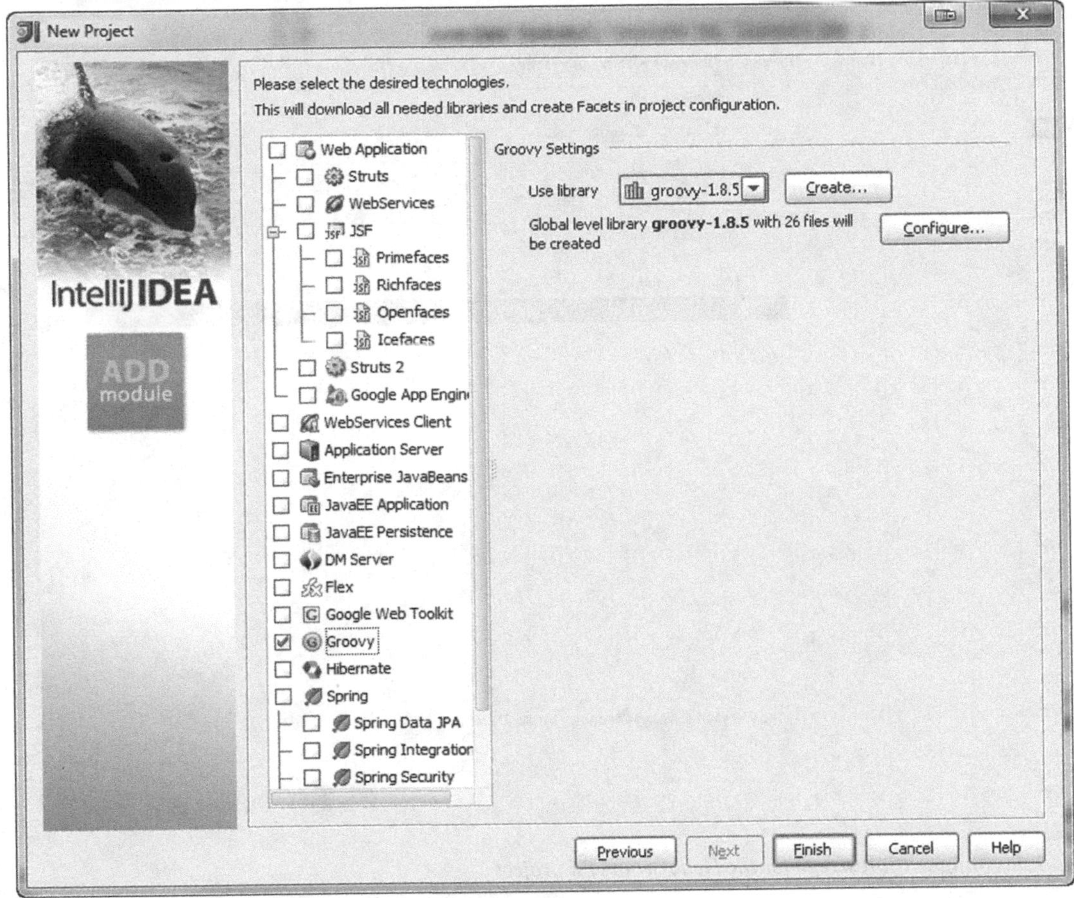

Figure 13-3. *IntelliJ New Project Wizard, second dialog box*

This is where you can select and enable Groovy support for your project. Find Groovy in the list on the left and select the check box. You also need to configure a Groovy runtime for it to work with in the right pane. If you don't already have a current Groovy runtime installation, you can grab the latest from the Groovy site at `http://groovy.codehaus.org/`.

The binary zip release should work fine. Extract this to a folder on your hard drive, and then go back to IntelliJ and set up the Groovy library by clicking the Create... button and selecting the folder to which you just finished extracting Groovy. To complete the project creation, click Finish and your new project will be opened in the current window.

We are almost done with the project setup, but are missing the dependent libraries for JavaFX and GroovyFX. To add these in, open the Project Structure... dialog box from the File menu, and navigate to the Modules section. This lets you configure the project settings in more detail than the New Project Wizard allows.

Click the Dependencies tab on the right side and the screen shown in Figure 13-4 appears.

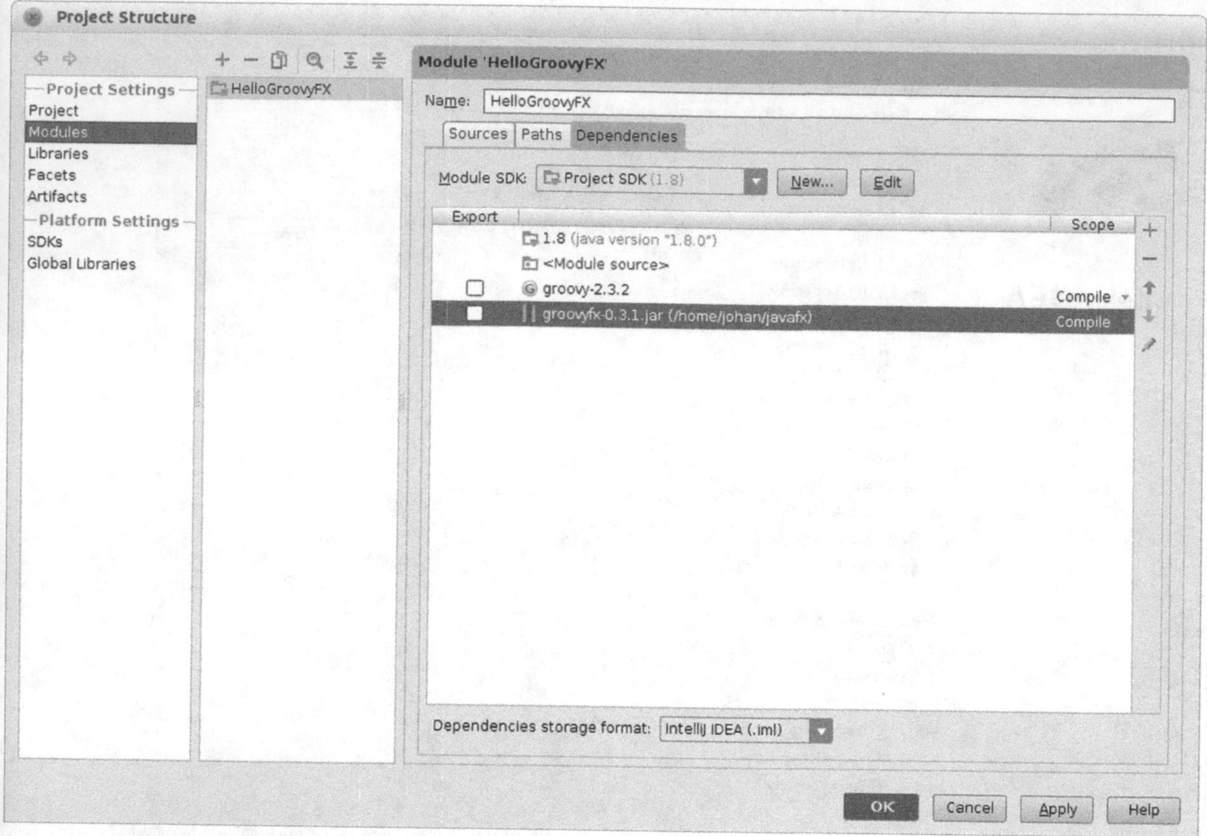

Figure 13-4. *Module configuration screen for the HelloGroovyFX project*

On the Dependencies tab, you need to configure one additional jar reference, as highlighted in the Figure 13-4. This is the GroovyFX jar file, which you can download from the GroovyFX site. The URL for the GroovyFX site is `http://groovyfx-project.github.com/`.

Now to create the HelloGroovyFX application, we need to add a new Groovy script to the project. Right-click the src directory of your project and choose New ➤ Groovy Script from the context menu. This opens a script creation dialog box where you can type the name of your script file and click OK to create it, as shown in Figure 13-5.

Enter name for new Groovy Script
Name: HelloGroovyFX
Kind: Groovy script
OK
Cancel

Figure 13-5. *Groovy Script creation dialog box*

Now you are finally ready to get started with some coding. The HelloGroovyFX application is very short, so you can grab the code from the source bundle that comes with the book, or just type in the code shown in Listing 13-4 yourself.

Listing 13-4. Hello GroovyFX Code

```
import groovyx.javafx.GroovyFX
import groovyx.javafx.SceneGraphBuilder

GroovyFX.start {
  new SceneGraphBuilder().stage(visible: true) {
    scene {
      stackPane {
        text("Hello GroovyFX")
      }
    }
  }
}
```

To run the application, simply right-click the class and choose Run "HelloGroovyFX" from the context menu. This gives you the application shown in Figure 13-6.

Figure 13-6. *Output from running the Hello GroovyFX application in IntelliJ*

Congratulations! You have created and run your very first JavaFX application in Groovy. In the next few sections we go into more detail on the features and capabilities of GroovyFX, but remember that anything you can do in JavaFX is possible in GroovyFX, because it wraps the full JavaFX APIs.

Properties in GroovyFX

One of the features that would most benefit UI development in Java with JavaFX is having a notion of first-class, observable properties in the language. Because this does not exist today, the JavaFX team added properties at an API level, which is sufficient, but much more verbose than a native syntax can provide.

Fortunately, with dynamic languages such as Groovy, it is quite easy to add in powerful features including a native property syntax. Groovy already has a built-in notion of simplified getter/setter access, so you can retrieve and store JavaFX properties just as if they were normal variables. For example, to set the width of a Rectangle in Groovy, all you need to write is:

```
rectangle.width = 500
```

This will be automatically translated to a setter call, such as the following:

```
rectangle.setWidth(500);
```

The other part of the JavaFX property pattern that is even more tedious is the creation of new properties. To define a new property on your class in the same way that the JavaFX APIs define properties, you need a total of one field and three methods per property. The standard boilerplate for creating a `name` property on a `Person` object is shown in Listing 13-5.

Listing 13-5. JavaFX Property Pattern to Create New Properties in Java

```
import javafx.beans.property.SimpleStringProperty
import javafx.beans.property.StringProperty

public class Person {
  private StringProperty name;
  public final void setName(String val) { nameProperty().set(val); }
  public final String getName() { return nameProperty().get(); }
  public StringProperty nameProperty() {
    if (name == null) {
      name = new SimpleStringProperty(this, "name");
    }
    return name;
  }
}
```

■ **Note** The preceding code can be further optimized by checking whether the property has been created in the `getName` method, and returning null if it has not been created (and thus not initializing the `name` property).

Although this code is only a bit more verbose than the standard Java property bean pattern, multiply it by the number of properties you need to define in your application, and you have quite a bit of code to maintain and debug when there is something that is not working as expected.

GroovyFX has a very elegant solution to this using a compiler hook for AST transformations. Rather than copying and pasting the property boilerplate each time you want to define a new property, you can simply annotate a variable with the `@FXBindable` annotation, and GroovyFX will take care of the rest. It generates exactly the same optimized code you would write by hand, but does it behind the scenes during the compile phase so that your source code is not cluttered with the additional logic.

Listing 13-6 shows what the `name` property would look like in Groovy.

Listing 13-6. GroovyFX Property Pattern to Create New Properties in Groovy

```
import groovyx.javafx.beans.FXBindable

class Person {
  @FXBindable String name
}
```

The GroovyFX `@FXBindable` annotation also supports handling the case where a property has a default initialization value:

```
class Person {
  @FXBindable String name = "Guillaume Laforge"
}
```

It also has a convenient shortcut syntax for converting all the variables in a class to properties:

```
@FXBindable
class Person {
    String name;
    int age;
    String gender;
    Date dob;
}
```

GroovyFX Binding

Binding in JavaFX is an extremely powerful feature, but the API-based syntax introduced in JavaFX 2 can often get in the way of understanding what the bind code is doing. GroovyFX solves this problem by taking advantage of the operator overloading feature of the Groovy language to provide an infix notation for common bind expressions.

For example, to bind one rectangle's width to the width of a second rectangle, you can write the following code in GroovyFX:

```
rect1.widthProperty.bind(rect2.widthProperty)
```

There is also an alternate version of the same code that you can use instead:

```
rect1.widthProperty.bind(rect2, 'width')
```

However, the real power of GroovyFX binding comes into play when you are combining multiple properties in a bind statement. As a second example, let's say that you want to bind one rectangle's width to the sum of two others. In GroovyFX you can write the following code:

```
rect1.widthProperty.bind(rect2.widthProperty + rect3.widthProperty)
```

This would translate to the following, much longer, JavaFX Java code:

```
rect1.getWidthProperty().bind(rect2.getWidthProperty().add(rect3.getWidthProperty()));
```

The GroovyFX distribution comes with an example of some binding code to animate the hands of an analog clock. This example was written by Jim Clark, and the relevant code showing properties and binding is shown in Listing 13-7.

Listing 13-7. Analog Clock Excerpt from the GroovyFX Demo Package

```
@FXBindable
class Time {
  Integer hours
  Integer minutes
  Integer seconds

  Double hourAngle
  Double minuteAngle
  Double secondAngle
```

```
public Time() {
    // bind the angle properties to the clock time
    hourAngleProperty.bind((hoursProperty * 30.0) + (minutesProperty * 0.5))
    minuteAngleProperty.bind(minutesProperty * 6.0)
    secondAngleProperty.bind(secondsProperty * 6.0)
  ...
}
```

The combination of automatic properties expansion via AST transforms and infix notation binding lets you express fairly complex logic without much code. The resulting Groovy analog clock graphic UI that you get when running the example is shown in Figure 13-7.

***Figure 13-7.** Groovy analog clock demo*

GroovyFX API Enhancements

In addition to the core language benefits of using Groovy instead of JavaFX, GroovyFX has taken many of the JavaFX APIs and Groovy-ized them to make them easier to use from a dynamic language. We cover three major ones in this section: the GroovyFX custom DSL for animation, a simplified table construction pattern, and streamlined JavaFX layouts. All of these provide significant benefits over the core JavaFX APIs, allowing you to write less code and do more.

Animation

GroovyFX supports building animations using a special DSL that has syntax for creating `Durations`, `KeyFrames`, and `KeyValues`, all with a concise syntax. We showed an example of the Groovy animation syntax earlier in the Vanishing Circles application, which looked like this:

```
timeline {
  at(3.s) { change e.source.radiusProperty() to 0 }
}.play()
```

The basic pattern is as follows, where you can have multiple at expressions in a timeline and multiple change expressions within an at.

```
timeline {
  at(duration) {
    [change property to value]
  }
}
```

Similar to binding, there is also a second format for referring to the property that makes up the change expression:

```
timeline {
  at(3.s) { change(e.source, 'radius') to 0 }
}.play()
```

The syntax also supports an optional tween that lets you provide a curve for the speed at which the animation proceeds:

```
timeline {
  at(3.s) { change e.source.radiusProperty() to 0 tween ease_both }
}.play()
```

With the preceding change, the animation would start out slow and speed up to its normal rate, and then slow down at the end the same way.

Compared to the full Java code, the Groovy animation syntax is a huge savings in characters and makes it much easier to see what your animation is actually doing.

Tables

Between the extra syntactic sugar for builders or imperative Java, and the need to specify Generic at multiple levels, building simple data tables in Java code can be quite a lot of code. Groovy simplifies this with a fairly intuitive builder format for creating tables, along with some conveniences, such as a built-in type converter that lets you specify a closure to change the output type for a field.

As a result, you can write fairly complex tables with very little code. The following example builds from the Person class that we created earlier to display a list of people in a tabular format. The full code is shown in Listing 13-8.

Listing 13-8. Code Demonstrating a Table in Groovy with Strings, ints, and Dates

```
import groovyx.javafx.GroovyFX
import groovyx.javafx.SceneGraphBuilder
import binding.Person
import java.text.SimpleDateFormat

def dateFormat = new SimpleDateFormat("MM/dd/yyyy")

def persons = [
  new Person(name: "Ada Lovelace", age: 36, gender: "Female",
             dob: dateFormat.parse("10/10/1815")),
  new Person(name: "Henrietta Swan Leavitt", age: 53, gender: "Female",
             dob: dateFormat.parse("7/4/1868")),
  new Person(name: "Grete Hermann", age: 83, gender: "Female",
             dob: dateFormat.parse("3/2/1901"))
]
```

```
GroovyFX.start {
  new SceneGraphBuilder().stage(visible: true) {
    scene {
      tableView(items: persons) {
        tableColumn(property: "name", text: "Name", prefWidth: 160)
        tableColumn(property: "age", text: "Age", prefWidth: 70)
        tableColumn(property: "gender", text: "Gender", prefWidth: 90)
        tableColumn(property: "dob", text: "Birth", prefWidth: 100,
          type: Date,
          converter: { d -> return dateFormat.format(d) })
      }
    }
  }
}
```

Notice that the code to display the table is almost as short as the code to set up the data. The converter in the last column to format the Date is a one-line operation in Groovy, but requires a CellValueFactory with an implementation of a Callback interface, which is several lines of Java code saved.

Figure 13-8 displays the result of running this table application in Groovy.

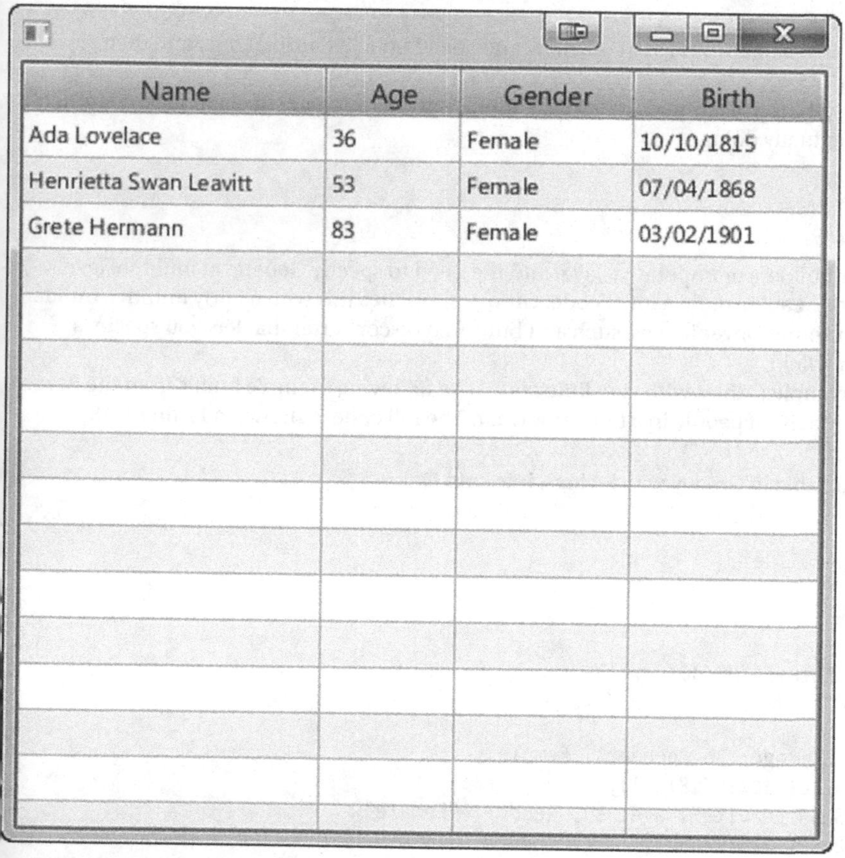

Name	Age	Gender	Birth
Ada Lovelace	36	Female	10/10/1815
Henrietta Swan Leavitt	53	Female	07/04/1868
Grete Hermann	83	Female	03/02/1901

Figure 13-8. Groovy Table demo with famous women in computers listed

Layouts

Another set of APIs that are relatively challenging to use in a declarative fashion are the JavaFX layouts. They have a powerful constraint system that you can use to give Nodes special layout behavior on a per-layout basis, but this also means that adding a Node to a layout involves two steps: (1) adding it to the container and (2) assigning constraints.

The GroovyFX APIs solve the layout problem with a very clean solution that involves annotating the node object with additional pseudo-properties for layout constraints. This allows you to define the constraints as you construct the scene graph, and then during the layout phase, the JavaFX layout system uses the constraints to control how the Nodes are positioned and sized.

Listing 13-9 shows an example of one of the more complicated layouts, GridPaneLayout, with the entire application written in a declarative style.

Listing 13-9. Example Code of a GridPane Layout in GroovyFX

```
import groovyx.javafx.GroovyFX
import groovyx.javafx.SceneGraphBuilder
import javafx.scene.layout.GridPane
import javafx.scene.text.Font

GroovyFX.start {
  def sg = new SceneGraphBuilder()

  sg.stage(title: "GridPane Demo", width: 400, height: 500, visible: true) {
    scene {
      stackPane {
        imageView {
          image("puppy.jpg", width: 1100, height: 1100, preserveRatio: true)
          effect colorAdjust(brightness: 0.6, input: gaussianBlur())
        }
        gridPane(hgap: 10, vgap: 10, padding: 20) {
          columnConstraints(minWidth: 60, halignment: "right")
          columnConstraints(prefWidth: 300, hgrow: "always")

          label("Dog Adoption Form", font: new Font(24), margin: [0, 0, 10, 0],
              halignment: "center", columnSpan: GridPane.REMAINING)

          label("Size: ", row: 2)
          textField(promptText: "approximate size in pounds", row: 2, column: 1)

          label("Breed:", row: 3)
          textField(promptText: "pet breed", row: 3, column: 1)

          label("Sex:", row: 4)
          choiceBox(items: ['Male', 'Female', 'Either'], row: 4, column: 1)

          label("Additional Info:", wrapText: true, textAlignment: "right",
              row: 5, valignment: "baseline")
          textArea(prefRowCount: 8, wrapText: true, row: 5, column: 1, vgrow: 'always')
```

```
            button("Submit", row: 6, column: 1, halignment: "right")
          }
        }
      }
    }
  }
```

Notice that the code is succinct and clean, and it closely models the UI that it is trying to build. The result of running this application looks exactly like what you would expect from a typical UI form, as shown in Figure 13-9.

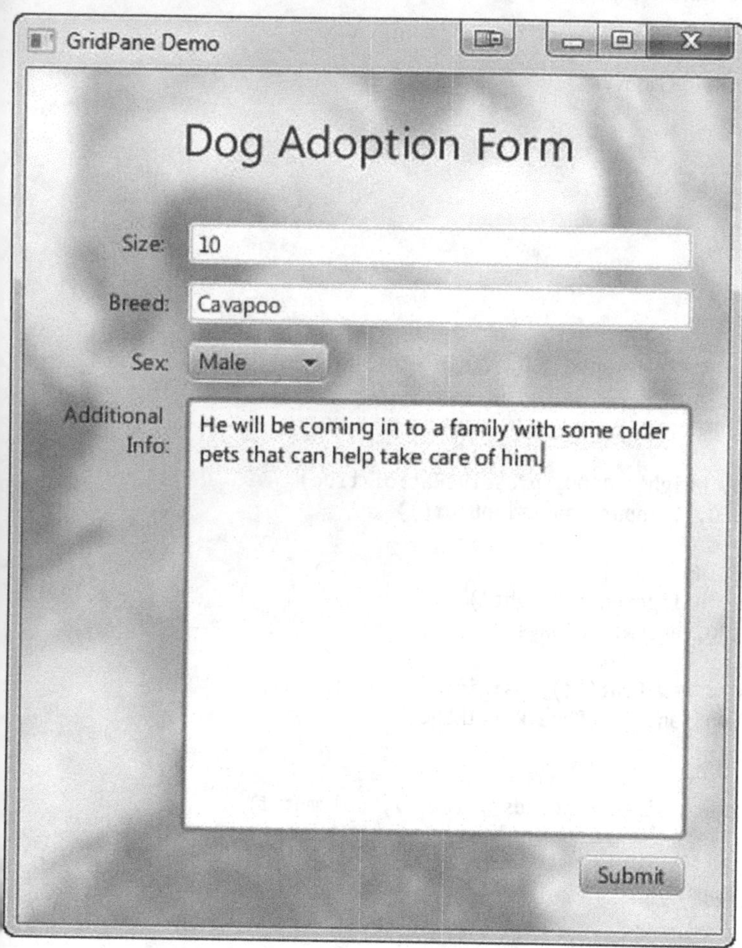

Figure 13-9. *Running Dog Adoption Form example with a Cavapoo (cross between Cavalier King Charles Spaniel and Poodle) in the background*[3]

[3]Public domain picture from Wikimedia Commons: `http://commons.wikimedia.org/wiki/File:Image-Cavapoo_puppy.JPG`

Scala and JavaFX

Scala is a powerful JVM language combining the best features of functional and object-oriented programming in a single language. As do the other JVM languages discussed in this chapter, it compiles source files directly to Java bytecodes and all the existing Java language libraries commonly used are compatible with it. However, Scala adds powerful, type-safe collections, an elegant actor model for concurrency, and functional language features including closures, pattern matching, and currying.

Scala was started by Martin Odersky in 2001 at the École Polytechnique Fédérale de Lausanne (EPFL), and has grown in maturity and popularity over the years. Odersky has actually been the genius behind the scenes working on Java compilers for many years, including the Pizza language that extended Java and GJ, which became the grandfather of the modern Java compiler after its adoption by Sun in Java 1.3. By developing an entirely new language on the JVM, Odersky was able to overcome several of the inherent design limitations of Java.

Scala is used today in many large enterprises such as Twitter, LinkedIn, Foursquare, and Morgan Stanley. There is also commercial support available from the creators of the language via TypeSafe, a Scala language company. Also, Scala has been hailed as the successor to Java by James Gosling, the father of Java; James Strachan, creator of Groovy; and Charles Nutter, JRuby Core Developer, among others. With all this support behind the Scala language, it makes a great candidate for also providing superior APIs for JavaFX development!

Although you can code in Scala directly against the JavaFX APIs, the end result will look very similar to the Java code we have been writing up to this point and will be unable to take full advantage of the language. The ScalaFX project was started to provide a more Scala-friendly API for doing JavaFX development and is what we use in all the examples throughout this book.

ScalaFX is an open source project created by Stephen Chin, one of the authors of this book, and has numerous additional contributors who have helped with the design and testing of the library. It is very similar to the GroovyFX library described earlier in this chapter, because it is also an open source library that constitutes a bridge between a JVM language and the JavaFX APIs. However, ScalaFX is different in that it prioritizes type safety and consistent semantics, which is in keeping with the spirit of the design goals of the Scala language.

Many of the constructs in the ScalaFX library were inspired by the JavaFX Script language that was used in JavaFX releases prior to 2, so for those of you familiar with JavaFX Script, the syntax will feel quite comfortable. It takes advantage of many of the advanced features available in Scala, but does not expose or burden the end user with understanding these to build great-looking UI applications.

Making you an expert Scala developer is beyond the scope of this book, but we do describe the Scala features as we use them in our ScalaFX code, so this should also serve as a gentle introduction to Scala for anyone who is already a proficient Java developer.

Getting Started with ScalaFX

To write your first ScalaFX application you need to download and install Scala as well as the ScalaFX library Because ScalaFX code is a DSL written in the Scala language, you can use any IDE that supports Scala development, such as IntelliJ, Eclipse, or NetBeans, although you might want to start with the Scala IDE for Eclipse because that is the one supported by the Scala language team at TypeSafe. We demonstrate the basic setup of an Eclipse environment for ScalaFX in this chapter, although the concepts apply to other IDEs as well.

To start, install the latest version of Eclipse and launch it. From the Help menu choose Install New Software… and paste the Scala IDE update URL into the Work with field. You can get the latest updated URL for Scala IDE from their web site at `http://scala-ide.org/download/current.html`.

This lets you select the Scala IDE for the Eclipse plug-in as shown in Figure 13-10.

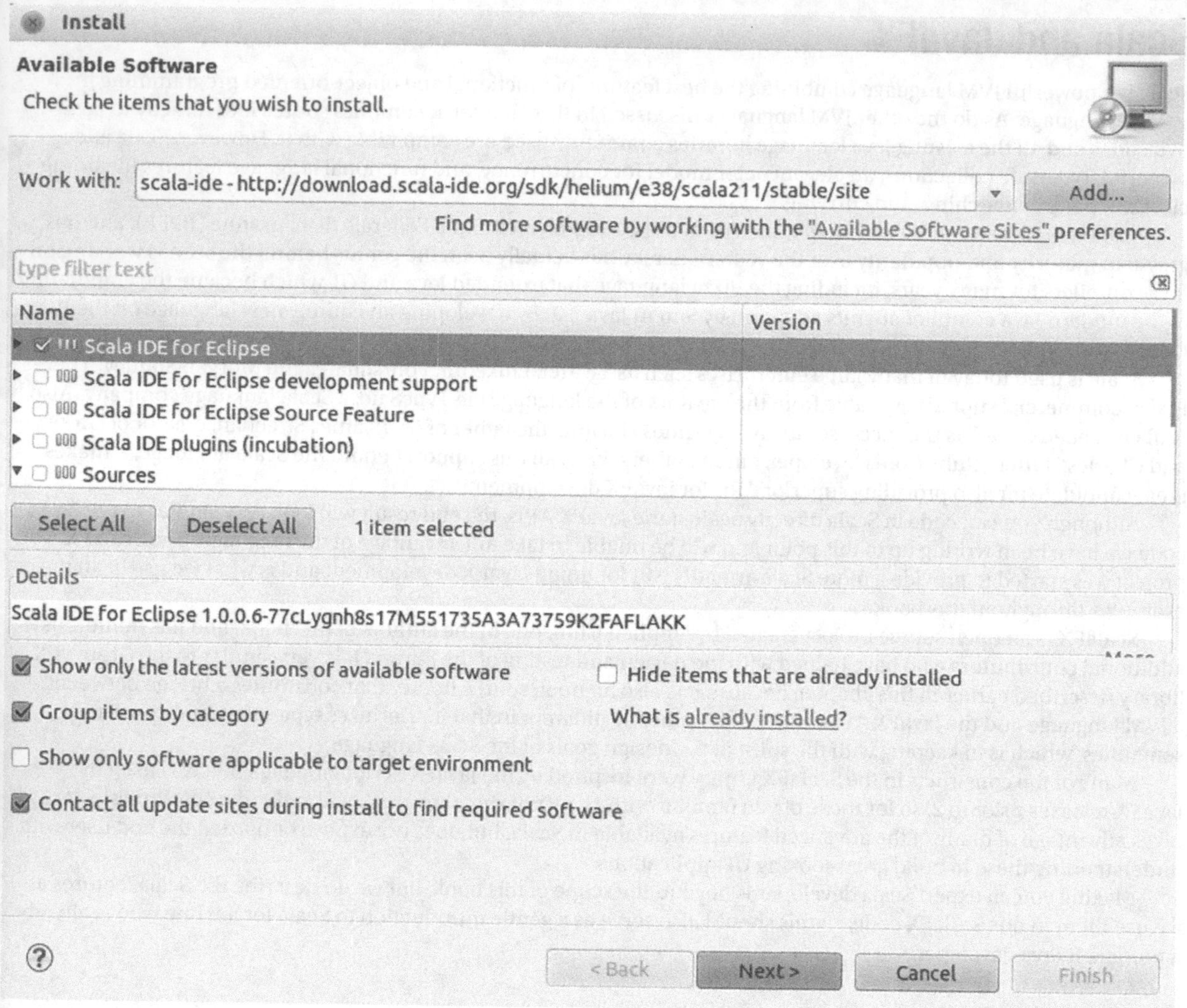

Figure 13-10. *Scala IDE installation in Eclipse*

Continue with the wizard, accepting the license agreement and default settings. After downloading and installing the plug-in and restarting Eclipse, you will be ready to begin Scala development.

To start with, we create a new Scala project. Go to the File menu and choose New ➤ Project... to open the New Project Wizard shown in Figure 13-11. Choose Scala Wizards/Scala Project from the list of choices and click Next.

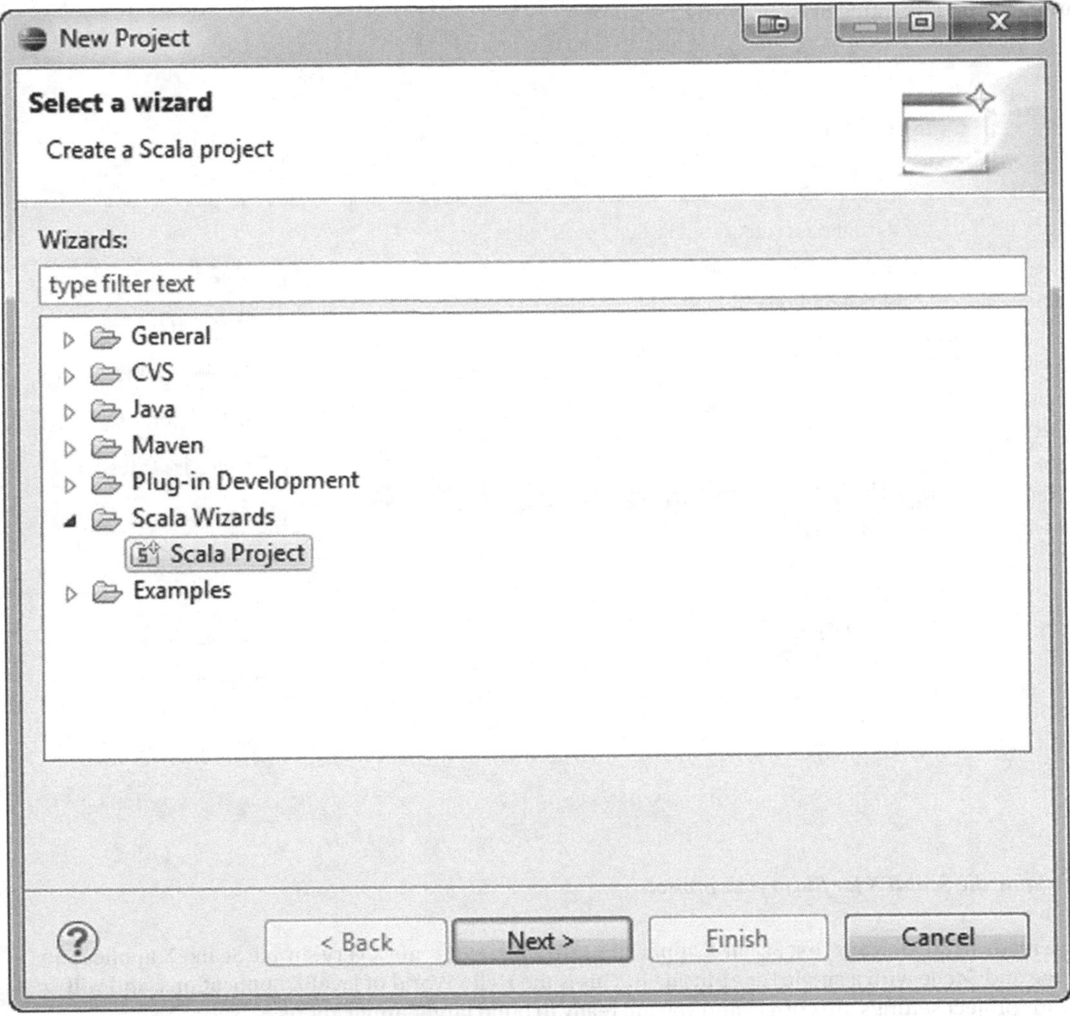

Figure 13-11. Scala project creation in Eclipse

We name our project Hello ScalaFX and use the default project settings. When asked to switch to the Scala Perspective, choose Yes and you will be in the proper view for editing Scala code.

In addition to the standard project setup, we also need to add in the ScalaFX and JavaFX libraries to code using this DSL. ScalaFX can be downloaded from the Google Code web site here at `http://code.google.com/p/scalafx/`.

You already have the JavaFX libraries installed as part of the JavaFX runtime and SDK. To install ScalaFX, simply download the latest distribution as a jar and add it to your project as a dependent library. The easiest way to do this is as follows.

1. Copy the `ScalaFX.jar` file to a `lib` folder under your project root.
2. Right-click your project and choose Properties... from the context menu.
3. Navigate to the Java Build Path entry, select the Libraries tab, and click Add Jars.
4. Select the `ScalaFX.jar` file you added to your project in Step 1.

Steps 2 through 4 are illustrated in Figure 13-12.

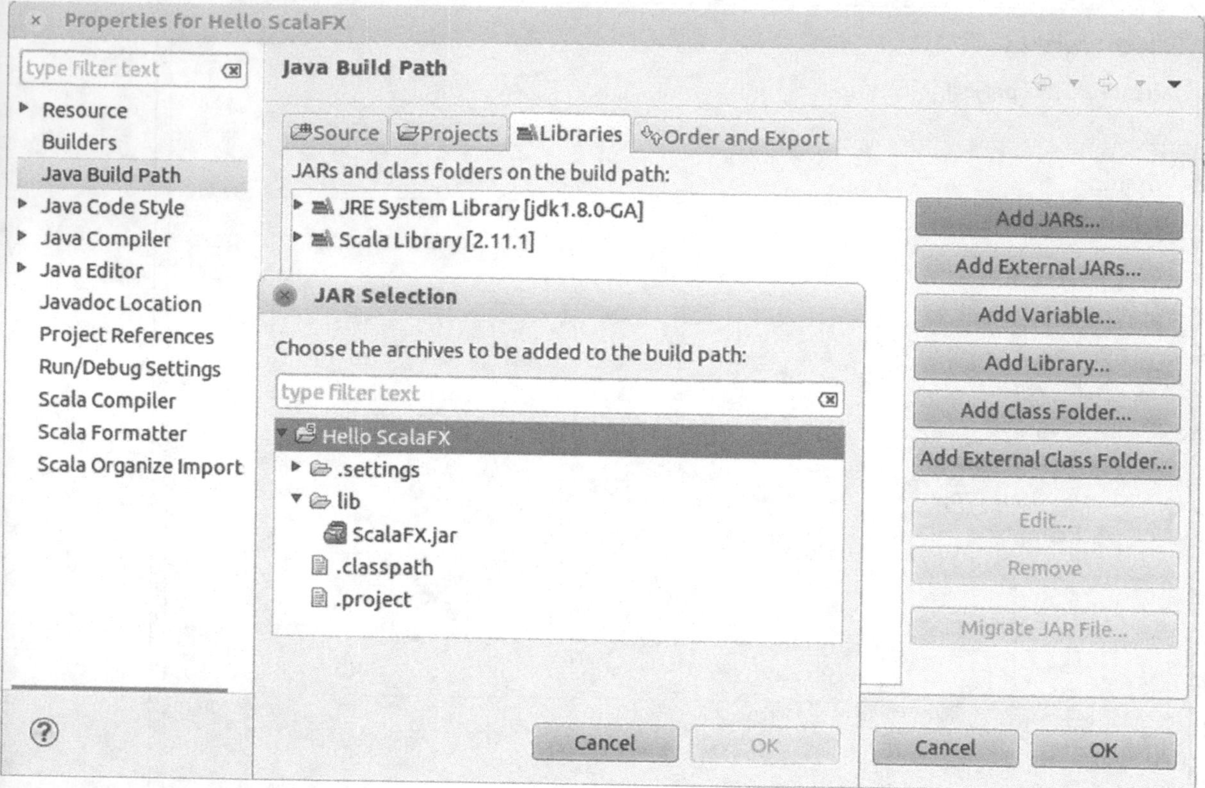

Figure 13-12. *Adding the ScalaFX jar file to your project*

Now you are ready to create your first ScalaFX application. To start, we create a very simple ScalaFX application that shows a `Stage` and `Scene` with a single `Label` inside it. This is the Hello World of JavaFX applications, and will ensure that all your project settings are correct and you are ready to build larger applications.

To create a new ScalaFX class, choose New ➤ Scala Object from the File menu. This opens a wizard in which you can set the name of your class to `HelloScalaFX` and select the `scalafx.application.JFXApp` class from which it should extend. On completing the wizard, Eclipse will create a stub class for you.

To complete the example, you need to add a `Stage`, `Scene`, and `Label` to your application. The full code for the Hello ScalaFX application is shown in Listing 13-10.

Listing 13-10. Hello ScalaFX Application to Test Your Newly Created Project

```
import scalafx.application.JFXApp
import scalafx.application.JFXApp.PrimaryStage
import scalafx.scene.Scene
import scalafx.scene.control.Label
```

```
object HelloScalaFX extends JFXApp {
  stage = new PrimaryStage {
    scene = new Scene {
      content = new Label {
        text = "Hello ScalaFX"
      }
    }
  }
}
```

You probably noticed some obvious differences from Java code. In Scala, semicolons are almost always optional where a line break would otherwise indicate that a statement has ended. This is why there is no semicolon on the import statements or the assignment to text. Also, Scala has both classes and objects, either or both of which can be defined in a given file. In this case we are creating an object that subclasses `scalafx.application.JFXApp`, which serves as a way of both defining our application and launching it in one step.

Creating an `Object` that extends `scalafx.application.JFXApp` is the fundamental pattern for building JavaFX applications using ScalaFX. This base class has all the core functionality to instantiate a JavaFX application, freeing you from the usual boilerplate required. All you have to do is take care of whatever initialization you need and override the stage variable with your own ScalaFX stage object.

This same pattern is followed for the `PrimaryStage`, `Scene`, and `Label`, all of which are ScalaFX objects that have properties on them for each of the available JavaFX properties of the same class. If you notice from the imports, we are not actually referring to JavaFX classes, but instead working with proxy classes in a parallel set of ScalaFX classes. These proxies are interchangeable with the equivalent JavaFX classes using a feature in Scala called implicits, but have additional functionality that supports this nested object-literal-like syntax.

To run this application, right-click the file and choose Run As ➤ Scala Application. On execution, this application opens a window with the words Hello ScalaFX as shown in Figure 13-13.

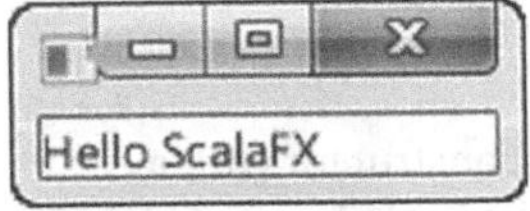

***Figure 13-13.** Hello ScalaFX application launched from Eclipse*

Congratulations! You have successfully run your first ScalaFX application. We now dig more into the design and features of ScalaFX, showing you how you can build more complex JavaFX applications in Scala.

ScalaFX Proxies and Implicit Conversions

For almost every JavaFX API class, there is an equivalent ScalaFX proxy class. The ScalaFX proxy classes are in a parallel package structure where `javafx` is replaced by `scalafx` and provides additional functionality on top of the JavaFX APIs. The proxy classes each include one or more of the following.

- *Delegate object*: Each proxy contains a reference back to the JavaFX class that it extends and wraps.
- *Property aliases*: For all properties, rather than referring to them as fooProperty, you can instead directly access them as foo.
- *Property assignment*: To support an object-literal-like syntax, the assignment operator is overloaded to allow you to set writeable properties directly.

- *List access*: All JavaFX ObservableLists are wrapped with a property to access the list that lets you treat it as a Scala collection.
- *API enhancements*: Some of the JavaFX APIs were not designed with the Scala language and object-literal construction in mind, so the API authors have taken some liberties in adding strategic enhancements.

For most uses, you can actually ignore the fact that there is a parallel set of classes, because the Scala implicits feature allows you to use them interchangeably. Anywhere you have an API that expects a JavaFX class, you can pass in the ScalaFX proxy and it will automatically get converted back to the JavaFX version. Similarly, if you have an API that expects the ScalaFX version, there is a Scala implicit conversion that will automatically wrap the JavaFX class in a ScalaFX proxy.

For example, you can change the Hello ScalaFX code to use a JavaFX label directly and the code will compile and run fine. The modified version is shown in Listing 13-11.

Listing 13-11. Hello ScalaFX Application to Test Your Newly Created Project

```
import scalafx.Includes._
import scalafx.application.JFXApp
import scalafx.application.JFXApp.PrimaryStage
import scalafx.scene.Scene
import javafx.scene.control.Label

object HelloScalaFXImplicits extends JFXApp {
  stage = new PrimaryStage {
    scene = new Scene {
      content = new Label("Hello ScalaFX Implicits")
    }
  }
}
```

Notice that we have changed the import to the normal JavaFX one and used the standard constructor with a String argument. Even though the Scene content is defined as a collection of ScalaFX Nodes, the Scala implicit kicks in and automatically converts the JavaFX object to a ScalaFX proxy.

The ScalaFX implicit conversions require that you import scalafx.Includes._, which has been the first line in all the programs we have shown. This is a special syntax for Scala that is equivalent to a static import in Java, and will automatically include several utility methods and all the JavaFX to ScalaFX implicit conversions. For the purposes of ScalaFX development, you should simply treat it as a preamble and include it on all your ScalaFX source files.

JavaFX Properties in Scala

Although we have been using ScalaFX properties directly, we have not directly shown how they work. In particular, notice the absence of the usual getter/setter pattern found in JavaFX. This is possible because ScalaFX lets us override the behavior of operators and assignment to substitute more efficient versions of the same operations. To understand this, let's take a look at the JavaFX property pattern again.

When creating properties for JavaFX in Java, each property definition consists of one variable and three different accessor methods as shown again in Listing 13-12.

Listing 13-12. JavaFX Property Pattern to Create New Properties in Java

```
import javafx.beans.property.SimpleStringProperty
import javafx.beans.property.StringProperty

public class Person {
  private StringProperty name;
  public void setName(String val) { nameProperty().set(val); }
  public String getName() { return nameProperty().get(); }
  public StringProperty nameProperty() {
    if (name == null) {
      name = new SimpleStringProperty(this, "name");
    }
    return name;
  }
}
```

Direct access to the property is restricted to allow it to be lazily created on the first use. The initialization occurs in the `nameProperty` method if it is null, and then the get and set simply delegate the call to the same named method on the property.

In ScalaFX, you get the same benefits of lazy initialization in a single line, as shown in Listing 13-13.

Listing 13-13. Simplified JavaFX Property Pattern Adapted Using ScalaFX APIs

```
import scalafx.beans.property.StringProperty

class Person {
  lazy val name = new StringProperty(this, "name")

  // this is optional, but supports the object-literal construction pattern:
  def name_=(v: String) {
    name() = v
  }
}
```

The first line that defines the property is sufficient to do everything that the preceding Java code does. Declaring `name` as a `val` tells Scala that it is a constant variable. The `lazy` keyword that precedes the declaration indicates that it should not be initialized until the first use. As a result, you can directly access this variable from user code and the initialization logic is automatically invoked when needed.

■ **Tip** Scala supports three different types of variable definitions: `val`, `var`, and `def`. The `var` keyword behaves most closely to what you are familiar with in Java, and defines a variable that can be modified in place. The `val` keyword, which we used here, declares a constant variable, and is most similar to final variables in Java. The last keyword, `def`, declares an expression that is reevaluated each time it is called, so it behaves just like a method in Java.

The second definition of a `name_=` method is special syntax for overloading the assignment operator in Scala. This is how the object-literal-like syntax we used earlier works; however, it is just a shortcut for accessing the property and assigning the value. It also demonstrates the basic pattern for how properties are used in ScalaFX.

Table 13-1 compares all the different combinations of how you access and set properties in Java and ScalaFX.

Table 13-1. Property Operations in ScalaFX Versus Java

Operation	Java	ScalaFX	Description
Get Property	`getFooProperty()`	`foo`	Get the raw property (typically used for setting up binds or listeners)
Get Property Value	1: `getFoo()` 2: `getFooProperty.get()` [long form]	1: `foo()` 2: `foo.get()` [long form]	Get the value of the property
Set Property Value	1: `setFoo(val)` 2: `getFooProperty.set(val)` [long form]	1: `foo() = val` 2: `foo.set(val)` [long form] 3: `obj.foo = val` [object literal shortcut]	Set the value of the property

Once you get used to the ScalaFX syntax, it is quite natural. In general, if you refer to a property directly, you will be accessing the full property object, which has all the methods for binding, listeners, and so on. However, if you follow the property name with parentheses, you will get (or set) the property value.

■ **Tip** This use of parentheses is supported via the Scala apply and update syntax, which is commonly used for `Arrays` and `Lists`, but in ScalaFX is used to differentiate between the raw properties and their values.

One exception to this rule is in the object literal case (third example of Set Property Value), where you can use the assignment operator directly to set the value of a property (no parentheses needed). An unambiguous case, this is allowed because JavaFX properties references are read-only, and it significantly cleans up the syntax of the user code.

If you ever get confused between properties and values, Scala's type system will come to the rescue. In general, the ScalaFX APIs have been designed to preserve strong typing and produce type errors anywhere the developer's intent is ambiguous. Therefore, if you use a property where a type is expected, or vice versa, the compiler will most likely catch the error before you even run the application.

ScalaFX Bind APIs

Binding is arguably one of the most innovative features in the JavaFX library; however, the APIs can be a bit cumbersome to use, especially in cases where you have complicated bind logic. The fluent API provided is quite powerful and expressive given the constraints of the Java language, but lacks a lot of the elegance that made bind so powerful with JavaFX Script.

The ScalaFX Bind APIs sit on top of the JavaFX binding support, but wrap them in a programming language syntax that is natural to write and understand. By taking advantage of operator overloading and infix notation, you can write complex ScalaFX bind expressions without even knowing all of the bind API methods that come with JavaFX.

For example, here is how you bind the height of one Rectangle to the sum of the heights of two others:

```
rect1.height <== rect2.height + rect3.height
```

Other than the special bind operator (<==), and lack of parentheses to convert from properties to values, this is the same code that you would write to add up the heights statically. However, once the bind is in place, any updates to `rect2` or `rect3` will dynamically change the height of `rect1`.

What this expression actually translates to is the following JavaFX code in Java:

```
rect1.heightProperty().bind(rect2.heightProperty().add(rect3.heightProperty()));
```

Even for a simple bind expression such as this, it is easy to get lost in all the parentheses and method calls that Java requires.

You can also do aggregate operators in ScalaFX. Rather than having to use the static methods on the JavaFX `Bindings` class, the ScalaFX Includes import gives you all these functions as methods you can call directly, such as the following code to bind the width of one rectangle to the max width of three others.

```
rect1.width <== max(rect2.width, rect3.width, rect4.width)
```

The other type of bind expression that is extremely common is conditional statements. Creating conditionals with the JavaFX APIs is possible, again by using the static `Bindings` class, but much simpler using the ScalaFX APIs. The following code changes the `strokeWidth` based on whether the cursor is hovering (just as we did in the Vanishing Circles application earlier).

```
strokeWidth <== when (hover) then 4 otherwise 0
```

The expressions passed in for the conditional value and result clauses can be arbitrarily complicated. The following example combines Boolean logic, String concatenation, and a conditional expression.

```
text <== when (rect.hover || circle.hover && !disabled) then textField.text + " is enabled"
otherwise "disabled"
```

In all of these examples, because you are writing code that sits directly on top of the JavaFX bind APIs, you get all the same benefits, such as lazy evaluation. Also, because Scala is a statically typed language like Java, you get these benefits without giving up type safety as you do with other dynamic languages. In fact, you get better type safety with the ScalaFX APIs, because it also supports type-safe dereferencing of subproperties. For example, in ScalaFX to bind the width of a rectangle to the width of a `Scene` you would simply write:

```
rect1.width <== stage.scene.width
```

This works even if the `Scene` has not been created yet, such as during initialization of the `Stage` object. You can also accomplish the same thing in Java, but it requires a non-type-safe property selector:

```
rect.widthProperty().bind(Bindings.selectDouble(stage, "scene.width"));
```

Underneath the covers, the ScalaFX calls this exact JavaFX API, but it protects the application developer from accessing a property that might be misspelled or of the wrong type.

Finally, a discussion of binding would not be complete without an example of bidirectional binding. This is similarly easy in ScalaFX, and can be accomplished using a slight variation on the bind operator as shown in the following example.

```
textField.text <==> model.name
```

This creates a bidirectional binding between the `name` property in the model and a `TextField`, such that if the user edits the text field, the model object will automatically be updated, too.

Although most of the ScalaFX operators are fairly intuitive, there are a few cases where it was not possible to use the standard operators. These include:

- `if/else`: These are Scala language keywords, so as demonstrated earlier, these have been replaced with `when/otherwise`, just as in the corresponding JavaFX APIs.
- `==/!=`: Directly using the equality and inequality operators produces some unwanted interactions with the same operations on the core Scala object base class. Instead use `===` and `=!=`, both of which were carefully chosen to have the same precedence rules as the operators they are replacing.

As an added bonus, you can specify the precision of the `===` and `=!=` operators for numeric comparison by using the following syntax.

```
aboutFiveHundred <== value1 === 500+-.1
```

This would test that `value1` is less than `.1` away from 500.

API Enhancements

By this time, you should have a pretty good feel for how the JavaFX applications you have been building translate to equivalent ScalaFX code. In general the ScalaFX APIs mirror the JavaFX APIs, providing equivalent functionality. However, in some cases it was actually possible to provide an improved API or alternative choice that matches the declarative style of programming that ScalaFX encourages. In this section we cover a few different areas in which ScalaFX improves on the JavaFX APIs.

Closures

One of the features that is new to Java 8 is lambdas or closures. This simplifies the case where you are creating event listeners or similar callbacks where you need to implement an interface that contains a single method.

Most modern JVM languages have had closures as a core language feature for quite a while, as does the Scala language. This means that anywhere you would normally have to implement an event or property listener, you can instead use a closure to simplify your code.

Earlier in the Vanishing Circles application we showed an example of a closure to set a mouse click handler:

```
onMouseClicked = {
  Timeline(at (3 s) {radius -> 0}).play()
}
```

The closure part is really that simple; all you have to do is surround your method logic with curly braces and assign it to the property for the event handler. There is another variant of this if you also need access to some of the variables passed in, such as the `MouseEvent`:

```
onMouseClicked = { (e: MouseEvent) =>
  Timeline(at (3 s) {radius -> 0}).play()
}
```

Layout Constraints

The layout constraint mechanism introduced in JavaFX 2 is very flexible, because it lets layout authors define their own constraints that get stored on `Node`, but is also not ideal from an application developer standpoint. It forces your code into an imperative pattern where you add children in one step and then set constraints following that.

Because the set of interesting layout constraints is fairly small, the ScalaFX APIs simply add the common ones onto the Node class directly. This lets you specify constraints such as alignment, margin, and grow declaratively as you are creating your object tree.

For example, to add a margin to the Label in our Hello ScalaFX example, it is as easy as setting the margin property on the Label:

```
object HelloScalaFXMargin extends JFXApp {
  stage = new PrimaryStage {
    scene = new Scene {
      content = new Label {
        text = "Hello ScalaFX Margin"
        margin = new Insets(20)
      }
    }
  }
}
```

This adds 20 pixels around the Label to space it out in the window. Without this ScalaFX feature, you would have been required to save a reference to the Label and later call the following.

```
StackPane.setMargin(new Insets(20));
```

An added benefit of the ScalaFX Node Layout Constraints is that they apply across all JavaFX layouts regardless of which type of container you are using. With the normal JavaFX Layout Constraints, you need to use the static method from the right layout type, otherwise the constraint will not work.

■ **Tip** For layout authors who want to make use of the ScalaFX Node Layout Constraints, ScalaFX also stores the layout constraint in an unprefixed form that you can directly access. For example, to get the margin constraint, simply call `node.getProperties().get("margin")`. For alignment you get your choice of accessing it as "alignment," "halignment," or "valignment," all of which get updated anytime the user sets the alignment property.

Animation

ScalaFX provides a shortcut syntax for expressing timelines that was inspired by the same syntax in JavaFX Script. It lets you specify the duration, keyframes, keyvalues, and tweens in a shortcut syntax that fits on a single line. We used this earlier in the Vanishing Circles example to specify an animation that shrinks the circles when they are clicked:

```
Timeline(at (3 s) {radius -> 0}).play()
```

This code is equivalent to the following Java code using the JavaFX animation API.

```
KeyValue collapse = new KeyValue(circle.radiusProperty(), 0);
new Timeline(new KeyFrame(Duration.seconds(3), collapse)).play();
```

As you can see, the ScalaFX variant is much more concise and readable even in this simple example. The basic syntax for animations in ScalaFX is:

```
at (duration) {[property -> value]}
```

This statement translates to a KeyFrame that can be added to a Timeline directly. You can pass in multiple KeyFrames to a Timeline or use multiple property->value pairs in the preceding syntax, giving you the flexibility to specify arbitrarily complex animations.

Breaking down this example further, notice that we used a shortcut syntax to create the Duration and the KeyValue. For the former, ScalaFX has an implicit conversion that adds a function to Doubles for ms(), s(), m(), and h(), allowing you to create a new Duration simply by calling the respective function. By using the postfix operator shortcut syntax in Scala, rather than calling "3.s()" or "3.s," you can further abbreviate it to "3 s" (where the space between 3 and s is required).

For the latter, ScalaFX properties have an overloaded operator of "->" that takes a value and returns a KeyValue object. In fact, not only can you specify the target value, but you can also add in a tween expression as shown here:

```
radius -> 0 tween EASE_OUT
```

This addition causes the animation to slow down as it approaches the end, resulting in a smoother transition.

Summary

As we have shown you in this chapter, you have a lot more options for writing JavaFX code than just using the Java language. There are already several DSLs available written in popular JVM languages such as Groovy and Scala.

The great thing is that you have the choice to use the language and markup that best suits your project needs. All of these technologies integrate cleanly with JavaFX code written in Java, and have their own benefits that you can take advantage of based on the needs of your project.

Resources

For more information about Groovy and GroovyFX, consult the following resources.

- Groovy Home Page: http://groovy.codehaus.org/
- GroovyFX Home Page: http://groovyfx-project.github.com/
- GroovyFX Announcement Blog Entry: http://pleasingsoftware.blogspot.com/2011/08/introducing-groovyfx-it-about-time.html

Additional information on Scala and ScalaFX can be found here:

- Scala Home Page: http://www.scala-lang.org/
- ScalaFX Home Page: http://code.google.com/p/scalafx/
- ScalaFX Announcement Blog Entry: http://javafx.steveonjava.com/javafx-2-0-and-scala-like-milk-and-cookies/

Index

■ D

E

F

G

H

I

J

K

L

M, N

O, P, Q

R

T

U, V

W, X,Y, Z

Apress®
THE EXPERT'S VOICE™